CONFRONTING THE CONSTITUTION

CONFRONTING THE CONSTITUTION

THE CHALLENGE TO LOCKE, MONTESQUIEU, JEFFERSON, AND THE FEDERALISTS FROM UTILITARIANISM, HISTORICISM, MARXISM, FREUDIANISM, PRAGMATISM, EXISTENTIALISM...

Edited by Allan Bloom
with the assistance of Steven J. Kautz

THE AEI PRESS
Publisher for the American Enterprise Institute
Washington, D.C.

The editor wishes to acknowledge the valuable assistance of Robert Licht, William Schambra, and Art Kaufman.

"Jefferson's Pulse of Republican Reformation" is reprinted from Ralph Lerner: *The Thinking Revolutionary: Principle and Practice in the New Republic*. Copyright © 1979, 1987 by Cornell University. Used by permission of the publisher, Cornell University Press.

Grants from the National Endowment for the Humanities provided substantial funding for this book.

Distributed by arrangement with

National Book Network
4720 Boston Way
Lanham, MD 20706

3 Henrietta Street
London WC2E 8LU England

Library of Congress Cataloging-in-Publication data are in the back of the book.

AEI Studies 496

The AEI Press
Publisher for the American Enterprise Institute
1150 17th St., N.W., Washington, D.C. 20036

Printed in the United States of America

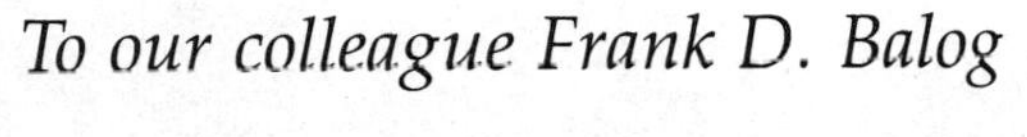

To our colleague Frank D. Balog

Contents

Contributors

FRANK D. BALOG was special assistant to the deputy director for data analysis, Bureau of Justice Statistics, U.S. Department of Justice. He was formerly assistant professor of political science at Nazareth College in Rochester, New York, and also taught at the University of Toronto. His articles have appeared in the *Canadian Journal of Political Science, Cooley Law Review,* and *European Review of the Social Sciences.* Mr. Balog died in 1989.

FRED BAUMANN is assistant professor of political science at Kenyon College. He was formerly director of the Public Affairs Conference Center at Kenyon and edited, in that capacity, *Democratic Capitalism?* and *Crime and Punishment: Issues in Criminal Justice.* He translated Leo Strauss's early work, *Philosophy and Law.*

ALLAN BLOOM, a professor in the Committee on Social Thought at the University of Chicago, has previously taught at Yale, Cornell, the University of Toronto, Tel Aviv University, and the University of Paris. He is also codirector of the John M. Olin Center for Inquiry into the Theory and Practice of Democracy. Professor Bloom translated Plato's *Republic* and Rousseau's *Emile* and wrote *The Closing of the American Mind.*

WERNER J. DANNHAUSER, professor of government at Cornell University, has also taught at the University of Chicago, the University of Toronto, and the Hebrew University of Jerusalem. A former editor of *Commentary,* he is the author of *Nietzsche's View of Socrates,* as well as numerous articles, reviews, and translations.

DAVID F. EPSTEIN is deputy director of net assessment, Office of the Secretary of Defense. He has taught political science as a member of the Graduate Faculty, The New School for Social Research, and is the author of *The Political Theory of The Federalist.*

JOSEPH HAMBURGER is a professor of political science at Yale University. His books include *Troubled Lives, John and Sarah Austin* (coauthor), *Intellectuals in Politics—John Stuart Mill and the Philosophic Radicals*, and *James Mill and the Art of Revolution*.

RALPH LERNER, a professor in the Committee on Social Thought at the University of Chicago, has also taught as a visitor at Stanford and Cornell. He is the author of various studies in medieval political philosophy as well as in American political thought. He coedited *The Founders' Constitution* and wrote *The Thinking Revolutionary: Principle and Practice in the New Republic*.

HARVEY C. MANSFIELD, JR., is the Frank G. Thomsen Professor of Government at Harvard University. He is the author of numerous books and articles, including *Statesmanship and Party Government, The Spirit of Liberalism*, and *Taming the Prince: The Ambivalence of Modern Executive Power.*

W. R. NEWELL is associate professor of political science at Carleton University in Ottawa, Canada. His articles on ancient, contemporary, and Renaissance political theory have appeared in journals, including the *American Political Science Review* and *Political Theory.*

JAMES H. NICHOLS, JR., is associate professor of government at Claremont McKenna College, Avery Fellow at Claremont Graduate School, and a research associate of the Salvatori Center. He has also taught at McMaster University in Hamilton, Ontario, and at the Graduate Faculty of the New School for Social Research in New York City. His writings include *Epicurean Political Philosophy* and essays, articles, and translations.

CLIFFORD ORWIN is associate professor of political science at the University of Toronto and has taught as a visitor at Harvard and Michigan State. He is the author of numerous articles on classical, modern, and contemporary political thought and is currently completing a book on Thucydides.

THOMAS L. PANGLE is professor of political science and chairman of the American studies committee at the University of Toronto. He has also taught at the University of Chicago, Dartmouth College, and Yale University. He is the author of numerous articles and books, including *Montesquieu's Philosophy of Liberalism* and *The Spirit of Modern Republicanism*.

MARC F. PLATTNER is the director of program at the National Endowment for Democracy. Previously, he was a fellow in residence at the National Humanities Center in North Carolina; adviser on economic and social affairs at the U.S. Mission to the United Nations; program officer at the Twentieth Century Fund; and managing editor of *The Public Interest*. He is the author of *Rousseau's State of Nature: An Interpretation of the Discourse in Inequality* and the editor of *Human Rights in Our Time*.

JOEL SCHWARTZ is managing editor of *The Public Interest*. He has taught political philosophy at the University of Michigan and the University of Toronto. He is the author of *The Sexual Politics of Jean-Jacques Rousseau*, as well as articles on Freud, Hobbes, Spinoza, and Tocqueville.

SUSAN SHELL is associate professor of political science at Boston College. She is the author of *The Rights of Reason: A Study of Kant's Philosophy and Politics*, numerous articles in periodicals and journals, and is currently completing a book on Hegel's logic.

JAMES R. STONER, JR., is assistant professor of political science at Louisiana State University.

NATHAN TARCOV, a professor of political science at the University of Chicago, recently served as the secretary of the Navy Research Fellow at the U.S. Naval War College. He has also served as a member of the Policy Planning Staff at the U.S. Department of State and has written extensively on political theory, American political thought, and American foreign policy. He is the author of *Locke's Education for Liberty*.

1
Introduction

Allan Bloom

Almost a decade ago, Robert Goldwin and Walter Berns persuaded a group of us to discuss the proper way to celebrate the approaching bicentennial of the Constitution of the United States. We were, perhaps, not a typical group, but all of us agreed that the only way for us was to *think* about the Constitution.

Aside from the fact that this should be the response of serious men and women to serious things, the Constitution, of all public documents, invites rational discourse. It was written by a group of wise statesmen who believed in the necessity, goodness, and power of reason in the establishment of just regimes. Their task was to establish the framework within which the natural rights announced in the Declaration of Independence would be protected. Moreover, in the debates of the Constitutional Convention and in *The Federalist*, they gave their detailed reasons for their doings. Their authority was founded not on tradition or revelation but on nature grasped by reason. This was a new beginning, a liberation from prejudice, legitimized by reference to principles of justice assented to by man's most distinctive and most common faculty and persuasive to a candid world. The Framers were not prophets, poets, or heroes in the old sense but were, rather, reasonable men. Other men were not required to believe what they heard from the Framers but had merely to look at what they pointed to and judge for themselves. Convinced that they had the best of any discussion about the good regime, the Framers, as it were, challenged the world to meet them on the field of reason. To test their conviction is to honor them.

This is the peculiarly American form of patriotism. With us it is not, at least not essentially, the instinctive and unquestioning love of our own—the burning passion that consumes all doubts, that sacrifices reason to dedication to the community. The genius of this country—which cannot and does not wish to treat its citizens like plants rooted in its soil—has consisted in a citizenship that permits reflection on one's own interest and a calm recognition that it is satisfied by this regime. And this reflection does not end in mere mean-spirited calculation, as is often alleged by critics from the Right and the Left, but leads to the peaks of philosophy. Our regime is founded on arguments, not commands. Obedience to its fundamental law is not against reason, and it can claim to have resolved what was thought to be the unresolvable tension between good citizenship and philosophizing.

In sum, in America, thoughtful citizenship is good citizenship. All of us involved in this project know ourselves to be modern men and women, which means that our education did not at first lead us toward the Constitution and the philosophic position underlying it. When we were young, we were taught, and were attracted by, thought that was in the air. Marx, Freud, Weber, and Nietzsche were "where it was at." And historicism was already effective enough to make us think that earlier thought could not be truer than later thought, that eighteenth-century opinions could not help us to answer twentieth-century questions. Like most people in this case, we remained attached to liberal democracy and the institutional structure given to it by the Constitution without asking whether a Marxist, an existentialist, or, for that matter, a utilitarian can do so consistently. Can any "state" be anything other than an instrument of class domination? Can irrational man also be the democratic voter? Is contempt for natural rights consistent with democratic justice?

These are obvious and necessary questions, but they arise only to those who seek for comprehensiveness and coherence, as did the Framers. That the Framers were such men is something most of us learned later, as graduate students, when we came to see that they had reasoned arguments that are defensible, if not true a priori. It required a certain de-ideologization to meet them fresh and listen to them without condescending from the heights of the twentieth century. The Framers had a keen sense of the relation between theory and practice; and their political founding was grounded in teachings about nature and the relation of justice to it. Their Bacon, Locke, and Montesquieu are worthy interlocutors—on the level of Kant, Hegel, Marx, and Nietzsche, who inspired less impressive political achievements. The Framers held that the rational conviction of the truth of the principle of natural right was essential for fighting the American Revolution, for establishing a constitution, and for preserving it. That conviction is undoubtedly not what it once was.

Does it deserve to be? That is our question. Since the framing of the Constitution many waves of thought have washed over our intellectual shores, most of them serious, each claiming to be a progress over earlier thought. This book's table of contents provides a survey of most of the notable ones. Some of them might have been predicted by the Framers; others would probably have surprised them. Some were directly critical of the solution to the political problem provided by the Constitution of the United States; others were not thinking of it, although their views of human nature and politics implicitly made them its critics and opponents. All have been seductive, and all have provided lenses through which Americans look at the world and by means of which they articulate its phenomena.

The authors of this book each proposed to take one of these schools of thought that had particularly interested him or her, to try to make precise what its view of constitutional politics is, and to reflect on whether the Framers' thought can make a convincing response to it. This effort was intended to be an exercise in our own self-awareness, but one that is in conformity with America's most fundamental tradition. We wished, without prejudice, to see what can still rationally be believed of the thought of the Constitution. This means that that thought had to be presented by those of us who knew it best, and then the various schools addressed by the rest. How well the thought of the Constitution would do in this contest was not presupposed. I suppose the results have been different for different ones of us. But the Constitution has been deepened and freshened for us all in seeing how it meets theoretical challenges unknown to its Framers.

When we first planned this volume, we were keenly aware that the discussion of the really interesting issues concerning our founding documents—whether popular government is a desirable form of government, whether the Constitution gives sufficient power to the people, whether religion is given a sufficient place to ensure a moral citizenry, and others—had been subordinated to secondary concerns such as the economic interests or the psychological peculiarities of the Framers, their historical situation and its intellectual limits, or their inability to distinguish value judgments from fact judgments. In other words, a new discipline, intellectual history, with newer methods—themselves related more or less consciously to new philosophies—gives priority to new kinds of questions, which prove to be endless. Thus the questions, and the answers, of the Framers—or those of any writer—can never be addressed and begin to be irrelevant, for they are alleged to have been unaware of the real questions. Their texts are thus not paths to be followed but symptoms to be diagnosed. Their arguments are judged to be untrue before being put to the test, as scholars devote themselves to explaining why they were wrong. It was precisely in response to this contempt for the text that we planned this volume. We hoped to demonstrate in deed that there is greater intellectual excitement, as well as greater political responsibility in adopting the perspective of the Framers rather than that of the trends of contemporary scholarship.

But the course of events intellectual and political since our first meeting has made efforts such as this all the more urgent. A new school of thought, derivative from the others, has overwhelmed the humanities during this decade and is making considerable inroads in the social sciences and the law. This approach has appeared to be just the thing for today's radicalism in America, which, in adopting it, has given it a life unwarranted by its intrinsic merits. Its thesis is that writers determine "values" or "world views," that they are unconsciously motivated by "the will to power," and that they are the sources of the domination of men by men. There are no theoretical human beings, and there is no objectivity, only commitment and subjectivity. Writers' apparently rational interpretations of a truly meaningless world provide the foundation for systems of domination and prevent the full flowering of individuals. Writers found legitimacy, and they spawn a race of interpreters or priests who are themselves legitimized by the sacred text they interpret. The focus on texts as the essential cause of political facts reverses the old Marxist relation between infrastructure and superstructure. Writers are conceived of as autonomous and given a new weight in the understanding of things. Of course, their autonomy rests not on their reason but on their irrational, creative unconscious. A new kind of liberating interpreter is conceived to do battle with the priestly interpreter and to destroy his foundation. The priest disappears with the Bible. The new interpreter "deconstructs" the sacred text, showing that its author could not know his own motives, that his text is incoherent and explodes, when pressured by the critic into the chaotic elements lying beneath its smooth rationalized surface. Race, gender, and class are the favorite prejudices of the unconscious' ruse in its quest for power.

Texts are the enemies, according to this school, and there is no need to insist on its threat to a political tradition that rests on fundamental texts. It was the pride of the Framers that for the first time in history a nation was founded on written documents that all can read and study and that appeal to the reason of each. It is a grave undertaking to undermine the credibility of such a legacy, although the deconstructionists approach it with levity. In a perverse way the deconstructionists agree with the Framers about the importance of their writing, but they insist that the Framers wrote to impose their rich, white, male, logocentric (or Eurocentric) selves on the poor, the females, and the nonwhites of the world. One can see why the deconstructionists appeal to certain kinds of extremists. They deny each of the premises of the Framers, especially those concerning nature, reason, and concern for the common good. Their influence now extends well beyond the academy into real politics. Deconstructionism has colored the public discussions about "original intent" as the guide for judges' interpretation of the Constitution and influenced the terms of the controversy surrounding Robert Bork's nomination to the Supreme Court. Deconstructionism must be studied, but the texts must be studied first to avoid beginning from parodies of them, parodies that are easy prey for the critics. In their digging, deconstructionists may well discover what they themselves have buried. This is easy to do when objectivity no longer prompts second thoughts.

This is how the American intellectual scene looks. Much greater events occurring outside the United States, however, demonstrate the urgency of our task. Those events are epitomized by the Statue of Liberty erected by the Chinese students in Tiananmen Square. Apparently, after some discussion whether it should be altered to have Chinese features, there was a consensus that it did not make any difference.

I write this at the moment when the terror in China has begun, and we cannot yet know what will become of those courageous young persons. But we do know the justice of their cause, and, although there is no assurance that it will ultimately triumph, their oppressors have won the universal execration of mankind. With Marxist ideology a wretched shambles everywhere, nobody believes any longer in Communist legitimacy. Everywhere, in the Communist world what is wanted is rational liberal democracy that recognizes men's natural freedom and equality and the rights dependent on them. The people of that world need and want education in democracy, which means study of the philosophy that explains the grounds of democracy and of the constitutions that actualize it. That education is one of the greatest services the democracies can offer to the people who live under Communist tyrannies and long for liberty. The example of the United States is what has impressed them most, and their rulers have been unable to stem the infection. Our example, though, requires explanations, the kind the Founders gave to the world. And this is where we are failing: dominant schools in American universities can tell the Chinese students only that they should avoid Eurocentrism, that rationalism has failed, that they should study non-Western cultures, and that bourgeois liberalism is the most despicable of regimes. However, this is not what they need. They have Deng Xiaoping to deconstruct their Statue of Liberty. We owe them something much better.

All of the contributors to this book are, with the exception of

Joseph Hamburger, students of, or students of students of, Leo Strauss. This great man reinterested us in America by teaching us how to read our country's political texts and demonstrating how wise they are. Suddenly we discovered how much there is at home to attract our best intellectual efforts. This was at a time when almost all of what appeared philosophically attractive engendered contempt for the Framers or what they stood for. From Strauss we learned that high adventure awaits those who wished to confront the Declaration of Independence, the Constitution, and *The Federalist*. His example made us ashamed of our smug sense of superiority to them.

Strauss was a refugee from Germany; hence, it was not choice that brought him to the United States. His life had been, and remained, dedicated to the question, What is reason? His was an unceasing quest for clarity about ancient and modern rationalism and the various kinds of antirationalism or irrationalism. One result of this quest was his rediscovery of the Socratic sense of political philosophy as the beginning point for the understanding of the place or fate of reason in human life. Thus, when he came to America, he discovered that it was most congenial to him. The American regime was friendly to him as Jew and philosopher, and, of course, the protections of these two aspects of his being were related in the rational universality of liberal principles. He had had experience, both theoretical and practical, of the German critique of those principles, and he unhesitatingly, unlike many refugees, preferred not the mystifying old cultures, however splendid, but a regime that in its founding faced the issues of reason and revelation. Our origins, properly understood, are more fundamental than theirs. Strauss began his study of the American regime from its highest claims for itself and, cutting through the overgrowth, went unerringly to the Founding thought that informed American reality. And he studied Lincoln as the authoritative interpreter of the liberal regime in its inevitable crisis over slavery. The United States, perhaps alone among regimes, merited philosophic examination because of its self-conscious attempt to solve the political problem, particularly in its relation to the two crucial elements—religion and philosophy—and because its founding documents were philosophic and derived from the great philosophers. He left this legacy to his students and gave us much to do.

PART ONE

The Intellectual Foundations of the Founding

2
The Philosophic Understandings of Human Nature Informing the Constitution

Thomas L. Pangle

The American Constitution is a product not of philosophers but of statesmen and lawgivers. Its chief aim is obviously the articulation, in precise and straightforward language, of a frame of government. Nevertheless, this institutional structure and the rules by which it is to operate are devised and promulgated in order to advance certain overarching moral goals. Contrary to what is sometimes claimed, the Constitution is not meant to be merely "procedural" as opposed to "substantive." In setting down the fundamental "rules of the game," the founders intend to determine in broad but definite terms the political culture and thereby the way of life of the future nation.

The Constitution, therefore, is the product of a prior, architectonic political reflection on the part of the founders. In the records they left behind of their comprehensive reflections on the character of the new and future society, the founders show themselves firmly rooted in a specific political philosophy. This deeper dimension of their lawgiving is unmistakably pointed to in the lapidary phrases of the great preamble to the Constitution. There the founders make it clear that their Constitution presumes, and partly for this reason does not discuss or argue for, a profound and lucid consensus on the nature of "justice," the "general welfare," and, preeminently, the "blessings of liberty." As *Federalist* 39 insists,[1] the American Constitution must be understood as growing out of and intending to advance "the fundamental principles of the Revolution."

That the American Revolution was in fact a revolution for the sake of principles, indeed for the sake of new philosophic principles, was a view widely attested among thoughtful Americans at the time of the founding. To quote Thomas Paine's *Rights of Man*, "The Independence of America was accompanied by a revolution in the principles and practice of Governments. . . . Government founded on a moral theory . . . on the indefeasible hereditary Rights of Man, is now revolving from west to east."[2]

At the time of the revolution, this appeal to the "moral theory" of human rights was still a fresh phenomenon on the stage of history. These newly discovered "rights of man" were of a fundamentally different character from the various sorts of local, traditional, and divinely revealed rights men had invoked since time immemorial as the legitimating grounds for their rule over others or for their rebellion against rule. In the first place, the rights to which appeal was made in the American Revolution were rights understood to inhere in all men simply as men. Second, these rights were understood to be knowable by all men capable of fully developed, unassisted reasoning. In particular, the rights were not understood as dependent on or derivative from divine revelation. Third, these rights were not regarded as having been granted or created by any human act or agency or historical process. They therefore could not be superseded, revoked, or even surrendered. They were, in Paine's words, "indefeasible" or, as the Declaration of Independence has it, "unalienable." But the rights were not merely *asserted* to be unalienable, inherent in all men, and knowable by reason; they were held to be so because and only because they were "natural"—the essential and undeniable endowments of human nature. While it was readily conceded that the nature and hence the natural rights of man are better recognized in some times and places than in others, the rights were nonetheless understood to be in principle derivable, in all places and at all times, from the rational or scientific study of human nature. The rights were the product not of revelation, "history," "culture," or "creativity" but of "nature and nature's God." Insofar as earlier theorists, in particular the classical political philosophers, had neglected to invoke these natural rights, they were exposed as having failed to discover their own nature as human beings.

It is true, of course, that the founders drew for their understanding of natural rights on a previous English and continental tradition of political philosophy and civic discourse. But that tradition did not confine itself to tradition—history or precedent—as the source of legal and constitutional standards. No one grasped the distinctive character of the new, theoretical appeal to nature as contrasted with older appeals to tradition, history, or practice better than Edmund Burke. In his "Speech on Conciliation with the Colonies," Burke reminded his audience of the true genealogy of the colonists' demand for "no taxation without representation." The conception of liberty or of rights that underlay this demand was, Burke insisted, an innovation in the history of the idea of liberty. Indeed, the new conception of liberty possessed no counterpart anywhere in classical republicanism. The new conception had roots in late medieval England and reached self-conscious maturity in modern England. Although the new notion of rights first came to prominence in English political life, it certainly did not rest, in the final analysis, on any particular determination of the facts or traditions of English history:

> It happened, you know, Sir, that the great contests for freedom in this country were from the earliest times chiefly upon the question of taxing. Most of the contests in the ancient commonwealths turned primarily on the right of election of magistrates; or on the balance among the several orders of the state. The question of money was not with them so immediate. But in England it was otherwise. . . . In order to give the fullest satisfaction concerning the importance of this point, it was not only necessary for those who in argument defended the excellence of the English constitution, to insist on this privilege of granting money as a dry point of fact, and to prove, that the right had been acknowledged in ancient parchments, and blind usages, to reside in a certain body called a House of Commons. They went much farther; they attempted to prove, and they succeeded, that in theory it ought to be so . . . whether the old records had delivered this oracle or not.[3]

What exactly is the modern philosophic conception of nature—conceived as the source of rights—that grounds and gives the guiding purpose to the founders' Constitution? What exactly does it mean to appeal, as do the Declaration of Independence and *Federalist* 43, to "the transcendant law of nature and of nature's God"? What are the full implications of and the arguments or evidence for the new conception of human nature? It is these most basic questions about the American Constitution that the following pages are intended to begin to answer. The aim is not merely to reproduce the views held by the founders or even by the few most thoughtful of the founders. The aim is, following the framers' lead, to ascend beyond the stated views to their philosophic sources. There, if anywhere, can best be discerned all that is at stake in the theoretical alternative embraced by the founders. There can best be laid out the full logic of the decisive arguments underlying the founders' vision of a good society. Yet in trying to trace the clearest and deepest version of the thinking that dominated the founders' minds, we must not forget that the founders were not themselves philosophers. The theoretical arguments were, in the minds of the founders (and even more in the minds of their followers), mingled with, qualified by, and often contradicted by other arguments and considerations. The exigencies and opportunities of the colonists' previous history taught lessons that were not to be found in treatises; the Bible, although increasingly interpreted in the light of Locke's extraordinarily influential Biblical commentary, remained a challenge to modern rationalism; and glowing embers of the old fires of classical republican political theory still lived, though in an embattled and senescent condition.

The Leading Theoretical Achievement in the Eyes of the Framers

To understand the founders' own conception of what marks their political theorizing as new and distinctive, we may best begin with this question, What was the gravest problem of principle the founders believed themselves to be facing as lawgivers? James Wilson's great speech in the Pennsylvania Ratifying Convention is in this respect most helpful.[4] While Wilson speaks of the problem of federalism—the difficulty of designing a proper balance between the national and the state governments—he treats this problem as subordinate or secondary. Federalism never posed much of a difficulty in principle: "It was easy," he says, "to discover a proper and satisfactory principle on this subject." The truly baffling or puzzling issue of principle, the only issue Wilson in fact calls "very important," is that which arises "from comparing the extent of the country to be governed, with the kind of government which it would be proper to establish in it." As Wilson proceeds to explain,

> It has been an opinion, countenanced by high authority (Montesquieu, *Spirit of the Laws* Bk. 8, chap. 20), "that the natural property of small states, is to be governed as a republick; of middling ones, to be subject to a monarch; and of large empires, to be swayed by a despotick prince; and that the consequence is . . . the spirit of the state will alter in proportion as it extends or contracts its limits." This opinion seems to be supported, rather than contradicted, by the history of the governments in the old world. Here then the difficulty appeared in full view. On one hand, the United States contain an immense extent of territory, and, according to the foregoing opinion, a despotick government is best adapted to that extent. On the other hand, it was well known, that, however the citizens of the United States might, with pleasure, submit to the legitimate restraints of a republican constitution, they would reject, with indignation, the fetters of despotism. What then was to be done? . . . Permit me to add, . . . that the science even of government

> itself seems yet to be almost in its state of infancy. . . . The ancients, so enlightened on other subjects, were very uninformed with regard to this.

Wilson here limns the founders' most salient break with previous experience and philosophic tradition. For at the time of the founding there prevailed widespread doubt about the viability—the very possibility—of a large-scale republic. Those who opposed or looked with a skeptical eye on the new Constitution started from the conviction that the Americans had only two likely avenues of future development: either the new nation could (and should) remain a loose confederacy of small republican states; or the nation would become unified and as a natural consequence would drift slowly but inevitably toward a centralized, authoritarian hierarchy and eventually despotic rule. This opinion was grounded in part on the universal experience of history. Never had there existed a stable republic encompassing more than one city or a loose federation of several cities. There had indeed existed aggressively imperalisitic republics that had succeeded in acquiring vast territories and subject populations (Rome being the premier example). Their successful expansion of dominion, however, had always sounded the death knell for their republican institutions.

Equally compelling was the near-unanimous testimony of the great tradition of political philosophy, ancient and modern. At least at first glance, the great political philosophers manifested firm consensus that the very nature of republican government demanded a small-scale, urban society—the polis or its equivalent. As James Wilson indicates, this apparent consensus was present to the founders' minds most vividly and authoritatively in the pages of Montesquieu's *Spirit of the Laws,* the most frequently cited work of political theory at the time of the American founding. Yet it was also the *Spirit of the Laws* that provided the most telling, if not so immediately obvious, refutation of this old tradition and its consensus. It is to the *Spirit of the Laws* that we need to turn first in order to begin to see the older arguments—about republicanism and human nature—that the founders had to attack and the new, Montesquieuian arguments that (in suitably modified or improved versions) they used as their weapons in this attack.[5]

Ancient and Modern Republicanism in Montesquieu

Montesquieu begins his analysis of the nature of republicanism by provisionally adopting the perspective of classical republicanism. To find models of successful republics and their characteristics, Montesquieu turns first to the great cities of Greco-Roman antiquity as well as to the city-republics that flourished in northern Italy in the Middle Ages. In trying to articulate systematically the requisites of the republican form of government as epitomized in such examples, Montesquieu initially accepts the key assumption underlying the classical city. According to that fundamental postulate (a postulate Montesquieu eventually shows to be erroneous),[6] "the liberty of the people" is synonymous with "the power of the people"; therefore "republic" must mean a government in which the people or some substantial portion of the people holds directly in its own hands the reins of power and responsibility. For large numbers of citizens to have direct access to sovereign office and to be under a duty to perform the functions of such office, the government must remain close to the people. The people must participate directly in the sovereign decisions that shape their lives. Such closeness or participation is by itself only a minimal precondition, however. There are other more arduous conditions of healthy republican politics.

A society whose supreme policy deliberations and decisions are entrusted to committees and assemblies composed, in rotation, of ordinary citizens is a society that requires in its citizens an intense public spirit. Each individual must in some measure dedicate himself to the good of the whole; he must sacrifice or risk time, energy, material prosperity, and—in war—even life itself, for the "fatherland." Republican government requires virtue as its "spring," as the "modification of the soul" that characterizes and animates each citizen. Virtue, according to Montesquieu, is the "principle" of republican government.

Virtue here means, first and foremost, patriotism—but not as an abstraction; patriotism in a sound republic means fraternity or a sense of solidarity that unites the citizenry to such an extent that each conceives of himself as truly a part of the larger and more significant whole that is the city. Virtue so understood is a characteristic of the heart rather than of the mind. It is a matter of feeling or sentiment and of lifelong habituation or custom, rather than of deep thought or intellectual education. Human beings do not *think* or *talk* themselves into brotherhood; they grow into such a relation by participating on rather intimate terms in a common way of life. Only those who share the same religion, the same education, the same family and sexual mores; only those who have enjoyed the same music and the same festivals; only citizens who have experienced the same victories and defeats, the same joys and sadnesses, can look upon one another with an authentic sense of identification and communion. Virtue is therefore the love of equality and homogeneity—the love of like for like in a society that prevents sharp distinctions or pronounced diversity.

From all this it follows that a sound republic cannot be "liberal." A sound republic must not decline into what Henri Bergson was to call "an open society" but must instead remain "closed"—characterized by a considerable degree of intolerance and a strict if "community-enforced" censorship. The government, in the hands of popular assemblies and their directorates, must severely restrict such dangerous sources of diversity as luxury, conspicuous consumption, economic inequality, travel, and erotic experimentation. Religious and artistic as well as political and philosophic innovation must be discouraged. The personal lives of citizens, especially their family lives—where the crucial early education and character formation of the children take place—must be closely watched by fellow citizens and neighbors.

An aristocratic republic seen from this perspective is an inherently defective form of republic. The virtue, which is the principle of aristocratic republics at their best, is not virtue in the full civic sense but is only "moderation"—a "lesser virtue" or, more precisely, the quality that in an aristocracy takes the place of true virtue.[7] This moderation, while it involves control of the passions and feelings, is an affair of the mind to a greater extent than is true political virtue. Moderation, as Montesquieu means the term in this context, is the shrewdly calculative self-control by which the few wealthy and powerful in an aristocracy restrain themselves and thus maintain the consent or acquiescence of the poor majority of citizens who are largely excluded from office.

Against the traditional republican forms of government Montesquieu poses the alternative of monarchic government, an alternative whose potential superiority gradually becomes more and more evident as the *Spirit of the Laws* unfolds. Monarchy, as Montesquieu understands it, is to be sharply distinguished from despotism or tyranny. Monarchy is the relatively recent historical product of the evolution of feudalism in Europe, whereas despotism is a global phenomenon as old as society itself. Monarchy is the institutionally limited rule under law of one man, who inherits his title. A true monarch is hemmed in by legitimate rival centers of power: an established clergy; a rule-governed bureaucracy and judiciary that do not serve simply at the will of the king; in the cities, strong local magistrates who represent powerful groupings of merchants and tradesmen; in the countryside and at court, deeply rooted and geographically diverse hierarchies of noble families and their client or patronage networks. Because power in a true monarchy is distributed into competing noble families, classes, estates, and regions, monarchic government is restrained or moderate in the sense of being checked and balanced. Monarchy usually places little if any political power in the hands of the people or the vast majority; but the people, though exploited, are nonetheless in some measure protected by the conflicts among the different centers of power. Besides, while the spirit and principle of despotism is fear, the spirit and principle of monarchy is honor or pride of place. With such pride goes a noblesse oblige among the upper classes—a sense of responsibility for the well-being and the dignity of subordinates.

The stability and, to a greater extent, the vigor of monarchic government depend on more than the structural checks and balances of competing centers of power. Monarchy to be successful must be infused from top to bottom with a sense of self-esteem, pride, or vanity that is at once assertive and deferential—depending on the relative rank of the individuals who come into relation to one another in every case. Honor dictates a meticulous attention to each individual's status and prerogatives. But honor, replacing republican virtue as the spring of society, requires almost no devotion to the society as a whole. Men's loyalty in a monarchy is to themselves, to their particular group, to the king as to a kind of father of the nation, and to their pride in self, family, and class.

Accordingly, monarchy tolerates, nay, promotes and thrives on, a diversity that would be anathema to healthy republicanism. Monarchy can be much more permissive, much more indulgent of luxury, love, the arts, individual eccentricity, selfishness, and competitiveness than can republicanism. In addition, monarchy not only allows but requires a large nation-state; it promotes greater security in foreign policy for its inhabitants and possesses much more potential for the development of commerce and all the prosperity that attends a strong commerce.

Montesquieu was convinced that in the most recent or advanced stages of its historical development monarchy was only beginning to reveal its full promise. Montesquieu looked to modern England as the model or at any rate as the foreshadowing of all that monarchy could become. England after the Glorious Revolution of 1689 combined many of the advantages of older European monarchies with a radical new openness to commerce and scientific technology accompanied by a sensible skepticism toward the traditional Christian opposition to worldly prosperity and comfort. Even more important, the English Constitution put together old-fashioned noble and clerical elites with a House of Commons that gave legislative power to a substantial portion of the people—not directly, as in traditional republicanism, but through the new and very indirect vehicle of "representation." As a result, one could see emerging in England a new form of republicanism: England was, in fact, "a republic hiding under the form of monarchy."[8]

The new synthesis of monarchy and *representative* republicanism required very little virtue and could even prosper with a much diminished or sensibly moderated sense of honor among its populace and rulers. To a degree never before seen, England substituted the checks and balances of institutions—the "separation of powers," a bicameral legislature, the jury system, political parties—for pristine or heroic qualities of character as the spring of government. The English form of government was the first dedicated to liberty in the truest sense of the term: not the right or duty to participate in rule, but the security of each individual as he pursued the objects of his most powerful personal needs or passions. In a world of scarcity, where men had been enlightened or educated so as to be no longer obsessed with trying to prepare for life in "the next world," this liberation issued in an unbounded, almost limitlessly productive, commercial and economic zeal.

Montesquieu was very modest in his hopes for the transplantation of English government or English political institutions. But he believed that the commercial spirit that those institutions liberated and encouraged could be promulgated and spread universally with great likelihood of success. In the "spirit of commerce," guided by the emerging science of economics, Montesquieu discerned the great engine of human liberation. The books of the *Spirit of the Laws* devoted to commerce—its past history and world-historical future implications—reveal the truly revolutionary thrust of Montesquieu's philosophic "legislation." In those books it is argued that commercialism, which can spread to many climes and infect many diverse political cultures, tends to cure human beings of the prejudices that veil their true, worldly needs. In recognizing the common material neediness that constitutes its basic nature, mankind discovers a sense of compassionate "humanity" that blurs previous religious, ethnic, national, and party sectarianisms. Once capitvated by the allure of peaceful trade, men look with increasing disgust at military exploits and the risks of war. They experience and learn to appreciate the spiritual as well as the material charms of exotic international diversity and individual singularity. If commerce threatens to vulgarize or trivialize the arts, it promises to release them, along with everything else, from parochialism and hence from the restraints of moral censorship.

The neediness, soft dependency, and cosmopolitanism that inevitably follow in the train of commerce certainly threaten austere traditional virtue, both religious and civic. But commerce brings virtues of its own: "frugality, economy, moderation, work, prudence, tranquillity, order, and rule."[9] More precisely, the spirit of commerce "produces in men a certain spirit of exact justice, opposed on the one hand to brigandage, but opposed on the other hand to those moral virtues which both restrain one from always pressing one's interests with rigidity, and allow one to neglect one's interests for the sake of the interests of others."[10] Above all, commerce brings the new virtue of "humanity": "one can say that the laws of commerce perfect the manners and morals, exactly as they destroy the manners and morals. Commerce corrupts pure manners and morals: this was the subject of Plato's complaints; it polishes and softens barbaric manners and morals, as we see it doing every day."[11]

Montesquieu admired and even extolled the classical republic, with its noble sense of the common good and near monastic self-sacrifice; but, for reasons that we will explore, he ultimately rejected classical republicanism for placing demands on men that run contrary to human nature. A comparative historical study of the workings of monarchy and classical republicanism reveals, according to Montesquieu, the key truth about human nature. Because human nature is what it is, republics of the classical sort are so fragile as to be mostly impracticable and so austere as to create unhappiness even where they are feasible. Before we descend more deeply into Montesquieu's analysis of human nature, let us consider how his critique of the classical republic, in the name of a new kind of republic devoted to individual liberty, was taken up, modified, and radicalized by the American founders. In order to understand this transmission, we must pay some attention to the intervening influence of David Hume—that younger contemporary who was perhaps the greatest of Montesquieu's intellectual heirs and who was, along with Montesquieu, so emphatically appealed to in the pages of *The Federalist*.

Hume's Attack on Classical Republicanism

Hume's political essays present a simplified and more straightforward version of the central argument of the encyclopedic *Spirit of the Laws*. The most notable change is the marked diminution of reverence for the ancient city. When treating some of the personal moral virtues in the course of his *Enquiry Concerning the Principles of Morals*, Hume is willing to give the ancients considerable credit; but their *political* theory and practice he regards with a gimlet eye: "These people were extremely fond of liberty; but seem not to have understood it very well."[12]

Like Montesquieu, but even more explicitly, Hume locates the root of the ancients' ignorance of political science in their imprudent partiality for direct popular government, together with their unrealistic insistence on a spirit of virtuous fraternity or community. Because they could not see or fully admit that the spirit of faction cannot be extirpated in a participatory republic, the ancients in effect countenanced permanent or recurrent revolution, as one after another of the inevitable classes or factions (especially the rich and poor) insisted on attempting to impose its will on the whole of society. "The maxims of ancient politics contain, in general," Hume observes, "so little humanity and moderation, that it seems superfluous to give any particular reason for the acts of violence committed at any particular period."[13] Even their most successful democracies were necessarily short-lived—doomed from the start because of two great flaws of political design. On the one hand, their founders or lawgivers tried to refine popular initiative by impractical or ineffectual attempts at moral education and exhortation, while remaining largely ignorant of those representative governmental institutions that alone can be relied upon to elevate and temper raw public opinion. On the other hand, the ancients were insufficiently aware of the ways in which all political power can and should be limited by means of countervailing factional representation in distinct and competing institutions: "The *balance of power* is a secret in politics, fully known only to the present age."[14] "In those days," he writes elsewhere, "there was no medium between a severe, jealous Aristocracy, ruling over discontented subjects; and a turbulent, factious, tyrannical Democracy."[15] Underlying the ancients' misconception of political institutions and political practice was their misapprehension of the true ends of civil society. In elevating the freedom and honor of republican politics as the chief end of civil society, the ancients promoted the militarization of life and quite failed to appreciate the extent to which the individual and social happiness of human beings depends on their safety and comfort. It has been the discovery of modern political economy that these more natural ends of humanity require the active promotion of avarice, private commerce, and extensive manufacture:

> Trade was never esteemed an affair of state till the last century; and there scarcely is any ancient writer on politics, who has made mention of it. . . . Ancient policy was violent, and contrary to the more natural and usual course of things. . . . They were free states; they were small ones; and the age being martial, all their neighbours were continually in arms. Freedom naturally begets public spirit, especially in small states; and this public spirit, this *amor patriae,* must encrease, when the public is almost in continual alarm, and men are obliged, every moment, to expose themselves to the greatest

> dangers for its defence. . . . Could we convert a city into a kind of fortified camp, and infuse into each breast so martial a genius, and such a passion for public good, as to make every one willing to undergo the greatest hardships for the sake of the public; these affections might now, as in ancient times, prove alone sufficient spur to industry, and support the community. It would then be advantageous, as in camps, to banish all arts and luxury; and by restrictions on equipage and tables, make the provisions and forage last longer than if the army were loaded with a number of superfluous retainers. But as these principles are too disinterested and too difficult to support, it is requisite to govern men by other passions, and animate them with a spirit of avarice and industry, art and luxury. . . . The harmony of the whole is still supported; and the natural bent of the mind being more complied with, individuals, as well as the public, find their account in the observance of these maxims.[16]

Hume was even more inclined than Montesquieu to suppose that the continued improvement in the design of limited monarchy would make this latter form of government more and more attractive to sensible observers. But, inspired by the example of the Netherlands (and following the footsteps of Spinoza's *Theologico-Political Treatise,* the first work to endorse and develop a theory of liberal democracy as a large-scale republican alternative to classical republicanism), Hume experimented in his mind's eye with a large-scale republican version of the regime based on an institutional balance of power and animated by the spirit of commerce. Hume went so far as to suggest that "the common opinion, that no large state, such as FRANCE or GREAT BRITAIN, could ever be modelled into a commonwealth, but that such a form of government can only take place in a city or small territory" was not only false but that in fact "the contrary seems probable." Hume admitted that it is much easier to *establish* a republic in a single city than in a far-flung nation: "a city readily concurs in the same notions of government, the natural equality of property favors liberty, and the nearness of habitation enables the citizens mutually to assist each other." But "these same circumstances, which facilitate the erection of commonwealths in cities, render their constitution more frail and uncertain." For "however the people may be separated or divided into small parties, either in their votes or elections; their near habitation in a city will always make the force of popular tides and currents very sensible." By contrast, in a large republic, if it "is modelled with masterly skill," there is "compass and room enough to refine the democracy" by representative and indirect government. What is more, the size and geographical dispersion of the populace make it less likely that a majority faction will be able to form: "the parts are so distant and remote, that it is very difficult, either by intrigue, prejudice, or passion, to hurry them into any measures against the public interest."[17] As Douglas Adair perceptively suggested, here is the germ of Madison's justly famous argument in *Federalist* 10.[18]

The New Republicanism of 'The Federalist'

Yet the authors of *The Federalist* are the celebrators of a great revolution against the English monarchy, the regime which Hume had championed and had held up as a model unrivaled by ancient republicanism. Because they are such rebels against England and its monarchy, they are allowed or compelled to take more seriously Montesquieu's presentation, in which the liberal English monarchy must to a greater extent vie for the stage with the illiberal and flawed, but still noble, classical republic. Accordingly, in contrast to Hume, the authors of *The Federalist* endorse a more confederal and more democratic or populist version of the modern liberal political system and lay greater stress on the kinship between the virtues such a system requires and the admittedly much sterner virtues found in the ancient republics.[19]

The pen name with which the authors chose to conclude every *Federalist*—"Publius"—testifies to their intention to establish a highly visible link with the Greco-Roman tradition of republicanism. As Madison later remarked (in his letter to Paulding of July 23, 1818), the name was taken from Plutarch's life of Publius Valerius Publicola, one of the founders of the Roman republic. More substantively, Hamilton and Jay open *The Federalist* by calling for a reinvigoration of the moral qualities displayed during the revolution: a genuine sense of fraternity, a capacity for individual self-sacrifice, and a dedication to

> one united people—a people descended from the same ancestors, speaking the same language, professing the same religion, attached to the same principles of government, very similar in their manners and customs, and who, by their joint counsels, arms, and efforts, fighting side by side throughout a long and bloody war, have nobly established their general liberty and independence.[20]

The Federalist moves to its conclusion with Hamilton declaring that "the only solid basis of all our rights" is "public opinion, and the general spirit of the people and the government."[21] In the Virginia Ratifying Convention, Madison spoke in a more purely classical tone when he said (June 20, 1788), "I go on this great republican principle, that the people will have virtue and intelligence to select men of virtue and wisdom. Is there no virtue among us? To suppose that any form of government will secure liberty or happiness without any virtue in the people is a chimerical idea."[22]

Nevertheless, while bowing to the classics and invoking, to some extent, their republican virtues, the new Publius also expresses severe, Humean criticism and a proud sense of innovation in republican theory and practice:

> It is impossible to read the history of the petty republics of Greece and Italy without feeling sensations of horror and disgust at the distractions with which they were continually agitated, and at the rapid succession of revolutions by which they were kept in a state of perpetual vibration between the extremes of tyranny and anarchy. If they exhibit occasional calms, these only serve as short-lived contrasts to the furious storms that are to succeed. If now and then intervals of felicity open themselves to view, we behold them with a mixture of regret, arising from the reflection that the pleasing scenes before us are soon to be overwhelmed by the tempestuous waves of sedition and party rage. If momentary rays of glory break forth from the gloom, while they dazzle us with a transient and fleeting brilliance, they at the same time admonish us to lament that the vices of government should pervert the direction and tarnish the luster of those bright talents and exalted endowments for which the favored soils that produced them have been so justly celebrated. . . . If it had been found impracticable to have devised models of a more perfect structure, the enlightened friends to liberty would have been obliged to abandon the cause of that species of government as indefensible.[23]

In *Federalist* 9 and 10, Hamilton and Madison trace the reasons for these drastic deficiencies of classical republicanism. The virtuous republic is necessarily short-lived because it is impossible to repress for long, without resorting to fear and violence, the natural diversity of mankind. This diversity is in the first place one of opinions or of opinions combined with passionate attachments—religious, moral, and political. But the cause of diversity on which Madison dwells is economic: inequality and heterogeneity inevitably arise from mankind's "different and unequal faculties of acquiring property." To the extent that men are allowed to express their talents and qualities, they will inevitably divide into classes, sects, and parties or factions—and as these emerge a small republic becomes more and more the scene of fierce conflict.

Yet, as the Federalists are led to stress in their polemics against the Antifederalists, the mixed regime that Montesquieu and Hume favor as an alternative is not possible in America—at least not in the form they depict and praise. Americans will not submit to an established religion or church; the nation lacks both a landed aristocracy and a royal family with hereditary title to occupy the chief executive office; America is infused with an egalitarian spirit that reflects the character of its agricultural and frontier yeoman society; and Americans are keenly attached to the dignity of their separate states. America must, therefore, devise a new species within the genus of modern, mixed, republican, or quasi-monarchic government.

It is this truth, the Federalists insist, that the opponents of the new Constitution fail to recognize. The Antifederalists refuse to confront the real problem, the new problem, America faces. They still think in terms of the old categories, alternatives, and choices—which no longer quite fit the new situation. On the one hand, the Antifederalists evoke nostalgia for the virtuous republics and republican confederations of old. But at the same time they are avid promoters of commercial growth and of the natural rights and liberties of individuals. They celebrate the private life of the individual property owner, independent of and unregulated by others. They do not seriously long for the total political commitment of the ancient Greeks and Romans: in fact, they wish to minimize the sphere of politics or government. On the other hand, leading Antifederalists like Patrick Henry look to the British Constitution as the only model for a strong and free government. Yet they know, and are compelled to admit, that this model is inapplicable to the social conditions and beliefs of Americans. As a result, they can offer no constructive suggestions. They call for simple government, kept close to the people, and seem to detect the threat of oligarchy or aristocracy looming in every effective feature of national government. But they cannot show that the existing *state* governments are or will remain small and simple enough to be truly close to the people. Most Antifederalists resist the idea of breaking up the existing states into smaller sovereign entities and concede the need for a national government that will to some extent police the possibly tyrannical tendencies of the states. They certainly admit the need for some sort of national government supervening over the states. But they fail to show how the national government can be made either strong enough to perform the tasks all agree it must perform or balanced enough to ensure that it will not become oppressive in the wrong hands. These unanswered questions are answered, adequately and even well, by the new Constitution the Federalists propose.

David Epstein will show in detail, in another chapter, precisely how the founders understood their Constitution to meet and master the new political conundrum or the new variation on the age-old conundrum. Our focus here is more preliminary and foundational. We seek to understand better the moral goals the founders had in view as they erected their great institutional and political structure. We have seen that the founders' unprecedented emphasis on protection of competitive diversity, especially regarding economics and property, and their elevation of the rights of men as private individuals, grow out of a comprehensive historical reflection on the experience of ancient republicanism and modern monarchy. Let us now turn back to Montesquieu and his systematic presentation of the character of the moral principles that derive from his empirical study of the workings of the various major types of political system that have emerged in history.

The Laws of Nature and of Nature's God in Montesquieu

The *Spirit of the Laws* opens with a compressed discussion of "laws in general" or "the necessary relationships that derive from the nature of things." We are assured at the very outset that even God as creator, and certainly God as ruler, is governed by such necessary relationships: "Thus the creation, which might seem an arbitrary act, presupposes rules as invariable as the fatality taught by atheists." What is more, "the laws according to which [God] created are those according to which he preserves." It is true that God created even these laws; but it would appear that he had no choice but to create some such invariable laws if he were to create anything that would subsist: "He acts according to these laws, because he knows them; he knows them because he made them; he made them, because they have a relationship with his wisdom and power. Since we see that the world . . . subsists always, it is necessary that its movements have invariable laws; and, if one could imagine another world than this one, it would have constant rules, or it would be destroyed." Existence or being necessarily entails invariable principles, "and, in this sense, all the beings have their laws." Nature and nature's God present an unbroken continuum of rationally knowable necessity.

Montesquieu states, one is tempted to say, a version of the principles that every intransigently rational account of life and of the world must necessarily embrace. For if the universe contains or may possibly contain a being capable of suspending or defying knowable necessity, then that being—and its potential past or future "miraculous" interventions—if it exists, necessarily confounds, and if it might exist, necessarily renders radically provisional all our plans and projects. In either case the knowable or "nature" must cease to be a wholly trustworthy guide. Prayerful hearkening to scriptural revelation and expectant or fearful waiting for further guidance would seem to be at least as reasonable or sensible as any attempt to rely on science in order to "go it alone." Above all, the Biblical account of the original condition or state of mankind—the miraculous Garden of Eden, the unfathomable Fall, and the mysterious contagion that defines our present worldly existence as sinful and in need of divine redemption—remains a great unanswered challenge or alternative to any simply rational or scientific attempt to explain the origin, cause, and nature of the human situation.

We can and should be grateful to Montesquieu for having stated so prominently and lucidly what may be called without exaggeration the fundamental hypothesis of modern rationalism, hence of modern natural right, and hence of the philosophy underlying the American Constitution. Yet Montesquieu's admirably bold and forthright declaration necessarily draws attention to the questionable character of that hypothesis. How Montesquieu knows—or thinks he knows, or could ever know—that the origins of the universe are governed by necessities, rather than by, as he puts it, "an arbitrary act," Montesquieu does not explain.[24] Indeed, one cannot help but be taken aback by the lighthearted or tongue-in-cheek character of Montesquieu's discussion of this very grave issue. The only theological authority to which Montesquieu has reference in this context is the "pagan" Plutarch.[25] Now Plutarch is a writer who, whatever his other estimable merits, has never before or since been regarded by any serious person as the last word in matters of theology or metaphysics. Has Montesquieu taken this whole issue with the seriousness it deserves and demands? Has he even stated the issue with the required caution and precision? Certainly one may question whether Montesquieu has not made his position much more extreme or boastful than he need have done: is it necessary, in order to defend the life guided by unassisted reason, to assert that we know or can know the necessitated character of the origin of all things? If so, the cause of rationalism might well seem to be very shaky, not to say doomed. The example of Maimonides suffices to prove that the cause of rationalism, in its medieval or ancient manifestation at least, is not so dependent and hence not so shaky or doomed.[26] But in regard to Montesquieu, we can wonder whether this philosopher does not, at the very outset of his endeavor, leave a large question mark looming over all his conclusions and surmises about the human condition. We may wonder the same thing about Montesquieu's modern philosophic peers.

But let us descend with Montesquieu from nature's God to nature itself. The laws of nature are the necessities of nature. The natural laws of each animal species will then be the principles of its behavior dictated by its permanent needs. The natural laws of the human species will be the principles of human behavior dictated by the inescapable needs of the human organism. These inescapable needs are visibly at work underneath the amazing and at first confusing heterogeneity of the many types of human societies and customs:

> I began by examining human beings, and I believed that, in this infinite diversity of laws and manners and morals, they were not conducted solely by their fantasies.
>
> I have laid down the first principles, and have watched the particular cases unfold as if by themselves; the histories of all the nations are but the consequence of them. . . .
>
> When I was called back to antiquity, I tried to take on its spirit, in order not to regard as similar, cases which are really different; and in order not to miss the differences between cases that appear similar.
>
> I have not taken my principles from my prejudices, but from the nature of things.[27]

Yet the "infinite diversity of laws and manners and morals" shows us that in human beings necessity operates in a manner different from the manner in which it operates in all other beings. The human species is distinguished from both the divine and the merely animal because its existence is left mainly to the guidance, not of instinct or infallible reason, but of a very fallible "intelligence," whose power of reasoning remains almost totally undeveloped unless it is wrenched into motion by accident or external pressure. Insofar as the human reasoning power does develop, it is evidently, in most men, a feeble and rather crude instrument. Reason affects human existence only in combination with passion and through the distorting filter of imagination, custom or habit, and belief. The human being is that malleable creature whose experience of its natural needs is such that, while susceptible of great change and diversity in behavior, it can usually change or be changed in its ways only very slowly over generations. Human beings feel, at bottom, the same fundamental necessities, the same fixed needs (for honor, secure preservation, and procreation, for example), but they frequently cannot discern the best—or even very adequate—ways to satisfy those always pressing natural needs. "Man," says Montesquieu, "this flexible being, bending himself, in society, to the thoughts and impressions of others, is equally capable of understanding his proper nature when it is shown to him, and of losing sight of it, even in his feelings, when it is hidden from him."[28] In their groping and more or less inadequate attempts over the ages to satisfy their basic needs in widely different natural and social environments, men to some extent alter the character, or at least the subordinate characteristics, of those needs. They feel the needs and seek to satisfy them in diverse ways. The enormous range in the way humans manifest and try to satisfy their sexual needs is for Montesquieu one of the most telling indications of the peculiar way in which human existence, as a fallible rational existence, is bounded, determined, and simultaneously differentiated by its response to the same underlying natural necessities.[29]

Mankind almost everywhere dwells in societies. From this follows the conclusion that man is "made to live in society."[30] But, considering the enormous historical diversity in, and contradiction among, human societies, we are forced to recognize how perplexing and equivocal man's sociability is. Man is surely not sociable in the way that bees, deer, birds, or indeed any other animal is sociable. In what sense or in what way is man "made" to live in society? What necessity or necessities, operating in what manner, "make" humans congregate in radically dissimilar societies? To begin from the assumption that man is by nature a social being is to paper over the deeply problematic and questionable character of the very sociability man exhibits. The further this assumption is questioned, the greater the need to try to rank in order of priority or primordial power the necessities or "laws" governing social behavior—in order to try to reconstruct the chain of necessity that makes man live in society.

Even Aristotle, the seminal exponent of the great anti-Montesquieuian doctrine that "man is by nature a political animal," feels the need to demonstrate the necessary emergence of the political association from the incompleteness of earlier, prepolitical associations. According to Aristotle, there could be a time when there are no political associations. But Aristotle's argument, at least as it appears on the surface and as it is usually or traditionally construed, is not intransigent enough. The argument too readily assumes that some form of the household or family is natural. The argument relies too much on the assumption that whatever can be observed occurring most or all the time is natural and, furthermore, that the natural in the fullest sense is the completed, fulfilled, or healthy condition of an animal. These assumptions assimilate the nature and natural condition of man too much to the nature and natural condition of other animals. The empirical evidence does not justify assuming that just because nature gives man a passion (fear, or a sexual itch, for instance), it also provides him with an unambiguous object of the desire or with a proper and clearly intelligible way of satisfying the desire.[31] Aristotle's presentation does not stick stubbornly enough to his first identification of the natural with the necessary.[32] Aristotle seems to assume that nature is more orderly or beneficent than is warranted by the evidence of the extraordinary historical diversity of human ways.

But let us not forget that the diversity of human societies is for Montesquieu only the least of the grounds for doubting the proposition that man is inclined or directed by nature to live in a small urban republic (polis). As we have seen, the actual life of such republics, studied in their various historical manifestations and in comparison with other types of society, proves on examination to be a life that manifestly cuts against the grain of the human animal. Like the grim order of a monastery (and even somewhat like despotism—though in a very different way and to a much lesser degree), the classical republic must war continuously against the natural proclivities of its citizens.[33] The obvious signs are the classical republic's instability, its need for repression and watchfulness, its incapacity to maintain its standards or aspirations, its consequent hypocrisy or self-delusion, its tendency to vent citizens' passions in unjust and ultimately suicidal foreign wars, the uneasiness citizens manifest toward the conflict between brotherly compassion for one another and the inhuman cruelty toward slaves and noncitizens, and, last but not least, the eagerness with which the classical republic's citizens and youths embrace the "corruption" of peace, commerce, luxury, private love, and personal vanity. As for monarchy, animated by the principle of honor, it is only somewhat less evidently engaged in a repression of and struggle against deep and abiding human desires.

Every previous or traditional type of civil society can be seen to depend for its functioning on a particular spring or principle that is the very soul of each type of civil society: this principle proves, on closer examination, to be a specific passion or structure of passions, a veritable "modification of the soul," that must be instilled and made to predominate in the heart of each citizen or subject.[34] In the emerging commercial republic governed by the checks and balances of the separation of powers, the animating force is of an entirely different kind: "all the passions being liberated there, the hatred, the envy, the jealousy, the ardor to enrich and distinguish oneself, would appear in all their full extent: and if it were otherwise, the State would be like a man struck down with illness, who has no passions at all because he has no powers at all."[35] The new kind of commercial society emerging in England and elsewhere is one in which the inhabitants are least coerced, least "modified" in their souls, least artificially "educated": "each individual, always independent, would follow to a great extent his caprices and fantasies."[36] It is from the comparative study of how men are beginning to behave in England, as opposed to the way they have behaved in previous types of society, that we arrive at the true science of human nature.

The primary clue, according to Montesquieu, is the observation that human society, unlike all other animal society, is constituted by laws and conventions and that these laws and conventions are the products of intelligence or reason, of however meager and incomplete a development. Men are not by nature or necessity directed to any one sort of society; they are at most impelled to try to figure out and construct some sort of society. But reason by itself does not do the impelling. Reason by itself moves nothing, not even itself. Reason is set to work in response to desire.[37] But then truly to understand what makes the human being tick, to know man "from the ground up," must we not try to peer down beneath reason and thought, before reason and thought, to see "in the raw" the forces or desires that awaken reflection? Apparently gripped by some such train of thought, Montesquieu is moved to make the very questionable assumption that it is intelligible to speak of human passion apart from or strictly before reason. Accordingly, Montesquieu avoids speaking of passion in the terms employed by Aristotle or the Latin-Aristotelian tradition of his time: Montesquieu does not use the terminology of "inclination" (inclinatio or *orexis*). He talks only of passions whose aims or objects are *not* very clearly given in the nature of the emotions themselves.[38] Such passions, and the behavior they generate, are what Montesquieu means by the "laws of human nature" in the strictest sense of the term.

It follows that the natural laws of human existence are prior to, and must be distinguished from, what may be termed "natural right," or "the relationships of equity anterior to positive law"[39]: for equity, or justice, presupposes some kind of more or less permanent and structured society and some developed intelligence. In contrast, the laws of nature are "thus named, because they derive solely from the constitution of our being," and, "in order to understand well" these laws, "we must consider a human being prior to the establishment of societies," a human being in a "state of nature."[40] "Man, in the state of nature," according to Montesquieu, "would have the capacity to form conceptions, rather than any actual conceptions." (In particular, man would not have "the idea of a creator"; man by nature has no conception of God and a fortiori no conception of obedience or disobedience to God.[41]) "Such a human being," Montesquieu believes, "would feel at first only its weakness; its timidity would be extreme." The strictly necessary core of the human constitution in each of us is a radically unconnected individuality filled with a dim but powerful awareness of its own exposedness.[42] Left strictly to nature or necessity, a human being's first ideas would lead it to "give thought to the preservation of its being." Montesquieu does not unambiguously indicate whether any human beings have ever actually been left for long in the state of nature, but he does refer to the evidence of very primitive forest dwellers, who he evidently thinks are at least much closer to the state of nature than literate men: "If one should have need of experience of this, there have been found wild men in the forest: everything makes them tremble, everything makes them flee."[43]

Foreshadowing Rousseau, Montesquieu rejects the Hobbesian state of nature, with its warlike desires for honor and dominion, as still too rational and sociable to qualify as the fundamental or strictly necessitated human condition and experience. Against Rousseau, and in more basic agreement with Hobbes, Montesquieu teaches that the state of nature is a state of terror and misery. By nature men are at peace, to be sure; but at peace because engulfed in cowering, impotent, impoverished, and isolating fear. Peace, understood as an expression of primordial fear, is the first law of human nature.

Inactive or retiring fear and the peace it brings are the primary law or necessity of human nature; but hunger and the activity it induces are almost equally fundamental: "Thus another natural law would be that which inspires man to look for food."

While man by nature lacks knowledge or conceptions *(des connoissances),* he possesses by nature a capacity to acquire knowledge or form conceptions *(la faculté de connoître).* In the beginning, or in its undisturbed essence, this capacity lies dormant; but men, responding to the spur of accident, "eventually arrive at a condition of having knowledge." The gradual accretion of knowledge changes human behavior. The state of nature, though it has no *telos* or developmental goal, is nonetheless a dynamic or changing condition. By their first natural impulse, men flee one another, prompted by the most powerful necessity, fear. But "the signs of a reciprocal fear move them soon to approach one another." Besides, "they would be carried in this direction by the pleasure that an animal feels at the approach of an animal of its species." Fear is the most powerful and primordial passion, but it is counteracted by another, weaker, but also primordial passion: in natural human relations, a weak natural pleasure (shared with other animal species) qualifies the almost overwhelming natural pain (peculiar, in its intensity, to the human species that is insufficiently equipped with guiding instincts). In addition, "the charm that the two sexes inspire in one another by their difference, would augment this pleasure; and the plea that they always make to one another, would be a third law" of our nature. Montesquieu pointedly refrains from characterizing sexual congress as a social bond. Men and women do not get married by nature, but by contract; fathers do not by nature necessarily know, let alone care for (or, for that matter, avoid as sexual partners), their offspring; and the family, like every society, requires for its stable existence positive law, which alone can "establish" "relations of equity" (for example, incest prohibitions).[44]

Eventually, man's capacity to learn and to adapt his behavior in the light of what he learns allows or compels him to acquire an incipient awareness of the pleasures and advantages that accrue from living in society. There finally appears as a fourth natural law—that is, as the fourth necessary consequence of the primordial human experience and the internal and external developments triggered by that experience—"the *desire* to live in society" (emphasis added). The desire does not, of course, guarantee or necessarily bring into existence the object that would satisfy the desire. After all, men by nature desire not to die—but they all eventually die. Yet men may—and are sooner or later by their passions prompted to—figure out artifices that postpone or even soften the rigors of death. Similarly, although men cannot make themselves into truly or spontaneously social beings (like bees), although they cannot make society natural in the sense of a strict and automatic necessity, they can (and are by their passions "made" to) take some giant steps in such a direction.

Unfortunately, however, the primary outcome of the desire to live in society is destructive: taking humanity out of the pure state of nature, this natural desire plunges our species into "the state of war."[45] Once we lose our overwhelming fear of other men to such an extent that we seek permanent relationships or a life together, our selfish needs for security, pleasure, honor, and material welfare tend to predominate, leading us to try to exploit our fellows or to protect ourselves, by anticipation, from our fellows' attempts to exploit us. The state of war is the elemental condition of human sociability.

Given the fact that men outside the reach of effective coercive government naturally tend toward a state of war, the distinction between the state of nature and the state of war begins to blur on closer inspection. Indeed, for practical purposes it would not seem misleading to identify the state of nature and the state of war.[46] At any rate, after having made very clear the distinction between the two states, in their strictest sense (and after having taken advantage of this distinction to trumpet, in the opening or most visible pages, his disagreement with the unpopular and politically dangerous teaching of Hobbes), Montesquieu, in a late and very unobtrusive chapter, comes around to speaking of the state of war as the "state of nature" or at least the "state of nature, so to speak." A social condition without

right may or should be relaxed. For example, natural right dictates that "an intelligent being, who has done evil to an intelligent being, deserves to receive the same evil."[60] But the strict rule of retaliatory justice, as opposed to various versions of the principle of reciprocity according to which "the punishment must fit the crime," is reasonable only in a despotism or among a primitive, warlike people—and even there requires some mitigation.[61] "A good lawgiver will be concerned less with punishing crimes than with preventing them."[62]

In other words, the science of politics and lawgiving depends on normative principles that extend beyond both the law of nature and the law of the natural light; the real heart of political science is political right, comprising in the first place "general political right, which has for its object that human wisdom that has founded all political societies," and in the second place "particular political right, which concerns each society."[63] Reason in politics must look to the ultimate goal of all civil life, the security of the citizenry, and then adapt that goal to the particular circumstances of each nation. Humanity as we know it in society is the product not merely of human nature, but of habit ingrained by ancient customs invented by fallible human intelligence responding to or trying to deal with vastly different historical and extrahuman, natural environments. Over generations, the general spirit of each nation gives its people a second, quasi-natural stratum of needs or a unique way of expressing and responding to the needs they share with all men. In society, humans have discovered the life of the mind, whose needs, while never divorced from or as urgent as the needs of the body, nonetheless supplement those needs and to some extent qualify or redefine the needs of the human being. The meaning of "security," while its core is unchanging, includes a rich periphery that differs from one people to another. The adaptation and modification of reason's goals and precepts in the light of the "general spirit of each nation" is what Montesquieu means by and intends to teach as the science of "the spirit of the laws."[64]

Nature, or the state of nature, shows us the deepest needs that give all society its fundamental *raison d'être.* Nature provides the standard for evaluating every political system and situation. Nature teaches us that despotism is worst and that a form of government dedicated to liberty understood as security is best. The essence of legitimate law is the rule of reason devised with a view to that security and peace that truly salves the individual's anxiety as much as possible. "Law, in general, is human reason, insofar as it governs all the peoples of the earth; and the political and civil laws of each nation ought to be nothing else but the particular cases which exhibit the application of this human reason." But perspicacious reasoning about the human condition reveals the absence of any strict universal rules or laws of justice beyond the minimal grounding of relations of equity anterior to the positive law that establishes them. Accordingly, Montesquieu goes on at once to add that "they [the particular laws and institutions that exhibit the application of this human reason] ought to be so proper to the people for which they are made, that it is a very rare chance if those of one nation can apply to another."[65] Given the diversity of the human condition, reason does not even provide us with a universally applicable principle of legitimacy like the social compact or the consent of the governed. There are unfortunate places and times when some form of despotism is the best possible form of society; despotism is therefore, in that time and place, the just society by nature and reason. The classic example, for Montesquieu, is China.[66] There are places and times where slavery may be unavoidable if a society is to produce enough food to allow its inhabitants to survive. Indeed, nothing better illustrates Montesquieu's somewhat melancholy rejection of all doctrinairism in politics than his teaching on slavery:

> Since all men are born equal, it is necessary to say that slavery is against nature, although in certain countries it may be founded on reasoning based on nature; and it is necessary to distinguish carefully these countries from those where reasoning based on nature rejects slaves, such as the countries of Europe, where slavery has been so happily abolished. . . . It is necessary, then, to limit slavery by nature to certain particular countries of the earth . . . and yet, perhaps there is no climate on earth where one couldn't rely on the labor of free men.[67]

The Relation between Montesquieu and Locke

While Montesquieu never mentions Locke by name, he begins the *Spirit of the Laws* by acknowledging a debt to unnamed "great men, in France, England, and Germany."[68] In decisive respects, the *Spirit of the Laws* pays silent tribute to Locke, if only by way of correction of a worthy predecessor. The two thinkers lay down almost identical foundations—the state of nature and the consequent identification of the end of government as individual liberty, understood as individual security. Both thinkers oppose Hobbes in strongly criticizing absolute monarchy and endorsing instead a government whose internal checks and balances would protect individuals from government oppression. Both advocate a way of life in which commerce and economic growth are at the very center of attention. The links of kinship are deep and manifest and yet, precisely on the basis of these links, one cannot help but be impressed by the remarkable secondary differences between the two thinkers in terms of the emphasis, tenor, and even substance of their teachings. In one of his minor educational writings (written in 1703 and published posthumously in 1720) Locke draws a fundamental distinction that may help us better understand the differences between his and Montesquieu's published writings: "politics contains two parts very different the one from the other, the one containing the original of societies and the rise and extent of political power, the other, the art of governing men in society."[69] Locke goes on to state that his own *Two Treatises of Government* deals with the first, but not the second, of these two great focuses of political theory. This characterization accords with an explicit indication given in the text of the *Second Treatise:* the one reference Locke makes to "the great art of government" is followed by an emphatic indication that this is a digression from his theme in the *Two Treatises.*[70] Montesquieu, one is tempted to say, decided to devote his efforts to an elaboration of that "great art of government" that Locke had left barely adumbrated. Still, it will not quite do to say that Montesquieu simply completes the unfinished work of Locke. By the difference in his choice of focus, Montesquieu indicates a difference in his understanding of the relation of theory and practice, or a difference in his understanding of how reason may best serve as a guide for political life. Montesquieu's teaching on the character of the norms nature provides and on the circumspection with which reason must apply those norms might well appear to be an attempt to correct the excessive universalism or doctrinairism of his great modern predecessors—above all John Locke. No one appreciated this aspect of Montesquieu's teaching more profoundly than Rousseau: "freedom, not being a fruit of every climate, is not accessible to all peoples. The more one ponders this principle established by Montesquieu, the more one senses its truth. The more it is contested, the more opportunities there are to establish it by new proofs."[71]

While Montesquieu speaks of a natural right to defense, he does not speak, except by implication, of a natural right to private property. While he shows that the family is a product of convention, he does not teach that patriarchy is contrary to natural right; he therefore does not explicitly deny the moral foundation of the traditional family, the place it assigns women, and the inheritance laws (especially primogeniture) on which it depends.[72] While Montesquieu applauds representative institutions, he does not trace all legitimate government to the consent of the governed and he never mentions the social compact. Accordingly, Montesquieu never declares that the principle of "no taxation without representation" is an unqualified and absolute law of nature.[73] Above all, Montesquieu does not teach that the majority has a right to commence a "revolution" with the aim of violently overthrowing duly constituted authority if and when that authority evinces a settled design to impose taxes without the consent of the people.[74] At the root of what we may call Montesquieu's conservatism is to be discerned the sort of reservation that was made more explicit by Hume. Montesquieu doubts whether the philosophic emphasis on the "rights" and consent of the individual as the sole basis for political authority will allow government to retain the reverence it must command if it is to demand—as from time to time it must—true devotion and sacrifice on the part of the individual for the sake of the common good.

Some of the American founders, and certainly the authors of *The Federalist* (in contrast to Jefferson), were alive to this difficulty.[75] Yet the founders were revolutionaries: the teachings of Montesquieu and, all the more, of Hume, remained in their eyes too cautious or undemocratic. Few went as far as Jefferson, who excoriated Hume and actively promoted the publication and circulation of Destutt de Tracy's attack on Montesquieu.[76] But *The Federalist* does speak emphatically of the "Social Compact"; it declares in no uncertain terms that "the people are the only legitimate fountain of power."[77] In his speeches during the ratification debates, James Wilson stressed that "the nature and kind of that government, which has been proposed for the United States, by the late convention [is] in its principle purely democratical." Underlying this Constitution is "the revolution principle" of "Mr. Locke": the new Constitution will establish the first government in history grounded unambiguously on the true principles of natural right, and "the great and penetrating mind of Locke seems to be the only one that pointed towards even the theory of this great truth."[78] If we are to appreciate the full reach of the basic moral principles to which the American founders explicitly appealed, we must move on from the conservatism of Montesquieu to the radicalism of Locke.

Locke's Peculiar Presentation of His Philosophy

To gain access to the heart of John Locke's political theory, we must begin by paying attention to and trying to grasp the reasons behind his strange manner of writing. Few philosophers have presented their doctrines in as dialectical or polemical a manner as Locke. The *Essay Concerning Human Understanding* grows out of an attack on "an established opinion amongst some men, That there are in the Understanding certain *innate Principles*."[79] The *Two Treatises of Government* is a work devoted in large part to a textual interpretation of and an assault on the writings of the political theorist Robert Filmer. Yet while Locke's combative stance and tone is unmistakable, he makes it difficult for the reader to discern the full reasons why he regards it as so important to undertake the attacks he mounts. That this obscurity is part of a deliberate rhetorical strategy becomes apparent once one peruses Locke's works with a view to discovering his theory of communication. Locke speaks repeatedly and emphatically of the need reformers and innovators have to hide the full thrust of their teachings in order to avoid persecution for themselves and their followers and to conciliate and attract the mass of readers, who, always enslaved to the reigning moral and religious authorities, are willing to entertain new moral and religious ideas only if they are dressed in the garb of the old and familiar.[80] Locke certainly follows his own advice in this respect. He writes in such a way as to make it extremely difficult for anyone to find unambiguous textual evidence that might form the basis for accusations of departure from traditional piety and moralism. Yet he also allows and prompts readers who share his sense of the need, excitement, and danger of independent moral thinking to join him in a voyage through previously uncharted intellectual seas.

Thus a careful reading of the opening chapters of the *Essay Concerning Human Understanding* leads one to see that the attack on innate ideas is in fact aimed principally at the notion of the conscience and hence constitutes a tacit destruction of the cornerstone of all traditional notions of natural law. The true purport of the attack on Filmer in the *Two Treatises of Government* is somewhat more difficult to decipher. Indeed, for many readers, the puzzle is never really confronted. Locke is clever enough to allow his readers to view only the positive superstructure of his political theory, while avoiding the laborious and difficult task of examining the deep dialectical or polemical foundations. Locke achieves this feat by dividing his chief work of political theory into two treatises or "books," the first of which supplies much of the foundation and the second of which builds on or presupposes what has been established in the first. The reader may discover at least the public face of most of Locke's politically most significant conclusions by reading only the second book or treatise. But, as Locke stresses in the preface, the two treatises taken together constitute "the beginning and End of a Discourse." Locke further notes in the preface that he has omitted publishing the middle or central portion of the discourse. The full message of each treatise becomes intelligible only if the reader studies the two treatises in constant conjunction and takes it on himself to supply the missing center, or the crucial reasoning that ties the whole together.

To such a reader it eventually becomes apparent that Locke's attack on Filmer is the inlet to and the covering excuse for a much broader attack on both the classical and the orthodox Biblical conceptions of the human condition. Filmer had based his argument for the divine right of kings on a appeal to Holy Scripture and to the patriarchal authority upheld in that Scripture. Locke quickly moves beyond a discussion of the texts of Filmer to a detailed examination of the Holy Scriptures themselves. In the course of that examination, Locke shows what he regards to be the enormous difficulties encountered by any political theory that attempts to take its bearings by the Scriptures alone; if the Bible or revelation are to make any sense, they must be read so as to make them strictly accord with what can be determined by human reason. Locke proceeds to read into the Scriptures a strikingly untraditional, liberal, or individualistic interpretation. He makes it clear that his new reading of the Bible opposes not only Filmer, but the tradition of Christian Aristotelianism most readily available in the great works of Grotius and Hooker. Yet Locke is clever enough to invoke Hooker even as he quietly underlines the extraordinary divergence between his own new teaching on human nature and Hooker's old Christian-Aristotelian teaching. Locke thus encourages the majority of his less thoughtful readers to assimilate his new conception of humanity to the old. He insinuates his corrosive and transformative theory in such a way as to leave standing the shell, if only the shell, of traditional moral and religious discourse. In the very act of destroying the traditions of natural law and Biblical Christianity, Locke establishes himself as the apparent natural law philosopher and as the guide to the interpretation of Scripture, or "the reasonableness of Christianity." To apply to Locke his own words, "like a wary physician, when he would have his patient swallow some harsh or *corrosive Liquor,* he mingles it with a large quantity of that, which may dilute it; that the scattered Parts may go down with less feeling, and cause less Aversion." Locke "chose rather to content himself with doubtful and general terms, which might make no ill sound in Mens Ears, who were willing to be pleas'd with them."[81]

Space does not permit me to restate here the detailed account I have presented elsewhere of Locke's critique of Scripture and of classical philosophy.[82] For present purposes it must suffice to sketch the outcome of Locke's quarrel with tradition—as regards property, human psychology, the family, and finally, government.

The Natural Right to Property

The radically new and anti-Biblical implications of Locke's teaching on property are signaled by Locke's focus, in the *First Treatise* especially, on meat or flesh as the paradigm and root of property: "Property, whose Original is from the Right a Man has to use any of the inferior Creatures for the Subsistence and Comfort of his Life, is for the benefit and sole advantage of the proprietor, so that he may even destroy the thing, that he has Property in by his use of it, when need requires."[83] By stressing that the human right to property is a right rooted in the need to destroy other living things, Locke brings to the fore his understanding of man as so situated in nature that he must, in order to survive or achieve security, not merely appropriate, but radically transform and destroy or negate (consume), what is given in nature or by nature's God.[84] In contrast, the Bible—read on its own terms and prior to its reinterpretation by Locke—attempts to remind man of an original condition in which he was prohibited from eating flesh. As Locke himself points out near the beginning of the *Two Treatises,* Noah and his sons were the first humans given "Liberty to use the Living Creatures for food."[85] During the many centuries prior to the flood man "could not make bold with a Lark or a Rabbit to satisfie his hunger, and had the Herbs but in common with the beasts, as is plain from 1 Gen. 29 and 30." The "propriety" originally given to individuals in the Biblical account was certainly not a property right as Locke understands "property."[86] The dominion given to mankind was a very narrow and scanty sort of property—a bare stewardship of the sort a hired hand has; man was told *"Subdue the Earth,"* but was not permitted to take "a Kid or Lamb out of the Flock, to satisfie his hunger," and hence cannot have been "Proprietor of that Land, or the Cattel on it."[87] The Bible teaches that humans are under the care and tutelage of a beneficent God who alone has true proprietary rights and with whose creation or property men were intended to live in peaceful harmony. Humans do not need to slaughter or destroy in order to survive, and insofar as man does engage in such behavior he acts by the sufferance and indulgence of the only true Owner of things.[88]

In the light of such passages, the Bible was taken as the fountainhead of a way of thinking about property according to which exclusive private ownership was conceived as a form of stewardship—an uneasy compromise between private property rights in the strict sense and an original (and future) divinely intended communism and charitable brotherhood. The compromise became necessary because of the sinful lusts and competitiveness brought on by man's fall from an innocent golden age. The compromise remained provisional and strictly subordinated to the duty of charity and the higher virtue of poverty. This pre-Lockean tradition, one of whose last great representatives was Grotius,[89] invoked as its paradigm the famous analogy employed by the Stoics Seneca and Cicero: possessing something as private property is like occupying one's seat in the public theater; the right to this property we possess is exclusive but only temporarily so; we gain the right not merely by our own efforts, luck, or inheritance but also by the consent of all others who use this vast but ordered natural whole; as owners, we are not ourselves the source of the natural goods we enjoy (though with the help of heaven, we may improve upon them), and we are under a reciprocal obligation to try to pass on the natural goods or their equivalents so that they may be enjoyed and improved on by others; and finally, the number of seats, the number of shares in nature's beneficence, is basically fixed—he who has a seat should not seek to acquire another that he does not need, but, by the same token, the many who have no seats, or who have poor seats, are unlikely ever to improve their lot and should not entertain much hope of doing so.[90]

Locke substitutes the notion of nature's God, a God who makes himself and the proper posture toward his creation known to man by reason alone: "The Law that was to govern *Adam,* was the same that was to govern all his Prosperity, the *Law of Reason.*"[91] And reason as Locke conceives it discovers no purpose for and no limitation on man's appropriation and transformation or destruction of nature except comfortable preservation. Despite his initial acknowledgment of the Bible's surface or explicit teaching, Locke soon shows that he intends to ignore or treat as figurative all the Bible's talk about a paradise, a fall, a curse, a centuries-long prohibition on the eating of flesh, a punitive flood and a subsequent covenant, and the promise or expectation of a messianic age in the future:

> The plain of the case is this. God having made man, and planted in him, as in all other Animals, a strong desire of Self-preservation, and furnished the World with things fit for Food and Rayment and other necessaries of Life, Subservient to his Design, that Man should live and abide for some time upon the Face of the Earth, and not that so curious and wonderful a piece of Workmanship by its own Negligence, or want of Necessaries, should perish again, presently after a few moments continuance: God, I say, having made Man and the World thus, spoke to him (that is) directed him by his Senses and reason . . . to the use of those things which were serviceable for his Subsistence, and given him as a means of his *Preservation.* And therefore I doubt not, but before these words were pronounced, 1 *Gen.* 28, 29 (if they must be understood literally to have been spoken) and without any such Verbal *Donation,* Man had a right to a use of the Creatures, by the Will and Grant of God. . . . And thus Man's *Property* in the Creatures, was founded upon the right

> he had, to make use of those things, that were necessary or useful to his being. This being the reason and Foundation of *Adams Property* gave the same title, on the same ground, to all his children . . . an equal Right to the use of the Inferior Creatures, for the comfortable preservation of their Beings, which is all the *Property* Man hath in them. . . .[92]

Yet Locke never ceases to mute and veil his innovative teaching by weaving into it ambiguous and traditional-sounding formulations. Nowhere is this rhetoric more evident than in the very exposed opening of the *Second Treatise,* where Locke presents his first elaboration of the state of nature. To an even more remarkable extent than in Montesquieu, the state of nature in Locke comes to sight as a state of peace, which in practice is always on the brink of turning into a state of war. The natural condition of human beings is one of "uncontroleable liberty" and "perfect Equality, where naturally there is no superior or jurisdiction."[93] "But though this be a *State of Liberty,* yet it is *not a State of License,*" because it is governed by a law of nature or by "reason, which is that Law," and which dictates peaceful collective preservation rooted in self-preservation.[94] Yet a law must be enforceable: someone must have the "executive power" of judgment and punishment. The god of nature, who is the source of the law of nature, has in practice left its execution entirely in the hands of each and every individual. The "appeal to heaven" is always an appeal to war between men.[95] By natural right, every single human being is vested with full executive authority to judge any and all other humans and to impose punishment, including capital punishment, on any whom he, in his opinion, finds guilty—even where he has suffered no direct personal injury or threat.[96] No wonder Locke immediately refers to "the Inconveniences of the State of Nature, which must certainly be Great, where Men may be Judges in their own case," and concedes that "the State of Nature is therefore not to be endured."[97] The state of nature is "full of fears and continual dangers."[98] In following the steps of Locke's teaching on property and the family we will come to understand better the nature and grounds for the fearful competitiveness and precariousness of the natural condition of men.

The first example of property in the *Second Treatise,* the only important example before chapter 5, is God's property in mankind.[99] As the property and workmanship of God, men are "sent into the world by his order and about his business . . . made to last during his, not one anothers Pleasure"; this is the reason why "no one ought to harm another." In addition, a man has not the right to destroy "so much as any Creature in his possession, but where some nobler use [unspecified] calls for it." The state of nature thus starts off sounding like the meatless antediluvian epoch described in the Bible, if not the age of innocence or the garden of Eden. Certainly this is the passage most frequently cited by all those who would try to find in Locke a conception of the sanctity and dignity of human life rooted in creation and ownership of mankind by the Biblical God. But in fact this passage makes no reference to the Bible or to human dignity: man is as much or more the property of God as are the other animals; and the powerful, wise God who is said to own us is not said to be either good or bountiful.[100] What is more, before the paragraph is finished Locke has begun quietly to disclose the grossly un-Biblical message lying immediately under the Biblical-sounding surface. Just as in Book One, section 86, so here, the only business or design we hear of God or nature having is preservation, above all preservation of individual human beings. (Accordingly, the nobler use to which we may put the animals turns out to be, among other things, breakfast.[101]) The solemn duty God's law of nature imposes is simply to preserve oneself. To be sure, "by the like reason" each of us ought to preserve the rest of mankind. But for the same reason this "ought" is operative for each person only "when his own Preservation comes not in competition"; the law of nature or reason forbids a human being to quit his station and risk his life for another human being.[102] One may be absolutely forbidden by the law of reason to risk one's life for another, but two chapters later we learn that even the duty to preserve oneself is not absolute: when a man enslaved feels life is worse than death, he may "draw on himself the Death he desires."[103] We further learn that human beings can be treated like animals or worse than animals. In the state of nature whenever in my personal opinion I discover persons with designs against anyone's life, the persons I judge guilty "may be treated as Beasts of Prey" or "noxious creatures."[104]

These observations prepare us for the opening of chapter 5 of the *Second Treatise*, the chapter devoted to the elaboration of the doctrine of property. Locke begins by substituting for God's ownership of man the ownership of each individual by himself.[105] Each man, by owning outright and exclusively his own person, owns his own labor, implicitly defined as the rational, destructive, or transformative action a human being takes with regard to external things in order to secure animal flesh and other means of comfortable subsistence.[106] To mix one's labor with anything not already possessed by another is to acquire that thing as exclusively one's own.[107]

Yet the fully individualistic character of the property right and the justification for that individualism in terms of the common good or the collective interest emerges only gradually. Locke proceeds cautiously, partly to mute his innovations but also to lead the thoughtful reader step by step through an argument that demonstrates the compelling need to abandon traditional moralism for the sake of rational clarity or truth. While Locke rejects at the outset the traditional notion that private appropriation depends from the beginning on "explicit consent of every commoner,"[108] he agrees that original appropriation arises as the alteration of a prior community of ownership in the earth among all men and he leaves open the possibility that some sort of tacit consent of at least the other commoners in the vicinity may be required or presupposed.[109] And while he innovates in asserting as unqualifiedly as he does that property rights antedate government, he does not explicitly base his discussion on the state of nature (a term he avoids in chapter 5). Locke's most radical departure from traditional views is the one that goes most easily unnoticed since it is made in silence: his thematic discussion of property ignores the duty of charity and the qualification of absolute proprietary right that such a duty had traditionally implied.[110] Nonetheless, even in this respect Locke seems to retain a link to traditional views insofar as he contends that labor can give a man title in what was originally common only "where there is enough, and as good left in common for others."[111]

In Book Two, section 31, Locke anticipates an objection, the response to which compels him to begin to lay bare the crucial consequences of his premises. The objector insists that Locke's doctrine imposes no effective, intrinsic restrictions on acquisitiveness. Locke replies, not that avarice and unrestricted acquisition are intrinsically sinful or base or evil, but rather that such behavior is imprudent and is therefore against natural law or "reason, which is that law." The most obvious reason unlimited laborious acquisition is irrational is spoilage: the only reasonable purpose of property is its enjoyment or advantage for the owner; each individual therefore has a right to acquire, through labor, "as much as anyone can make use of to any advantage of life before it spoils." But "whatever is beyond this, is more than his share." The deeper and more decisive reason appears when we hearken to the "Voice of Reason confirmed by Inspiration": "*God has given us all things richly,* 1 Tim. vi. 17." As long as we have faith in the description of the human condition given in the New Testament, we may rest confident that the "plenty of Natural provisions" found in God's nature makes it unnecessary for us to worry and sweat over material possessions.

Locke, however, presents this response only in order to lay out the naive or irrational and irresponsible view whose fabric he intends to unravel. Locke's first step in this unraveling is to point out that what is to be justifed is not merely the appropriation of fruit, venison, and water, but the enclosure and exclusive use of land "as that which takes in and carries with it all the rest" and is the "chief matter of property."[112] Such a radical transformation of the originally common land is justified by reflection on the penury of the human condition. Until man has labored long and hard on it, the earth is not bountiful or even fruitful. Human labor as the original title to ownership can by no means be understood as the mere appropriation of nature's bounty. To labor on the earth is to subdue the earth—to master and dominate it by wrenching it from its spontaneous or natural and inhumanly inhospitable course.[113] Now reasonable men will not undertake such painful labor unless they are confident they will be the ones to enjoy its fruits. One must therefore severely qualify the notion that "God gave the World to Men in Common"[114]: the God whose voice is the voice of reason cannot be supposed to have meant it should always remain common, and therefore waste. But this means it was never really given to all indiscriminately but only to some—"to the use of the Industrious and Rational, (and *Labour* was to be *his Title* to it;) not to the Fancy or Covetousness of the Quarrelsome and Contentious." The former was under no obligation whatsoever to ask or gain the consent, express or implicit, of the latter, even if the latter was in the vicinity or stretched out in stupid and nasty idleness on top of the land in question. As for the other industrious and rational folks, since there was in the beginning plenty of land left over after each appropriation, they needed not complain.

At this point, Locke implicitly raises a new objection to the drift of his argument. He reminds us of what is in fact the status of landed property "in England, or any other Country, where there is Plenty of People under Government, who have Money and Commerce"[115]: there is no more free land, because at some point enclosure continued beyond the point where there was "as good left" for others. "In the beginning," the voice of reason or of nature's God declares, "it was quite otherwise. The Law Man was under, was rather for *appropriating*." Locke compels the attentive reader to wonder what this implies about the legitimacy of the law men are under in England, or "any other Country" like it. Has the positive law not drifted into violation of the original natural law?

This is the impression Locke gives at first, as he launches into a praise of "the first Ages of the World" as described in the Bible, beginning with "the Children of *Adam*, or *Noah*," and extending through the age of the Patriarchs Abraham, Lot and Esau.[116] During those many centuries men lived within "the measure of Property, Nature has well set." And "this measure did confine every Man's

Possession, to very moderate Proportion, and such as he might appropriate to himself, without Injury to any Body." What destroyed this "Golden Age," as Locke later calls it?[117] "The *Invention of Money* and the tacit Agreement of Men to put a value on it." Once desire "had *agreed, that a little piece of Yellow Metal,* which would keep without wasting or decay, should be worth a great piece of Flesh," mankind had the power to circumvent nature's spoilage limitation on acquisition (and slaughter). But why should mankind so comfortably situated fall prey to such foolishness, to "the desire of having more than Man needed," to "the temptation to labour for more than [a man] could make use of"?[118]

Traditional Christianity answers that the whole system of private property based on money and commerce is a painful and dangerous, if to some extent necessary, compromise with the effects of original sin.[119] Locke allows those readers who are pious, careless, or both to assimilate his account to their outlook. If his account is examined with any close scrutiny, however, it becomes clear that Locke rejects the notion of original sin.[120] In Locke's account, "the Children of *Adam,* or *Noah*" are described as being uncorrupted by original sin, partaking of the "unforeseeing Innocence of the first Ages," the "Innocence and Sincerity of that poor but vertuous age" before vices "had corrupted Mens minds."[121] Once one reads the Biblical account according to this "reasonable" interpretation, one is compelled to wonder whether the invention of money really marked such a sinful and unnatural break in man's history or whether the invention was not rather a leap forward in a progressive social evolution that responded to pressing natural needs. If the latter, then is not every unavoidable step in that progressive process, including the stage now reached in England and countries like it, justified by "Reason, which is the Law of Nature"?

In the midst of his paean to the first Ages of the World, Locke parenthetically notes that nowadays in Spain, where land is in some areas as unenclosed as it was in the beginning, "the Inhabitants think themselves beholden to him, who by his Industry on neglected, and consequently waste land, has increased the stock of Corn, which they wanted."[122] In the very next section Locke asks leave "to add, that he who appropriates land to himself by his labour, does not lessen but increase the common stock of mankind. For the provisions serving to the support of humane life, produced by one acre of enclosed and cultivated land are (to speak much within compasse) ten times more," nay (Locke soon adds), a hundred times more than those produced by "Land, of an equal richness, lyeing waste in common." The truth about nature's so-called plenty comes within our grasp only if we read the Biblical narrative in the light of what we know about "the several

Nations of the *Americas*"—those "needy and wretched" folk who are now still living in the condition of early man. They "are rich in Land, and poor in all the Comforts of Life . . . Nature having furnished [them] as liberally as any other people, with the materials of Plenty, i.e., fruitful Soil."[123] When we look more closely into the sources of the difference between their poverty and our "ordinary provisions," we begin to comprehend "how much *labour makes the far greatest part of the value* of things, we enjoy in this World: And the ground which produces the materials is scarce to be reckon'd in"; "Nature and the Earth furnish only the almost worthless Materials, as in themselves."[124] Contradicting what he first seemed to say, Locke now affirms that so long as "Men, at first, for the most part, contented themselves with what un-assisted Nature Offered" and, in particular, so long as men lived or live in an environment where there is not sufficient incentive to enclose and secure for private gain all arable land, the human beings so situated are in a parlous state.[125]

From all this we recognize "how much numbers of men are to be preferd to largenesse of dominions."[126] But the "Increase of People and Stock" goes "with the *Use of Money.*"[127] By the time Locke is ready to discuss in detail the nature and origin of money, he has already stripped away every rational ground for the opprobrium associated with lucre and the love of lucre. Prior to the invention of money, men had no "hopes of commerce with other Parts of the World" and therefore no incentive to enclose more land than they and their families needed in the short run.[128] This means they had no way to ensure survival, let alone comfort, in the long run: "Thus in the beginning," the voice of nature's God teaches, "all the World was America, and more so than that is now; for no such thing as *Money* was any where known."[129]

By tacitly agreeing to money and thus commerce, men "have agreed to disproportionate and unequal Possession of the Earth."[130] As the division of labor proceeds, mankind tends more and more to become organized in hierarchies of increasingly mobile, competitive individuals who trade not only their products but their labor power. As a consequence, the few most rational and industrious tend to come to the top and become far wealthier than the majority. By his repeated references to masters and servants, Locke makes it plain that he is presenting a justification of the system of contractual wage labor, among other things.[131]

Against the later Marxist criticism, Locke is confident that this system, whose spirit he tries to clarify and intensify, improves vastly the lot of even the lowliest worker. For in America a "King of a large fruitful Territory there feeds, lodges, and is clad worse than a day

Labourer in England."[132] So when the general run of men agree to money and all it entails they are not swindled. Land that is not yet enclosed is owned by all but good for none: it is, as Locke repeatedly says, *waste*.[133] The original prohibition on appropriating where there is not "as good left over" simply ceases to apply once money enters the picture, because every enclosure has the potential to increase the good for everyone if it is in the main carried out by the rational and industrious—that is, the reasonably and energetically greedy rather than the covetous and lazy. This requires that the rational and industrious be protected from the covetous, that they be given the freedom and security to pursue a reward proportionate to their efforts. What Locke means by "the protection of property" as the *chief* end of government is not just the protection of the present holdings and holders of property, but also the protection and encouragement of nonholders who have the energy to acquire and improve property.[134] Locke's conception of rational man is not so much a conception of man as a possessive, but rather as an acquisitive and productive individual.[135]

The constant goal of a society suffused with the Lockean spirit is to increase the productivity of human labor without limit by extending to more and more individuals the promise of unlimited accumulation of exchangeable value in direct proportion to their industry, frugality, and rationality. In this way, the Lockean spirit promotes justice in two fundamental senses (and brings those two often competing senses into concord): the common good, or at least the good of almost all industrious and rational men, is advanced through the "increase of the common stock of mankind"; fairness, or distributive justice, is furthered by bestowing on "every Man a Title to the product of his honest Industry," measured in money or exchange value.[136]

As Locke indicates in his recounting of the division of labor in section 43, and even more explicitly in section 44, the labor by which man "subdues" the earth and liberates himself from nature's bondage is only initially the sweaty toil of physical labor; more important are invention and the arts, including the arts by which men learn to organize the collective labor of other men. Locke's insistence on the exponential increase in value brought by labor should be taken together with his insistence in the *First Treatise* on the exponential increase brought about by the cultivation of the sciences.[137]

One could receive the impression that the most important role played by politics in the Lockean system is a preliminary one: protecting the market by maintaining peace and order and liberating market forces from the constraints of old-fashioned institutions and customs. Once the free market is in operation it governs itself, to a considerable extent, by quasi-autonomous "laws of value"[138]—the full discovery and elaboration of which is left to Locke's successors. Unlike some of the more narrow and dogmatic of those successors, however, Locke in his political economy evinces an acute awareness of the need for governmental regulation including, in some cases, governmental ownership.[139] Locke advocates charity, in the common sense of the term, when he talks about *government* action: "common charity teaches, that those should be most taken care of by the Law, who are least capable of taking care for themselves."[140] It is *government* that must, by established laws of liberty, "secure protection and encouragement to the honest industry of Mankind against the oppression of power and narrownesse of Party."[141]

Yet in chapter 5, Locke abstracts not only from the art of governing but even from the discussion of the need for government. By temporarily downplaying the political, Locke makes it clear that property has neither its source nor its purpose in politics (though it depends on politics for protection and regulation). Lockean property does not exist in order to provide the equipment with which man as the political animal may pursue fulfillment in civic life and noble leisure.[142] Lockean politics emerges secondarily as a means to the preservation of sound economic activity: "Government has no other end but the preservation of Property."[143]

Even in chapter 5, however, Locke leaves clear hints that the evolution of property and commerce proceeds under constant threat of strife and therefore requires some sort of government from the very beginning.[144] The same penury that makes productive labor and commercial competition reasonable will often make cunning or violent exploitation seem—even be—reasonable for many. From this we must not rush to conclude, however, that all conflict springs from material scarcity and laziness or stupidity—and hence that sound economic policy is sufficient remedy for all fundamental social problems.[145]

Human Psychology and the Pursuit of Happiness

Locke presents most clearly the underlying psychological basis for his doctrine of human nature and the moral law deduced from that nature in the *Essay Concerning Human Understanding*. His starting point is a severe denial that man possesses any innate or self-evident moral rule or law, not even "that most unshaken Rule of Morality, and Foundation of all social Virtue, *That one should do as he would be done unto.*" Against the traditional natural law doctrine espoused by Thomas Aquinas and Richard Hooker, which identified the conscience as the source of humanity's innate sense of right and wrong, Locke argues that "conscience . . . is nothing else, but our own Opinion" and any "who have been but moderately conversant in the History of Mankind, and look'd abroad beyond the Smoak of their own Chimneys" must admit that "some men, with the same bent of conscience, prosecute what others avoid": "View but an Army at the sacking of a Town, and see . . . what touch of Conscience, for all the Outrages they do."[146] "The breaking of a rule, say you, is no Argument, that it is unknown. I grant it: But the *generally allowed break of it anywhere,* I say, *is a Proof, that it is not innate.*"[147] Locke appeals to the extraordinary diversity of human moral beliefs to demonstrate that if we "look abroad, to take a view of Men, as they are, we shall find, that they have remorse in one Place, for doing or omitting that, which others, in another Place, think they merit by."[148]

It is decisive, in Locke's eyes, that men can always, without absurdity, ask the reason for any moral rule or duty (which is not the case with truly self-evident principles such as that of contradiction or the axioms of arithmetic): *"there cannot any one moral Rule be propos'd, whereof a Man may not justly demand a Reason."*[149] This shows that "the truth of all these moral Rules, plainly depends upon some other antecedent to them, and from which they must be deduced, which could not be, if either they were innate, or so much as self-evident."[150] The rules that constitute morality come to sight as somehow derivative from some more fundamental imperative. That imperative is HAPPINESS. "Power and riches, nay Vertue it self, are valued only as Conducing to our Happiness."[151] According to Locke it is self-evident that all men have by nature an innate and all-consuming drive to be happy. "Mankind . . . are and must be allowed to pursue their happiness, nay, cannot be hindered."[152] Men are "constant in pursuit of happiness"; it is "happiness and that alone" that moves desire.[153] And "hence naturally flows the great variety of Opinions, concerning Moral rules, which are to be found amongst men, according to the different sorts of Happiness, they have a Prospect of, or propose to themselves."[154]

Mankind agrees, in a general or formal way, as to what happiness means. Happiness "in its full extent is the utmost Pleasure we are capable of."[155] In fact, "things are Good or Evil, only in reference to Pleasure or Pain." But while humans can agree on the supreme goodness of pleasure, they cannot agree on which specific modes of pleasure are most intense or greatest. Indeed, "even what they themselves have enjoyed with great pleasure and delight at one time, has proved insipid or nauseous at another."[156] From this follows the mortal failing of classical political philosophy: "The mind has a different relish, as well as the Palate; and you will as fruitlessly endeavor to delight all men with Riches or Glory . . . as you would to satisfy all Men's Hunger with Cheese or Lobsters . . . hence it was, I think, that the Philosophers of old did in vain enquire, whether *Summum Bonum* consisted in Riches, or bodily Delights, or Virtue, or Contemplation . . ."[157]

The problem of finding some kind of common, objective ground for human evaluation consists not only in the diversity, mutability, and contradictory character of human tastes or pleasures. The unhappy fact is, human beings have strong proclivities that lead them to find pleasure in what gives pain to others. These proclivities are revealed most nakedly in the behavior of very small children. In them one discovers that the primordial natural root of the desire for property itself is not physical or economic need but a desire for power and dominion over others:

> I told you before that Children love *Liberty* . . . I now tell you, they love something more; and that is *Dominion:* And this is the first Original of most vicious Habits, that are ordinary and natural. This love of *Power* and Dominion shews it self very early, and that in these Two Things. We see Children as soon almost as they are born (I am sure long before they can speak) cry, grow peevish, sullen, and out of humour, for nothing but to have their *Wills.* They would have their Desires submitted to by others. . . . Another thing wherein they shew their love of Dominion, is their desire to have things to be theirs; they would have *Propriety* and Possession, pleasing themselves with the Power which that seems to give . . . these two Roots of almost all the Injustice and Contention, that so disturb Humane Life . . . Covetousness, and the Desire of having in our Possession, and under our Dominion, more than we have need of, being the Root of all Evil . . . we are all, even from our Cradles, vain and proud Creatures. . . .[158]

Locke does not deny that humanity has discernible innate practical principles of a kind:

> Nature, I confess, has put into Man a desire of Happiness, and an aversion to Misery: These indeed are innate Practical Principles, which (as practical Principles ought) do continue constantly to operate . . . I deny not, that there are natural tendencies imprinted on the Minds of Men . . . Principles of Action indeed there are lodged in Men's Appetites, but these are so far from being innate Moral Principles, that if they were left to their full swing, they would carry Men to the over-turning of all Morality. Moral Laws are set as a curb and

> restraint to these exorbitant Desires, which they cannot be but by Rewards and Punishments . . . *Robberies, Murders, Rapes,* are the Sports of Men set at Liberty from Punishment and Censure.[159]

Locke reproduces on the level of psychology, or internal nature, the teaching about man's relation to nature that he elaborated as regards external nature, in his discussion of property. He shows "Man's Power and its way of Operation to be muchwhat the same in the Material and Intellectual World."[160] Nature or nature's God gives man only the almost worthless materials, out of which he must construct for himself a rational psychological order and objective rules of social behavior.[161] The law of nature as Locke understands it is a law of reason in the sense that it is constructed, not merely discovered, by reason. Like his successor Montesquieu, Locke understands morality or natural law to have something resembling the ontological status of the principles of geometry.[162] Reason, or natural light, uses its creative powers of abstraction and combination to devise objective, permanently valid normative principles that allow mankind to subdue and control the chaos of the passions into which humanity is plunged by inhospitable nature and that nature's uncharitable God. Yet even more than in the case of geometry, mankind's realization of its true situation and its devising of the intellectual tools that allow it to master that situation have been agonizingly slow. Reason and its normative code must combat not only the chaos of nature but the intensification of that chaos by the historical creation of mad, foolish, and self-destructive conventions and myths:

> The busie mind of Man [can] carry him to a Brutality below the level of Beasts, when he quits his reason, which places him almost equal to Angels. Nor can it be otherwise in a Creature, whose thoughts are more than the sands, and wider than the ocean, where fancy and passion must needs run him into strange courses, if reason, which is his only Star and compass, be not that he steers by. The imagination is always restless and suggests variety of thoughts, and the will, reason being laid aside, is ready for every extravagant project; and in this State, he that goes farthest out of the way, is thought fittest to lead, and is sure of most followers: And when Fashion hath once Established, what Folly or craft began, Custom makes it Sacred, and 'twill be thought impudence or madness, to contradict or question it. He that will impartially survey the Nations of the World, will find so much of their Governments, Religions, and Manners brought in and continued amongst them by these means,

> that he will have but little Reverence for the Practices which are in use and credit amongst Men. . . .[163]

In order to comprehend reason's "geometry" of morals, we must first liberate ourselves from the attempt, associated with classical philosophy, to orient ourselves by a fulfillment, completion, or "highest good" that nature or God is supposed to reveal. We must recognize the disconcerting but ultimately saving truth: what *"determines the Will in regard to our Actions"*

> is not, as is generally supposed, the greater good in view: But some (and for the most part the most pressing) *uneasiness* . . . we constantly desire happiness; and whatever we feel of *uneasiness,* so much, 'tis certain, we want of happiness . . . even in *joy* itself, that what keeps up the action, is the desire to continue it, and fear to lose it . . . as long as any *uneasiness,* any desire remains in our Mind, there is no room for *good,* barely as such, to come at the *Will,* or at all to determine it . . . till every *uneasiness* we feel be perfectly removed: which in the multitude of wants, and desires, we are beset with in this imperfect State, we are not like to be ever freed from in this World. . . . Desire is always moved by Evil, to fly it.[164]

Locke does not reduce the meaning and experience of pleasure to the removal of pain but he does insist that the strong allure of future or even present pleasure is due to the pain or uneasiness caused by its absence or conceivable loss. Even when we are absorbed in present pleasure, the intervention of pain or anxiety easily dispels the absorption and overwhelms the pleasure: "we have so great an abhorrence of Pain, that a little of it extinguishes all our Pleasures . . . our whole Endeavors and thoughts are intent, to get rid of the present Evil, before all things."[165] To the extent that human beings grasp and accept these truths of human psychology, their understanding of pleasure—of true joy—comes into sharper focus. What most comforts us as rational beings, what we most desire, is not the temporary forgetfulness brought about by consuming present pleasure; more solid and satisfying is the prospective consciousness of our power over and possession of things that we can deploy at some unspecified time in the future, whenever we might decide to produce pleasure or diminish pain. "*Joy* is a delight of the Mind, from the consideration of the present or assured approaching possession of a Good; and we are then possessed of any Good, when we have it so in our power, that we can use it when we please."[166] From this we begin to understand better why the practically limitless drive for power—hence property, dominion, prestige, and triumph—is so natural to man. From this we can also begin to discern the path reason can construct to lead us out of nature's state of conflict among passions and individuals.

Locke's reflections on the "careful and constant pursuit of true and solid happiness . . . the care of ourselves, so that we mistake not imaginary for real happiness"[167] lead to the awareness that the positive pole of life—pleasure—is far less arresting, less important, less endowed with independent and stable reality than the negative pole: pain, uneasiness, anxiety. For this, we can be grateful. Because while men cannot agree on any fixed positive goals of life (any greatest pleasures, or least uneasiness), our species can agree, especially as it becomes more reasonable and self-conscious, on what is most important, most gripping, the greatest evil we all seek to avoid or postpone.

The most unremitting and powerful uneasiness for human beings is the fear of death and of the physical suffering that attends or intimates death. Human beings share with "all other animals" a "strong desire of Self-preservation."[168] But in man the desire for preservation is guided by imagination and reason rather than instinct; as a result, man possesses a true self or personal identity constituted by his coherent consciousness of individual existence over time.[169] The distinctly human desire for the continuation of the self as the cockpit of personal existence is in man the strongest desire.[170] The desire for preservation is not only "planted" in men, as it is in the other animals; it is a natural inclination, "wrought into the very Principles of their Nature."[171] To begin with, the full strength of this inclination is somewhat shrouded in most men. Preservation needs the assistance of reason to become the explicit core of the natural inclination to the pursuit of happiness. But it is never entirely unilluminated by reason; it is always endowed with foresight: the human desire to survive is a desire for "comfortable Preservation," for "the comfortable Provision for this Life"; it is the desire not merely to subsist but "to subsist and enjoy the conveniences of life."[172] Man's desire for self-preservation directly entails the desire for property and protection of the opportunity to acquire and increase property. Finally (and especially after money and large property accumulation enter the picture), man, in his desire for preservation, can readily see that he needs the aid of other, similarly insecure and farsighted men: the rational desire for comfortable self-preservation conjoins all men, or all men insofar as they are rational, into "one Community of Nature," "one Society distinct from all other Creatures."[173]

A human being belongs to this community inasmuch as he makes it manifest to other human beings that he regards his strong desire for comfortable preservation (property) as something more than a mere personal desire: that is to say, inasmuch as he uses his powers of abstraction and combination of ideas to express his desire in terms of natural right. A "natural right," in Locke's most fundamental sense, is a claim that expresses a desire or need that is so deeply planted in individuals, so overwhelming, that they cannot but demand or claim the freedom to satisfy it. To express my desire as a natural right is to express publicly a solemn calculation that arises from my clear perception of this state of things: it is to express first, a claim that I be allowed to pursue the satisfaction of my desire as much as possible; second, a concomitant promise or commitment (or "duty") to grant the same prerogative to the same desire in all others (who respond to my claim in a congruent fashion); and third, a promise, on the basis of some further additional calculation, to assist other rational men as much as possible in our mutual defense against those who refuse to recognize our natural rights. All animals have strong natural desires; only a rational animal who recognizes his and others' lack of clear instinctual or natural restraints can express or make known certain of his desires as natural rights. By the same token, whenever anyone threatens any innocent person in a way that manifests ignorance or disregard of this fundamental equality as regards the right to self-preservation, he is to be treated by any and all others as a wild, clever, and therefore very dangerous animal, to be destroyed (if necessary) in order to safeguard the rest. For when a man quits rational calculation, he lays aside the "common Rule and Measure, God hath given to Mankind . . . and therefore may be destroyed as . . . one of those wild Savage Beasts, with whom Men can have *no Society*."[174]

Thus we see that the self-preservative drive is expressed by reason primarily as a right; but that there follows immediately from this expression of right a duty, a law of nature, the right or duty of whose execution is vested in every rational human *"by the Fundamental Law of Nature, Man being to be preserved, as much as possible."*[175] This is the fundamental principle on which reason erects its normative code: "The preservation of all Mankind," Locke avers, is "the true Principle to regulate our Religion, Politicks, and Morality by."[176]

Yet while rational preservation, as the highest principle and strongest desire, regulates all other desires and principles, it does not extinguish the other components in the pursuit of happiness. Even the most rational human beings continue to have distinct tastes or continue to be moved differently by different sorts of uneasiness. Lockean natural law and the community founded on that law does not for a moment mean to ignore or extinguish this individuality and diversity. On the contrary, the Lockean community is self-consciously a community of individuals pursuing their diverse individual goals in legal and rational harmony. Yet the commitment to that harmony and the principles on which it depends cannot help but affect the substantive goals or tastes of the members. Locke does not aim at a society that would cultivate limitless diversity.

The substantive standards of the Lockean community become clearer when we take note of the enormous importance of education, or of what we might call "socialization," in the Lockean vision of a free society. Locke's psychological doctrine implies that there is by no means an automatic or necessary harmony between the pursuit of happiness, which characterizes all human beings without exception, and natural law, which defines the rational pursuit of happiness. The imagination and the passions must be brought into a created order—they must be checked, harnessed, and structured by conventional habits, laws, institutions, and beliefs that embody and enforce the specific rational rules which make up the code of the natural law. The most essential of these rules define the systems of behavior by which man can best minimize his greatest natural uneasiness. The code starts from such rules as "one should do as he would be done unto." "Men should keep their Compacts," "Parents preserve and cherish your Children"; it leads to such rules as "there must be property if there is to be justice," "no taxation without representation."[177] It follows that childhood education—meaning the formation or construction of moral character—takes on a new and awesome significance. Locke is the first great philosopher to devote an entire treatise to education, focusing on the moral education of very young children.[178] Precisely because the human mind has no natural order, it possesses, at least when young, a malleable openness to being brought into order by human manipulation. As Locke says at the commencement of his educational treatise, "I imagine the minds of children as easily turned this way or that way, as Water it self." Or, as he says at the conclusion, the child he has had in view he has "considered only as white Paper, or Wax, to be moulded and fashioned as one pleases." Through the shaping of the sentiments and feelings of its "dear little Ones" mankind can shape itself and its future to a degree undreamed of by the Christians, with their doctrine of original sin, or by the classical philosophers, with their belief in a natural order of the soul: "You cannot imagine of what Force Custom is"; "Custom" is "a greater power than Nature," for "white Paper receives any Characters."[179]

The self-conscious goal of the new education must be to instill in the mind of the child the "power" to "master," "subdue," and "deny" its natural inclinations, its "Natural wrong inclinations."[180] The principal spring of the psychological power that conquers nature is shame, "the only true restraint belonging to Virtue."[181] Shame is "the true principle" or the "great Secret of Education."[182]

To grasp the full import of Locke's stress on the educative function of shame, we need to pursue further his account of child psychology. Locke finds at the primordial core of the human passions not only a desire for the pleasures that accompany the satisfaction of our appetites and an aversion to the pains that signal the frustration of those appetites, but in addition, a spontaneous love of liberty and free activity. This "spirit," as Locke calls it, is a spur to industry in the pursuit of objects of desire and the avoidance of objects of aversion, but it also has an independent and original status. It manifests itself in resistance to all restraints, in delight in variety, and, above all, in joy in mastering or believing ourselves to master our environment. We have already taken note of the warlike and dangerous natural bent of human spiritedness; but Locke insists that, if properly directed and channeled from a very early age, this psychological spring can become the strongest support for sociable reasonableness. The desire for power and dominion can easily be shaped into a desire for prestige and recognition. This desire entails a sense of shame that can be worked on in little children to convert the raw love of triumph into a reasonable love of reputation, especially reputation for reasonableness and hence for true or rational freedom and dignity.[183]

In a teaching that brought forth Rousseau's respectful but far-reaching protest, Locke contends that the child's radical dependence on the opinion of others liberates, rather than enslaves, the child. For it is only by way of shame, vanity, or *amour propre* that a child can be reliably brought along the path toward rational self-control over an innately savage and even self-destructive human nature. Locke has no sooner brought home the importance of instilling the capacity to deny and master the natural inclinations than he hastens to correct what he fears may be a false impression: education must not "humble" the mind of the child; it must not abuse the child's spirits. An education based on shame, properly managed, should socialize or rationalize, but certainly not repress, the child's spirited sense of independence; such an education should make the child see its power and liberty as expressed in respect for, and rooted in respect from, other similarly "independent" men.[184]

Once we have Locke's new conception of education in view, we are in a position to appreciate how much depends on what happens to children in their first years and how much depends on the relations of parents to one another and to their children within a family life that should take early child-rearing far more seriously than has been the case in most traditional upper classes.[185] This in turn means that education will proceed according to reason only insofar as the human family is organized on rational principles that compel mothers and fathers to take a keen interest in the early education of the "dear little ones"; and the organization of the family is, to say the least, deeply affected by municipal law.

There is more than one good reason why Locke devotes so much of the *Two Treatises of Government* to the family. He does so not only to clarify and ground his argument for the radically free or unattached and anomic condition of man by nature; he also demonstrates how the family can be understood as an artificial, historical human construction—and shows the way to a new and much more reasonable version of this construction. He sketches the outlines of a vast, if gradual and semi-hidden, reformation of the human family. Last but not least, Locke impresses on us the fact that the political order must be conceived as an artificial ordering not of human individuals as such, but rather of individuals who are also, or were previously, artificially ordered in families, to which they owe their most important education.[186]

The Family

In the case of the family even more than in the case of property, Locke's teaching in the *Second Treatise* grows out of the critique of Filmer in the *First*. Filmer based his argument for absolute monarchy on the notion that a king is properly understood as the divinely ordained father of his people; and fatherhood, Filmer argued, must be understood as embodying the absolute power and responsibility that is exemplified in the Biblical God's grant to Adam in regard to Eve.[187] According to Filmer, the right of Adam, and of all subsequent husbands, to rule over their wives and the children sprung from those wives is ordained by God in Genesis 3:16, where God unambiguously places Eve in subjection to Adam. This interpretation of Genesis 3:16 was by no means an innovation of Filmer's; certainly as regards paternal authority within the family, and even to some extent as regards political authority of monarchs, such a reading of the Scripture was close to being a commonplace of the scholastic natural law tradition. Accordingly, Filmer appealed for authoritative support for his notion of patriarchy within the family not merely to the Old Testament but also to the natural law tradition, especially to its great recent secular exponent, Grotius.[188] This tradition taught that the attachments, duties, and rights or powers of parents over children and of husbands over wives are dictated by a human nature that is ordered in more than merely a mechanical or even animal way. Human beings are endowed with innate, universal, and permanent natural inclinations, which, together with the conscience, direct them toward a hierarchy of specific sorts of rational and emotional fulfillment within family and civil society. Humans by nature are ordered in families constituted by the loving, monogamous, and permanent tie of spouses whose children are the permanent responsibility of and the obedient subordinates to their mother and, above her, their father. This patriarchal family structure is not only ordained by the New Testament,[189] these relationships, inclinations, and innate principles of conscience have been expressed in the behavior and codified in the consensus of civilized nations down through the ages.[190]

By now it should come as no surprise to hear that Locke rejects this tradition, root and branch. As regards Genesis 3:16, Locke does not leave it at cutting the ground from under Filmer's tendentious (if eminently traditional) attempt to read into this passage political sovereignty; Locke goes on to claim that there can be found in these words of the Bible ("he shall rule over thee") no grant of any authority whatsoever: "God, in this Text, gives not, that I see, any Authority to *Adam* over *Eve*, or to Men over their Wives."[191] Even more radical are the doubts Locke raises about the natural foundation for the authority and responsibility of fathers to their children. Not content with rejecting the notion of an absolute authority of fathers,[192] Locke goes on to raise the question why mere "Copulation" should give a human male any right over (and implicitly, any duty toward) his offspring: "What Father of a Thousand, when he begets a Child, thinks farther than the satisfying his present Appetite?"[193] It is not human males, but nature or nature's God alone who "makes" babies, "often against the Consent and Will of the begetter"; and this God's "Fatherhood is such an one as utterly excludes all pretence of Title in Earthly Parents."[194]

Before the full import of these remarks can ring too many alarm bells, Locke backtracks: "But grant that the Parents made their Children, gave them Life and Being, and that hence there followed an Absolute Power." Still, no body can deny but that the Woman hath an equal share, if not the greater." "The rational Soul . . . if it must be supposed to derive anything from the Parents, it must certainly owe most to the Mother."[195] If there is any sense in which adults become by nature (i.e., spontaneously, necessarily, by an innate impulse) attached to offspring in a relationship of authority and responsibility, it is the mother who most likely does so. The question remains: how and to what extent does the human male by nature come to be in such a relationship to the children he happens to beget? If we consider that marriage is a matter of contract—i.e., of conventional rather than natural right[196]—we begin to see how Locke came to wonder what natural need obligates a woman to subordinate herself and her children to her mate; what is there to "oblige a Woman to such Subjection, if the Circumstances either of her Condition or Contract with her Husband should exempt her?"[197]

Locke goes yet further in the *Essay Concerning Human Understanding*. There he makes it clear that his refutation of the existence of innate ideas is meant in particular to demonstrate the nonexistence of any innate parental sense of responsibility. Of those "Rules, which . . . fewest people have had the impudence to deny. . . . If any can be thought to be naturally imprinted, none, I think, can have a fairer Pretence to be innate, than this; *Parents preserve and cherish your Children*"; but we need not "seek so far as *Mingrelia* or *Peru*, to find instances of such as neglect, abuse, nay and destroy their Children; or look upon it only as the more than Brutality of some savage and barbarian Nations, when we remember, that it was a familiar, and uncondemned practice amongst the *Greeks* and *Romans*, to expose, without pity or remorse, their innocent Infants."[198] Indeed, Locke insists there is evidence showing that some cannibal peoples raised their own children on a systematic basis for food, "and served the Mothers after the same fashion, when they grew past Child bearing": "thus far can the busie mind of Man carry him to a Brutality below the level of Beasts . . . *nor can it be otherwise* in a Creature, whose thoughts are more than the Sands, and wider than the Ocean, where fancy and passion must needs run him into strange courses, if reason, which is his only Star and compass, be not that he steers by."[199]

Locke's account of the family begins, therefore, from the demonstration that humans are not prevented by any innate moral sense from widespread and even systematic child abuse. But from this he does not mean for us to conclude that humans have no natural impulses that urge them toward loving parenthood. Quite the contrary: in most cases parents are "taught by Natural Love and Tenderness to provide for" their offspring.[200] It is "conformable to the natural Inclination of the greatest part of Men" that they cherish their children.[201] The great difficulty is, these tender impulses—like other natural and weaker benevolent impulses—are neither reliable enough nor well enough aimed by nature to constitute a steady monitor of human behavior. Locke apparently is sure that it is the evidence of cruel abuse that will most impress his readers; but he himself is at least as troubled by the less shocking but more routine neglect and corruption that is the product of excessive parental fondness:

> Parents, being wisely ordain'd by Nature to love their Children, are very apt, if reason watch not that natural Affection very warily, are apt, I say, to let it run into Fondness. . . . The Fondling must . . . have what he Cries for, and do what he pleases. Thus Parents, by humoring and cockering them when *little,* corrupt the Principles of Nature in their Children, and wonder afterwards to taste the bitter Waters, when they themselves have poisoned the Fountain. For when their Children are grown up . . . and their Parents can no longer make use of them, as Playthings; then they complain, that the Brats are untoward and perverse . . . And then perhaps too late, would be glad to get out. . . Try it in a dog or an horse, or any other Creature . . . And yet none of those Creatures are half so wilfull and proud, or half so desirous to be Masters of themselves and others, as Man.[202]

To arrive at a precise understanding of Locke's conception of the problem of the family, we do best to begin from the following crucial text:

> The first and strongest desire God Planted in Men, and wrought into the very principles of their Nature being that of Self-preservation, that is the Foundation of a right to the Creatures, for the particular support and use of each individual Person himself. But next to this, God Planted in Men a strong desire also of propagating their Kind, and continuing themselves in their Posterity, and this gives Children a Title, to share in the *Property* of their Parents, and a Right to Inherit their Possessions.[203]

Here Locke teaches not only that the desire to propagate is secondary to the desire for self-preservation in man, but also that in humans the desire to propagate their kind is inseparably mingled with the desire to continue their *selves:* the "Natural Love and Tenderness" of human parents is directed not to their offspring unconditionally (as in the case of other animals) but to their offspring "as a part of themselves."[204] This distinguishing characteristic of human parenthood is fraught with far-reaching and ambiguous consequences. It is natural, according to Locke's teaching, for a parent's love to vary enormously, depending on the extent to which custom, habit, and the "association of ideas" leads to a convincing sense of identification with a child. Parents may come to love all, or some, or one of their children much more—or much less—than animals ever love their nameless, numberless broods.[205] From this we may understand why, according to Locke, human parenthood is by nature so unreliable—despite, or rather because, humans can be very loving parents. In sum, nature or nature's God poses to mankind's reasoning power the following challenge: What can be introduced into human society by contrivance that will knit together human parent and child in a surer union, so as to promote not only procreation and increase of the species (which nature blindly wills), but also attentive and strict parental education of children in rational and industrious habits (which man figures out for himself he needs far more than indiscriminate population growth)?

The answer emerges in an important dimension of Locke's doctrine of property that we have until now left in the background. Pervading the *Two Treatises of Government* is a discussion of inheritance, a discussion that Locke frequently interrupts or appears to drop but to which he returns again and again. That discussion gradually discloses an altogether new, rational (that is, natural) law of inheritance. As usual, Locke makes his radical new teaching sound superficially like the accepted or traditional teaching.[206] Like Grotius, Locke insists on the child's natural right to inherit his parents' property.[207] But Grotius and the traditional authorities assembled by him derive this right from a prior natural duty—the duty of parents to provide for their offspring. Locke, in contrast, derives the child's right not from any duty at all, not even from another right, but from a desire—the parent's desire to continue his or her self. As a consequence, Locke stresses that in his theory of inheritance the parent's duty to husband and transmit property to the child is to be understood as not at all in tension with the principle that property is "for the particular support and use of each individual person himself"; or the principle that "Property . . . is for the benefit and sole Advantage of the Proprietor, so that he may even destroy the thing, that he has Property in"; or the principle that a man's title to property "is founded wholly on his own private good and advantage."[208] Whereas traditional natural law theorists argue that by nature all children who have not been disowned have an unconditional right to inherit from parents what they need for their support, Locke teaches that the child's right is severely conditional. It is only a right "before any other man"; that is, the child's natural right to a parent's property obtains only if the parent "dispos'd not otherwise of it by his Positive Grant"[209]; "a Father may dispose of his own Possessions as he pleases, when his Children are out of danger of perishing for want."[210] Natural law poses no strict moral bar to rich parents leaving any or all of their children paupers.[211] Locke makes clear the full thrust of his teaching when he devotes a section to explaining why he has devoted so much space to the question of inheritance: he has done so not only to refute what Filmer says about the descent of royal authority from Adam, but also to show that primogeniture, although generally established by the municipal laws of civilized nations (the *ius gentium*), and particularly by English municipal law, has no basis whatsoever in natural or divine right.[212]

It is at first difficult to discern how Locke's revolutionary teaching on the moral basis of all inheritance might help knit the family together more securely. Does not the new latitude given to parents in the disposal of their property after death intensify the uncertainty whether parents will provide for their young? Locke unfolds the answer in the sequel, in the chapter of the *Second Treatise* "Of Paternal Power."

At the very outset of this chapter Locke voices the fear that he "may be censured" for what he will now have to say. The fear is not misplaced. For, building on what he has established in the *First Treatise,* Locke begins by boldly denying that there is any such thing as "paternal power," at least in anything like the sense ordinarily given to the phrase. "If we consult Reason or revelation," we will find that the mother has "an equal Title."[213] But then "without looking any deeper into the matter," we see that "parental power" (as it should be called) is a shared if not a divided power and hence a limited and uncertain power in any one individual.[214] How then are the distinct, equal, and potentially clashing authorities of naturally independent mother and father to be coordinated by reason?

Temporarily leaving this question, Locke forges on to present his positive teaching on what he evidently regards as a more primary or basic issue: the natural relationship between parent and child. All human beings are by nature free and equal; but paradoxically, no human being (since Adam and Eve) has been in this equality. All children are born in "Bonds" of "Subjection" to the "Rule and Jurisdiction," the "Government" (though certainly not the "Civil Government" or government by consent) of their parents.[215] What guides or limits this despotic governmental power of parents over children? Suddenly switching to quasi-Biblical language, Locke lays down the edifying principle that all adults who become parents are "by the Law of nature, *under an obligation to preserve, nourish, and educate*" their children—"not as their own Workmanship," but rather as the "Almighty's," "to whom they were to be accountable for them." Locke would appear to be reverting to an appeal to a revealed and unconditional duty that obliges parents to cooperate with one another and to sacrifice their own interests for the good of their children. But in the following section, while the reader is still suffused with the warm glow of this noble appeal, Locke affirms more distinctly than ever that the one and only law governing man is the law of reason. This law applies only to those to whom it is promulgated; and it is "promulgated or made known by *Reason* only." Above all, "*Law,* in its true Notion," is "*the direction of a free and intelligent Agent* to his proper Interest, and prescribes no further than is for the general Good of those under that Law." Children, since they are not come to the use of reason, "cannot be said to be *under this Law.*" These solemn asseverations necessarily imply that the sole law obliging a parent is a law that commands him to use his children for his own proper interest (and the proper interest of other rational adults). What then, in the law of nature or reason, protects the interests of the prerational child?

Locke next draws our attention to that trouble parents must take if they assume "that Duty which is incumbent on them."[216] Then, almost in passing, Locke notes that a father may with perfect legitimacy be replaced by a "Guardian"; or may himself "substitute a Deputy" or at least a "Tutor" (and thus somewhat more easily acquit himself of "that Duty" or trouble). Locke does not yet inform us of the extent to which, in cases where the tutor or deputy takes charge while the father is still alive, the father retains legitimate authority over and a corresponding right to obedience from his young children. He does declare, however, that after the child has attained the age of reason, "the father and Son are equally *free* as much as Tutor and Pupil . . . without any Dominion left in the Father . . . whether they be only in the State and under the Law of Nature, or under positive Laws."[217] Locke thus compels the reader to wonder what "proper interests" of mature, rational children should lead them to look after their elderly parents—just as he previously compelled the reader to wonder what proper interests of parents should lead them to look after their troublesome offspring.

Having provoked in his readers an insistent demand for answers to some very grave and touchy questions, Locke begins in section 60 to provide the materials out of which the readers may construct his responses. Locke remarks on the wretched state of the brutes and contrasts with this the inclinations of tenderness and concern God has placed in human parents. Human tenderness is superior to the often much stronger *feelings* of parental tenderness seen in dumb animals because human tenderness can be checked and guided by reason.[218] When so checked and guided, human parents educate their young "to be most useful to themselves and others." This education includes making "them work when they are able for their own Subsistence."[219] A parent who is rational may well find the trouble involved in raising and educating children justified not so much by unreliable good feelings as by solid economic calculation. This kind of parental love obviously requires that the rational parent achieve a certain unsentimental clarity of vision concerning his or her dear little one. Inclinations of tenderness and a sense of identification with one's child may be a spur to a kind of farsightedness, but these feelings may also be something of an obstruction if they are not truly enlightened.

Locke next reminds us that in the male parent inclinations of tenderness are not reliable enough to guarantee great concern for offspring. Not only do we see all-too-much evidence of fathers shirking their responsibilities—educational and otherwise—but, to probe the roots of this deplorable behavior, we must reflect on what men would be like if left even freer than they are under English municipal law: "What will become of this *Paternal Power* in that part of the World where one Woman hath more than one husband at a time? Or in those parts of *America* where when the Husband and Wife part, which happens frequently, the children are all left to the Mother . . .?"[220]

In almost the same breath Locke shows the remedy reason can begin to provide. Reason concludes that we need to make fathers realize that they are not, as fathers, automatically endowed with any parental authority: "Nay, this *power* so little belongs to the *Father* by any particular right of nature, but only as he is Guardian of his Children, that when he quits his Care of them, he loses his power over them, which goes along with their Nourishment and Education, to which it is inseparably annexed."[221] Reason teaches us that fathers can and should be taught that practically nothing may be taken for granted in the way of respect, assistance, or even companionship from their grown children; they need to be brought to the realization that every hope they might have in this regard—for conformity to their wishes, for comfort in old age, for remembrance after death—depends strictly on the amount and effectiveness of the educational effort they expend on each child. They need to have these austerely reasonable lessons instilled into their hearts and reflected or reinforced in the opinion of the society that surrounds them. It is such lessons that Locke quietly but incisively begins to cultivate:

> The *honour due from a Child,* places in the Parents a perpetual right to respect, reverence, support, and compliance too, more or less, as the Father's care, cost and kindness in his Education, has been more or less.
>
> And 'tis plain, all this is due not to the bare Title of Father; not only because, as has been said, it is owing to the Mother too; but because these Obligations to Parents, and the degrees of what is required of Children, may be varied, by the different care and kindness, trouble and expence, which is often imployed upon one Child, more than another.

Yet Locke's attempt thus far to supply a rational support for (and modification of) natural tenderness between parents and children is exposed to a rather obvious prudential difficulty: the parents deliver on what we may call their part of the bargain but, in order to receive many of the reciprocal benefits, they must wait until their children mature, and then they must trust to their children's "gratitude"[222]—at a time when the children are likely to be more attentive to their own children, for the same reasons their parents were once so attentive to them. This is not to mention that "there is not one passage in the *Two Treatises of Government* in which Locke says that children have feelings of love or tenderness or affection (or anything like these) for their parents."[223] The well-brought up child owes "*honour* and respect, support and defence, and whatsoever gratitude can oblige a Man to for the highest benefits he is naturally capable of." But none of this entails obedience to the father's wishes. The most that can be said as regards the aging father's will is that "it may become his Son in many things, not very inconvenient to him and his Family, to pay a Deference to it."[224] It is precisely here that Locke deploys the new doctrine of inheritance he developed in the *First Treatise*—and it is at this point in the *Second Treatise* that we discover the full purpose and, if you will, elegance, of that doctrine:[225]

> There is *another Power* ordinarily *in the Father,* whereby he has a tie on the Obedience of his Children: which though it be common to him with other Men, yet the occasions of shewing it almost constantly happening to Fathers in their private Families, and the Instances of it elsewhere being rare, and less taken notice of, it passes in the world for a part of *Paternal Jurisdiction*. And this is the power Men generally have to *bestow their Estates* on those, who please them best . . . as the behavior of this or that Child hath comported with his Will and Humour.
>
> This is no small tye on the Obedience of Children. . . .

And, we may add, the need to acquire and strengthen this tie is no small incentive for a father to accummulate as much property as possible. This same tie, Locke immediately adds, is a key means by which children are induced to become and remain citizens of the civil society in which they grow up.[226] Inheritance, especially in land, distributed not by primogeniture but by the favoritism of the father and mother, proves to be the tie that binds maturing young people to society, both familial and civil.[227]

Locke completes his teaching on the family when he finally treats, in chapter 7 of the *Second Treatise,* the topic we saw he left in suspense: the true, natural foundation of the attachment between husband and wife, and the rational or natural laws that are deducible from that foundation. Locke chooses to discuss this theme in a very broad context: it is here that Locke treats thematically, if compendiously, the nature of the most elemental human sociability. This weighty chapter happens to be the only chapter in the *Two Treatises* that opens with the word "God." The wording of the opening sentence recalls in a striking way the wording of Genesis 2:18–24. The Biblical God, Locke reminds us, no sooner created man than He judged that "It is not good that the man should be alone"; on the basis of this divine judgment, God "formed every beast of the field and every bird of the air"; finally, in order that there would be a fit helper for man, He created out of man's flesh woman—to whom, as a wife, man "cleaves" so that they become "one flesh." (" 'For I hate divorce,' says the Lord God of Israel"—Malachi 2:16.) In contrast, Locke's (or nature's) God "made man such a Creature," that in this creature's "own Judgment, it was not good for him to be alone." Or, as Locke also puts it, nature's God put man "under strong obligations of Necessity, Convenience, and Inclination to drive him into *Society*."[228]

The "first Society" mankind was driven into "was between Man and Wife." This "*Conjugal Society* is made by a voluntary Compact between Man and Woman."[229] Even the first society is a matter of convention; there is no simply natural, spontaneous, or instinctual human society. This first, contractual relationship is the basis for those other societal bonds, including that of parents and children, which go together to make up the family, ruled by a "Master or Mistress."[230] As Locke makes clear in the sections that immediately follow,[231] he has not forgotten that the male and female can procreate by the mere act of copulation: there can be children where there is no contract. Moreover, throughout much of the rest of the animal kingdom there exists not only "*conjunction between Male and Female*," but also "*Conjugal Bonds*" and even "Conjugal Society"[232]—all without any contract, of course. Yet in the case of human beings, where there is no contract between male and female, there is no society. Locke's strange teaching becomes intelligible if we recognize that his use of the term society is rather precise at this point: he means a reliable, stable, lasting relationship among animals of the same species, defined by and adequate to specific purposes or goals. In the human species such relationships can exist only on the basis of calculated, voluntary, and specific conventional agreements.

For while "we find the inferiour Creatures steadily obey" a "Rule, which the infinite wise Maker hath set to the Works of his hands," a rule that keeps the male joined to and helping the female "so long as is necessary to the nourishment and support of the young Ones,"[233] the situation of human beings is very different. On the one hand, the length of time the young remain dependent and the difficulty of hunting makes the period during which the female needs the assistance of the male considerably longer than in the case of the other beasts of prey among the mammals; the problem is compounded by the fact that when the male does stay around, the female is likely to conceive and give birth again long before the previous child can fend for itself. On the other hand, we cannot find and admire any strong, clear instinct God has given human males and females as a guide to the correct manner of providing the needed cooperation. We can admire the "Wisdom of the great Creatour" only to this extent: having created a massive problem or having "made it necessary, that *Society of Man and Wife should be more lasting*, than of Male and Female amongst other Creatures," He has "given to Man foresight and an Ability to lay up for the future."

Naturally, it took mankind a long time to begin to deploy its foresight effectively in devising rules and sanctions that would prevent "uncertain mixture, or easie and frequent Solutions of Conjugal Society" that mightily disturb the laying up of goods for the sake of the offspring. "In the beginning," we recall, "all the world was *America*, and more so than that is now,"[234] and in parts of America, the husband and wife part frequently, leaving the children wholly under their mother's "Care and provision."[235] By and large, the patriarchal family emerged as the most obvious solution to the natural conundrum of human sexuality and sociability; and this solution had some reasonable ground. Given that husband and wife "will unavoidably sometimes have different wills" and that "the last Determination" must be placed somewhere, it "naturally falls to the Man's share, as the abler and the stronger."[236] But the patriarchal family goes far beyond anything entailed in this reasonable observation.[237] The patriarchal family, in emerging out of the original savagery, has woven thick veils of superstition that obscure the true, fundamental needs that underlie and alone justify the marriage contract. Mankind has lost sight of the fact that the chief, if not the only reason why husband and wife should stay together any longer than other animals is the upbringing and education of the offspring.[238]

There is in the first place "no necessity in the nature of the thing" that prevents marriage from being dissoluble, either by mutual consent or simply after a fixed term, as long as the children's education and inheritance are provided for;[239] nay, the so-called power of the husband is "so far from that of an absolute Monarch, that the Wife has, in many cases, a Liberty to *separate* from him"—usually by provision of the contract, but in some cases purely by natural right, that is, with a view to the nature of the thing marriage is. "The Children upon such Separation fall to the Father or the Mother's Lot" as "the Contract does determine."[240] There is therefore no reason why the wife and mother should not be allowed and encouraged to contract in such a way as to maintain very considerable economic and personal independence: "Community of Goods, and the power over them, mutual Assistance, and Maintenance, and other things belonging to *Conjugal Society,* might be varied and regulated . . . as far as may consist with Procreation and the bringing up of Children."[241] The cardinal principle based on nature and reason that ought to govern law and public policy in this crucial matter is this: all should be arranged between husband and wife "so their Industry might be encouraged, and their Interest better united, to make Provision, and lay up Goods for their common Issue."[242] A dose of uneasiness about the permanence of the marriage, not to mention the expectation of its likely dissolution after a time, may well instill a very productive uneasiness in both spouses and will doubtless heighten in each the awareness of the need each has to secure by material accumulation and careful moral education the support of the children in future years. This obviously carries great implications for the education of daughters as well as sons. In his treatise on education Locke bows to contemporary convention and discusses almost exclusively the education of boys, but near the outset he quietly makes clear that this bow is only perfunctory: as regards daughters, "I will take the Liberty to say, that . . . the nearer they come to the Hardships of their Brothers in their Education, the greater Advantage will they receive from it all the remaining Part of their Lives."[243]

Locke revolts against the patriarchal family, not merely because he sees the illusion underlying it, but because he sees this particular illusion as pernicious to the happiness of mankind. In his detailed speculations (in chapters 6 to 8 of the *Second Treatise*) on the historical origins of patriarchal monarchy, Locke makes vivid the degree to which the patriarchal family depends on and cultivates a deep trustfulness in the "Goodness and Vertue," the "Honesty and Prudence" of fathers and leaders as father-figures.[244] But men do not by nature deserve trust of this kind. Such trust induces negligence in and tempts the insolence of the ruler; it tends to keep the ruled in a childlike state of dependency and innocence that renders them the easy victims of tyranny. At the same time, the traditional family with its laws of ownership and inheritance instills a resigned complacency in men and women regarding their economic condition; it veils and stifles the rational uneasiness that can alone spur individuals to the industry and science that might relieve humanity's natural condition of miserable insecurity.

The Meaning of Locke's "State of Nature"

We are now in a position to give a synoptic statement of what Locke means by his famous and extraordinarily influential doctrines of the "natural freedom and equality of men" and the "state of nature." These terms, taken in the strictest sense, signify the fundamental and disorderly constitution of man or the human passions, the drastic economic scarcity of the natural environment in which man is situated, and the social condition toward which man drifts as a result of his constitution and condition—until or unless his reasoning power gathers itself to react in a decisive and comprehensive fashion against this drift.

By nature man is a social animal for Locke. By nature men may live peacefully for a time with other men; they are driven, especially after the invention of money with the attendant inequalities of accumulated wealth, to construct a variety of more or less reasonable institutions and relationships pertaining to property, money, marriage, inheritance, education, rules of war, and religion. They construct certain kinds of government—usually outgrowths of the family. But all such peaceable acquisitions and conventionally ordered relationships remain extraordinarily fragile until reason takes a radical step. Reason is prepared to take the decisive step when it becomes self-conscious about the true gravity of the human condition. Then reason comprehends both the deep economic and psychological sources of conflict among men and the fact that it has such unreliable support from the passions that the human animal cannot be trusted to understand or, if it understands, to follow the dictates of reason. Reason sees that even those few who do, at least for a time, follow and support it are likely (precisely because of their knowledge of the strength of the passions in their neighbors) to wield the "executive power" of enforcement in such a way as to escalate violence—or they are likely to be frightened (reasonably) into exercising the executive power erratically.[245]

Having arrived at this point, man understands and feels in his very bones the key rational rule, law of reason, or natural law. That law is the imperative to join or help set up a government that possesses a virtual monopoly of coercion and uses that monopoly to supply the sanction that divine intervention, the conscience, and spontaneous human nature fail to provide: "the Magistrates Sword being for a *Terror to Evil Doers* and by that Terror to inforce Men to observe the positive Laws of the Society, made conformable to the Laws of Nature."[246] The rational terror is obtained when every person who makes up the commonwealth resigns to the commonwealth his executive power to enforce the rules of reason, but at the same time gives the commonwealth the right to employ his force in its executive enforcement. At this moment, for the first time, mankind creates a *civil* society, ruled by civil government.

Precisely at the moment when mankind and its political theory stands on the brink of the solution, however, it also teeters on the brink of disaster. For it can become bewitched all over again—partly on account of the age-old heritage of the patriarchal family, partly on account of the deceptive clarity of Hobbes's terrible misstep: mankind can fall prey to the idea that the terror should be in the hands of a fatherly government or an absolute monarch who alone will be left with all the executive power of reason originally vested in the individuals who united themselves into the commonwealth. This means that instead of obtaining a neutral "known Authority . . . which every one of that Society ought to obey,"[247] men in fact put themselves in a "worse condition than the state of Nature,"[248] a condition "much worse, than the state of Nature, or pure Anarchy."[249] The government of absolute monarchy is so far from being a rational solution that it "is indeed *inconsistent with Civil Society,* and so can be no Form of Civil Government at all."[250]

The state of nature, then, can be imagined or understood to take many different forms or to include many diverse ways of life. What unites all these forms, what strictly speaking defines the state of nature, is what it lacks rather than what it contains: "where-ever there are any number of Men, *however associated,* [my italics], that have no such decisive power to appeal to, there they are still *in the state of Nature.*"[251] Yet while the state of nature or natural freedom and equality is defined negatively and reveals itself to be a condition of manifold possibilities, all of which reason tells us to quit as definitively and as soon as possible, we must not forget that in addition to being "full of fears and continual dangers,"[252] the condition also contains or reveals that for the sake of which all legitimate and rational law or public policy exist. Life, liberty, and estate and the family knitted together by its individual members' concern for their private property, all come to be more rationally and stably ordered by the regulations of civil society. But the ultimate purpose and nature of these basic goods in no way derives from or is altered by civil society.

The state of nature, therefore, is not so much a historical condition that men dwelt in at some time in the past, as it is—to use Hobbes's helpful expression—an "Inference, made from the Passions."[253] Or, in Locke's terminology, the idea of the state of nature is a mixed mode put together by the mind to clarify the natural bent of the passions.[254] This means to say, however, that the idea reveals a latent reality that lies just beneath the surface of all civil existence and explains the *raison d'être* of that existence. The latent becomes actual when law and order break down or when men find themselves temporarily beyond the reach of the "terror" of civil government. In addition, since no civil authority has jurisdiction over all men or over any man at all times, natural freedom always remains in existence at the frontier, as it were. International relations take place in a permanent state of nature.[255] Every individual, at the time he reaches the age of reason and until he swears allegiance to or accepts the authority of some civil society, "is a Free-man, at liberty what Government he will put himself under."[256] The right to emigration at this point in a person's life is inalienable. Resident aliens, even those who own land, while "not being in a state of War," are no more members of the society to whose laws they temporarily submit than are guests the members of a family with whom they peacefully and temporarily lodge.[257] To put it generally, as regards civil society, "nothing can make any man" a *"member of that Society"*—not family, not land ownership, not even tacit consent—"but his actually entering into it by positive Engagement and express Promise and Compact." Be it well noted, though, that once a pledge of allegiance is made in public by an adult legally acceptable to the community, he who pledges is "perpetually and indispensably obliged to be and remain unalterably a Subject . . . never . . . again in the liberty of the state of nature; unless by any Calamity, the Government, he was under, comes to be dissolved; or else by some publick Act cuts him off."[258] Nothing brings home more vividly the remarkable combination of freedom and bonds,[259] the revolutionary element of radical commitment, the voluntary leap and transformation of the individual as individual that is at the foundation of rational, legitimate citizenship for Locke.

In Locke's scheme, there is no basis for supposing that human nature requires or inclines toward a government that defines for its subjects their happiness, virtue, or salvation:

> The commonwealth seems to me to be a society of men constituted solely for the preservation and advancing of civil goods. Civil goods I call life, liberty, the integrity and freedom from pain of the body, and the possession of external things, such as estate, money, furniture, and so forth. . . . In truth the whole jurisdiction of the magistrate reaches only to these civil goods, and all civil power, right, and dominion terminates in and is limited to the care and promotion of these things alone.[260]

We find a mighty echo of this basic principle of liberal law at the outset of Blackstone's *Commentaries:*

> By the absolute *rights* of individuals we mean those which are so in their primary and strictest sense; such as would belong to their persons merely in a state of nature, and which every man is intitled to enjoy whether out of society or in it. But with regard to the absolute *duties,* which man is bound to perform considered as a mere individual, it is not to be expected that any human municipal laws should at all explain or enforce them. For the end and intent of such laws being only to regulate the behaviour of mankind, as they are members of society, and stand in various relations to each other, they have consequently no business or concern with any but social or relative duties. Let a man therefore be ever so abandoned in his principles, or vitious in his practice, provided he keeps his wickedness to himself, and does not offend against the rules of public decency, he is out of the reach of human laws. . . . But, with respect to *rights,* the case is different. Human laws define and enforce as well those rights which belong to man considered as an individual, as those which belong to him considered as related to others. For the principle aim of society is to protect individuals in the enjoyment of those absolute rights. . . .[261]

These passages do indeed imply that the fundamental compact gives the magistrate some legitimate supervision over the morals of the citizenry—but only insofar as is necessary to keep the peace and secure the lives, liberty, and property of the citizenry. Moreover, if he is to secure liberty, the magistrate must beware of trying to protect men from themselves.[262] Civil society at its founding moments does not require and should not bow to statesmen who claim to possess some special insight into the meaning or purpose of life. No government should be dedicated to any goals that cannot reasonably be supposed to be perfectly intelligible and on that basis acceptable to every citizen in his sober moments.[263]

Nor does the consent of the people that rests at the base of all legitimate public policy remain merely imputed or hypothetical. Locke's principles make straight the way for that new force in politics that Jefferson hailed as "the mighty wave of public opinion."[264] The people retain and should know they retain, in the final analysis, the supreme say regarding the rightful exercise of the powers delegated to government.[265] The majority's armed, violent resistance to authority it regards as oppressive is the most vivid, nonhypothetical expression of the sovereignty of the people. As Goldwin points out, Locke candidly admits that the majority's judgment as regards such resistance is based not on its wisdom or reason or even its considered opinion but rather on its feeling and perceiving.[266] The majority, to be sure, is hardly the same as the people. But so powerful is humanity's tendency to disagree and so lacking is mankind in any natural mode of establishing consensus, that in order to have any capacity to act or express a will the people (and every one of its members) must from the outset agree that every decision after the initial compact will be determined by simple majority rule. The majority's title does not derive from any claim to superior virtue or prudence (for example, "two heads are better than one"), but from sheer "greater force."[267] This means, of course, that while the majority retains supreme political power it does not retain and never had unlimited power. The supreme (irresistible) power governing every rational person's behavior is the desire for self-preservation and every individual retains the inalienable right to resist perceived threats to his property and existence, no matter what the source of those threats.[268]

Locke makes it his goal to enlighten the people—the ordinary people, the mass of men and women; he sees it as his vocation to awaken their spirit as individuals and as a people, to teach them their right and duty to appeal to heaven and go into the streets if it finally comes to that. Granted, Locke seems to envisage a populace more deferential to tradition and royal authority than that for which the American founders legislated; but he legitimates, and thus prepares the way for, the sort of popular prickliness that was later to characterize the Americans. Let us listen again to the words Jefferson paraphrased in the key section of the Declaration of Independence:

> Such *Revolutions happen* not upon every little mismanagement in publick affairs. *Great mistakes* in the ruling part, many wrong and inconvenient Laws, and all the *slips* of humane frailty will be *born by the People,* without mutiny or murmur. But if a long train of Abuses, Prevarications, and Artifices, all tending the same way, make the design visible to the People, and they cannot but feel, what they lie under, and see whither they are going; 'tis not to be wonder'd, that they should then rouze themselves, and endeavour to put the rule into such hands, which may secure to them the ends for which Government was at first erected. . . .[269]

Locke shows he is not under the illusion that by preaching the right of popular resistance one can forestall the right's ever having to be exercised. The Lockean right to resistance is not like nuclear deterrence. While Locke is not, unlike Machiavelli and Marx, exhilarated by the spectacle of a people in arms, neither does he fear it in the manner of Hobbes. It is true that the first stated purpose of the *Two Treatises* as a whole is "to establish the Throne of our Great Restorer, Our present King William; to make good his Title, in the Consent of the People"—sound Hobbesian doctrine; but the second stated purpose is "to justifie to the World, the People of *England*, whose love of their Just and Natural Rights, with their Resolution to preserve them, saved the Nation when it was on the very brink of Slavery and Ruine."[270] Locke publishes in the afterglow of what he—in striking contrast to Hume[271]—presents as a glorious popular revolution. More generally, it is characteristic of Locke that when he speaks of popular uprisings he rarely if ever blames the people and instead almost always blames the rulers. He in fact teaches that wherever one finds a popular, seditious rising one can assume there was oppression that justifies that sedition: *"una est quae populum ad seditionem congregat: oppressio"* ("one thing only gathers the people in sedition: oppression").[272] In these words we hear Locke at his farthest from Hobbes; we hear the Locke who is a key source of the modern sympathy for revolutions and revolutionaries; we hear the Locke whose teaching frightened Hume and Blackstone and delighted Jefferson and Wilson. This is the Locke who not only celebrates revolution for Englishmen at home but is willing to encourage wars of liberation abroad:

> Who doubts but the Grecian Christians descendants of the ancient possessors of that Country may justly cast off the Turkish yoke which they have so long groaned under when ever they have a power to do it? For no Government can have a right to obedience from a people who have not freely consented to it: which they can never be supposed to do, till either they are put in a full state of Liberty to chuse their Government and Governors, or at least till they have such standing Laws, to which they have by themselves or their Representatives, given their free consent, and also till they are allowed their due property, which is so to be Proprietors of what they have, that no body can take away any part of it without their own consent. . . .[273]

The intellectual genealogy of Locke's revolutionary teaching is indicated in the epigraph from Livy that Locke affixed to the *Two Treatises*. Locke's deliberate cultivation of salutary fear in the governors and vigilance verging on distrust in the populace would appear to be a kind of tamed version of Machiavelli's thesis according to which constant strife between populace and rulers is the elixir of civic health. But Locke has no interest in producing a populace capable of being formed into invincible legions, honed by an endless struggle against a ruthless senatorial class, with both populace and leaders crowded together in the pressure cooker of a single small civic republic. What Locke aims at instead is a spirit not unlike that which Jefferson celebrated as the spirit that broke forth so admirably—and then subsided even more admirably—in what Jefferson regarded as his temporary political party:

> As the storm is now subsiding . . . it is pleasant to consider the phenomenon with attention. . . . For this whole chapter in the history of man is new. The great extent of our republic is new. Its sparse habitation is new. The mighty wave of public opinion which has rolled over it is new. But the most pleasing novelty is, its so quietly subsiding over such an extent of surface to its true level again. The order and good sense displayed in this recovery from delusion, and in the momentous crisis which lately arose, really bespeaks a strength of character in our nation which augurs well for the duration of our republic. . . . There was no idea of force, nor of any occasion for it. . . . This peaceable and legitimate resource [the calling of a Constitutional Convention], to which we are in the habit of implicit obedience, superseding all appeal to force, and being always within our reach, shows a precious principle of self-preservation in our composition, till a change of circumstances shall take place, which is not within prospect at any definite period. . . .[274]

This popular strength of character, animated by "a precious principle of self-preservation," is not a heroic spirit. It does not bespeak the civic patriotism of the Romans, the honor of the nobles who made the Fronde, or the religious zealotry of Cromwell's Puritans. Yet it is a spirit that evinces a capacity for protest, resistance, even risk. Such a spirit depends on a sober sense of individual self-respect, bolstered by or rooted in the possession of private property and the reasonable hope of bettering one's condition through private enterprise. Locke envisaged, and in his wonderfully influential writings helped to foster, a new conception of the property-based dignity of man as human being and citizen. In America that conception became predominant, in part directly through the impact of Locke's own writings, in part through the intermediary influence of thinkers such as Trenchard and Gordon, Blackstone,[275] and, perhaps most important, the representatives of the "Scottish Enlightenment" who adapted and modified, while still fundamentally continuing, the Lockean heritage.

3
The Political Theory of the Constitution

David F. Epstein

What is the best form of government? For Americans today this question may appear impossible to answer and unnecessary to ask. The question seems to require a judgment among competing values that is impossible in principle as well as a science of political facts that is, at least so far, incomplete. And the question appears entirely academic, since our 200-year-old government seems (at least) so firmly entrenched that fundamental revision is unlikely or (at best) successful enough that such revision is unnecessary.

But the Americans of 1787 found it necessary to ask this question. In order to "institute new Government," a people must decide what arrangements are best or at least "seem to them" best.[1] Their deliberation on this question was guided by self-evident truths concerning man's natural rights and the origins and purposes of government. Today those principles may no longer be thought self-evident, or even true, but seem to be of historical interest as an ideology or myth that shaped the events of 1787–1788. It seems that later Americans need not believe the thoughts of the founders in order to perpetuate the government they created. Perhaps the question of that government's goodness will not be raised by a generally satisfied population or by the sophisticated, but apolitical, minds who recognize political myths as myths. But it is not clear that such an unreflective posture can satisfy a thoughtful citizen; it is also not clear that this combination of theoretical skepticism and practical complacency is durable. For one thing, some who dispute the Constitution's original principles also dislike its institutional practice and seek its revolutionary overthrow; and perhaps one cannot assume that this view will remain that of a small, frustrated minority, if the claim that our form of government needs no argument in its defense poorly conceals a belief that no convincing argument is available. Second, the perpetuation of our constitutional institutions without reference to their principles may permit the Constitution to "evolve" in accordance with more recent principles whose intrinsic merit, popular acceptability, and compatibility with the rest of the Constitution are uncertain, so that the Constitution may insensibly be transformed into something the population no longer feels complacent about.

My purpose in this chapter is to explain the thought that guided the Constitution's founders' choice of political institutions and to consider to what degree a rejection of that thought changes or endangers those institutions.

It should be obvious that no compact and relatively unified account of the thought underlying the Constitution's political institutions can do justice to the variety of opinions, particular issues, and compromises that figured in its writing and ratification. I have taken my bearings by those speeches and writings that reflect most directly on the broad principles at issue and do not insist that each framer or ratifier agreed on all points or even thought through all points. In case of disputes, I have tried to state the view that prevailed, that is, the opinion that recommended the provision adopted; but I have often borrowed from the losing side statements of principles I believe were shared by both sides or that put the prevailing side's position in sharper relief. Quotations from the founders and from philosophic writings known to them should be regarded as illustrative, since I cannot in this essay document how widely each view was shared or fully explain the particular circumstances in which it was expressed.

The variety of opinions and disagreements of 1787–1788 did not call into question the fundamental political principles asserted in the Declaration of Independence. According to the Declaration, the self-evident truth that all men are created equal in their inalienable rights poses an end and standard for government ("to secure these rights"); it shows the necessity of government ("governments are instituted among men"); and it identifies the source of government's authority ("deriving their just powers from the consent of the governed"). These self-evident principles set the bounds of the debate on what form of government should be adopted. That the best form of government is not also self-evident reflects the fact that these principles offer somewhat contradictory political guidance.

Man's rights are natural and inalienable, but they are not secure by nature. In a "state of nature, any one individual may act uncontrolled by others," but "every other individual may act uncontrolled by him," resulting in "dissensions and animosities,"[2] and "rude violence."[3] This means that government, while unnatural, is an "indispensable necessity"[4] and its "introduction" is "universal."[5]

Natural liberty also sets a standard for government. Government's purpose is to secure the rights to life, liberty, and pursuit of happiness, and it deserves abolition if it fails to do so. Of course, the recommendation that a government be abolished if it misbehaves seems to contradict the view that government is absolutely necessary. Accordingly, although Thomas Hobbes, the writer who most strongly emphasized the natural necessity of government, indicated that there are natural standards for government, he refused to allow anyone to enforce those standards. By contrast, James Madison sought to enforce the standards without denying the necessity and saw the paradox as a "great difficulty" in devising government: "You must first enable the government to control the governed; and in the next place oblige it to control itself."[6]

Natural liberty also specifics a source for government: only the consent of the governed confers legitimate powers on government. Because all men are by nature free, no one can claim any natural right to rule another even if he sees the necessity of government or knows how to achieve its purpose. Only consent can confer authority. Perhaps in recognition of the necessity of government, this principle is interpreted to permit a majority to institute a particular government for a people that has unanimously decided to have some government (by deciding to be a single society). Even so, the principle of consent may be in tension with the natural necessity for government and the natural standards for government. What if a people chooses a government that is too strong or too weak to secure their rights? The Declaration says they can institute the government that seems best to them, but it also admits the need and asserts the standard for government.

Thus the self-evident truth of man's natural liberty defines for those choosing a form of government the problem of reconciling or combining the several implications of that principle. My discussion will consider how the founders interpreted and applied each of those implications in the construction of political institutions. In the first section, I will discuss the founders' view of the purpose of government and their efforts to "enable the government to control the governed." The subject of the second section is how the Constitution attempted to "oblige [the government] to control itself" by a combination of popular elections and auxiliary precautions. In the third section, I will consider the founders' argument for and their practical interpretation of "the consent of the governed."

Controlling the Governed

While the questions of limited government and popular government were in some measure peculiar to the thought underlying the American Constitution, the question of effective government, of government's ability to control the governed, was not. Thus, for example, in creating powers to raise armies and levy taxes, the founders followed not some specifically liberal or republican theory but the "customary and ordinary modes practiced in other governments."[7] Topics such as the necessary qualities of rulers and the basis for obedience to them were also traditional ones. But the founders' principle of man's natural freedom put these matters in a different light. In contrast to those who took the existence of government for granted, the liberal philosophers who asserted that man is naturally free raised thereby the question of why government exists at all; but they immediately and emphatically offered an answer. Whereas rulers by force, nature, or divine right make broad but questionable claims of authority, the liberal philosophers tried to demonstrate the basis for a political authority that is narrow in scope but unassailable in legitimacy. The characteristics that enabled past governments to control the governed had therefore to be reevaluated in light of government's newly limited ends and reconstituted from scratch in light of the rejection of any inherited or traditional basis for authority.

I will consider in this section the American founders' view of the purposes of government, the powers and qualities necessary in rulers, and the basis for obedience by citizens.

The Purpose of Government. Considering men in a state of nature without government makes clear the necessity of government. Men's natural passions place them at odds with one another, leading to continuing fears of robbery or homicide that poison the enjoyment of natural liberty.[8] "If men were angels, no government would be necessary," but men are not angels; "the passions of men will not conform to the dictates of reason and justice without constraint."[9] Even though some men "would be glad to be at ease within modest bounds" and would simply "plant, sow, build, or possesse a convenient seat" for themselves,[10] their "possessions or enjoyments" may be sacrificed to the "views and designs" of others who are "strong" or "more crafty and designing."[11] The "corruption, and vitiousness of degenerate Men"[12] require good men in a state of nature to anticipate or punish invasions by the wicked (and thus, from different motives, virtually imitate their behavior).[13]

Government might become unnecessary in a "golden age . . . of perfect wisdom and perfect virtue,"[14] not (as Marx suggests) in a golden age of perfect equality and perfect plenty. Scarcity and inequality of material goods are not the only cause of war or impulse to government; more fundamental are man's (or some men's) non-angelic, "ambitious and designing," "wicked and overgrown"[15] tendencies (remediable only by perfect virtue), as well as modest men's anticipation of aggressions by others (remediable only by a perfect wisdom that understands the perfect virtue of others). Equality and plenty do not result in perfect virtue because they may not quench men's desire for the material goods of others; and, in any case, they do not abolish some men's "pleasure in contemplating their own power in the acts of conquest."[16] The permanent problem posed by this spirited, ambitious side of human nature is neglected or denied by those who expect economics to permit the withering away of politics.

A particular people institutes government not only to protect "against the violence of wicked and overgrown citizens" among themselves but also to protect against "invasion by the rest of mankind."[17] "Did there ever exist a nation which, at some period or other, was not exposed to war?"[18] Certainly in a world of ambitious monarchs, and even in a world of competing commercial republics, war would remain a possibility.[19] There is a sharp distinction between *government* on the one hand—a "DISCRETIONARY SUPERINTENDENCE" that rules a people—and leagues or alliances or treaties on the other, which may be useful but are "subject to the usual vicissitudes of peace and war, of observance and nonobservance, as the interests or passions of the contracting powers dictate."[20] While government can establish peace among the people who institute it, the best it can do with respect to other peoples is to "prevent wars or render them less expensive or bloody"[21] by marshaling the society's force and controlling its behavior. Just as some badly behaved men make government necessary for society's internal peace, those who act unjustly toward other nations[22] or lag in contributing resources to a common defense[23] make a coercive government the necessary means for a people's external defense. The possibility of war and the necessity of a government that can prevent or conduct it are permanent.

For Americans in 1787 the practical question was not the necessity of government as such but whether America as a whole needed *one* government. The "advantages and necessity of a federal government among states" resemble, in American circumstances, the "advantages and necessity of civil government among individuals in society."[24] A federal government would prevent a state of war between the states that would otherwise result from particular disputes or simply from the "nearness of situation" that "constitutes nations natural enemies";[25] and it could marshal America's resources and conduct its policy so as to make war with other countries less likely and less devastating. This is not strictly necessary in the way that "civil government" is necessary to end the state of war among individuals. The fact that war remains possible between disunited states is not as urgent a cause of "misery" as is war among "particular men,"[26] nor is it a situation that a federal government can fundamentally alter unless it is a world government. Thus the choice of the new Constitution was not the single-minded quest for social peace that a state of war among individuals ought to inspire.[27] The relatively greater ability of a "more perfect Union" to "insure domestic Tranquility" and "provide for the common defence"[28] was an important advantage but not a conclusive argument that union is a "necessity."[29]

What men wish to secure when they institute government is not merely the life and limb that were imperiled in the state of nature but the freedom they have imperfectly enjoyed there. Without freedom, men are unlikely to be or feel truly safe, a fact that vindicates but does not by itself explain men's love of freedom. Indeed, the prospect of "occasional wars," which kill people, compares favorably with the "fangs of despotism," which merely inflict "the most abject servility":

> As passing clouds obscure for a time the splendour of the sun, so do wars interrupt the welfare of mankind; but despotism is a settled gloom that totally extinguishes happiness, not a ray of comfort can penetrate to cheer the dejected mind.[30]

While seeking to preserve their freedom, "Individuals entering into society, must give up a share of liberty to preserve the rest,"[31] because the freedom of each depends on government's ability to restrain all others. "It is at all times difficult to draw with precision the line between those rights which must be surrendered, and those which may be reserved. . . ."[32] Statements that attempted to sketch that line suggested that government secures freedom when it protects men from "unreasonable exactions,"[33] when it protects the "free and generous exercise of all the human faculties, so far as . . . is compatible with the publick welfare,"[34] when it permits men to do what they ought to wish to do.[35] These formulations reflect the fact that government must make some reasonable exactions (for example, impose taxes) so that it can prevent unreasonable ones; it must restrain men wishing to do what they ought not (for example, steal) so as to protect men who wish to do what they ought.

Government adopts laws to specify men's rights and provides for the execution of laws in order to protect each man's rights from interference by other men; this ends the state of nature and "establish[es] Justice."[36] Justice is established in the sense that men can now reasonably feel confident that their rights are secured by the laws, police, and courts. Justice is not an "ideal" to be progressively pursued or promoted by government; it is an arrangement established from the beginning. Or rather it should be. The Constitution of 1787 offered those held as slaves no protection against the men who violated their rights, and in this respect failed to establish justice. Yet even if a government is established whose laws and enforcement will protect all men from each other, justice remains at risk because the government's own power to repress private injustice can be used as an instrument of injustice. Accordingly, the most that can be "established" is not justice itself but a government able to restrain injustice and unlikely to commit injustice.[37] The founders' insistence that government not simply achieve some semblance of tranquillity or generally serve the public interest, but rather impartially protect the rights of each citizen, is their most exacting demand on government.

Prominent among the rights government is instituted to protect is the right to acquire property. Property was sometimes listed with "life" and "liberty" as the objects of government; and Gouverneur Morris went so far as to assert that

> property was the main object of Society. The savage State was more favorable to liberty than the Civilized; and sufficiently so to life. It was preferred by all men who had not acquired a taste for property; it was only renounced for the sake of property which could only be secured by the restraints of regular Government.[38]

James Madison's formulation was that the protection not exactly of property itself but of the "faculties of men, from which the rights of property originate" is the "first object of government."[39] Men use their faculties to acquire property, and government makes it possible and attractive for them to do so by securing to them the fruits of their labors. The "political Creed . . . that as the Earth was given to the Children of Men, . . . every Man ought to go Share and Share alike, let the Industry, Services or Merit of some be what it may"[40] neglects the fact that the earth as given does not include "those things that are necessary to the comfortable support of our lives," "fit and prepared for our use."[41] "We have no reason to expect any climate or soil will be found, or any age take place, in which plenty and wealth will be spontaneously produced."[42] Thus government's task is not to distribute available material goods according to need or merit but to secure each man's right to *create* those goods, by "preserving men in the possession of what honest industry has already acquired, and also . . . preserving their liberty and strength, whereby they may acquire what they further want."[43]

To secure for each man the fruits of his own labor, government must punish theft. In more recent views, government should also prevent more subtle means by which one man might exploit another's industry. While the founders doubted the practicality of political efforts to ensure a perfect correlation between men's exercise of their acquisitive faculties and what they in fact acquire, a more fundamental dispute between the founders and some recent thought concerns men's right to the product of their own faculties. If men's faculties are not themselves earned, but appear to be a kind of gift or accident, how can they confer a right?[44] While this objection is made particularly to men's possession of talents, it can also be made to their possession of a propensity to exert themselves. At bottom, this objection amounts to a denial of Locke's assertion that each man is the owner of his own person, that is, his own body, and that "no Body has any Right to [it] but himself."[45] More recent thought may find our claim to our own body unprovable or unreasonable, although skepticism on this point calls into question each man's right not only to the acquisitive faculties he has not earned but also to the life and liberty he has not earned. Self-ownership may seem more like a proud assertion than a reasonable moral claim, but Locke's point remains: are there any other claims to our body that are more reasonable? Can other men or society or mankind in general claim a right to our body, when no human being has earned his membership in the society or species any more than he has earned his own body?

On the founders' own principles, however, government can adopt laws that "regulate the right of property"[46] and regulate the "various and interfering interests" of men who acquire property in different ways and in different degrees.[47] The simple necessity of taxation alone means that the right to property is not immune to political decision. But in the founders' view the object of such regulation was neither to distribute property according to need or desire nor to restrict the acquisition or use of property so as to save men from vice; it was to establish conditions under which men would be free to acquire what they want by "honest industry." Some founders recommended measures that would quietly moderate the extremes of wealth and poverty in order to preserve a broad opportunity to acquire without diminishing men's incentive to do so.[48] But excessive taxes would "prey upon the honest and industrious part of the community";[49] and "equal division of property" would be an "improper or wicked project."[50]

A different type of regulation of property would be concerned not with improving the material lot of the less affluent but with improving the moral well-being of the more affluent. If "industry is most favourable to the moral virtue of the world,"[51] the protection of men's right to acquire appears morally unobjectionable; but the right to acquire appears to carry with it the right to possess and use one's acquisitions in a manner unfavorable to virtue. At the Constitutional Convention, George Mason proposed to authorize Congress to enact sumptuary laws (that is, restrictions on consumption) that could give "a proper direction" to men's "love of distinction."[52] The proposal was rejected. Gouverneur Morris objected that other men's opportunity to acquire property would be inhibited if men with landed wealth were prevented from squandering their fortunes. Elbridge Gerry insisted that "the law of necessity is the best sumptuary law," implying that government ought not restrain men's freedom to consume as they wish and are able. In both arguments, what men do with their wealth is less important than their freedom to acquire it in the first place. Similarly, Madison suggested in a later essay that men's right to a "free choice" of occupation is more important than the better or worse effect that different occupations have on their minds and bodies.[53] A just government leaves men free to choose; it "secures the fruits of industry and virtue; but the best system of government cannot produce general happiness unless the people are virtuous, industrious and œconomical."[54] The Convention went only so far as to form a committee to encourage by example what sumptuary laws would command by law,[55] and the committee appears to have done nothing.

Men use their faculties in pursuits other than the acquisition of property, and these too are part of the civil liberty government is instituted to protect. James Wilson "could not agree that property was the sole or primary object of Govérnt. & Society. The cultivation & improvement of the human mind was the most noble object."[56] "Where tyranny reigns, there is the country of ignorance and vice—where good government prevails, there is the country of science and virtue." And "the most important of all the blessings of good government," Wilson suggests, is its enabling men to pursue the "heaven-descended science" that directs men's souls toward "the next [world]."[57] Wilson makes clear that government's role in these regards is simply to secure the freedom that naturally fosters human excellence. Just as the security of religious freedom, not the imposition of religious practice, is what allows men to save their immortal souls, good government secures the conditions that make men free to improve themselves but cannot require them to do so without abridging the freedom that is perhaps the precondition of excellence and may in any case be more highly valued by men than the excellence it makes possible. Human happiness is not guaranteed by government.[58] While unwilling to use sumptuary laws to "give . . . a proper direction" to the "natural" "love of distinction," the founders hoped that a proper direction would be the uncoerced result of a republican form of government that stimulated men's ambitions for political office (see below, "Popular Government"). Voluntary human improvement might also be encouraged by a national university Congress could establish in the federal district it would rule.[59]

Although what has been said so far suggests that government's fundamental task "is to protect the *liberties, lives,* and *property* of the people governed, from foreign and domestic violence,"[60] the assertion that "this, *and this only,* is what every government should do effectually"[61] is confounded by the Constitution's statement of an additional purpose, to "promote the general Welfare." Indeed the general welfare or the "public good"[62] is a traditional formulation of the object of government in writings that did *not* assert the primacy of individual men's rights. What is the relation between this object and the Constitution's concern to secure individual rights (that is, to "establish Justice")?

One connection is the dependence of private rights on a common defense. National defense (and even, on a smaller scale, support of the officers that preserve domestic peace) requires taxation. Taxation requires that there be something to tax. Therefore not just the safety of the community but its prosperity may be a necessary condition for the protection of an individual's rights. This is suggested by Noah Webster's argument that for the national government to lack any powers necessary for "the general *interest*" of the Union is "inconsistent with the *safety* of the United States."[63] According to Blackstone, laws that "constrain our conduct in matters of mere indifference" are "destructive of liberty," but

> if any public advantage can arise from observing such precepts, the control of our private inclinations, in one or two particular points, will conduce to preserve our general freedom in others of more importance; by supporting that state, of society, which alone can secure our independence.[64]

Likewise, according to Locke, it is "necessary" that a man entering political society "part . . . with as much of his natural liberty in providing for himself, as the good, prosperity, and safety of the Society shall require."[65] Thus it appears that the dependence of men's private rights on the existence of a society requires that government be able not barely to secure society's immediate safety but to serve the "interest" or "prosperity" that makes the continuing preservation of society most likely.

In addition to being, in some measure, instrumental to the preservation of rights, the general welfare is also a positive good in itself. Men's rights are necessary but not always sufficient to achieve or maximize their "welfare," and if government can contribute to welfare without violating rights, that is a desirable bonus. According to Adam Smith, when government has secured its "first and chief design" of maintaining "justice" (that is, "maintaining men in what are called their perfect rights"), it "will next be desirous of promoting the opulence of the state."[66] Edmund Randolph argued that a revised American government should not only secure America against foreign invasion and internal conflict, but also "p[ro]cure . . . various blessings."[67] The promise of economic advantage was conspicuous in the ratification debate.[68] A new national government could bargain advantageously with foreign powers for commercial advantage and could secure free trade among the American states. Noah Webster wrote that "on the adoption of this constitution, I should value real estate twenty per cent. higher than I do at this moment."[69]

The general welfare that government promotes does not mean welfare in a general or vague sense but the general welfare of America as a whole as distinguished from the particular welfare of individual persons or states.[70] The "public good" means "the good of every particular Member of . . . Society, as far as by common Rules, it can be provided for."[71] Not "care applyed to Individualls" but "a generall Providence" favoring "lawfull Industry" conduces to the general welfare.[72] By creating conditions in which men's exercise of their right to acquire property will be more fruitful, above all by promoting commerce, government serves the general welfare:

> The prosperity of commerce is now perceived and acknowledged by all enlightened statesmen to be the most useful as well as the most productive source of national wealth, and has accordingly become a primary object of their political cares. By multiplying the means of gratification, by promoting the introduction and circulation of the precious metals, those darling objects of human avarice and enterprise, it serves to vivify and invigorate all the channels of industry and to make them flow with greater activity and copiousness. The assiduous merchant, the laborious husbandman, the active mechanic, and the industrious manufacturer—all orders of men look forward with eager expectation and growing alacrity to this pleasing reward of their toils.[73]

The invigorated exercise by individuals of their private rights is the primary engine of a general prosperity.[74] For example, if creditors lack "confidence" that their rights are secure, "property will sink in value, and there will be no inducement or emulation to industry,"[75] whereas protecting the rights of writers and inventors by copyrights and patents stimulates their contributions to the "public good."[76]

The fact that men's exercise of their rights leads to national wealth may provide a kind of confirmation that human beings are indeed best understood as individuals with natural rights, and even today persuades many that rights exercised in a free market are an efficient means of creating material well-being. But one should not attribute to the founders the view that rights are simply a means to welfare and, by implication, dispensable if other means are discovered. Man's freedom is bounded by nature's not having provided those things necessary to the comfortable support of our lives, but he resists claims by other men or by government that would restrict his freedom within that broad necessity. The protection of rights is more fundamental than the promotion of welfare; it is the "first object of government," indeed it is the "end of civil society."[77]

This fundamental importance of private rights does not change the fact, already mentioned, that private rights depend on the existence of a public whose general welfare or at least common defense is necessary to their protection and may in some cases take priority over them; nor does it make clear exactly what expanses of human activity should be considered part of men's rights. The founders' problem was less to answer this question fully themselves than to create a government that would be most likely to give the right answer (see below, "Obliging the Government to Control Itself"). And in many cases the precise division between private rights and public regulation would not need to be settled by the national government at all. The continuing existence of separate state governments meant that, however limited the scope of government altogether, the national government created by the Constitution would have even narrower purposes. The central government was to "legislate in all cases to which the separate States are incompetent, or in which the harmony of the United States may be interrupted by the exercise of individual Legislation."[78] The federal government's promotion of the general welfare would not include promoting the particular welfare of each state; it

> cannot interfere with the opening of rivers and canals; the making or regulation of roads, except post roads; building bridges; erecting ferries; establishment of state seminaries of learning; libraries; literary, religious, trading or manufacturing societies; erecting or regulating the police of cities, towns or boroughs; . . . nor . . . do any other matter or thing appertaining to the internal affairs of any state, whether legislative, executive or judicial, civil or ecclesiastical.[79]

In these internal affairs would arise most occasions for men to decide the relative scope of private rights and of the public undertakings that tend to make men's rights secure and fruitful. While this discretion was limited by constitutional injunctions against certain specific state practices (ex post facto laws, for instance), it remained up to the states to determine how to use their broad range of powers in a way that both protects the rights of individuals and promotes the public good.

There remains one purpose of the Constitution announced in the preamble that I have not yet mentioned: "to secure the Blessings of Liberty for ourselves and our Posterity." "Liberty" in this context evidently means not safety and enjoyment of private rights (these were already mentioned: "secure domestic Tranquility"; "establish Justice"), but rather the political liberty that exists when a people is ruled only by their own consent or that of their elected representatives.[80] One could infer that this final clause of the Preamble merely asserts that the blessings already listed flow from political liberty and announces a determination to transmit them to posterity. But it is also possible that not all the objectives previously listed depend on liberty or that liberty confers some blessing distinct from or in addition to the previous list. I will return to this subject later, considering the Constitution's character as a popular government and the degree to which that character serves other ends or is an end in itself.

Powers of Government. Despite the founders' intention to limit the purposes of government, and especially of the national government, the most formidable *powers* of government could not easily be limited. Although government's proper object is not conquest of other nations but only "happiness at home," that is, the "civil & religious liberty" of its citizens, government cannot serve this modest objective without being "respectable abroad."[81] Even if founders can foresee and define the purposes of government, *"it is impossible to foresee or to define the extent and variety of national exigencies"*; so the power to raise armies and the revenues to support them must exist "without limitation."[82] The new government was even granted the power to maintain a standing army in peacetime[83] so that it could prepare in advance for "the gathering storm."[84]

Thus, despite its limited ends, the new government's *powers* appeared to "extend to every case that is of the least importance," to "every thing which concerns human happiness."[85] Taxation "is the great mean of protection, security, and defence, in a good government," but it is "the great engine of oppression and tyranny in a bad one."[86] However necessary they are, standing armies have a "malignant aspect to liberty."[87] I will consider in the next section the question of how the Constitution hoped to oblige rulers with such formidable powers to control themselves rather than tyrannically abuse those powers.

Government's contribution to "happiness at home" consists primarily of protecting men's rights by adopting *laws*—"settled standing Rules, indifferent, and the same to all Parties"[88]—and arranging for their *execution*. Rule by law is made practical by the principle that government's purpose is to secure rights. The greater flexibility and precision with which a ruler might decide individual cases is unnecessary because the ruler's task is not to direct citizens individually toward whatever excellence or happiness they might personally be capable of but only to secure the right of all to exercise their own faculties freely within the general limits that make freedom possible. Laws enable men to know in advance what is permitted and what is forbidden; a government that issued decrees would leave men with the same uncertainty that distressed them in the state of nature. And the laws themselves must be stable if men are to enjoy that mental "repose and confidence . . . which are among the chief blessings of civil society."[89] Stability permits men to reap the natural fruits of the industrious use of their own faculties, while sudden changes in the law serve the schemes of sharp speculators but injure elaborate enterprise as well as steady labor.[90]

For this reason, it would be pleasing to think that the legislature might settle the main points of law that define men's rights, leave their enforcement to other officers, and then have little to do.[91] But "there are tides in [the affairs of men]";[92] new exigencies beyond the legislature's control may require new laws, treaties, declarations of war, or taxes. The stable laws that protect men's rights cannot be entirely permanent but should change relatively infrequently. To this end, a senate whose members serve overlapping six-year terms can blunt the "mutability in the public councils" that results from "a rapid succession of new members" in the House of Representatives.[93]

Even the most reasonable taxes and most impartial laws that impinge on no man's rights will impinge on some men's inclinations. So laws must be enforced, and on this point the Articles of Confederation were particularly defective. Congress's "requisitions" of money from the states often went unheeded; the United States could "DECLARE every thing" but "DO nothing."[94] But the solution was not to give the government a "small number of armed vessels"[95] or allow it to "call forth the force of the Union agst. any member of the Union failing to fulfill its duty under the articles thereof."[96] Instead of addressing laws to the *states*—and seeing them ignored or fighting a war to compel obedience—the government needed to exercise a "national

Legislation over individuals"[97] that could be enforced against individuals. Individuals, unlike states or other groups of men, cannot contemplate successful resistance by force and so need not be subdued by force. They respond to the "arm of the ordinary magistrate" in "courts of justice."[98]

Force will still be necessary against foreign armies and against individuals who band together in seditious or criminal conspiracies, and that force must be directed by an executive power. The Convention decided to make the executive a single person rather than a committee. "Energy in the executive" comes from one man's ability to deliberate secretly, decide unanimously, and act quickly.[99] A single executive is especially important to command armies in war. George Mason admitted these advantages of a single executive but asked

> whether there is not some pervading Principle in Republican Governments which sets at Naught, and tramples upon this boasted Superiority—as hath been experienced, to their cost, by most Monarchys, which have been imprudent enough to invade or attack their republican Neighbors. This invincible Principle is to be found in the Love the Affection the Attachment of the Citizens to their Laws, to their Freedom, and to their Country—Every Husbandman will be quickly converted into a Soldier, when he knows and feels that he is to fight not in Defence of the Rights of a particular Family, or a Prince; but for his own.[100]

The founders chose a single executive, unwilling to forgo "this boasted Superiority" of monarchy, weighing more heavily the importance not only of eventually restoring society's tranquillity by tenaciously defeating enemies but of decisively acting to discourage or repel such assaults in the first place.

Those who boasted of monarchy's superiority in energetically securing the people's safety and tranquillity did not confine themselves to praising its ability to enforce laws. Hobbes recommended that a monarch act as the "Soveraigne" who can "do whatsoever he shall think necessary to be done," including making, changing, or violating laws.[101] Locke distinguished domestic policy ("the *Laws* that concern Subjects one amongst another, being to direct their actions, may well enough *precede* them") from foreign policy ("what is done in reference to *Foreigners*, depending much upon their actions, and the variation of designs and interests, must be *left* in great part *to* the *Prudence* of those who have this Power committed to them");[102] and even in domestic affairs defended the king's "*Prerogative*," a power to do good without or even against the authority of law.[103] Hamilton described how the need for energy led the Roman republic "to take refuge in the absolute power of a single man, under the formidable title of dictator."[104] The American president "shall take Care that the Laws be faithfully executed"; this means, among other things, acting as "Commander in Chief" to "repel sudden attacks"[105] that might prevent the law from being executed; and using the "Power to Grant Reprieves and Pardons"—that is, choosing some cases where the law will not be executed—if at "critical moments" in "seasons of insurrection or rebellion" he needs to bend the laws for a dangerous faction if he is to preserve the laws at all.[106] These aspects of what the Constitution tersely calls "the executive Power" indicate that he is not an automaton carrying out the legislature's written instructions but do not make clear whether he is endowed with Lockean prerogative or Roman dictatorial powers. The notion of a prerogative to do good even against the law was not unknown to the founders, as is evidenced by their own willingness to look beyond the law so as to revise the Articles of Confederation.[107]

The formidable powers the founders thought necessary to enable government to control the governed have won less admiration from subsequent thinkers than have the founders' precautions to oblige the government to control itself. Unlimited powers, armies, police, and executive prerogative are sometimes seen not as harsh necessities imposed by the facts of life but as outmoded conclusions from an excessively pessimistic or "Hobbesian" view of man. This criticism takes its most extreme form in Marx's argument that the full development of man will eventually coincide with the withering away of the state. Government can become a sanitized and predictable "administration of things," free of the violence or potential violence of an energetic executive trying to wrest tranquillity from an unruly human situation.

But while the necessities that justified powerful government to the founders appear potentially less pressing in light of hopes for human progress, more recent thought invigorates some of government's powers by its denial that those powers should be confined to the limited ends the founders envisioned. (By diminishing the sense of necessity and enlarging the range of choice, both in the name of progress, such thought may tend to support legislative more than executive powers.) For example, Federalists claimed that an unlimited power of taxation was an unavoidable necessity because it would be needed in wartime. Anti-Federalists predicted that such a power would lead the government to find new objects for all the revenue it could command: *"in Government what may be done will be done."*[108] Impressed as they were with the necessities that might be imposed by extraordinary events,[109] the Federalists thought it imprudent to limit government in the Constitution to the powers that should ordinarily be exercised. They thus appear to have depended on the climate of opinion to distinguish between ordinary and extraordinary circumstances. As opinion came to understand government's purposes more broadly than the founders did, powers that could be of service were already at hand.

Qualities of Government. Whether government serves its purposes depends not only on its formal powers but also on how well those powers are used. The difficulty of planning or anticipating whether rulers will use power well leads to the sentiments expressed by Alexander Pope:

> For forms of government let fools contest—
> That which is best administered is best.

Hamilton calls that maxim "political heresy."[110] A people choosing a form of government must act on some opinion about what form of government is likely to be best administered; it cannot resign itself to the uncertainty inherent in the question. The Constitution thus not only grants powers but also arranges offices so as to encourage those powers to be used well. For example, as discussed earlier, senators have lengthy terms to foster "stability," and the executive is singular for the sake of "energy." But the qualities most clearly conducive to good government are "wisdom" and "virtue." Compared with wisdom and virtue, energy and stability appear to be qualities whose goodness is more specific to a particular office and that are good only as a general rule. A wise legislator would appreciate the value of stability but would know when the common good requires a change in the laws; a virtuous executive's energetic assault on criminals and conspirators would be guided and sometimes moderated by his love of the common good (as in the case of pardons, discussed above). Madison states this high standard for the qualities of rulers:

> The aim of every political constitution is, or ought to be, first to obtain for rulers men who possess most wisdom to discern, and most virtue to pursue, the common good of the society; and in the next place, to take the most effectual precautions for keeping them virtuous whilst they continue to hold their public trust.[111]

The precautions intended to keep rulers virtuous will be discussed in the next section; here I will consider the Constitution's attempt to "obtain" wise and virtuous rulers, or some useful approximation thereof.

The political importance of wisdom is a venerable theme of political thought. Wisdom was regarded by classical authors as an independently valid claim to rule, not as something an otherwise legitimate political constitution ought to aim to "obtain." The philosopher who understands what is good for human beings is best equipped to direct them toward it.[112] But such an extravagant claim for the political importance of wisdom (or, alternatively, of divine inspiration) springs from an extravagant understanding of the proper purposes of political authority. Rulers who enforce peace and protect rights do not need precise knowledge of the good but only a clear understanding of how to avoid what all men know to be bad. The "wisdom" needed is more precisely a "knowledge of the *means*" to well-known ends.[113]

But even this is no small task. Simply to prevent a nation from becoming entangled in pointless wars (not to mention the task of fighting and winning unavoidable wars) requires rulers of "wisdom and prudence."[114] Modern political writers did not underestimate this requirement and suggested how to meet it. Hobbes thought a king should obtain the "Counsell" he needed from private advisers; public debate would be led astray by passion and eloquence.[115] Although popular government relies on public debate, Montesquieu suggested that a small republic is better equipped for that than a large republic because its "public good is better sensed, better known, closer to each citizen."[116] In a large country the public good is complicated and distant from everyday observation. Even though the public good may be defined as "the permanent and aggregate interests of the community," the aggregated opinions of people who do not "always *reason right* about the *means* of promoting it" will not necessarily serve the public good.[117] A large republic needs rulers with the "wisdom to discern" the complicated "common good" of a diverse society, and *elections* are the "characteristic" means by which republican government seeks to obtain such rulers.[118] Indeed, a noteworthy feature of the new Constitution as compared with earlier, small republics was its "*total exclusion of the people in their collective capacity* from any share in" the government;[119] the people were entitled to choose rulers and to judge their policies or the results of their policies but were not required themselves to adopt policies.

The quality of rulers might be influenced by their mode of selection, number, length of experience in office, and opportunity to engage in careful deliberation. There was disagreement at the Convention about what system of elections would choose the best rulers: indirect elections for a "refined" choice by knowledgeable electors, or direct elections so as to avoid cabal and horse-trading in an electoral body and obtain persons of widely distinguished reputation rather than popularity among political colleagues. The Convention settled on a mixture, moved partly by other considerations;[120] but both methods were defended for their tendency to select meritorious persons rather than "representative" in the sense of average or ordinary persons. The *number* of officers to be elected and number of people doing the electing were also considered in this context. While some Anti-Federalists insisted that in the small districts of state legislatures the people were better acquainted with the qualities of the candidates and so better able to choose the best,[121] Madison argued that a national legislature's necessarily larger districts would increase the probability of a fit choice by making bribery less practical and drawing from a larger supply of suitable candidates.[122] The same principles of supply and demand would tend to provide presidents more talented than, say, state governors.[123]

Relatively long terms permit the acquisition of knowledge and experience, qualities which if not identical to wisdom are nonetheless useful to men's ability to judge how to serve the public good. A two-year, rather than the more obvious one-year, term for representatives gives them a chance to learn things they had no occasion to learn in their private lives. And a longer term gives representatives "full freedom of deliberation"[124] because they will not be hastily judged by their constituents on the basis of a single decision. The small size and long term of the Senate were thought especially conducive to mature deliberation.[125]

The founders' thoughts about how to obtain wise rulers centered not simply on these institutionalized opportunities afforded to the exertion of talent but more fundamentally on the human motives that would stimulate such exertions. The problem was not only to select but also to attract meritorious rulers to office—and not only to give them the opportunity to exercise their wisdom but also to give them a motive to do so. One incentive that might attract able congressmen was the possibility of being appointed to executive offices. Attempts to exclude such appointments so as to prevent an executive from corrupting the legislature by dispensing or promising such favors were resisted by James Wilson and others because that would discourage men of "talents" from entering Congress.[126] In reply, George Mason said he

> cd. not suppose that a sufficient number of Citizens could not be found who would be ready, without the inducement of eligibility to offices, to undertake the Legislative service. Genius & virtue it may be said, ought to be encouraged.

> Genius, for aught he knew, might, but that virtue should be encouraged by such a species of venality, was an idea, that at least had the merit of being new.[127]

Wilson in turn

> animadverted on the impropriety of stigmatizing with the name of venality the laudable ambition of rising into the honorable offices of the Government; an ambition most likely to be felt in the early & most incorrupt period of life, & which all wise & free Govts. had deemed it sound policy, to cherish, not to check.[128]

"Venality" or "avarice" may move some but not most men who aspire to high offices; the more ordinary motive is a "laudable ambition" that loves office or honor or power for its own sake. Even so, does that impulse encourage "virtue"? Mason appears to agree with Montesquieu's description of republican virtue as a pure, patriotic love of the public good that limits each citizen's ambition to "the sole desire, the sole happiness of doing greater services to his country than the other citizens."[129] Even Montesquieu's severe formulation suggests that virtuous men do not entirely forget themselves. And according to James Wilson and other founders, government needs the services of men who think much about themselves. An able lover of power can be a useful servant of the public good. If the prospect of higher office will draw such people into the legislative body, one should be careful not to bar that prospect. "The impulse to the Legislative service, was evinced by experience to be in general too feeble with those best qualified for it."[130] "If [patriotism] be the only inducement, you will find a great indifferency in filling your legislative body."[131]

This argument assumes that service in Congress is not a sufficiently exalted "reward" for someone of "laudable ambition." The love of power is frustrated when its object is widely shared, as it is in the House of Representatives. Conspicuous executive offices may be more attractive, and the Senate's small size gives each senator a "sensible degree of the praise and blame" for successes and failures.[132] But the presidency is where the conjunction of "constitutional means" and decidedly "*personal* motives"[133] comes into sharpest focus. The single executive stands alone, and the "responsibility" to praise or blame, reward or punishment, is his alone. No colleagues obstruct his opportunity to act or dilute his credit for the results.[134]

The president's personal motives were considered in the debate over whether to make him eligible for reelection. George Mason said no:

> He held it as an essential point, as the very palladium of Civil liberty, that the great officers of State, and particularly the Executive should at fixed periods return to that mass from which they were at first taken, in order that they may feel & respect those rights & interests, Which are again to be personally valuable to them.[135]

Mason recommended a seven-year term, so he was not simply opposed to a fairly lengthy stay in office; but the executive should look forward to again being a private citizen—a prospect that will make him more sympathetic to the rights and interests of the citizens he will rejoin. To borrow the distinction already quoted, Mason is concerned with "virtue" or faithful intention, rather than with "genius" or talents. But the Convention ultimately took a contrary view, holding that the president should be able to look forward to again *being president*. The possibility of rejection would make him sufficiently concerned with the interests of private citizens, but the hope of continuation could spur him to do good works. At a minimum, the hope for reelection would discourage oppressive measures or graft that would arouse the people's antipathy, and it would offer an alternative for criminally ambitious men who might, if excluded by the Constitution, try instead to overturn the Constitution.[136] But the hope for reelection could spur more than the "negative merit of not doing harm."[137] In the best case, the "love of fame," "the ruling passion of the noblest minds,"[138] the "great spring to noble & illustrious actions,"[139] would

> prompt a man to plan and undertake extensive and arduous enterprises for the public benefit, requiring considerable time to mature and perfect them, if he could flatter himself with the prospect of being allowed to finish what he had begun.[140]

In contrast to Mason's hope that officers should closely identify themselves with the people, the prevailing view saw advantages in officers who would think more about their own personal prospects for power or fame. The people are better off employing, and controlling by reward and punishment, men whose personal motives make them receptive to those controls, rather than hoping to elevate men who do not think about themselves at all. The founders looked not to a self-abnegating virtue to guarantee public-spirited intentions but to a self-aggrandizing spirit that would provoke public-benefiting actions. They hoped to attract genius and hoped various checks built into the political institutions would safeguard—or if necessary "suppl[y] . . . the defect of"[141]—the rulers' virtue.

The founders intended that the quality of rulers should in some respects rise above the quality of the people, but entirely on the basis of the people's own choice. While this meant that "in the general course of things, the popular views, and even prejudices, will direct the actions of the rulers,"[142] the "exceptions to this rule" would give scope to the particular qualities of rulers. These exceptions may be significant in practice but are neglected by political analysts who understand or wish elected officials to be only transmitters and aggregators of their constituents' impulses. More common today than the apparently obsolete, elitist theme of "wisdom" is a recognition of the place of "expertise" located in specialized bureaucracies. This may seem more acceptable because it is so clear that such experts really are the hired servants of the people and subordinate to them—an assertion that might appear questionable when applied to a leading political figure. The opinion that government should be (intellectually) as good as, not better than, the people has largely displaced the founders' view, although it may be that the institutional opportunities the founders created for wisdom to exert itself are not seriously impaired by a climate of opinion that denies its necessity.

While on the whole less willing to admit the role of rulers' wisdom than were the founders, contemporary thought at the same time seems to make that wisdom more important by its denial that government's ends are limited. Rejecting the principle that government's task is limited to securing those rights that are men's by nature prior to government, contemporary thought appears to restore something of the open-ended character of politics that made wisdom appear in preliberal thought a decisive claim to rule.

Contemporary thought may affect the founders' expectations for the quality of rulers in one more respect if a new climate of education and opinion diverts men from the political impulses that the founders mistakenly ascribed to human nature. Does the love of power animate a sufficient supply of able men, or can the desire for comfort and income make men averse to the risk either of entering politics or of undertaking anything other than the preservation of their place once in office? Does the love of fame permanently grip some noble minds, or can the charms of momentary acclaim or comfortable anonymity displace it? Altogether, the founders did not bend much effort to "conform the principles, morals, and manners of our citizens to our republican forms of government,"[143] because they thought the particular republican form they devised could accept human nature in a rawer, purer form than could the strict, high-minded, virtuous republic celebrated in earlier thought. Virtue, they judged, was too corruptible to be the main foundation of their regime;[144] to the extent that the passions the founders thought more solidly implanted in man were in fact the product of a specific climate of thought, they too are corruptible.

Obedience to Government. Some Anti-Federalists thought that, if an effective national government depends on attracting talent by indulging ambition and perhaps also on a standing army to enforce its laws, America would be better off relying on state governments. The people would be rightly suspicious of the "ambitious views" of rulers of a large country, while in a small republic the rulers are close at hand and can win the confidence and cooperation of citizens more familiar with them.[145] Noting Montesquieu's observation that despotic government, with force as its principle, was the type suited to large empires, they insisted that only the continued primacy of state governments would win the voluntary obedience of citizens. In this view, state governments should both rule their own internal affairs and be relied on to carry out the central government's policies.[146]

The Constitution's intention to preserve the state governments with an independent sphere of action reflects the influence of this argument (and of other arguments to be discussed later). But the Convention did not rely on the states to enforce federal laws, because state officers might lead a trusting people in resisting the federal laws rather than win the people's trust for those laws.

The Federalists agreed that government's ability to control the governed would depend not only on the powers and talents of the rulers but also on the dispositions of the ruled. The Federalists hoped to win popular confidence in the new government by the reputation of its framers, by the evident trustworthiness of its structure, and perhaps most conclusively by its performance. For the people to ratify the government would of course be a sign of some confidence in it, so the problems of voluntary obedience and ratification overlapped. Praises of the wisdom and patriotism of Washington, Franklin, and the Philadelphia Convention's membership in general were common in Federalist campaign literature. More substantive were arguments that the "wholly popular" character of the new government, the arrangement of its offices so that the dangerous ambitions of rulers could be checked, and (paradoxically) the very fact that a suspicious people led by their jealous state governments would be watching it closely, all made the Constitution "safe" and therefore trustworthy. Once the new government was in operation, it would be able to win popular allegiance and obedience by its performance. The states might benefit from men's natural or habitual affection for what is nearby, but the national government could win respect and obedience by being "better administered" than the states.[147] "Public attachment" is fostered by "a train of prosperous events, which are the result of wise deliberation and vigorous execution."[148]

This source of attachment and obedience depends partly on the opinions of the people about what constitutes good performance by a government. Perhaps "all governments rest on opinion."[149] Seeing the importance of opinion in fostering or discouraging men's obedience to government, Hobbes insisted that the sovereign's "generall Providence" for the people's safety would consist not only of good laws and their execution but also of "publique Instruction, both of Doctrine, and Example."[150] Quite apart from the need to educate citizens or rulers who will be deliberating about how to rule, some kind of public instruction appears necessary merely to secure obedience to government.[151]

The founders agreed that education of citizens would help preserve free government but (as their endorsement of free speech and free press indicates) did not believe government would need to restrict the content of public teaching. While Hobbes feared that unscientific doctrines might dissuade the people from their duties as revealed by Hobbes's political science, the American founders appear to have been confident that the self-evident truths that supported the American form of government would indeed be evident to the people. When men yield only the proper portion of their natural rights so as to establish a government, "the government is really strengthened; because wherever the subject is convinced that nothing more is required from him, than what is necessary for the good of the community, he yields a chearful obedience."[152] Thomas Jefferson (commenting on the proposed Constitution) suggested that

> information to the people . . . is the most certain & the most legitimate engine of government. educate & inform the whole mass of the people. enable them to see that it is their [interest to?] preserve peace & order, & they will preserve it. and it [requires no very?] high degree of education to convince them of this.[153]

Man's natural taste for the enjoyment of his natural rights is a valuable crutch for a government that protects those rights. Because the Constitution did not rest on a noble lie or on "arrogant pretensions" of some "self-appointed" rulers,[154] the citizens' education need not be controlled to support a lie, nor need it be so highly refined as to understand difficult truths.

But even if the natural ends of government are naturally attractive to man, man is not immune to error; man's nature can be concealed from him.[155] Another difficulty is that attractive ends are served by necessary means (an energetic executive, for example) that are not themselves attractive. And even the best government may not enjoy uninterrupted success in serving popular ends. The people's modestly educated appreciation of their rights may not make them always tranquilly contemplative of the long view or understanding of insurmountable difficulties.

One approach to these problems was to try to educate the people about the ends, means, and problems of government. One purpose of a bill of rights was to make prominently and permanently clear to the citizens the rights they should expect. Some supporters of ratification probably had educational purposes in mind when they joined a rather comprehensive public debate on the principles of government rather than confining themselves to superficial campaign slogans. They regarded it as important that the "popular creed" not embrace political doctrines that "would utterly unfit the people of this country for any species of government whatever."[156] But the founders doubted that such reasoning would be entirely sufficient; except in a "nation of philosophers," "the most rational government will not find it a superfluous advantage to have the prejudices of the community on its side." Such prejudices in the government's favor would be cultivated by "that veneration which time bestows on everything."[157] If the Constitution lasted "through succeeding ages,"[158] it would acquire a reservoir of good will among the people. An additional and more immediate source of popular obedience and attachment was the procedure by which the Constitution was put into effect. The principle that popular consent is the foundation of government (and even the specific, questionably legal application of that principle in the procedures of 1787) was virtually unchallenged in the ratification debate. The belief that such consent gives this government and no other the right to rule serves as a bulwark against discordant or fluctuating opinions about how well this government is serving its purposes. The doctrine of government by consent distinguished government's right to rule from the goodness of its rule in recognition that the latter point would be too controversial to be a lasting basis for peace.

But each of these foundations for obedience appears vulnerable to later shifts in thought. The founders' arguments may lose their influence on the popular creed. The people may judge government more harshly if its responsibility for their happiness is not limited by an accepted opinion of government's limited ends. And the government's right to rule may become questionable if the principle of an original, popular ratification is seen not as the binding foundation of legitimate government but as a merely formal or outdated token of the people's wishes or as morally meaningless altogether (see below, "Founding by Consent").

Obliging the Government to Control Itself

> If men were angels, no government would be necessary. If angels were to govern men, neither external nor internal controls on government would be necessary. In framing a government which is to be administered by men over men, the great difficulty lies in this: you must first enable the government to control the governed; and in the next place oblige it to control itself.[159]

For the same reason that men need government to restrain them, government itself needs some source of restraint. Men institute government to secure their rights, but government can become destructive of their rights; a government that can control the governed might find it as easy to oppress the innocent as to restrain the wicked. And, because it is a government "by men," it may find that course attractive:

> Rulers have the same propensities as other men; they are as likely to use the power with which they are vested for private purposes, and to the injury and oppression of those over whom they are placed, as individuals in a state of nature are to injure and oppress one another.[160]

Thus "almost every page of the history of nations" proves "that power, lodged in the hands of rulers to be used at discretion, is almost always exercised to the oppression of the people, and the aggrandizement of themselves."[161]

While some founders quoted Montesquieu's statement that virtue is the principle or activating spring of republican government, and even regarded "some degree of virtue"[162] or "sufficient virtue"[163] as indispensable, they did not think virtue a sufficient control on the behavior of rulers. Virtue can stimulate good service by rulers, but cannot reliably prevent bad behavior. Either because even rulers with the "most virtue" are corruptible or because a constitution that aims to obtain such rulers cannot consistently do so, such a constitution must also "take the most effectual precautions for keeping them virtuous whilst they continue to hold their public trust."[164]

Protecting the people from oppression by rulers was an important concern of the framers, but the principle of man's natural freedom posed an additional complication. Not merely the welfare of the people in general but security for the rights of each individual is the object for which government is instituted. Thus "it is of great importance in a republic not only to guard the society against the oppression of its rulers, but to guard one part of the society against the injustice of the other part."[165] The problem of obliging the government to control itself thus has a double character. Before discussing the knotty problem of guarding the rights of each part of society, I will outline the Constitution's attempts to guard the people as a whole from oppression by their rulers.

Guarding the Whole Society. One means of restraining rulers was to adopt a constitution whose language conferred only limited authority upon them. In adopting the Constitution, the people make a "positive grant" of "authority," and "every thing which is not given, is reserved" by the people.[166] But while "an [enumeration] and definition of the powers necessary to be exercised by the national Legislature" would be desirable, its "practicability" was doubted.[167] Thus the Constitution enumerates not exactly the powers of the legislature but the objects or ends of the legislature.[168] Its *powers* in the service of those objects are as complete as the states' powers to serve their objects[169]—as one might judge from the expansive power to "make all Laws which shall be necessary and proper for carrying into Execution" the powers granted in the Constitution. Since not all powers given could be spelled out, it was not simply redundant or contradictory to spell out some powers the people wished reserved; thus a bill of rights would limit the powers or means that the government could use in service of its specified ends. The Constitution as submitted for ratification already contained some prohibitions on government (for example, "No Bill of Attainder or ex post facto Law shall be passed"), and thereafter additional provisions of a bill of rights were judged "proper to restrain and regulate the exercise of the great powers necessarily given to rulers."[170]

Some Federalists were doubtful that such "parchment stipulations"[171] would have much practical effect against ambitious rulers; and some thought such restraints imprudent, because it "is possible that in the infinite variety of events, it might become improper strictly to adhere to any one provision that has ever been proposed to be stipulated."[172] Even though Hamilton was reluctant to "disarm the government of a single weapon, which in any possible contingency might be usefully employed for the general defense and security,"[173] the Constitution as amended clearly determines that even where abridging liberty of the press or punishing criminals without a trial would be useful to the public safety, it is not allowed. If, however, a proscribed power is not merely useful but indispensably necessary to the public safety, the prohibition cannot be regarded as absolute. A "great and over-ruling necessity" excuses an "extraordinary exercise of power" that the Constitution explicitly forbids.[174]

Nonetheless, the prevailing view held that a clear and prominent "declaration of our rights" would prevent their being "hereafter . . . unknown, forgotten or contradicted by our representatives, our delegates, our servants in Congress."[175] Still, not all limits the people wish to impose on government can be written into the Constitution. As was noted earlier, an enumeration of powers cannot omit, nor a bill of rights forbid, the legislature's very dangerous powers to lay taxes and raise armies; these powers must be granted "without limitation" in order to meet national *"exigencies"* that cannot be foreseen or defined in advance.[176] The people nonetheless intend that Congress shall not adopt unreasonably high taxes or maintain an unnecessarily large army, that is, that Congress shall do only what is "necessary and proper," or what serves the public good. While the Constitution's language could indicate this intention in a general way, the proper conduct of policy could not be defined in clear grants or denials of specific "powers." Some Federalists thought that constitutional language guaranteeing "liberty of the press" was no more appropriate than language declaring "that taxes ought not to be excessive"[177] or that government could not forbid "matrimony, or . . . burial of the dead"[178] or "eating and drinking."[179] Those who adopted the Bill of Rights over this objection did not wish to imply that *all* intended limits on government were written there (see the Ninth Amendment).

The efficacy of either written or unwritten limits on government depends fundamentally on what the *form* of the government is:

> The only real security that you can have for all your important rights must be in the nature of your government. If you suffer any man to govern you who is not strongly interested in supporting your privileges, you will certainly lose them. If you are about to trust your liberties with people whom it is necessary to bind by stipulation, that they shall not keep a standing army, your stipulation is not worth even the trouble of writing. No bill of rights ever yet bound the supreme power longer than the *honey moon* of a new married couple, unless the *rulers were interested* in preserving the rights.[180]

Thus Anti-Federalists' objections to "the extent of the powers" granted to government were "inflammatory declamations and unmeaning cavils"; the true subject for debate was whether the "internal structure" of the government was "modeled in such a manner" as to be trusted.[181]

Elections are the most obvious way of interesting rulers in preserving the rights of the people:

> The greatest possible Security that a people can have for their civil rights and liberties, is, that no laws can be made to bind them, nor any taxes be imposed upon them without their consent by representatives chosen by themselves.[182]

This means of controlling the government operates even in a mixed government such as England's; the government as a whole is controlled because it cannot act without the consent of its representative part (the House of Commons). The American Constitution goes further, putting the "whole power" of the government "in the hands of the representatives of the people" so as to secure the people's "rights and privileges."[183] The short term, direct election, and relatively large size of the House of Representatives make it the branch most immediately dependent on the people and therefore seemingly "more immediately the confidential guardians of the rights and liberties of the people."[184]

But the representation promised by the American Constitution did not satisfy those who thought "that those who are placed instead of the people . . . should bear the strongest resemblance of those in whose room they are substituted."[185] Anti-Federalists argued that a "considerably numerous" body of representatives would be necessary to simulate the people's qualities and win their trust:

> The people of this state will have very little acquaintance with those who may be chosen to represent them; a great part of them will, probably, not know the characters of their own members, much less that of a majority of those who will compose the fœderal assembly; they will consist of men, whose names they have never heard, and of whose talents and regard for the public good, they are total strangers to; and they will have no persons so immediately of their choice so near them, of their neighbours and of their own rank in life, that they can feel themselves secure in trusting their interests in their hands. . . . [The representatives'] station will be elevated and important, and they will be considered as ambitious and designing.[186]

These objections, which conclude that only in much smaller republics (that is, the states) will elected representatives be properly dependent on the people, set in sharper relief the quite different principle of representation that prevailed in the Constitution. The Federalists emphasized not the resemblance between represented and representative, but the distinction between them that allows the former to choose, second-guess, and depose the latter. Indeed the "closeness" of a trusted local representative could be a trap; dangerous powers "had better be in those hands of which the people are most likely to be jealous than in those of which they are least likely to be jealous."[187] Representatives should be seen not as a sample or microcosm of the people but as carefully selected agents of the people who are commissioned to deliberate on their own and can be held responsible for the results of their decisions. The Federalists suggested that even if voters did not personally know the person they voted for, they would know whether the candidate has an "extensive reputation for talents and other qualifications";[188] and if the constituents' characteristic disposition toward incumbents was suspicious watchfulness rather than blissful, neighborly confidence, that would be a useful guard against betrayal. The people can control the government best if they judge from a cool distance rather than wholeheartedly identify with representatives they regard as close neighbors or personal friends.

The people can use elections to oblige the rulers to control themselves; they also retain the right to alter or abolish the entire government by means of revolution. The possibility of such a revolution may deter rulers from contemplating innovations that deprive the people of their ordinary means of control. The Constitution attempts to make revolution unnecessary by giving the people a way to amend the Constitution even if their incumbent elected national officials oppose the amendment.[189] The people may be united and inspired in their own defense by a bill of rights that serves as an "ensign, to which . . . the asserters of liberty may rally."[190] And the people's ability to control the government by election, amendment, or revolution is enhanced by the existence of state governments, whose separate (and rivalrous) elected officials will watch the national government's deeds and serve as agitators and leaders of a people abused by them. State officials can do this formally, in electing senators or passing on constitutional amendments;[191] informally, by influencing popular elections;[192] or illegally, by leading a revolution.[193]

While a dependence on the people "is, no doubt, the primary control on the government,"[194] the "means relied on in this form of government for preventing [the rulers'] degeneracy are numerous and various."[195] Elections cannot completely secure the people against overbearing rulers, if rulers between elections misuse their powers for that limited time—making their personal "harvest as abundant as it was transitory";[196] or concoct deceptions that an inattentive people fails to detect; or baldly usurp powers by canceling future elections. Certain "auxiliary precautions"[197] were built into the government's internal structure to help guard the people against these dangers.

The first of these is the Constitution's arrangement for government to rule by means of laws and its division of the activities of this mode of ruling among distinct legislative, executive, and judicial departments. This arrangement obliges rulers to control themselves in several respects. It not only provides the people the security of knowing in advance what the rulers forbid but also assures them that they personally will be coerced or punished not by a ruler who rules as he pleases but only by an "executive" who carries out the rules made by others. And the executive is confined to this modest task of law enforcement by the existence of a separate judiciary, which permits individuals to dispute the executive's application of the law to their case before an independent third party. The separation of powers also has an important controlling effect on the legislature itself, as was most clearly explained by John Locke:

> And because it may be too great a temptation to humane frailty apt to grasp at Power, for the same Persons who have the Power of making Laws, to have also in their hands the power to execute them, whereby they may exempt themselves from Obedience to the Laws they make, and suit the Law, both in its making and execution, to their own private advantage, and thereby come to have a distinct interest from the rest of the Community, contrary to the end of Society and Government: Therefore in well order'd Commonwealths, where the good of the whole is so considered, as it ought, the *Legislative* Power is put into the hands of divers Persons who duly Assembled, have by themselves, or jointly with others, a Power to make Laws, which when they have done, being separated again, they are themselves subject to the Laws, they have made; which is a new and near tie upon them, to take care, that they make them for the publick good.[198]

If the legislators are liable to have the law executed against them, they share with the rest of the population an interest in laws that serve the public good; this "has always been deemed one of the strongest bonds by which human policy can connect the rulers and the people together."[199]

This prescription for rule by the impartial and independently reviewed execution of laws that serve the public good is incomplete in three respects. First, some of government's activities (for example, the executive's power as commander in chief) are not carried out according to this formula and must be controlled by other means. Second, the effects of rule by law depend heavily on the goodness of the laws, which is encouraged but not guaranteed by their applying to the legislators; so the founders conceived of several other precautions to control the laws. Third, a separation of the powers of legislation, execution, and judging is vulnerable to the "encroaching nature" of power; [200] so a constitutionally prescribed separation cannot by itself keep rulers from usurping powers from the other departments and destroying the security that separation was meant to achieve. One or more of these difficulties explain a set of constitutional arrangements that supplement the separation of powers: the executive veto, the bicameral legislature, judicial review of legislation, and impeachment.

The success of separation of powers depends on some "practical security" to keep each department confined to its own job.[201] One security is to make each department as independent of the others as possible. Because the executive must not be under the legislature's control when he decides against whom to execute the legislature's laws, "making the Executive the mere creature of the Legislature" is "a violation of the fundamental principle of good Government."[202] The Convention devised the Electoral College so that the president would not depend on Congress for his election or reelection.

Neither should the legislature be under the control of the executive, as in England where the king "by his influence" (from dispensing lucrative offices to legislators) "in a manner dictates the laws."[203] Restrictions on the president's appointment of congressmen to executive offices were designed to prevent this. And the judiciary must be independent of the executive to be able to control his enforcements. While judges owe their appointment to the president and confirmation to the Senate, their term of "good Behaviour" frees them from dependence.

One branch could undermine separation of powers not only by subtly influencing a dependent branch but also by boldly usurping the powers of a weaker branch. To protect the president's authority against a Congress that wished to seize his power and act as its own executive (or appoint a different executive), the Convention provided a means of self-defense, a qualified veto on the legislature's acts. By using his veto to defend his independent authority to execute the laws, the president preserves the legislature's incentive to make laws that they would not mind having applied to themselves.

But it was recognized that the veto does more than protect the president from the legislature: it virtually makes the president a branch of the legislature. Laws cannot easily be passed without him; he can influence the laws, although his influence falls short of the

"Power of making Laws" that must not be combined with "the power to execute them."[204] Still, the veto that protects the president's power also adds greatly to his power and offers a new means by which government is obliged to control itself. The president can veto not only laws that encroach on his authority and tend to create a tyrannical concentration of power in the legislature that would eventually redound to the people's detriment; he can also veto any particular laws that would be to the people's detriment even if enforced by an impartial executive. "Col Mason Observed that the defence of the Executive was not the sole object of the Revisionary power"; it would also hinder or deter the enactment of "unjust and pernicious laws."[205]

This second purpose was also to be served by the bicameral arrangement of the legislature. I have already noted the particular qualities of the Senate that were intended to raise the quality of government, but the mere fact of two distinct branches to "watch & check each other"[206] would, it was hoped, make it more difficult to enact oppressive laws. The decision " 'that the national Legislature ought to consist of two branches' was agreed to [by the Convention] without debate or dissent."[207]

Some founders envisioned the judiciary as one more safeguard against oppressive laws. Courts are most obviously a restraint on the executive, because they judge whether his executions conform to the law; but the doctrine now known as judicial review makes courts also a restraint on the legislature, because they can judge whether its legislation conforms to the Constitution. In applying the law to particular cases, judges are obliged to interpret and reconcile the law that the people enact in the Constitution together with the law that the legislature enacts under the Constitution. Since the legislature's own authority derives from the Constitution, the laws it makes give way to the Constitution's own provisions in case of a conflict. In this way, a people's original intention to create a limited government can be enforced against a legislature that tries to break through those limits. Indeed, the people's original intention can even be enforced against their own later inclinations, if those inclinations provoke or support overreaching legislation.

This judicial control on legislation was given an impressive exposition and defense by Hamilton in *Federalist* No. 78 but was not very clearly discussed or formally enacted by the Convention itself. Several delegates spoke against such a power.[208] But in the ratification debate Brutus, opposing judicial review, and Hamilton, defending it, both asserted that the Constitution implied that power.[209] The judiciary's independence *of the people* distinguishes its review of legislation from that by the Senate and the executive, making its role more controversial than those other "auxiliary precautions."[210] But the judiciary's role in limiting the legislature is also distinguished by its application of only the written and not the unwritten limits on government. In contrast to the Senate's and the president's authority to resist measures they believe unnecessarily intrusive on the people's free choice, or contrary to the public good, or unjust, judicial review enforces only the Constitution's specific written restraints on government.[211] And those restraints were few (and rather clear cut) before the Bill of Rights was added. The Convention repeatedly rejected a proposal by Madison and Wilson to give the judiciary a share in the "Revisionary power," that is, the power to veto laws. This proposal would have enabled the Supreme Court to help control laws that, while not unconstitutional, were unwise or unjust or tended to infringe on the judiciary's authority. The proposal was defeated on the grounds that it would make "Statesmen of the Judges," corroding the impartiality necessary to the Court's primary role as interpreter of the law.[212] The Convention also did not support the position that the Court would judge legislation by unwritten standards of natural justice, rejecting Ellsworth's view that "ex post facto laws were void of themselves" even if not prohibited in writing.[213]

Judicial review is justified not as adding another ambitious competitor to the policy-making process but as an enforcement of the Constitution as *law.* To the extent that government can be controlled by the creation of offices whose occupants will look out for their own powers by virtue of their human nature, that effect appears relatively invulnerable to future changes in political understanding. The founders expected the president to defend his power because he is ambitious, not necessarily because he understands or loves the Constitution. But to the extent that the control of government rests on the Constitution's being enforced as law, it appears dependent on future opinion about the Constitution's principles. If those principles are regarded as dated or false, their judicial enforcement as law will seem obnoxious. One result is that if judges wish to exercise the impressive powers ascribed to them in *Federalist* No. 78, they will feel a strong personal motive to promote belief in the continuing vitality of constitutional principles, either for their intrinsic excellence or for their having been solemnly adopted by the people and not solemnly amended or repealed by the people. Judges doubtful of some of the Constitution's principles or of their ability to promote continued public belief in them have seen two alternative ways to adjust to a changing climate of opinion. One approach is "judicial restraint," whereby the Court decides to impose constitutional principles prudently and sparingly so as not to offend present-day opinion by enforcing as law the full weight of past principles. A second approach is "judicial activism," whereby the Court itself reinterprets and revises constitutional principles even while strongly insisting on their binding character. Ambitious judges are thus still required to promote the idea of constitutional principles but must devise skillful rhetoric to make plausible their creative substitutions.

So much for the auxiliary precautions designed to prevent the legislature from usurping the powers of the other departments or abusing the power that properly belongs to it. The provision for impeachment is designed to control the executive and judicial branches in these same respects. Impeachment can preserve the separation of powers against a criminal president who tries to rule by fiat in defiance of the law or the courts, or against a judiciary that, pretending to enforce the Constitution, substitutes its own wishes for constitutionally acceptable legislation.[214] But preserving separation of powers does not prevent all abuses of power, such as those by a judge who simply renders unfair decisions in civil disputes properly before him. More important are the presidential powers that do not depend on the guidance of law or the consent of a judge. As commander in chief of the armed forces, the president could suppress an insurrection, and those who did not survive the battle could not appeal to the judiciary for a second opinion. A president's treasonous conduct of foreign policy or embezzling supervision of the Treasury would not depend on a court's consent. The "energy" of a single, formidable executive is not sufficiently controlled by a "parchment" prescription of a judicial procedure that does not always come into play. Nor is he sufficiently controlled by his "dependence on the people," because his corruption or treachery could be quite consequential in the time before the next election and he might corruptly contrive his reelection (and even his initial election).

The nature of some of the executive's tasks makes them controllable only after the fact. The constitutional provision for impeachment gains force from the fact that the executive is "single" rather than plural; he cannot shift blame to a council of colleagues but can be held personally responsible.[215] Besides serving as an auxiliary precaution against the slowness or vulnerability of the electoral process, impeachment can also result in the *punishment* of the guilty, which the denial of reelection may not do sufficiently to deter the crime or satisfy the victims.[216] Impeachment is preferable to the alternatives that discontented men might resort to if it were unavailable: insurrection or

> assassination in wch. [the chief Magistrate] was not only deprived of his life but of the opportunity of vindicating his

> character. It wd. be the best way therefore to provide in the Constitution for the regular punishment of the Executive when his misconduct should deserve it, and for his honorable acquittal when he should be unjustly accused.[217]

Impeachment thus controls not only rulers but also private citizens who might try to control rulers by drastic means, providing a formal channel for them to make their case and depriving them of an excuse to resort to violence.

The Convention assigned the impeachment power to the legislature with some reluctance, not wanting to make too dependent on the legislature an executive who is relied on to control the legislature's excesses. The Convention tried to mitigate this problem by separating the House (for indictment) and the Senate (for conviction), by requiring a two-thirds vote to convict, by providing a rather narrow definition of impeachable offenses ("high crimes & misdemeanors" rather than "maladministration"), and by putting senators on oath, with the chief justice presiding, to impart a more judicial and less political character to the proceedings.[218] While the executive's control of the legislature (the veto) is a political weapon he may deploy as he thinks best (and which the legislature can in turn override), the legislature's control of the executive is distinguished as a legal or quasi-legal procedure by which the Constitution's grant of power is enforced as law.

Guarding the Parts. Thus far I have considered those controls on government exercised by or on behalf of the people as a whole. The people can exercise their electoral power to protect themselves against abusive rulers and can expect some of the ambitious officers they directly or indirectly elect to stand up against other ambitious officers who try to serve themselves rather than the people. But the whole people includes within it diverse parts—groups and individuals who are diversely affected by government's interventions. A government whose policies tend to serve the "great body of" the people,[219] some more and some less, might seem the best one could hope for; but the fundamental status of the *rights* of each individual makes that less than some founders insisted upon. "Justice is the end of government. It is the end of civil society."[220] Each man's primary object in joining others in civil society is to secure his own rights; this requires a government that is not only favorable to the "happiness" of "the whole Society" but also "sufficiently neutral between the different interests and factions, to controul one part of the Society from invading the rights of another."[221] Such neutrality cannot be ensured by representation, because a minority will be represented by only a minority of representatives. Thus although taxation without representation was tyranny in 1776, any American representatives in the British Parliament could have been outvoted in any case, leaving American rights insecure.[222] Nor is neutrality inherent in the fact that laws are "settled standing Rules, indifferent, and the same to all Parties,"[223] because the parties themselves are different and therefore differently affected.[224]

The constitutional arrangements that divide and control the power of lawmaking were thought likely to encourage laws more neutral between the different interests and factions than those a single assembly might adopt. For one thing, a majority's attempt to violate private rights may result from a "sudden" impulse that is also "transient"[225] and succeeded by regret. The relatively slower three-part legislative procedure might allow heads to cool; and the Senate and the president in particular "might seasonably impose agst. impetuous counsels"[226] with the expectation that by the time their longer terms had expired, a chastened people would gratefully reward their initially unpopular firmness. Because violations of private rights tend not to serve the public good in fact, it is not unreasonable to hope that the people would before too long come to understand this tendency in a particular case.

Constitutional officers would also have the opportunity to practice virtue without expecting an eventual electoral reward. A "magistrate possessing only a common share of firmness" would probably not seize the opportunity, but "there are men who, under any circumstances, will have the courage to do their duty at every hazard."[227] A concern for glory or reputation may cause an executive "who has the Eyes of all Nations on him" to exercise his veto as "a just Judge."[228] The judiciary's term of good behavior allows judges to defend individuals against illegal executions or unconstitutional legislation; thus the enumeration of rights in the Constitution and the Bill of Rights "may do good . . . because the Judges can take hold of it."[229] The judiciary "will consider themselves in a peculiar manner the guardians of those rights" and resist legislative and executive encroachments on "rights expressly stipulated."[230] Nevertheless, only judges with an "uncommon portion of fortitude" would "do their duty" against the passionate opposition of "the major voice of the community,"[231] and not all possible forms of injustice will be illegal or unconstitutional.

While honorable officers' willingness to lose elections, suffer opprobrium, or be impeached may increase the possibility of their defending justice, if they are not then rewarded or vindicated by a calmer people, their deeds will not permanently avert an injustice the majority remains determined to commit. Unlike regimes in which "an hereditary or self-appointed authority" "independent of the majority" might simply defy a majority's unjust intentions, the American Senate, executive, and judiciary possess only enough "stability and independence" to delay the majority's schemes.[232]

As against the hope for a neutral, nonpartisan officer who will defend justice, we may distinguish an entirely different approach to the same problem—that is, to expect the distinctive parts of the society to defend themselves, acting as their own partisans rather than looking to someone else's nonpartisanship. This intention can be seen in the way some founders understood representation in the legislature and, even more, in proposals to apportion the legislature not simply according to population but so as to protect those whose rights might be endangered if numbers alone prevailed.

But arrangements that encourage individuals and groups to defend their own rights may permit them to cross the line from self-protection to self-promotion. While every man's *rights* deserve to be protected ("Justice is the end of government"), men use their rights to pursue interests that cannot all be protected and indeed are mutually "interfering" and therefore require "regulation" by government. Particular interests may need to be sacrificed or partly thwarted to serve "the permanent and aggregate interests of the community."[233] If some part of society, for example, a state, "should insist on claims evidently unjust, and pursue them in a manner detrimental to the whole body," then it "ought to be injured for the sake of a majority of the people."[234]

Some founders thought each part of society could best secure its rights by electing its own representative. Anti-Federalists in particular objected that the proposed House of Representatives would not represent the "variety of classes, each having distinct and separate concerns, to which some respect would most certainly be due."[235]

> In this assembly, the farmer, merchant, mecanick, and other various orders of people, ought to be represented according to their respective weight and numbers; and the representatives ought to be intimately acquainted with the wants, understand the interests of the several orders in the society, and feel a proper sense and becoming zeal to promote their prosperity.[236]

This formulation leaves unclear whether the acquaintance and understanding desired is to inhere in the individual representative with respect to his own constituents, or in all representatives with respect to all "orders in the society" whatever their electoral district. The

Federalist reply to this criticism stressed the role of representatives not as spokesmen or agents for their particular constituents but as "impartial umpires & Guardians" of the public as a whole.[237] Each representative should *report* or "state" the interests and sentiments of those who elected him, so that those can be understood by the other representatives; but a good representative should "act" in the interest of the whole.[238] While "some partiality for constituents is always expectable,"[239] the founders did not mean to promote logrolling, that is, "secret combinations from local views,"[240] but rather a "coalition" on "principles . . . of justice and the general good."[241] This purpose requires not a minute representation of every particular part of society but a knowledgeable representation by men who understand society's variety and can judge how to combine and reconcile various interests and opinions. To the extent that this happens, even the people's most immediate representatives contribute to the purpose of a "sufficiently neutral" government that I have described earlier with respect to the other branches.

There is, after all, a limit on what a representative can do to promote a minority's interest, or even to protect its rights, because such attempts can simply be outvoted by other representatives not elected by that minority, and that becomes more probable as the representation becomes more minute. For the parts of society to protect themselves, they need not just their proportional share of agents in the legislature but an ability to block decisions unfavorable to them.[242] At the extreme, "the controlling powers must be as numerous as the varying interests, and the operations of government must therefore cease."[243] A more moderate proposal was "to increase the number of votes necessary to determine questions in cases where a bare majority may be seduced by strong motives of interest to injure and oppress the minority of the community, as in commercial regulations."[244] This approach had been embodied in the Articles of Confederation, which required that nine states agree to important decisions; but "what at first sight may seem a remedy, is in reality a poison." If a majority cannot rule, "a pertinaceous minority" can impose "tedious delays; continual negotiation and intrigue; contemptible compromises of the public good"—or even keep the government "in a state of inaction."[245]

Notwithstanding these objections to giving every part of society its own veto, or even modestly inflating its weight (by requiring more than a majority to decide), one might try to give certain specific minorities a veto with which to protect themselves, or at least modestly inflate their weight (by a share in the legislature disproportionate to their numbers). England's House of Lords was a model of the first approach, giving "men distinguished by birth, wealth or honors" a separate share in rule, and thus "a right to stop the enterprises of the people, as the people has a right to stop theirs."[246] In America, the minority that seemed most likely to need special protection was not a hereditary aristocracy but rather property holders in general. Although the right to acquire and preserve property is an important object men seek in instituting government,

> An increase of population will of necessity increase the proportion of those who will labour under all the hardships of life, & secretly sigh for a more equal distribution of its blessings. These may in time outnumber those who are placed above the feelings of indigence. According to the equal laws of suffrage, the power will slide into the hands of the former.[247]

One plausible solution would be a mixed government, with one branch of the legislature democratic and one branch mildly oligarchic:[248]

> Persons and property being both essential objects of Government, the most that either can claim, is such a structure of it as will leave a reasonable security for the other. And the most obvious provision of this double character, seems to be that of confining to the holders of property, the object deemed least secure in popular Governments, the right of suffrage for one of the two Legislative branches.[249]

Indeed some suggested that voting for the *entire* government could be limited to freeholders.[250] But neither a mild oligarchy nor a mixed government was adopted by the Convention, despite the protection they would seem to promise for the right of property. For reasons that I will discuss later, a "wholly popular" government was chosen instead, and protections for property judged by their compatibility with that choice.

Thus no minority was awarded a separate share in rule with which to "stop" the "enterprises" of the majority. But two minorities did receive the lesser protection of weight in the legislature disproportionate to their numbers: states with relatively small populations and slave-holding states.

Delegates from small states argued that an equal number of seats in the legislature should be allotted to each state. Their primary argument was that representation proportional to population would leave the small states grossly outnumbered and unable to protect themselves from being "swallowed up" by the large states.[251] Opponents who did not object to the principle of an apportionment that would protect the parts of society did object to the application of that principle to the case of the small states. There is nothing distinctive about small states, they said, that requires protection; the large states are more likely to be rivals to one another than to band together against the small states.[252] The Connecticut Compromise, which provided for equal representation of each state in one branch of the legislature, was in the eyes of some of its proponents a useful device for the protection of the rights of each part of society; but it was regarded by some leading founders who strenuously opposed it not as a compromise but as a triumph of extortion by the small states.

A different argument for equal representation of states looked on it not as a means of protecting individuals within the small states but as a means of protecting the existence and importance of the states as such. The decision to give each state an equal vote in one legislative branch

> was expressly made upon this principle, that a territory of such extent as that of United *America,* could not be *safely and advantageously governed,* but by a combination of republics, each retaining all the rights of supreme sovereignty, excepting such as ought to be contributed to the union; that for the securer preservation of these sovereignties, they ought to be represented in a body by themselves, and with equal suffrage; and that they would be annihilated, if both branches of the legislature were to be formed of representatives of the people, in proportion to the number of inhabitants in each state.[253]

Individuals within small states may not have rights that are particularly in danger, and the states themselves have no natural rights of their own; but because the division of the Union into states is favorable to the public happiness, the parts that preserve the division deserve protection.

The decision to count three-fifths of the slave population in apportioning the House of Representatives was similarly controversial. Some who doubted that small states constituted a distinctive part of society admitted that the slave states did;[254] yet the slave states were not exercising a right but perpetuating a wrong that certainly deserved no special protection. While some argued that this part of society should be protected for its value to the whole (that is, its production of wealth available for taxation),[255] this appeared absurd to those who thought slavery creates a danger of insurrection, has "the most pernicious effect on manners," and would "bring the judgment of heaven on a Country."[256] Even more clearly than the Connecticut Compromise, the three-fifths clause illustrates in the act of a founding by consent a fact that also applies to the operation of a government by consent. Those whose consent must be obtained do not confine themselves to insisting on their rights; their right to consent can also be used as a means to promote their interests. These two decisions on apportionment, in a sense the least democratic of the Constitution's provisions, were also those most obviously the result of the founders' wish to put the Constitution on the democratic foundation of popular ratification.

The difficulty of securing the rights of each part of society without giving those parts the strength to promote themselves at the expense of the public good suggested to some that the best political arrangement requires a society with as few distinct parts as possible. To the extent that a society has a real "uniformity of interests," the precise mode of apportionment becomes inconsequential;[257] and if it lacks that uniformity, any mode of apportionment will appear problematic. Against the view that requiring a two-thirds vote of the Senate would protect the various parts of America against treaties unfavorable to them, Wilson said that "if the majority cannot be trusted, it was a proof . . . that we were not fit for one Society."[258] If a society does not have a fundamental unity of interest or purpose, then majority rule will be only the involuntary subjection of the few to the many, and attempts to check or modify majority rule will be only the involuntary surrender of the many to the few.

Accordingly, there was good reason for the diverse American states to act in most respects not as "one Society" but as separate societies, in each of which a relatively small, local, homogeneous population should undertake the primary activities of government. Anti-Federalists especially insisted that America's diversity was incompatible with a consolidated government. For "six millions of white inhabitants in a republic one thousand miles long" to be "all reduced to the same standard of morals, or habits, and of laws, is in itself an absurdity, and contrary to the whole experience of mankind."[259] Although "by endeavouring to suit both extremes" government would tend to injure both of them,[260] such fruitless impartiality is not probable. The people of each part will inevitably feel strong affections and attachments that do not extend to more distant parts,[261] and there will be constant contention on behalf of the different interests and customs of the different parts.[262]

This case against uniform national rule over diverse states was also embraced by Federalists, who insisted that the Constitution would preserve the primary role of state governments and limit the central government to a few necessary tasks:

> The immediate security of the civil and domestic rights of the people will be in the governments of the particular states.

> And as the different states have different local interests and customs which can be best regulated by their own laws, it would not be expedient to admit the federal government to interfere with them, any farther than may be necessary for the good of the whole.—The great end of the federal government is to protect the several states in the enjoyment of those rights, against foreign invasion, and to preserve peace and a beneficial intercourse among themselves; and to regulate and protect their commerce with foreign nations.[263]

Because "each state still retains its sovereignty in what concerns its own internal government, and a right to exercise every power of a sovereign state not particularly delegated to the government of the United States,"[264] the United States appeared to correspond to Montesquieu's description of a confederation: "Composed of small republics, it enjoys the goodness of internal government of each one; and, in regard to the outside [world], it has, by the force of the association, all the advantages of large monarchies."[265]

But while some Federalists thought the argument for a small republic could support the proposed Constitution, the argument itself was fundamentally challenged by James Madison. Madison admitted that if the people in a society with "narrow limits" "all" had "precisely the same interests, and the same feelings in every respect," then public affairs could indeed be "most accurately managed" "within a small sphere." But "no Society ever did or can consist of so homogeneous a mass of Citizens,"[266] and this unavoidable diversity provides occasions and motives for a majority to oppress a minority. Madison's recommended solution to this problem is not to approximate homogeneity as closely as possible but to embrace the diversity of an extensive country, which makes it less likely that any single faction will compose a majority of the population—and therefore less likely that a faction can use the form of popular government to oppress other parts of the society.[267]

Madison's view that national diversity is a security for the rights of each part recommended institutions that would permit the national government to control the state governments. The opposite view, that local homogeneity is a security for the rights of each part, recommended institutions that would permit the state governments to defend their independent authority against national encroachment. Election of senators by the state legislatures would serve this latter purpose. "If [the State Govts.] are to be preserved as [Mr. Mason] conceived to be essential, they certainly ought to have this power [of self-defence], and the only mode left of giving it to them, was by allowing them to appoint the 2d. branch of the Natl. Legislature."[268] Madison unsuccessfully opposed that decision on the grounds that the Senate should help control the factious spirit of the state legislatures, not be controlled by it.[269] Madison also advocated a national legislative power to veto state laws, thinking this the only reliable way that national diversity could overrule local injustice. The Convention rejected this proposal, so as to preserve the state governments' independent authority to serve their own distinct purposes. But it did not quite adopt the localist view that "within the State itself a majority must rule, whatever may be the mischief done among themselves."[270] In specifically denying the states the power to issue paper money, impair the obligation of contracts, or pass ex post facto laws and in allowing the national judiciary to enforce those prohibitions, the Convention reflected Madison's view that the nation should protect individual rights against the states.[271]

On this point, then, the Constitution appears to embody two opposite theoretical premises: on one hand, the preservation of an autonomous role for state governments so as to protect the parts of the United States from being bluntly homogenized by a central government and, on the other hand, the creation of a central government, the diversity of whose constituents would tend to make each part safer from the oppressions of the others. Subsequent amendments (particularly the Fourteenth and the Seventeenth) weakened the localist and strengthened the nationalist view of how to secure rights.

What effect do subsequent changes in belief have on the constitutional scheme for controlling the government? More recent thought tends to accept the idea that government should be controlled from any tendency to injure the public in general but suggests that the founders' various auxiliary precautions are excessive for this purpose and prevent a coherent government that could best serve the public good. While this criticism is consistent with the founders' own concern that government not be stalemated and that it show the "positive merit of doing good," it takes less seriously than the founders did the difficulty and importance of ensuring that government have the "negative merit of not doing harm."[272] Government's "enlarged plans of public good,"[273] while desirable, are a less important contribution to human happiness than its securing men's natural rights against injury by others (either private citizens or oppressive rulers). Government's goodness is "of the greatest importance" in "emergencies,"[274] and government's ability to act when necessities make themselves felt is more important than its ability readily to adopt schemes that are pursued from a spirit of improvement. Dropping the starting point of natural rights, later thought is more taken with the positive good that might be done by a government with less constricted processes. This change in belief results in some dissatisfaction with the Constitution, although as long as dissatisfaction does not result in constitutional amendment even unadmired institutions can exert the intended control on government. Perhaps some persistent level of dissatisfaction with the Constitution is intrinsic to the founders' intention that some rulers would entertain ambitions that other rulers would thwart.

Later thought is divided about the founders' intention to protect each part of the society. On one hand, dispensing with the idea of natural rights makes any special protection for a part seem like an unjustified obstruction of the majority's ability to impose policies that serve the greatest good of the greatest number. Yet the same partiality that is criticized is also invigorated, as a change in belief about government's proper purposes makes "special interests" more able to benefit themselves by means of government and more anxious to protect themselves from suffering the expense of government's care for someone else. If government's promotion of "the general Welfare" is understood to include promoting the welfare of particular parts, or what Hobbes called "care applyed to Individualls," then the parts of society face a more consuming political task of self-protection and more numerous political opportunities for self-promotion. Thus the claims made by society's parts lack both the dignity and the limits provided by the idea of rights.

Another strand of contemporary thought insists on the importance of protecting minorities' rights but (unlike the founders) looks chiefly to the courts to serve that purpose. The founders doubted that the natural rights of men could be exhaustively and precisely stated in a legally enforceable form, although the Bill of Rights was a step in that direction. How human faculties can be protected will depend to some extent on circumstances, and thus their protection will depend more on political processes that inhibit oppressive measures than on legal provisions that define them. In a more recent (Kantian) view, human reason has knowledge of rights that are binding independent of circumstances or consequences and thus are better suited to an inflexible judicial enforcement. In this view, the Constitution's broad intention of securing rights is served by judges who rely on contemporary thought rather than the constitutional text to determine the content of those rights. The tendency in our time not to look to the nonjudicial institutions for protection of rights is probably connected to the shift from a doctrine of natural rights, which it was thought were naturally attractive to human beings and would generally be supported by a people not distracted by some passion or interest that impels them to oppress others, to a view that rights are founded in reason but not in nature and so accord with man's capacity for a priori reasoning but not necessarily with most men's self-attachment. Thus when John Rawls's theory of justice asserts that men faced with a "veil of ignorance" about their own particular interests and circumstances would consent to its commands (regarding distribution of wealth, for instance), it admits that actual men, even in moments of calm deliberation rather than passionate rage, would not be attracted by the rights prescribed. If separated powers and social diversity inhibit their momentary schemes, angry or covetous men tempted to violate natural rights may return to their senses; but that prospect will not suffice for moral doctrines that require pure reason to overrule men's senses.

Consent

It might seem strange, rather than a self-evident truth, to say that a government with sufficient powers designed to encourage the energetic but stable rule of wise and virtuous men limited to their proper purposes and unlikely to abuse any part of the people nonetheless lacks "just powers," if it does not also have "the consent of the governed."[275] To some extent, of course, consent can be understood not as an additional requirement but as a means of achieving the intentions already discussed—most obviously as a means of limiting government to its proper purposes. But the requirement of consent is in other respects an obstacle to good government. The Philadelphia Convention "must follow the example of Solon who gave the Athenians not the best Govt. he could devise; but the best they wd. receive."[276] And in addition to establishing the government by an initial act of popular consent, the Convention was determined to create a government that would depend on the continuing consent of the governed in regular elections—even though the numerous officers and frequent elections that are the "genius of republican liberty" are in some tension with the energy and stability that characterize good government.[277] These difficulties suggest two questions: Why is consent of the governed required, and what is a sufficient manifestation of that consent? I will consider first the popular consent by which the Constitution was introduced and then the place of popular consent in the continuing operation of the government created by the Constitution.

Founding by Consent. The men who wrote the Constitution submitted it for approval by popularly elected conventions in each state. This procedure recognized "the People" as the "pure, original fountain of all legitimate authority," whose "Right" it is to "institute new Government."[278] The old governments—the Articles of Confederation and state governments—provided no legal basis for the procedures of

1787–1788, and the Articles' requirement of unanimity for amendment posed a legal barrier. The people were therefore exercising not a legal right but a natural one.

According to John Locke's argument for that natural right, a society created by unanimous consent of naturally free individuals institutes a government by consent of its majority. Governments that come into being without this sanction rely on false claims that God or nature appoints some man or men to rule over others, or simply rule by "Force and Violence," the "Rules . . . of Beasts."[279] The majority's right to choose a government derives from the fact that "the consent of every individual" is "next impossible ever to be had" (due to absences, various opinions, and contrary interests), so that "where the *majority* cannot conclude the rest, there they cannot act as one Body, and consequently will be immediately dissolved again."[280] This reflects a kind of natural democracy but does not necessarily imply that the majority will or should institute a democratic government, that is, perpetuate its own authority. It should choose whatever government is "most likely to effect [the people's] Safety and Happiness."[281] A people could retain the original democracy, or choose a specific person or group of persons to rule—the choice between democracy, monarchy, and aristocracy that Hobbes offered;[282] but Americans did none of these things, instead instituting a "constitution" specifying in the abstract what kind of ruling offices would exist, how they would be filled, and what powers they would exercise.

The fact that the ruling offices are both created by popular choice (at the founding) and will be filled by popular choice (in elections) should not obscure the fact that "providing a Constitution for future generations"[283] is an attempt to limit the people's choice. The people who adopt the Constitution and the generations that follow are of course permitted (if not necessarily encouraged) to amend the Constitution; but "until the people have, by some solemn and authoritative act, annulled or changed the established form, it is binding upon themselves collectively, as well as individually."[284] By establishing a constitution instead of merely perpetuating a democracy, the people make a solemn and authoritative choice of purposes other than popular choice; they establish a mode of rule that both creates their own role in choosing officers and policies and discourages oppressive and encourages good government. This intention requires that the people's role as constitutional authorities be distinct from their role as political participants and that the former role be not too frequently undertaken. The Constitution's elaborate procedure for amendment both recognizes the people's right to alter the government as they see fit and makes such action especially "solemn and authoritative" to preserve the distinction between a chosen, binding constitution and a continuing, formless plebiscite.

The founders' practice of instituting government by popular consent may also be contrasted with two other rejected views on the subject. Some influential writers supported a less literal-minded practice of consent, the "tacit consent" visible in a country with a long-standing and well-regarded government. According to William Blackstone, "long and immemorial usage" is evidence that "the general consent of the people" has "vested" England's executive power in a single king.[285] David Hume thought the kind of actual consent the American framers required unlikely ever to be practical and likely to institute a bad government if it were practiced.[286] Consent should not be understood as an original formality but as a continuing atmosphere.

The principle of tacit consent was implicitly recognized in the Declaration of Independence. While the people have the right to "institute new Government" if they find it necessary to overthrow the old one, existing governments that had been "instituted among Men" might "deriv[e] their just powers from the consent of the governed" without having been instituted *by* the governed. Only when a government loses that consent, in revolution, must a new government be instituted *by* the governed. The first American governments—the state governments and the Articles of Confederation—could not in general claim to have been formally adopted by the people themselves; but had their performance been satisfactory, it might have been sufficient to say that they had "been too long acquiesced in, to be now shaken."[287] The argument that "we exist at present, and we need not enquire how, as a federal Society, united by a charter"[288] was offered in support of obeying that charter's prescribed procedures for amendment. But this principle of tacit consent implied by example that a new constitutional transformation could be carried out by whoever thought they could succeed (the Philadelphia Convention or the Continental Congress, for example), in the expectation that a future, generally satisfied people "need not enquire how" their government had been created. But, as the Declaration of Independence indicates, tacit consent once withdrawn is hard to restore in a tacit manner. In the American case, an additional complication was the existence of separate state governments that might also claim to enjoy tacit consent to authorities potentially in conflict with the new Constitution's claims. To avoid this "uncertainty," the Constitution "should be ratified in the most unexceptionable form, and by the supreme authority of the people themselves"[289]—"the most certain means of obviating all disputes & doubts concerning the legitimacy of the new Constitution."[290]

Even further than tacit consent from the American principle of formal consent is the denial that government needs the people's consent at all. More precisely, this view concedes that the people's tendency to accept or rebel against a government is one factor among many that a government must manage so as to preserve its authority, but popular consent confers no special legitimacy on a ruler. The noblest version of this view suggests that government may serve ends that a people might not understand or approve of if asked, but which are for their own happiness properly understood. A philosopher-king or his imperfect facsimile may need to consider how his measures will be received by a people, but if he rules well without their approval, he is justified by the good that he does rather than illegitimate for the consent that he lacks. A different and simply amoral view of politics holds that force and fraud are the basis of rule, that neither consent nor public-spirited policies confer any right to rule, and neither is a practical necessity for a ruler's success. Rulers gain power however they can, for whatever ends they wish, and are replaced by whoever finds the means to do so. The people cannot expect to control this process; they can quietly accept whoever rules them or join in insurrection, but they can just as well be deceived or betrayed as rewarded for their role. They are at the mercy of "accident and force."[291]

The vagueness of tacit consent and the elitism or immorality of no consent tend to make the American doctrine appealing to present-day thought. But those alternative doctrines have reappeared in surprisingly seductive forms in influential schools of thought.

The doctrine of tacit consent finds its present-day equivalent in the notion of a "living Constitution." According to this view, constitutional principles evolve to keep pace with changing historical conditions, not by the awkward formality of constitutional amendment but by judicious reinterpretation by statesmen and particularly judges sensitive to the moral and practical imperatives of the times. This adaptation preserves the respectability of the Constitution, preventing it from becoming a dead hand of the past obnoxious to men of the present; it also borrows from the respectability of the Constitution, as new procedures and new ends are insensibly amalgamated with the old. The people consent to this only implicitly or tacitly. Political scientists observe the rate at which citizens vote in elections, express confidence in the government in opinion polls of "representative" respondents, and refrain from insurrectionary violence. These *informal* measures of tacit consent support judgments of whether the American regime enjoys "legitimacy."

The doctrine of no consent finds its present-day equivalent in the notion of postponed consent. To insist on explicit consent as the American founders did is to limit the political possibilities to those that a people's majority will voluntarily consent to in advance of any influence those political arrangements might have. The founders' approach puts the choice of government in the hands of a people not possessed of perfect wisdom or virtue, who may lack knowledge of their own highest possibilities for happiness. Although there is hope for a further improvement in the people's understanding that would impel them to amend the Constitution later, their understanding may be limited by the experiences open to them living under the Constitution they chose at first. Thus no radical transformation seems possible if consent is required; there is no opportunity to "change, so to speak, human nature."[292] According to Rousseau, such a transformation is required for a good political order, and it cannot be initiated by the people themselves—because that would require that "men be prior to laws what they must become by means of [laws]."[293] Genuine political freedom will therefore not be freely chosen but must be the work of a lawgiver who persuades the people of his divine inspiration.

Some so-called Marxists also interested in man's radical transformation saw this same difficulty, but Marx himself denied it. Unlike Rousseau, who recognized the importance of politics in changing human nature to suit it to a just regime, Marx asserted that economic forces would by themselves change social conditions and opinions so that political improvement would win overwhelming consent. The revolution would be made not merely by the majority of the people but by the almost universal class of proletarians. Unwilling to wait for Marx's prediction to come true, Lenin described "false consciousness" as an impediment to revolution by general consent; the noble future Marx described would result only from conspiracy and insurrection by a few. Consent would come later, so universal that it need never be formal.

The observation that a people might not give their consent to the best political arrangements was also made by some American founders. Several delegates at the Convention who thought the British limited monarchy an excellent form of government regretted that it could not be established by popular consent.[294] "Preconceived jealousies"[295] among the people made them "adverse to the very semblance of Monarchy,"[296] distrustful of "the vigor of government,"[297] and attached to annual elections and existing state governments.[298] The people's tendency to favor or even venerate the governments to which they have become accustomed[299] is normally a healthy prop to stability and an impediment to usurpers who would make things worse.[300] But that tendency makes the voluntary choice of a substantially new government more difficult. Some founders stressed the need to accommodate the people's opinions on many points,[301] while others thought the plan would have most chance of winning popular consent if the Convention's members could honestly defend its merits: "We ought to consider what was right & necessary in itself for the attainment of a proper Governmt."[302] Informal leadership by "some patriotic and respectable citizen or number of citizens"[303] who could prudently make concessions to or impressively argue against popular prejudices was admittedly important in making a founding by consent possible. But the fact that "the people commonly *intend* the PUBLIC GOOD" and that their defect is rather that they do not "always *reason right* about the *means* of promoting it"[304] makes such efforts to obtain consent for good government plausible. The fact that the proper ends of government are naturally attractive to the people, rather than something that only superstition or habituation could support, means that the educative efforts of informal leaders will not be impossibly difficult.

Apart from the problem of popular prejudice in general, individual men have particular attachments and interests that may divert them from seeking a government that serves the public good as a whole. In some cases concessions had to be made to those impulses, so the proposed Constitution was not "the most perfect One that the Deputies cou'd devise for a Country better adapted to the reception of it, than America is at this day, or perhaps ever will be."[305] But the problem of particular interests appeared less radical to the founders than it did to Rousseau, because they did not wish to transform fundamentally man's natural propensity to prefer himself and his own interests. If government's proper purpose is to protect the free exercise of man's natural faculties, the transformations a clever Rousseauist legislator might achieve to make men less individual and more social would be unjust. The problem for founders is rather to persuade particular interests that they will be protected and prosper under the general conditions of freedom the Constitution will secure, and to resist, or merely moderate (that is, in some cases, partly accommodate) the tendency of particular interests to seek some special protections or advantages for themselves beyond the impartial protection of their and others' rights that they are entitled to expect. This fact of partiality (or of differing opinions about what constitutes impartiality) is one reason that a people cannot "spontaneously and universally . . . move in concert" in creating a new government; they rely on the assistance of a few persons who, working in secret, can fashion compromises and propose a completed package for acceptance or rejection.[306]

The "spirit of Accommodation" to particular interests[307] detracted from the Constitution's intrinsic excellence but was thought to be a price of winning consent. The most egregious example of a particular interest at work was the slave states' insistence on counting slaves in apportionment, preserving the slave trade for twenty years, and requiring fugitive slaves to be "delivered up on Claim of the Party to whom [their] Service or Labour may be due." The fact that such provisions were "inconsistent with the principles of the revolution and dishonorable to the American character"[308] gave way to the apparent "necessity of compromise."[309] While some delegates who believed that the southern states would never "confederate on terms that would deprive them of [the slave] trade" preferred to accept that result rather than "doing injustice . . . to human nature,"[310] the Convention did not and decided to "leave the matter as we find it."[311] The rejected alternatives were to divide America permanently—leaving the South to do as it pleased regarding slavery—or to attempt to impose by force a regime of freedom that could at some subsequent period enjoy the consent of a people no longer insistent on a right to own slaves.[312]

The obstacles of prejudice and partiality did not persuade the founders that establishing government by consent was impossible, only that it was difficult. Some saw the circumstances of 1787–1788 as a rare opportunity, when a "fortunate coincidence of leading opinions" (including that of the revered George Washington) might dispose the people to follow that lead, and the nation's circumstances provided a momentary inducement for states to sacrifice some of their particular interests.[313] The other side of the coin was the prospect that a failure to agree on a government at that time would lead to disunion, anarchy, and eventual acquiescence in a usurpation that could restore order.[314] Thus while the people's right to choose their own form of government was agreed, their ability to exercise that right successfully appeared fragile and fleeting.

Having noted some of the difficulties posed by the attempt to institute government by consent of the governed, I will now recapitulate its advantages. First, it affords a greater likelihood of good government than does the alternative origin of government, "chance, war and conquest."[315] While one can imagine a benevolent founder whose force or fraud imposes good government, one could hardly count on it. In "the old world . . . governments are the children of force or fraud, and carry with them strong features of their parent's character," that is, an indifference to the happiness of the people they rule.[316] "The science of politics has very seldom had fair play," as founders more often look to "the particular advantages or necessities of a few individuals, than to the permanent good of society."[317]

Second, a formal, popular choice of government was meant to

place authority in an unambiguous and indisputable location. Self-appointed rulers of all kinds are more likely to provoke challenge by others who wish to appoint themselves as replacements. The divisions in society that make consent difficult to practice at the same time make it a crucial means by which those divisions are subdued. A government that could claim authority only by virtue of its good policies is undermined by the inevitable disputes about those policies. A doctrine of tacit consent to a living constitution muddies the clarity about the Constitution's legitimate authority that a formal act of consent is designed to create. Innovations insensibly introduced and tacitly consented to may be the object of discontent by part of the people or by most of the people immediately or eventually. When that happens, the Constitution as a whole appears to have lost its legitimacy, but there is no formal means by which it can regain its legitimacy. Its legitimacy can be endlessly controversial since no formal act by the people can determine what form of government the people's majority consents to (unless there is a new constitution whose principle of formal consent is respected and perpetuated).

The right of the majority to choose a government for a whole people depends on that people's prior agreement to be one people—"the fundamental compact by which individuals compose one Society, . . . which must in its theoretic origins at least, have been the unanimous act of the component members."[318] America's "one Society" had a double or ambiguous character. It was both a society of individual persons, united since before 1776 (the Declaration of Independence speaks for "one people"[319]), and a "society of societies,"[320] composed by the unanimous act of the states that were its component members. Accordingly, Madison argued that ratification should depend on the consent both of a majority of states and of states containing a majority of the American population.[321] The Convention's simpler nine-state provision ("a respectable majority") was recommended as more "familiar to the people" from practice under the Articles of Confederation[322] but it was roughly consistent with Madison's principle.[323] Even this consent by a majority of states and a virtual majority of population would not impose the Constitution on the states that rejected the plan (although it would impose the effective dissolution of the Articles of Confederation). In this respect, ratification would be the "unanimous act" of whatever nine or more states agreed to be "component members" of this new form of union.[324]

In departing from the legal framework of the Articles of Confederation, the founders put into practice their revolutionary principle of consent in a manner quite cautiously deferential to the people's explicit choice. The Convention did not assert that it already represented the people and could thereby ratify its own work, and it insisted on approval by conventions elected to decide this particular issue, not state legislatures elected for other purposes. It did not assume that all states were so wedded to the Union that a majority of them could bind the rest nor that the existence of an American society obliterated the distinct society of each state so that a majority of the large society could overrule all majorities of the small societies.

The Constitution's provision that three-fourths of the states must consent to amendments can be understood as virtually ensuring that a majority of the entire country's population consents, and as a compromise between the principle that a majority of the states must consent and the principle that the states must unanimously consent. The provision defers less to the separateness of the states than did the ratification process, because all states are bound even if only three-fourths ratify. Thus the Constitution attempts to cement what imperfectly existed before its adoption: a united American society that must thereafter act as one in choosing or rejecting constitutional innovations.

Popular Government. The American framers made consent not only the principle of constitutional creation but a prominent feature of government's operations under the Constitution. In periodic (direct and indirect) elections the people could choose who would hold the offices whose existence the people consented to in 1787–1788. And popular consent was not "mixed" with authorities independent of the people, as England mixed the House of Commons with the House of Lords and the king; popular consent was made the only source of political authority under the Constitution. All officers were to be selected by the people or by persons selected by the people. The Constitution could therefore be described as a "wholly popular" or "wholly elective" government.[325]

The argument for popular government gains an initial advantage from the assumption that forms of government should be judged by their propensity to serve the "Safety and Happiness" of the people as a whole.[326] Other claimants to rule assert that government's purposes are those they are peculiarly qualified to serve—for example, the rich can claim to be the best at getting and preserving wealth, the warrior at achieving conquests, the virtuous at practicing and teaching virtue, the pious at promoting religion. But the people as a whole can plausibly claim to be the rulers most likely to serve the democratic ends announced by the Declaration of Independence. It is they who "commonly *intend* the PUBLIC GOOD."[327]

But democratic ends do not conclusively justify democratic means, if nondemocratic contenders for rule can show their usefulness or necessity in serving democratic ends. Although popular government makes some important contributions to government's ability to control the governed, and to its being obliged to control itself, those requirements do not unequivocally recommend popular government.

A popular government is at an advantage in controlling the governed because the people's trust of its good intentions makes them more likely to grant it sufficient powers[328] and to obey its commands voluntarily.[329] On the other hand, "the requisite stability and energy in government" do not flow naturally from the "genius of republican liberty" that assigns power for short terms to many hands:

> Stability, on the contrary, requires that the hands in which power is lodged should continue for a length of time the same . . . whilst energy in government requires not only a certain duration of power, but the execution of it by a single hand.[330]

Furthermore, wisdom is a quality that the people as a whole cannot supply but can only try to locate and employ. According to Blackstone, of the three desirable qualities of government—"wisdom, to discern the real interest of the community; goodness, to endeavour always to pursue that real interest; and strength, or power, to carry this knowledge and intention into action"—only "goodness" is characteristic of democracy, hence the advantage of England's mixed government, which combines that goodness with the wisdom of an aristocracy and power of a monarchy.[331] The British government's advantage in wisdom appeared doubtful to Americans who thought elections could choose persons of "virtue, good sense and reputation," preferable to the "supercilious haughtiness" and "emptiness" of Britain's Lords,[332] and ensure that, in contrast to a hereditary monarch, the president "cannot be an idiot, probably not a knave or a tyrant."[333] Nonetheless, monarchy appeared to have advantages both in promoting stability and in possessing what Blackstone called "strength, or power" and what the founders called "energy": "There is an idea, which is not without its advocates, that a vigorous executive is inconsistent with the genius of republican government."[334] The founders tried to supply popular substitutes for some qualities less typical of popular governments that enable government to control the governed, but this effort indicates that it was not with a view to these qualities that popular government appeared desirable to begin with.

Popular government appears in a more clearly favorable light in relation to the requirement that government be obliged to control itself. Elections enable the people to restrain rulers' temptation to serve their own good rather than the public good. But popular government is less well suited to protecting the rights of each part of the community—an end that, as has been discussed, is both fundamental in itself and also generally a necessary condition for the public good as a whole. Concern that a popular government would be dangerous to the rights of a few, and in particular to the rights of property, led some at the Convention to favor property qualifications for voters or officeholders.[335]

But such restrictions were not finally adopted. The Constitution deferred to each state's practice, so that those eligible to vote for the more popular branch of each state legislature could vote in congressional elections. The Convention rejected proposals to be more restrictive than the states. Despite assurances that the "great mass" of Americans (even "9/10 of the people") were themselves freeholders and "will be pleased with" a provision denying suffrage to non-freeholders, Madison expressed concern about the "probable reception such a change would meet with in States where the right was now exercised by every description of people."[336] He and others appear to have been concerned not with the Constitution's prospects for ratification but with the people's morale or spirit. Franklin argued that "it is of great consequence that we shd. not depress the virtue & public spirit of our common people; of which they displayed a great deal during the war, and which contributed principally to the favorable issue of it."[337] Franklin's argument centers not on how a certain set of people would affect the tendency of government by their votes but on how having or not having a vote would affect those people's own tendencies. When Britain restricted suffrage to freeholders, "the consequence was that the residue of Inhabitants were disgraced. . . . The English common people from that period lost a large portion of patriotism."[338] Hamilton argued that the main advantage of "Free Government" over "absolute monarchy" was its "tendency . . . to interest the passions of the community in its favour [and] beget public spirit and public confidence."[339] According to Mason, the fact that "Republican Governments" attract "the Love the Affection the Attachment of the Citizens to their Laws, to their Freedom, and to their Country" enables such governments to "perfor[m] . . . Wonders" "in time of war."[340]

A similar line of reasoning was applied to the question of property, age, and residency qualifications for officeholders. Immigrants barred from office "would feel the mortification of being marked with suspicious incapacitations though they sd. not covet the public honors."[341] With only minimal (and no property) qualifications for office, the Constitution left every "place of *power or profit* . . . open *to the whole body of the people*."[342] "Every individual is a fair candidate for the highest seat in the empire, which is a matter unknown to every other nation in the world, which must be a most powerful incentive and spur to every laudable exertion to be virtuous and learned. . . ."[343] Even age qualifications might "damp the efforts of genius, and of laudable ambition."[344] The "strongest stimulus to public virtue" is "the hope of honor and rewards. The acquisition of abilities is hardly worth the trouble, unless one is to enjoy the satisfaction of employing them for the good of one's country."[345]

Unlike Montesquieu, who seemed to suggest that virtue is a precondition for popular government, these founders suggested that the political opportunities of a popular government would tend to encourage a "laudable ambition," which, if not quite the virtue Montesquieu described, would produce some of the same effects. But even without such optimistic expectations, a broad field for political opportunity seemed important so as not to "debase the spirit of the common people."[346] "To be appointed to a place may be a matter of indifference. To be incapable of being appointed, is a circumstance grating, and mortifying."[347] In answer to Anti-Federalist objections that the relatively small number and long terms of offices under the new Constitution would sharply limit the number of people to whom office was in practice accessible,[348] Aristides pointed to the continuing existence and importance of the state governments as a rich source of political opportunity:

> If there be men, who delight in parliamentary warfare; who choose a fair wide field for displaying their talents; who wish to see every servant of the public prostrate before them; whose ears are soothed by humble supplication; they may still enjoy rich sources of gratification. Are not the regulations of property, the regulations of the penal law, the protection of the weak, the promotion of useful arts, the whole internal government of their respective republics; are not these the main objects of every wise and honest legislature? Are not these things still in their power; and, whilst free from invasion or injuries abroad, are not these almost the only things, in which sovereignty is exercised?[349]

Aristides' mocking tone reflects his view that gratifications for the ambitious are less important than "advantage . . . to the public."[350] But his argument, like those urging relaxed qualifications for voters and officers, makes clear that government cannot be understood purely as an instrument for "protection & security," because it is also a source of "honors and privileges."[351] Arrangements for suffrage and officeholding cannot be constructed with a view only to their tendency to protect men's private rights, if such provisions would be grating, mortifying, odious, or disgraceful to men's public ambitions. Aristotle's *Politics* makes this point, in response to the same kind of practical considerations of "protection & security" that seemed to some founders to require that suffrage or officeholding not be open to all:

> That all of these things [the wealthy plundering the poor, and the poor plundering the wealthy] are bad and unjust, then, is evident. But should the respectable rule and have authority over all [matters]? In this case, all the others are necessarily deprived of prerogatives, since they are not honored by [filling] political offices. For we say that offices are honors, and when the same persons always rule the others are necessarily deprived of [these honors or] prerogatives.[352]

I have noted earlier how those who claim a right to rule do so on the basis of a peculiar skill or qualification that makes them likely to rule well. A somewhat different claim can also be made: that the would-be ruler or ruling group has some quality that deserves the *honor* of ruling because of its intrinsic importance to the community, rather than a quality that is specifically capable of ruling. For example, if only those "whose sex made them capable of protecting the state"[353] were admitted as citizens, this is not because bodily strength is a plausible indicator of ability to contribute to political deliberation but because it is of peculiar value to the community's protection and therefore can claim the honor of ruling even if it cannot claim the ability to rule. Similarly, Rufus King advised the Convention not to exclude from office "the monied interest"—not because its members were qualified to rule but because it would be imprudent to offend men "whose aids may be essential in particular emergencies to the public safety."[354] In the case of the people as a whole, their qualification to rule is their "goodness," that is, their tendency to "*intend* the PUBLIC GOOD." But the people's general attachment to the good of society is only a partial qualification to rule (because rule also requires an ability to "*reason right* about the *means* of promoting it"[355] and a respect for the rights of all of society's parts, rather than just for society in general), and might seem to entitle them only to a partial share in rule (as Blackstone argued). It appears that the people's honor, rather than their ability, underlies the case for a *wholly* popular government. A monarchy's deference to a single man's superiority, whatever its utility in serving men's interests, offends their pride. The problem with elective monarchy is that "men [are] unwilling to admit so decided a superiority of merit in an individual as to accede to his appointment to so preeminent a station."[356]

Some founders saw the regime's respect for men's honorable political impulses as a matter of *justice*. Madison unsuccessfully pressed this argument in the apportionment debate. According to him, those who opposed apportioning Congress by population admitted that "it would not be *just to allow Virga.* which was 16 times as large as Delaware an equal vote only" but claimed only that "it would not be *safe for Delaware* to allow Virga. 16 times as many votes."[357] Proportional representation may appear unsafe in that minorities (for example, small states) are in danger of having their private rights violated by laws that favor the majority (for example, large states); it can lead to injustice but is not itself unjust. Equal representation of states, on the other hand, is objectionable on its face, that is, apart from its likely policy consequences, because it unjustly dishonors the voters in the large states by giving them a smaller share in rule than voters in the small states enjoy.[358] And on the question of suffrage, Ellsworth thought "there is no justice in supposing that Virtue & Talents, are confined to Freeholders,"[359] referring, I believe, to the injustice to *individual* meritorious nonfreeholders who, whatever the tendency of their class as compared to the class of freeholders, are unjustly denied the opportunity to display their individual talents if barred from voting or officeholding. In the same vein, Davie thought "an insuperable difficulty" with a certain electoral scheme was that "the larger Counties or districts thrown into a general district, would certainly prevail over the smaller Counties or districts, and merit in the latter would be excluded altogether."[360] This objection is offered not on behalf of the community's need for meritorious rulers (which might be satisfied from the larger counties) but on behalf of the individual meritorious candidate who might be unfairly excluded.

It was thus important as a matter of principle that in America, unlike either Great Britain or the ancient republics, "the whole community will enjoy in the fullest sense that kind of political liberty which consists in the power the members of the State reserve to themselves, of arriving at the public offices, or at least, of having votes in the nomination of those who fill them."[361] But the "honorable determination . . . to rest all our political experiments on the capacity of mankind for self-government"[362] did not insist on precisely the kind of political liberty experienced in direct democracy. The American governments (state and federal) were characterized by *"the total exclusion of the people in their collective capacity,* from any share" in them.[363] According to Benjamin Rush,

> It is often said, that "the sovereign and all other power is seated *in* the people." This idea is unhappily expressed. It should be—"all power is derived *from* the people." They possess it only on the days of their elections. After this, it is the property of their rulers, nor can they exercise or resume it, unless it is abused. It is of importance to circulate this idea, as it leads to order and good government.[364]

According to Hamilton, ancient democracies "in which the people themselves deliberated, never possessed one feature of good government";[365] and in a remark to the New York ratifying convention that Hamilton implied might be too impolitic for others to make, he singled out the problem of foreign policy: "The branch of administration, especially, which involves our political relation with foreign states, a community will ever be incompetent to. These truths are not often held up in public assemblies; but they cannot be unknown to any who hear me."[366]

The people are not, of course, excluded in their *individual* capacities as voters; and James Wilson argued that this is "a momentous part" that "every citizen will frequently be called to act," because "all the derivative movements of government must spring from the original movement of the people at large." But when Wilson restates his point "without a metaphor," that "original movement" consists in the people's taking "care to choose none but representatives that are wise and good," so that, derivatively, "their representatives will take care, in their turn, to choose or appoint none but such as are wise and good also."[367] If the people are simply choosing others to rule them on the basis of "personal merit alone,"[368] their role may seem a rather humble one.

But in judging which rulers are "wise and good," the people inevitably judge the wisdom and goodness of their policies, if only by judging the apparent results of past policies. The diversity of men's opinions and interests causes them to hold different opinions "concerning government" and to form different attachments to "leaders ambitiously contending for pre-eminence and power."[369] Except if there is a universal alarm for the public safety, a people free to choose their rulers will be divided into parties: "an extinction of parties" "ought to be neither presumed nor desired."[370] The fact that the people judge potential and experienced rulers periodically rather than rule themselves continually does not keep them from being politically opinionated, and their opinions are known or anticipated by rulers.

While Hamilton, who was most outspoken about the people's limited deliberative abilities, foresaw certain "conjunctures, when it may be necessary and proper [for rulers] to disregard the opinions which the majority of the people have formed," he concluded that "in the general course of things, the popular views, and even prejudices, will direct the actions of the rulers."[371]

Elective government is intended to raise the quality of popular government without abandoning its spirit. A "republican form of government" gives "every man . . . a consciousness of a personal equality and independence. Let him look at any part of the continent;—he can see no superiors." As a result, the people have a "high spirit" that makes them resist any abuse of power by rulers.[372] But because the people's spiritedness is directed to the task of judging rulers, they escape certain temptations and vulnerabilities they would face if they ruled themselves as in an ancient democracy. A people that is "dispersed" rather than "assembled" is neither as likely to be carried away by passion nor as capable of "cabal and intrigue" for corrupt purposes.[373] In contrast to popular assemblies where a "single orator, or an artful statesman" could rule in effect although not in name as a king,[374] the American regime sets ambitious orators in competition with one another and lets the people judge from a distance. But opinionated citizens may feel fully entitled to their opinions because of their authority as choosers and judges of the rulers. And, to repeat, while the people as a whole does not rule directly, any ambitious member of it who wishes to try is allowed to seek office.

The most obvious tendency of more recent thought is to fault the founders' version of self-government as insufficiently democratic. One form of this critique, stated best by Rousseau, sees in the occasional, electoral political life of Americans a poor substitute for the inspiriting activity of participatory citizenship. Benjamin Rush's admission that the people possess power "only on the days of their elections" can be compared with Rousseau's judgment that the English people "is not [free] except during the election of the members of Parliament; as soon as they are elected, it is a slave, it is nothing."[375] But no serious program for direct democracy has been suggested, so democratic reforms adopted or envisioned can only attempt to weaken the independent judgment of rulers and shorten their leash. In these efforts one can see part of the Constitution's own logic, coupled with a forgetting or denial of other parts. For example, themes such as the importance of wisdom are today even less "often held up in public assemblies."

But this dogmatic determination in favor of self-government is accompanied by an understanding of human beings and politics that makes the case for self-government questionable and departures from it excusable. Neither Rousseauian participation nor American voting is now thought of as the fundamental meaning of freedom; freedom means freedom from government's rule, not a share in it. Men have no distinctively political impulses, at least none that deserve respect. Politics is simply a means by which men bargain for private protection and advantage. Voting is not understood as judging the rulers' performance in serving the public good but rather as one form of lobbying—and not necessarily the most effective form. This economic view of politics reaches one logical conclusion in Marx, according to whom an advanced stage of economic development makes protection and advantage available to all without their own or anyone else's political exertions. The same tendency is visible in a deference to regulatory agencies and activist courts. If electoral politics is a form of lobbying for private advantage, more professional or principled adjustments may be available from nonelected officials, with more convenience to the people. Without an honorable determination to rest all our political experiments on the capacity of mankind for self-government, self-government may come to seem a dispensable means to nonpolitical ends.

It could be said that both of these departures from the founders' view of self-government merely amplify the two contradictory halves of the founders' own view. Or perhaps one should say they separate and radicalize the contradictory psychological impulses that the founders aptly characterized and tried to reconcile: men's proud claim to a share in rule and their desire for a safe and comfortable private life.

Thought and the Constitution

The political institutions created by the Constitution were the practical deductions from their inventors' understanding of the human condition—that is, not only the condition of Americans in 1787 but more generally the natural rights of mankind and the "natural and necessary progress of human affairs."[376] Human nature was understood to provide a standard for good government, impose a requirement of limited government, and require that government be by consent. The debate among the Constitution's framers and opponents centered on whether the specific political choices made properly combined and practiced those principles.

The Constitution's framers anticipated that future generations might improve upon the institutions of 1787, if only because experience with those institutions would permit further progress in the science of politics. And amendments have been adopted in reaction to or anticipation of the results of the Constitution—for example, the prospect that states largely unregulated in their internal police would not secure the rights of former slaves or that a popular executive might repeatedly win reelection.

The debate of 1787–1788 amply demonstrated that different men could propose modified institutions even on the basis of shared premises, and one might expect revision of the premises to suggest even more radically revised institutions. But the questioning or rejection of the Constitution's theoretical premises has not in fact led to a wholesale revision of its institutional conclusions. This can be explained in several ways: the apolitical character of much recent thought, the immunity from theoretical assault conferred on the Constitution by "that veneration which time bestows on everything,"[377] or the possibility that the Constitution is defensible on grounds other than those assumed by its framers. Or what the framers regarded as theoretically sound principles may now be deprived of that status but nonetheless given a certain credence; thus, for example, the notion that rulers must be controlled need not be understood as a "reflection on human nature"[378] but merely as a rough and ready maxim for practical purposes, even if it describes only a culturally relative phenomenon induced by transitory socioeconomic conditions.

New ideas that do not result in amendment of the Constitution (or its overthrow) may taint the Constitution's reputation, perhaps weakening the "prejudices" in its favor that "the most rational government will not find . . . a superfluous advantage."[379] And such ideas may change the Constitution. To the extent that the Constitution's operation depends upon men's understanding of and sympathy with its principles, it may operate differently when different opinions prevail. This can be understood as progress, and the Constitution congratulated for its flexibility and hospitality to new ideas, unless the new ideas are inferior to the old ideas or incompatible with the institutions founded on them.

Because the founders could not enumerate all of government's powers or men's rights, new opinions concerning the purposes of government may have particular influence. An influential opinion today holds that the proper objects of the federal government are more extensive than the founders asserted. In this view, government serves human happiness by a variety of efforts to correct or compensate for the unequal or unfortunate constraints that chance and society impose on man. These efforts cannot be left to state governments, which might not undertake them equally or at all. From the founders' perspective, such aspirations to remake society can be expected among the ambitious, those in office or seeking it, but would be restrained by the "high spirit" of a republican people defending themselves against an ambitious government. But the founders' very success in creating a government that wins the people's confidence may calm their spirit of resistance and make them more receptive to the new projects and promises offered by the ambitious. By a similar process, the founders' success in rescuing popular government "from the opprobrium under which it has so long labored"[380] may result in an opinion less appreciative of the "more perfect structure" that remedies popular government's vices.[381]

But the founders did not leave the operation of American institutions entirely at the mercy of later men's understanding of them. For example, neither a study of the founders' ideas about the proper separation of powers nor an obedience to "parchment" provisions that briefly expressed those ideas was expected to preserve that separation in practice. The "personal motives" put to use by the founders' institutions need not be understood to be effective. If the Constitution was built on certain truths about human nature that later men denied, it might endure anyway, proving by its durability the soundness of the (now unbelieved) opinions that created it. Nonetheless, ambitious officers' actions will be constrained by their own opinion about what they may properly do, as well as by their view of the opinions of competing ambitious officers who may resist them and of the people whose votes can ultimately decide which officer to restrain (that is, vote out of office) and which to indulge. Those opinions may shift partly in response to current events and perhaps cyclically as, for example, concern about an "imperial presidency" leads to effects that provoke concern about an "imperial legislature." The institution that appears weakened may be able to fight another day, with new officers with their own "personal motives" taking possession of "constitutional means" that remain intact. On the other hand, the constitutional means may be altered by amendment or the personal motives dulled by habit and belief. For example, whether today's expansive understanding of the federal government's proper objects represents a permanent change in the Constitution depends on whether the people or the states retain the means[382] and develop the inclination to reverse that result.

The variety of contemporary thought may dilute, and at least obscures, its practical influence on the American Constitution. Contemporary thought encompasses both derision of "rights" and long lists of rights; a wish to change human nature, and a belief in democracy; an indifference to wisdom, and a desire that government transform society; a skepticism toward government's moral authority, and a distaste for an energetic executive; an enthusiasm for government's benefiting individuals and groups, and a lament for the self-interested influence of those individuals and groups. Individual thinkers cannot be charged with these paradoxes because individual thinkers have tended to address questions narrower or broader than the comprehensive practical question that faced the founders: what form of government is most likely to serve the people's safety and happiness? Because the founders' answer to that question included the principle of self-government, their successors have opportunities to shape the operation and fate of the American Constitution. Those opportunities cannot be used wisely without a fair consideration of the founders' own reasons for establishing thc form of government they did.

4
Jefferson's Pulse of Republican Reformation

Ralph Lerner

Thomas Jefferson's striking assessment of his life's work is inscribed for all to see and contemplate. His achievements and motivations were equally objects of his anxious care, so much so that he sought to preserve the materials with which later generations might make their own assessments. Accordingly, Jefferson became the Americans' preeminent archivist-founder. But lest the sight of the forest be lost for all the trees, he also marked with studied simplicity those actions by which he wished to be remembered. The inscription he prescribed—"& not a word more"—may still be read on the plain obelisk over his grave at Monticello. He was satisfied to let his fame rest on this: that he had been the "Author of the Declaration of American Independance[,] of the Statute of Virginia for religious freedom & Father of the University of Virginia." These would suffice to establish his singularity. As for the rest—his high offices, his astonishingly varied other accomplishments—these, he apparently thought, did not reach to the core meaning of his life's work.

It is not altogether obvious why Jefferson singled out these three, and only these, as his final claim to fame. Although Jefferson was indeed "Author" and "Father," in none of these cases was he acting alone. Each of these noteworthy acts was accomplished through the medium of a committee, and at that not always in a manner that gratified its moving spirit. Each depended on the consent of a legislative body and on the political skills and labors of others who secured that consent. Yet of course each was unmistakably a production of Jefferson's mind and pen, and each formed a part of his singular vision of what America and its people might become. That vision of his, I here argue, made of those parts a whole.

It was not enough for the Declaration to proclaim—and, in proclaiming, to trace—the separate career of this people. Large principles, especially grand-sounding principles, had to be brought down to earth, translated into the institutions, procedures, and habits of mind that go to make a political regime actual. All the more was this the case if the object in view was a self-governing people. Confusing right and capacity might be fatal. If self-governance were not to become a hollow or a bitter joke, a people had to be prepared, qualified to rule itself. It is, then, in the context set by the principles and aspirations of the Declaration of Independence that we may seek the larger meaning of those other achievements that Jefferson singled out as testimonials that he had lived.

The founding of the University of Virginia was in fact Jefferson's second (and second-best) attempt at putting higher education in America on a proper footing. His earlier effort, for the thorough reformation of the College of William and Mary, disappointed his expectations but nonetheless deserves pride of place here, for that prior project was conceived by Jefferson as part of a vastly ambitious scheme, one encompassing the statute for religious freedom as well. Both were parts of Jefferson's grand design to make the promise of the Declaration a reality.

That design was much on Jefferson's mind even while he was composing the Declaration. In the full flush of his revolutionary ardor in the summer of 1776, he could hardly wait to be excused from the Continental Congress to return to Virginia and tend to the urgent business at hand. A great deal needed doing. Virginia's initial surge of legislative activity—among other things, abolishing entail and exempting dissenters from compulsory contributions for the support of the established Anglican church—was indeed only a beginning. Those enactments showed something of "the strength of the general pulse of reformation" but by no means all that could and should be done. Jefferson was fired "in the persuasion that our whole code must be reviewed, adapted to our republican form of government, and, now that we had no negatives of Councils, Governors & Kings to restrain us from doing right, that it should be corrected, in all it's parts, with a single eye to reason, & the good of those for whom it was framed."[1] Here was a project to engage his ardor, learning, persistence, and principles.

At his prompting the Virginia General Assembly in late 1776 appointed a committee of luminaries to undertake a sober review and revisal of the entire legal legacy that had up to then shaped life and institutions in colony and commonwealth. This Committee of Revisors, composed finally of Jefferson, Edmund Pendleton, and George Wythe, would labor for two and one-half years before reporting 126 bills for legislative consideration and possible enactment.[2] The result, if approved, would be the reformation—better, the virtual transformation—of an emerging republican society. On this project Jefferson lavished his astonishing concentrated energy.

To speak of this revisal as Jefferson's revisal is not to denigrate the contributions of his weighty fellow committeemen or to ignore the extent to which he had to accommodate his notions to theirs. Yet the fact remains that close to half of all the bills proposed by the committee can plausibly be held to be the products of Jefferson's drafting, that all or nearly all of the most striking bills bear his distinctive stamp, and that his dedication to this arduous project was second to none. Indeed, his singularity might seem to be confirmed by another fact: the revisal's rough journey through the Virginia General Assembly testifies to the political and psychic barriers separating Jefferson from those fellow planters in whose midst he lived and on whose votes his measures depended.[3]

Interesting as these perspectives may be, they do not take in the core of Jefferson's project. It is possible to consider the revisal as offering a rare and comprehensive view of how a founder envisioned an actual republican society. Without floating off into the fantasies of the philosophes or sinking into a morass of sociological minutiae, Jefferson through his revisal showed the character of an emerging republican society as it was and as it might yet be. The grandness of the goal must not, however, obscure the obvious. Although an entire society was indeed to be reformed and transformed, that great work was to take place within certain legal constraints. The three revisers, representing the best legal learning in Virginia, would approach the common law with caution; they would build on existing English and colonial legislation. Precisely because the chosen instrument of change was a work of *revisal,* within a legal tradition, it presupposed that the meaning and effect of many of its prescriptions would have to be worked out in a long course of interpretation. As a whole, then, the proposed bills testify—sometimes eloquently, sometimes mutely—to a world of high aspiration and intractable circumstance, to a sense of open possibilities and cherished constraints. Wishing to soar, but obliged as sober legislators always to touch Virginian soil, the revisers came forward with a singular project for their colleagues to enact and their successors to ponder. In acting or failing to act as they did, each group would reveal something of itself and thereby enable us to limn a world distinguished by extraordinary equality and inequality, by complex demarcations of public and private realms, and by elaborate efforts to form and sustain a people capable of governing itself.

Unequals in a Republic of Equals

Most manifestly, that Virginian world is a society of heterogeneous parts. Its deeply ingrained habits and institutions are touched by the revisal, but only with caution. Those givens form a somber background to the revisal's efforts to accommodate equal rights and social inequality among whites; indeed, they make those efforts seem especially fragile and tenuous. We are, on the whole, more apt to be impressed by the longstanding inequalities the revisal preserves and confirms than by its often muted reforms. Yet a fuller account would have to acknowledge that the revisal does more than merely accept and somewhat mitigate existing conventional inequality. For in his elaborate education bills Jefferson showed that he thought the active promotion of natural inequality was fully compatible with, even indispensable for, a regime of republican equals.

It is a republic with a sharp eye for making distinctions and discriminations. There are citizens and aliens, rich and poor, masters and servants, slaveowners and slaves, and what can be called anomalies. Thus, while only whites may be citizens in Jefferson's Virginia (No. 55), free nonwhites are to be denominated not aliens but rather outlaws or potential outlaws (No. 51).[4] And while "all infants wheresoever born" may derive citizenship from either parent (No. 55), women otherwise remain outside the politically relevant part of the population (Nos. 2*, 118*). White males and even male citizens are further differentiated according to the task or end in view. To qualify as an elector of members of the General Assembly, one must be a male citizen, over twenty-one, and possessed of a certain amount of property or (if a townsman) have served as an apprentice to some trade for five years (No. 2*). Electors are a larger population than the class of potential members of grand juries or trial juries (No. 118*); but the suffrage, to Jefferson's later publicly expressed chagrin, is markedly narrower than the qualifications for service in the state militia.[5] Bill No. 5* not only enrolls "all free male persons, hired servants and apprentices, between the ages of 16 and 50 years" but even takes pains to specify the non-arms-bearing employment of "free mulattoes," however evanescent that category may seem in the light of the bill concerning slaves (No. 51).

Notwithstanding this highly unequal treatment of the inhabitants of Virginia, the entire body of laws may be seen as forming a mantle of procedural safeguards for all. At Jefferson's prompting the legislature's initial call for revisal had stressed the need to accommodate the existing system to the new constitutional circumstances created by a republican revolution. The "republican spirit" and "liberty and the rights of mankind" had to be reflected in and secured by appropriate laws.[6] Jefferson's revisal seeks to achieve that end by employing a mass of insistent, detailed, sometimes apparently petty particulars whose cumulative effect might be to find a place for unequals in a society dedicated to the equal enjoyment of rights. This intention is seen as readily in a proposed system by which popularly elected aldermen nominate justices of the peace "with open doors" (No. 95*)[7] as in the preservation of a freshly articulated "natural right, which all men have of relinquishing the country, in which birth, or other accident may have thrown them, and, seeking subsistance and happiness wheresoever they may be able, or may hope to find them" (No. 55).

This note of hope and promise is much diminished, however, by the likes of the bill for the support of the poor (No. 32). In the accents of the English poor law—at once threatening and threatened—it speaks of a workhouse and of an overseer "for the government, employment, and correction of the persons subject to him, restraining him from correcting any of them with more stripes than ten, at one time, or for one offence." The bill further provides for the forcible removal of emigrants from other counties, of whom aldermen are "apprehensive" lest they become public charges. Provisions such as these view the poor as a menace to public order and to public and private funds. Yet this is not the whole story, for quite apart from that threat, and not simply derivative from it, is a challenge to which the revisal tries to rise.

Bill No. 32 authorizes local alderman to "raise competent sums of money for the necessary relief of such poor, lame, impotent, blind, and other inhabitants of the county as are not able to maintain themselves." While hardly an invitation to lavishness, these provisions are at least a public response to private distress—and without the customary badges of shame.[8] The children of the destitute, and most particularly poor orphans, are to be put out as apprentices but only after having attended "the school of the hundred" for three years and having been clothed and boarded at the public expense if need be (Nos. 32, 60*). The whole takes place in a context of some, albeit limited, public accountability and regulation and with the understanding that such children-apprentices may grow up to be qualified voters in Williamsburg or Norfolk (No. 2*). Lest their duties be overwhelmed by their poverty, the revisal provides for public purchase of arms for those members of the militia who cannot supply their own (No. 5*). And lest their rights and the interest of "indifferent justice" be similarly frustrated, courts are given the discretion to waive fees for writs, to assign free "counsel learned in the laws," and otherwise to "help and speed poor persons in their suits" (No. 112). If this is not relief on a generous scale, perhaps it is because the poor laws are seen mainly as a charitable remedy for particular misfortune. The large remedy for poverty lay elsewhere. Given a broad land of natural plenty, its opportunities for modest sufficiency and individual independence might best be placed within most people's reach by republican policy and republican laws: land grants of up to fifty acres "in full and absolute dominion" to "every person of full age," inheritance laws encouraging the equal treatment of all brothers and sisters, and the general abolition of feudal impediments.[9]

The revisal perpetuates the traditional system of white bondage for limited periods, with its heavy penalties for misconduct, refusal to work, and running away. But the changes, such as they are, give some reason to hope for greater fairness. The contractual freedom of neither masters nor servants is absolute (No. 52). A mitigation of the rigors of servitude is effected by the revisers' provisions for the capture and return of runaways. Under Bill No. 53* the apprehender delivers the fugitive to the owner or owner's agent. This replaced a system whereby the justice of the peace of the county where the fugitive was captured sent the hapless servant on the way back with a warrant to the neighboring constable to receive and pass along the fugitive "and give him or her such a number of lashes, as the said justice shall think fit to direct, not exceeding thirty nine, . . . and so from constable to constable, until the runaway be delivered to his or her owner or overseer" (6 Hening 363). Under both the old and new provisions for runaways, the difference between servants and slaves tended to collapse.

Needless to say, Jefferson's bill concerning slaves (No. 51) bristles with complications.[10] Its opening paragraph proclaims that "no persons shall, henceforth, be slaves within this commonwealth," even while excepting present slaves "and the descendants of the females of them." It frees all "Negroes and mulattoes which shall hereafter be brought into this commonwealth" after they have lived in Virginia for the equivalent of one year; but then, if they have not departed the state after a further year of grace, it would put them "out of the protection of the laws." Had these proposals been enacted, they would have constituted a policy of very slow attrition, rendered speedier perhaps by the rate of lawful private manumissions. Without replenishment from abroad or from neighboring states and with the harsh threat of outlawry hastening every free or newly freed "negro or mulatto" out of Virginia, the proportion of blacks to whites would alter.[11] Here, indeed, was the core of Jefferson's policy toward blacks.[12]

It is no simple matter to assess the reach or even the full intentions of this bill. While the wish may be father to the deed, public wishes more often than not find expression in "short methods," in measures that even their proponents may come to rue. In this respect Jefferson's views on slavery bear a strong resemblance to Edmund Burke's wrestlings with the slave trade: "Taking for my basis, that I had an incurable evil to deal with, I cast about how I should make it as small an evil as possible, and draw out of it some collateral good. . . . I am persuaded that it is better to allow the evil, in order to correct it, than by endeavouring to forbid, what we cannot be able wholly to prevent, to leave it under an illegal, and therefore an unreformed, existence." Still, it has been argued that Jefferson's Bill No. 51 displays a more than Burkean caution and gradualism; indeed, that unlike Burke's proposals, it deliberately shuts its eyes to slaves as human beings and to the very prospect of their enjoyment of human liberties.[13]

We are, I think, as little entitled to trace the ambiguities of the bill to its author's supposed truculence toward blacks as to its author's supposed timidity toward whites. Some of the harshest features of the bill were rejected by the legislature, but on grounds we can only surmise. That bare fact may be attributed as well to a fear that such strictness would indeed portend a major change in the numbers and character of Virginia's labor force as to a compassionate revulsion against the bill's proposed outlawry. Furthermore, however one understands the legislature's reaction to Jefferson's bill, the Virginians' perpetuation of slavery displays yet again the general truth that it is always easier to act on right principle when viewing from afar.

As a statement of the proposed policy of republican Virginia, then, Bill No. 51 holds out little hope and still less generosity for present slaves and their descendants, slave or free. Virginia can be no fit home for free men or women of color; they must find their own place elsewhere if they are to live as they should and as becomes "a free and independant people."[14] Within Virginia the black has only the hard option of servitude or outlawry. But the bill directing the method of trying slaves charged with treason or felony (No. 104*) preserves or introduces certain safeguards. The most notable of these is the provision that a defendant who has commenced an action to assert his or her freedom "shall be prosecuted and tried for any such crime, in the same manner as a freeman ought to be prosecuted and tried." Where the servitude itself is in question, the procedural presumption is in favor of freedom.

Beyond this, Jefferson's revisal either would not or could not go. In his own eyes the failure to provide a direct, if long-term, remedy to the blight of chattel slavery left a profound contradiction in the system and spirit of the laws and a source of future catastrophe. For all its proponents' brave hopes, the revisal could not transcend conditions and feelings on a matter that, if unresolved, would doom the whole republican enterprise.

The Public and the Private Realms

A regime dedicated to the emancipation of the private pursuits of happiness from needless, meddlesome authority could not simply avert its eyes from the social consequences of those pursuits. Large matters might be no one's particular concern and yet, for all that, demand public attention and thought. So although the enjoyment of private freedom is a great good in Jefferson's *nomoi* (laws), it is by no means a simple good. In the jarring or rubbing of private desire against public need, his laws detect a continuing problem, a continuing challenge. Their response, as is true of any legal system's accommodations, is evidence of a complex underlying judgment of what constitutes a just social and political order. In the case of Jefferson, that most public of our private men and most private of our public men, the judgment and the accommodations are especially complex. It is unlikely that anyone felt more keenly than he the conflicting impulses to enjoy one's own, to tend to one's proper business in peace and quiet, and yet also to take one's turn in "the commonplace drudgery of governing a single state"[15] (or, for that matter, in the arduous labors of revising its laws).

These contending impulses are clear enough in the revisal's discussions of public duties but with the additional complication introduced by republican orthodoxy. Thus not only ought a qualified voter to vote, an elected representative to attend, but each can properly be penalized for failing to vote, failing to attend (No. 2*). The integrity of the representative body requires that its members be (in George Mason's vexed characterization) more than "the Choice of a Handful, a Neighbourhood, or a Junto," for the prime beneficiary of general indifference is the type seen often enough in "our late Assemblies"—"a factious, bawling Fellow, who will make a noise four or five miles around him, and prevail upon his party to attend" the election and thereby triumph over the more weighty, modest, and deserving.[16]

Ideally, then, elections ought to be so contrived as to bring forth the best the community can offer, not the worst. But even so those choices, fine as they might be, ought not to be held hostage by the public. Thus no one who shall have served a total of seven years in the state legislature shall be afterward compellable to serve therein (No.

2*). A somewhat different concern animates the prohibition on anyone's serving as a delegate to the Continental Congress for more than three years in any term of six years (No. 10). Here the problem appears to be a possible "danger which might arise to American freedom" and a likely loss of "the confidence of their friends" should the distant continental legislature fail to be infused regularly with new faces.[17]

The most diverse-seeming bills ring the changes on this common theme: just as there are duties owed the public, so are there rights assertable against it; but in a decent society neither claim holds undisputed sway. The salaries and fees of public officials ought to be matters of public record and posted prominently in offices and courts so as to be "visible to persons resorting thither" (No. 33*). Far from being a private matter or a public license to private enterprise, appointment to public office now is inseparable from accountability to that public.[18] In his militia bill (No. 5) Jefferson added to the list of those exempt from duty "the Presidents, Professors, and students of the College of William and Mary, and Academy of Hampden-Sidney," as well as "quakers and menonists." Even a political society at war could still afford to harbor its learned and its tender consciences.[19] That society could, with equal right, make sure that no one "shall desert wives or children, without so providing for them as that they shall not become chargeable to a county" (No. 32). In general, able-bodied persons who lack "wherewithal to maintain themselves" are forbidden to "waste their time in idle and dissolute courses, or . . . loiter or wander abroad." Proclaimed vagabonds by the law, they are impressed with a sense of their obligations to others by a confinement of up to thirty days in the poorhouse.

Not all private inclinations or passions are displayed as enemies to be overcome; some are exhibited as supports to sound policy and the public good. Thus the bill for licensing counsel, attorneys-at-law, and proctors (No. 97*) seeks to generate causes based on ordinary human drives in order to promote desired effects. It gratifies the passion of a favored class of lawyers for wealth and leisure by restricting access to the general courts. It excludes those who enjoy a comparative advantage, local county attorneys ("an inundation of insects") whose convenient and familiar access to clients enables them to "consume the harvest" while leaving general court lawyers weary with "incessant drudgery." In making it easy for the better sort of attorneys to earn a comfortable living and still "have leisure to acquire science," Jefferson hoped to raise the competence of the bar and make it "an excellent nursery for future judges."[20]

These features of Jefferson's socioeconomic legislation were overshadowed in his and contemporaries' eyes by the bills concerning the transmission of wealth, the inheritance of estates. Here Jefferson saw himself as striking a mighty blow against the haughty pretensions of the privileged rich and in favor of those conditions that might best "make an opening for the aristocracy of virtue and talent, which nature has wisely provided for the direction of the interests of society, & scattered with equal hand through all it's conditions." This self-consciously republican campaign saw the enemy as the unnatural, irrational, unjustifiable restrictions embedded in the feudal common law. To rid Virginia and America of these would enlarge "natural right" by giving scope and expression to natural feeling.[21]

Some such intention lay in the foreground of Jefferson's decision to leave Congress and go back to Virginia. One of the first products of his legislative draftsmanship on that occasion was the bill enabling "tenants in fee-tail to convey their lands in fee-simple."[22] Its intention and effect are perpetuated in the simpler language incorporated in the bill for regulating conveyances (No. 22*). With one stroke the bill does away with all restrictions placed by fathers or fathers' fathers on the sale or further bequest of land—to the advancement of good policy, family tranquillity, and the better use of the time of a legislature that would no longer have to trouble with petitions for special exemptions.[23] A system whereby an earlier generation's fancies or dreams of founding patrician dynasties lay heavy upon the desires and even necessities of their offspring could be defended by no sound principle of political economy or of political science, to say nothing of republicanism.

Equally obnoxious and hence equally fit for rapid extirpation was the common law directing the course of descents in the case of those dying intestate. Its discrimination in favor of the eldest son and his issue in preference to any other heirs is overturned, as is its rule that a bastard can inherit nothing. The general discrimination in favor of male heirs is replaced by a rule of equal division among all descendants of the same degree of consanguinity. The common-law rule that inheritance shall never lineally ascend in default of lineal descendants but shall rather escheat to the lord is rejected in accord with John Locke's reasoning on the matter: "If his Son dye without Issue, the Father has a Right in Nature to possess his Goods, and Inherit his Estate (whatever the Municipal Laws of some Countries, may absurdly direct otherwise)."[24] Indeed, it is against this whole array of what he too saw as feudal absurdities that Jefferson aimed his bill directing the course of descents (No. 20). He thought it one of the most remarkable of the revisers' proposals, and with good reason, for here was yet another instance of using the revisal of ordinary legislation to elaborate on what ought to be the fundamental principles of the regime.[25] By deflating and rejecting the grandiose claims of feudal usurpations "& such fooleries," the revisal guards against the public realm's engrossing all it sees.[26]

Yet there are of course instances, all too frequent, when the government acting in the name of the public must take private property, liberty, even limb and life. When "wicked and dissolute men [resign] themselves to the dominion of inordinate passions," no one's life, liberty, and property can be safe, and the very reason for men's entering into society is put in jeopardy. A government that stood mute or helpless in the face of such domineering "would be defective in it's principal purposes" (No. 64). Of the many occasions in the revisal for reconciling the tensions between public needs and private wants, between enlightened calculations and passionate urgings, few have the immediacy and drama of this.

The purpose of Bill No. 64 is to proportion "crimes and punishments in cases heretofore capital" by arranging each "in a proper scale" with a view to enlisting men's natural inclinations in the aid of duty. Jefferson turned to this task with special enthusiasm, prompted (in the language of the preamble) by "the experience of all ages and countries . . . that cruel and sanguinary laws defeat their own purpose by engaging the benevolence of mankind to withhold prosecutions, to smother testimony, or to listen to it with bias." Rather than needlessly affront this natural fellow feeling, Jefferson sought wherever possible to replace punishments that "exterminate" with punishments that reform and restore "sound members to society." Instead of warring with their passions, citizens could then convict and punish with a clear, calm conscience, and those "contemplating to perpetrate a crime would see their punishment ensuing as necessarily as effects follow their causes." Jefferson's objections to capital punishment did not, however, carry him to advocate its total abolition. It still "should be the last melancholy resource against those whose existence is become inconsistent with the safety of their fellow citizens."[27]

As a whole, however, Bill No. 64 presents itself as the studied, even artful, attempt of reason and experience to find alternatives to mindless cruelty. Julian P. Boyd's inclination is to view the bill as less a reform than a restatement of generally accepted practices concerning capital offenses; that, indeed, in its reliance on the *lex talionis,* it contrasts "shockingly" with the liberal thought of the age. The evidence he adduces of Jefferson's dissatisfaction with the bill, both at the time of its drafting and later, lends support to this judgment. But as Boyd also points out, the absence of any statement in favor of the *lex talionis* in any of the surviving documents of the revisers' proceedings is noteworthy and raises questions about Jefferson's account of its inclusion. Our efforts to take the measure of this bill are not helped much by the little we know of contemporary reactions to it. There does not appear to be any clear evidence of what the House of Delegates found obnoxious in this bill or of what amendments to render it less so they proposed during their protracted deliberations. James Madison attributed its defeat, in large measure, to the legislature's "rage against Horse stealers." His bitter complaint that "our old bloody code is by this event fully restored" makes it hard to join Boyd in asserting that the "harsh features of the Bill undoubtedly contributed to its defeat." This much at least seems likely: an enlightened republican hope of measured punishment and reform foundered because the legislature took offense at what it detected behind the bill's learned citations. Lurking there was not so much the spirit of Exodus 21 as that of Beccaria.

That very spirit informs Jefferson's companion bill (No. 68) prescribing the treatment of prisoners and suffices to explain why this bill too was spurned by the legislature. Modern doctrine warns against succumbing to either cruelty or compassion when correcting the wicked. Malefactors condemned to hard labor are to be "marked out to public note," "constantly shaven," distinguished in dress from "the good citizens of this commonwealth," and this not only with a view to rendering fugitives more visible. The bill also seeks to secure equal justice by forbidding prisoners any clothing, money, property, or service beyond that supplied by their keepers, lest "the opulence of the offender, or of his friends, or the indiscreet [b]ounties of individuals . . . disarm the public justice, or alleviate those sufferings." Procedures for reviewing the behavior of jailers and the treatment of prisoners are established and assigned to some local person of "discretion, humanity and attention." The bill repeatedly seeks to guard against gross partiality or cruelty, each in its way subversive of the rationale for public punishment.

With these varied efforts at evenhandedness Jefferson and his fellow revisers hoped to strike a tolerable balance between the passionate, interested forces they meant to free and the requirements of the polity, economy, and society within which those private forces would need to be contained.

Opinion and Knowledge in Republican Society

Nowhere is the confrontation of public need and private wish more troubling and threatening than in matters relating to belief, opinion, and thought. Few issues of public policy held equal significance for

Jefferson, and to none did he devote more sustained reflection and care. All the more striking is it, then, that in these very matters his revisal should contain such disparate and apparently warring elements. Some of the conflicts can perhaps be understood as inadvertent, the results of somewhat mechanical salvage and incorporation of earlier legislation or practice of long standing (and assumed to be unproblematic) in juxtaposition with novel departures. Some, but not all. What, for example, is to be made of that provision in Bill No. 64 that punishes with ducking and whipping ("not exceeding 150 stripes") "all attempts to delude the people, or to abuse their understanding by exercise of the pretended arts of witchcraft, conjuration, inchantment, or sorcery or by pretended prophecies"? One might say with Blackstone that this is "a crime of which one knows not well what account to give." Even more might one say this of its inclusion in *Jefferson's* bill. Artfully decked out with its elaborate and ancient supporting citations in Anglo-Saxon, Latin, Old French, and English, this is no merely routine copying of Virginia precedent. As matters stand, Blackstone's soft-spoken reproof of the whole business is more intelligible than the fact that the author of this provision is one who steadfastly and publicly exploded the notion that Christianity is a part of the common law.[28]

Other provisions are not so mystifying. While days of "public fasting and humiliation, or thanksgiving" were far less common in Anglican Virginia than in Congregationalist New England, the notion was familiar enough.[29] Bill No. 85* allows for such proclamations by executive order in cases where the legislature is not in session and requires further that "every minister of the gospel" preach a suitable sermon in his church on such an occasion "on pain of forfeiting fifty pounds for every failure, not having a reasonable excuse."

Much more familiar to Virginians were the provisions of Bill No. 84 punishing those who conduct business as usual on Sundays. These restrictions stem from an old line of Sabbatarian legislation, although the talk is no longer of "the holy keeping of the Lords day."[30] The bill promotes both religion and religious diversity by securing "any minister of the gospel" from arrest while engaged in public preaching or worship and by restraining and punishing those who disturb others in their worship. As enacted in 1786, this protection is extended to "any minister of religion."[31] For a licensed minister to enjoy this immunity, the bill requires as a prior condition that he swear (the act, that he swear or affirm) fidelity to the commonwealth.

Religious interests are both protected and readjusted in other ways as well. In the matter of the property of the once-established church, Bill No. 83 preserves the glebe lands, buildings, and other property of the "English church," conforming in this way more closely to the legislature's point of view than to Jefferson's.[32] The bill also compels the church vestries to distribute as poor relief the excess funds levied by them in the past. Although the administration of poor relief is rendered a purely civil matter by Bill No. 32's transfer of jurisdiction from the vestry of the parish to the aldermen of the county, the vestries themselves are not touched.[33]

Not only poor relief is given a civil face. The registration of vital statistics (No. 63*) is no longer a responsibility of parish minister or parish clerks, nor apparently are fees to be charged for this service, as required under the prevailing law of 1713.[34] The law of marriage, too, receives a strongly secular cast. Although retaining the Levitical law regarding forbidden degrees of union, Bill No. 86* quietly does away with any need for religious solemnities. In rendering ecclesiastical authority superfluous in these matters, the revisers would also be putting an end to longstanding agitation over the Anglican clergy's monopoly over marriages, the resentment over the required threefold posting of banns, the need for special exemptions for Quakers and others, and the grudging licensing of dissenting ministers and even of "sober and discreet laymen" in the "remote parts of this commonwealth . . . on the western waters." Secularization and domestic tranquillity proceed apace.[35]

Yet Jefferson's goal, one need hardly add, was something much grander than a society of placid, comfortable burghers, squires, or yeomen. To render men unlikely candidates for murderous and suicidal crusades was one thing, to dispose and fit them for the demands of self-governance another. Here Jefferson brought more than his formidable legislative skills to bear on the work at hand. Theme, commitment, and art joined to produce a burst of concentrated reasoning and rhetoric that could not be contained by the dull opening formula, "Be it enacted by the General Assembly." Nothing less than a proem would do to set legislator and ordinary citizen in mind—now and forever—of the reasons for, and hence the ends of, this particular legislation. Since this part of the revisal (Nos. 79–82) had to do with the freeing of the human mind, eloquent statement of those reasons would equally be a support for a politics of reason. No tolerably alert reader of these preludes could miss that intention.[36] It is not far-fetched, then, to view two of these preambles as testaments of Jefferson's republicanism. Therein he pronounced the principles and reasons of his practical program, leading the reader from effects back to causes and then from whys to hows. By considering these preambles together with their bills' detailed provisions, we may better grasp the political science through which Jefferson hoped to make republicans.

Bill No. 79 does more than nod smilingly in the direction of republican government. Without Jefferson's needing to mention that favored form by name, we know that it is surely among those that are "better calculated than others to protect individuals in the free exercise of their natural rights, and are at the same time themselves better guarded against degeneracy." Despite this favorable prospect, Jefferson's sequel turns out to be less an expression of congratulation than of concern, caution, even alarm, for experience testifies to the gradual corruption of public trustees and to their perversion of even the best forms into tyranny. To forfend what has happened everywhere and always is the objective of the "bill for the more general diffusion of knowledge."

The best preventive, it is believed, "would be, to illuminate, as far as practicable, the minds of the people at large." Being forewarned, as it were, by the exhibits of history, they would be forearmed. By coming to "know ambition under all its shapes," they would be "prompt to exert their natural powers to defeat its purposes." The most famous gloss on the revisal puts it best: "Of all the views of this law none is more important, none more legitimate, than that of rendering the people the safe, as they are the ultimate, guardians of their own Liberty."[37] Yet by itself this precautionary instruction cannot suffice, at least if one has in mind something more than frustration of potential tyrants. More is wanted, and more is possible; not only the free exercise of natural rights—not only the pursuit of happiness, one is tempted to say—but the real happiness of the people is to be sought. And that search (Jefferson's preamble asserts) compels one to look beyond the people at large to "those persons, whom nature hath endowed with genius and virtue." Without this better sort to form wise laws and to administer them honestly, the people cannot be as happy as they might be. The bill for the more general diffusion of knowledge is thus inevitably also a bill for the "liberal education" of the indispensable few who will thereby become better "able to guard the sacred deposit of the rights and liberties of their fellow citizens." To find those few, then, is a public necessity and a public charge.

Precisely because the public need for them is so great and precisely because so few are worthy of receiving such an education, sound public policy dictates that the joining of promising genius and proper education not be left to chance. To the extent that barriers of wealth, birth, or other accidental circumstances might prevent that happy conjunction, they ought to be overcome. Jefferson took for granted as basic social facts both "the indigence of the greater number" and the random distribution of rare genius. To identify, nourish, and educate those children "whom nature hath fitly formed and disposed to become useful instruments for the public" requires a social policy at once generous and tough. The preamble defends that generosity on grounds of political economy. Without some form of public assistance, the able children of the poor will not receive the education of which they are worthy—to the public's own great loss: "It is better that such should be sought for and educated at the common expence of all, than that the happiness of all should be confided to the weak or wicked." The toughness of the policy is clear enough from the bill. The annual selection of scholarship students for the next higher stage, "after the most diligent and impartial examination and enquiry," constitutes what Jefferson characterizes elsewhere as raking the best geniuses from "the rubbish."[38] In creating a system whereby a poor man's gifted son would deservedly receive what any rich man's son could afford, Jefferson held to a totally unsentimental view of entitlement.

One of the striking features of Bill No. 79 is its great detail in prescribing the manner of defining school districts, determining the location of the schools, prescribing the modes of condemning property for public use, and the like. Almost two-thirds of the bill proper is devoted to administrative details of this kind, descending even to the minutiae of the grammar school steward's job description and the exact time and manner for selecting scholarship students. The details bespeak an intention to impress upon local electors, aldermen, and overseers the gravity of their educational responsibilities; if the legislature takes such pains with every detail, imparting to each an almost ritual significance, every detail of educational administration must indeed be somehow terribly important for the success of the whole. Electors of the hundreds are charged with determining where the local schoolhouse shall be located or relocated. Alderman are charged with determining and regulating the boundaries of local districts; further, they are to conduct the public interrogation of nominations for grammar school scholarships. Overseers have the "business and duty" of appointing and (if necessary) removing teachers, examining the scholars, and fixing a centrally situated place for a grammar (or secondary) school. Visitors of the grammar schools are charged with hiring and firing the master and steward of the school, setting tuition, and examining the school, its staff, and its students. Both the overseers of the schools of the hundreds and the visitors of the grammar schools are charged with seeing to it that any general instructional plan recommended by the visitors of William and Mary College shall be observed. Teachers are accountable for their performance, just as they are for their fidelity to the commonwealth; overseers are accountable for their recommendations and appointments; scholars are accountable for making the best of whatever genius they have. In short, the entire scheme for establishing and maintaining an educational system constitutes in itself an education in responsible self-governance. In lavishing these details on the bill, Jefferson also gave his fullest explanation by example of what he meant by self-government. The scheme's elaborations thus make it of a piece with a curriculum that would teach the three R's to all the free boys and girls of the commonwealth by drawing on useful lessons from Greek, Roman, English, and American history. For their own safety and that of others, for their own happiness and that of their children, a free people must be qualified "as judges of the actions and designs of men."[39] Jefferson's bill encompasses that intention at every level.

"In order that grammar schools may be rendered convenient to the youth in every part of the commonwealth," Bill No. 79 arrays all the counties of the state into twenty fairly compact districts. In each of these is to be established a school where students would be taught "the Latin and Greek languages, English grammar, geography, and the higher part of numerical arithmetic." With half of these districts entitled to a choice every other year, those ten among the select grammar school seniors adjudged annually to be "of the best learning and most hopeful genius and disposition" would be sent to William and Mary College, there to be educated, boarded, and clothed for three years at the public expense. But the college they would attend, along with fifty or so sons of the well-to-do, would differ significantly from the William and Mary of Jefferson's undergraduate days (1758–1760), or George Wythe's (1746). To effect that change and to justify it is the object of Bill No. 80. Doing so takes no few words; indeed the preamble of this bill for "amending the constitution of the college of William and Mary and substituting more certain revenues for its support" is about the length of all the other six preambles combined. It begins by telling a long story in a tone and style that have been found unworthy of its author.[40] It is a narrative of hopes and frustrations, of generosity and misguided intentions, all told with tedious particularity by a man who detested pleonasms and legalistic involutions, who was obliged to follow the revisers' general rule of draftsmanship "not to insert an unnecessary word, nor omit a useful one," and who was more adept than most at saying much in few words.[41]

One need not puzzle long over this departure from pithiness, especially since Jefferson in effect accounted for it all when drawing the necessary and useful lessons from this history of the college. The narrative of "the experience of near an hundred years hath proved" that, as constituted, William and Mary can only continue to disappoint; further, that its defects are fundamental and hence beyond the ordinary powers of its trustees to remedy; still further, that its reliance on public exertions and public benefactions going back to its very origins and foundation entitles one to view that endowment as "no wise in nature of a private grant."[42] Accordingly, the present General Assembly and governor of Virginia, acting as the public's "legal fiduciary for such purposes," not only may but of right ought to reconstitute the college's charter "until such form be devised as will render the institution publicly advantageous, in proportion as it is publicly expensive." To dispose of any lingering misgivings or scruples that might impede full consent to this project to alter a private corporation's charter, the preamble ends in an appeal to the revolutionary moment and its revolutionary promise:

> The late change in the form of our government, as well as the contest of arms in which we are at present engaged, calling for extraordinary abilities both in council and field, it becomes the peculiar duty of the Legislature, at this time, to aid and improve that seminary, in which those who are to be the future guardians of the rights and liberties of their country may be endowed with science and virtue, to watch and preserve the sacred deposit.

It is only after all this necessary justification that Jefferson permitted the enacting clause to hover into sight.

What follows in the body of the bill may seem only to reinforce the initial impression that the whole effort is overwrought, out of proportion, and therefore out of character with its author. But Jefferson took pains within the overall confines of the bill to depict the "after" as vividly as the "before" of William and Mary. In fact the "after," the potentially far-reaching effects of the revolutionary changes being legislated for a private Anglican foundation, can be said to be emphasized by the very intermixture of details large and small. Consider, for example, the provisions specifying procedures for removing professors "for breach or neglect of duty, immorality, severity, contumacy, or other good cause"; for replacing the college's revenue from state duties on skins, furs, and liquors with a more reliable and steady "impost of 9d on every hogshead of tobacco to be exported from this commonwealth by land or water"; for authorizing, indeed directing, the visitors to engage "that greatest of astronomers, David Ryttenhouse," to make and erect a mechanical model of the solar system "that this commonwealth may not be without so great an ornament, nor its youth such an help towards attaining astronomical science." In such and such ways, prescribed by law, shall the visitors, chancellors, and faculty perform their offices. As in the case of the lower schools, the legal detail exemplifies a conception of republican governance applied to a central institution. The visitors or governors of the college are now to be appointees of the state legislature. Their sworn assurance of fidelity to the commonwealth, their tenure of office at the legislature's pleasure, their liberation from the original charter's restrictions based on "the royal prerogative, or the laws of the kingdom of England; or the canons or constitution of the English Church"—all these point to a public, politically accountable superintendence over the college's principal policies.

Most prominent, partly owing to the typographical arrangement of the bill's appendix, is Jefferson's reconstitution of the college's curriculum. Here especially lay the heart of Jefferson's project to take a training school for Anglicans, "to enlarge its sphere of science, and to make it in fact an University." The old arrangement of six professorships into four schools (Sacred Theology, Philosophy, Latin and Greek, Indian) is no more. Holy Scripture falls out of the curriculum, as do "the common places of divinity, and the controversies with heretics," and the teaching of metaphysics. Ecclesiastical law and ecclesiastical history are folded into those larger disciplines of which they are now seen to be only a part. The teaching of Latin and Greek is transferred to the grammar schools where it belongs, thereby ridding the college of "children," freeing the college's resources, which had been "exhausted in accommodating those who came only to acquire the rudiments of science," and giving those "young and tender subjects" enrolled in the grammar schools a program of secular studies more suited to their powers and needs.[43] The Indian school, founded on the private bequest of the pious chemist Robert Boyle and dedicated to teaching Indian boys the three R's and the Christian catechism, is abolished and its professor replaced by "a missionary, of approved veracity," who is charged with collecting anthropological and especially linguistic materials for the college library.

The description of the eight professorships as given in the bill's appendix is hardly a New Organon, but it does display clearly enough what Jefferson found wanting in the existing arrangement. The old professorship of rhetoric, law, and ethics is replaced by one of ethics (moral philosophy, law of nature, law of nations) and fine arts (sculpture, painting, gardening, music, architecture, poetry, oratory, criticism). Present necessity might compel a union of subjects that future legislative leisure and generosity would subdivide, but this particular joining is far from arbitrary or accidental.[44] An altogether new professorship of law and police is established, encompassing

"Municipal" law (the teaching of common law, equity, and mercantile, maritime, and ecclesiastical law) and "Oeconomical" law (the teaching of politics and commerce). Also altogether new are three professorships of anatomy and medicine, of natural philosophy and natural history, and of modern languages (French, Italian, German). Whereas Hebrew was earlier taught by the professor charged with expounding the holy scriptures in the School of Sacred Theology, now it is in the domain of a professor of ancient languages, "oriental and northern." This philological polymath is responsible for teaching Hebrew, Chaldee, Syriac, Moeso-Gothic, Anglo-Saxon, and Old Icelandic.

The implications of this reorganization for the kinds of questions to be asked and the kinds of answers to be sought are no mystery. If the William and Mary of the 1693 charter faithfully exhibited the contours of a prelatical establishment and the hopes and vision of its royal or pious benefactors, so too would the new William and Mary exhibit the new contours of the republic of learning and the hopes and vision of its learned republican benefactor. The "liberal minded" impulse that first led Virginians to petition their rulers for a college would now at last be fulfilled in a seminary of science, rights, and liberties.

The third of Jefferson's bills to free the human mind proposes the establishment of a public library (No. 81). Its particulars are rather sparse and, at that, somewhat at odds with his two glosses on the bill. As presented in the "Autobiography," the library would be the third stage of an educational system that rose from elementary schools to colleges to "an ultimate grade for teaching the sciences generally, & in their highest degree." In *Notes on Virginia* the bill is described as proposing "to begin a public library and gallery, by laying out a certain sum annually in books, paintings, and statues." The text of the bill, however, says nothing that would suggest an art gallery or a teaching institute of advanced studies. It speaks instead of books and maps, intelligently selected and properly preserved; of a noncirculating collection "made useful by indulging the researches of the learned and curious, within the said library, without fee or reward." The library is public in the sense that two thousand pounds per annum are to be paid out of the state treasury for its acquisitions and operations. It is public in the sense that access to its riches is to be without charge or favor. But this is not a library *for* the public. Admission is to be limited to the qualified; furthering *their* already advanced researches is the great object in view. In proposing to devote substantial public funds to the advancement of rare private minds, Jefferson displayed his confessed "zeal of a true Whig in science." The sight of such splendor, like the sight of beautiful buildings, might enlarge and enrich an entire country. A people boasting such adornments would be worthy of self-respect and of the respect of others.[45]

Finally there is Bill No. 82, whose enactment by the General Assembly Jefferson accounted as one of the three pillars on which he was content to rest his everlasting fame. Its enacting clause relieves everyone from compulsory attendance in or compulsory support for any form of religious worship and from any manner of penalties on account of religious opinions or belief. At the same time it guarantees to all the freedom "to profess, and by argument to maintain, their opinions in matters of religion," having equated religious opinions with "opinions in physics or geometry" as matters independent of civil rights.[46] With such simplicity and directness would Jefferson establish religious freedom in Virginia. But that plain prose, far from standing alone and austere (and, for all that, memorable), is encased in a text of throbbing eloquence and conviction. The bill's opening and conclusion may stand as definitive statements of Jefferson's republican creed, inviting one to consider No. 82 as a capstone of those bills in the revisal directed to freeing the human mind.[47]

Singularly, the preamble dispenses with the customary "Whereas" and seems to begin in the very midst of an argument: "Well aware that the opinions and belief of men depend not on their own will, but follow involuntarily the evidence proposed to their minds."[48] All the fourteen or so parallel clauses that follow depend on that awareness or common knowledge, or lend credence to that assertion, or trace the evil consequences of ignoring that truth. In sum they show that it is futile or impious or tyrannical, or some combination of all these, to coerce others in matters of opinion, belief, religion, persuasion, or worship. Echoing Milton, the preamble suggests that reason is but choosing and holds "that truth is great and will prevail if left to herself . . . unless by human interposition disarmed of her natural weapons, free argument and debate." Echoing Locke and Shaftesbury, the preamble proclaims "that the opinions of men are not the object of civil government, nor under its jurisdiction." And echoing Adam Smith, it holds that monopolistic privileges corrupt minister and religion alike. For in depriving parishioners of "the comfortable liberty" of contributing to whomever they please, the old law of compulsory religious assessments simultaneously withdraws "from the ministry those tempora[l] rewards, which proceeding from an approbation of their personal conduct, are an additional incitement to earnest and unremitting labours for the instruction of mankind."[49]

Equally singular is the presence in Bill No. 82 of a coda. As though loath to part and leave the enactment to stand on its own, Jefferson showed plainly enough that this bill, if any, would be his candidate for an irrevocable law. Put once and forever beyond the tamperings and temporizings of future generations, this law would confirm and secure most precious "natural rights." But such a wish is absurd: "We well know that this Assembly, elected by the people for the ordinary purposes of legislation only, have no power to restrain the acts of succeeding Assemblies, constituted with powers equal to our own." The proper bottoming of republican society requires the authorization of a power greater than that of "this Assembly" but other than that of "Almighty God," "the holy author of our religion."[50] Yet however more secure and solemn such a guarantee may be as compared with an ordinary enactment, even a constitutional provision grounded on explicit popular consent would still be subject to later revision by another convention. Would "the natural rights of mankind" then be proof against a constitutional majority's desire to repeal or narrow the enjoyment of those rights? The coda suggests that there are fundamentals, such as the rights asserted in this bill, that are beyond the legitimate reach of laws or even constitutions. The argument for establishing natural rights by law and constitution is not that the latter are sufficient but that they are indispensable for helping to educate the people in the principles of their regime. Thus, even while guarding Virginians against any imminent infringement of their rights, the bill for establishing religious freedom helps educate a society that will cherish such guarantees now and in the future.

The Philosophical Legislator's Long View

Jefferson's *nomoi* display in all their richness and complexity the intersections of his intelligence, principle, and circumstance. The society they portray and prescribe is at once harsh and tender, calculating and lofty. It whips bodies and cossets consciences; it honors genius from behind a wharf of tobacco hogsheads. It cherishes institutional safeguards not of its making, while finding the past instructive mostly for its failures and disasters.

Above all Jefferson's *nomoi* anticipate a society that faces forward. That society is invited to raise its hopes, even while mired in a system of chattel slavery that promises to swamp or befoul every brave plan. Those hopes are centered on itself, its land, and the finest of its children. Here all is promise, another kind of promise, a promise anchored in a sense of past achievements and present dedication. The indeterminacies of the present and of the distant future seem hardly to matter. In the midst of a war of uncertain duration and outcome, the revisal's preoccupation is with the kind of society Virginia means to be.

That society, if it is to be at all worth forming and preserving, must be self-governed by truly free men. The simple directness of that stipulation cannot conceal the complexity of the means needed to realize it. For Virginia to become a commonwealth in fact and not merely in name, all segments of the body politic need to be instructed. Schooling is only a part of that instruction and (I am inclined to believe) not even the greater part. The three years of common schooling that all would get, the few years in secondary school that some would enjoy, even the college instruction of the privileged handful—all that could only alert and forewarn, cajole and predispose a people to wish to be their own best guardians of their rights. To make that wish a fact, lessons learned would have to be applied. Institutions had to be contrived that would draw individuals together, compel them to speak and listen to one another, accustom them to judging men and measures, confirm them in the habits of being accountable for their acts. With apparently hopeless circularity, the problem seemed to demand simultaneously that society be made worthy of free men and that individuals be made fit for free society. Here was a challenge that would drive a Rousseau to seek an unspoiled people on an island by themselves; only such a people would be fit for the best a philosophical legislator could contrive. Jefferson, in contrast, needed no mythic Corsica to elicit his greatest efforts. The ground he stood on, the people in whose midst he had always lived—these would be, had to be, the makings of the promising society.

More than his hopeful temperament sustained Jefferson in this bold project. For to a greater degree than the revisal allows (or my account discloses), Jefferson assumed a people already long accustomed to the forms and habits of English law, "a people fostered & fixed in principles of freedom."[51] Similarly, he could take for granted that the extensions of public accountability and local self-government called for in the revisal would be perceived as precisely that—extensions of what had in one form or another existed in Virginia for over a century and a half, not bewildering or alien novelties. What *was* new and in need of careful explanation and ardent justification was a heightened spirit of dedication. To legislate that spirit in matters large and small was the great challenge to which Jefferson tried to rise.

Here was a goal worthy of his revolutionary impulse. Making the people aware of what it took to be and to remain their own masters was a considerable undertaking. Each type of person had to be addressed in a manner suitable to its capacities, even while those capacities were themselves being stretched and developed. Furthermore, all this was to be done in a setting where a thousand daily circumstances drew citizens' thoughts and energies earthward and inward, where the enticements of immediate material reward threatened to drain public life of the indispensable involvement of the many and the indispensable contribution of the best. For Jefferson such wholesale indifference would be the very hemorrhaging of public life. A nation of private calculators with short memories would forget the long-term consequences of not tending to the public business. More than anything else they needed to be instructed and confirmed in their present resolve not to be the wards of others.

In seeking to effect that outcome, the revisal nowhere carelessly takes for granted an easy harmony of public need and private interest, not even when suggesting their congruence. To establish a network of connecting secondary postal service for "the more general diffusion of public intelligence among the citizens of this commonwealth and the maintenance of correspondence between friends and merchants" requires, after all, an act of legislation—and is no simple matter at that (No. 19). To be sure, the revisal does not eschew using private interest no further a public purpose (as when licensing counsel, No. 97*), but it would hardly mistake such support for the bedrock of a self-governing society. More is needed.

Here enter the great proems that introduce those bills most critical to Jefferson's project and most characteristic of his legislating art. Inspiring and inspired, they could rouse a people to a sense of what that people might be. They could remind a people of the evils self-governance helps them avoid—and of the possibilities for good and ill it puts within their reach. Commercial opportunities and free consciences, public accountability and participation in public duties, the freeing of private life and the public utility of private excellence—here were benefits to be cherished by all, both atop Monticello and in the valleys below. It took a rare, long perspective to make that evident and point out the way.

5
The Social Theory of the Founders

Nathan Tarcov

Our founding is political rather than social. We celebrate the bicentennial of the political institutions established by the Constitution as we celebrated that of the political independence proclaimed by the Declaration of Independence. To a remarkable degree, we remain governed by those political institutions, however modified by amendments and accretions. Perhaps even more remarkable is the degree to which our understanding of those institutions and of political life generally remains governed by the political theory of our founding: the equality of individuals and peoples; rights to life, liberty, and the pursuit of happiness; consent of the governed; separation and division of power to secure liberty; energetic government to preserve the Union, ensure domestic tranquility, provide for the common defense, and promote the general welfare; and the authority of the people and their Constitution. We do not celebrate with similar clarity the social institutions and mores of our founding. Our society has changed far more than our polity during the two centuries since our political founding: changed in its forms of property and commerce, its class structure, its religious life, its science and art, its family life, and the characters and mores of its members. But perhaps even more important, we do not adhere to a social theory established by our founding as we do in great part to its political theory.

This discrepancy between the continuity of American political practice and theory and the transformation of American social reality and theory reflects the *political* character of our founding. The founding was not exclusively concerned with political *institutions*—*The Federalist* argued not only for the Constitution itself but also for a "political creed" compatible with it (end of No. 23, beginning of No. 26). But it did not establish an equally conspicuous *social* theory or delineation of the characteristics of a free society. It is therefore not entirely an accident that while we have remained relatively faithful to the political institutions and principles of the founding, we have adopted a variety of new social practices and theories. The political emphasis of the founding permitted this result; it was, in a sense, even designed to do so. The theory of the founding made the distinction between government and society that underlies this later discrepancy and made it the business of founding or constitution making to establish political institutions and declare political principles, not to freeze social facts or aspirations. Indeed the founding tended to leave society free to develop outside the purview not only of constitution making but of government altogether. In this way the American founders differed both from the classical models of sociopolitical founders or lawgivers, such as Theseus, Romulus, Solon, or Lycurgus, and from the modern sociopolitical founders or revolutionaries, such as Lenin, Mao, Castro, or Pol Pot, who alike were creators or destroyers of social classes as well as of political institutions.

Our adoption of later social theories while we retain earlier political theory reflects not only the political emphasis and intention of the founding but also the social emphasis of later thought. The past two centuries have not been as fruitful as the Enlightenment, the era of the founding, in political theory or the design of political institutions. But they have given birth to a variety of social theories and notions of what various aspects of society should be like. Thus it seems almost logical that we should take our politics from the Enlightenment and our society from the schools of thought of the succeeding centuries.

The symmetry between our political fidelity to the founding and our social innovations, on the one hand, and the political emphasis of the founding and social emphasis of later thought, on the other, may suggest that we have chosen the complementary best from both worlds and consummated a happy marriage. But can we happily mate republican government, individual rights, and the Constitution with class struggle, the inner-directed man, and psychotherapy? Although the founders did not establish a social theory or social institutions as conspicuous as the Constitution and political creed they bequeathed us, they made strenuous efforts to reform various social practices in ways that fit their political achievements, and they gave careful thought to the kind of free society that is compatible with republican government. We have an uneasy sense that our inherited political institutions and principles are inappropriate to our new society and social understanding. Must we therefore abandon our political inheritance and reconstitute our polity to fit our social practices and goals? Can we possibly return to the society or social understanding of 1787? Can we continue indefinitely to muddle through with more or less understanding of our mixed condition?

A Republican Society

Before we can begin to answer those questions, the first requirement is not a sociological examination of the actual circumstances of American society at the time of the founding but a theoretical conception of the sort of society appropriate to the republican institutions established by the Constitution. The social circumstances of two centuries ago need not and cannot be the norm for American republican society; departures from them may be movement toward rather than away from the social implications of the founding. Slavery is only the most obvious social contradiction of the principles of the founding.

The republican character of the Constitution is proclaimed not only by the guarantee of a republican form of government to every state in the Union (Article IV, section 4) but above all by the representative, that is, directly or indirectly elective, character of the legislative and executive branches of the federal government. These representative institutions presuppose a society in which there is no hereditary nobility or royalty to constitute a legislative house or a chief magistracy.

The implications of the Constitution's representative institutions for republican social structure emerge from the debate at the Constitutional Convention. John Dickinson expressed the wish that the Senate should "consist of the most distinguished characters, distinguished for their rank in life and their weight of property, and bearing as strong a likeness to the British House of Lords as possible" (June 7).[1] Dickinson, however, was somewhat old-fashioned, the product of a British legal education, known for his refusal to sign the Declaration of Independence, and of an older generation than the bold young men of the founding. His own former student in the law, James Wilson, responded to him that "the British government cannot be our model. We have no materials for a similar one. Our manners, our laws, the abolition of entails and of primogeniture, the whole genius of the people, are opposed to it" (June 7).

Far from "the superior classes of society" constituting a hereditary aristocracy, George Mason remarked that "however affluent their circumstances, or elevated their situations might be, the course of a few years, not only might but certainly would, distribute their posterity throughout the lowest classes of society" (May 31). Charles Pinckney expressed his confidence that

> the Constitution of Great Britain . . . will not or can not be introduced into this Country, for many centuries . . . the peculiar excellence, the distinguishing feature of that government can not possibly be introduced into our System . . . we

> neither have or can have the members to compose it, nor the rights, privileges and properties of so distinct a class of Citizens to guard. (June 25)

The distinctively American view of what distinguished American society was that the absence of an aristocratic social structure made republican institutions necessary and possible.

Dickinson must have clearly recognized that even the strongest likeness to the House of Lords that could be constitutionally arranged would fall far short of a genuine nobility. He had admitted that "a House of Nobles . . . were the growth of ages, and could only arise under a complication of circumstances none of which existed in this Country" (June 2). Later in the convention he opposed property qualifications for members of Congress because he "doubted the policy of interweaving into a Republican constitution a veneration for wealth. He had always understood that a veneration for poverty and virtue were the objects of republican encouragement" (July 26). The poverty he would have us venerate, however, was that of virtuous freeholders, not that of "those multitudes without property and without principle with which our Country like all others, will in time abound" (August 7).

Thus even one of the strongest admirers of the British constitution among the founders reluctantly recognized that it was not applicable here because of our republican social structure and conversely that our political model was instead a republic composed of poor and virtuous freeholders. For Dickinson the salutary alternative seemed to be either a mixed constitution for which we lacked the aristocratic social structure or a republic that required a simple social structure. He may have needed "consolation for the future fate of his Country" and worried that we might read its fate in the history of "ancient republics . . . found to flourish for a moment only and then vanish for ever" (June 2), in part because he thought it less likely that time would bring us the aristocracy needed for a mixed constitution than that it would bring us the dangerous propertyless multitudes destructive to republics.

"Equality of Condition"

A republican social structure or the absence of hereditary royalty or nobility was not understood simply as the prior condition for a republican government, as if the social determined the political. The founders took their task more seriously than that. The representative institutions of the Constitution presuppose the absence of an hereditary aristocracy to begin with, but the constitutional prohibitions against either the federal or state governments granting any titles of nobility were meant to ensure that one would not be established later (Article I, Sections 9, 10). *The Federalist* presented those prohibitions as among the most decisive proofs of "the republican complexion of this system" (No. 39; see also No. 84). We have seen that Wilson presented the absence of the "materials" for British or mixed government not simply as a matter of social facts existing before and beyond the reach of the political activity of founding but in part as a result of our laws, particularly the abolition of entails and primogeniture, the legal and economic bulwarks of aristocracy.

Similarly, although Pinckney attributed our distinctive "equality of condition" in part to "that vast extent of unpeopled territory which opens to the frugal and industrious a sure road to competency and independence," he also recognized that "the destruction of the right of primogeniture and the equal division of the property of intestates will also have effect to preserve this mediocrity; for laws invariably affect the manners of a people" (June 25). Pinckney thus included what we might consider the fundamental social fact of class structure within the moral category of manners shaped by the political acts of legislation.

The same view was expressed later by Alexis de Tocqueville in *Democracy in America.* He helped to found modern sociology by his hypothesis that social condition may be considered as the source of most of the laws, customs, and ideas that control the conduct of nations and that one must first study a people's social condition to understand their laws and mores. But that hypothesis was for him more a means of organizing his material than a limit on the ability of founders to organize their material. Tocqueville stated that hypothesis only immediately after stating that social condition is sometimes the result of laws; he quickly went on to emphasize that laws of inheritance have an incredible influence on the social condition so that lawgivers can rest for centuries once they have fixed such laws (volume 1, part 1, chapter 3). It might have been partly for this reason that he proclaimed that every fresh generation is new material for the lawgiver to mold (volume 1, part 1, chapter 5).

Even J. Franklin Jameson's attempt to support the doctrine that economic phenomena are the cause of political institutions and arrangements, and that "political democracy came to the United States as a result of economic democracy," shows in fact that political acts of legislation, especially the abolition of entail and primogeniture, helped to bring about "economic democracy" or the social structure that the founders believed appropriate to republican government.[2] A republican social structure, like the other aspects of republican society, is in part the prerequisite and in part the product of the political institutions of the Constitution.

It is harder to state positively what was the relation of social classes that the Constitution's republican institutions implied for the founders than to state the negative implication, the absence of hereditary royalty and nobility. The debate at the convention reveals competing visions. Pinckney, for instance, emphasized American equality (June 25). He contrasted the United States, which "contain[s] but one order that can be assimilated to the British Nation—this is the order of Commons," with Great Britain, which "contains three orders of people distinct in their situation, their possessions, and their principles."

This view of America as comprising only one social order of people might conjure up a vision of a classless society defined in economic terms, but Pinckney's analysis was neither fundamentally economic nor classless. The equality he emphasized ("a greater equality, than is to be found among the people of any other country") was in the first place legal and political and only secondarily economic. This equality arises from the legal and political facts that "every freeman has a right to the same protection and security; and a very moderate share of property entitles them to the possession of all the honors and privileges the public can bestow." Economic equality entered this argument indirectly: only as long as there were "few poor, and few dependent" would the legal and political facts of low property qualifications to vote or hold office have the effect that "every member of the society almost, will enjoy an equal power of arriving at the supreme offices and consequently directing the strength and sentiments of the whole Community."

Since the equality Pinckney emphasized is primarily political, it is compatible with some economic inequality and the existence of economic classes, just as it requires some economic equality (few, if any, poor and dependent) and the absence of distinct social orders or ranks (royalty and nobility). Just as republican equality permits only a few, if any, poor men for the political reason that the poor are dependent, so it permits only a few rich men defined in a political sense and for a political reason since "by rich men I mean those whose riches may have a dangerous influence." Pinckney admitted that there were such rich men in America ("less than a hundred") but the crucial point for the political question of the "representation and protection" of wealth was that the country's riches were not in their hands but in those of "the great body of the people." The point of republican equality is not an economic notion of just distribution, whether based on equal need or unequal effort, but a political notion of the social structure suitable to maintaining political equality and liberty.

Pinckney's denial of distinct social orders did not prevent him from concluding that "the people of the United States may be divided into three classes": professional, commercial, and landed. None of these classes are likely to give rise to a new order of nobility. Their "weight in the political scale" differs and, far from being a social given beyond the reach of politics, depends on whether "wise or injudicious commercial policy is pursued." Whereas the professionals must have "a considerable weight" as long as the government remains popular or republican, it depends on what policy is adopted whether the landed interest will remain "the governing spring in the system," as it ought, or the commercial class will have much weight, as it ought not. Pinckney's vision of American society as one social order therefore has a specifically agrarian slant. In common with views that emphasize American equality from other perspectives, however, his vision claims that despite the different political weights of the classes, their members are "individually equal in the political scale" and, owing to their mutual dependence, "have but one interest." The arguments that American classes are so united in interest that they constitute almost a classless or one-class society compared with traditional European social structures and that the political and legal equality and geographical and social mobility of American individuals matter more than any class divisions later became the creed of American capitalism although they were originally agrarian (and even anticapitalist).

"The Few and the Many"

Alexander Hamilton offered the convention a very different social picture from Pinckney's. Whereas Pinckney found equality "the leading feature" of the United States (June 25), Hamilton maintained "that nothing like an equality of property existed" (June 26). Whereas Pinckney hoped that America could avoid either a dangerously influential rich few or a dangerously dependent poor many (June 25), Hamilton declared that "in every community where industry is encouraged [presumably not only by the effectual provision of individual security but also by the sort of commercial policy Pinckney considered injudicious], there will be a division of it into the few and the many" (June 18). Unlike Pinckney, who hoped to preserve our distinctive equality, Hamilton explained "that an inequality would exist as long as liberty existed, and that it would unavoidably result from that very liberty itself. This inequality of property constituted the great and fundamental distinction in Society" (June 26). For Hamilton, inequality, not equality, characterized a free society. American social structure was not fundamentally different from that of other free societies, perhaps because fundamental inequality was the product of the same passions of "avarice, ambition, interest, which govern most individuals" (June 18).

Whereas Pinckney took heart from the "vast extent of unpeopled territory" as "the means of preserving that equality of condition which so eminently distinguishes us" (June 25), Hamilton repeatedly "confessed he was much discouraged by the amazing extent of Country" to be governed and almost came to "despair that a Republican Government could be established over so great an extent" (June 18). He feared that it would be difficult to establish a national government able to provide the "desired blessing." The government would have to enjoy "such a compleat sovereignty" as would win over the interest, ambition, avarice, habitual attachment, and legal and military force of the extended community.

For Hamilton, the inequality of property or fundamental class division of a free society made it possible to solve the problem of establishing a republican government for a vast territory as well as the problems posed by that social division itself. He explained in his famous daylong speech at the convention (June 18): "Give all power to the many, they will oppress the few. Give all power to the few, they will oppress the many. Both therefore ought to have power, that each may defend itself against the other."

Tenure for Life or Good Behavior. The division between the few and the many therefore not only posed the problem of oppression but offered the solution of a republican government that represented the few as well as the many. Hamilton's speech culminated in his proposing a Senate and executive serving for life or good behavior to defend the few. He held up the House of Lords as "a most noble institution" and the English hereditary monarchy as "the only good model" on the subject of the executive. But he insisted that his proposal was still for a republican government since "all the Magistrates are appointed, and vacancies are filled, by the people, or a process of election originating with the people." Both the need to make republican government strong enough to govern a vast country and the demand of liberty or justice that oppression be prevented dictated "that we ought to go as far in order to attain stability and permanency, as republican principles will admit." Republican government would be most likely to achieve success (the prospects for which remained dubious to Hamilton) if it expressed and arbitrated rather than repressed or neglected the fundamental social division between the few and the many.

The convention did not seriously consider Hamilton's plan as such. Its striking elements, a Senate and executive serving during good behavior, were separately proposed by others later in the convention—his plan was not so isolated or beyond the pale as is sometimes thought—but the records leave the weight of those later proposals questionable. On June 25 George Read moved that the Senate serve during good behavior. According to James Madison's notes the motion was seconded by Robert Morris, but according to Robert Yates's notes it was not seconded, which would explain why there were no recorded discussion, no vote, and no evidence of the motion in the official journal. More interesting was the proposal on July 17, during Hamilton's six-week absence, by Dr. James McClurg, seconded by Gouverneur Morris, to let the executive serve during good behavior. Mason opposed this proposal as a step away from republican principles, from which the next would be "an easy step to hereditary Monarchy." Madison and Gouverneur Morris nevertheless defended it as a way to preserve republicanism.

This remarkable proposal is best understood in the context of the preceding and succeeding events at the convention. It was made shortly after a decision to let the national legislature elect the executive and immediately after a decision to let the executive be eligible for reelection. The net effect of these decisions had been to make the executive dependent on the legislature, as McClurg pointed out in making his proposal. During the debate he explained that "it was an essential object with him to make the Executive independent of the Legislature; and the only mode left for effecting it, after the vote for destroying his ineligibility for a second time, was to appoint him during good behavior." Madison added a footnote that "the probable object of this motion was merely to enforce the argument against the re-eligibility of the Executive Magistrate, by holding out a tenure during good behaviour as the alternative for keeping him independent of the Legislature."[3]

The point of the proposal therefore seems to have been to preserve executive independence from the legislature, not any Hamiltonian intention to make the executive independent of the many and the ally of the few. Whereas McClurg's object seems to have been to overturn or compensate for the decision to let the executive be eligible for reelection, Gouverneur Morris had been more concerned about overturning or compensating for the decision to let the legislature elect the executive, which he had vigorously opposed. Although the motion failed, with four states in favor and six against, it seems to have made its point and led at once to unanimous agreement to reconsider the executive's ineligibility and to adjournment for the day. On July 19 Morris succeeded in broadening the reconsideration to the whole section about the executive, which led rapidly to a temporary decision to substitute electors for the legislature in the election of the executive. The result seems to confirm the indications of the arguments that this consideration of perhaps the most striking element of Hamilton's plan concerned executive independence from the legislature rather than the need to defend the few against the many in the fundamental social division.[4]

An Executive to Guard the People. Gouverneur Morris supported this Hamiltonian proposal for an executive for life not only out of an institutional concern with executive independence but also out of a social intention that, though in itself directly opposite to Hamilton's, reveals a social analysis that may be considered a variation on the Hamiltonian theme. His impressive speech that opened the reconsideration of the executive (July 19) advocated an executive independent from the legislature not as a bulwark of the few against the many but precisely the opposite, as "the guardian of the people, even of the lower classes, against Legislative tyranny, against the Great and the wealthy," as "the great protector of the Mass of the people." He warned: "Wealth tends to corrupt the mind and to nourish its love of power, and to stimulate it to oppression. History proves this to be the spirit of the opulent." Against the love of power of the wealthy, "who in the course of things will necessarily compose the Legislative body," he countered with the strong and independent executive's "love of fame," which he considered "the great spring to noble and illustrious actions."[5]

Other advocates of executive tenure during good behavior seemed to aim at overturning the immediately preceding decision to leave the executive reeligible. Morris, however, led by this view of the love of fame and the importance of keeping open a "road to Glory," supported the decision for executive reeligibility so as to preserve "the great motive to good behavior, the hope of being rewarded by a reappointment" (July 17). (Perhaps this mention of "good behavior" as the consequence of reeligibility suggested a tenure of good behavior to McClurg.) Thus ruling out nonreeligibility, he saw "no alternative for making the Executive independent of the Legislature but either to give him his office for life, or make him eligible by the people." When faced with an executive elected by the legislature, he had therefore advocated tenure during good behavior, but during the reconsideration he expressed his preference for an executive elected by the people (with a short term, reeligible, and not impeachable by the legislature) in accordance with the executive's function as guardian of the people. Morris seemed to have agreed with Hamilton that the few and the many were the fundamental social division but presented himself on this occasion as more concerned with guarding the many against the few.

Morris considered it necessary to prevent oppression by the wealthy few because "his creed was that there never was, nor ever will be a civilized Society without an aristocracy. His endeavor was to keep it as much as possible from doing mischief" (July 6). He was thus no American exceptionalist of the nobody-here-but-us-commoners school. He feared that the rich "will have the same effect here as elsewhere if we do not . . . keep them within their proper sphere" (July 2). And that result would be "a violent aristocracy or a more violent despotism." Even the vast territory that Pinckney found a preservative of exceptional American equality Morris found an opportunity for oligarchy: "The schemes of the Rich will be favored by the extent of the Country. The people in such distant parts can not communicate and act in concert. They will be the dupes of those who have more knowledge and intercourse." On the basis of his analysis of social classes and their tendencies to domination, he emphatically rejected the hopes of American exceptionalism: "Thus it has been the world over. So it will be among us. Reason tells us we are but men: and we are not to expect any particular interference of Heaven in our favor."

Gouverneur Morris's desire to prevent domination by the rich is paradoxically confirmed by his advocacy of a Senate of the rich (July 2). He wanted the Senate to serve for life (the other element in Hamilton's plan to defend the few) and without pay (so that none but the rich could compose it) and to be appointed by the executive (so as to avoid "a dependence on the democratic choice"). He argued that it should "have great personal property, it must have the aristocratic spirit," in part so that it would have "a personal interest in checking the other branch," in defending the few against a democratic House. Just as Morris argued that the strong and independent executive's love of fame must counter the wealthy's love of power, he argued that "abilities and virtue" were insufficient and "vices as they exist, must be turned against each other," that the Senate "must love to lord it thro' pride" so as to counter the pride of the many and their representatives. The general postulate of his social psychology seems to have been that "pride is indeed the great principle that actuates both the poor and the rich. It is this principle which in the former resists, in the latter abuses authority."

The crucial motivation was more political than economic, concerned with power and freedom not wealth as such. Morris did not think that any social class, rich or poor, was the pure expression of disinterested love of liberty, let alone, as Thomas Jefferson had claimed, God's "peculiar deposit for substantial and genuine virtue,"[6] or as Karl Marx was to claim, the class designated by history to do away with all class antagonism. But Morris argued for a Senate of the rich only in part to defend the few; he also contended that "the proper security" against the efforts of the rich "to establish their dominion and enslave the rest" is "to form them into a separate interest. . . . By thus combining and setting apart, the aristocratic interest, the popular interest will be combined against it. There will be a mutual check and mutual security." Otherwise, he warned, "let the rich mix with the poor and in a Commercial Country, they will establish an oligarchy." Putting the rich in a senate of their own where they could be watched and counteracted and excluded from a democratic house was not an eccentric idea peculiar to Morris. John Adams in the preface to his *Defense of the Constitutions of Government of the United States of America,* circulated in 1787 before the convention, had written:

> The rich, the well-born, and the able acquire an influence among the people that will soon be too much for simple honesty and plain sense in a house of representatives. The most illustrious of them must, therefore, be separated from the mass and placed by themselves in a senate; this is, to all useful and honest intents, an ostracism.[7]

A more positive aspect of Morris's expectation that a house of their own would render the rich safe for republicanism is indicated by Yates's notes, which have Morris saying in this same speech, "Give them the second branch, and you secure their weight for the *public good.* They become responsible for their conduct." Similarly, Madison records him as saying a few days later (July 6) that responsibility is "the great security for good behavior," in arguing against depriving the Senate of joint responsibility for originating money bills. This more positive side reached its acme at the conclusion of this speech, in which Morris hinted that "the only security against encroachments will be a select and sagacious body of men, instituted to watch against them on all sides," not simply a body of domineering rich to defend or isolate themselves. The possibility of disinterested wisdom seems an extra fillip on top of the more solid considerations of class interest, human pride, and institutional responsibility.

Morris's fear that without an aristocratic Senate the rich would dominate the House of Representatives was consistent with his warning later, when he failed to achieve the sort of Senate he advocated, that "the Constitution as it is now before us . . . threatens this Country with an Aristocracy. The aristocracy will grow out of the House of

Representatives." Those more simply democratic perspectives, eighteenth-century or later, that would find Morris's means of restraining the rich (a president and Senate for life) themselves suspiciously oligarchic, would also find his diagnosis of this aristocratic danger and his prescription for it undemocratic. His diagnosis or prognosis pertains more to our century than to the eighteenth: "We should not confine our attention to the present moment. The time is not distant when this Country will abound with mechanics and manufacturers who will receive their bread from their employers." Morris doubted that such men would be "the secure and faithful guardians of liberty" or "the impregnable barriers against aristocracy" and warned, "Give the votes to people who have no property, and they will sell them to the rich who will be able to buy them."

Morris's solution was to limit the suffrage to freeholders. Whereas he supposed that enfranchising the propertyless would permit the rich to exploit them and achieve political domination, we tend to suppose rather that his solution of excluding them would have that effect. This difference is explained only partially by the rise of the secret ballot. We may regard his proposed restriction as somewhat less undemocratic when we consider, as Morris pointed out and later scholarship has laboriously confirmed, that this same restriction that excluded the vast majority of people in Britain, whence it came, would enfranchise 90 percent of free adult males in America at that time. But Morris's point was precisely to deal with a later time when the propertyless would abound. And Martin Diamond pointed out that "the legal exclusion from the franchise of even a very small portion of the adult population may have enormous significance for the politics and life of a country."[8] We should not therefore minimize the significance of this proposed restriction, but we should recognize that its intention was not oligarchic but republican, motivated by fear less of the propertyless themselves than of the rich who would exploit them.

Theory of Social Diversity

Madison offered the convention a third vision of the social structure appropriate to American republican institutions, distinct both from Pinckney's picture of unprecedented social homogeneity and from Hamilton and Morris's ancient division between rich and poor. Madison admitted that "it was true as had been observed (by Mr. Pinckney) we had not among us those hereditary distinctions of rank which were a great source of the contests in the ancient Governments as well as the modern States of Europe, nor those extremes of wealth or poverty which characterize the latter" (June 26). But he nevertheless immediately noted (June 26) that "we cannot however be regarded even at this time, as one homogeneous mass, in which every thing that affects a part will affect in the same manner the whole."

Earlier in the convention (June 6) Madison presented his theory of social diversity as the democratic remedy for the defects of democracy, developed during the preceding months in his observations on the "Vices of the Political System of the United States," further refined in a letter to Jefferson after the convention (October 24, 1787), and made famous in *Federalist* No. 10. In this speech, in defense of popular election of the House rather than election by the state legislatures, Madison rejected the view of Roger Sherman that restricted the objects of the Union to defense against foreign danger and against internal disputes, foreign treaties, and foreign commerce. Madison insisted instead on the necessity of "providing more effectually for the security of private rights, and the steady dispensation of Justice." Interferences with these, he warned, threatened the very survival of republican liberty. The federal government, representing a larger and more diverse society, could provide more effectually for the security of private rights and the steady dispensation of justice than the smaller, more homogeneous states, and thus could minimize the danger that liberty would be surrendered in the pursuit of justice. While the size of the American republic dismayed Hamilton, appeared to Morris to favor the schemes of the rich, and seemed to Pinckney to offer the frugal and industrious a route to economic independence and to preserve homogeneity and equality of condition, size promised Madison a social diversity conducive to a successful republic.

Social diversity was the basis of threats to private rights and justice in republics, but, Madison argued, more extensive social diversity could also be the basis of their republican salvation. Madison started from the observation that "all civilized Societies would be divided into different Sects, Factions, and interests, as they happened to consist of rich and poor, debtors and creditors, the landed, the manufacturing, the commercial interests, the inhabitants of this district or that district, the followers of this political leader or that political leader, the disciples of this religious Sect or that religious Sect." If a majority in a republic is united by a Common interest or passion adverse to the rights of other citizens or to the permanent and aggregate interests of the community, the form of government allows the majority to violate private rights, commit injustice, and disregard the common good; one cannot expect prudent regard for the common good, concern for reputation, or conscience to prevent them from doing so. The only remedy, Madison concluded, was "to enlarge the sphere, and thereby divide the community into so great a number of interests and parties, that in the first place a majority will not be likely at the same moment to have a common interest separate from that of the whole or of the minority." Through extent and diversity Madison hoped not to prevent majority rule or to establish logrolling pluralism but to form majority coalitions on the principles of justice and the general good, to make a society more duly capable of self-government (*Federalist* No. 51).

In a republic simply divided between rich and poor, the poor majority would use government to rob the rich unless civil war broke out or the republic was overturned in the hope that monarchy or despotism would better safeguard property and ensure stability. Madison worried that a future America would see such a poor majority:

> An increase of population will of necessity increase the proportion of those who will labour under all the hardships of life, and secretly sigh for a more equal distribution of its blessings. These may in time outnumber those who are placed above the feelings of indigence. According to the equal laws of suffrage, the power will slide into the hands of the former. (June 26)

Madison voiced that fear in arguing for a nine-year term for the Senate since one of the means to guard against leveling attempts in such circumstances was "the establishment of a body in the Government sufficiently respectable for its wisdom and virtue, to aid on such emergencies the preponderance of justice by throwing its weight into that scale." That solution, however, seemed admittedly designed to meet transient emergencies rather than to counter a lasting shift in social structure.

Property Qualifications for Suffrage and Election

A more direct response to the danger of a poor majority was limitation of the equal laws of suffrage. Later in the convention (August 7) in response to Morris's motion to limit the suffrage for electing the House to freeholders, Madison expressed a political reservation: "Whether the Constitutional qualification ought to be a freehold, would with him depend much on the probable reception such a change would meet with in States where the right was now exercised by every description of people." Nevertheless, "viewing the subject in its merits alone," he judged that "the freeholders of the Country would be the safest depositories of Republican liberty." As with the Senate's term, Madison was concerned with future social change: "In future times a great majority of the people will not only be without landed, but any other sort of, property."

The political danger he discerned in such social change was double-edged, encompassing both Hamilton's and Morris's concerns: that the propertyless majority

> will combine under the influence of their common situation; in which case, the rights of property and the public liberty, will not be secure in their hands: or which is more probable, they will become the tools of opulence and ambition, in which case there will be equal danger on another side.

The propertyless thus would pose a political danger not only from their lack of respect for the rights of property and public liberty, but from their dependence on the propertied and their susceptibility to the ambitious.

Madison's views on this occasion were shared by Morris, who invoked the danger of aristocracy. Morris rejected the applicability of the argument of no taxation without representation on the grounds that "the man who does not give his vote freely is not represented. It is the man who dictates the vote" who is in fact represented. Dickinson too, we recall, feared "the dangerous influence of those multitudes without property and without principle with which our Country like all others, will in time abound." And Mercer argued that without a freehold qualification, townspeople could unite their votes in favor of one candidate and thus prevail over countrypeople, who, being dispersed, would scatter their votes among several candidates.

The convention nevertheless overwhelmingly rejected the proposal to restrict the suffrage for the House to freeholders (Madison merely recorded Virginia as opposed without indicating whether he or any other of its delegates voted for it). Opponents invoked not only the likelihood of popular opposition (Wilson, Oliver Ellsworth, Mason, Pierce Butler, and John Rutledge) but the practical difficulty of forming any uniform rule for defining a freehold (Wilson, Ellsworth); the impropriety of excluding any taxpayers, wealthy merchants and manufacturers as well as landholders (Ellsworth), or even any man "having evidence of attachment to and permanent common interest with the Society," parents as well as merchants and married men (Mason); the tendency of franchise restrictions toward establishing aristocracy (Butler, though admitted also by Madison); and the importance of keeping up the virtue and public spirit of the common people (Benjamin Franklin).

Shortly before and after this suffrage debate similar issues arose in the debates about a property qualification for members of the national legislature. Mason (who would oppose a landed property qualification for the electors) and Pinckney proposed a landed property qualification for those elected (July 26). Morris, Dickinson, and Madison preferred qualifications in the electors rather than the elected. Madison nonetheless successfully moved (and Morris seconded) to strike only the term "landed" so as to leave a broader property qualification. Madison argued that "landed possessions were no certain evidence of real wealth," but he did not argue simply for the representation of wealth. The argument he made for a broader property qualification, indeed, seemed to cut in principle against any property qualification: "It was politic as well as just that the interests and rights of every class should be duly represented and understood in the public Councils."

Despite Madison's inclination toward a freehold qualification for electors, his social vision was not agrarian. He pointed out that many landowners owed more than they were worth and sought election to the legislatures to pass unjust laws against their often landless creditors, who deserved protection and representation. While Madison invoked justice, Rufus King warned that the public safety in particular emergencies might require the aid of the monied interest, who therefore could not be safely excluded. Madison argued that the commercial and manufacturing classes also needed representation so that their interests should not be left entirely to the care of the landed class—the most important immediate implication of his more general argument for extent and diversity. Dickinson, as we have seen, argued apparently more radically against any property qualification for legislators in the austere accents of a more traditional republicanism:

> He doubted the policy of interweaving into a Republican constitution a veneration for wealth. He had always understood that a veneration for poverty and virtue were the objects of republican encouragement. It seemed improper that any man of merit should be subjected to disabilities in a Republic where merit was understood to form the great title to public trust, honors and rewards.

Yet typically of that republicanism, Dickinson, while arguing against property qualifications for legislators, presumed that the suffrage would be limited to freeholders. Traditional republican veneration for poverty over wealth was also veneration for property, that of the freeholders, and fear of the propertyless.

These issues were finally settled after the Committee of Detail reported to the convention without drafting a clause for property qualifications, as the convention had instructed. The committee left to the legislature the authority to establish such property qualifications for the members of each house as to them shall seem expedient (August 6). Pinckney complained that the national legislature might set them either too high or too low, either establishing an undue aristocratic influence or failing to assure members of sufficient property to be independent and respectable (August 10). He proposed setting specific qualifications in dollar amounts, but Ellsworth pointed out the difficulty of setting amounts appropriate for both North and South or for both present and future; Pinckney had to leave blank the amounts in his own motion. Franklin again expressed his dislike of everything that tended to debase the spirit of the common people, pointed out that wealth did not ensure virtue, and warned that a constitution partial to the rich would disappoint the "most liberal and enlightened" men in Europe and discourage the common people there from immigrating. Pinckney's motion was overwhelmingly defeated. Madison nonetheless expressed his opposition to leaving this power to the legislature since "the qualifications of electors and elected were fundamental articles in a Republican Government and ought to be fixed by the Constitution." Wilson pointed out that the legislature would probably never fix a uniform property qualification (presumably for some of the same reasons the convention could not do so in the Constitution). The whole section was finally dropped.

A Propertyless Majority

Fear of future social change toward a majority without property or respect for property made property qualifications tempting. But all efforts at embedding them in the Constitution came to nothing partly from deference to the spirit of the common people, partly from the complexity already introduced by sectional and social diversity, and partly from deference to future social change. Madison was thus able to argue more or less in good faith in *Federalist* No. 57 that the electors of the federal representatives were to be "not the rich, more than the poor; not the learned, more than the ignorant; not the haughty heirs of distinguished names, more than the humble sons of obscure and unpropitious fortune," but "the great body of the people." Similarly he could proclaim there that the objects of popular choice would be "every citizen whose merit may recommend him to the esteem and confidence of his country" with "no qualification of wealth, of birth, of religious faith, or of civil profession."

The problem of property qualifications and the danger of a future propertyless majority nevertheless continued to trouble Madison. To his speech (August 7) that favored on its merits the restriction to freeholders of the suffrage for the House, he added a note sometime after the convention. In this later note he argued that since both persons and property are essential objects of government, its structure should provide both with reasonable security.[9] The "most obvious provision of this double character" would be to confine the suffrage for one house to propertyholders. This solution, however, still did not seem necessary or proper for the United States since the country had not yet "reached the stage of Society in which conflicting feelings of the Class with, and the Class without property, have the operation natural to them in Countries fully peopled." Madison concluded his note with his favorite solution of enlarging the sphere as "the best expedient yet tried for solving the problem," a better expedient than suffrage restrictions and one that would not be limited to the present social structure.

In a fuller note written around 1821, Madison further explored the problem of property and suffrage.[10] Here Madison explained that the United States had "a precious advantage" not merely in "the actual distribution of property, particularly the landed property" but also in "the universal hope of acquiring property," which "can generally inspire a sympathy with the rights of property." Equal distribution of property was less crucial than perceived social mobility. The future danger was accordingly amended to that of the majority being not only without property but also "without the means or hope of acquiring it." Although still interested in the possibility of confining the right of electing one branch of the legislature to propertyholders, Madison suggested that

> should Experience or public opinion require an equal and universal suffrage for each branch of the Government such as prevails generally in the United States, a resource favorable to the rights of landed and other property, when its possessors become the Minority, may be found in an enlargement of the Election Districts for one branch of the Legislature, and an extension of its period of service.

Large districts would be favorable to the election of persons of probable attachment to the rights of property, and longer terms would render the branch "more capable of stemming popular currents taking a wrong direction, till reason and justice could regain their ascendancy." Finally, even if large districts and long terms should prove unacceptable, Madison reflected that

> the security for the holders of property when the minority, can only be derived from the ordinary influence possessed

by property, and the superior information incident to its holders; from the popular sense of justice enlightened and enlarged by a diffusive education; and from the difficulty of combining and effectuating unjust purposes throughout an extensive country.

While Madison remained convinced of the importance of widespread property ownership for a healthy republic and correspondingly was preoccupied with the political dangers of a future propertyless majority, he did not despair or succumb to a social determinism. He continued to put his hope in extent and diversity, political institutions, and education.

Madison's emphasis on the salutary political effects of extent and diversity transformed the social question from the simple proportion between propertyholders and propertyless to the complicated relations among the different kinds of property. It was not enough for property ownership to be widespread so as to prevent the propertyless from either oppressing the propertyholders or becoming their dependent instruments. Property also had to be diverse enough to prevent one kind of propertyholder from oppressing others or driving others to abandon republicanism.

The logic of Madison's convention speech on extent and diversity (June 6) and *Federalist* No. 10 seems to imply that the crucial diversity was that none of the major social classes defined by kinds of property (landed, commercial, manufacturing, and monied) should constitute a majority. The problem posed by this interpretation, however, is that landed property then constituted a clear majority in the United States. Madison observed in his speech moving to broaden the qualification for legislators from landed to property generally (July 26) that "the three principal classes into which our citizens were divisible, were the landed, the commercial, and the manufacturing. The second and third class, bear as yet a small proportion to the first." He concluded somewhat lamely that

> these classes understand much less of each other's interests and affairs, than men of the same class inhabiting different districts. It is particularly requisite therefore that the interests of one or two of them should not be left entirely to the care, or the impartiality of the third.

He thus required merely that no class be entirely excluded from the legislature, and apparently left the landed majority in a position to oppress the others. Madison noted in his major speech on extent (June 6) that

> the landed interest has borne hard on the mercantile interest. The Holders of one species of property have thrown a

> disproportion of taxes on the holders of another species. The lesson we are to draw from the whole is that where a majority are united by a common sentiment, and have an opportunity, the rights of the minor party become insecure.

If Madison's theory of extent and diversity required a balance among the great classes of property, then the United States seemed condemned to majority faction. Conversely, it seemed as if the United States could achieve the requisite diversity only through the development of commerce and manufacturing. Madison remarked in *Federalist* No. 56:

> At present some of the States are little more than a society of husbandmen. Few of them have made much progress in those branches of industry which give a variety and complexity to the affairs of a nation. These, however, will in all of them be the fruits of a more advanced population.

It is therefore easy to see Madison's argument for extent and diversity as decisively dependent on future commercialization and industrialization.

There is, however, no definite indication that Madison regarded the predominance of agriculture as an insuperable obstacle to healthy politics or its reduction to minority status in a commercial-industrial economy as the desideratum for the success of popular government. On the contrary, he feared that the replacement of the dominant status of agriculture by commerce and industry would produce precisely that propertyless majority that threatened all forms of private property and public liberty. Madison recognized at the convention that the proportion of the commercial and manufacturing to the landed classes would "daily increase" until the United States resembled the populous countries of Europe in this respect (July 26). In a note prepared during the Virginia constitutional convention of 1829, he explained that by "a law of nature, now well understood," the application of labor-saving improvements to agriculture would reduce the proportion of the population devoted to it.[11] Like Marx, Madison further believed it to be "the lot of humanity" that a large proportion of the growing rest of the population would be "necessarily reduced by a competition for employment to wages which afford them the bare necessaries of life. That proportion being without property, or the hope of acquiring it, can not be expected to sympathize sufficiently with its rights, to be safe depositories of power over them." Specifically, Madison calculated that the United States might attain such a dangerously crowded state of population of 192 million in a century, in 1929. He soberly cautioned that "to the effect of these changes, intellectual, moral, and social, the institutions and laws of the Country must be adapted, and it will require for the task all the wisdom of the wisest patriots."

Madison feared not only lack of respect for the rights of property on the part of impoverished wage earners but, as he explained in his late note on his convention suffrage speech, the dependence of indigent laborers on wealthy capitalists in manufactures and commerce.[12] The ultimate dilemma of Madison's social theory seems to be that the very process of commercialization and industrialization that promises to replace an overbearing landholding majority with greater social balance threatens instead to produce a more dangerous propertyless and dependent majority. Madison did not despair at the prospect of the concentration of wealth in the hands of great capitalists and the impoverishment of their dependent laborers. America's equalizing republican laws of inheritance could reduce the opportunities for and defeat the permanence of the concentration of capital, and even diminish the availability of capital for large labor-saving industrial establishments. The practical conclusion of his remarkable social analysis circulated at the Virginia constitutional convention in 1829:

> This view of the subject makes it proper to embrace in the partnership of power, every description of citizens having a sufficient stake in the public order, and the stable administration of the laws; and particularly the House keepers and Heads of families; most of whom "having given hostages to fortune," will have given them to their Country also.[13]

For Madison, the capacity of a society for self-government entailed the adaptation of its institutions and laws to social changes precisely to render social changes compatible with its continued capacity for self-government.

Subdivision of Interests

Not only did Madison try to transform the intractable conflicts between rich and poor to the more manageable rivalry between landed, commercial, manufacturing, and monied interests, but also he suggested a further diversification of those classes or great interests into smaller subdivisions.[14] His convention speech on extent and diversity (June 6) left the economic division at "rich and poor, debtors and creditors, the landed, the manufacturing, the commercial interests"; but *Federalist* No. 10 added "a moneyed interest, with many lesser interests." His presentation of the argument for extent and diversity to Jefferson (October 24, 1787) is the fullest on this point: "There will be rich and poor; creditors and debtors; a landed interest, a monied interest, a mercantile interest, a manufacturing interest. These classes may again be subdivided according to the different productions of different situations and soils, and according to different branches of commerce, and of manufactures."[15]

Similarly, at the convention Madison argued that the large states had no common interest distinguishing them from the others since the staple production of Massachusetts was fish, that of Pennsylvania flour, and that of Virginia tobacco (June 28). In a draft of a letter in 1833 he observed:

> As a source of discordant interests within particular States, reference may be made to the diversity in the applications of agricultural labour, more or less visible in all of them. Take for example Virginia herself. Her products for market are in one district Indian corn and cotton; in another, chiefly tobacco; in another, tobacco and wheat; in another, chiefly wheat, rye and live stock. This diversity of agricultural interests, though greater in Virginia than elsewhere, prevails in different degrees within most of the States.[16]

Although Madison did not explicitly make the argument, this subdivision of the great interests might prevent any one of them, in particular the majority landed interest, from oppressing the others. At the convention Pinckney argued that the five distinct commercial interests (the fisheries and West Indies trade of New England; the New York interest in free trade; wheat and flour of the Middle States; tobacco of Maryland, Virginia, and North Carolina; and rice and indigo of South Carolina and Georgia) would be a source of oppressive regulations if a bare majority could regulate commerce; Sherman replied that "the diversity was of itself a security" (August 29). Hamilton asked in *Federalist* No. 36:

> What greater affinity or relation of interest can be conceived between the carpenter and blacksmith, and the linen manufacturer or stocking-weaver, than between the merchant and either of them? It is notorious that there are often as great rivalships between different branches of the mechanic or manufacturing arts as there are between any of the departments of labor and industry.

Hamilton admitted, however, in *Federalist* No. 35 that the landed interest is in a political view, particularly in relation to taxes, "perfectly united from the wealthiest landlord to the poorest tenant." Madison in *Federalist* No. 10 also treats the landed interest as a unit when he writes: "Shall domestic manufacturers be encouraged, and in what degree, by restrictions on foreign manufacturers? are questions which would be differently decided by the landed and the manufacturing classes, and probably by neither with a sole regard to justice and the public good." The subdivision of the great interests increases the power of the argument from extent and social diversity, but we might be guilty of dangerous complacency if we relied on it confidently when Madison stopped short of doing so.

The founders emphasized the protection of property as an object of government because its secure possession made men independent and capable of republican citizenship and encouraged them to improve their own condition and that of the community—and because it was a right deserved by free and rational creatures. But paradoxically from the perspective of some later theories, this emphasis on protecting property also led them to desire its continued widespread dispersion through a society of relatively equal social condition.

Even Hamilton could argue at the New York ratifying convention that a relatively equal division of property was the basis of republican politics: "While property continues to be pretty equally divided, and a considerable share of information pervades the community; the tendency of the people's suffrages will be to elevate merit even from obscurity." Accordingly, he worried that "as riches increase and accumulate in few hands; as luxury prevails in society; virtue will be in a greater degree considered as only a graceful appendage of wealth, and the tendency of things will be to depart from the republican standard." He offered no preventative; on the contrary he lamented: "This is the real disposition of human nature: it is what, neither the honorable member nor myself can correct. It is a common misfortune, that awaits our state constitution, as well as all others."[17] A desire for relatively equal distribution of property based on respect for property could not be effectuated by direct government action in violation of the rights of property.

Conclusion

Given the diversity of views among the founders, it would be unpersuasive and disingenuous to claim that the founding endorses a single model of the social structure appropriate to America's republican political institutions, let alone one directly applicable to American society two hundred years later. It is therefore misleading to characterize the effect of later social theories, themselves diverse in content, as the replacement of one such model by another. It is somewhat misleading to try to isolate the social theory of the founders as if their views of social structure could be understood otherwise than as a segment of their emphatically political theories. The contrast with later thought tends to be between different views of the relation between politics and society, different emphases on politics or society.

It is misleading, for example, to isolate Madison's argument about extent and social diversity without noting that he includes not only socioeconomic divisions but divisions based on political as well as religious opinions and leaders. Avarice is rivaled by ambition. He always pairs his argument about diversity with his complementary remedy of representation. Madison's version of republican politics is not a mere reflection of contending social forces but an arena in which responsible representatives may have the wisdom to discern the true interest of their country and the patriotism and love of justice to pursue it. Despite his deep awareness of the power of faction, Madison remained far from those Anti-Federalists and later theorists and historians who would reduce every claim of wisdom or justice to economic interest or social pretension.

What the social aspect of the political theories of the founders may have to offer us is an emphasis on the political consequences of social questions. We might well follow them in asking whether social structures are conducive to republican liberty, personal independence, and a stake in the common good and in judging less according to abstract standards of just distribution than according to an explicitly republican distribution. The founders recognized that social structures would change, but they hoped their successors would remain determined to rest their political experiments on the capacity of societies for self-government.

6
The Scottish Enlightenment and the Liberal Political Tradition

Frank D. Balog

The bicentennial of the U.S. Constitution has provoked a renewed interest in the intellectual and historical foundations of the American regime. Among the candidates for important influences upon the founders of the republic are the philosophers and thinkers of eighteenth-century Scotland, a period that has come to be known as the Scottish Enlightenment. These thinkers have been heralded by many contemporary scholars as the true source of much of the distinctive character of American political thought.[1] But what precisely is meant by the Scottish Enlightenment? This chapter will attempt to clarify some of the conceptions and misconceptions that have developed around the use of this term and will seek to locate the particular characteristics of the major Scottish thinkers in light of the broader development of classical liberal political theory.

The Scottish Enlightenment was, indeed, a rich and fertile period for philosophy, economics, political thought, and history. Among the most influential Scottish thinkers were Francis Hutcheson, David Hume, Adam Smith, Thomas Reid, Adam Ferguson, and Dugald Stewart. To what extent, however, did this diverse group of philosophers constitute a unified movement or school? Many suggestions have been put forward that attempt to isolate the specific ideas that these thinkers shared. Empiricism, deductive rationalism, common sense, "true individualism," communitarianism, and civic republicanism are only some of the characterizations that have been offered to define the Scottish Enlightenment.[2] The fact that many of these characterizations are mutually contradictory should not be completely surprising given the variety of thinkers that this period encompasses.

As one examines the thought of these men on their own terms, rather than as representatives of an historical epoch, the conception of a unified school of thought becomes problematic. On a number of vital questions regarding metaphysics, morals, and politics there was considerable disagreement and in some cases bitter opposition among the members of the Scottish Enlightenment. Thomas Reid, for example, actively opposed the religious skepticism of David Hume, and Adam Smith totally rejected the economic protectionism of Sir James Steuart.[3] Thus, in the opinion of one commentator: "When one speaks of the influence of the Scottish Enlightenment, one is speaking of a rich and various body of thought, united by tone and origin rather than by doctrine."[4] There is general agreement, however, that the thinkers of the Scottish Enlightenment were united by a commitment to approach the study of man and society in the scientific spirit of Bacon and Newton.[5] While they often disagreed upon the correct answers to philosophical and political questions, they shared a common outlook and a common commitment to reason and science.

Although the Scottish Enlightenment lacks a unity of doctrine, much of the recent scholarship emphasizing its importance seems to be unified by a common objective, namely, to rescue the Scottish thinkers from the liberalism of John Locke. Garry Wills, for example, sees the Scottish Enlightenment as a "communitarian" and "egalitarian" alternative to the individualism of Locke and thus a more solid theoretical foundation for understanding the American regime.[6]

Another group of thinkers, influenced by the writings of J. G. A. Pocock, have similarly argued that the Scottish Enlightenment is best understood as an extension, and perhaps a modification, of a tradition of political thought and discourse known as "civic humanism."[7] This tradition emphasizes civic virtue, political participation, material equality among citizens, and selfless service to the public in opposition to the liberal tradition that stresses private rights, private liberty, and commercial activity. While Locke is identified as the best exponent of the civic humanist tradition, it is said to derive from Aristotle, Machiavelli, and the seventeenth-century British commonwealthmen Harrington, Sydney, and Neville.

Interestingly enough, recent work among these scholars has led some of them to dispute the supposed civic humanist context of eighteenth-century Scottish thought and to introduce a new conceptual "paradigm," the school of natural jurisprudence, as the major influence of the Scottish Enlightenment. This tradition includes such continental thinkers as Grotius, Pufendorf, and Vattel, as well as Hobbes and Locke in England. Thus, while Locke the liberal individualist is dismissed, Locke as a member of the natural jurisprudential tradition is reintroduced as an influence, if not necessarily the decisive one.[8]

Earlier scholars, however, had a much different opinion of the significance of John Locke for the Scottish philosphers. To quote James McCosh, whose *The Scottish Philosophy* in 1857 was the first English work to present the thought of Scotland as a unified school: "The Scottish metaphysicians largely imbibed the spirit of Locke, all of them speak of him with profound respect; and they never differ from him without expressing a regret or offering an apology."[9] If a source even closer to the times be desired, one can hardly do better than Dugald Stewart, the last great figure of the Scottish Enlightenment, disciple of both Adam Smith and Thomas Reid. In his *Dissertation: Exhibiting the Progress of Metaphysical, Ethical, and Political Philosophy, Since the Revival of Letters in Europe* of 1815, he wrote: "In Scotland, where the liberal constitution of the universities has been always peculiarly favourable to the diffusion of a free and eclectic spirit of inquiry, the philosophy of Locke seems very early to have struck its roots, deeply and permanently, into a kindly and genial soil."[10] And in a later passage, he notes: "How many are the threads which, even in Catholic countries, have been broken by the writings of Locke! How many still remain to be broken, before the mind of man can recover that moral liberty which . . . it seems destined to enjoy!"[11]

As indicated in the remainder of this chapter, the pivotal position of Locke is decisive for an accurate understanding of the issues and controversies of the Scottish Enlightenment. Whether in metaphysics or in moral and political philosophy, Lockean categories and concepts were fundamental. Despite the divergences that existed among the various Scottish thinkers, their thought is best understood as an extension and modification of Lockean liberalism, rather than as an alternative, either a pre-Lockean civic humanism or a post-Lockean benevolent communitarianism.

Moral Sense and Moral Sentiment

If one could identify one substantive conception or distinctively original idea that distinguishes the Scottish Enlightenment, it would probably be the notion of a "moral sense." All the major thinkers of the Scottish Enlightenment—Hutcheson, Hume, Smith, Kames, Reid, and Ferguson—speak of moral sense or sentiment.[12] Their treatments of this idea, however, diverge in many important respects. To identify the Scottish Enlightenment with the advocacy of a moral sense is thus problematic because of the variety of theories grouped together under this term. There was in actuality no single conception of what the moral sense was, how it operated, and what objects it recommended to the individual for his approval. Thus, while one can identify a common language among the Scottish thinkers on questions of moral philosophy, no common *doctrine* regarding the moral sense was shared by all or even by most of them.

There was, however, a set of issues that each of these thinkers felt compelled to address. The most important of these issues were the following: (1) Was human nature capable of disinterested and unselfish feeling and actions? (2) Was the faculty that recommended objects as morally praiseworthy or blameworthy a function of reason or passion? and (3) Was that faculty itself capable of being explained and analyzed into more basic psychological principles or passions, or was it an independent and irreducible faculty of the mind? While all the Scottish moral philosophers answered the first question in the affirmative and on the whole considered the moral faculty akin to the passions rather than to reason (Thomas Reid and Adam Ferguson excepted), they seriously disagreed on both the scope of those benevolent feelings and on the origin of the moral faculty itself. Thus, serious differences regarding the ultimate status of morality and its political significance permeated the Scottish Enlightenment. Moreover, the concept of the moral sense was transmitted in the protean form to the American continent and thus affected the thought of the founders in various ways.[13]

The origin of the term *moral sense* to refer to a faculty of the mind that perceives the difference between virtue and vice and that prompts the individual to pursue the former and avoid the latter is owed to the Third Earl of Shaftesbury, tutored by John Locke himself. Shaftesbury coined this term in his "Inquiry Concerning Virtue or Merit" as part of a general refutation of the Hobbesian teaching that morality was derived by a rational calculation of self-interest.[14] The term was adopted by Francis Hutcheson, professor of moral philosophy at the University of Glasgow.

In his writings, Hutcheson transformed Shaftesbury's general and somewhat diffuse comments into a rigorous doctrine of the moral sense. Hutcheson writes of "an original determination in our nature" by which we approve of certain actions as good or virtuous and condemn others as bad or vicious, just as the sense of taste approves of certain foods and disapproves of others.[15] It is by these original determinations of human nature that mankind is essentially guided. The ultimate ground of virtue, then, is an immediate, internal sensation that cannot be explained any further than to identify its existence as an empirical fact. Although reason may later indicate the utility of virtue, either for the individual or for mankind in general, one does not initially approve of it from a rational understanding of its consequences. While reason may later add force to the desire to perform acts of virtue, the pleasing character of virtue is immediately sensed by the mind as something desirable in and of itself. Hutcheson thus argues that approval of virtuous actions is initially rooted in the sentiment of benevolence, rather than in a rational perception of the good, as the Cambridge Platonists believed, or in calculations of self-interest, as Bernard Mandeville, the radical disciple of Thomas Hobbes, argued. For Hutcheson, moral approval is a disinterested passion that recognizes the beauty of benevolence and thus recommends it to all observers as intrinsically desirable.

The moral sense is also the mental faculty that ought to regulate and control all the other passions, particularly self-love. Self-love is the immediate inclination of the individual to pursue the "natural" goods of health, strength, wealth, and bodily pleasure. Such goods are desirable either for their own sake or as means to other ends. The moral sense, in contrast, is the capacity of the mind to perceive the desirability of benevolent and *disinterested* actions as good and thus to limit and to define the conditions for the pursuit of the natural goods. Hutcheson argues that although we may often pursue the natural good at the expense of the moral good, we know, by virtue of the strong feelings that the moral sense implants in us, that it is better and more noble to limit the pursuit of the natural good for the sake of accomplishing benevolent deeds. All morality, therefore, is interpreted by Hutcheson to be a form of benevolence, or disinterested concern for others. The individual virtues are all forms of or means to benevolent affections and actions. Self-love and the actions it prompts the individual to perform are not part of the essence of morality.

Hutcheson's emphasis upon a morality of benevolence, however, does not lead him to argue in favor of complete self-abnegation or for a total overcoming of self-love. Although he opposes the moral sense to self-love, he also asserts that when properly understood they are in harmony with one another. Thus he writes that "every mortal's acting within these bounds for his own good, is absolutely necessary for the good of the whole, and the want of such self-love would be universally pernicious . . . And thus a neglect of our own good may be morally evil and argue a want of benevolence toward the whole."[16] In other words, Hutcheson argues that our benevolent sentiments indicate the good to the whole that the proper pursuit of self-interest achieves. The moral sense thus approves of self-love as necessary and good.

This ambiguous treatment of the relationship between benevolence and self-love can be seen even more clearly in another passage. He writes: "Were there any good proposed to the pursuit of an agent, and he had a competitor in every respect only equal to himself, the highest benevolence possible would not lead a wise man to prefer another to himself, were there no ties of gratitude, or some external circumstance to move him to yield to his competitor."[17] There seems, then, to be a limit to the proper scope of benevolence. In computing the morality of one's actions, one should consult one's own good as well as the good to others. To do evil to oneself, such as to endanger one's life or safety or perhaps one's property or livelihood, in the name of doing good to others is contrary to both interest and morality, when the good sacrificed is greater than the good accomplished. A rich man is morally obliged to engage in greater acts of charity than a poor man, but neither is obliged to impoverish himself or risk becoming a burden to others in the name of benevolence. Similarly, sacrificing one's life for others makes sense in only very limited circumstances because it eliminates the possibility of accomplishing any future good. Hutcheson thus attempts to demonstrate that self-love and the moral sense are not in any fundamental conflict. While self-love is not per se moral, it does not necessarily conflict with morality.

It seems clear, then, that Hutcheson is not seeking to return to classical principles of morality. Although he states that the primary "laws of nature" are "loving God" and "promoting the universal happiness,"[18] a formulation that appears similar to the teaching of the New Testament, Hutcheson also asserts that the primary *right* of nature is the right of self-preservation.[19] The moral sense, whatever else it may do, does not invalidate this primary right. Rather, it recommends or permits the pursuit of self-interest in a manner that is consistent with the right of all others to do the same. Rights rather than duties are, in fact, the primary moral phenomena in Hutcheson's philosophy. The political teaching constructed upon this foundation also emphasizes the primacy of rights, particularly the right to property and to its full use and enjoyment. Hutcheson's moral philosophy is thus not a rejection of the individualism of Locke, but an attempt to soften some of its more radical implications.

The true import of Hutcheson's teaching is perhaps most clearly revealed in the following passage:

> Thus not only the Prince, the Statesman, the General, are capable of true heroism; but when we find in an honest Trader, the kind friend, the faithful and prudent advisor, the charitable and hospitable neighbor, the tender husband, and affectionate parent, . . . the promoter of love and good understanding among acquaintances, we must judge this character really as amiable, as those whose external splendor dazzles an injudicious world into an opinion 'that they are the only Heroes in Virtue.'[20]

The "honest trader" is thus the moral equal to the statesman or general. Even the most ordinary member of a commercial society may be heroic because virtue does not require either great and noble self-sacrifice or uncommon wisdom. An amiable disposition towards others, a respect for the rights of men, and a prudent regard for one's own interest are sufficient to guarantee one's morality. Hutcheson's moral teaching is thus substantially more egalitarian than that of the ancients because its goals and expectations are considerably lower.

Hutcheson's treatment of the psychological foundations of conscience is also far removed from the teaching of classical philosophy. Whereas for Thomas Aquinas, for example, conscience is a habitus of rational principles directly implanted in man by God, Hutcheson's moral sense is an instinctive, irreducible passion, and reason is a tool for determining the most effective means for its satisfaction. To appreciate this novel argument fully, we must view it against the background of seventeenth-century philosophy. Thomas Hobbes, and later Locke in his *Essay Concerning Human Understanding,* had subjected human consciousness to a rigorous scientific analysis that appeared to leave no room for conscience in the traditional sense of the term. The reconstruction of human psychology upon an empiricist and sensationist foundation had eliminated the possibility of innate practical principles of morality or intuited principles of right reason.[21] Reason was henceforth to be understood as the slave of the passions, as David Hume would later express it. The foundation of human behavior, its ends or goals, could not be discerned by reason, but was rooted in the passions, namely, the desire for pleasure and the aversion to pain. Such a view of human psychology seemed, however, to leave no room for morality, justice, and benevolence. Only refined calculations of self-interest could justify morality, if it was to be more than a mere convention invented by some to control others. Laws of justice, to have any binding force, must be rational deductions or "theorums," as Hobbes had argued, derived from the strongest natural impulse to avoid pain and death. This utilitarian view of the nature of morality and justice, however, seemed to deny or tarnish its dignity and beauty.

Hutcheson's unique doctrine of the moral sense was intended to rescue the phenomenon of morality from its modern debunkers, but to do so in a manner consistent with the new Lockean psychology. Reason, for Hutcheson as for Locke, does not discern the ends of moral actions. The ends are immediately sensed, a given of the passions. The desirability of benevolence is sensed in a manner analogous to the perceptions of taste or sight. Reason's role is to discern the most appropriate means for satisfying these various desires. Reason is thus seen as a passive principle, not an active one, because it does not move to action. Only passion or the uneasiness that arises from the need to gratify the passions can lead to action.

In accordance with these premises of modern philosophy, Hutcheson holds that all causality is efficient.[22] Reason discerns the "relations" among things; it uncovers "efficient" but not "final" causes. Hutcheson's attempt to defend the existence of conscience as a *natural* phenomenon should not, therefore, be seen as a return to pre-Lockean or premodern categories of thought. Rather, his teaching is a reinterpretation of the foundations of conscience and virtue that is compatible with the new Lockean science of human nature and the epistemological foundations on which it rested.

Whatever the merits of this attempt, many of Hutcheson's fellow Scotsmen were not entirely persuaded by his notions of virtue and conscience. Although subsequent Scottish thinkers continued to use the language of moral sense or sentiment, its meaning underwent considerable revision, particularly in the hands of the two most famous Scotsmen, David Hume and Adam Smith. Both Hume and Smith were dissatisfied with the restriction of virtue to benevolence because it appeared to leave insufficient room for a variety of other qualities generally deemed praiseworthy, such as courage, as well as those qualities associated with the care for one's own well-being, such as frugality, industry, and moderation. While some of these characteristics might be interpreted as forms of benevolence, or regard for the public good, it seemed more reasonable to define virtue so as to include those qualities "useful and agreeable to ourselves" as well as those useful and agreeable to others and to emphasize the importance of "awful and respectable" virtues as well as the amiable and benevolent ones.[23] Thus, for Smith, "propriety" rather than benevolence is the true foundation of virtue. All qualities that are praiseworthy, for whatever reason, should be deemed virtuous, not merely the benevolent affections. Such a notion enlarges the scope of those qualities that Hutcheson had excluded from the moral sphere, and it reduces the tension between self-interest and morality that had created difficulties for Hutcheson's theory.

Furthermore, Hume, and more explicitly Smith, did not find the doctrine of an independent moral sense as the source of moral judgment to be fully convincing. While they agreed with Hutcheson that conscience could not be explained as a form of self-interest, they attempted to account for it in terms of more fundamental and elementary passions.[24] Smith's *Theory of Moral Sentiments* is an elaborate effort to explain the existence of moral impulses by revealing their underlying roots in the psychological principle of "sympathy." Sympathy, in Smith's usage, should not be understood as benevolence. In Smith's view, human beings have a natural, almost automatic tendency or inclination to experience the various passions of others, or to duplicate in their own imaginations the feelings and situations of others. This tendency for the passions of one individual, his joys, griefs, fears, and anger, to be communicated to others is the true basis upon which judgments of propriety and impropriety, or virtue and vice, are formed. As Smith writes: "We either approve or disapprove of the conduct of another man according as we feel that, when we bring his case home to ourselves, we either can or cannot entirely sympathize with the sentiments and motives which directed it."[25] The conscience or sense of moral duty comes into being when we develop the habit of judging our *own* passions and actions from the point of view of others' perceptions of ourselves. Smith writes:

> We endeavor to examine our own conduct as we imagine any other fair and impartial spectator would examine it. If, upon placing ourselves in his situation we thoroughly enter into all the passions and motives which influenced it, we approve of it, by sympathy with the approbation of this supposed equitable judge. If otherwise, we enter into his disapprobation and condemn it.[26]

In other words, the standards we apply to others, when we observe them impartially, we come to apply to ourselves.

Conscience, then, is a social phenomenon, the natural foundation of which rests upon sympathy, a passion that is, in itself, not specifically moral. The inclination to conform to the dictates of conscience is, according to Smith, derived from the love of mutual sympathy or the desire to have others sympathize with oneself. Smith writes that "nothing pleases us more than to observe in other men a fellow-feeling with all the emotions of our own breast; nor are we ever so much shocked as by the appearance of the contrary."[27] The ground of morality for Smith, therefore, is a passion, but one that seems to have much in common with the passion that Locke referred to as the "love of credit" or that Rousseau called *amour-propre* or vanity. Out of the natural inclination of human beings to compare themselves to others and to place themselves in others' situations, social standards of propriety and virtue emerge and impress themselves upon men's minds.[28]

Smith, then, building upon certain elements in Hume's thought, believed he could account for morality in a manner that was more genuinely scientific and empirical, and more in accordance with the psychological categories of modern philosophy, than had Hutcheson. Like Hutcheson, Smith held that morality is not simply reducible to rational calculations of interest. Nevertheless, the moral sentiments are not founded solely upon disinterested or benevolent principles but upon the desire for a particular kind of pleasure and aversion to a particular kind of pain. The psychological impetus to morality for Smith does not seem to be entirely unrelated to the "uneasiness" and anxiety that pervade Locke's portrait of the human condition.[29] Thus, while Smith and Hume continued to use the language and categories of moral philosophy that Hutcheson had developed, they radically revised their character. Such a revision, needless to say, was not entirely acceptable to many of their contemporaries, who perceived in these changes a dangerous slide toward skepticism and even atheism.[30]

The State of Nature

The various doctrines of moral sense and moral sentiment that characterized Scottish thought in the Enlightenment are thus best seen as attempts to deepen and enrich the understanding of human nature that the new political thought of the seventeenth century had established. With varying degrees of theoretical success, the Scottish thinkers sought to demonstrate that some foundation for morality and justice could be found in human nature and that human society was held together by more than calculating self-interest. The wider implication of this was that society itself was not simply an artificial construct of reason but was the natural condition of human beings, a product of immediate inclination and not merely of interest or necessity. For the Scottish thinkers, the state of nature is a social state. Man's historical origins do not suggest isolated autonomy or asocial animality, as Hobbes's teaching, and later Rousseau's, argued; rather, rude and primitive social life is man's earliest natural state.

One must, however, examine the thought of the Scottish philosophers more carefully to determine the political consequences that they derived from this view of man's natural sociality. Just as the doctrine of the moral sense and its variants were articulated within an essentially Lockean psychological framework, so too the political teachings of the Scots did not depart radically from that of the *Second Treatise on Government*. Francis Hutcheson, the thinker most credited with developing an alternative political teaching to Locke, a teaching emphasizing "virtue" and "community," is in fact virtually a direct disciple of Locke in matters political.[31] A brief examination of the major political themes discussed in his *System of Moral Philosophy* should be sufficient to reveal the parallels, if not identity, between Locke's politics and his own.[32]

Although, as has been shown, Hutcheson altered the basic Lockean psychology to give conscience and morality a more prominent role than they seemed to have for Locke, when he turned to the groundwork of social and political life, Hutcheson adopted in explicit terms the doctrines of natural rights and a prepolitical state of nature. The state of nature, or "the state of natural liberty," exists among those who have no common superior and are only subject to God and the laws of nature. He writes: "'Tis no fictitious state, it always existed and must exist among men, unless the whole earth should become one empire."[33]

Hutcheson, however, argues against the Hobbesian theory of the state of nature as necessarily a state of war, and he defends the notion of the natural sociality of the human species and thus the possibility that the state of nature is potentially a state of relative social peace. In the state of nature, men are capable of grasping the fundamental principles of justice, which enable society to exist in rudimentary form. Men possess a "moral faculty which points out the rights and obligations of this state, and shews how far any appetite or passion can be indulged consistently with the inward approbation of our souls."[34] Further, men possess "reason which clearly points out our external interests in this matter, and shews that we cannot gratify our selfish desires, except by an innocent and friendly deportment toward others."[35] This reasoning is strengthened by "the delicacy and weakness of our frame." Thus, "a friendly, just, kind deportment . . . is the only probable method of obtaining security, and all the external advantages and pleasures of life."[36] This combination of rational self-interest, natural weakness, and the moral sense enables social life without government to exist.

The state of nature is also a state of "natural equality" among men. Hutcheson argues that although human beings "differ much from each other in wisdom, virtue, beauty, and strength," all men "have strong desires of liberty and property, have notions of right, and strong natural impulses to marriages, families, and offspring." Consequently, all men equally possess the right to pursue such objects, "by the laws of God and nature." These laws "prohibit the greatest or wisest of mankind to inflict any misery on the meanest, or to deprive them of any of their natural rights, or innocent acquisitions, as well as their large ones to master the strong and artful."[37]

In the state of nature, therefore, men are equal in their natural liberty and in their right to acquire property. This does not, however, imply a substantive equality of condition. The amount of property that any person may rightfully possess is a result of his own exertions. More precisely, the original, natural titles to the ownership of property are "occupation" and "labor." Thus, Hutcheson writes: "If great occupation and much labour employed entitles the vigorous and active to great possessions, the weak and indolent have an equally sacred right to the small possessions they occupy and improve."[38]

The right to acquire property is based upon the more fundamental right of "self-preservation" and is confirmed by the fact that "men are naturally solicitous about their future interests and those of such as are dear to them."[39] "Security for future enjoyment" is the natural ground of the right of private acquisition. The existence of this right is further confirmed because it encourages "industry" rather than "indolence." This is conducive to the common good, which requires universal industry for the "support of mankind." Without private property benevolence would be the only motive to industry, a motive that is too weak to be relied upon to excite diligence and labor. Hutcheson notes that "the most extensive affections could scarce engage a wise man to industry, if no property ensued upon it."[40] Self-interest and the common good thus seem to be in a natural harmony with respect to the acquisition of wealth. While Hutcheson occasionally echoes traditional objections to limitless acquisition, the thrust of his teaching, like that of Locke, is to liberate the acquisitive impulses in the name of public prosperity.

In the state of nature, the "perfect rights" that all individuals possess to life, liberty, and property, including the right to freedom of thought and conscience and the right to marry and to associate with those who consent to it, may be defended from encroachment by force. To use Locke's term, all men possess the "executive power" of the laws of nature. Hutcheson also identifies a class of "imperfect rights," such as the right to equal treatment by others, to gratitude for favors, and to relief from distress. He asserts that these rights are all suggested to us by our moral sense. These rights, however, "though truly sacred in the sight of God," are "not of such absolute necessity to the subsistence of society among men" and "are not matters of compulsion."[41] Enforcement of these imperfect rights must be left "to men's honour and conscience." No one may compel another to perform these duties or to fulfill the claims of the imperfect rights of others. Acts of injustice, or violations of an individual's perfect rights, may be punished according to the laws of nature, but ingratitude, illiberality, or lack of compassion may not be.

Although the state of natural liberty is not by definition a state of war, the necessity of government arises "either from the imperfection or depravity of men, or both."[42] Hutcheson writes:

> As many are covetous, or ambitious, and unjust and oppressive when they have power, or are moved more by present prospects of gain, than deterred by any moral principles or any distant prospects of future evils to redound to them from their injustices; a remedy must be provided against the evil dispositions of such men; a remedy that is present and sensible, and no other can occur so effectual as a civil power with force sufficient to maintain justice and inflict present punishment on such as are injurious.[43]

The state of nature, or "anarchy," is thus an imperfect state, possessing "dangers" and "miseries" because the laws of nature, or the laws of justice, are only imperfectly enforced. Because men, even those with just intentions, are often "under the secret influence of self-interest," they use excessive force to defend their rights. Civil government thus becomes necessary to maintain the laws of justice.

Hutcheson, like Locke, holds that government is an artifice or convention. It is a product of reason and deliberation, a voluntary contract among free individuals. Man is by nature social, but he is not by nature *political.* As Hutcheson writes,

> When many of the ancients speak of man as a species fit for civil society, they do not mean that men as immediately desire a political union, or a state of civil subjection to laws, as they desire the free society of others in natural liberty, or as they desire marriage and offspring, from immediate instincts. 'Tis never for itself agreeable to any one to have his activities subject to the direction of others, or that they should have any power over his goods or his life.[44]

There is no substantive human perfection that political life as such is uniquely destined to provide. It is a disagreeable remedy for the defects of the state of nature.

Because men in the state of natural liberty are all equal to one another in their rights, no one has the natural right to rule over another. "Consent" is the only legitimate foundation for political union. The power of a civil authority extends only so far as the people who created it wish, and they may alter that power whenever it conduces to the general happines of society. Hutcheson forcefully defends the "right of resistance" and argues that there "is no hope of making a peaceful world or country, by means of such tenets as the unlimited powers of governors, and the unlawfulness of all resistance."[45] Although there is a moral obligation to obey lawfully constituted authority, the "public rights of governors" exist for the sake of protecting "the private rights of subjects," which are "more sacred and important" than the rights of governors.[46]

The grand purpose of government is to establish "civil liberty," or "the right of acting as one inclines within the bounds of the civil laws, as well as those of nature." Natural liberty cannot remain completely unlimited, but under "our modern plans of law, where little regard is had to the education and discipline of the subjects," liberty "is little confined in any sense, and a people is demonstrably free, when their important interests are well secured against any rapacious or capricious wills of those in power."[47] Civil liberty, as here defined, rather than civic virtue, is the goal of political union and the limit to its power over individuals.

Nevertheless, Hutcheson also argues that "the happiness of a people depends on their virtue."[48] Specifically, piety, justice, sobriety, industry, and fortitude are qualities necessary to social happiness. Government must seek, by "education, instruction, and discipline," to inculcate these qualities in the citizenry. Hutcheson identifies several appropriate measures for accomplishing this, such as providing instruction for the young, discouraging the excessive consumption of luxuries, mandating universal military training for all able-bodied men, rigorously punishing criminals, and maintaining independent and honest courts of law. Hutcheson does not entirely neglect the issue of civic virtue of civic education, but its role is not prominent or central to his politics. If anything, he seeks to minimize the coercive role of the state in regulating the morals and consciences of the people. Thus, he defends the freedom of worship and the freedom of inquiry, even for atheists and subversives. As he notes, "There has been much gross abuse of this power of restraining men from publishing the tenets which magistrates have reputed dangerous, that it is no wonder many good men are unwilling to allow it."[49] Hutcheson trusts to the free marketplace of ideas and to the good sense of the people to discern truth from falsehood and good from evil.

On the whole, therefore, Hutcheson's moral philosophy does not provide a substantive public purpose for government beyond protecting the equal rights of men. Moral virtue is displayed primarily in the social and familial spheres, and it does not require political activity for its completion. While government can and should encourage certain virtues among the people, particularly those virtues necessary for maintaining liberty, it cannot compel its citizens to perform those moral duties that are correlative to "imperfect rights," such as gratitude, liberality, or benevolence. All the rights of men are intuited by the moral sense, but only those rights that are essential for the subsistence of society and, one might add, that an enlightened self-interest most clearly discerns, are to be protected by government. Hutcheson, therefore, modifies the Lockean view of human nature, while not breaking decisively with Locke's notion that society, or the voluntary realm of natural liberty, is superior to the coercive realm of politics and that politics is at best a necessary means for the protection of private rights.

This conception of the moral foundations of government can be said to form the common core of the political writings of the Scottish philosophers. In this sense they were all disciples of Locke. Scottish thought after Hutcheson continued to articulate the themes of the legitimacy and purpose of government in terms of the protection of individual liberty, the right to acquire property, and the advancement of commerce. Nevertheless, certain elements of the Lockean teaching that Hutcheson had accepted, specifically the doctrine of the social contract and the right of resistance to government, began to undergo modification in the writings of some of the Scots, such as Hume, Smith, and Adam Ferguson.

David Hume, for example, in his essays "Of the Original Contract" and "Of Passive Obedience" criticizes these two Lockean doctrines on the grounds that they are unhistorical and subversive to the good order of society.[50] With respect to the right of resistance, Hume does not deny its existence altogether; however, he cautiously circumscribes its usefulness for real political life. He argues, "I shall always incline to their side, who draw the bond of allegiance very close, and consider an infringement of it, as the last refuge of desperate cases, when the public is in the highest danger from violence and tyranny." Yet he also openly disagrees with those who carry "the doctrine of obedience to such an extravagant height, as not only never to mention the exceptions in extraordinary cases . . . but even positively to exclude them."[51] Prudence rather than theory seems to underlie Hume's retreat from the doctrine of the right of resistance, which figured so prominently in Locke's and Hutcheson's writings.[52]

In place of the doctrine of an original compact or contract as the foundation of legitimate government, Hume, and even more prominently Smith and Ferguson, focuses upon history and custom, or the slow process by which principles and habits of authority and obedience are introduced "naturally" into society. Hume does not deny that some form of compact at a distant point in history may have established the first governments, but he is intent on arguing that obedience to *existing* governments is not derived from such contracts. Rather, the *utility* of regular government for the protection of life, liberty, and property is the true, rational ground of a citizen's obedience to existing authority. Further, he and Smith argue that the people's habit of venerating existing authority is essential to maintaining peace and order, an observation that at least some of the founders of the American regime shared.[53] Thus, for Hume and Smith, the citizen's obligation to his government derives not from a presumed historical compact but from that government's continued commitment to the protection of the rights of its citizens, whatever its historical origins. The actual willingness to obey authority, however, is generally not the product of reason but of custom, tradition, and habit.

The growing emphasis upon the historical evolution of political practices and institutions in the writings of many of the Scottish philosophers after Hutcheson reflects the development of liberal political theory in the late eighteenth century and, particularly, the influence of Montesquieu upon it. History becomes a primary theme of political philosophy after Montesquieu, a shift clearly discernible in the work of Hume, Smith, Ferguson, and John Millar. History, however, is not viewed as the rival or alternative to nature; rather, it is studied as a fund of empirical evidence about human nature and society from which to draw generalizations regarding the operation of natural laws in human affairs. Through the use of the historical method, or what the Scots called "conjectural history," a better and truer grasp of nature and natural right could be achieved. Although this might intimate the development of the historicism of the nineteenth century, for the Scottish thinkers history confirms the truths of nature; it does not replace them.[54]

The influence of Montesquieu can be further noted in the attempts by several of the Scots to develop a sophisticated *science* of politics. This science was understood to include a science of legislation and constitution making as well as a science of commerce or political economy, and it took its bearings by men's passions rather than their moral perfection or virtues. The channeling of ambition and avarice, the encouragement of the "desire of bettering one's condition" within the limits of law, and the structuring of competitive political and social institutions to protect liberty and to promote commerce and peace were all hallmarks of this science, which owed much to Montesquieu's *Spirit of the Laws*.[55]

It is tempting to view these changes within the liberal tradition as the beginning of a new, conservative strain of liberalism, centered around the concern with the unsettling political consequences of the doctrines of individualism and natural rights and with the character of the new commercial society that embodies these ideas. To be sure, there is in the writings of some of the Scots an awareness of the defects as well as the opportunities inherent in the liberal commercial society. Both Adam Smith and Adam Ferguson expressed concern over the debilitating effects of the division of labor and urbanization on the human character, and they both feared the decline of the martial spirit, so essential for the defense of society and the preservation of liberty. Smith's discussion of these issues in the last book of *The Wealth of Nations* in many respects suggests the more extended treatment of the limits and decay of modern society that one finds in the writings of Tocqueville and even Marx.[56] The qualifications that Smith and others had about modern society were simply that, however; and whatever limitations they may have perceived in the liberal project, they did not hesitate to embrace it as genuine progress over other political alternatives.[57]

Conclusion

As the preceding analysis has suggested, the Scottish Enlightenment was neither a communitarian nor a traditionalist rejection of the political philosophy of Locke. Although none of the Scottish thinkers accepted all the details of Locke's teaching, his language and philosophical categories provided the framework within which they analyzed moral, political, and theoretical questions. Contrary to the views of Garry Wills, Pocock, and others, none of the Scottish thinkers sought to return to a preliberal civic republicanism or to a regime of virtue. The major Scottish thinkers—Hutcheson, Smith, and Hume—all believed that the essential goals of political life were personal liberty and a free commercial order, not virtue, selfless citizenship, and material equality.

The Scottish philosophers, however, differed with Locke on one fundamental issue, the nature of conscience and morality. Although they provided different answers to the question of the origins of man's moral sense, they generally rejected the most radical implications of the teachings of Hobbes and Locke. Yet none of the major Scottish thinkers attempted to return to a pre-Lockean, classical understanding of human psychology and virtue. Rather, they sought an understanding of virtue and conscience that would be compatible with Lockean psychology and with a society based upon commerce and the acquisition of property.

The common hope of the Scottish Enlightenment, therefore, was that a liberal society, in conjunction with the natural operation of men's moral sentiments, would provide at least a modicum of virtue and decency in men's social relationships; and in a free, prosperous, peaceful world, virtue, understood as benevolence and generosity, might even flourish. Such is the intellectual heritage that this diverse group of thinkers bequeathed to the founders of the American republic, a heritage that continues to shape our way of life.

PART TWO
Challenges to the Intellectual Foundations

7
Rousseau—The Turning Point

Allan Bloom

At the moment the Framers wrote "We the people of the United States . . . ," the word "people" had been made problematic by Jean-Jacques Rousseau.[1] How do you get from individuals to a people, that is, from persons who care only for their particular good to a community of citizens who subordinate their good to the common good? The collective "we" in the Preamble might well be the voice of a powerful and wealthy few who coerce and deceive the many and make their consent meaningless. Or the many who consent to the use of "we" may do so innocently, not realizing how much of their "I" they must sacrifice, or corruptly, intending to profit from the advantage of the social contract and evade the sacrifice it demands. It is difficult beyond the belief of early modern thinkers, so Rousseau teaches, to turn men free and equal by nature into citizens obedient to the law and its ministers. "Man was born free. Everywhere he is in chains," he observes. Rousseau's task is not to return man to his original condition but to make the results of force and fraud legitimate, to persuade men that there is a possible social order both beneficial and just.

On the basis of these preliminary remarks, it should be evident that Rousseau begins from an overall agreement with the Framers and their teachers about man's nature and the origins and ends of civil society. Man is born free, that is, able to follow his inclinations and to do whatever conduces to his preservation or comfort, and equal, that is, with no superiors who have a valid claim to command him. He has no obligations. Government is, therefore, not natural but a construction of man, and the law is a thing strictly of his making. The

---

This essay is based on a few relatively short writings of Rousseau: *Discourse on the Arts and the Sciences, Discourse on the Origins of Inequality, Political Economy,* and *Social Contract.* These readings can be supplemented by his longer books: the educational novel *Emile;* the romantic novel *La nouvelle Héloïse;* and *Confessions.*

natural state is wholly distinct from the civil state, and the only way from the one to the other is consent. All other titles of legitimacy, divine or human, derived from appeals to the ancestral or exclusive wisdom, are neither binding nor believable. In *the state of nature* rights are primary; duties are derivative and become binding only after *the social contract* is freely made.

All this and much more provides the common ground of modernity where Rousseau walks arm and arm with his liberal predecessors and contemporaries. He does not reject the new principles, but he radicalizes them by thinking them through from the broadest of perspectives. In his eyes the epic battle of his Enlightenment fellows against throne and altar, which had lasted for two centuries, had simply been won. Monarchic and aristocratic Europe was, he correctly predicted, on its last legs. There would soon be great revolutions, and it is the visage of the political orders that were to emerge that concerns him. He could even afford a few generous gestures of recognition toward the defeated nobles and kings (though rarely the priests) whose moral and political greatness was hardly recognized by those who had been locked in battle with them. The new world would be inhabited by individuals who know they are endowed with rights, free and equal, no longer treading the enchanted ground where rights and duties were prescribed by divinities, now recognizing no legitimacy with higher sources than their own wills, rationally pursuing their own interests. Might they become the victims, willing or not, of new despotisms? Might they not become as morally questionable in their way as the unthinking patriots or fanatic believers who were the special objects of modern criticism and whose place they were to take?

Rousseau's reflections had the effect of outflanking the Framers on the Left, where they thought they were invulnerable. Their enemies were the old European orders of privilege, supported by the church and monopolizing wealth and the ways of access to it, and their revolution was the movement from prejudice to reason, despotism to freedom, inequality to equality. This was a progress, but not one that was to be infinite, at least in principle. The dangers were understood as coming from the *revanchisme* of throne and altar in various forms. There were many opponents of Enlightenment and its political project—in the name of tradition or the ancestral, in the name of the kings and the nobles, even in the name of the ancient city and its virtue. But Rousseau was the first to make a schism within the party of what we may call the Left. In so doing he set up the stage on which the political drama has been played even until this day. The element that was so much more extreme in the French Revolution than in the American Revolution can be traced, without intermediaries, to Rousseau's influence on its principal actors. And it was by Rousseau's standard that it was judged a failure and only a preparation for the next, and perhaps final, revolution. The camp of radical equality and freedom has very few clear political successes to show for itself, but it contains all the dissatisfactions and longings that put a question mark after triumphant liberalism.

Rousseau gave antimodernity its most modern expression and thereby ushered in extreme modernity. It is a mistake to treat him as only the genius of the Left. His concentration on the people, the corporate existence of individual peoples, provided the basis for the religion of the nation in the nineteenth and twentieth centuries. His assault on cosmopolitan civilization prepared the way for the assertion of national cultures, unique and constitutive of their individual members. His regret of the lost happy unity of man was the source of the romanticism that played at least as much of a role on the Right as on the Left. His insistence on the centrality of religion to the life of the people gave a new content to theology and provided the impulse for the religiosity that is one of the salient traits of the nineteenth and twentieth centuries. The contempt for the new man of liberal society that Rousseau articulated lent itself to the projects of both extremes of the political spectrum, and his Left informed the new Right, which constituted itself on the intellectual shambles of the old Right. His influence was overwhelming, and so well was it digested into the bloodstream of the West that it worked on everyone almost imperceptibly. Even the mainstays of democratic liberalism were affected by Rousseau; they were impressed by his critique of the harshness of the political and economic relations characteristic of the modern state and sought to correct them on the basis of his suggestions. The influence was direct on Alexis de Tocqueville, indirect, by way of Wordsworth, on John Stuart Mill. The Thoreau who for America represents civil disobedience and a way of life free from the distortions of modern society was only reenacting one part of the thought and life of Jean-Jacques.

It is this ubiquity of his presence, often where Conservatives or Leftists would least like to recognize him, that makes him the appropriate introduction for this second part of *Confronting the Constitution.* He is the seedbed of all these schools and movements that enrich, correct, defend or undermine constitutional liberalism. His breadth and comprehensiveness make it impossible to coopt him completely into any single camp. The schools that succeed him are all isms, intellectual forces that inform powerful political or social movements with more or less singleness of purpose. Rousseau resists such limitation. For him the human problem is not soluble on the political level; and although he, unlike Socrates, suggests practicable solutions, they are tentative and counterpoised by other solutions and temptations. One can always find in him the objections to each school that depends on him. Therefore Rousseau did not produce an ism of his own, but he did provide the authentically modern perspective. His concern for a higher, nonmercenary morality is the foundation of Kant's idealism. His critique of modern economics and his questions about the legitimacy of private property are at the root of socialism, particularly Marxism. His emphasis on man's origins, rather than his ends, made anthropology a central discipline. And the history of the movement from the state of nature toward civil society came to seem more essential to man than his nature—hence historicism. The wounds inflicted on human nature by this process of socialization became the subject of a new psychology, especially as represented in Freud. The romantic love of the beautiful and the doubt that modern society is compatible with the sublime and pure in spirit gave justification to the cult of art for art's sake and to the life of the bohemian. The longing for rootedness and for community in its modern form is part of Rousseauean sensibility, and so is the love of nature and the hatred for nature's conquerors. All this and much more flows from this inexhaustible fount. He possessed an unsurpassed intellectual clarity accompanied by a stirring and seductive rhetoric.

The Bourgeois

The bourgeois is Rousseau's great invention, and one's disposition toward this kind of man determines one's relation to modern politics inasmuch as he is the leading human type produced by it. The word has a strong negative charge, and practically no one wants to be *merely* a bourgeois. The artists and the intellectuals have almost universally despised him and in large measure defined themselves against him. The bourgeois is unpoetic, unerotic, unheroic, neither aristocrat nor of the people; he is not a citizen, and his religion is pallid and this-worldly. The sole invocation of his name is enough to legitimate revolutions of Left and Right; and within the limits of liberal democracy, all sorts of reforms are perennially proposed to correct his motives or counterbalance them.

This phenomenon, the bourgeois, is the true beginning point of Rousseau's survey of the human condition in modernity and his diagnosis of what ails it. The bourgeois stands somewhere between two respectable extremes, the good natural man and the moral citizen. The former lives alone, concerned with himself, his preservation, and his contentment, unconcerned with others, hence wishing them no harm. The latter lives wholly for his country, concerned solely with the common good, existing only as a part of it, loving his country and hating its enemies. Each of these two types, in his own way, is whole—free of the wasting conflict between inclination and duty that reduces the bourgeois and renders him weak and unreliable. He is the individualist in society, who needs society and its protective laws but only as means to his private ends. This does not provide sufficient motive to make the extreme sacrifices one's country sometimes requires. It also means that he lies to his fellow countrymen, making conditional promises to them while expecting them to abide by their promises unconditionally. The bourgeois is a hypocrite, hiding his true purposes under a guise of public-spiritedness. And hence, needing everyone but unwilling to sacrifice to help others reciprocally in their neediness, he is psychologically at war with everyone. The bourgeois' morality is mercenary, requiring a payoff for every social deed. He is incapable of either natural sincerity or political nobility.[2]

The cause of this dominant new character's flaws is that he took a shortcut on the road from the state of nature to civil society. Rousseau's thinking through of the new political science, which taught that man is not by nature political—a thinking through that led much further in both directions, nature and society, than his predecessors had believed necessary or possible—proved to him that natural motives cannot suffice for the making of social man. The attempt to use man's natural passions as the foundation of civil society fails while it perverts those natural passions. A man who never says "I promise" never has to lie. One who says "I promise" without sufficient motive for keeping his promise is a liar. Such are the social contracts proposed by Hobbes and Locke, requiring binding promises from their participants, who are concerned solely with their own well-being and whose contracts are therefore conditional on calculations of self-interest. Such social contracts tend toward anarchy or tyranny.

In essence, Rousseau's bourgeois is identical to Locke's rational and industrious man, the new kind of man whose concern with property was to provide a soberer and solider foundation to society. Rousseau sees him differently—from the perspective of morality, citizenship, equality, freedom, and compassion. The rational and industrious man might be an instrument of stability, but the cost of relying on him is human dignity. This contrast between two ways of seeing the central actor in modernity summarizes the continuous political debate of the past two centuries.

The Enlightenment and Virtue

Rousseau's earliest formulation of this critique of modernity was in his *Discourse on the Arts and the Sciences,* which exploded on the European scene with a force hardly credible to us today. In it he made the first attack on the Enlightenment based on the very principles that motivated Enlightenment. Simply put, he argued that the progress and dissemination of the sciences and the arts, their emancipation from political and religious control, are noxious to decent community and its foundation, virtue. By virtue he appears to mean the republican citizen's self-forgetting devotion to the common good, a common good established and preserved by freemen, which protects the equal concern for and treatment of all the citizens. In this definition of virtue, Rousseau follows Montesquieu, who calls virtue a passion and says it was the principal, or spiritual mainspring, of ancient democracies, as fear is of despotism or honor of monarchies. Virtue, of course, was not a passion in any ancient account of it, and it was certainly not especially connected to democracy. Rousseau apparently accepts Montesquieu's account of virtue because he, like the rest of the moderns, believed that passion is the only real power in the soul and that there is nothing in it capable of controlling the passions. Passion must control passion. Virtue must be understood as a special kind of complex passion. However that may be, Rousseau comes out squarely in defense of those ancient "democracies," early republican Rome and especially Sparta, in opposition to Montesquieu, who in harmony with the general tendency of Enlightenment favored the commercial republic or monarchy (with some indifference as to the choice between the two) because he thought the price for ancient virtue too high. Rousseau chooses patriotism, a motive tinged with fanaticism, because it alone can counterpoise the natural inclination to prefer oneself over everyone else, an inclination much intensified and perverted by man's social condition, where men are interdependent and self-love turns into *amour-propre,* the passion to be first among them, to be esteemed by them as he esteems himself. Patriotism is a sublimated form of *amour-propre,* seeking the first place for one's country. Without such a counterpoise society turns into a struggle for primacy among individuals or groups who unite to manipulate the whole.

Thus it is as the solvent of patriotism that Rousseau objects to Enlightenment. The fabric of community is woven out of certain immediate habits of sentiment. They are vulnerable to reason, which sees clearly only calculations of private interest. It pierces veils of sentiment and poses too powerfully the claims of perservation and comfort. Reason individualizes. In this Rousseau picks up the old assertion of classical political philosophy that there is a tension between the theoretical and practical lives that renders their coexistence at best uneasy. Or, to put it otherwise, Enlightenment proposed a parallelism between intellectual and moral or political progress, which the ancients regarded as very doubtful, a doubt recapitulated and reinforced by Rousseau, who expresses the opposition in the contrast between Sparta and Athens. He, of course, categorically preferred the former. Enlightenment wished to convert the selfishness of man in the state of nature into the enlightened self-interest of man capable of joining civil society rationally on the basis of the natural and dependable natural passions. It is this conversion Rousseau regarded as noxious and the source of moral chaos and the misery of man. He first comes to light as the defender of the old moral order against the spirit of philosophy to a degree unparalleled by any previous philosopher, doing so perhaps because modernity had more systematically attacked the moral order than had any previous thought. Rousseau is the first philosopher to appear as morality's defender *against* reason. He insisted that the movement from the natural state to the social one could not be made in the direct and almost automatic way Enlightenment claimed.

More concretely, the arts and sciences can flourish only in large and luxurious countries, which means from the outset that they require conditions contrary to those required by the small, austere, tightly knit communities where moral health prevails and the individuals have no objects of aspiration beyond those of the community. For some to be idle, others must work to provide the surplus necessary for them. These workers are exploited for the sake of the few privileged who no longer share their condition or their concerns. The fulfillment of unnecessary desires, begun as a pleasure, ends up being a necessity; the true necessities are neglected and their purveyors despised. Desire emancipated becomes limitless and calls forth an economy to provide for it. The pleasures are exclusive and are pleasant in large measure because they are exclusive. The sense of superiority follows from the practice of the arts and sciences and is also part of the reason they are pursued. Following from the general principles of modernity, it may be doubted that the intellectual pleasures are natural rather than affects of vanity. They almost always have some of the latter mixed in with them, which suffices to render them antisocial. The spirit of Enlightenment philosophy, perhaps of all philosophy, is to denigrate the simple feelings of common humanity that cause men to forget their self-interest.

In fine, the arts and sciences tend to increase inequality and fix its throne more firmly within society. They give more power to the already powerful and make the weak ever more dependent on the powerful without any common good uniting the two parties. The effective freedom of the state of nature, where man could choose what seems to him good for himself, has been replaced by the imposition of arbitrary authority over him, which has no concern for his good. Freedom was the first and most important of the natural goods, as means to live as one pleases, also as end in itself. Equality meant that in right nobody can command another and in fact nobody wished to do so because men were independent and self-sufficient. The civil condition means, in the first place, mutual dependence, physically and spiritually, but without order, each struggling to maintain the original freedom, failing to do so as relations of force or power take the place of freedom. The purpose of life becomes trying to find an advantageous place in this artificial system. Freedom is lost, not only because there is mastery and slavery but mostly because it becomes absorbed in commanding or obeying, in moving the wills of others rather than in fulfilling the objects of one's own will. The loss of freedom is best expressed in the fact of inequality, that some men are strong, others weak, some are rich, others poor, some command, and others obey. The primary fact of the state of nature as described by all teachers of the state of nature is that men are free and equal. But the bourgeois state, which in speech affirms the primacy of natural freedom and equality, in practice does not reflect that primacy. Natural right, as opposed to merely conventional right, demands the continuation or restoration of the original equality of man.

In this all regimes fail, but Rousseau judges that the ancient city came closest of all to real equality and collective freedom. Although the ancient city looks, with all its restraints, traditions, austerity, harsh duties, and so on, to be much further away from the natural state than does a liberal society where men apparently live pretty much as they please, it comes close to the essence of what really counts for man. The study of the state of nature permits Rousseau to see that essence, but such study cannot result in a plan for building a civil state that protects that essence. That must be a purely human invention, and the easy solutions that seem to preserve or to be most faithful to nature are specious. Rousseau's analysis leads to a much stricter insistence on freedom and equality within civil society than the thought of Locke or Montesquieu. Against their moderation, Rousseau adds a dose of extremism to modern politics from which it cannot easily recover. What began as an attempt to simplify politics ends up as a program for reform more complex and more imperative than anything that had preceded.

Rousseau introduced the taste for the small, virtuous community into the modern movement toward freedom and equality. Here freedom becomes less each doing what he pleases than each equally taking responsibility for making and preserving the law of the city. Ancient politics used freedom as the means to virtue; Rousseau and his followers made freedom, the natural good, the end and virtue the means to it. But, in any event, virtue, morals, and character become central again to politics and cannot, as the moderns would have it, be peripheral to the machinery of government, to institutions that channel men's passions instead of educating, reforming, or overcoming them.

Property

This point is made most forcefully in Rousseau's reflections on economics or, to put it more precisely, on property, the cornerstone of modern politics. "Ancient political writers spoke constantly about morals and virtue; ours speak only about commerce and money."[3] A man's attachment to his property, always threatened by the poor and the rapacious, is the special motive used by Locke and his followers to get his consent to the making of a social contract and the establishment of government. This is the means of achieving mutual recognition of property rights as well as protection for them from a whole community capable of punishing aggressors. The rational and the industrious who provide for themselves by labor rather than by war are the foundations of civil society, and its purposes are elegantly defined and limited by their needs. They preserve themselves comfortably, following their most powerful inclinations, and produce peace and prosperity for the whole. Their wills assent to the arrangement that their reasons determine best for their interest. This is so manifestly superior to the condition of war that prevails before the contract that it fully engages the hearts and minds of those who profit from it.

The right to property is society's golden thread, the right that emerges as the ground of consensus of the free and equal. "Work and you shall enjoy the fruits of your labors." For Hobbes, whose civil society emerges out of fear of death alone, property rights are left to the prudence of the sovereign, who can arrange them in whatever way seems fitting for the most secure establishment of peace. But for Locke, who taught that property is the true means to peace, property rights are more absolute, and the economic system governing the increase of property, what is now called the market, must as much as possible be respected by the sovereign. Government protects the individual best by protecting his property and leaving him as free as possible to care for it. The naturalness of property and government's special concern for the protection of the pursuit of it are Locke's novelties and become the hallmark of the serious projects for the reform of governments.

For all of the plausibility and even practical effectiveness of this scheme, Rousseau observes, there is something immediately shocking about the assertion that equal men should freely consent to great inequalities of property. The rich have lives that are so much freer, so much easier, so much opener to the enjoyment of life. They are so much more powerful. They can buy the law, and they can buy men. Why should the poor accept this willingly? No, the poor must have been forced to agree, or they must have been deceived. This is not natural right. The property relations that prevail in the nations are so many acts of violence against the poor, which they are too weak to prevent. There is no legitimacy here. The opposition between Locke and Rousseau is measured by the fact that the establishment of private property is for Locke the beginning of the solution to the political problem while for Rousseau it is the source of the continuing misery of man.[4]

This does not mean Rousseau is a communist or that he believed that it is possible or desirable to do away with private property. He is far too "realistic" to follow Plato's *Republic* and abandon the sure motive of love of one's own things. It does mean, however, that he strongly opposes the emancipation of acquisitiveness and that he argues against laissez faire. For him the business of government is to supervise the pursuit of property in order to limit the inequality of fortunes, to mitigate the harshness of economic competition, and to moderate the increase of desire among the citizens. Adam Smith's book *The Wealth of Nations,* which is very much in the spirit of Locke, is in large measure a presentation of the iron laws of the increase of property. Rousseau's book *Political Economy* is a treatise devoted to moral education. A modern reader who picks up *Political Economy* finds himself at sea, wondering what in the world this has to do with economics. The science of economics as we know it is predicated on the emancipation of desire, an emancipation Rousseau is concerned to prevent. In no point does Rousseau's analysis of the meaning of freedom and equality differ so much from Locke's as in the property question. The most practically radical opposition to liberal constitutionalism comes from this direction. The property right, which Locke wished to establish solidly, becomes the most doubtful of all things.

Again, though, this difference begins in an initial important agreement between Locke and Rousseau. Property is in its most primitive form that with which a man has mixed his labor. Neither God nor nature gives man directly what he needs. He must provide for himself, and his appropriation of things necessary for preservation is an extension of the original property that all have in their own body. The man who has planted beans and wishes to eat them is universally recognized to have a better right to do so than the one who without planting takes away the other's beans. There is an original of simple justice here, accessible to men of good sense. And Locke follows it through its fullest development and most complicated expressions in commercial societies. The reciprocal recognition of this right to what one has worked for constitutes property, and this solution unites self-interest with justice. The ancient view that property is constituted by a combination of what one has worked for with what one can use well is reduced to the single principle, for the classical formula implies that property is based on political determinations that can be regarded as subjective and arbitrary.

Rousseau parts company with Locke on the question of scarcity. The man who has no beans concerns him. The economist responds, "He didn't plant any, so he doesn't deserve them." But his hunger obliterates his recognition of the property right of the other, and the essence of the right is in the recognition. This malcontent can be controlled by the union of those who have provided themselves with beans, or who have inherited them, and wish to live in security from the attacks of him and his kind. So force must be introduced to compel the idle and contentious to keep away from other's property and to work to provide for themselves. The civil union is really made up of two groups: those who freely recognize one another's property rights and those who are forced to comply with the rule of the property owners. The latter are used for the collective private interest of the former. *Class* is decisive in civil society, and there is no common good without radical reform.

Thus the liberal view is that society consists in the opposition between, to repeat, the rational and industrious and the idle and quarrelsome. The former produce peace and prosperity for all, while the latter produce penury and war. Rational men must recognize and consent to the order that favors the dominance of the propertied. Rousseauean economics, however, views the social opposition as existing between the selfish, avaricious rich, exploiting nature and men for the sake of the increase of their personal wealth, and the suffering poor, unable to provide for their needs because the land and the other means of production are monopolized by the rich. As the perspective shifts, those who were once objects of execration become objects of pity.

Locke found the source of prosperity in the transformation by labor of the naturally given. This labor is motivated by need, by desire for comfort, and by anxiety for the future. For the satisfaction of all that man might possibly want, there is never enough. Once the imagination has been opened out beyond the merest physical need, the desire for acquisition becomes infinite. Rousseau concludes from this that those who are ablest at getting land and money end up possessing all the means of gaining wealth. They produce much wealth, but they do not share. For those who do not succeed, there is ever greater scarcity, and they must live their lives at the mercy of the rich. In the beginning their simple needs did not require much for their satisfaction, but that little disappears, for example, when all the land is enclosed and they have no place to plant their beans. The best they can do is sell their labor to those who have land in return for subsistence, which depends no longer on their own efforts but on the wills of the rich or the impersonal market. The scarcity that Locke asserts existed at the beginning was really, Rousseau asserts, a result of the extreme extension of desire, and Locke's solution increases scarcity within wealth, a scarcity that could be corrected by moderation, a return to a simple economy directed to real needs. The expanding economy can never keep up with the expansion of desire or of longing for the means of satisfying future desire. The economy that was instituted to serve life alters the purpose of life, and the activity of society becomes subservient to it. The present is sacrificed to a prosperous future that is always just beyond the horizon. Actually nature was not such a stepmother as the moderns thought, and it is not so unreasonable to seek to live according to nature as they teach.

As politics turns into economics, the qualities requisite to the latter come to define the privileged human character. Selfishness and calculation have primacy over generosity and compassion. Dealings among men are at best contractual, always with an eye to profit. Differences of talent at acquisition do exist; but, Rousseau asks, does a decent society privilege them at the expense of differences in goodness and decency? The social arrangement of property that he asserts should follow from the study of man's natural condition is not that of commercial societies but that of agricultural communities, where production requires only simple skills, where the division of labor is not extreme, where exchange is direct and the virtuosos of finance play little role, where inequalities of land and money are, if not abolished, limited, where avarice has little opportunity for activity, and where the motive for work is immediate necessity. The scale should not become such that men are abstractions while money is real. A modest sufficiency of goods and a moderate disposition, not the hope of riches and their perpetual increase, should be the goal of political economy. The natural equality of man can tolerate only a small amount of the inequality produced by society.

Rousseau confronts Locke's assertion that liberal economies make all members of society richer and, therefore, palpably better off than they were in the natural condition with the counterassertion that freedom can never properly be put in the same balance with riches and comfort. Perhaps the day laborer in England is better clothed, housed, and fed than a king in America. Unimpressed by the moral qualities Locke finds in the English day laborer, Rousseau turned back toward the proud dignity and independence of the king. Locke took it that his argument is sufficient to persuade the rational poor to accept the inequalities present in society in preference to the neediness of the state of nature. Rousseau uses the same argument to make men rebel against the state of dependence and anxiety caused by the economies of civilized society. He goes further. In depicting the degradation of the bourgeois, the new kind of ruler, in comparison with the greatness of the ancient citizen, he makes the life of the advantaged in liberal society appear to be as despicable as the life of the disadvantaged is miserable.

The delegitimization of property's emancipation from political control, that is, from the will of all, was one of the most effective and revolutionary aspects of Rousseau's thought. His great rhetoric was used to make compassion for the poor central to relations among men and indignation at their situation central to political action. With all the freshness of original insight, before this kind of analysis became routine and tired, he outlined all that is negative about excessive concern for self-preservation and the means of ensuring it. But for all that, Locke was simply right in one decisive aspect. Everybody, not just the rich, gets richer in a system of liberal economy. Gross inequalities of wealth persist or are encouraged by it, but the absolute material well-being of each is greatly enhanced. Rousseau, followed by Marx, taught that the inner logic of acquisition would concentrate wealth in fewer and fewer hands, completely dispossessing the poor and alienating them from the means of becoming prosperous. Locke's great selling point has proved to be true. Joining civil society for the sake of protection and comfort is a good investment. This fact has been widely accepted by Americans for a long time; it is only now becoming fully recognized by Europeans. Intellectuals committed to the revolution are the last to resign themselves to the facts. The grinding sense of necessity has been alleviated and with it most of the revolutionary fervor. One may continue to believe, as somber critics still do, that the way of life of such a society is repulsive and that the motives for association are inadequate and corrupt. But that is not quite the same as the progressive impoverishment and enslavement of mankind at large. Most of all, the poor, the many, the masses—however they are now qualified—become supporters of "the system," out of crass self-interest, and that destroys the revolutionary movements. The humanness of life may be lessened, but that is not accompanied by starvation.

Locke taught that the protection and increase of property guaranteed by government based on consent are both efficient and just. The justice is harsh natural justice—the protection of unequal natural talents for acquisition from the depredations of the idle, the less competent, the envious, and the brutal. The argument for efficiency remains; but since the full effect of Rousseau penetrated the bloodstream of Western thought, hardly any of the economists who are capitalism's most convinced advocates defend the justice of the inequalities in which it results. It is at best an effective way of increasing collective and individual wealth. Rousseau's arguments for the primacy of natural equality have proved persuasive. The construction of civil society based on inequalities of property-producing gifts is seen to be a contradiction of what is most fundamental. As a matter of fact, natural inequalities of any sort—whether of strength, beauty, or intelligence—must not have any privileges in civil society because they did not in the state of nature. This is a step away from the sway of nature that Rousseau was the first to make. Nature mandates political inventiveness for the attainment of equality in civil society. Coarse pragmatism can live with a system that "works," as long as it works. But we find ourselves, at least partly because of Rousseau, in the interesting situation where we do not entirely believe in the justice of our regimes.

The General Will

Since man is naturally free, the only political solution in accordance with nature is for Rousseau one where man governs himself.[5] This does not mean that man consents to let others govern for him. Practically, he cannot accept the dictates of other men. He experiences them merely as wills opposing his will. Other men may force him to act against his wishes, but this is force, not right. Law is not essentially force. For law to be law, the one who obeys it must do so with the assent of his will; and in the absence of a fully wise and just ruler, other men cannot be trusted. The human law worthy of obedience is the law one has made for oneself. Only this formula combines freedom with obligation. Self-legislation is the true meaning of a decent political order.

This Rousseau contrasts with the liberal formula that one gives up a bit of freedom to enjoy the rest undisturbed. This leaves everything unresolved. Just how much is this bit? How is the ever-present possibility of opposition between what the individual wants and the demands of the collectivity to be mediated? The arrangement contains no element of morality or obligation, only contingent calculations of immediate interest. Utilitarian morality is no morality at all. Analysis reduces it at best to long-range self-interest. Real duty, the un-self-regarding moral deed, becomes a will-o'-the-wisp. The struggle between inclination and duty, obstinate and irreconcilable, is the psychological price paid for the liberal social contract. Only the man whose private will wills only the common good would experience no tension between his individuality and society, freedom and duty.

This analysis is the source of the general will, Rousseau's most famous innovation, his attempt to establish a moral politics that does not degrade man or rob him of his freedom.[6] The will of individuals is, by definition, individual and is therefore not concerned with the good of others. But man is capable of generalizing. His rationality consists in it. The simple operation of replacing "I want . . ." by "we want . . ." is typical of reasoning man. The man who wills only what all could will makes a community of shared, harmonious wills possible. The society of men who will generally together dissolves the virtual war of all against all with respect to which liberal society is only a truce. General will is the common good.

Man's dividedness is not overcome by the general will, but its character is transformed. It is no longer experienced as an opposition between self and other, inside and outside. The struggle is now between one's particular desire and one's general will, a will recognized as nonarbitrary and good. Self-overcoming is the essence of the moral experience, and it is this capacity that Rousseau believed he had discovered, a discovery only dimly perceived by ancient politics and entirely lost in modern politics. Willing generally constitutes a new kind of human freedom, not the satisfaction of animal inclination but real choice. It is the privileged and profound form of rationality as opposed to the calculation of personal benefit. It is a transformation of nature that preserves what is essential about nature. Obedience to the general will is an act of freedom. This is the dignity of man, and a good society makes possible and encourages such dignity.[7]

The passage from the particularly willing savage to the generally willing citizen is the triumph of civilization, and it is man's historic activity to construct the bridge between the two. The distance is great. The soul has no such natural order, and its development is not a growth but a willful making, a putting in order of man's disordered and incoherent acquisitions during the course of time. Education is this activity of construction, which Rousseau presents in all its complexity and richness in his greatest work, *Emile.* The putting into political practice of this education is really the work of the Legislator, who must be an artist. Beginning from the first needs and desires of a limited and selfish being, passing through all the experiences requisite to learning how to preserve itself, he ends with the man who thinks of himself as man simply, controlling his wishes by the imperative of their possibility for all men.

All this is abstract. For such a man to exist really, there must be a community into which he is woven so tightly that he cannot think of himself separately from it, his very existence formed as part of this whole. The public business is identical to his private interest, and he thinks of it when he wakes in the morning and when he goes to bed at night. It does not suffice that he be an unquestioning part of a traditional society governed by ancestral ways. He must understand himself as guiding his own destiny, as a lawmaker for his city and thereby for himself. Every decision, act, or decree of the city must be understood to be the result of his own will. Only in this way is he autonomous and does he maintain his natural inalienable freedom. The citizen as understood by Rousseau combines the competing charms of rootedness and independence.

It follows immediately that the citizen must choose to practice the severest virtues of self-control, for if his private bodily needs or desires are imperious, he will be too busy tending them. Moderation for the sake of freedom is his principle. This is different from the bourgeois' delay of gratification, which still has as its motive the private needs of the individual and looks toward infinite increase as the end. The citizen's efforts are connected with present satisfactions that constitute their own reward. Concern with public business in the assembly of citizens is the core of his life. He works and cares for his property with a view to maintaining a modest competence, setting aside great private indulgences and personal anxieties about the future. The whole organization of community life inclines him toward generality in a substantial way. The choice of individuality would be difficult to make, whereas in a commercial society the public-spirited way of life has no support. Rousseau's city provides little opportunity for private consumer expense and imposes severe sumptuary taxes on itself.

The simplest political requisite of healthy politics is, therefore, a small territory and a small population.[8] The whole body of citizens must be able to meet regularly. Moreover, they must know one another. The extension of human sentiments is limited, and caring requires acquaintance. Love of country and one's fellows cannot be abstract; they must be continuously experienced. Perhaps the most remarkable difference between Rousseau's politics and the politics of Enlightenment concerns this question of size. The commercial republic tends to favor large territories and large populations. Large markets encourage production and exchange, hence increase of wealth. Moreover, only large countries can counterbalance large and powerful enemies. And they offer all kinds of advantages for the machinery of modern governments that rely less on the good character of men than on various counterpoising forces, on checks and balances. What is sacrificed, according to Rousseau, is autonomy and human connectedness. Concentration on local community and responsibility is part of Rousseau's legacy, a concentration that goes against all the dominant tendencies of commercial republics in modernity. Rousseau connects large size with despotism. As Montesquieu looked to great nations like England as the models for modern regimes directed to freedom, Rousseau looks to modern cities like Geneva as well as to Sparta to demonstrate the possibility of what he prescribes.

Small size is also necessary to avoid the modern democratic device of representation, which for Rousseau epitomizes the halfway modern solution to the problem of freedom.[9] Without transforming natural freedom into civil freedom, that is, without abandoning the habit of living as one pleases and doing what is necessary to become a part of a sovereign body, men hope that others will take the responsibility of governing for them while remaining loyal to their will. The effort of determining general wills is to be left to the representatives without having a citizen body that wills generally. This is a prescription for interest politics or the compromising of particular, selfish wills. The idea of the common good disappears, and the conflict of parties takes its place. Worst of all, representation institutionalizes divided modern man, no longer really free, hopelessly dependent on the wills of others, believing himself to be master but incapable of the effort of moral autonomy.

Thus, in broad outline, Rousseau rejects most of the elements of modern constitutionalism including those that make up the U.S. Constitution. The principles of enlightened self-interest as well as the machinery of limited representative government only exacerbate in his view the tension between individual and society and lead to ever greater egotistical individualism accompanied by dangerous arbitrary abuses of centralized governmental power. The very notion of checks and balances encourages the selfishness of partial interests. Good institutions in this sense are predicated on the badness of men. Whether the institutions function or not, they give way to and encourage moral corruption.

The foundings of government Rousseau wishes to encourage are those that make the virtue of all the citizens necessary to their functioning, and they are very complicated affairs. In most modern political philosophy after Machiavelli, there is little talk of founders or legislators. Lycurgus, Solon, Moses, Theseus, Romulus, Numa, and Cyrus were previously the common currency in discussion of the origins of political regimes. It was taken for granted that the union of disparate individuals into a community of goods and purposes is the most difficult of political deeds and requires men of surpassing greatness to achieve it. A way of life that engages all the members had to be instituted. But the new political discoveries seemed to indicate that the foundation of civil orders was more like the striking of a business contract, where all that is required is individuals who are clear about their personal interests and where they intersect with those of others. The transition into the civil state was understood to be almost automatic, certainly not requiring common agreement about the good life. This hardly perceptible transition indicated the naturalness of the new politics. All that was necessary to the founding of a political order was enlightenment or an instruction manual. Hobbes thought that the advantages of the civil order could be made evident to men before its establishment. The ancients thought that the most far-seeing statesmen alone could know those advantages and that the individual citizens could know them only afterward. The foundings require persuasion, deception, and force as well as an elaborated plan for a way of life adapted to the particular people that is to be founded. The ultimate goals of justice may be universal, but the ways to them are almost infinitely diverse. The Legislator must combine particular and universal, taste and principle. Prudence rather than abstract reason is his instrument. Such was the view of ancient politics, and Rousseau partially returns to it, though further encumbering the Legislator with the abstract demands of modern legitimacy. All of this underlines Rousseau's view of the great distance between the natural and the civil states.[10]

This treatment of Legislators may be useful in thinking about the American Framers, whose position is anomalous in modern political thought. Their role was at least halfway between the Enlighteners and Rousseau. Their founding activity was not based on any explicit teaching about founding in the philosophies of Locke or Montesquieu.

They were, as is Rousseau's Legislator, without authority, acting as they did before the legislation that founds all authority, and their task was almost limitless. Surely they thought not only of the abstract contract but of how it would fit the people they were founding. And they reflected—individual members of the founding group more or less coherently—on the moral character of the citizens and the national life requisite for the success of their project. They were for a time and in their way almost princes, legislating for egalitarian rule, preparing their own extinction, acting out of motives of a vastness and selflessness far transcending those they expected of the citizens. All this is discussed by Rousseau, and it provides a link between the petty egotism attributed by Rousseau to the classical liberal model of politics and the sublime morality Rousseau sought and insisted on.

Conclusion

Rousseau's description of what the Legislator must accomplish might make the modern reader think that he is speaking of culture rather than politics. The very word "culture," first employed in the modern sense by Kant, stemmed from an interpretation of Rousseau's intention. He was looking for a harmony between nature and civilization, civilization meaning all the historically acquired needs and desires of man and the means of satisfying them discovered by him. Civilization had shattered man's unity. Although the foundation of civil societies and the discovery of the arts and sciences might appear to be simply a progress, if progress is measured by actual happiness rather than the production of the means for the pursuit of happiness, the advantages of civilization become doubtful. The restoration of the unity of man is the project of politics taken broadly. Politics in its narrow modern sense concerns the *state,* the minimal rules for human intercourse, not the happiness of man. Culture is where we think man as a whole lives; it frames and forms man's possible ways of life and his attainment of happiness. It is thought to be the deeper phenomenon. Rousseau appears to us to combine the concerns of culture and of politics. For him they are really not separable. The nineteenth-century idea of culture was completely separated from politics. It ceased to be understood as a conscious founding within the power of men to construct. It came to be understood as a growth, a result of the mysterious process of history. But however far the notion moved from its roots in Rousseau, it continued to express Rousseau's concern for the "organic" character of human association. The habitual way of using the word "culture," as something admirable, as opposed to mere cosmopolitan, superficial "civilization," reflected and still reflects Rousseau's contempt for bourgeois society and modern liberal constitutionalism as well as the critique of civilization he launched with the *Discourse on the Arts and the Sciences*.

So it is perhaps helpful for us to describe Rousseau's Legislator as the founder of a culture, and this makes more evident the magnitude of the task imposed on him by Rousseau. To succeed he must charm men with at least the appearance of divine authority to make up for the human authority he lacks and to give men the motives for submission to the law that nature does not provide. He not only needs authority from the gods, he must establish a civil religion that can support and reward men's willing the common good. What is called the sacred today and is understood to be the summit of culture finds a place in Rousseau's project more central than the very ambiguous one it has in liberal legislation, where religion may be understood to be unnecessary or even dangerous to the civil order. As one looks at what the Legislator must do, it is hard to resist the temptation to say it is impossible.[11]

This impression was confirmed for Western consciousness by one highly visible experiment, the legislative activity of Robespierre, or the Terror. The attempt to institute citizenship was a bloody business, which was sufficient to repel most observers. As Locke and Montesquieu were the presiding geniuses of Adams, Madison, Hamilton, and Jefferson in their moderate founding, Rousseau was the presiding genius of the excesses of the French Revolution. Edmund Burke's overwhelming description of the events and Rousseau's influence on them is unforgettable.[12]

In spite of Rousseau's dangerous impracticality, he could not be put aside as just another failure. His articulation of the problem of democratic politics was just too potent. His views about what effect his thought should have on practical politics are difficult to penetrate. Locke and Montesquieu would certainly in general have approved of the handiwork of their great pupils, and Rousseau would just as certainly have disapproved of Robespierre. Although his teaching is full of fervent aspiration, it is also full of bleak pronouncements about the possibility of correcting the tendencies of modernity. Whether or not he thought his kind of city could actually come into being is uncertain. But if it were possible, it would be so only in a few small places with very special circumstances, like Corsica. The universal applicability and possibility of actualization that is the hallmark of modern political science disappears in Rousseau. In this again he is more like Plato and Aristotle than a modern. But Plato and Aristotle made a distinction between the just regime and acceptable ones that permitted men to live with the less than perfect, whereas Rousseau insists that only the simply just regime is legitimate, thereby making almost all real political life unacceptable. He somehow combines the high standards of the ancients with the insistence on actualization of the good regime of the moderns, thus producing the ultramodern political disposition.

The origins of this are in Machiavelli's turning away from the imaginary cities of the old philosophers toward the way men really live. He intended to reduce the disproportion between the is and the ought, in favor of the is, so as to achieve the modest goals given by men's real needs. A lowering and simplification of the understanding of man's nature would make the satisfaction of that nature possible. But somehow this moral reductionism does not work. Man's longing for justice and dignity will not accept it, and with Rousseau the old tension reasserts itself in the form of the opposition between the real and the ideal. The state-of-nature teachings, which were elaborations of Machiavelli's intention, taught that man is naturally a brute concerned exclusively wth his preservation. Civil society was in those teachings only a more prudent way of realizing the most primitive goals. Its establishment is a progress in that sense alone, not in the sense of a movement from brutishness to humanity. Freedom in the state of nature was only the means to preservation, and equality was only the absence of the authority of any man over any other man to prevent the exercise of his freedom. Civil society uses freedom and equality merely as means to the basic end of comfortable self-preservation. Therefore they could be greatly attenuated in the service of that end. Freedom and equality could be signed over to civil society, which adopts the responsibility for the more effective fulfillment of the goal for which they were the imperfect natural instruments. So it seems. But experience and reflection teach that, once man knows himself to be naturally free and equal, it is impossible to avoid the demand that men in society be free and equal in the most absolute sense. The freedom of man is recognized to be his essence, and civil freedom is not possible without factual equality. In practice all of society's laws remain doubtful until they can really be understood to be self-imposed, and every inequality appears intolerable. The easygoing solution of the satisfaction of the basic needs is overturned by constant demands for greater freedom and equality. They become insistent in practice as men are informed of their natural rights and act as perpetual goads to reform and revolution. What later came to be called a dialectic was set in motion, and natural freedom tends to civil freedom. Only when law is the expression of rational universality and all men are equally recognized by all as moral agents and as ends in themselves is the process complete. The chapter in the *Social Contract* where Rousseau describes the difference between natural animal freedom and moral freedom describes the two terms of the process.[13]

Whatever the consequences, once the principles appear to be self-evident, this aspiration toward ever greater freedom and equality follows, tending to challenge all prudential stopping points or efforts to counterpoise it by other principles or by traditions. The problem can be epitomized by the idea of social contract. All thinkers are in agreement that consent is requisite to the establishment of laws. But, Rousseau argued, none of them before him found any kind of rule of consent that binds the individual when the law is believed by him to be contrary to his interest, that is, in the extreme case, his life, liberty, and property. Only Rousseau found the formula for that, distinguishing self-interest from moral obligation, discerning an independent moral interest in the general will. He discovered the source of moral goodness in modern political principles and provided the flag under which democracy could march. So, at least, it was understood. Regimes dedicated to the sole preservation of man do not have the dignity to compel moral respect.

Although the attempt to incarnate the moral democratic regime in a modern nation appeared worse than quixotic to sober men after the French Revolution, they all agreed that Rousseau had to be taken account of, that his thought had to be incorporated into the theory and practice of the modern state.[14] Kant and Hegel are only the two most notable examples of this, giving an account of moral dignity in freedom based on Rousseau while using it to reinterpret and sublimate bourgeois society. Thus they hoped to reconcile Rousseau with the reality of modernity rather than permitting the impulse transmitted by him to lead to ever greater extremes in rebellion against triumphant modernity. Failing that reconciliation, Rousseau's persuasive depiction of humanity shattered and fragmented by the apparently irresolvable conflict between nature and society authorizes many different kinds of attempts to pick up the pieces: on the political Left, new Revolutions and new Terrors to install the regime of democratic virtue; on the Right, immersion in the rootedness of local cultures without the justification of rational universality; then there are those who, like Thoreau, flee the corruptions of society in an attempt to recover natural self-sufficiency.

Taking Rousseau seriously, however, does not necessarily mean despising and rejecting the regime of the U.S. Constitution, as the example of one of the most serious of those thoughtful men influenced by Rousseau proves. That is Alexis de Tocqueville, whose very obvious Rousseauism is masked to contemporary eyes by his conservative admirers, who refuse to admit that he could have any connection with Rousseau, the leftist extremist. He turned from the spectacle of European egalitarian disorder to the United States, which he saw as the model of orderly liberty. He affirmed without hesitation the justice of equality as over against the unjust privileges of the past. He interpreted the United States as a vast educational undertaking, instructing citizens in the political exercise of their rights. He treated the Founders as men whose characters expressed a higher morality that may not have been contained in their principles. He, of course, could not believe that the United States simply solved the political problem. His view of American democracy is tinged with the melancholy Rousseau induces when one looks at real political practice. He casts respectful glances at American savages and at the great souls of some aristocratic men. He recognized the danger that the regime might tend toward materialism, to mere self-interest on the part of the citizens, and to atomizing individualism. He concentrated on the importance of local self-government, which approximated the participation of the independent city, and saw the New England town as the real foundation of American freedom, the core around which the larger government aggregated. Moreover, he introduced compassion, a sentiment alien to Locke and Montesquieu, as the corrective to the harshness of economic relations in the commercial society. Compassion he took to be the core of democratic feeling and the ground for something more than connections of interest among men. He also concentrated as liberals did not on the connectedness between man and woman and their offspring as constituting an intermediate community, a bridge between individual and society. He simply reproduces Rousseau's reflections on the family in *Emile.* And he looks to a gentle, democratic religion to mitigate the American passion for material well-being. Rousseau makes Tocqueville alert to the dangers of liberal society and allows him to reinterpret it in such a way as to encourage the citizen virtues that can emerge out of the principles of freedom and equality rightly understood.

I have adduced the example of Tocqueville to indicate the kind of meditation about politics that men of Rousseauean sensibilities might have. Rousseau's specific projects were quickly exploded. But he infected most of us with longings for freedom and virtue that are difficult to get over. He is that modern thinker of democracy who had the depth and breadth in his vision of man found in Plato and conspicuously absent in those who propounded our principles. He does not simplify man to get results. He can talk about love and God and the sublime in revealing the fullness of the human potential. Most of all Rousseau concentrates not so much on what threatens life as on what makes life worth living, taking his orientation from the positive rather than the negative. He more than any of his predecessors tried, on the basis of what moderns believe to be true about man, to describe and recover the fundamental sweetness of existence. This complicates things but proves irresistible to all those who seek for the good. This generation must come to terms with his understanding of our democratic life, as have all those who lived since he wrote.

Above all Rousseau's criticism of liberalism must be tested against the original and authentic voices of liberalism to see whether they can meet his objections. Is Rousseau perhaps like Machiavelli, who subtly parodied Plato and made him appear to be an idealist to later ages? Is liberalism as coarsely materialistic as Rousseau alleges, or did Locke, Montesquieu, and the *Federalist* anticipate his objections? Did triumphant liberalism forget its own profound moral sources and replace them with oversimplified arguments in favor of itself, leaving itself open to Rousseau's assault? Have we not adopted Rousseau's characterization of us and thereby weakened our self-respect? This confrontation between Rousseau and the great liberals will enhance our self-awareness and make us recognize the profundity of the antagonists. This part of the book is in large measure tribute to the richness of Rousseau's influence. He may be a charm to be overcome. But to do that, his charm must first be experienced.

8
Utilitarianism and the Constitution

Joseph Hamburger

The newly created nation in North America was "one of the most enlightened, if not the most enlightened, at this day on the globe."[1] So said Jeremy Bentham, the most notable of the utilitarians, in 1789. And three decades later he called the American government "the first of all governments to which the epithet of *good* . . . could with propriety be attached."[2] This admiration developed against a background of considerable dissatisfaction with British institutions.

Bentham and most of the other utilitarians were radical critics of the monarchy, the church, aristocratic nepotism in political life, the common law, and the administration of justice.[3] Looking across the Atlantic, they could see that the young American republic differed markedly from what was familiar on the domestic scene, and Bentham and his followers held it up as a model. Bentham regarded the United States as an open society unhampered by the weight of tradition. His admiration was unbounded from the first, in spite of his regret that the colonies rebelled, but it became wildly enthusiastic twenty years or so after the founding when his judgments were shaped not only by his radicalism but also by his new belief in democracy. Now he regarded the United States as a land of "democratic ascendancy" and virtually universal suffrage, and in his arguments against antidemocrats in England he responded to their fears by pointing out that in America, although it was a "*total* democracy," private property and religious minorities were perfectly secure.[4] So favorable were his judgments that he described himself as "at heart more of a United-States-man than an Englishman."[5]

Such encomiums, however, did not prevent the utilitarians from criticizing the American Constitution, including the principles on which it was founded and many of the institutions that it established. Although Bentham praised *The Federalist* for its sound reasoning, he also said it wanted clearness, its reasoning was desultory and unmethodical, and its definition of the end of government was inadequate.[6] *The Federalist,* together with the Declaration of Independence, provided a weak and confused foundation for a regime that he approved. Thus he regarded America as a wholesome place despite its formative documents. "Who can help lamenting," Bentham asked, "that so rational a cause should be rested upon reasons, so much fitter to beget objections, than to remove them?" It was a case, he added, "where the conclusion has supported the premises, instead of the premises the conclusion."[7]

Utilitarian criticism of the Constitution was expressed in many ways. First, I will show that this criticism was directed against constitutionalism itself and all the devices and institutions used to limit government and reduce the opportunities for the emergence of despotism. Next I will turn to the differences between the utilitarians and the framers about underlying assumptions and basic principles. Then I will examine the way Publius arrived at his political judgments in order to contrast it to utilitarian politics. Finally I will turn to the place of liberty in the regimes promoted by the framers and by the utilitarians to show how much they differed in their understanding of liberty and in the value they attached to it.

Constitutional Limitations

The utilitarians opposed the very idea of constitutional limitations. They were even reluctant to allow that constitutional limitations had legal status. For John Austin constitutionalism was a matter of morality and opinion, not law; therefore, what were called unconstutitional acts were not infringements of law and could not be called illegal. It was the character of a sovereign body to be "incapable of *legal* limitation." This held for both free and despotic governments, and thus persons that distinguished between them used language that was "inappropriate and absurd."[8] Bentham's view was similar. The power of the supreme body was without bounds; for one "to say there is any act they *cannot* do,—to speak of any thing of their's as being *illegal,*—as being *void;*—to speak of their exceeding their *authority* (whatever be the phrase)—their *power,* their *right,*—is, however common, an abuse of language." This was true even under a so-called free constitution. Therefore, any attempt to establish constitutional limits was pointless, and all talk about limitations could be reduced to such "arguments as are drawn from the principle of *utility*"; such talk amounted to saying "that the tendency of the law is, to a greater or a less degree, pernicious."[9]

Utilitarian opposition to constitutional limitations was based not only on an analysis of the realities of sovereignty and law but also on the belief that constitutional limitations were mistaken. There was no good purpose served by tying the hands of future legislators.

> I would sooner [Bentham said], were the power of sanctioning in my hands, give my sanction to a body of laws framed by any one else, how bad soever it might appear to me, free from any such perpetuating clause, than a body of laws of my own framing, how well soever I might be satisfied with it, if it must be incumbered with such a clause.[10]

With the considerable literature of constitutionalism evidently in mind, Bentham alluded to the many well-meant recommendations in ingenious books that endeavored "to restrain supreme representative assemblies from making laws in such and such cases, or to such and such an effect." What these proposals really expressed, however, was the assertion, "Your laws shall become ipso facto void, as often as they contain any thing which is not to my mind." But "a perfect acquaintance with the dictates of utility . . . would, in many, if not in most, of those instances, discounsel the attempt." Such unhappy attempts to limit the power of legislatures were not uncommon, but they were made most frequently in that newly created, enlightened nation across the Atlantic.[11]

Utilitarian opposition to constitutional limitations was reinforced by a powerful faith that a science of legislation could be developed. The utilitarians differed in their understandings of the method and character of science, but Bentham, James Mill, Austin, and John Stuart Mill shared a great faith in it. Bentham entertained the ambition to play Newton's role for a science of law. Extrapolating from the example of scientific political economy, James Mill spoke confidently about the science of government and the science of jurisprudence.[12] Austin was convinced that the principle of utility could generate a science of ethics that would maximize human happiness. He shared the hope and prediction of John Locke (whom he quoted) that "ethics would rank with the sciences which *are capable of demonstration*."[13] For Austin the science of ethics included the science of legislation, and it was its scientific status that made constitutional limitations objectionable. Since science could discover how to maximize general happiness, Austin argued, sovereign authority guided by such a science ought not to be limited by constitutional checks. Such checks Austin called positive morality. They originated in opinion, moral beliefs, and tradition; they did not have legal status, and they were binding only to the extent that morality and opinion were felt to be compelling. The constitutional limitations and norms of constitutionality that were known to Austin originated in a prescientific age, and he argued that it would be undesirable to allow such norms to check laws made in the light of the science of legislation.[14] Austin, like the other utilitarians, wanted to emancipate sovereign power from all limitations in order to maximize opportunities to confer benefits by legislative means.

This outlook led to the utilitarian critique of the main features of the Constitution, including the devices used to limit political power. The first of these was the claim for the existence of individual rights. Publius himself, it should be acknowledged, was uneasy, or perhaps only reticent, about the assertion of rights, but he accepted the Bill of Rights and argued that "the constitution is itself, in every rational sense, and to every useful purpose, *A Bill of Rights*."[15]

Bentham criticized all use of language that suggested the existence of natural or inalienable or universal rights, whether they were general rights or particular rights to liberty or to property or to security or to resist oppression and whether the language was found in American or in French declarations. This meant that he rejected all rights not created by a sovereign power and therefore not legally established. He recalled that when as a student at Oxford he heard Blackstone's lectures he "immediately detected his fallacy respecting natural rights." Throughout his life Bentham held there were "no such things as natural rights—no such things as rights anterior to the establishment of government." Such claims were nonsense; they followed from the misuse of language; they came from imaginary laws, from laws of nature, fancied and invented by poets, rhetoricians, and dealers in "moral and intellectual poisons." All this amounted to the "nothingness of the . . . rights of man." The French in creating their Declaration of Rights were "deluded by a bad example—that of the American Congress."

Yet there was a more serious objection: natural rights diminished the authority of government and encouraged insurrection. Thus Bentham said they were proclaimed in "terrorist language." When Bentham encountered the passage in the Declaration of Independence that asserted that all men are created equal and that they are endowed with certain unalienable rights, he decided that "in these tenets [the Americans] have out done the utmost extravagance of all former fantatics," and he compared them to the German Anabaptists. All declarations of rights, he concluded, were "rights asserted as against government in general, [and they] must be . . . the rights of anarchy—the order of chaos."[16] This was not Bentham's view alone. It was shared by Austin, and John Stuart Mill in *On Liberty* made it clear that he did not ground his argument on an assertion of individual right.[17]

The utilitarians were also critical of most institutions generated by the American Constitution. Federalism itself was hardly compatible with the utilitarian theory of sovereignty. Bentham said that federal government would lead to collision with state governments and that it was "like a watch with two main springs."[18] Austin especially went into detail regarding this. In every independent political society, he said, the sovereign "is *one* individual, or *one* body of individuals"; if this were not the case, the society "is either in a state of nature, or is split into two or more independent political societies." Furthermore, in his view of sovereignty, all authorities that were not supreme were subordinate and existed at the single sovereign's pleasure. This was tantamount to denying the realities of American government, as became evident when he applied his definitions to the United States, for he concluded that "the common or general government is not sovereign or supreme." Austin's position led to distorted accounts of American government as he attempted to reconcile American realities with his theory of sovereignty.[19]

The depreciatory attitude to federalism was also reflected in discussions of centralization. Like Bentham, Austin enthusiastically advocated centralization. He regarded it as a necessary feature of indivisible sovereignty, which would be diminished by the rival authority of local governments. Austin regarded the term "centralization" as a metaphor for the inherently hierarchical relationships of authorities in political society. Shared or divided authority was inconceivable; one had to be supreme and all others subordinate, as "they may be said to radiate from [the supreme authority] as from their common centre." Thus it is not surprising that he characterized the American Union as "held together by a merely federal tie" and said the absence of centralized government was a "structural defect."[20]

Even John Stuart Mill, whose utilitarianism deviated considerably from the views of Bentham, Austin, and his father, James Mill, was somewhat critical of federalism. As so often, however, he was equivocal. He thought that the benefits of centralization were great but that the principle of local self-government had been undeservedly discredited. Despite his lip service to the idea of local self-government, however, Mill asserted that the mode of administration of the New Poor Law, which was modeled on Bentham's plan and provided for a high degree of centralization, was "in its general conception almost theoretically perfect."[21] In his *Considerations on Representative Government* (1861), Mill called *The Federalist* "the most instructive treatise we possess on federal government," and he defended local representative bodies (called sub-parliaments), but not for the reasons that justified them to Publius. For Mill they provided a division of labor and encouraged participation, and thus they promoted political education and self-management of one's affairs. In any case, as "a mere local body" the sub-parliament was denied important functions, was denied discretion even when functions were left to it, and was subject to dissolution by the central government.[22] The position of Mill's sub-parliaments did not differ much from local governments as regarded by Austin; Mill also thought they were necessarily subordinate and that they existed at the pleasure of the sovereign.

Utilitarians had another occasion to reveal their views on the Constitution when they considered the principle of separation of powers. This was a matter, Publius noted, that continued to "puzzle the greatest adepts in political science."[23] But not Bentham.

> As to the not absolutely nonsensical, but only very obscure clause, about a society's having "the separation of powers determined," it seems to be the result of a confused idea of an intended application of the old maxim, *Divide et impera:* the governed area to have the governors under their governance, by having them divided among themselves. A still older maxim . . . I am inclined to think a truer one, is, that a house divided against itself cannot stand.[24]

For Bentham only one branch would have the power of decision: "In my view of the matter the administrative and the judiciary are two authorities employed to give execution and effect to the will of the Legislative."[25] Bentham did not share Publius's belief that the accumulation of executive, legislative, and judicial powers was "the very definition of tyranny" and that the principle of separation was a truth "stamped with the authority of [the] more enlightened patrons of liberty."[26]

The utilitarian response to the principle of separation of power was also evident in discussions of mixed government—a notion, associated with Montesquieu, Blackstone, and De Lolme, that a government, such as the British, might combine monarchy, aristocracy, and democracy. Such a combination, according to Blackstone, would yield the benefits while reducing the disadvantages of each of these simple forms.[27] Unlike the division into branches of government under the separation principle, in mixed government the three forms were not differentiated according to function, but the division of power was justified in terms of checks and balances, as it was with the separation of power. James Mill, following Bentham, reacted to this with disbelief. Since all persons actively sought their own advantage, he argued, two of the recipients among whom power was divided would combine to dominate and exploit the third. It was a visionary supposition to believe "they balance one another, and by mutual checks produce good government."[28]

Utilitarian response to the separation of powers can also be found in opinions about a division of the legislature into two chambers. The Senate, Bentham said, was "a separation of power without any utility." He objected on several grounds—it caused delay and checked the power of the more democratically elected House. Most important, however, it violated his belief in a unified, all-powerful legislature. The Senate was useless and a hurtful encumbrance, and he looked forward to the progress of civilization, which would "lop off that unnecessary complication of power and make the Legislature one and indivisible."[29]

Judicial review was another matter considered by utilitarians that revealed their views on separation of powers. Bentham was opposed to allowing judicial limitations on the legislature. "Give to the Judges a power of annulling [the legislature's] acts; and you transfer a portion of the supreme power from an assembly which the people have had *some* share, at least, in chusing, to a set of men in the choice of whom they have not the least imaginable share."[30] Austin disagreed with Bentham, but without contradicting his position on supreme legislative sovereignty. "I by no means disapprove of what Mr. Bentham has chosen to call by the disrespectful . . . name of judge-made law." Austin thought such law was necessary and that in lawmaking judges were superior to the avowed legislators. But he decided—and this is how he avoided self-contradiction—that when "judiciary law" was made the judges were acting as a "subordinate source" of sovereignty. In doing this the judges were "exercising *legislative,* and not *judicial* functions." When judges did this, Austin regarded them as interpreting and extending already existing law, not as evaluating and possibly overruling statute law.[31] Thus, while allowing judges to make law, Austin, like Bentham, was not opening a door to judicial review. With John Stuart Mill, however, the utilitarian position eroded considerably. He praised the founders for establishing the Supreme Court and approved the principle of judicial review, but he recognized the significance of the Court's decision in the Dred Scott case in bringing about the Civil War.[32]

Another feature of the Constitution that led to differences with utilitarians was its inclusion of parts of English common law. There were many such borrowings, especially common-law procedural rights, including habeas corpus, protection against ex post facto laws, protection from general search and seizure, the right to confront witnesses, and especially trial by jury. Publius even made explicit the wish "to recognize the ancient law" and referred to "the judicious Blackstone."[33]

Utilitarians generally rejected common law, and this implied criticism of those parts of the Constitution that incorporated it. For the utilitarians the common law reflected tradition and the dead hand of the past, and therefore it was regarded as an obstacle to reform. In Bentham's view, common law was based "on some random decision, or string of frequently contradictory decisions, pronounced in this or that barbarous age, almost always without any intelligible reason, under the impulse of some private or sinister interest, . . . without thought . . . of any such circumstances or exigencies, as those of the people . . . at the present time." It created uncertainty and uncognoscibility, Bentham complained, and it gave arbitrary power to judges, "with the semblance of a set of rules to serve as a *screen* to it," and, furthermore, it was incorrigible.[34] Austin also held common law to be a chaos that arose from "savage and stupid ages"; it made a people "the slaves of custom," which indicated that they were "in the infancy of reason."[35] James Mill, also following Bentham, looked on the common law as "the barbarous product of a barbarous age"; he was astonished that it was "handed down to a later and civilized age in a state of more perfect preservation, than any other monument, not physical and indestructible, of rude antiquity."[36]

The utilitarians would have replaced common law with codes. They were enthusiasts for codification (a word Bentham invented), and this was the occasion for Bentham's proselytizing among Americans, including James Madison, John Quincy Adams, Andrew Jackson, and the governors of most of the states. In 1811 to Madison he offered to draw up a complete body of statute law for the United States—what he called a Pannomion. This would remove the shapeless, unwritten common law, which was still a yoke around Americans' necks, causing them to be perplexed and plagued. Madison, it hardly need be said, was skeptical. He allowed five years to elapse before replying, explaining that the war had made communication between them unseemly and mentioning that he also had other occupations. He esteemed Bentham's work, but he gently hinted that Bentham's project was impracticable and unlikely to achieve all that was claimed.[37]

Underlying Assumptions and Basic Principles

The utilitiarians were harsh judges of important features of the American Constitution and the institutional framework established by it—

individual rights, federalism and local government, separation of powers, judicial review, the Senate, and the incorporation of common-law protections. But they did not stop here. Many of the assumptions and principles underlying the Constitution were also targets for utilitarian criticism, including the understanding of human nature, the role of interests in politics, the place of conflict and faction, and the attitude to the populace and majoritarianism.

The utilitarian view of human nature can be traced to Hobbes. According to Bentham, each individual seeks to maximize pleasure and minimize pain. Those who understood motives differently "deal in sounds instead of sense, in caprice instead of reason, in darkness instead of light." The "selfish and dissocial passions" were necessary, the first for the very existence of each individual, the second to his security.[38] James Mill described the implications of this view for politics. Each person desired to render the person and property of others subservient to his pleasure, and "the desire of the object implies the desire of the power necessary to accomplish the object." The desire of power for this purpose, therefore, was "a grand governing law of human nature."[39]

Publius would not have disagreed entirely with this outlook. *The Federalist* includes frequent references to human selfishness and the ambitious, vindictive, and rapacious character of men. Because of these things, because men were not angels, government was necessary. The passions of men will not conform to the dictates of reason and justice. Moreover, "the fiery and destructive passions of war reign in the human breast with much more powerful sway than the mild and beneficent sentiments of peace." No wonder Publius said that "there is a degree of depravity in mankind which requires a certain degree of circumspection and distrust." But he revealed his ambivalence by indicating that there was more to human nature than this. The "supposition of universal venality in human nature is little less an error in political reasoning, than the supposition of universal rectitude." Thus while there was some, perhaps a preponderance of, depravity, there were also "other qualities in human nature which justify a certain portion of esteem and confidence." Republican government especially presupposed the existence of these better qualities. Were they not to be found—which was what the utilitarians argued—"the inference would be, that there is not sufficient virtue among men for self-government; and that nothing less than the chains of despotism can restrain them from destroying and devouring one another."[40]

Different conceptions of interest and class and conflict accompanied these different views on human nature. For Publius, since there was some self-seeking in human nature, there would also be discordant interests. These had many sources. There would be differences of opinion arising from the fallibility in man's use of reason; from zeal for different opinions concerning religion, government, and many other points; and from attachment to different leaders ambitiously contending for power; perhaps most important, there were differences over property. Men had different faculties, manners, habits, and these led to the possession of different degrees and kinds of property. As a consequence, there ensued "a division of society into different interests and parties" and also into different classes. But even if none of these differences over property or if none of the other occasions for differences existed, "so strong is this propensity of mankind to fall into mutual animosities, that where no substantial occasion presents itself, the most frivolous and fanciful distinctions have been sufficient to kindle their unfriendly passions and excite their most violent conflicts." So great was the diversity in the faculties of men that there was "an insuperable obstacle to a uniformity of interests."[41]

The utilitarians' view of human nature produced an altogether different understanding of interests. Whereas Publius regarded interests as inherently varied, the utilitarians regarded them as uniform, that is, as universal and therefore shared by the entire populace. This was not easily observable, however, when political arrangements were defective, for they allowed the formation of sinister interests, which were particular and separate, the very opposite of universal. Any persons, given an opportunity, would, as James Mill said, "sacrifice the interests of other men to their own."[42] If political arrangements did not prevent such things, there would be sinister interests. In response to a prevailing doctrine of parliamentary representation that called for representation of a variety of propertied and professional groups (merchants, manufacturers, landed proprietors, military officers, lawyers), James Mill argued that each of these groups had sinister interests.[43] Such sinister interests did not have to prevail, however; when they were not allowed to establish themselves, only the universal interest of the entire populace remained. To promote this, of course, required democracy.

This belief in the underlying reality of the universal interest implied that conflicts of interest were unnecessary, even that they were undesirable, for such conflicts were obstacles to the recognition of the underlying reality of shared interests. This outlook was evident in Austin's explanation of "the healing principle of utility": by consulting the criterion of utility, contestants would recognize that they could come closer to reaching their goals by compromising differences than by refusing to do so, and thus they would approach mutual understanding. The healing principle of utility would make civil war and revolution much less likely.[44] Austin's disapproval of conflict was carried so far as to lead him to say that the Reformation had "on the whole, been an evil to mankind," for it popularized theological questions, made the multitude quarrelsome, and produced a divisive sectarianism.[45] Bentham held the same view of conflict. "Men, let them but once clearly understand one another, will not be long ere they agree. It is the perplexity of ambiguous and sophisticated discourse that . . . stimulates and inflames the passions." Contestants "would stand a much better chance of being adjusted than at present, were they but explicitly and constantly referred at once to the principle of *utility*." Here was "a plain and open road . . . to reconcilement at the last."[46]

These views assumed that shared values could be recognized and that potential near unanimity of opinions and the universal interest could be established. They also meant that there was no necessity for permanent cleavages in society, including those involving social and economic classes. When the utilitarians turned to politics, they claimed to write and act on behalf of "the people," that is, those in whom the universal interest was located. "The People, that is, the Mass of the community," James Mill wrote, "are sometimes called a class; but that is only to distinguish them from the aristocratical class. In the proper meaning of the term class, it is not applicable to the People. No interest is in common to them, which is not in common to the rest of the community."[47] Any particular class, including the middle class, would have had a separate and sinister interest.[48] Thus whereas Publius accepted class divisions, the utilitarians rejected them. What were inevitably different interests for Publius were for the utilitarians unnecessarily separate and sinister interests. Whereas the promotion of shared, universal interest was for Publius (in a famous passage in *Federalist* No. 10) either impracticable or unwise and a remedy worse than the disease it was meant to treat, for the utilitarians it was an important goal in politics.

From these views on interests, the identification of the most important political problem and its remedy emerged. For the utilitarians the problem was to establish obstacles to sinister interests and to promote the universal interest, and the remedy was to provide for representation of all the people by means of universal suffrage. Bentham advocated this in his *Plan of Parliamentary Reform* and *Constitutional Code,* and most of his disciples also did so. Bentham called this "democratical ascendancy." Without it there was "corrupted influence [which] . . . separate, partial, and sinister interests . . . obtained over the democratical interest."[49]

Publius recognized greater complexity, and he especially had qualified views about majoritarianism. This is not to say that there was no similarities in the democratic rhetoric used by him and by the utilitarians. Publius held that "the people are the only legitimate fountain of power" and that the fabric of American government "ought to rest on the solid basis of *the consent of the people*. The streams of national power ought to flow immediately from that pure, original fountain of all legitimate authority." He also argued that representatives should be dependent on and in sympathy with the people and that, to achieve this, frequent elections were required.[50]

Such similarities in rhetoric, however, disguised important differences, especially regarding the power of majorities. Publius's difficulty with majorities arose from his concern with faction, which was a "poison" that could be found in both a minority and a majority. Thus even a majority could consist of a group of citizens who were united and actuated by some common impulse of passion or interest and who were adverse to the rights of other citizens or to the permanent and aggregate interests of the community. Even a majority could "display the infirmities and depravities of the human characater," and majorities could also be hurried "into improprieties and excesses." This was made more problematic because the government was popular, which enabled the majority "to sacrifice to its ruling passion or interest both the public good and the rights of other citizens." The framers therefore sought to protect against the dangers of majority faction but without violating the republican principle of popular government. "To secure the public good and private rights against the danger of such a faction, and at the same time to preserve the spirit and the form of popular government, is then the great object to which our inquiries are directed."[51] This required practical ingenuity and theoretical clarity, and the political judgments made by Publius relied on a recognition of complexities that was notably absent from the vision of pure democracy produced by the utilitarians.

Publius argued that the two imperfectly compatible purposes could be reconciled by referring to the varied interests that were to be found in the populace, especially if it was the populace of a large, extended republic. By recognizing diversity, that is, "by comprehending in the society so many separate descriptions of citizens as will render an unjust combination of a majority of the whole improbable, if not impracticable," the problem might be solved. Thus, "Whilst all authority . . . will be derived from and dependent on the society, the society itself will be broken into so many parts, interests and classes of citizens, that the rights of individuals, or of the minority, will be in little danger from interested combinations of the majority." Had the

Federalists, like the utilitarians, perceived the populace as uniform in interests and motives, they would have been incapable of the "inventions of prudence," as Publius called them, which allowed for the reconciliation of popular government with protection against factious majorities.[52]

The Ways of Making Political Judgments

Apart from differences about institutions and substantive principles and underlying assumptions, the framers were also different from the utilitarians in their manner of arriving at political judgments. The framers' purpose was to understand how new political institutions would work. Thus it was necessary to succeed in "calculating [their] probable effects" and to form "a just estimate of their real tendency to advance or obstruct the public good." For this the framers had to understand political conduct not only as they observed it but also as it was found in historical experience and as it might occur in conceivable circumstances in the future. "Constructions of civil government are not to be framed upon a calculation of existing exigencies, but upon a combination of these with the probable exigencies of ages, according to the natural and tried course of human affairs." Consequently the framers' thinking was based on a "rational calculation of probabilities," and in this sense it was consequentialist and can be regarded, in a very loose sense of the term, as "utilitarian." This kind of thinking required an appreciation of the imponderables in the making of political judgments, and therefore it proceeded cautiously and with moderation. In this respect it contrasted markedly with Bentham's and Austin's precise definitions of their subject and their boldness and self-confidence.[53]

To evaluate the new institutions, the framers began by looking to the past. *The Federalist* contains frequent appeals to history. Publius drew examples from the history of Greek cities, the Roman republic, Renaissance principalities, and the experience of Great Britain. History was a source of "political lessons, both of the monitory and exemplary kind." This was part of his general empiricism: "Let us consult experience, the guide that ought always to be followed whenever it can be found."[54] History had its limitations, however, for the experience of other nations might not have a bearing on American circumstances. American popular government had to be different from the republics of Sparta and Rome, and this rendered "extreme circumspection necessary." Moreover, although history might help identify the causes of problems, it "can therefore furnish no other light than that of beacons, which give warning of the course to be

abstract thinking, used the word "utopian" disapprovingly. He also rejected the perfectionism that was associated with such intellectual tendencies. A perfect work was not to be expected from imperfect man; it was difficult to avoid imperfection in deliberations that were the result of compromise of dissimilar interests and inclinations. A choice, he explained, had to be made, "if not of the lesser evil, at least of the *greater, not the perfect,* good."[62] Moreover, the framers had a greater wish to avoid known and not improbable evils like anarchy and tyranny than to achieve conditions infinitely superior to what had ever been established before. In addition, the Constitution they drafted was intended to allow change only in small increments, and this was something not acceptable to utopians.

The utilitarians, in contrast, sometimes displayed symptoms of the opposite kind. Bentham had the utopian's aspiration to explain everything in terms of one simple principle. The principle of utility, he said, "is itself the sole and all-sufficient reason for every point of practice whatsoever."[63] He also rejected the ideas (exemplified by Blackstone) that he regarded as justificatory of the existing order, and he believed that a new, reformed, rational, and democratic regime could be readily established if only bad motives could be frustrated so that clear thoughts might prevail. He also justified his belief in the viability of his ideal regime by assumptions and principles that many others regarded as utterly unrealistic.

This outlook was adopted by some of Bentham's disciples, notably James Mill and John Stuart Mill as a young man. James Mill argued that there was no difference between theory and practice; those who depreciated theory and upheld practice were merely trying to berate philosophy.[64] John Stuart Mill, on reading Bentham on law and morals, reported "the feeling [that] rushed upon me, that all previous moralists were superseded, and that here indeed was the commencement of a new era in thought." The principle of utility, he said, "gave unity to my conceptions of things. I now had opinions; a creed, a doctrine, a philosophy; in one among the best senses of the word, a religion." Mill also reported that with regard to the political application of Bentham's principle, "the French *philosophes* of the eighteenth century were the example we [including his like-minded friends] sought to imitate, and we hoped to accomplish no less results." He also acknowledged his "youthful fanaticism."[65] These were the characteristics that provoked Macaulay's well-known attack on the utilitarian theory of government in which he particularly criticized the unrealistic and abstract and deductive character of James Mill's political reasoning.[66] John Stuart Mill in 1835, still not emancipated from his doctrinairism, defended the making of governments "by preconceived and systematic design"—what he called "the practicability of Utopianism."[67]

The Meaning and Value of Liberty

The differences between the utilitarians and the authors of the Constitution went beyond institutions and underlying principles and the ways of making political judgments. They would also have disagreed about the meaning and value of liberty. The structure and substance of the defense of the Constitution offered by Publius indicates that liberty had central importance. His purpose was to avoid both tyranny and anarchy: tyranny because it would obviously be incompatible with liberty and anarchy because it would allow the assertion of power by factions and therefore threaten the liberty of others and ultimately turn into tyranny. It was in the middle ground between tyranny and anarchy that liberty could be established, and it was the purpose of the "confederated republic"[68] to combine the self-government that came from republicanism with the boundaries within which liberty could flourish that were provided by the federal idea.

The utilitarians, despite their prominence in the liberal tradition, were often indifferent to liberty or equivocal about it. Bentham, with his preference for precise and coldly neutral language, was deeply suspicious of the very word:

> At the mention of liberty every man conceives it to be his right, and many a man conceives it to be his duty to fall into a passion. . . . the less the use that is made of [the word liberty], the better. I would no more use the word liberty in my conversation when I could get another that would answer the purpose, than I would brandy in my diet, if any physicians did not order me: both cloud the understanding and inflame the passions.[69]

When he turned to argument, Bentham held that liberty was inversely proportional to law: liberty was necessarily diminished by law. Therefore maximizing liberty created a threat of anarchy.[70] Since he regarded law as the main instrument for promoting individual and collective happiness (that is, utility), liberty, the very antithesis of law, was subordinated to it. This conclusion was shared by Austin, who noted that it was only "to the ignorant and bawling fanatics who stun you with their pother about liberty, political or civil liberty seems to be the principle end for which government ought to exist," and he added, "Political or civil liberty has been erected into an idol, and extolled with extravagant praises by doting and fanatical worshippers." He also said, "political or civil liberty is not more worthy of eulogy than political or legal restraint."[71]

In yet another argument about liberty that revealed his implicit disapproval of the Constitution, Bentham held that free government did not depend on limitations; power was supreme, in free no less than in despotic governments. A regime was made free, he continued, by virtue of wide participation made possible through the distribution of power among several ranks, frequent and easy changes of position between governors and governed, the governor's obligation to give reasons for his public acts, and the possibility of expressing grievances through liberty of the press and public association.

The emphasis on participation is clear, but it is difficult to reconcile Bentham's mentioning of liberty of press and association (here and elsewhere) with his insistence that even in a free government the supreme power was without legal limitations.[72] There is no question that Bentham recognized the utility of liberty of the press as a way of communicating between citizens and government and as a way of discouraging abuse of power.[73] Yet his rationale for liberty of the press was always subordinated to his theory or sovereignty and his promotion of the greatest happiness. Its most important function was to encourage discussion as a means of sifting out error so that utilitarian calculations would be uniformly used. Bentham characteristically

> planned to make use of freedoms relating to the press and to public discussion in order to secure, in a seemingly paradoxical way, a more punctual and complete obedience on the part of citizens under a 'government of laws.' His purpose remained manipulative in spite of his endorsement of specific sorts of liberty.

For Bentham liberty was a means of obtaining security, and throughout his writings it was repudiated as an end in itself.[74] Consequently he reduced the significance of liberty as a constitutional issue, and "he abandoned Hume's position that society must everywhere and always be the arena for 'a perpetual intestine struggle . . . between authority and liberty.' "[75]

Much of the utilitarians' response to the Constitution is reflected in the contrast between their views and Tocqueville's in *Democracy in America,* for there were affinities between this work and the framers' thought, especially regarding liberty. If Bentham, who died in 1832 at eighty-four, had lived another three years, he would have been able to read the first part of *Democracy in America.* Bentham, with his theory of sovereignty, would have had no sympathy for Tocqueville's favorable treatment of federalism, separation of powers, and constitutional checks generally or with his belief that unlimited power was dangerous and contained the germ of tyranny.[76] With his view of democracy, Bentham would have been skeptical about Tocqueville's greatest concern, that democracy could be combined with tyranny. In keeping with this, Bentham also had no sensitivity to the problem of the tyranny of the majority (a notion that Tocqueville seems to have derived from the concept of majority faction in *Federalist* No. 10). Tocqueville's belief that juries were useful for the opportunity they provided citizens to participate in governing and for their educational function would strike no sympathetic chord in Bentham, who was highly critical of the ignorance and inefficiency of juries. And Tocqueville's approval of the legal profession for its respect for precedent and the common law, which allowed it to contribute to the mitigation of the tyranny of the majority, would have enraged Bentham. In Bentham's view lawyers were "indiscriminate defender[s] of right and wrong"; they were "a class of persons against whom he certainly [had] a most inveterate hatred."[77]

The distance between Bentham and Tocqueville was even greater than indicated by these considerations. Tocqueville's belief that religion served as a welcome restraint on ambition and passion and that it was perfectly compatible with recognition of the principle of separation of church and state would have been rejected by Bentham, who regarded religion as incompatible with rational politics.

A difference of even greater significance would have arisen had Bentham been able to consider Tocqueville's conception of individualism. It was the unwholesome condition of isolation that left individuals without the attachments to others and to larger communities, and when it existed, according to Tocqueville, a society was ripe for despotism. Although Publius used different language to describe it, his references to the reverence and attachment required of citizens indicate that he was aware of this feature of a good regime, as did his insistence that "other qualities" than mere selfishness in human nature were necessary for republican government. But to Bentham Tocqueville's conception of individualism would have been a correct description of all individuals in their relationships to others, for he insisted that the community was a fictitious entity and that utilitarian applications could be made only with regard to individuals.[78]

Austin also disagreed with Tocqueville in ways that reflected his dissatisfaction with the Constitution. Austin, with a theory of sovereignty similar to Bentham's, could not have shared Tocqueville's views on federalism and constitutional limitations. His greatest difference with Tocqueville, however, concerned centralization. In contrast to Tocqueville's appreciation of decentralization as a condition favorable to liberty, Austin was an aggressive defender of centralization and in 1846 wrote a long article to set forth its advantages. The contrast with Tocqueville's well-known position was so evident that Austin probably had Tocqueville in mind when he wrote it. Although he did not mention him, there are clear allusions to Tocqueville. Austin had contempt for those with "silly regrets for the former [French] provinces and their privileges," and he mentioned the "tyranny of the majority" only to ridicule the notion.[79]

John Stuart Mill was also critical of Tocqueville in ways that revealed what he thought about the Constitution, particularly its provision for liberty. When in 1835 he published his largely favorable review of part one of the *Democracy,* Mill depreciated Tocqueville's concern that a tyranny of the majority might undermine individual liberty. He even avoided an exact repetition of Tocqueville's pungent phrase and instead referred to "the omnipotence of the majority," although there is a more direct allusion when he observed that "it is not easy to see what sort of minority it can be, over which the majority can have any interest in tyrannizing." Mill concluded that "we see nothing in any of these tendencies from which any serious evil need be apprehended."[80]

When in 1840 he reviewed part two of the *Democracy,* he was willing to use Tocqueville's famous phrase but complained that it was "susceptible of a Tory application." He also tried to save democracy from association with tyranny and insisted that it was the middle class that tyrannized and that one should hold responsible not democracy but commercial civilization. Mill did appreciate Tocqueville's notion of individualism, but he did not discuss Tocqueville's argument that it might lead to the new and dreadful kind of despotism that democratic nations especially had to fear.[81]

In the famous essay *On Liberty* Mill continued to show how much he differed from Tocqueville (and, by implication, from Publius). The difference here is perhaps most striking in view of the superficial similarities, which have led to a commonly held opinion that Mill and Tocqueville thought alike on matters relating to individual liberty. After all, both gave the highest priority to individual liberty, and both feared the intrusion of social pressures; Mill even acknowledged in this essay that " 'the tyranny of the majority' is now [1859] generally included among the evils against which society requires to be on its guard."[82] This common ground, however, conceals a vast difference about the conditions that would allow liberty to flourish. Whereas for Mill custom and religion and the expectations of one's peers in associations and other groups were oppressive and, in the case of custom, despotic, for Tocqueville these were the things that would serve as obstacles to tyranny and would allow liberty to flourish. What for Mill was an ideally free society was Tocqueville's nightmare, that is a society without custom and religion and therefore vulnerable to democratic despotism. And the American regime, which despite its defects Tocqueville welcomed with hope because it promised liberty in a democracy, was, from Mill's point of view, one in which there was the despotism of custom, the oppressiveness of religion, submission of individuals to group pressures in their associational activities, and obstacles to improvement.

These differences between Mill and Tocqueville arose from divergent conceptions of liberty. Mill looked for liberation from the rules and expectations of conventional social life, whereas Tocqueville, while appreciating the value of individuality, above all wished to secure that essentially political liberty that could exist only by the avoidance of despotism. In this, as in so many things, Tocqueville and Publius came to similar conclusions. Mill, however, thought that political liberty was unproblematic but that a claim to freedom in the social realm was still to be established. "Protection . . . against the tyranny of the magistrate is not enough: there needs protection also against the tyranny of prevailing opinion and feeling." About liberty in the public realm Mill felt no uneasiness; to believe that the tyranny of the majority operated chiefly through public authorities (an allusion to the concern with majority faction in *Federalist* No. 10) was vulgar.[83] Mill was complacent about the problem that most worried Publius.

In view of the differences between Bentham and Mill, one cannot attribute a single view of liberty to utilitarian thought. Whereas Bentham and Austin reduced the importance of individual liberty, Mill wished to extend its boundaries so that the individual would be emancipated not only in the political realm but also from social, religious, and customary moral restrictions. The utilitarians represented the extremes of insensitivity to the importance of liberty and hypersensitivity to restrictions on it. In contrast, the framers, like Tocqueville, took a middle position, sharing neither Bentham's complacency nor Mill's belief that custom and religion posed a threat to individuality.

Conclusion

One might ask why the utilitarians and the framers, both associated with liberalism, differed so much. For despite their shared acceptance of economic individualism and high expectations from commerce and capitalism and their similar though not identical understandings about human nature, they had vast differences about rights and individual liberty and the separation of powers and constitutional limitations and a host of other matters. Although both are connected with the liberal tradition, it is evident that they were fundamentally different in the ways they related liberalism to their constitutional thought.

The framers did not share the utilitarians' ambition to establish an ideal regime by designing political institutions in light of their philosophic understanding. They were prepared to settle for much less: they regarded it as sufficient to avoid abhorrent conditions, particularly tyranny and anarchy. Publius noted the alternation of calms and furious storms and the continual agitation that led to "a state of perpetual vibration between the extremes of tyranny and anarchy."[84] They were familiar with this phenomenon from reading Thucydides, Polybius, and Aristotle.[85] They had also read Blackstone's warning that liberties were sometimes "depressed by overbearing and tyrannical princes; at others [that is, other times] so luxuriant as even to tend to anarchy."[86] John Adams, whose *Defense of the Constitutions* (1787) was dominated by this understanding, observed that "the pendulum was for ever on the swing," and he warned against "perpetual altercations of rebellion and tyranny, and butcheries of thousands upon every revolution from one to the other." On the one hand, there would be a move to the extreme of anarchy with "everlasting fluctuations, revolutions, and horrors, until," on the other hand, "a standing army, with a general at its head, commands the peace," that is, there is a move to tyranny.[87]

This was not a matter of historical imagination, for anarchy and tyranny were regarded as real possibilities. Publius was hypersensitive to "tumult and disorder" and quite nervous about anarchy and rebellion. This was evident in his frequent allusions to Shays's Rebellion, in his assertion that "seditions and insurrections are, unhappily, maladies as inseparable from the body politic as tumors and eruptions from the naural body," and in his observation that wars and rebellions were the "two most mortal diseases of society." Madison thought that "the insurrections in Massts. admonished all the States of the danger to which they were exposed,"and he believed the country was "rapidly approaching to anarchy."[88] Turning to the other extreme, tyranny was also an authentic problem. The framers had a lively sense of its possibility, and the threat of it was often on their lips, especially as political philosophy and history showed that it was the most likely growth from the soil of anarchy. Publius foresaw the possibility of "the same engines of despotism which have been the scourge of the Old World," and already in the first of the papers he warned that there was an easy move from demagogic zeal for liberty to despotism and tyranny.[89]

The framers, because they so emphasized the importance of avoiding the abhorrent extremes of tyranny and anarchy, developed an understanding of the way principles should be connected with institutions that distinguished them from the utilitarians and that also helps explain why they differed about so many other matters.

To avoid both extremes of tyranny and anarchy, it was necessary to establish middle ground where there would be stability without tyranny and liberty without anarchy. This required balancing and combining opposing powers, interests, and institutions and also recognizing the different principles with which the spokesmen for those powers, interests, and institutions sought to establish the validity of their claims. Publius acknowledged the difficulty of blending stability and liberty, especially as each required different things, but the solution was made possible by recognizing that a constitution could embody and mediate among opposing principles.[90] Whereas the doctrinaire utilitarians endorsed simple democracy based on a coherent theory that was unacceptable to the framers, American constitutional thought, with its emphasis on a balance of discordant principles, exemplified what James Mill contemptuously called "a perpetual system of compromise, a perpetual trimming."[91]

The framers' remedy for the twin threats of anarchy and tyranny was in keeping with their practical cast of mind. Wanting stability but not tyranny and liberty but not anarchy, they went in for mixing and balancing and the artful improvisations that were the novelties for which they are best known. This approach—and accomplishment—was the very opposite of the simple remedies put forth by the utilitarians. The unchecked democracy of the utilitarians was a perfect exemplification of the simple government that was the antithesis of the balanced and mixed regime defended by the Americans. By institutionalizing complexity the framers obscured their philosophic origins and perhaps opened the door to the actualization of unexplored philosophic assumptions, but this was the price of not adopting political arrangements, such as those recommended by the utilitarians, for which abhorrent consequences were foreseeable.

9
Idealism

Susan Shell

The idealist, as popular usage would have it, is a moralist: a person guided by ideals or visions of how things ought to be. Of course, anyone who is not utterly vicious can be said to be guided by a sense of *ought*. The idealist is typically distinguished, in popular usage, by the degree to which he distinguishes his ideals, his *ought*, from what is and by the optimism with which he pursues that ought. He is likely to view the world with indignation and yet at the same time with hope. For, again typically, the distance between his visions and the world does not lead him to turn away from the world in resignation or despair. His visions are not symbols of acceptance but calls to action; he sees them not as mere wishful models but as practical goals.

At the same time, the idealist is not simply an activist. Again typically, he is more concerned with rightness of intention than with certainty of result, and he perceives his own rectitude as largely constituted by the purity of his ideals, their lack of taint by or compromise with the world he would transform. Idealism harbors an uneasy tension between external (or this worldly) concern for results and an often overriding internal (or otherworldly) concern for purity of conscience. For some, faith in Divine Providence, belief that so long as one does one's duty "God will provide," has helped to relieve the tension. For others it has been eased through a secular faith in "progress" or "history."

Idealism understood in this popular sense has served as a counterpoint to the dominant materialist and worldly trend in American life, sometimes enhancing that trend, more often opposing it. Tocqueville, fearing the power of materialism in our young democracy, looked to religion to maintain a sense of the spiritual or ideal; later Henry Adams, in his own discussion of the ideals of the early Americans, spoke of commercial and technological expansion, the very stuff of worldly success, as itself a national ideal, able to rouse in Americans a sublime enthusiasm and willingness for sacrifice that narrow self-interest alone could never inspire. In matters domestic, there have been traces of idealism both in Americans' celebration of worldly success (be it about the locomotive or the moon landing) and, more typically, in recurrent efforts (be they on the part of transcendentalists in the nineteenth century or hippies in the twentieth) to transcend the material goals of a commercial society. In matters of foreign policy, traces of idealism have appeared in a recurrent faith (bordering on the jingoistic) in the expansive historical destiny of America and, more typically, in a concern with (putative) moral goals as distinguished from mere national interest, that is, as an abhorrence of *Realpolitik.* To the extent that idealism implies an unwillingness to dirty one's hands or conscience with improper or unpleasant means, however seemingly desirable the results, it also finds an example in World War II pacifists for whom the good of defeating Hitler could not outweigh the evil of engaging in war itself and in radical abolitionists who preferred withdrawal from the Union (and retention of slavery in the South) to continued dealings with the slave power, even if such dealings might ultimately mitigate slavery, or end it.

A portion of this idealist strain in America may be traced to religion; a portion may be traced to extraneous social causes. But a portion undoubtedly stems from the American founding itself and the tradition associated with it. For the Declaration of Independence explicitly presents itself as deriving from universal and self-evident principles of justice and, hence, as constituting a potential model to the world. For its part, the U.S. Constitution is neither a cold contract of prudence nor an effusive assertion of *Volkgeist,* but the foundation of what Abraham Lincoln once called our "political religion," the core beliefs that constitute us as a country and as a nation.

We are here confronted with a paradox: as earlier chapters of this volume have argued, the Constitution derives its fundamental principles largely from the regimen of the reduced moral expectations characteristic of the liberalism of Montesquieu and Locke. It begins with the equal rights of individuals, each assumed to be moved by a strong and generally overriding concern for self-preservation and, secondarily, for comfort. And yet, in enshrining these concerns as rights, worthy to be upheld even at cost of life, the Constitution seems to lift these concerns above themselves. There is, it appears, a tension at the heart of liberalism between the self-interested character of the rights it claims and the sacrifices of self-interest it must call upon if those rights are to be properly upheld—indeed, if civil life is to be possible at all. To the extent that this tension informs the civic tradition that the Constitution has inspired, it helps to explain the ongoing appeal of idealism in American life as an expression of a yearning for spiritual nourishment beyond the resources of a liberalism too narrowly and egoistically defined.[1]

Philosophical Idealism

A philosophical school or tradition principally associated with Immanuel Kant, Johann Gottlieb Fichte, and Georg Wilhelm Friedrich Hegel speaks directly to this issue.

The philosophical idealism that now concerns us differs from, although it also has many affinities with, the popular idealism just described. The idealism of Kant, Fichte, and Hegel is not the same as moralism. Nor is it identical with the belief that action should be guided by a higher spiritual purpose. Still less is it the simple opposite of materialism. The term *idealism,* it is true, is often used to denote any or all of these things. In modern times, however, idealism has also come to assume a unique political and philosophic meaning, informed by a series of theoretical and moral problems that previous chapters of this book have charted.

Idealism in the special sense that now concerns us emerged on the modern scene as one of many heirs of Rousseau's revolutionary understanding of freedom. The philosophical idealists' appropriations of this understanding vary—yet all share in the (skewed) Rousseauian legacy of viewing freedom as divided from nature in a particularly unambiguous and emphatic way. Idealism begins with dualism, with the assertion of a radical distinction between nature and freedom, matter and will, what the mind or self encounters and what the mind or self projects.

For all their doubts about the moral sufficiency of classical liberalism, the philosophic idealists share with liberals a general optimism—lacking in Rousseau (but surely attractive to many Americans)—concerning both the desirability of scientific progress and the ultimate solubility of the political problem. The idealists take to heart Rousseau's questioning of the liberal natural rights doctrine while retaining a liberal faith in the power of man to conquer nature. Thus they tend to ignore or miss the more pessimistic implications of Rousseau's teaching. Where Rousseau looked ambiguously to nature or to precivilized society as the best condition possible for man, Kant and Fichte seek it in the civilizing future, while Hegel claims to find it in the here and now. Justice for these philosophers is not a problematic dream but a rational goal, while science and the civilizing arts are not the enemy of morality but its tool. Others took Rousseau's thought in the direction of melancholy resignation or subdued acceptance of the necessity of imperfection in human affairs. Kant and Fichte, however, find in his thought a call to political action and basis for moral hope.

The philosophical idealists' optimistic reading of Rousseau has important consequences for their treatment of liberalism. Where Rousseau rejected a politics based on enlightened self-interest at the expense of public-spirited citizenship, the idealists find much in such a politics to endorse. Where Rousseau rejected commercial society and representative government as inadequate and corrupting arenas for political freedom, the idealists seek in one way or another to retain and redeem them. In philosophical idealism, liberal optimism concerning the desirability of technological progress and the viability of a society based largely on the satisfaction of private wants combines—sometimes jarringly—with Rousseauian pessimism concerning the moral and spiritual sufficiency of such a society.

A final feature of the philosophical idealists' relation to Rousseau deserves mention. The idealists embrace not only Rousseau's longing to fill the moral and spiritual vacuum left by the new science but also his conviction that the mind can fill this vacuum. For Rousseau, imagination was to be the vehicle of this renewal of spiritual plenitude. For the philosophical idealists, reason itself serves to fill the void. Unable to find a basis in nature for the sublime, all these thinkers sought exaltation in the emanations of the self. For Rousseau, who linked the self's creative power with imagination, the products of the self never entirely transcended the status of mere appearances or pleasant delusions. For the idealists, on the contrary, who linked the self's creative power with "reason" or "will" or "spirit," the products of the self are ultimately more objective and substantial than nature itself.[2]

In a sense, the philosophical idealists seek to overcome the moral and spiritual crisis posed by modern science by a kind of mental operation bootstrap (suspended, some would say, by sky hooks). The ultimate failure of their ambitious project, if failure it be, does not, however, detract from the instructive earnestness and rigor with which they pursue it. For Kant, Fichte, and Hegel, the problem of reconciling the insights of modern science with the claims of common sense morality becomes thematic. If, in the face of modern science, the tenets of popular idealism retain a serious claim to our secular allegiance, a part of the reason at least is likely to be found in the teachings of these three thinkers.

Kant and the Appeal to Human Dignity

For Immanuel Kant (1724–1804), Rousseauian freedom meant primarily moral freedom or accountability—the capacity to merit moral praise or blame. Kant had begun his career as a philosopher of nature, pursuing a course influenced both by the German rationalist tradition and by the Newtonian school newer to Germany. Moved by the explanatory power of modern science, he was also struck by its apparent lack of support for human moral aspirations and concerns. What especially alarmed him was the seeming disappearance, in Newton's mechanistically determined universe, of human freedom, our power to act and be held accountable for our deeds. The moral implications of this lack seemed to Kant enormous. Newtonian science appeared to Kant essentially correct in its description of the world. If science and morality could not be reconciled, science must prevail. Kant's moral misgivings over such an outcome led him to begin his "critical" project, a philosophical undertaking that was to set both science and morality in a new light.[3]

Rousseau, or Kant's selective reading of him, helped Kant resolve the conflict between morality and science by suggesting that freedom might be conceived not as in conflict with nature but as apart from and above it. Kant developed this suggestion in his famous doctrine that nature (or science) and freedom (or morality) constitute separate and independent realms of which freedom is the higher. The realm of nature is constituted by mere phenomena or appearances; for our access to it comes by way of the distorting forms of sensible intuition.

It is not as scientific observers but only as moral agents that we have access to things independent of the senses, things as they are in themselves. This access, to be sure, lacks the cognitive status of scientific knowledge. But it is not for that any the less morally real, coming to us by way of our individual consciousness of duty or the "moral law." Thus for Kant the validity of science, in its own realm, is maintained, while the independence and indeed preeminence of freedom and morality are upheld. Although science cannot discover freedom, neither can it deny it. And freedom, invisible to science, is confirmed by morality, as a necessary corollary of our sense of duty. For to acknowledge oneself to be morally obliged is to assume one's freedom to meet that obligation. "Ought," as Kant puts it, "implies can."

This very brief sketch of Kant's underlying philosophic strategy raises many difficulties that cannot here detain us. It must suffice to note that, despite these difficulties, Kant's reconstitution of philosophy proved an extremely attractive if controversial one; repeated attempts to get or make it right were to inspire not only Fichte and Hegel but also such philosophic movements of the later nineteenth and twentieth centuries as positivism and existentialism.

Our primary concern, however, is not with Kant's importance to the history of philosophy and science but rather with his moral and political teaching, especially with a view to its bearing on the American constitutional tradition. It is well to say at the outset that Kant was an admirer of the American Constitution and of the republican principles that it embodies. He was also a firm supporter of the liberal doctrines underlying much of constitutional thought, carrying some of these doctrines, such as the inviolability of contracts and private property rights, further than the founders did themselves. At the same time it must be stated that Kant did not think these principles had been sufficiently well established, or to use a Kantian phrase, "rationally grounded" by the classical liberal thinkers on whom the founders chiefly relied.

Part of Kant's impatience with classical liberalism stemmed from his belief that necessary truths must be knowable a priori, or without regard to nature or empirical experience. Being always subject to future revision, empirical knowledge is radically contingent and finally uncertain. For Kant, the contingent status of empirical knowledge seriously undermined the foundations of the older liberal natural rights teaching. By seeking to base rights in nature, this teaching limited them to a realm our knowledge of which could never be more than empirical and hence inconclusive. If this were all there were to human rights, they could be recognized as the transitory customs of a given age, but they could not be grasped as transcendent necessities. To provide rights with a rational and certain foundation, Kant was forced on another track, permitting him to ground them not in nature with all its vagaries but in the absolute dictates of morality and the dignity it confers upon the moral subject.

This anchoring of rights in moral dignity goes together with a detachment of rights from the down-to-earth empirical concerns with which classical liberalism associates them. To grasp the nature of this detachment we must look briefly at Kant's understanding of morality.[4]

Perhaps the most striking feature of Kantian morality is its emphasis on universality, on the rights and duties that belong universally to men as men. As something that we experience as absolute and unconditional, our sense of moral duty, according to Kant, cannot rest on natural contingencies but must find its basis in reason alone. The moral law must therefore apply not just to this or that individual (as it might were it based on such contingencies) but to all (finite) rational beings as such. And since Kant identifies rationality with freedom, or the capacity for morally imputable action, this means in human terms (Kant does not discount the possibility of rational extraterrestrial life) that it must apply to all individuals capable of being held accountable for their deeds, say every sane person over the age of ten.[5]

Corollary to this emphasis on universality is a similar stress on "universalizability," a more rigorous version of the common habit of testing the legitimacy of an act by asking, "What if everybody did it?" It is Kant's much disputed contention that the *content* of our duties can be spelled out on the basis of such a formal test, which (putatively) derives its validity, not from contingent facts about the world but from the a priori and necessary universality of the moral law.

If universality is one striking feature of Kantian morality, its emphasis on intentions over results is another. This emphasis follows from the seriousness with which Kant takes the notion of moral freedom and his corollary assumption that one can be morally praised or blamed only for that which is fully under one's control. Hence good will, not good results, is the final measure of moral worth.[6] Kant's doctrine expands upon the popular view that would reward effort and striving ahead of inborn ability and talent, and it provides a secular or nonreligious basis for the traditional religious argument that conscience matters more than consequences.

The roots of Kant's dissatisfaction with classical liberalism are perhaps best indicated in his determination to set right and duty above the morally questionable ground of prudent selfishness. This elevation is possible only, according to Kant, if virtue is wholly severed, at least in principle, from the desire for happiness. Once again, it is Kant's radical understanding of moral freedom as the basis of human dignity that makes necessary this rigid separation. For to act out of a desire for happiness is, according to Kant, to submit to natural impulse and thus to be implicated in the natural causal chain governing the realm of appearances. It is only when one acts for the sake of duty rather than happiness that one definitively transcends the dictates of nature and assumes the mantle of freedom in all its glory.

Kant calls this transcendent freedom—or action according to, and for the sake of, the law of reason—"autonomy," which he defines as submission to self-made law.[7] Rousseau's definition of freedom as self-legislation is thus pulled from its social and political moorings to a new seat in the private will. Self-legislation means for Kant in the first instance an internal act of moral resolve rather than external participation in the deliberations of a political body. At the same time, in exercising his autonomy, the individual conforms to a law that ought to govern every other rational being. Where Rousseauian self-legislation subsisted in the relation between the citizen and his particular society, Kantian autonomy bypasses earthly politics, linking the private individual directly to a universal and transcendent fellowship of reason.

How does Kant's demanding and austere moral teaching translate juridically? Curiously, Kant's moral demands upon the political order are in many respects no higher than were those of earlier liberals whose reduced moral regimen Rousseau criticized. Missing are those appeals to citizen virtue and patriotic sentiment that inflame the rhetoric of Rousseau. As Kant sees it, the central purpose of the law is not to foster public spirit or a particular virtuous way of life but rather to regulate conflict between competing wills pursuing their own personal ends. Kant hopes that these ends will be morally good ones and that the habits encouraged by civil order will help make them so. The state's main purpose, however, remains the avoidance of outer conflict, not the fostering of inner virtue.[8]

Men's status as subjects of the moral law, the foundation of their priceless dignity and worth, also gives them a primary right to protection from the lawless interference of others. Where earlier liberal thinkers spoke of a "natural right" to life, liberty, and property, Kant speaks more abstractly of an "innate right" to pursue one's private ends, whatever they may be, so long as they are compatible with the rights of others.[9] Although the coercive apparatus Kant would establish to protect these rights resembles that of Hobbes or Locke, Kant is at pains to rest it, not on empirical factors, such as natural scarcity or human greed, but on the formal requirements of freedom expressed as universal law.

Kant does hold, with Locke, that rights are mainly asserted through the possession of private property. But this is so, for Kant, not because property conduces to security or life, still less because it promotes human happiness, but rather, more formally and abstractly, because it provides men with a "means in general" to achieve their ends whatever they may be. In his efforts to dissociate his justification of rights both from the dictates and from the vagaries of nature, Kant feels compelled to sever rights from the natural bodily urges that earlier liberal thinkers intended them to serve and hence to deny any intrinsic connection between justice and human satisfaction or happiness. Justice, according to Kant, "has nothing to do with the end men have by nature, the end of achieving happiness."[10] Where Locke justified private property and the inequality it promotes through appeal to the general prosperity it also promotes, Kant attempts to rest his rights doctrine on formal considerations alone. "Justice ought to prevail," he asserts, "though the world perish," and not for the sake of enhancing men's worldly prospects, however much it may incidentally serve them.[11]

The formality of Kant's concept of rights has several important—and disturbing—political consequences. In the private sphere, it supports an almost limitless degree of material inequality unchecked by the (earlier liberal) concern with general prosperity. Locke had defended the accumulation of private wealth partly on the grounds that it increases mankind's common stock and improves the living conditions of the poor who are willing to work.[12] Kant on the contrary argues that the formal equality of men (all that justice requires) is compatible with "the greatest degree of inequality in their material possessions," whatever its effect on the general welfare.[13]

In the public sphere as well (or what Kant calls the realm of public law) his formalism has troubling implications. For Kant, as for liberal thinkers preceding him, civil society is established by a contract into which each member of society at least tacitly enters and by which he is bound. But whereas earlier liberals held that contract to be a historical or quasi-historical event, exacting men's real consent at some specific point in time, Kant treats it as frankly "ideal," a necessary demand and construction of moral reason rather than an actual past occurrence. He freely admits that the real foundations of any state almost always rest on violence and injustice. For securing men's ideal rights first requires a usurption of real power. Justice is almost invariably preceded by force. It would, of course, be well, Kant believes, if matters were otherwise and states were founded through the voluntary mutual consent of their citizens. But the injustice surrounding a state's origin does not relieve one of the obligation to obey its laws: civil law, however imperfect, is always preferable to the lawless anarchy that disobedience would in principle sanction.

What applies to the origin of civil law applies equally to its form or constitution. Ideally, the constitution of the state is always republican, the law's legitimacy deriving from the consent of the governed. What is true ideally, however, need not (though Kant hopes it will) be duplicated in the empirical institutions of a given state. For purposes of justice, it is not necessary that a people actually consent to the laws but merely that the laws be such that a rational people "could" consent to them. Kant believes no rational people, for example, would consent to the arbitrary elevation of a few to the ranks of feudal privilege.[14] A rationally administered monarchy, though, may be perfectly acceptable, so long as it rules in a "republican spirit," that is, with a view to what rational people could approve. Self-government for Kant is less a function of actual participation in the legislative process than of ideal inclusion in a hypothetical construct made up of abstract rational beings. Real political representation is eclipsed and to some extent replaced by rational administration, and the way paved for what came to be called the *Vernunftstaat* (reason state) in the nineteenth century, bureaucratic or administrative justice in the twentieth. Even today, for some Kantianized liberals, rights are to be primarily secured, not by guarding the workings of a representative political process, but by the administrative and judicial imposition of "just standards" themselves determined through appeal to "neutral principles" and other abstract models of "rational social choice."[15]

To be sure, Kant holds that his administrative "republicanism in the spirit" ought ultimately to be accompanied by a legislative republicanism "in the letter." Empirical institutions ought to reflect their ideal form, and Kant hopes that through the mutual enlightenment of princes and peoples the world can gradually be so transformed. Morality finally demands a world of peace, justice, and true republican self-government and lays upon us all the duty to work obediently and peacefully toward those ends.

It becomes important, then, for Kant to show that these moral goals, though "ideals" or free projections of reason, are not impossible to realize in the world. No amount of moral zeal, Kant believes, could weather that discouraging knowledge. Although ought implies can, men seem to need more to buttress their practical faith than the austere dictates of an a priori moral logic. Although good intentions are what count, no one can be expected to intend what he regards as impossible. Thus Kant comes to seek in nature and history a morally reassuring trajectory of progress. And here the morally undemanding forces of classical liberalism, greed and fear, come again to the fore, providing a curious sort of moral comfort. For it appears that the central goals of a morally inspired politics—peace and republicanism—can be achieved without morality. "Sooner or later," Kant avows, "the spirit of war is overturned in every state by that of commerce and enlightenment."[16] Enlightened self-interest alone can finally secure justice.

If there is a utopian element in Kant's thought, it lies less in his moral hopes per se (for man, as he acknowledges, echoing Luther, "is made from crooked wood") than in his expectation that the dictates of self-interest and those of morality can be made to coincide. Moral statecraft, he believed, can be fully reconciled with *raison d'état,* while self-interest alone can secure the peace and justice that morality demands.

Kant says "can" and not "will" secure peace and justice. Kant's edifying "conjectural history" is meant to assure the morally serious that their efforts are not in vain, not to prove that their efforts are superfluous. Later thinkers, eager to find in Kant a practical and easy guide to world peace, have often forgotten the tentative quality of his hopes. And in any case, Kant's "realistic" resort to a dependable immorality or amorality, is not without its moral difficulties and dilemmas. If the goals of a morally inspired politics can be achieved without morality, if a world of justice and peace can be brought about through the selfish dealings of immoral men, what is the moral status of such a world? "The problem of organizing a state," Kant says in his famous essay on perpetual peace, "can be solved for a nation of devils if only they are intelligent."[17] In his effort to support morality, Kant finds himself returning to the credos of Locke, Mandeville, and Montesquieu. Having culled his moral ideals a priori and apart from nature, Kant feels morally compelled to show that these ideals are workable within it. And this, ironically enough, he finds he can most easily do by returning to the very regimen of low moral expectations that his great teacher Rousseau had so adamantly rejected.

Why, one may well wonder, do Kant's political goals remain so limited? Why should not the state be expected to generate virtue as well as secure peace? One answer lies in the rigidity of his dualism, itself a product of his radical understanding of moral freedom as the foundation of human dignity. Kant does offer the hope that the habit of external law-abidingness promoted by a just state will encourage men to make the inner leap to moral goodness. He cannot, however, press this claim too far without calling into question the free and unconditioned character of that inner leap. Virtue, precisely because it depends on a radically independent inner choice, cannot be externally forced. However strong his support for moral education, its ultimate status remains problematic for Kant.

A second answer lies in the absolute priority that Kant assigns to moral over political community. Like earlier liberals and unlike Rousseau, Kant deems political participation at best a chore rather than the activity in which the citizen can be most fully free. Having transformed Rousseau's notion of political self-legislation into private moral terms, the most important community becomes for Kant the universal ethical community, a "kingdom of ends" uniting every rational being.[18] From such a vantage point, the divisions of class and nation, rulers and ruled on which politics depends must come to seem secondary at best.

Kant attempts to provide liberal principles with a morally satisfying foundation, a foundation that the earlier natural rights teaching leaves obscure. He does so by deriving human dignity from moral freedom—that is, by grounding rights not in a morally discredited nature but in the capacity of all rational persons to submit themselves to reason's law. The rhetorical attractiveness of this move, however, finally seems more compelling than its logical persuasiveness. Generations of scholars and critics have questioned the possibility of an a priori morality and have puzzled over the application of its abstract principles to concrete human affairs. Nowhere is this difficulty more evident than in the relation in Kant's thought between morality and politics. Kant's doctrine of human rights culminates in a politics that is rigidly moral in its foundations, ambiguously so in its consequences. His teaching does lend the liberal idea of rights a kind of sanctity lacking in earlier liberal formulations. But his political teaching also echoes these formulations, in some cases even exaggerating them. Although he hopes that the state will play a morally educative role, its central purpose remains for him the upholding of contracts and the preservation of private property. The attenuated "political" dimension of classical liberalism is in Kant's thought even further diminished. Kant's moral enshrining of human rights tends to eclipse the political institutions and practical safeguards earlier liberals thought necessary to secure those rights. The right to republican self-government threatens to shrink to a right to be governed in a "republican spirit."

Finally, in elevating what were originally conceived as sturdy and practicable standards into timeless and sublime ideals, Kant's moralized liberalism has its own political dangers. If Kant's idealized politics runs the risk of lowering liberal standards (for example, by transforming current expectations of representative government into future goals), it also runs the greater risk of raising them too high. On the one hand, implementation of these standards can be put off indefinitely, rule by an enlightened elite becoming an indefinite substitute for true self-government. On the other hand, these standards can become so absolute and rigid that any breach of them becomes a reason for questioning the legitimacy of the political order. Kant was too cautious to grasp any but the first alternative. Later epigoni, however, from Fichte to Baader-Meinhof have been at least equally inclined to choose the second.

While Kantian formalism finds an echo among some Americans (for example, civil and economic libertarians), many more have embraced the appeal to universal human dignity that Kant meant it to serve. Historically speaking, the combined experiences of slavery and multi-ethnic immigration surely heightened the attractions of the Kantian appeal to human dignity. How better to counter Calhounian claims that America belonged essentially to the white Anglo-Saxon descendants of the signers of the original compact than by ballasting the universalism of the Declaration of Independence with Kantian freight?

The appeal to human dignity, however, for all its moral attractiveness, has also had its cost. Freed from the rigorism that for Kant gave it substance and bite, the notion tends to grow ever broader and more vague. "Dignity" becomes a basket that any "new idea" can fill. Nor is formalism alone the answer. For one thing, it is hard for most to believe in the purely formal definition of freedom and equality (or freedom and equality consistent "with the greatest degree of inequality among men in their material possessions") on which Kant himself insisted. For another, in its disdain for the merely empirical and contingent, Kantian formalism tends to slight the real if contingently based distinctions by which actual communities are defined. This tendency can result in a salutary opposition to fanatical nationalism (as in the transcendentalists' opposition to the Mexican War) but also in a less healthy attachment to distant and dubious moral causes at the expense of the legitimate interests of one's own country and community. America more than most nations can be said to have begun as an idea based on an appeal to universal principles. As the erratic moralism of our foreign policy might suggest, however, there is an unavoidable and even "Kantian" tension between our foundational claims ("We hold these truths to be self-evident, that all men are created equal. . . .") and our particular requirements as a nation, a tension that has perhaps not yet been adequately resolved.

Fichte and the Demand for Equality

Johann Gottlieb Fichte (1762–1814), Kant's student and critic, set himself the task of bringing to Kant's moral vision a due regard for the particular and material facts of human experience. Specifically, he turned from an early "Kantian" preoccupation with formal freedom, to a concern with material satisfaction and equality as the sine qua non of human dignity. He came to believe, moreover, that such freedom and equality required (in the short run at least) a stringent moral pedagogy only possible in small, coercively homogeneous or "closed" communities. His modification of Kantian universalism arises, then, not from a prudent regard for the limitations of politics, but from a heightened—and indeed radical—optimism concerning its moral possibilities.

There are a variety of reasons for Fichte's heightened optimism. Kant, who began his career as a natural scientist and one of whose early works took as its subject the awesome destructive force of the

Lisbon earthquake, never lost his respect for the power of nature to cancel any and all human plans. An errant asteroid, as he reminds us in a late work, could destroy the world tomorrow.[19] And this respect for nature's power leads him to doubt that mankind can ever conquer nature completely, can ever make it fully serve human ends. Progress remains for him a sporadic affair, mankind often gaining in one area (for example, by discovering new continents) only to lose in another (for example, by encountering new diseases). Fichte, on the contrary, treats the progressive overcoming of nature, so that it should be as much under our control as our bodies already are, less as a strictly scientific and technical project than as a moral one.[20] The conquest of nature for Fichte is not merely a matter of human happiness or convenience but an outright moral duty. And since ought implies can, this conquest must be regarded as possible unless conclusively proved otherwise.

Another cause of Fichte's political optimism stems from his transformation of Kant's understanding of human happiness. Kant regarded happiness as a problem that is ultimately insoluble for man. Following Hobbes and Locke, he held that human desire is infinite and hence always beyond the reach of human power. While our power can expand, our desires can always expand even faster. Fichte, on the other hand, following Rousseau, holds that desire can and should be held in check. The radical variability and contingency of human desire that for Kant implied the subjectivity and uncertainty of human happiness, for Fichte spells a malleability that ought to brighten our hopes. And the labor we expend to satisfy desire, which Kant held to be at best a burden and a cost, Fichte deems a positive and enduring source of dignity and joy. Happiness can be achieved according to Fichte both through the control of desire (along the lines of the present-day slogan "less is more") and through the recognition of labor itself as a complete and lasting satisfaction.

Fichte's conception of labor neatly rejoins the (material) pleasure and (moral) dignity and self-esteem that Kantian dualism kept asunder. To the moral dimension of freedom adapted by Kant, Fichte adds a new emphasis on work and practical "efficacy."[21] As for the later Marx, labor, be it that of the worker at his tool bench or of the scholar at his study, serves Fichte as the essential indicator and expression of human freedom.

Fichte's efforts to move beyond Kantian dualism without departing entirely from Kant's moral inspiration affect his political teaching in a variety of ways. Of these the most striking is his attempt to reintegrate formal right with material equality and happiness, while still preserving the a priori character of his argument. Where Kant is willing to accept "the greatest degree of material inequality" so long as formal equality is respected, Fichte insists that formal and material equality must go hand in hand. In place of the liberal right to the *pursuit* of happiness, Fichte substitutes the right to (equal) happiness itself. His egalitarian vision calls for a society in which "each must work, but all who are willing to work must be able to live,"[22] and live, he later adds, as agreeably as possible up to a level equal to that of their fellows. If Kantian idealism finds its echo among present-day defenders of laissez-faire capitalism, Fichtean idealism finds one among present day Socialists and left-leaning liberals.

The securing of "equal enjoyment" requires, to be sure, an extensive state apparatus, one which, in order to ensure that enough people enter the right trades and produce the right goods in correct quantities to be sold at an appropriate price, must allow authorities to "know pretty much what everybody is doing at every time of day."[23] What people lose under such a yoke by way of freedom of choice, they make up, according to Fichte, through freedom from uncertainty. It is not prosperity as such that Fichte seeks so much as the avoidance of risk. His aim is an environment in which there are no surprises, in which no plan rationally conceived can fail. It is only one of many ironies of Fichte's thought (and of later revolutions he helped to inspire) that he is willing to risk everything in pursuit of the elimination of all risk.

Fichte does reestablish the connection, severed by Kant, between justice and the satisfaction of human need. This restoration comes, however, at heavy cost. The effort to address human need through the vehicle of a priori argument renders Fichte's account of rights more rigidly mechanical, less sensitive to human variation than its Kantian counterpart.

A similarly crude optimism hounds his understanding of the state's role in moral education. Fichte restores to the state the morally educative function that Kant and earlier liberals were forced to minimize or deny. Fichte's primary association of freedom with activity rather than (in the manner of Kant) with imputability allows him to slur over the Kantian insistence that virtue cannot be compelled, making possible an aggressively activist—indeed coercive—moral pedagogy. Fichte's attempt to overcome the rigid dualism of Kant without forsaking his Kantian attachment to the power of freedom thus traps him in a graver sort of difficulty. For his attempt is premised on a dogged moral hope that precludes the modest pragmatic accommodations that tempered Kantian idealism. The extremity of Fichte's moral demands is matched by the extremity of means necessary, Fichte believes, to meet those demands. For his attempt rests on the optimistic assumption that the difference between nature and will can finally be overcome by will and so, by implication, that all human difficulties can be so overcome.

The abstract character of Fichte's argument has the added effect of further reducing the role of politics, in the sense of active citizen participation in the making of law and policy. If Kant was willing to allow the monarch to govern "in a republican spirit" at least for the indefinite future, Fichte is happy to leave to experts, in quasi-perpetuity, the exacting regulations that are to shape people's lives. Kant's hypothetical republicanism is by Fichte further rarified. It is not a far step from Fichte's idealized "rational citizen" to later models of bureaucratic rationality, along with the claim, by now all too familiar, that "false consciousness" renders popular self-government less democratic than rule by a right-minded elite.

To be sure, Fichte argues, this machinery will not always be necessary. When the state has educated all its citizenry up to the level of the most cultivated, all will undergo rational restrictions willingly, and coercive government will disappear. Unlike Kant, who held that even the best of men will "disagree about what is good" and so require coercive laws, Fichte (anticipating Marx) extends the promise of a state that finally "withers away," as the mechanism of government is replaced by the free movement of a wholly voluntary ethical community.[24]

It might seem that Fichte's abstract constructs would push him even further than Kant in the direction of cosmopolitan universalism. In an ultimate ethical sense this is true. Along with the withering away of separate states, Fichte envisions the final ascendance of a universal ethical community, a "unity of race" in which the individual is not only included but subsumed. The road to this universal ethical embrace, however, is for Fichte emphatically particularized. For the morally educative functions that Fichte assigns to the state can best—indeed only—be carried out in communities that are nationally and culturally homogeneous. National and even racial exclusivity (Fichte has in mind linguistic groupings) becomes for Fichte the rational historical vehicle (ominous in the light of twentieth century developments) to moral universalism.

While the direct historical influence of Fichte in America (as opposed to his indirect influence through Marx) has been slight, he does represent an early and instructively extreme example of a familiar (local) type—the intellectual bent on teaching the people to know their own will grasped in "progressive" terms.

Where Kant sought to solve the problem of material equality by denying its juridical significance (the legal equality of citizens is compatible with the greatest degree of material inequality), Fichte begins with the sensible observation that material inequality pushed beyond a certain point effectively robs the citizen of both his liberty and his dignity. Fichte's own sort of rigorism, however, soon pushes him to conceive material equality in absolute and not relative terms and as constituting not merely one precondition of a free community but as virtually constituting its defining goal, with obvious costs to "freedom" as originally conceived. However perverse, the paradoxes of Fichte's political pedagogy merely state in a more extreme fashion the dilemmas of a regime (resembling in some ways our own) that attempts to account for the public good in purely private terms. Unchecked private selfishness and indignation born of the suffering to which it may give rise are thus two sides of the same coin. In its emphasis on individual rights to property and arguable slighting of concomitant duties to the community, the American project too can come to seem all too venal. The perpetual (if ultimately limited) appeal of socialism and other "progressive causes" in America is thus predictable, as is their continuing failure to seize the high ground. Like the "free-marketeers" they criticize, those on the "progressive left" tend, like Fichte, to exaggerate the importance of material well-being and so fail to transcend the essentially private perspective they mean to rise above.[25] Like Fichte, they fail to see that the pursuit of material well-being, whether that pursuit is rooted in resentment or in greed, cannot itself support the sense of common purpose by which a political community is sustained.

Hegel and the Interests of Community

No one saw the essential connection between the rigid libertarianism of classical liberalism and the rigid egalitarianism that opposes it more clearly than Georg Wilhelm Friedrich Hegel (1770–1831). And no one saw more clearly the need, in the very interests of freedom and equality properly conceived, to give an adequate account of political community, an account, according to Hegel, that Kant, Fichte, and classical liberalism all fail to provide.

Hegel's thought emerges out of and pursues many themes shared by his idealist predecessors. Hegel was concerned with reintegrating the radical oppositions laid out by Kant and Fichte. And he claimed to see both in philosophy and in history the path by which these oppositions are overcome, and reason and freedom fully realized in the world. The final moment of historical reconciliation coincides, according to Hegel, with the synthetic achievement of his own thought. The last pages of Hegel's *Phenomenology of Mind* are finished within earshot of Napoleon's advancing troops. With the completion of Hegel's thought and the emergence of the modern state out of the ashes of feudalism and excesses of the French Revolution, it can at last be said, according to Hegel, that "the rational is actual and the actual is rational."[26] Where Kant and Fichte projected the ideals of reason into the indefinite future, Hegel claims to find them realized in the here and now.

Hegel's astonishing claim to stand at the end of both philosophy and history is supported by a rich and complex argument to which justice cannot be done here; it must suffice to note that this claim has a persuasiveness that no abstract summary, as Hegel would have been the first to insist, can adequately convey.

In turning an earlier idealism on its head before Marx ever did, in locating the ideal or rational in the present, Hegel's thought conveys a practical message quite different from that of Kant and Fichte. Their ethical fervor, their call for moral resolve in the face of an opposing and often dispiriting present, gives way to the counsel to accept the present and give up as misconceived those elements of moral hope that cannot be reconciled with it. Kant's call for world peace based on an abstract and limited notion of right, along with Fichte's rigidly egalitarian visions, is to be seen, as is the French Revolution, which is their material counterpart, as deriving from concepts incompletely grasped and developed. There is melancholy as well as exaltation in Hegel's assertion that "reason is the rose in the cross of the present."[27]

That aspect of Hegel's thought that here especially concerns us is his appraisal of the liberal tradition that undergirds the American Constitution. Hegel tends to see in Kant and Fichte less a critical break with that tradition than its at times inverted continuation, their excesses growing out of the very deficiencies in liberal thought that they wish to correct. Where Kant stresses the moral emptiness of liberalism and Fichte its failure to appreciate the nobility of labor or truly provide for the satisfaction of human need, Hegel insists (with his own bow to Rousseau) on a new understanding of community that both "preserves and overcomes" *(hebe auf)* the abstract and one-sided remedies of its idealist critics. This project of understanding appears early in Hegel's thought. Already in 1803 (three years prior to the completion of the *Phenomenology of Mind*) his essay *Natural Law* shows that he perceives the problem to be one of reconciling those who would base right or law on reason alone and those who would acknowledge and respect it as an empirical or historical occurrence.[28] As Hegel sees it, the earlier idealists were correct to insist that right and law are more than contingent events and yet wrong to sever them entirely from the historical and communal context from which they derive their support and concrete meaning. Hegel allied himself with Kant and Fichte by denying that rights properly conceived ought to be called "natural" except, perhaps, in that special sense in which history (path and product of freedom) can be called a "second nature"; but he also denied that reason, understood as something wholly separate from the historical process, could give an account of rights that is satisfying and complete.

What Hegel saw in Kant and Fichte was less a critical reappraisal of liberalism than its culmination, liberalism's outward and ultimately empty egoism matched by idealism's inward and ultimately empty moralism. What was lacking for Hegel both in liberalism and in its inverted idealist extension was an adequate appreciation of the "concrete," of the individual who is not merely isolated and abstract but who participates in what Hegel called the "universal life of the spirit." The clearest example of such a life for him was the "ethical community" of ancient Greece. But Hegel, for all his admiration of the Greek polis, did not think we could return to it or should wish to. Missing from the world of ancient Greece was an appreciation of inward or "subjective" freedom and with it the possibility of full self-consciousness, a lack ultimately responsible for that world giving way. It is, according to Hegel, the "right of subjectivity" that serves as the pivot between the ancient and the modern world.[29] Hegel is with the moderns in insisting that individual rights—both inward, as moral conscience, and outward, as property—are the necessary means by which the will imposes itself upon and so transforms the world. The modern citizen is a free subject, conscious of and finding his satisfaction in the recognition of rights of which his ancient counterpart never knew.

The integration of the duty-bound citizen and the free subject is, according to Hegel, accomplished by the modern state in a variety of ways. The external aspects of individual rights are most obviously expressed in what Hegel calls "civil society." By civil society he means a "system of needs" (not unlike today's private sector or marketplace) in which each individual, in pursuing his own interests, serves (unwittingly) the interests of others and the whole. It was the hope of earlier liberals that such a system could take over many of the traditional functions of government, private selfishness proving a more potent means to public benefit than public exortations to self-sacrificing virtue. This hope, exaggerated by later liberals under the influence of economists such as Adam Smith, Hegel in part qualifies, in part rejects. The marketplace model of human community fails psychologically and politically, while the notion of individual rights that supports it gives way conceptually, Hegel argues, through an inner dynamic of contradictory logical demands. But to say that the marketplace model is inadequate is not to say that it has no place. Civil society and the arena for individual expression and freedom of choice that it provides are a necessary part of the modern state. It is a part, however, in need of radical supplement.

At one level, this supplement takes the form of professional and occupational associations that serve to draw the individual out of an otherwise unduly narrow interest in self into a fellowship, of however limited a scope, of common concern. It is to these associations or "corporations" that he assigns many of the welfare tasks, such as providing for members who meet with ill health or other misfortune, that were, as he notes, assumed in former times by the family.[30]

The modern family has for Hegel the more substantial task of providing the individual, who as a member of civil society engages in a continuous if bloodless struggle against others, with an immediate community of self-sacrificing love. This unifying task, however, requires a division of labor, more decisive than any in the marketplace, between man and woman, the former always reemerging out into that world of work and public recognition, the latter finding the horizons of her spiritual life within the home. It is the family's task to supply at the level of feeling a supplement to the one-sided individualism of the marketplace, in which the family at the same time also actively participates (through the husband) as holder of property or capital. Thus Hegel strives to absorb the market model of society while qualifying the undifferentiated, homogeneous individualism to which it seems to point. Hegel denies that marriage can be understood, as both Locke and Kant maintain, as a species of compact analogous to a commecial contract. For marriage involves the relinquishing of the private rights that commercial contracts presuppose. In marital love, spouses give up their property in themselves and only in so doing create a union in which each partner is substantiated and upheld.[31]

Hegel's discussion of marriage calls to mind Tocqueville's later discussion of the family in America, where, as Tocqueville notes, the equality of the sexes joins with a voluntary submission on the part of women to the confines of matrimonial domesticity, a submission more severe than that of their less liberated European sisters. Tocqueville registers puzzlement as well as admiration over this arrangement, as if the free submission of American women constituted a kind of paradox.[32] For similar reasons, perhaps, Hegel does not rely overly much on the strength of the family or weigh it down with the full burden of providing the unifying, ethical corrective to civil society. Unlike its ancient counterpart, the modern family is essentially a nuclear one, fated to a highly temporary existence. With the maturing of children and the death of parents, the individual family, for all practical purposes, passes away. Indeed, as Hegel observes in his discussion of divorce, the egoistic tendencies of civil society often themselves intrude upon familial unity, bringing upon it a premature demise.[33]

A third counterweight to the centrifugal forces of civil society is provided by divisions of the body politic into estates or classes. Against the crude uniformity of pure democracy, Hegel advocates a class system that incorporates a hereditary, landed element, along with other elements drawn from civil society and from what he calls "the universal class" or civil service. The unduly narrow and self-centered perspective of the "bourgeoisie" is to be offset by the stability of the landed class and by the universal and unifying perspective of the professional state official—without, however, compromising the free activity of the bourgeoisie within their proper sphere.

Finally, Hegel looks to the feeling of patriotism to bring the citizen out of an overly private and self-preoccupied existence into a fuller awareness of and participation in the life of the whole. Ordinarily, he assumes, it will be war or its threat that awakens this feeling. Unlike Kant and Fichte, along with earlier liberal figures for whom world peace was a political and moral goal, Hegel accepts modern warfare (conducted within civilized limits) as politically unavoidable and morally beneficial. It is politically unavoidable, because individual nations in their sovereignty and jealous dependence on one another's "recognition," will always find reason or excuse to quarrel. And it is morally beneficial because it interrupts the foul and corrupting calm, the decay of public spirit, that would be the result of a "prolonged, let alone a perpetual peace."[34] As for the mechanization and depersonalization of modern warfare—far from decrying its deemphasis on personal bravery and the ideals of chivalry, Hegel applauds it as an expression of the conscious participation of the individual in an "organic" and "objective" whole.

This far from exhaustive account of Hegel's treatment of the modern state is sufficient to suggest his overall aim. Hegel claims to see reconciled in the modern state the right to freedom, understood as private or subjective choice and given widest scope within what we might call the liberal marketplace, with the right of the state itself, understood as an "objective" whole, in which the merely negative freedom of the marketplace acquires positive content and purpose. The modern state gives subjective freedom its due without permitting it to deteriorate into mere arbitrariness and trival selfishness. That retreat of the individual into himself that Tocqueville feared in America, Hegel expects a fully developed rational state to resist and prevent. For if the state secures the individual in his private rights to life, liberty, and the pursuit of property, it also provides that life with a goal and "substance" without which it would not constitute that life of the spirit that freedom, according to Hegel, ultimately entails.

One must finally pause to consider whether the modern state succeeds in resolving, as Hegel claims, the conflicting demands of liberal right and polis-like community. Can any state combine, without undermining either or both, an ideal of private freedom with one calling for the submergence of the individual in a greater "organic" whole? One wonders, for example, to what extent a free market society will be able to flourish, given the constraints imposed by a centralizing bureaucracy and semifeudal class divisions. For the energy and genius of the free market seem to lie precisely in its opposition to such constraints, its encouragement of class mobility, and its resistance to unitary authority. To be sure, the emergence in modern commercial society of what Tocqueville called an "aristocracy of wealth," the development of large commercial corporations, and the growing interdependence of government and business all lend some credence to Hegel's position. The free market is less self-sufficient than some have imagined. And the sway of the market in a liberal republic imposes its own sorts of restrictions on individual freedom. But the failure of the market model to give an adequate account of political reality does not in itself vindicate the alleged Hegelian synthesis of individual freedom as understood by the modern rights tradition and civic virtue as practiced in the ancient polis.

A similar difficulty surrounds Hegel's claim to see in the modern state the perfection and surpassing of the ancient virtues. Hegel claims that the bureaucrat and the professional civil servant along with the housewife and the soldier, all represent in their very ordinariness a qualitative moral and spiritual leap beyond the always exceptional heroics of the ancient polis. These modern human types are not so much the heroes of the modern world as the proof that we no longer need heroes, that everything for which exceptional human beings have striven in the past is already essentially completed and achieved. The superiority of modern virtue lies not only on its democratic accessibility to all but also in its accommodation of the ordinary passions—greed, fear, even vanity—that the classical and Christian accounts of virtue held it necessary to check. Modern man, Hegel claims, need no longer live divided from himself.

Nor need he any longer live divided from the world. The modern citizen, according to Hegel, enjoys substantive satisfaction—not, of course, of his every whim but of the essential demands that he makes upon life. Different sorts of people will enjoy that satisfaction at different levels and in different ways, the scholar and civil administrator consciously participating in the state's rationality more fully than does the common laborer. But conscious participation in this rationality is in principle universally accessible to anyone who has penetrated it in thought as Hegel has done. Every individual may look out upon his social world as a kind of second nature, one into which, unlike the first, his mind can fully enter and in which he may feel fully at home. With freedom realized and the dynamic contradictions of history finally overcome, there is nothing left to long for, no "beyond" for which the soul need pine, or to which it need appeal: the state is the "march of God in the world."[35] And having seen history through to its effective end, mankind can now live at one with God and at peace.

That Hegel should nevertheless find it necessary to recur to war to forestall the "foul corruption" of too long a calm is one indication that his political conclusions may be more problematic than he is willing to admit. Hegel's claim to see integrated in the modern state the self-sacrificing virtue and unity of the ancient polis with the self-aggrandizing freedom and individuality of the modern liberal republic finally strains one's credulity. The conflicting demands of freedom and community do not seem so much resolved by the modern liberal state as left to lie in uneasy tension, with the forces of liberal freedom enjoying a preponderance of strength. Liberal rights and ancient duties, Locke and Cato, finally fail to mesh. One can admire and be grateful for Hegel's efforts to abate the powerful moral longings that propelled the utopian visions of his idealist predecessors. But one must also finally wonder if any understanding of history—even so rich and ingenious a one as that of Hegel—can lay all such longings to rest.

Least utopian of the idealists (or most utopian, insofar as he claimed that utopia has arrived), Hegel is also in an obvious sense the most political. At the same time, his understanding of the political is complicated, giving short shrift, as it must seem to us, to "abstract" demands (as it seemed to him) for universal suffrage and other efforts to represent and otherwise politically engage the citizen. For Hegel actual government is largely an administrative matter, the legislature accomplishing more as a symbol of unity than as a generator of specific laws. Indeed, the essentially (and arguably problematic) symbolic function of lawmaking for Hegel does much to qualify his—to our ears—offensively undemocratic endorsement of hereditary monarchy and noble privilege.

Hegel's greatest legacy, however, from an American perspective, lies less in discussions of the workings of government than in his treatment of the moral and spiritual requirements of a free community.[36] According to Hegel's understanding, a free people is essentially sustained not by self-interest alone—still less by traditional ties of "ethnicity" and religion—but by a shared ethos of political and moral belief that can withstand the test of reason, an understanding perhaps most fully echoed in America by Lincoln's evocation of the need for a "political religion" based on principles of equality and freedom.

For a short time in American history, the period immediately following the Civil War, Hegel seized the imagination of a small but dedicated group of self-taught Americans.[37] It was tempting to see in the figure of Lincoln and resolution of that great war, along with the heady westward expansion that followed, the last great act of world history, in which America would assume its rightful place on the world stage as the universal and rational state fully realized.

Later students of Hegel and of American politics have been slower to see the connection. And yet there remains something in Hegel's account, as in the thought of Kant and Fichte before him, that continues to attract the attention of thoughtful Americans. The recent success of books by John Rawls, Michael Sandel, and others, all based at least partially on Kantian or Hegelian grounds, is only the latest example of this appeal. In its fundamental acceptance of democracy and the technological conquest of nature, along with its efforts to enoble or spiritualize liberal freedom, philosophic idealism shares some of the aspirations of the American project.

The point, Abraham Lincoln once suggested, is not to pursue happiness, but to pursue it laudably. It is only on such a basis that the Constitution and the rights it would secure can become a "political religion," the only religion upon which a state pledged to upholding such rights can consistently depend. The founders implicitly acknowledged the need for such a "religion," some cohesive core to bind together a nation in which the centrifugal forces of private interest were otherwise to have so great a sway. The constitutional framers did not adopt liberalism unalloyed. In addition to liberal principles of "self-interest rightly understood" (to use Tocqueville's phrase) and the artful management of the private passions, their words and deeds reveal a concern with liberty, understood not merely as the freedom to pursue one's personal ends but as a right and power of self-government with its own intrinsic dignity.

Are, then, the framers and the German idealist philosophers who were their near contemporaries all to be seen as liberal revisionists, pursuing alternate paths to a similar goal? Implicitly, at least, the framers shared some of the idealists' dismay over the inadequacy of liberalism crudely construed. As practical men they could hardly do otherwise. A people had to be stirred to revolt and to make the sacrifices that revolt entailed. And war over, regional divergences—dictated in part by economic interest, in part by a fierce sense of local independence and loyalty—could not be meliorated by appeal to self-interest alone. Beyond the calculated alliances of the Articles of Confederation there was need to appeal to a higher common purpose, that the United States might be not merely a worried calculus of factions, Kant's "nation of intelligent devils," but also a moral beacon to the world. As Lincoln observed in mourning the passing of the generation that directly experienced the revolution and for whom its principles were most vividly alive, America must rededicate itself to these principles or risk degeneration into a means to private enrichment, to be discarded when it ceases so to serve. To this extent one may speak of an "idealistic" component in the American constitutional tradition or, alternatively, of a "political" component, embracing those appeals to shared belief and mutual sacrifice slighted by liberal theory too narrowly construed but without which no community—even a liberal one—can long thrive.

None of this should be taken as implying that the constitutional framers were unconscious or unwitting philosophical idealists. Too much separates their practical accommodations of liberal theory to political need from the speculative surgery of Hegel, Fichte, and Kant. It was not the theoretical divide between "will" and "nature" but practical exigencies that moved them to write and act.

To call the founders less speculative, however, is not to call them unreflective. The founders speak from a philosophic tradition that implicitly rejects the strict dichotomies (will/nature, ideal/real, morality/science) that philosophic idealism takes as its point of departure. Their understanding of practical life does not lead them to distinguish sharply between "is" and "ought": they assert a natural right to the pursuit of material and natural ends, and they hope for but do not necessarily expect an enlightened and virtuous leadership and citizenry.

In their politic appraisal of human nature, the framers seem to skirt many of the theoretical and moral difficulties with which the philosophic idealists, who combine the framers' high political hopes with Rousseau's high moral demands, so earnestly grappled. And yet problems remain. Given the prevailing scientific view of nature, the foundation or ground of natural rights continues for many to seem problematic. Hobbes and Locke left the final basis of their natural rights teaching in an obscurity unrelieved by any explicit clarification on the part of the founders. The Declaration of Independence holds the source of men's natural rights to be "self-evident." In an intellectual climate like our own, in which it has become easy to dismiss the liberal rights doctrine as an expression of cultural imperialism or bourgeois ideology or democratic decadence, the appeal to self-evidence may no longer be enough.

In pitching their tent on freedom defined over against nature, in placing their full reliance on "reason," "will," and "spirit" as emanations of the self, the philosophical idealists sought to secure the support for human rights and dignity that nature no longer seemed able to provide. It may well be, however, that their efforts were, in the final analysis, mutually incompatible, severing man, for the sake of a spurious theoretical certainty, from that realm beyond the self that is the true source of man's dignity.

Like idealists in the more popular sense, Kant, Fichte, and Hegel are invaluable as reminders of what liberalism, in striving to secure the rights to life and liberty, has lost or risks losing. It is neither the idealists' high moral demands nor their high political hopes but both together that render their doctrines finally unsatisfactory.

10
Historicism and the Constitution

Fred Baumann

Like most other regimes, the United States of America was created by particular acts of violence. Had Burgoyne won at Saratoga, it might not have survived its birth. Yet, unlike most other regimes, it was at the same time created through a claim to justice. The claim was not a particular, territorial one like, say, Frederick the Great's claim to Silesia. Rather, in the Declaration of Independence the revolutionary founders of the United States justified their particular revolution by reference to a right that holds universally and always. Recognizing the necessity of justification before the decent opinion of mankind, aware of the presumption of legitimacy that deemed them lawless rebels against king and Parliament, the signers sought to unmask the British sovereign's particular claim to authority by showing how it derived from a violated contract, which in turn derived its legitimacy from the origin of all politics out of nature and hence from the unalterable, permanent character of human beings who form societies to avoid death.

Historicism and the American Regime

Just as the authors of the Declaration appealed without reservation to "self-evident" truths applying to "all men" without exception, so too the drafters and interpreters of the Constitution were guided by assumptions about the unchanging nature of human beings. Thus Publius claims to know not only that men cannot be angels and so always need government[1] but also that the first purpose of legitimate constitutional government is to preserve the difference among human faculties for pursuing property[2] and that the failures of the polis would be repeated, centuries later, in America if certain geographical possibilities and institutional devices were not used advantageously.[3] Like the Declaration, the Constitution and thus the country they both founded stand firm on what are held to be permanent truths.

Faith in American principles as sure and true because universal reigned throughout American political life for most of the nineteenth century, from the level of common opinion described with tolerance by Tocqueville and exasperation by Dickens up to the sublime level of Abraham Lincoln.[4] With Lincoln we find the clearest possible identification of the legitimacy of the American regime with the universal principles of natural equality of right. To preserve that identification in principle, Lincoln seems to have been prepared to induce a civil war that would threaten the actual preservation of the nation.[5]

Yet our situation is no longer the same. We only have to look at how a much-renowned self-confessed defender of the natural rights tradition defines natural rights to see how far we have come. Ronald Dworkin tells us that "the assumption of natural rights is not a metaphysically ambitious one" and that it requires no more than the hypothesis that "the best political program . . . is one that takes protection of certain individual choices as fundamental." A right is an interest men are entitled to protect if they wish, Dworkin tells us, and the status of rights as natural comes as an assumption the philosopher makes to unite and explain "our political convictions."[6] Here natural rights, discovered (or invented) precisely to give political thought a surer grounding than the alleged captious dogmatism of premodern thinkers, are reduced to arbitrary choices, willfully made and dogmatically entertained. It is hard to know which is more striking: Dworkin's openness about his conventionalism or his impudence in daring to mask that openness nominally with the title of natural rights. Perhaps most instructive is that he thinks, apparently correctly for the most part, that such a blatant self-contradiction can pass.

What accounts for this curious situation, where the name of natural rights still has an efficient grace that can even shed itself benignly on their denial but where their substance can hardly be taken seriously anymore even, and especially, by those who speak in their name? What accounts for the dissolution of the robust confidence of the founders into the straightforward denials or the complex, defensive mumblings of their successors? Appropriately enough for a regime that from the outset sought its justification in theory, its legitimacy was undermined by perceived theoretical weakness. In sharp contrast to Marxist regimes whose practical failures (even and especially by Marx's own standards) have apparently not dimmed the allure of Marxist theory, the plain facts of American success have not protected the regime from the sharpest theoretical scrutiny.

Two fundamental doubts have been raised about the assumptions of the founders. First, are human beings, as such, as liberal theory describes them? Second, and even more fundamentally, are they "as such" at all? Is there a human nature or indeed even "nature" at all? Many of the movements of thought discussed in this volume have contributed to raising doubts on the first point. Chief among those that have struck at the second is historicism.

Historicism, which denies the possibility of universal human principles, has incited a number of characteristic American responses. Interestingly, they tend to take the form of both affirming and denying the regime's principles at the same time. The dominant and therefore most important version of the response to historicism is what I will call liberal patriotism. There is a companion conservative patriotism that has fared better in other countries like Germany than in the United States, which I will discuss briefly. Two readily available examples, however, of the ambiguity of contemporary liberal opinion about the American regime created by the influence of the historicist critique are the doctrine of the "living Constitution" and the way human rights issues are treated in the context of foreign policy. One example emerges from how we explain ourselves to ourselves, the other from how we explain ourselves to others.

The doctrine of the living Constitution is clearly an attempt to take into account the phenomenon of historical change while preserving allegiance to a Constitution that is meant to bind men over time. Thus Justice Benjamin Cardozo cited Arthur Corbin with approval to the effect that "it is the function of our courts . . . to keep the doctrines up to date with the *mores* by continual restatement and by giving them a continually new content."[7] The paradoxical and ambiguous content of this doctrine is perhaps best exemplified in the opinion of Justice William O. Douglas in *Harper* v. *Virginia Board of Elections*. There, citing Justice Oliver Wendell Holmes's warning against allowing the doctrines of the day to influence the Court's interpretation of the Constitution (thus suggesting that the Constitution is indeed something timeless), Justice Douglas takes Holmes to mean thereby that the doctrines of *Holmes's* day may not be allowed to govern the interpretation of the Constitution, thus clearing the way for the doctrines of *Douglas's* day to be given free rein.[8]

The problem created by the doctrine of the living Constitution for the legitimacy of the Constitution is obvious. It is that the Constitution then preserves only a formal existence, that it becomes a kind of moral capital on which the Supreme Court ceaselessly draws but that it can never replenish. As that capital is drawn down, it becomes ever clearer that it is not the Constitution that lives but only its name; consequently neither the Constitution nor the Court deriving its justification from the Constitution can enjoy further legitimacy. Yet the doctrine of the living Constitution is far from an effort to dissolve the Constitution in historical solvent. On the contrary, it is an effort to rescue the Constitution from historical relativization, to preserve, in a more sophisticated and flexible form, principles one fears can no longer be rigidly or simply maintained. For, as Douglas's opinion in *Harper* plainly implies in its reliance on Holmes's formally timeless Constitution, it is a necessary element of the doctrine that while the Constitution's "accidents," so to speak, may change over time, its "essence" must still be there and be recognizable as the evolved original. The doctrine of the living Constitution is thus ambiguous; it at once recognizes and denies the continuity and authority of the Constitution.

The parallel case of human rights doctrine faithfully reflects this ambiguity. Those for whom human rights are an important element in American foreign policy descend directly from the liberal universalism of Thomas Jefferson and Lincoln. Yet the disputes about the proper application of human rights in foreign policy between the two groups into which they divide reveals a common ambiguity about the very principles of the liberalism they advocate. The paradox is so well known as to be banal. Some are eager to apply standards of human rights to the Soviet Union and Nicaragua but less so to El Salvador and Chile. Some are eager to denounce South Africa or the elected government of El Salvador but less eager to denounce the governments of the Soviet Union, Iran, or Nicaragua. While a host of arguments, some more persuasive than others, involving national interest, ideological outlook, and assessments of historical developments, can always be adduced to justify particular distinctions, it is striking how frequently on both sides the justification for not imposing a strict human rights standard is the appreciation of cultural differences that separate us from them (whoever "them" happens to be). It is naive and unhistorical, we hear, to impose our peculiar Western standards on cultures, many of them quite ancient, that differ so greatly from our own. We are thus at times the confident bearers of universal principles of decency while at others we become acutely aware of ourselves as merely particular, as conditioned by a political culture, one among others, with no special claim to truth or justice. Here too liberal patriotism asserts its belief in the universal principles of the regime at the same time that it denies them. That the occasions when we assert the principles and when we restrain their assertion are determined by other political and ideological considerations is less interesting for present purposes than that we often want it both ways.

What are we to make of this ambiguity? If nothing else, it indicates how grudging has been the liberal response to the sophisticated self-knowledge forced on it by historicism. Historicism has not created cynicism or relativistic disbelief so much as a desire to have it both ways, to accommodate to the apparent demands of reason as little as possible (and perhaps less than necessary) while preserving our old forms of life as much as possible. One might, of course, viewing this historically, merely interpret the stubbornness of American devotion to an unchanging essential Constitution or to universal morality in foreign policy as a sign of America's particular national character, persisting through time.

Yet liberal patriotism when fully developed can claim to be more than an ambiguous response to the problem posed by historicism; it can claim to solve the problem. This solution is proffered perhaps most lucidly in the work of the late American historian Carl L. Becker. It animates, I believe, most decent liberal opinion today, although it is rarely stated as elegantly and self-consciously as it was over half a century ago by Becker. By examining his version of that solution we can see with greater clarity the problem that historicism poses for the American regime.

Becker was not only a ground-breaking historian but an influential theorist of the study of history as well. As such he had deep doubts about the possibility of transhistorical truths and thus about the liberal doctrine of natural right. In part his skepticism derived from his reflections on the craft of the practicing historian. Much like his contemporary R. G. Collingwood, he was too experienced in the wiles of historians to share the naive positivist confidence in the sanctity of the historical "fact." "The simple historical fact," Becker knew, is only "a *symbol,* a simple statement which is a generalization of a thousand and one simpler facts which we do not for the moment care to use."[9] In reality, "The historical facts are in his mind or in somebody's mind or they are nowhere,"[10] so that "the historian cannot eliminate the personal equation."[11] Hence historiography properly regarded becomes "a history of history subjectively understood (the 'fable agreed upon,' the 'pack of tricks played on the dead') rather than a history of the gradual emergence of historical truth objectively considered."[12] What then guides the historian in asking his questions and arranging his answers? Becker teaches Everyman that the historian is guided by nothing other than his purposes, whatever they happen to be, which is why, in the words of the title of Becker's most famous essay, Everyman is his own historian when he sets out to pay his coal bill.[13]

To contend, however irrefutably, that the study of history cannot itself discover transhistorical truths is not, however, to demonstrate that they cannot be discovered. Aristotle, who thought such truths existed, shared Becker's modest view of the possible attainments of history and consequently gave it a low rank among the sciences. Still,

Becker's skepticism about the transhistorical principles of natural right is only partly based on his self-knowledge as a historian. Most important, it emerges from his philosophic views.

Becker is perhaps best known as a historian for trumping the Enlightenment's ace by pointing to the dogmatic basis of its attack on dogma.[14] He follows the same strategy with the Enlightenment's child, the American founding. The initial epigraph of his classic work on the Declaration of Independence already answers the fundamental question about the truth of the Declaration's claims, based on natural right. "Nature is itself only a first custom," says Pascal, and with him Becker.[15] Becker argues that even to ask whether the natural rights philosophy of the Declaration is true or false is a "meaningless question"[16]:

> When honest men are impelled to withdraw their allegiance to the established law or custom of the community, still more when they are persuaded that such law or custom is too iniquitous to be longer tolerated, they seek for some principle more generally valid, some "law" of higher authority, than the established law or custom of the community. To this higher law or more generally valid principle they then appeal in justification of actions which the community condemns as immoral or criminal. . . . To them it is "true" because it brings their actions into harmony with a rightly ordered universe, and enables them to think of themselves as having chosen the nobler part.[17]

Although the question may be meaningless, the answer is not; the Declaration's claims are not true.

Becker treats all assertions of universal principle as rationalizations of desire. John Locke (a well-known apologist for the Glorious Revolution)[18] "made it possible for the eighteenth century to believe what it wanted to believe,"[19] and the colonists in turn "modified their theory to suit their needs."[20] Becker can know that universal claims about the nature of man or "a rightly ordered universe" are not true because, as his citation from Pascal indicates, "nature" is only custom that does not know itself. Strikingly, Becker's book on the American Declaration ends with a trenchant quip from that great enemy of the Enlightenment, De Maistre. He has known many kinds of men, he says, "but as for *Man,* I declare I never met him in my life."[21] What persuades Becker that nature is but custom misunderstood, however, is the triumph of historicism:

> The effectiveness of the historic rights philosophy was indeed precisely in this, that it encountered the natural rights

> philosophy of the eighteenth century on its own ground, and refuted it from its own premises. Admitting that rights were founded in nature, it identified nature with history, and affirmed that the institutions of any nation were properly but an expression of the life of the people, no more than the crystallization of its tradition, the cumulative deposit of its experience, the résumé of its history.[22]

It would seem that Becker's skepticism, learned from historicism, leads him simply to destroy the foundations of the American regime and with it chances for any intelligent patriotism. Yet, oddly enough, the reprinted edition of 1942 bears the marks of what appears to be some reconsideration of his earlier, clearer position. Stung by the "incredible cynicism and brutality of Adolf Hitler's ambitions," Becker cautiously entertains a "conviction" that " 'liberty, equality, fraternity' and 'the inalienable rights of men' are phrases, glittering or not, that denote realities—the fundamental realities that men will always fight for rather than surrender."[23] Yet—and this is essential—Becker says much less here than his rhetorical tone implies. The fact that men will fight for "realities" that they call "liberty" etc. is far from a judgment that their fight is worth supporting or indeed that it is substantively different from anyone's fight for some "reality," denoted by a phrase "glittering or not." Indeed, what Becker actually says here does not even allow us to distinguish the American Revolution from Hitler's "cynical" and "brutal" fight for what he called the liberty, say, of the Sudeten Germans. All Becker is saying substantively is that if there are Nazis there are also liberals who fight them. Despite the exalted tone, Becker does not in fact commit himself even slightly to partiality in the struggle. Yet it is hard to deny that Becker has something against "cynicism and brutality" and hence something to imply, if not actually to say, for "the inalienable rights of man."

In fact, Becker was somewhat less tongue-tied in the original edition in describing natural rights philosophy:

> Founded upon a superficial knowledge of history it was, certainly; and upon a naive faith in the instinctive virtue of human kind. Yet it was a humane and engaging faith. At its best it preached toleration in place of persecution, goodwill in place of hate, peace in place of war. It taught that . . . all men are equal in the possession of a common humanity . . . it invited men to promote in themselves the humanity which bound them to their fellows.[24]

In 1922 he assures us that "this faith could not survive the harsh realities of the modern world."[25] But in 1942, the realities having become distinctly harsher, Becker appears to find a renewed use for these illusions. But what is the reality behind the illusion he is striving, so guardedly, to express? If history teaches us that there is no being called Man, what is the point of appealing to the false or meaningless belief in common humanity to combat the harsh "realities"? Once one has subscribed to De Maistre's devastating sneer, is the attachment to liberal principles anything more than sentimentality?

Becker evidently preferred the illusion of humanity to the reality of nationality precisely because he preferred toleration to persecution. In this preference Becker reveals himself to belong to the liberal tradition and to the Enlightenment, which preached tolerance and humanity. He belongs to it heart and soul, but because he has learned its lessons too well, because his enlightenment extends to history, he cannot ground his preference for the Enlightenment.

To take the Enlightenment seriously is to learn that its principles are ungrounded, it appears. "What seems but common sense in one age often seems but nonsense in another. Such for the most part is the fate which has overtaken the sublime truths enshrined in the Declaration of Independence."[26] Yet to learn this is not, in fact, to abandon the Enlightenment but only to reveal that it is neither its principles nor the stories it tells that we must value but rather its "values" themselves, namely, tolerance and—despite the nonexistence of humanity—humaneness. It follows therefore that to criticize the Enlightenment for its rigid principles is to criticize in the name not only of historical sophistication but of the Enlightenment value of tolerance that historical sophistication brings. Thus criticism of the Enlightenment at one level is affirmation of the Enlightenment at a deeper level. Similarly, criticism of the naive Enlightenment universalism that informs American patriotism is, at another level, a superior form of American patriotism. Indeed, from this viewpoint, straightforward adherence to American principles is defective adherence to them, while their demolition is the higher loyalty.

This view, which not only is close to the surface in Becker but also, if a bit less explicitly, characterizes much contemporary liberal opinion, does not necessarily involve doublethink, but it does involve doubletalk. Liberal patriotism proceeds by the use of code, easily interpretable by initiates. By identifying the highest principles of the regime with the relativism born of historicism, it can criticize the narrowness of a regime that, like all regimes, claims universality but presents only particularity. Yet in the very act of making that criticism, liberal patriotism gives off unmistakable signals of preference for liberal regimes precisely because they are tolerant. Occasionally, in times of crisis, a Carl Becker may find it necessary to bend the rules a bit and let us in on what was never supposed to be such a secret, namely, that our historical relativism is not all that radical and that it stops at intolerance and inhumanity. But even Becker at his most indiscreet would violate the code were he to say so explicitly.

Liberal patriotism then responds subtly to the threat of annihilation posed by historical relativism: it appears to embrace it and by embracing it neutralizes it. It is a sly and enduring response, a kind of intellectual judo. It offers an accommodation for those who cannot naively accept the principles of the American founding but do not want to give it up. All it asks in return is a decent reticence, a mannerly complicity in not revealing its chosen strategy. If we refuse to contend on the battleground of principles, if we remain silent about what we really are, it turns out, delightfully, that not only can we go on being what we are with impunity but we can dismiss any competing claims, not even as false but as "meaningless."

Yet the price of reticence is perhaps a higher one than it at first seems. By refusing to argue about natural right, we may save tolerance, but then what shall we say for tolerance itself? Becker yearns to say something good about it but is constrained by the terms of his strategy to pointing mutely to the rights of men as "realities" that men will fight for. And if American patriotism, sincere belief in the "values" of the regime, is to be preserved through reticence, indicated only esoterically by pointing away from itself, is it not likely to be forgotten, or at least no longer understood?

This does not mean that liberal patriotism will wither away; on the contrary, the record of liberal patriotism seems to me a good one for preserving what it conceives to be American "values" among many who in other societies would be embittered opponents of the regime. It does mean that it is in many cases an unknowing patriotism, which often thinks itself to be opposed to the regime. More important, it means (however paradoxically for the heirs of the Enlightenment) that patriotism, acceptance of the "values" of the Enlightenment, becomes dogmatic. Precisely because the Enlightenment's chosen battlefield (to use Becker's phrase), on which it was defeated by historical consciousness, has been abandoned by its loving but cleverer children, precisely because its "values" and not its principles are cherished, it must be either affirmed or denied, willed or rejected, as an irrational act, an act of faith. This fideism is exactly what Becker charges against the eighteenth-century philosophers; it is precisely what historical sophistication is supposed to transcend. In fact Becker, and liberal patriotism with him, have merely radicalized it.

It would be odd if in the end liberal patriotism based itself on nothing more than an act of faith. But it cannot even do this. To know that you merely believe is already not quite to believe or at least not to believe as you did before you knew you merely believed.[27] The crafty silence that conceals faith is hard to tell from the crafty silence that conceals its absence. For silence has any meaning one chooses to give it; only speech defines possibilities, makes itself vulnerable to refutation, and hence is capable of producing solid conviction.

If liberal patriotism is the classic form for dealing with the threat of historicism in this, the liberal nation par excellence, it is not the only one. Conservative patriotism, though weaker here than in Germany, for example, and perhaps best exemplified in the writings of a scholar like M. E. Bradford, still presents a significant alternative.[28]

It is the essence of conservative patriotism to be explicit where liberal patriotism is silent. Like its robuster European siblings, it accepts and even insists on the contingent character of the regime—in this case the American founding—and derides any hint that the nation is based on universal principles of natural right. Following Edmund Burke (of whom more later), it contends that legitimacy comes only from tradition, from prescription. Perhaps the most extreme rhetorical formulation of this position is found, not surprisingly, in a German play, Friedrich Hebbel's *Agnes Bernauer.* There old Duke Ernst explains to his rebellious son Albrecht, who wants to marry for love, that because the angel who drove Adam and Eve from Paradise did not come along to guide them "we must put a stamp on what is as such worthless and ascribe to it a worth; we must exalt the dust over the dust."[29]

There is in general something paradoxical about this position. Like their model Burke, who urged the preservation of the "decent drapery" that covered presumably indecent realities (such as the origin of nations in rapine and conquest) and the employment of "politic veils" to mask impolitic unmentionables, conservative patriots cannot help tearing away that "decent drapery" or impoliticly unveiling precisely as they seek to preserve that drapery and those veils. For to acknowledge the drapery is to call attention to what it drapes; to admit to veils implicitly unveils. As Tom Underwood, then pitching for the Yankees, is reported to have remarked when asked by reporters whether he had followed an unwritten law of baseball in throwing a retaliatory beanball: "If it's an unwritten law, don't write about it."

If the general position of conservative patriotism in its own attempt to use judo on historicism is paradoxical or even self-contradictory, there is something especially odd about it when the decent drapery happens to be worn by Uncle Sam, that is, when the "myth," the "peculiar principle," is a founding based on natural right. The prescriptionist can, like Bradford, deny that the founding was based in any way on natural right and assert that it was simply an arrangement among certain Englishmen.[30] This amounts not only, first, to stripping off insufficiently decent drapery and reclothing the regime in fitter raiment but, second, thereby to weakening loyalty to the regime on any principle other than that loyalty is itself a good thing. Third, and worst of all, one must then contend, like Bradford, that the regime was stolen in effect and refounded (by Lincoln according to Bradford) on a basis he rejects.[31] Then, however, as a follower of prescription, the conservative patriot faces the classic embarrassment that if history prescribes it seems at least for the time being to have prescribed Lincoln's America and prescribed against his. Or when, at what precise date, will, say, the Fourteenth Amendment become prescriptive?

To take a non-American example, one would have to ask how long an Aleksandr Solzhenitsyn who put his faith in conservative patriotism (instead of the Christian God, as the real one seems to) could continue to defend the true Russia against the infamy of association with a foreign, Western Marxism? Given that his highest loyalty was to the historical culture of Russia, would he not at some point have to defend the form it had taken historically, however foul the means? Thus in the end the apparent advantage of conservative patriotism, its boldness and explicitness in going forward to greet historicism, proves to be an even greater disadvantage than the silence of liberal patriotism. Both contradict themselves, but conservative patriotism, in doing it more openly, cannot as easily resort to the deliberate missing of the point that is, such as it is, the salvation of liberal patriotism.

If, then, both liberal and conservative patriotism, for all their respective elegance and boldness, prove inadequate responses to historical consciousness, we need to look afresh at historical consciousness as it makes claims against the principles of the American regime. This means looking at the movement of thought called historicism.

Definitions and Roots of Historicism

What is historicism? As a category of intellectual history it seems to cover so much ground that some have plausibly despaired of its usefulness as a term of distinction. Defined most broadly, it includes those who think that history can simply substitute for philosophy as the path to truth, those who think that history provides a privileged moment at which it can be transcended and philosophy again becomes possible, and those who despair of the possibility of privileged moments as well as of the possibility of direct access to historical truth and who thus become either relativist skeptics or committed irrationalists. Thus, for example, the late Henry Pachter, writing about the great historian and historicist Friedrich Meinecke, rejects the term "historicism" for Meinecke's school, adopting instead the admittedly "ugly coining" of the German word "Historismus":

> Unfortunately Benedetto Croce and Karl Popper have preempted this latter term [historicism] for the Hegelian view that history is a perennial progression toward a predetermined goal and each period is a stage on the way to the next "higher" one. Historismus is the diametrically opposed view: that "all periods are equally close to God."[32]

While Pachter admits that "both historicism and Historismus deny any eternal nature of man and are both hostile to biological views of history," he asserts that they differ importantly in that

> historicism sees all human history as one and as subject to universally valid laws of development, applicable to all nations alike; Historismus stresses the unique individuality of each historical formation and assumes that each nation, each period, each individual, lives under its own star—"the law by which thou first wert formed" (Goethe).[33]

Nonetheless, the variants Pachter cites and the others, mentioned above, are all the product of the crucial decision to turn to history as the one subject matter that might possibly tell us how things really are. Consequently, I will define historicism here in the most general way, as the turn to the study of history as *the* study. To understand it as a whole means asking why the turn to the study of history was made in the first place.

Historicism began, modestly enough, within early modern natural rights rationalism, by attempting to give an account of something that was missing. Since what was missing—particularity—was supposed to be missing, indeed had to be missing if the natural rights project was to succeed, this initially modest supplement eventually produced a line of thought that swept natural rights rationalism entirely away. Yet, because historicism was born out of early modern natural rights thought, it was unable to return to earlier ways of thinking.

Classical thought had not only acknowledged the manifold variety of human types, characters, and ways of life, it had insisted on it. The laws of each polis, Aristotle argued, created a kind of citizen, a kind of human being, by means of the order of preferences they enjoined.[34] Spartans differed from Athenians, Greeks from Persians, as their laws differed. The one agreement shared by these regimes in their particularity was that there was a best possible arrangement, which each claimed to exemplify. Their very narrowness thus implied a universal perspective, which ancient political thought tried to occupy. Whether one was Athenian, Spartan, or even Persian, it ought in principle to be possible to figure out the best ordering of virtue and passions and hence of laws for human beings as such. Classical thought attempted to do precisely what Max Weber began by denying that social science could do, namely, to establish standards for regimes on the basis of ends.[35]

Early modern rationalism also tried to subject the varieties of human life to a rational standard but on a different basis. "The best life" known by reason had come to seem, for practical as well as theoretical reasons, a failed standard. It was discovered to represent dogmatism, masked by tautological formulas. Hobbes accused its teachers of making "the rules of *good* and *bad* by their own *liking* and *disliking*," creating in practice therefore no sustainable rational order but merely replicating "so great diversity of taste."[36] Reason could not authoritatively order the arrangements for living together because, while these arrangements were but instruments, so too was reason itself an instrument of the passions. Therefore, if there were to be an authoritative ordering of the varieties of human experience, it would have to find its axiomatic beginning in the fundamental reliability and uniformity of the passions.

By the doctrine of natural rights liberalism announced its solution. In the passion for self-preservation it had discovered the basic and reliable source of human action. Its fundamental character was acknowledged by the ascription of natural right to life and its auxiliaries, the rights to liberty and property. For example, Locke at one point appears to shrug his shoulders in bemusement over the infinite variety of human desires. Men seem like "a Company of poor Insects, whereof some are Bees, delighted with Flowers, and their sweetness; others Scarabes, delighted with other kinds of Viands."[37] Yet a page later he shows himself solidly on the side of the beetles: "As therefore the highest perfection of intellectual nature, lies in a careful and constant pursuit of true and solid happiness; so the care of our selves, that we mistake not imaginary for real happiness, is the necessary foundation of our *liberty*."[38] Similarly, it is Hobbes's main concern that man not forget the primacy of self-preservation; the cockiness that leads to disruptive pride needs liberal doses of fear to be reminded of the fundamental issues of life. Henceforth, any evidence of deep-seated desires or tastes that either do not readily reduce to self-preservation or might be stronger than self-preservation will prove problematic for liberalism.

Early modern liberalism's success in establishing order over multiplicity thus depended both on the reduction of reason to an instrument of passion and on the discovery of the primacy of the passion for self-preservation. The first significant crack in the structure is unsurprisingly an apparently modest one; it is found in the thought of David Hume.

Hume denies that moral distinctions can be derived from reason.[39] They might be if one could rely on self-interest as the fundamental and therefore privileged human passion. In his "Enquiry Concerning the Principles of Morals," he admits that "self-love is a principle in human nature of such extensive energy . . . that those philosophers were excusable, who fancied, that all our concern for the public might be resolved into a concern for our own happiness and preservation." These philosophers "denominated the objects of these sentiments [approbation or blame], *virtues,* or *vices*"; and "they found it simpler to consider all these sentiments as modifications of self-love."[40] Hume is confident that he can test this identification by the Baconian *experimentum crucis,* the test or experiment "which points out the right way in any doubt or ambiguity":

> We have found instances, in which private interest was separate from public; in which it was even contrary: And yet we observed the moral sentiment to continue, notwithstanding this disjunction of interests. And wherever these distinct interests sensibly concurred, we always found a sensible encrease of the sentiment, and a more warm affection to virtue, and detestation of vice, or what we properly call *gratitude* and *revenge.* Compelled by these instances, we must renounce the theory, which accounts for every moral sentiment by the principle of self-love.[41]

Here Hume is admittedly pointing to utility as "a principle, which accounts, in great part, for the origin of morality."[42] But utility is a relative term that must be grounded in an account of the nature of the being whose utility is being served.

Hume thus rejects the idea that morality can be known by reason. For reasoning is a matter either of comparing ideas or of inferring matters of fact. Yet look at the fact of a murder: "Examine it in all lights, and see if you can find that matter of fact, or real existence, which you call *vice.* In which-ever way you take it, you find only certain passions, motives, volitions and thoughts."[43] As for comparing relations, the relationship of incest is found among animals, where it is not vicious, and that of parricide among trees, where it is innocent.[44]

Hume thus finds the origin of morality in a moral sense, in human sentiments. Hence "twist and turn this matter as much as you will, you can never rest the morality on relation; but must have recourse to the decisions of sentiment."[45] While the direction of this discovery is self-evident, for Hume it did not require a plunge into radical relativism. We learn to adjust our passions, at least as far as our "general notions" go, to the consensus of others. "And tho' the *heart* does not always take part with those general notions, or regulate its love and hatred by them, yet are they sufficient for discourse, and serve all our purposes in company, in the pulpit, in the theatre, and in the schools."[46]

If we ask what lies behind this willingness to rule our heart by general notions learned from others, ascending at least to the level of hypocrisy, it would seem to be a combination for Hume of "calm judgment," which makes its appearance when passions are, through tenuousness of connection, not greatly aroused, and prudential self-interest, which counsels that "we every day meet with persons, who are in a different situation from ourselves, and who cou'd never converse with us on any reasonable terms, were we to remain constantly in that situation and point of view, which is peculiar to us."[47] Self-love therefore ultimately still seems strong enough for Hume to allow him to discover a practical resolution of the looming problem of relativism and moral incoherence. This is of course a particularly severe problem for liberal societies, which cannot simply impose from without, like Hebbel's Duke Ernst, a code of right and wrong that makes up in terror what it may lack in persuasiveness. But Hume is still enough of a believer in enlightened self-interest that he is not forced to the radical conclusions his discoveries point to.

Still, they do point somewhere. By undercutting the reliability of the passion of self-interest and hence the fundamental uniformity of the passions, Hume destroyed much of the power of the liberal argument for rational social arrangements based on natural rights, since those rights were nothing other than recognitions of fundamental and unalterable ("unalienable") passions. Most important, in pointing to the sentiments as the determinants of ideas of justice, he implicitly pointed to the question of the origins of those sentiments. The study of those origins is the study of cultures, societies, and regimes that develop and inculcate sentiments and patterns of preference, that is, the study of history. While Hume does not turn to history as *the* study, he prepares the way for that turn since after him there does not seem to be anywhere else to go for information on the proper arrangement of human things.

In Burke we find another attempt to supplement natural rights liberalism that ends by demolishing it or at least pointing to its demolition. In his case we find a much more explicit approach to historicism, even though Burke is held back by some sort of commitment to some sort (whether modern or ancient) of natural right; hence, "Far am I from denying in theory; full as far is my heart from withholding in practice (if I were of power to give or to withhold) the *real* rights of men."[48] So far so good. Nor is there anything new in Burke's insistence that "if civil society be the offspring of convention, that convention must be its law."[49] But Burke's emphasis on those conventions and their distance from natural right goes a long way to decoupling life in civil society from natural rights. "Government is not made in virtue of natural rights, which may and do exist in total independence of it. . . . Government is a contrivance of human wisdom to provide for human *wants.*"[50] It is not that rights no longer matter at all; it is that they do not seem to matter very much:

> These metaphysic rights, entering into common life, like rays of light which pierce into a dense medium, are by the laws of nature, refracted from their straight line. Indeed, in the gross and complicated mass of human passions and concerns, the primitive rights of man undergo such a variety of refractions and reflections, that it becomes absurd to talk of them as if they continued in the simplicity of their original direction.[51]

It is the dense medium, the intricate nature of man, the complexity of the objects of society, to which Burke directs our attention.[52] Thus it has been suggested that Burke's primary significance in political thought is the attempt to free political practice from the rule of abstract theory and hence, in a way, to return to Aristotle.[53] But crucially, and unlike Aristotle, Burke does not appeal to a reason superior to the abstractions of the political metaphysicians, nor, and unlike Hume, does he find in self-love on the whole a reliable practical guide. On the contrary, it is only in "opinion and sentiment"[54] that the naked selfishness of the rights theory (which Burke himself does not deny) can be transformed into the conditions of a stable and successful civil society. Even the French revolutionaries, who think they proceed by principles of natural right alone, are indebted, according to Burke, to irrational opinions that legitimize and glamorize ancient thefts. For by what title do they claim the soil of France for their revolution?

> Who are they who claim by prescription and descent from certain gangs of banditti called Franks, and Burgundians, and Visigoths, of whom I may have never heard, and ninety-nine out of an hundred of themselves certainly have never heard, whilst at the very time they tell me that prescription and long possession form no title to property?[55]

Leaving those opinions and sentiments in place is therefore good statecraft. One should imitate the statesmen of the Glorious Revolution who allowed the breach in the succession to be masked by a "politic, well-wrought veil"[56] and not those new revolutionaries who want to tear away "all the decent drapery of life."[57]

If the abstractions of the political metaphysicians cannot be imposed on the "dense medium" of human life, if no other form of reason will avail, if, like Hume, Burke directs us to the "opinions and sentiments" of men, to their beliefs in tradition and to the traditions that form their beliefs, then the path to historicism lies open. While Burke is not optimistic about the prospects for the study of history to achieve theoretical coherence, he clearly directs us to a study of particular histories:

> I doubt whether the history of mankind is yet complete enough, if ever it can be so, to furnish grounds for a sure theory on the internal causes which necessarily affect the fortune of a state. I am far from denying the operation of such causes: but they are infinitely uncertain, and much more obscure, and much more difficult to trace, than the foreign causes that tend to raise, to depress, and sometimes to overwhelm a community.[58]

In his emphasis on the irrational and traditional, in his insistence on the particular and its inherent resistance to the explanatory power of universal theories, in his appreciation of the complexity, intricacy, and diversity of human beings, Burke sounds some of the key themes of historicism that we shall find again in Johann Gottfried Herder and Leopold von Ranke. He is only being consequent when he points to history as the appropriate study for those seriously interested in human things because history is the study of the particular in all its complexity. And he is again only being consequent to his emphasis, if not his natural rights starting point, when he goes so far as to admit that his critique of the French Revolution will be disproved if the institutions it created manage to last.[59] With this he anticipates a crucial corollary of the turn to history from all the studies that claim to transcend it, namely, the teaching that there is no appeal from the verdict of history. Of course Burke is no worshipper of History with a capital *H;* he merely celebrates the "local and accidental." But one can only distinguish the two if there is still something that transcends both. If there is not, if there is only the local and accidental, our sole hope will be that it may amount to history, that is, either that its study becomes complete enough to allow us to theorize or that some privileged moment will emerge that will allow us to transcend the local and accidental.

The sharpest turn toward historicism within the natural rights tradition was taken by Rousseau, whom Allan Bloom treats elsewhere in this volume. We find this turn in essence in that passage of the *Second Discourse* where Rousseau turns upon the English natural rights theorists their own conceit of the state of nature and discovers that Hobbes's and Locke's "natural" men are actually unnatural, calculating, contemporary Englishmen.[60] But if human nature is not what Hobbes and Locke say it is, if we only have access to men formed by various regimes, we may not be able to know at all what nature is. More seriously, if by "nature" we mean something that is always the same fundamentally, no matter how differently it may manifest itself historically, man may actually have no nature at all, beyond the capacity to transform himself. It is of course the burden of the *Second Discourse* to give a historical account of human development on the basis of man's capacity for "perfecting" himself, which accounts for his irreversible transformation from a thoughtless beast into an envious man. In his ingenious efforts to find a variety of possible homes for man, whether in the *Emile* or in *The Social Contract,* Rousseau begins from the knowledge that man has made his old home uninhabitable by changing himself into a being that can no longer live there. Hence to know man necessarily comes to mean knowing his history.

The destruction of the props of liberal thought in Hume, Burke, and Rousseau seems to leave only one place to turn. If we do not have access to transcendent reason or to a reliable, uniform account of the passions or to a sufficiently useful account of human nature to serve practical purposes or to any account of human nature as such (not to mention any account of divine revelation that can be simply believed, separate from its historical provenance), there is nothing left to do but to look once more at the phenomena in an unbiased way, without preconceptions. It is either that, it seems, or give up entirely the enterprise of reflection on human life. To take this unbiased look means to look at the phenomena as they present themselves to us, as they come. This means that we have to turn to history.

Historicism—Herder and Ranke

In this chapter I concentrate almost entirely on early historicism, what Pachter calls Historismus. I have selected two figures, one of the eighteenth, one of the nineteenth century, who well represent both the theory and the practice of early historicism. The great philosophers of history like Hegel, who discovered in it a "privileged moment" that permitted them to begin to reason anew, and those who, like Nietzsche, rejected any such moment and despaired of finding meaning in history are far more important figures in the history of thought and showed a far deeper understanding of the problems inherent in the turn to history. Yet although they are giants, they stand on the shoulders of early historicism. Indeed, they seem to be looking down ever more uneasily, ever more aware of the epistemological problems they have inherited from the historical school's turn to history. By contrast, at least for me, it is early historicism's faith in and love of immediacy that at once allow what is most persuasive about historicism to be presented most persuasively and make it, within its horizons, so liberating to the student of human beings, so charming and so attractive.

It is initially attractive in its polemic. Thus Ranke—anticipating Becker, by the way—condemns the "new Scholasticism" of the Enlightenment for dogmatic arrangements of the real world.[61] Similarly Herder casts scorn on the Enlighteners' "universal doctrine" and celebrates the inexpressible individuality of a man or a nation.[62] There is a great joy in this radicalization of Enlightenment individualism, where the individual, no longer confined (and shielded) by a generalized understanding of human nature, now steps forth gloriously as the maker of his nature. For in rediscovering history we rediscover magnanimity. We are no longer bound to sneer at the unenlightened past or required pedantically to instruct it about its errors while implicitly celebrating our own unique (yet universal) excellence. Great pleasure as well as salutary humility lies in store for the student who, like Hoffmann's Anselmus, allows himself to learn what it is to be someone other than himself, who immerses himself in full faith in the strange writings of other times and cultures, and to whom every view or custom, however foreign to him, is for that very reason uniquely precious. For Herder, as indeed for most of the earlier generation of romantic nationalists, the celebration of particularity had its own tolerance and universality. (Perhaps the last great political monument to this sentiment is Woodrow Wilson's Fourteen Points.) In this universal love of the particular early historicism is part and parcel of the romantic movement. It shares with romanticism the assumption that essences could be intuited, lived into, by an observer willing to lose himself in close and sympathetic attention to the object. And it shares in the relief and joy in the immediate contact with things, whether intimately one's own or wildly exotic, that characterize early, confident romanticism.

Yet from the outset historicism did not and could not rest content with its claim to know the individual. For, as Ranke says, to understand a human being "according to [his] own point of view"[63] means to understand him according to his context, that is, his culture, his way of life, and the order of his judgments. Thus the study of the individual rapidly and necessarily becomes the study of the individuality of nations and cultures.

While the state is still a mechanism for Herder, since all culture is a product of human activity,[64] it is no longer merely a contractual mechanism, designed to facilitate in a neutral way the attainment of universally human desires that happen to achieve particular expression at a particular time and place but whose particularity is the least important thing about them. Now that the state is understood to create the point of view of the citizens by means of its laws, its gods, and even the tastes it inculcates, we would seem at first sight to have returned to Aristotle. Of course we have not, since for Aristotle there was still something beyond the horizon of the individual polis, some idea of the good life that conformed to the universal possibilities of human excellence and that therefore established a standard for all the particular worlds they created. Such an appeal was not possible for early historicism. What went for the individual went for the culture as well; it had to be understood immanently. Thus Herder calls for "another Montesquieu" who, unlike the first, would tell us about "the internal changes in the character and culture of a nation," by "tracing the historical process of these inner, and essentially traditional, forces."[65] But, like the individual, the individual nation's "point of view . . . its own inherent aspirations" cannot be wholly understood except by understanding its understanding of its context and hence by understanding its context.

Thus from the outset, both in Herder and in Ranke, historicism brings with it an explicit doctrine of world history (which, for example, for the Reformation period Ranke readily identifies with German history).[66] What this means is that sometimes a nation incites a "world movement," as did, for example, the Counter-Reformation papacy, and becomes so important for its time that its own history broadens, in effect, into world history.[67] There is of course an assumption here, namely, that a standard exists whereby one can know whether the Counter-Reformation papacy was indeed the crucial factor in early modern Europe or whether it was merely a surface appearance, masking the true universal history of, say, a rising bourgeoisie or gradual shifts in trade patterns. Yet how could such a standard be arrived at immanently, from within the study of a particular culture? Presumably it comes from studying all the phenomena according to all their viewpoints. Yet if such a study could provide a harmonizing universal perspective, there would be no need for the immanent viewpoint. Furthermore, presuming that the universal has its own point of view, what is our access to it? Thus the necessary extension of subject matter from the individual to the universal made it increasingly problematic whether history could replace philosophy merely by studying phenomena according to their own point of view.

Ranke does not seem to have been overconcerned by the problem his own claims raised. At times he appears to think that the facts speak for themselves, as if all we need to do is "to return to the positive."[68] Elsewhere he seems to rely on some sort of natural intuition vouchsafed to the elect: "The insightful of all ages knew what was good and great, what was permitted and just, what progress and decadence are. It is written in great characters in the human breast: a simple reflection suffices to conceive it."[69] At other times, though, he calls for prudent reflection *(Besonnenheit)* combined with daring of the spirit, in order "to take up in oneself the seed and the deepest secret of circumstances and to observe in one or another people how the human things are founded, grow and thrive."[70] But this again turns out to be a simple matter of "observing what lies before our eyes and from it, by reflection, to discover the secrets of far distant causes."[71]

In the passage for which Ranke is perhaps most remembered, where he rejects for history the tasks of judging the past and teaching the future in favor of showing "how it actually was," he distinguishes between two obligations. The first is strict presentation of the facts, the second development of the unity and progress of occurrences. At least this second task seems by its very nature to require interpretation and selectivity (as Becker and others have demonstrated, so does the first). Yet the question of the basis for interpretation and selectivity appear to pose Ranke no great problem: "In so far as the state is to be founded, a peculiar principle asserts itself, of equally spiritual nature, which also has its inner necessity, expresses itself in specific forms, incites special educations [and] claims an unlimited freedom."[72] The forms that the historian arranges and recounts, therefore, are already given by the peculiar principle the historian intuits. Perhaps, but if so, then the historian's perceptions are traceable to the "special educations" that are a product of his own state and its "peculiar principle." Hence any discovery of the peculiar principle of another state or culture becomes suspect because the discovery is perhaps as much a product of the historian's culture as of the culture he studies.

In short, if the confidence of early historicism is not to founder, the study of history must be separable from what history studies. Yet the possibilities for such an exemption are severely limited. The original claim that mere attentiveness to the phenomena would suffice proves inadequate once the historian self-consciously applies to himself the standard of cultural determination he finds in his subject matter. One alternative would seem to be straightforward scientific positivism. Distinguishing itself from Enlightenment rationalism by preferring the concreteness of "facts" to abstract theory, it finds out that it cannot do so because it merely reintroduces, through "scientific method" (that is, the theory of identification and arrangement of facts), the same transcendent reason that historicism begins to demolish.

A second alternative is discovering the already mentioned privileged moment as Hegel did (and as Marx perhaps also assumed he had done). The moment would be privileged because in it blind, meaningless history would finally arrive at self-conscious understanding. This, of course, would be possible only at the very end of history; otherwise one's sense of having discovered the meaning of all history would certainly be relativized by the future. The real would then coincide with the rational, and the historian, no longer relativized by his own position, would be outside history and once more a philosopher. Aside from the minor drawback of having to happen to be writing at precisely that moment (and of assuring oneself that one has not deluded oneself about this all too convenient piece of good fortune), this alternative solves the problem of historicism by transcending it and replacing it with a new (though historicized) philosophy.

A related alternative for those who are embarrassed by the cumbersome apparatus of the Hegelian philosophy of history is to argue in the fashion of Collingwood for a nonromantic reliving of experience.[73] Granted that the historian is caught up with his own questions, can he not still come to know his subject's questions? Can he not, by knowledge as complete as possible of the circumstances, enter into the experience of taking the action as a response to the historical actor's question? Thus, can we not relive the discovery of the Pythagorean theorem once we understand the line of thought that brought it forth?

The strength of this example shows the limits of the argument. After all, it is the abstract and universal character of mathematics that gives it certainty. Who needs historians to report on the intuitions of mathematicians? We ask historians to tell us about the contingent, about passions and above all about opinions. If we wish to relive Caesar's crossing of the Rubicon, understood as how that action appeared to Caesar, we must understand Caesar fully, understand from within his ambition, his courage, fears, daring, fatalism. Unless the historian were empowered to set up some other standard of what was important about the event, he would have to become Proteus, capable of becoming Caesar or any other human being who had ever lived. But to do this he would have either to be wiser than his subjects, that is, a philosopher who knew the whole, or to be capable of intuitively "living-into" the past. Here we seem to be back at the beginning with the rejected alternatives of nonhistorical reason and a romantic intuition that ignores its own cultural determination.

It is easy enough then to see why that current in historicism that refused the Hegelian temptation to philosophize and insisted on staying loyal to the study of history came in the end to the frank and courageous skepticism of a Carl Becker. And indeed Becker seems to me to be on strong ground as a practicing historian describing what historians actually do. But in renouncing the effort to make history replace philosophy, in choosing such a well-fortified if (and because) narrow position, he demonstrated that the burden of truth seeking so joyfully assumed by early historicism had proved too much to bear. Yet Becker's modest assessment of what historians could do was not accompanied by faith (or even agnosticism) about what other disciplines, and in particular philosophy, could do. If historicism had failed in discharging its positive burden, it had apparently succeeded beyond hope of appeal in its negative task. It seemed plain to Becker that historicism had permanently destroyed the possibility of returning to ways of thinking that failed to give decisive status to historicity and that naively hoped to find some transhistorical or natural standard for human things. Like history itself, historicism could only go forward, to the end.

The Consequences of Historicism

Historicism has had profound consequences for liberal democracies, particularly for the United States. Above all, in serving as the chief theoretical agent of the destruction of the traditional teaching of natural rights (the response to the depression doing much of the practical work of capitalizing on theoretical victories), historicism has paved the way for many of the movements of thought discussed in other chapters, among them pragmatism, "value-free" social science, cultural relativism, and the so-called rights revolution. As liberal patriotism begins to become uncomfortable with itself and as even the protean solidity of tolerance as the highest virtue begins to evaporate (for example, in contemporary feminism), resort to these schools of thought becomes attractive. Even the current orthodoxy in the humanities departments of the best universities, which combines egalitarianism with Nietzschean relativism, can be understood practically as a prosthetic aid to liberal patriotism rather than as a serious departure into uncharted political territory. These consequences I will therefore not discuss, even though they often offer more of intellectual interest than the matrix of liberal patriotism from which they emerge and into which, in this country, they always seem to return.

Here I want only to expand a little on the earlier description of liberal patriotism and its workings. For it does not rest with the anointment of tolerance as the sole virtue. In its early stages of self-consciousness, before fleeing to some new haven it has re- or deconstructed for itself, it undergoes notable modifications.

With tolerance and openness understood as the regime's highest and axiomatic goals, the actual intentions of the founders cannot be understood or respected. The reason is that the founders' sober, Lockean acceptance of the irreducibly self-loving and self-interested element of human beings must, to meet the new standards, be rejected and replaced with a kind of moralizing, denatured Kantianism. Where tolerance about large issues such as religion seemed laudable to the founders, it was to be achieved largely by allowing men to pursue their happiness, most typically in the form of property. Attaining heights of tolerant self-overcoming in the name of moral excellence was precisely the sort of thing they despaired of and sought to avoid.[74] Consequently, many elements of the American Constitution, above all guarantees of property rights, are incomprehensible and even an embarrassment to liberal patriotism. The "rights revolution" discussed by Clifford Orwin and James R. Stoner, which moves in the name of a rediscovery of natural rights toward a radical redistribution and the transformation of constitutional rights into bureaucratically assigned privileges (and which thus drastically weakens those rights James Madison thought it was government's first duty to protect), is not a direct consequence of the liberal patriotism encouraged, if not created, by historicism. But the requisite forgetfulness of liberal patriotism about the origin of those rights was a precondition for it.

In short, liberal patriotism saves the Constitution first by granting much to historicism and second by refounding the regime on a utopian moral basis. On a utopian basis limited, republican government will inevitably seem irksome, while problem-solving, "result-oriented," rule-making, and rule-breaking government will, at least in domestic politics, seem the norm. In other words, "prerogative," that necessary but dangerous power that Locke sought to fence in and the founders sought further to fence in by replacing it, in effect, with enumerated though still fairly general powers, reemerges as the common-sense procedural norm, legitimated by claims that it works to create some utopian good.[75]

If liberal patriotism tends to expand the power of the government domestically, it surely does not have that effect on foreign policy. There, in contrast to Locke's view that the "federative" power, that is, the foreign policy power, would need to be especially free to use whatever means were necessary for survival in the international state of nature, liberal patriotism tends to create paralysis. It does so by converting straightforward national interest into a complex operation of symbolism and moral omphaloskepsis. As the debate over the Mexican War demonstrated, the self-understanding of the United States as a liberal power that respects national self-determination was always likely to come into conflict with simple understandings of American self-interest. But that debate pales before contemporary versions. Liberal patriotism tends to understand enemies as not so much objectively hostile as opportunities for the exercise of virtuosity in tolerance. If one could only unmask, confess, and end one's intolerant behavior (which explains foreign enmity), one would improve oneself morally and earn new friends. Charles Fairbanks has called this the "hearty handshake" fallacy, which led the Carter administration to try to obtain the friendship of the Sandinistas despite their avowed Marxism-Leninism and anti-Americanism. Despite the failure of this sincere effort, the myth persists that only inveterate American hostility explains our unpopularity in Managua.

If liberal patriotism extends tolerance to regimes that the older liberalism would have felt good about despising, its tolerance is not universal. Characteristically, it stops at the gates of South Africa, guilty of a form of intolerance that reminds us of our own, and with increasing frequency at the gates of states like Israel, which are understood to be so closely linked to the United States that they can be given the high if dubious compliment of being judged by the excruciating standards of tolerance and meekness liberal patriotism reserves for its homeland.

It is a mistake, though, to conclude that liberal patriotism merely has a soft spot on its left side for regimes that, however repulsive in practice, still claim to have replaced liberal democracies as the true heirs of the Enlightenment. We need only compare a representative nineteenth-century liberal, John Stuart Mill, on the subject of Islam,[76] with a representative twentieth-century liberal, Richard Falk, on the subject of the Ayatollah Khomeini[77] to discern how much more tolerant the new tolerance is.

These examples already hint at the ultimate practical conclusions to which historicism leads. After all the ambiguities have been exposed and the tricks detected, after the fraud of "natural" rights founded on dogmatic assertion has been disclosed and the true "values" underlying "value neutrality" have been revealed, cynicism and its concomitant, vulgar success worship, emerge. Liberal patriotism is still doing a good job of concealing this from itself. Yet the woolen eyeshade is increasingly threadbare. For in the end, as the effort of conservative patriotism to embrace historicism shows, historicism makes it plain that nothing transcends, because everything is, action. The readiness of German "liberal" historicists like Treitschke to abandon liberalism for Bismarckian nationalism once the latter produced desired results is both emblematic and a tip-off. It is not that historicism introduces irrationalism. It merely radicalizes modern rationalism, which, to cite Leo Strauss, is "irrational" enough already.[78] But modern rationalism at least separated reason as an instrument of the passions from the passions it was to serve. Historicism collapses even this distinction, as Becker's explanation of Everyman's exercise in historical reasoning demonstrates. In dissolving the notion of a permanent human nature grounded in an order of the passions, historicism reduces us to saying that objectively certain things are happening and subjectively we are talking about them because we want things to go our way, whoever "we" may be. Whether it is the homely little example of paying one's coal bill or the less innocent example of willing the triumph of one's race, the principle is the same. Julien Benda's "treason of the clerks" was actually the "fidelity of the clerks" to their insight that, since reason's claim to transcend history was unmaintainable, there was nothing but history, that is, action, to guide them. But while there may be no right and wrong, there are still strong and weak, and us and them; the unguided choices we are likely to make among these are not difficult to predict.

Plainly, the identification of contemplation with action, the understanding that reason is merely another form of goal-directed activity, that philosophers and historians are like everyone else in pursuing ends of their own, and that "truth" has no special status as an end, can only undermine the legitimacy of liberal, constitutional democracy. The point goes beyond the dissolution of the theoretical basis of rights. For liberal democracy lives by the insistence on proper procedures, even at the risk of producing inefficient or wrong results.

It is notoriously not "result oriented," and it must claim priority for its procedural goals over the more obvious results that a democratic population may from time to time desire. Even more important, it depends on the understanding that there is a difference between reason and action, persuasion and compulsion, because democratic consent depends on the distinction between legitimate persuasion and illegitimate force and fraud. If the sophisticated, not to say sophistical, view that all persuasion is a form of manipulation were to become general in a liberal democracy, its citizens would necessarily come to despise as hypocritical and degrading the constitutional procedures of elections, deliberations, and appeals to public opinion without which liberal democracy is impossible.

In sum, then, historicism acts like a solvent on liberal democracy. A complex, deliberately questionable structure to begin with, its justification is that, unlike simpler and more apparently solid abodes like absolute despotism, it is the only way really to bring people indoors out of the state of nature, that is, of need, oppression, and feral conflict. But liberal democracy is dissolved at its foundations by the reduction of its principles to manifestations of culture and the consequent denial of the possibility of its claim of universal standing. Fortunately, we have for the most part responded prosaically enough to our interesting situation by patching up the structure with available bits. Or perhaps we have responded magically, like Donald Duck, who continues to walk on air even after running off the precipice because he hasn't noticed that he has. Eventually, of course, he notices.

Summary

Does historicism then relegate all forms of American patriotism, all principled allegiance to our Constitution, to wishful thinking and bad faith? One must begin by giving historicism credit. It is hard to deny that historicism revealed what was partial in the assumptions of the founders, in particular the assumption that there could be a uniform account of human nature based on the passion for self-preservation. But to admit this suggests that historicism made possible and even logically required another effort to return once more in an unprejudiced way to the phenomena. This is, in fact, what it thought it was doing, and to a large extent it succeeded. Historians in particular learned the need to be open to information gathered from every form of human activity and to every possibility of interpretation. Yet historicism shared one assumption with the rationalism it thought it had refuted and transcended, which lay so deep as not, apparently, to be recognizable as an assumption at all. This shared assumption is that reason could not transcend the passions but was merely their instrument.

It was this assumption, however, that eventually frustrated historicism's positive project, for it made it impossible consistently to rescue the historian from the history he examined or to give any special status to his conclusions. Becker's skeptical pragmatism exemplifies the problem; the historian's reason merely serves ends that are themselves not governable by reason. Hence historicism left its followers in the self-contradictory position of simultaneously believing and not believing in what they were doing.

To say this, though, is to raise the question whether the apparent success of historicism in destroying the possibility of anything but itself is really as maintainable, not to say as unquestionable, as Becker thought. To show that reason, conceived as a tool of the passions, cannot prescribe for all men because the passions are not uniform is not to refute the possibility that reason may be capable of transcending and ordering the passions.

This suggests that historicism may perhaps be met by a more consistent, radical, and indeed more skeptical version of itself. A "historicism" that sought to look at the phenomena as they present themselves, in an unbiased way, without dogmatic assumptions, would at least have held as unproved the subjection of reason to the passions. Such a "historicism" would in fact have made it possible to begin afresh the unprejudiced examination of human things that had begun, on similar terms, in classical Athens. What results such a "historicism" would have for the American regime one could not readily tell. Yet it is unlikely that it would end by pronouncing a condemnation of the regime that is in fact implicitly a self-condemnation and a confession of its own failure. For the historicist condemnation of the universal claim of the American regime is grounded on the same dogmatic dismissal of the power of reason that condemns the historian's own reasonings. In the end, it seems to me that historicism's enormous powers of destruction are finally powers of self-destruction; hence its despair need not be ours.

It may be argued, however, that the admitted strength of historicism, its power to make do on so little, its willingness, skeptical and ingenuous at once, to see only what is there and no more, contradicts the possibility of a special "rational faculty" being dragged in to help us out of our difficulties. Perhaps the skepticism shared by the Enlightenment and historicism about the transcendence of reason is not based on dogmatic assumption. Is not the burden really on those who would entertain the possibility to demonstrate it first?

In this regard, a passage in Herder's essay on the origin of language comes to mind. Herder wants to refute the Enlightenment view of Condillac that human language is derived from animal noises that express feelings. Imagining two children in a desert with no knowledge of the use of signs, Condillac argues that when brought together they will learn by mutual commerce to connect thoughts with the cries of passion whose natural signs they are. Herder has some fun with this, asking how these two children, who know even less than animals, begin to have "commerce" and then are capable of "learning" to connect thoughts with cries of passion.[79] As his parodic rendering of Condillac's argument continues into the derivation of prosody, rhetoric, music, dance, and poetry from animal noises, Herder demonstrates that Condillac is assuming something he has not presented. Either Condillac's argument makes no sense at all, or he is assuming "the whole thing, language, even before the first page of his book,"[80] or rather, "in short, words came about because there were words before they were there."[81] Rousseau's denial of the human capacity to invent language is not much of an improvement, Herder thinks, because it is based on the impossibility of Condillac's derivation and of there being any alternative to the animal noises theory.[82] (In fact it is striking how in the *Second Discourse* Rousseau repeatedly emphasizes the problematic character of deriving human language from his hypothesized natural man.[83])

Herder's alternative begins by considering the difference between human beings and animals. In short, he distinguishes between the specific occupations of animals for which very specific instincts suit them and the human lack of any clear determination and of any very specific instincts. Yet man has something corresponding to the instincts, he argues. One may call it what one will, "understanding, reason, reflection etc.," but it is this that enables man to create language, which is so necessary to him in undertaking the obligations of a biological generalist.[84] What makes Herder's argument relevant here is not the hackneyed point that man differs from the animals by having reason. Rather, it is Herder's insistence that he is not speaking about some "qualitas occulta" arbitrarily arrived at[85] or about some "separated powers" (or "mere elevated stages of animal powers").[86] Herder does not try to return to what he thinks Aristotle was doing; on the contrary, he wishes to meet the scientific moderns on their own ground. Like the founder of historicism he was, he wishes to look at the phenomena without prejudice, just as the scientists claim to do. When he does so, he recognizes that man is not just an animal like all the others with some curious differences but that as an object of study he turns out to be different in being rational.

One might argue that Herder was here merely demonstrating involuntarily how far he still had to go in breaking with metaphysical assumptions. The opposite seems truer to me. In stating perhaps naively a conclusion that Rousseau rejects while emphasizing the difficulties inherent in that rejection, Herder seems to exemplify what historicism could have been and what, if it had been, might have saved it from its self-annihilation. For in accepting reason as the defining difference between human beings and animals, Herder begins to make possible an account of human history that would leave room for historians too and would not doom them as historians to pretend they were indistinguishable from Everyman paying his coal bill or as citizens to pretend that their allegiances do not exist.

Neither the cleverness of liberal patriotism nor the bravado of conservative patriotism in their responses to historicism serves us adequately as citizens of the United States. Nor are we intellectually obligated to the relativism or nihilism of radical, but perhaps not sufficiently radical, historicism. True, on this showing we cannot claim that the founders were right about everything. Yet to recognize that there is something partial in the account of individuals founding a state for the protection of their natural rights, understood as their deepest passions, does not require us therefore to embrace it blindly as "ours," discard it angrily as false, or nervously affirm it by pretending to deny it. Instead, we can try to look at it without prejudice. We may well learn from such an examination that the regime and the principles it is based on approximate the necessary conditions of liberty and equality under the law in a decent regime. We may also come to learn that the American Constitution, while it may not be the only admirable one ever to have existed, is peculiarly suited to our times and circumstances. Even in comparison with others we may come to admire, which perhaps provided tighter bonds of community or more exalted opportunities for the excellent to display their greatness, we may well come to appreciate, cherish, and even prefer its success in making possible for most people a prosperous, decent, and worthy life.

11
Capitalism

Marc F. Plattner

Unlike the other "isms" discussed in this volume, capitalism refers primarily to a set of economic arrangements rather than to a body of thought. Accordingly, the adjective "capitalist" usually designates not the proponent of a particular doctrine but a man belonging to a certain economic class or having a certain economic function—an owner or employer of capital. It must also be noted that the term "capitalism" was popularized by its opponents and has often been avoided or even repudiated by its advocates. Nonetheless, there is little difficulty in identifying prominent thinkers whose teachings may reasonably be viewed as defenses of the economic system commonly labeled capitalism.

Thus Adam Smith is widely and properly regarded as the classic philosopher of capitalism. In the contemporary era, the thinkers who most readily come to mind as champions of capitalism are the so-called free-market economists, whose most prominent representatives—at least as regards more general defenses of a capitalist order—are Nobel Prize winners Friedrich A. von Hayek and Milton Friedman. Broadly speaking, then, we may identify the school of thought with which this essay is concerned as the tradition of political economy from Smith down through the economists of the present day.

This statement of focus must, however, immediately be qualified. In the first place, it would be more precise to speak of the tradition of bourgeois (or individualist or liberal) political economy. For we surely want to exclude Marx and other avowed socialists and their present-day disciples, who self-consciously stand apart from the mainstream of Western economic thought, viewing themselves as enemies rather than adherents of capitalism. But even with this exclusion it is misleading simply to identify bourgeois political economy (or contemporary economics) with the defense of capitalism. Marx himself distinguished the "scientific bourgeois economy" of Smith and David Ricardo (and to a lesser extent of John Stuart Mill) from the "apologetics" or "vulgar economy" of their successors.[1] The situation is even more ambiguous with respect to present-day economics. It has been said that today "most economists are agreed that economic theory as such can say little of general validity about the respective merits of capitalism and socialism."[2] Notwithstanding the claim and aspiration of modern economic science to be value free, it can be argued that its premises and approach are rooted in liberal individualism. Be that as it may, certainly very many non-Marxist economists today would bridle at the suggestion that they are defenders of capitalism. Therefore, in assessing the influence of capitalist thought on American opinion, we must remain attentive to the distinction between avowedly procapitalist doctrines and the implicitly capitalist assumptions of scientific economics.

Almost everyone would agree that the United States is a capitalist country and that its economic system has an enormous influence on the lives, habits, and views of its citizens. It is equally obvious that American thought about specifically economic matters has been decisively affected by the work of economists. But our inquiry here must be restricted to the influence of political economy on American opinion about broader questions of politics and morality.

If one looks at the contemporary scene, the broader influence of the economists is apparent in two ways. The first is the resurgence of the explicitly procapitalist doctrines of the free-market economists. Not very long ago thinkers of this school were typically regarded as a reactionary sect that was academically isolated and politically marginal. Today their academic respectability is unassailable, and since the election of Ronald Reagan to the presidency they have risen to a position of considerable political influence. This phenomenon is by no means confined to the United States, where "conservative" political forces have traditionally been allied (if sometimes uneasily) with admirers of free markets. In Europe, where conservative parties have frequently reflected traditional nationalist, religious, aristocratic, and statist antipathies toward capitalism, the growing prominence of free-market doctrines is even more striking. In Britain the Tories under the leadership of Margaret Thatcher are now dominated by this strand of thought, which seems also to be increasingly powerful in the conservative parties of the Federal Republic of Germany and even of France. With the welfare state everywhere in a period of retrenchment and with democratic left-of-center parties generally in a period of political and intellectual disarray, free-market advocates can plausibly claim that today their doctrines provide a critical source of support for liberal democracy.

A second important influence on contemporary public opinion may be ascribed to a more general "economism" that is not specifically procapitalist. In recent years economics has become the most imperialistic of the social sciences. Economic methods and approaches have infiltrated political science and sociology, and economic analysis has been applied to such seemingly noneconomic institutions as the criminal justice system and the family. Most significant politically has been the hegemony of economics over the new discipline of policy analysis. Not only academic journals but legislative chambers and op-ed pages today are filled with the language and concepts economists have brought to the discussion of public policy—costs and benefits, trade-offs, efficiency, maximization, optimal solutions, market mechanisms, externalities, public goods, incentives and disincentives, and so on.

These economic tools of policy analysis are meant in principle to be neutral not only as between economic systems but also as between political regimes. They could equally well be employed by a despot as by a democratically elected legislature. But precisely because they are tools meant to be useful within the context of the existing political arrangements, they are not likely to attract those who are fundamentally opposed to American liberal democracy. It is no accident, then, that non-Marxist economists (and policy analysts), when speaking as citizens rather than scientists, are almost universally supporters of the political liberties and institutions established by the Constitution of the United States.

Thus at first glance there is surely an apparent harmony between bourgeois political economy and the views of the American founders. The task of the remainder of this chapter is, first, to probe more deeply into the shared principles and outlook that account for this harmony between the teachings of the political economists and those of the founders and, second, to examine where these two sets of doctrines diverge and what the implications and consequences of these divergences may be. On this basis we should be able to reach some conclusions about the ways in which the teachings of political economy strengthen or imperil the theoretical underpinnings of the political regime founded on the Constitution.

Shared Principles

The very notion that a primarily economic doctrine could claim comparable theoretical rank with the political philosophy of the founders implies an extraordinary elevation of the importance of economic matters for the right ordering of human life. Before the eighteenth century economics was either a very practical subject discussed chiefly by men of affairs or, insofar as it was treated in a more theoretical fashion, a very subordinate part of political philosophy. This earlier subordination is recalled not only in the term "political" economy but also in the definition Smith gives the new science in *The Wealth of Nations*. Political economy, he states, is

> a branch of the science of a statesman or legislator [that] proposes two distinct objects: first, to provide a plentiful revenue or subsistence for the people, or more properly to enable them to provide such a revenue or subsistence for themselves; and secondly, to supply the state or commonwealth with a revenue sufficient for the public services. It proposes to enrich both the people and the sovereign.[3]

This statement makes it clear what the goal of political economy is—namely, riches, for both the individual and the government. It does not indicate, however, the relation of political economy and its goal to the other branches of legislative science. At the conclusion of his treatise on moral philosophy, *The Theory of Moral Sentiments* (1759), Smith laments the failure of philosophers to have established "a system of what might properly be called natural jurisprudence, or a theory of the general principles which ought to run through, and be the foundation of, the laws of all nations." He then states his own intention to write

> another discourse, endeavour[ing] to give an account of the general principles of law and government, and the different revolutions they have undergone in the different ages and periods of society, not only in what concerns justice, but in what concerns police, revenue, and arms, and whatever else is the object of law.[4]

Smith subsequently published his work on political economy, *The Wealth of Nations* (1776), but not a comprehensive discourse on natural jurisprudence. There are available to us, however, two records of notes taken from the lectures Smith gave on jurisprudence in his post as professor of moral philosophy at Glasgow University. As reported in both these accounts, Smith defined jurisprudence in the same broad manner as in the conclusion of *The Theory of Moral Sentiments* and divided it into the four parts there enumerated—justice, police, revenue, and arms.

According to the fuller of the two accounts (1762–1763), Smith in his opening lecture characterized the initial part of jurisprudence as follows:

> The first and chief design of every system of government is to maintain justice; to prevent the members of a society from encroaching on one another's property, or seizing what is not

> their own. The design here is to give each one the secure and peaceable possession of his own property.

He then went on to state:

> When this end, which we may call the internal peace, or peace within doors, is secured, the government will next be desirous of promoting the opulence of the state. This produces what we call police. Whatever regulations are made with respect to the trade, commerce, agriculture, manufactures of the country are considered as belonging to police.

With regard to revenue, the third branch of jurisprudence, Smith says he will

> consider the different methods which have been taken to raise the sum necessary for the expense of the state in different countries, and how far they are adapted to do this with the least loss or hindrance to the industry of the people, which ought to be the chief thing in view.

Finally, Smith explains the inclusion of the subject of arms by noting,

> Besides these three considerations of the security of property, the police, and the revenue of the kingdom or state, it must also be necessary to have some means of protecting the state from foreign injuries. Though the peace within doors be never so firmly established, yet if there be no security from injuries from without the property of individuals cannot be secure.[5]

By comparing this account of the branches of jurisprudence with the definition of political economy in *The Wealth of Nations,* it becomes apparent that political economy comprises police and revenue and that the remaining parts of the science of the legislator are justice and arms.[6] The latter two tasks of legislation, however, have as their goal the security of property. Thus, although internal justice and external defense may be the most basic and pressing concerns of the legislator, they seem in another sense to be ministerial or subordinate to the goals of political economy—namely, "to enrich both the people and the sovereign." Moreover, as between these two aims of political economy, Smith in the lectures makes it clear that the task of meeting the expenses of the sovereign ought to be carried out in the way that least hinders "the industry of the people"—in other words, that the end of revenue is subordinate to that of police.

The opulence of the people, then, appears to be for Smith the ultimate aim of jurisprudence. To appreciate the significance of this fact, it will be useful to inquire further into Smith's identification of the branch of jurisprudence concerned with enriching the people as "police." In the first of his lectures on police, he notes that this word "originally derived from the Greek *politeia,* signifying policy, politics, or the regulation of a government in general. It is now however generally confined to the regulation of the inferior parts of it." Smith indicates the range of police in the modern sense by recounting the instructions given to a newly appointed intendant of Paris—"to provide for the *netteté* (cleanliness), *sûreté* (security) and *bon marche* (cheapness of goods) in the city."[7] The first two of these—keeping the streets clean and the "proper form and regulation of town guards"—are said to be subjects "of too mean a nature" to be treated in his course. But cheapness (which is "a necessary consequence of plenty" or opulence) is not considered too mean to be the subject of very many lectures and subsequently of the greatest part of T*he Wealth of Nations*.

In his comments on the science of natural jurisprudence at the close of *The Theory of Moral Sentiments,* Smith had noted that the *Laws* of Cicero and of Plato "are laws of police, not of justice."[8] Here Smith is clearly using the term "police" in its ancient sense. For the *Laws* of Plato contains detailed regulations regarding the political and social institutions, education, religious beliefs, and way of life of the citizens. Among other things, these impose the strictest bounds on the pursuit of wealth—for example, fixed and inalienable allotments of land, narrow limits on the accumulation of property, the banning of gold and silver, and the forbidding of "vulgar" commercial occupations. For riches are held to be incompatible with virtue and friendship among the citizens.[9]

By explicitly reducing the object of police to promoting the opulence of the people, Smith makes plain his rejection of the ancient view that the goal of legislation is to promote virtue and public spirit on the part of the citizenry. Smith's contemporary Jean-Jacques Rousseau had deplored the fact that while "ancient political thinkers incessantly talked about morals and virtue, those of our time talk only of commerce and money."[10] In terms of this dichotomy, Smith clearly sides with modern political thought against Rousseau and the ancients. Once it is no longer believed that legislation must be guided by the requirement of civic virtue, the unlimited pursuit of wealth is free to emerge as the end of both the individual and the nation. With this change the way is paved for economics to be elevated from a subordinate or "inferior" part of political science to become its capstone. And with the acceptance of the goal of maximization of wealth, economics can come into its own as an autonomous field of knowledge both worthy of and amenable to theoretical or scientific study.

Smith's specifically economic prescription for "accelerating the progress of the society towards real wealth and greatness" is embodied in what he called "the system of natural liberty":

> Every man, as long as he does not violate the laws of justice, is left perfectly free to pursue his own interest his own way, and to bring both his industry and capital into competition with those of any other man, or order of men. The sovereign is completely discharged from a duty, in the attempting to perform which he must always be exposed to innumerable delusions, and for the proper performance of which no human knowledge or wisdom could ever be sufficient; the duty of superintending the industry of private people, and of directing it towards the employment most suitable to the interest of society.[11]

This advocacy of what became known as laissez faire and today is more commonly called free-market capitalism emerges primarily from a critique of the system of mercantilism—that is, government attempts to maximize national wealth by giving preferences to or imposing restraints on particular branches of industry. The attack on government intervention in the economy and the praise of the efficiency of free competition are no doubt Smith's most distinctive and original contributions to political thought. Yet in the present context we must be careful not to overemphasize the theoretical importance of the free market in Smith's overall political teaching.

In the first place, it is necessary to recognize that Smith was not as extreme or dogmatic in his advocacy of laissez faire as is sometimes believed.[12] Many remarks from *The Wealth of Nations* might be cited to demonstrate this point, but the following passage (in which Smith defends a prohibition on the issue of bank notes of less than five pounds) will suffice:

> Such regulations may, no doubt, be considered as in some respect a violation of natural liberty. But those exertions of the natural liberty of a few individuals, which might endanger the security of the whole society, are, and ought to be, restrained by the laws of all governments; of the most free, as well as of the most despotical. The obligation of building party walls, in order to prevent the communication of fire, is a violation of natural liberty, exactly of the same kind with the regulations of the banking trade which are here proposed.[13]

Second, it is clear that Smith never believed that the "system of natural liberty" he recommends would ever be implemented to its fullest extent: "To expect, indeed, that the freedom of trade should ever be entirely restored in Great Britain, is as absurd as to expect that an Oceana or Utopia should ever be established in it."[14] Yet this by no means led Smith to despair regarding the future prospects of his country, for he did not regard economic or commercial policy as the crucial determinant of prosperity:

> The security which the laws in Great Britain give to every man that he shall enjoy the fruits of his own labour, is alone sufficient to make any country flourish, notwithstanding these [the corn laws] and twenty other absurd regulations of commerce. . . . The natural effort of every individual to better his own condition, when suffered to exert itself with freedom and security, is so powerful a principle, that it is alone, and without any assistance, not only capable of carrying on the society to wealth and prosperity, but of surmounting a hundred impertinent obstructions with which the folly of human laws too often incumbers its operations.

Thus Smith notes that despite their adoption of similarly counterproductive mercantilist policies, Great Britain has grown rich while Spain and Portugal remain "beggarly." For

> this bad policy is not in those countries counterbalanced by the general liberty and security of the people. Industry is there neither free nor secure, and the civil and ecclesiastical governments of Spain and Portugal, are such as would alone be sufficient to perpetuate their present state of poverty, even though their regulations of commerce were as wise as the greater part of them are absurd and foolish.[15]

For Smith then, the essential condition for prosperity is a political order that provides the people with liberty and security and thus guarantees them the enjoyment of the fruits of their labor. This requires a government that not only prevents its citizens from oppressing or despoiling one another but also is itself restrained from oppressing or despoiling them. When these conditions are met, men's "universal, continual, and uninterrupted effort to better their own condition" can be allowed free reign.[16] The stability and good order of the society do not require that the citizens be imbued with a strict sense of moral duty or a strong devotion to the public good. In a commercial society people's self-interested and "vulgar" desire of "augmenting their fortune" is alone sufficient to produce that industriousness, sobriety, and frugality that Smith characterizes as "good conduct."[17] And this self-interested good conduct not only reinforces political stability but also, by promoting the steady accumulation of capital, leads to ever-increasing national wealth. This natural harmony between the individual's pursuit of his own economic advantage and the public good—understood as constituted by liberty, security, and prosperity for all—lies at the core of Smith's political thought. The idea that free competition is a more efficient commercial policy than government bounties and restraints is merely an extension and refinement of this more general view.

In viewing the security, liberty, and prosperity of the individual as the ends of civil society, Smith places himself squarely in the liberal tradition whose great founder was John Locke. It is altogether fitting that Locke was the first eminent philosopher to have written treatises wholly devoted to economic issues in the modern sense. In his *Some Considerations of the Consequences of Lowering the Interest and Raising the Value of Money* and *Further Considerations Concerning Raising the Value of Money,* Locke espouses a mercantilist approach to questions of economic policy. In this regard, of course, he may be reckoned an opponent rather than a progenitor of Smith's "system of natural liberty." Yet the respects in which Smith follows Locke are much more fundamental. For it is in Locke's political philosophy that we first find clearly enunciated not only the central importance of economic motives to political life but also the view that the individual's uninhibited pursuit of economic self-interest is both morally legitimate and conducive to the common good.

In a famous passage in his *Second Treatise of Government,* Locke states: "The great and *chief end* . . . of Mens uniting into Commonwealths, and putting themselves under Government, is the *Preservation of Their Property."*[18] How men come legitimately to acquire the property that government is dedicated to preserving (and increasing) is explained by Locke in a chapter entitled "Of Property." Although the earth has been given to men in common, each individual has by nature an exclusive property in his own labor. By mixing his labor with some part of what belongs to all in common, the individual converts it into his own private property. The reason why "the Property of labor . . . [is] able to over-ballance the Community of Land" is that "'tis labor indeed that puts the difference of value on everything." The immensely superior value of cultivated as opposed to uncultivated land is wholly owing to labor. Therefore, "he, that encloses land and has a greater plenty of the conveniencys of life from ten acres, than he could have from an hundred left to Nature, may truly be said, to give ninety acres to mankind." The individual's creation and accumulation of wealth through labor "does not lessen but increase the common stock of mankind." The self-interested quest for economic gain redounds to the advantage of all. With the progress of "Invention and Arts" and the division of labor that accompanies that progress, societies can attain a standard of wealth and comfort that renders contemptible the pittance that "un-assisted nature" provides. Although such societies may be characterized by great inequalities of wealth, even their poorest day laborer "feeds, lodges, and is clad" better than a king among the savage nations of the Americas.[19]

Locke's emphasis on labor as the source of wealth, on the role of division of labor, and on the possibility and desirability of economic growth is conspicuously reflected in the opening pages of *The Wealth of Nations.* In the introduction Smith notes that in "civilized and thriving nations . . . a workman, even of the lowest and poorest order, if he is frugal and industrious, may enjoy a greater share of the necessaries and conveniences of life than it is possible for any savage to acquire."[20] And he includes in chapter 1 a lengthy reflection on the "variety of labour" that is necessary to produce the simple commodities enjoyed by the "very meanest person in a civilized country"—a passage that strikingly echoes Locke's description in the *Second Treatise* of the manifold kinds of labor that contribute to the production of a loaf of bread.[21] Smith concludes from this reflection that

> it may be true, perhaps, that the accommodation of a European Prince does not always so much exceed that of an industrious and frugal peasant, as the accommodation of the latter exceeds that of many an African king, the absolute master of the lives and liberties of ten thousand naked savages.

In sum, it is in the thought of Locke that we find the basic premises elaborated on by Smith in the classic exposition of capitalism.

As is confirmed by Thomas Pangle's chapter in part one of this volume, Locke is also the most important philosophic source of the thought of the American founders. Like Smith, the founders embraced the protocapitalist elements of Locke's teachings. The authors of *The Federalist* unhesitatingly endorse a commercial society, one meant to encourage among its members the industrious pursuit of private gain. They regard "the protection of different and unequal faculties of acquiring property" as "the first object of government." Indeed, the vital importance of providing for the security of property was acknowledged by all sides in the debate over the adoption of the Constitution.[22]

Beyond these shared Lockean premises, the relationship of the thought of the founders to that of Smith is much more elusive. We know that Alexander Hamilton, James Madison, and Thomas Jefferson all read *The Wealth of Nations* during the 1780s. In a letter to Thomas Mann Randolph written in 1790, Jefferson remarked, "In political economy, I think Smith's *Wealth of Nations* the best book extant."[23] But although the founders' thought may have been influenced by Smith, it would be difficult to argue that any of them were strict adherents of the "system of natural liberty." Nonetheless, the unwillingness of the founders consistently to advocate commercial policies that went as far in the direction of laissez faire as *The Wealth of Nations* recommends does not indicate any incompatibility at the level of fundamental principle between Smith's teaching and their own. The Constitution of the United States does not establish the system of natural liberty, but neither does it forestall or hinder its adoption.

The relationship of the founders to the Smithian economic system of natural liberty is to some extent analogous to Smith's relationship to the republicanism of the founders. Smith was clearly a proponent of "free" as opposed to despotical or absolute government. That is, he favored a government that guarantees the personal liberty and security of the people and thus encourages the exercise of their industry and the attainment of prosperity. As means of securing personal liberty, Smith endorses the key elements of the new science of politics cited in *The Federalist:* the separation of powers, an independent judiciary, and elected representation in the legislature.[24] Yet despite his frequent praise for the "wise republic of Holland," Smith cannot be considered a champion of republicanism; for he bestows equal if not greater praise on the kind of mixed government exemplified by the limited monarchy of Great Britain.[25] It seems then that representation, separation of powers, and an independent judiciary are regarded by Smith as the crucial political desiderata; as long as these are provided for, the question of the republican or monarchical character of the regime is of secondary importance. It should be recalled, however, that neither the political teaching of Locke nor even the principles enunciated in the Declaration of Independence require a strictly republican form of government. Thus once again there seems to be no serious conflict at the level of principle between the republicanism of the founders and the political thought of Smith.

Divergences and Their Implications

Although both Smith and the American founders rest firmly within the tradition of Lockean liberalism, this does not mean that there are no significant theoretical differences between them. One noteworthy sign of divergence is that Smith, in his lectures on jurisprudence, follows the argument of David Hume in rejecting the doctrine of the social contract propounded by Locke and adopted in both theory and practice by the Americans.[26] Both Hume and Smith argue that in fact princes and subjects in almost all political societies do not base the duty of obedience on any notion of a social contract. Their opposition to this aspect of Locke's teaching derives in part from a conservative wariness about the revolutionary implications of making the consent of the people the sole foundation of legitimate government. Instead of contract or consent, Smith holds that "authority" and "utility" are the two principles of allegiance to the civil magistrate.

Those thinkers who reject the doctrine of the social contract typically also reject the associated Lockean doctrines of the state of nature and the natural rights of man. Thus Hume labels the state of nature a "mere philosophical fiction, which never had, and never could have any reality" and does not speak of men's natural rights.[27] Smith's position is more ambiguous. Although he speaks in the lectures of the natural rights to life and liberty, he seems to deny the Lockean view that the right to property is natural and to question the usefulness of discussions of the state of nature.[28] The clearest expression within eighteenth-century liberalism of this rejection of key elements of Locke's teaching is found in the thought of Jeremy Bentham. Bentham denies that there is a clear demarcation between the state of nature and the state of political society; he labels the social contract a "chimera" ("effectually demolished by Mr. Hume") and offers in its place the Humean principle of utility; and he ridicules the idea of "natural imprescriptable rights" as "rhetorical nonsense—nonsense on stilts."[29]

One may distinguish, then, two branches of liberalism deriving from the thought of Locke—the natural rights and the utilitarian traditions. The former would include the physiocrats and the French revolutionaries who composed the Declaration of the Rights of Man and the Citizen, Thomas Paine and certain other early British radicals, the American founders, John Marshall and other American jurists of the nineteenth century, and perhaps Herbert Spencer. Today the natural rights tradition, although it continues to exert a lingering influence over American popular opinion, is largely moribund among intellectuals. Apart from the followers of Leo Strauss, only Robert Nozick and a few other "libertarians" might plausibly claim to be the heirs of this tradition.

In the utilitarian tradition the most prominent figures are Hume, Smith (though in less clear-cut fashion), Bentham, and James and John Stuart Mill. This is clearly the branch of liberalism in which political economy—and, more distantly, present-day economics—have their theoretical roots. The importance of Smith and John Stuart Mill for political economy goes without saying. And although the significance of Bentham's strictly economic writings may be slight, his decisive impact on the subsequent course of economic thought is attested to by no less an authority than Alfred Marshall, who identifies Bentham as "on the whole the most influential of the immediate successors of Adam Smith."[30]

Despite jettisoning the natural rights foundation of Locke's teaching, the utilitarian tradition remained committed to such Lockean goals as individual liberty, the security of private property, and the emancipation of economic self-interest as a means of enriching both the individual and the nation. No less than the adherents of natural rights, the utilitarians of the eighteenth and early nineteenth centuries affirmed what may be called the bourgeois ethic. They regarded labor as the source of value and the ultimate basis for private property and were wholly dedicated to the proposition that the laws should seek to ensure to men the fruits of their labor. The two traditions differed on the grounds on which men ought to be rewarded with the fruits of their labor. Locke himself had supplemented his defense of the individual's natural right to property—that is, to the fruits of his labor—with the argument that securing this right would promote an increase in societal wealth ultimately benefiting all. It was this latter justification that the utilitarians seized upon and made the sole basis of their case for the security of private property.

The rejection of natural rights by utilitarians like Bentham by no means led them to waver in their support for the existing distribution of property. Indeed, some radical versions of the natural rights doctrine were much more hostile to the prevailing economic order, particularly with respect to landownership. For a doctrine that founded the natural right to property on labor could readily be interpreted and applied in a way that challenged the disproportion between productive labor and wealth in contemporary civil societies. For this and other reasons the natural rights teaching came to be associated in many quarters with Jacobinism. Thus Albert Venn Dicey has argued that "the unlimited scorn entertained by every Benthamite for the social contract and for natural rights" helped make Benthamism attractive to moderate English opinion by serving as "a guarantee against sympathy with Jacobinical principles."[31]

Bentham's own teaching, it is true, reckoned material equality as one of the four "subordinate objects" of legislation (subordinate, that is, to the general end—"the happiness of the body politic"). He argued that greater wealth brings greater happiness and that "the more nearly the actual proportion approaches to equality, the greater will be the total mass of happiness." Yet Bentham remained resolutely opposed to the redistribution of property because of the overriding importance he attached to security: "When security and equality are in opposition, there should be no hesitation; equality should give way." And "the grand principle of security," according to Bentham, directs the legislator to "maintain the distribution [of property] which is actually established. This, under the name of justice, is with reason regarded as his first duty: it is a general and simple rule applicable to all states, adapted to all plans, even those which are most opposed to each other."[32]

Alfred Marshall attributes Bentham's "passionate desire for security" to the impression made on his mind by "the terror of the French Revolution."[33] Yet the importance he places on the security of property and the reasoning he employs to defend it are entirely consonant with the teaching of Smith. Bentham holds that without the security of enjoying the fruits of one's labor afforded by the laws, human industry is paralyzed. The condition of savages and that of peoples living under "the absurd despotism of the Turk" are adduced as examples of the poverty that prevails where security is lacking. Poverty is the "primitive condition of the human race"; the creation of wealth is made possible only when the security of property is assured. "The Law does not say to a man 'Work and I will reward you'; but it says to him, 'Work, and by stopping the hand that would take them from you, I will ensure to you the fruits of your labor, its natural and sufficient reward, which, without me, you could not preserve.' "[34]

Bentham appears to entertain no doubts about the desirability—indeed, the justice—of laissez-faire capitalism on purely utilitarian grounds. Yet his arguments reflect the lingering influence of those aspects of Locke's thought that he explicitly rejected. Despite his contempt for the doctrine of natural rights, he invokes the naturalness of ensuring to men the fruits of their labor. And despite his reservations about the notion of the state of nature, his justification for the security of private property lays great stress on the contrast with a primitive or savage state of mankind in which no such security exists.

Only when these Lockean ways of thinking lose their hold is there a serious weakening of the connection between utilitarianism and the bourgeois ethic of laissez-faire capitalism. Such a weakening can be observed in the dominant economic work of the mid-nineteenth century—John Stuart Mill's *Principles of Political Economy*.

To be sure, Mill's massive treatise contains many echoes of the Benthamite viewpoint. He asserts, for example, that

> all laws or usages . . . which chain up the efforts of any part of the community, in pursuit of their own good, or stand between those efforts and their natural fruits—are (independently of all other grounds of condemnation) violations of

> the fundamental principles of economic policy; tending to make the aggregate powers of the community productive in a less degree than they would otherwise be.[35]

In several places he stresses the vital importance of security of property as a precondition of prosperity: "Industry and frugality cannot exist where there is not a preponderant probability that those who labor and spare will be permitted to enjoy."[36] His insistence on maintaining the connection between exertion and reward leads him to condemn trade union opposition to piecework as "one of the most discreditable indications of a low moral condition given of late by part of the English working classes. . . . Dislike to piece work in itself, except under mistaken notions, must be dislike to justice and fairness, a desire to cheat, by not giving work in proportion to pay."[37]

Yet in an earlier passage of the *Principles,* noting that most of the French socialist manufacturing associations that had begun by sharing the remuneration equally had subsequently adopted a standard of piecework, Mill concludes:

> The original principle [that is, equal remuneration] appeals to a higher standard of justice, and is adapted to a much higher moral condition of human nature. The proportioning of remuneration to work done is really just only in so far as the more or less of the work is a matter of choice: when it depends on natural difference of strength or capacity, this principle of remuneration is itself an injustice: it is giving to those who have; assigning most to those who are already most favored by nature. Considered, however, as a compromise with the selfish type of character formed by the present standard of morality, and fostered by the existing social institutions, it is highly expedient; and until education shall have been entirely regenerated, is far more likely to prove immediately successful, than an attempt at a higher ideal.

Along these same lines, Mill elsewhere speaks of "the true idea of distributive justice, which consists not in imitating but in redressing the inequalities and wrongs of nature."[38]

The opposing viewpoints expressed in these two sets of quotations coexist uneasily within Mill's *Principles.* The first set seems to regard rewarding individuals with the fruits of their labor not only as economically efficient but also as both natural and just. The second, by contrast, defines distributive justice as emphatically opposed to nature and to the natural connection between labor and its fruits. It also implies that the proper standard for judging the distributional consequences of capitalist society is not the insecurity and poverty of a precivilized state but some future and more enlightened era by whose higher and less selfish standard of morality capitalism will be found severely wanting.

This kind of shift in perspective would hardly be possible within the natural rights tradition. For the central role of the state of nature in this doctrine ensures that the precivilized past will remain as a key point of reference, and the very idea of a natural right to the fruits of one's labor requires that nature remain a guidepost for distributive justice. The utilitarian tradition, however, contains no intrinsic barrier to the adoption of the very different viewpoints that Mill seems to have absorbed from the philosophy of history and from socialism. Thus, despite its Lockean ancestry and the intimate association of its Benthamite version with laissez faire, utilitarianism proved highly susceptible to being turned in an anticapitalist direction.[39]

Noting that Mill's *Principles of Political Economy* was "the most successful and influential treatise of that age," Joseph Schumpeter remarks:

> Nothing can be more revealing of the character of bourgeois civilization—more indicative, that is, of its genuine freedom and also of its political weakness—than that the book to which the bourgeois accorded such a reception carried a socialist message and was written by a man palpably out of sympathy with the scheme of values of the industrial bourgeoisie.[40]

Schumpeter probably goes too far in suggesting that the confused and often contradictory "message" of the *Principles* can simply be classified as socialist. Yet he is surely on the mark in observing that this classic of bourgeois political economy calls into question the basic ethical premises of capitalist society. Having abandoned the theoretical underpinnings of the doctrine of natural rights, the utilitarian tradition of political economy winds up more or less grudgingly acceding to the moral critique of capitalist justice offered by its egalitarian and "progressive" opponents.

After Mill it is difficult to find a distinguished political economist who does not share to some degree his ambivalence toward the capitalist ethic and particularly his doubts about the justice of distribution in capitalist society. To be sure, most political economists reconciled themselves to the system of private property, but their objections to socialism tended to be practical rather than moral. Henry Sidgwick, for example, asserted: "I object to socialism not because it would divide the produce of industry badly, but because it would have so much less to divide."[41]

By 1923 the prominent American economist Frank H. Knight could write: "We find a fairly general agreement among serious writers that the principle of *need*, which would practically amount to equal sharing as a general rule, is the ideal basis of distribution."[42] Knight, a teacher of Milton Friedman, has been described by Hayek as "the American economist who has done most to advance our understanding of a free society."[43] Yet his essay "The Ethics of Competition," just quoted, is an almost unqualified attack on the bourgeois ethic and on the justice of distribution under capitalism. Knight specifically challenges the notion that labor supplies an ethically valid title to income, and he does so principally on the same ground as Mill: He argues that from an ethical standpoint "inherited [that is, natural] capacity," which he identifies as the most important source of more productive labor, "represents an obligation to the world rather than a claim upon it."[44]

The view that greater productivity stemming from greater natural ability is not morally deserving of larger rewards is now virtually universal among economists who have addressed this question. For thinkers of an egalitarian bent, this argument has become a crucial element in the moral justification of government policies aimed at the redistribution of income. Thus Arthur Okun, for example, defending the case for redistribution in his *Equality and Efficiency*, asserts that "society should aim to ameliorate, and certainly not to compound, the flaws of the universe" by deciding to "restrict prizes that bestow vastly higher standards of living on people with . . . greater innate abilities."[45]

A still more striking elaboration of John Stuart Mill's assertion that "the true idea of distributive justice . . . consists . . . in redressing the inequalities and wrongs of nature" is to be found in John Rawls's *A Theory of Justice*. The premise that natural ability, because it is undeserved and hence "arbitrary from a moral point of view," cannot provide a moral claim to greater reward is the very foundation of Rawls's entire theoretical structure.[46] That structure yields a doctrine of distributive justice labeled the "difference principle," which calls for redistribution to maximize the economic benefits of the least advantaged. The difference principle, according to Rawls, reflects an agreement to "regard the distribution of natural talents as a common asset."[47] In short, because individuals do not deserve their natural talents, these talents should in effect be collectivized and regarded as the common property of society as a whole.

It is difficult to imagine a view that runs more directly counter to the Lockean principle, affirmed by the American founders, that the individual has a natural right to the fruits of his labor. The foundation of this right according to Locke is that "every man has a property in his own person: this nobody has any right to but himself. The labour of his body and the work of his hands, we may say, are properly his."[48] From this perspective the question whether people deserve the particular body and hands (and brain) with which they are endowed does not arise; the individual's sole mastery and possession of his own person is the irreducible starting point of moral reasoning about property. Consequently, differences in wealth that flow from people's unequal natural endowments are in no way unjust, and the individual's pursuit of wealth is not rendered morally questionable by the fact that some are more successful than others.[49]

By contrast, for those who question the morality of rewards accruing to greater natural ability and therefore abandon the notion of a right to the fruit of one's labor, the justice of economic inequality and of the capitalist ethic is rendered highly problematic. This becomes apparent even in the thought of such apostles of the free market as Hayek and Friedman. Although both these authors reject the redistributionist conclusions drawn from it by Okun and Rawls, they fully endorse the argument that since individuals do not deserve the natural abilities they inherit, neither do they deserve in an ethical sense the rewards that flow from the exercise of these abilities.[50] As a consequence both Hayek and Friedman explicitly eschew any attempt to defend capitalism on grounds of distributive justice.[51] This of course does not lead them to the view that capitalism is morally indefensible. Instead, they seek to construct their case for a capitalist order by attributing the supreme moral value to individual freedom. It is in the name of freedom—and not of justice—that they defend the economic inequality generated by capitalism.[52] Hayek even goes so far as to say that a society based on the principle of distributive justice "in all essential respects would be the opposite of a free society."[53]

Individual freedom is of course an essential principle for the entire liberal tradition. But the radical divorce of freedom from justice constitutes a decisive departure from the teaching of Locke (and of the American founders), in which the rights to liberty and to property in the fruits of one's labor go hand in hand. This loss of belief in the justice of a liberal economic order even by its most eminent proponents is the ultimate consequence of the rejection of the doctrine of natural rights by the tradition of political economy.

The weakening of belief in the justice of capitalism poses severe practical dangers for liberal democratic societies. Considerable economic inequality must inevitably arise in a society that guarantees individual liberty, including men's freedom to pursue their economic self-interest. To the extent that this inequality is no longer held to be defensible as just, the better off are likely to be beset by guilt and the worse off by resentment. These symptoms are already apparent among America's more highly educated classes. Were it not for persisting popular attachment to the capitalist ethic, it is doubtful that the protection of private property essential to a liberal capitalist order could long be maintained. For the appeal to individual freedom, divorced from justice, is unlikely to prevail in the political arena against appeals to equality that emphatically claim to be on the side of justice.

If we shift our focus from the broader defenses of liberal society offered by thinkers like Hayek and Friedman to the mainstream of contemporary economics, we are no longer in a realm that admits appeals to principles of freedom or justice. For present-day economics typically defines itself as a science concerned with the choice among scarce means to achieve given ends. As Lionel Robbins puts it, "Economics is entirely neutral between ends. . . . [It] is not concerned with ends as such."[54] Clearly, to the extent that it conforms to this conception of its nature and role, economic science cannot be explicitly procapitalist or committed to the principles of liberalism.

Yet those Marxists and other radicals who attack mainstream economics as bourgeois are not wholly lacking in justification. For the characteristic assumptions and approaches of contemporary economics do reveal the traces of the liberal individualism in which the tradition of political economy was nurtured. The neutrality of economics regarding ends usually means in practice that it accepts as its goal the maximal satisfaction of the existing wants of individual consumers. And for achieving this goal the market is generally the most efficient mechanism. Thus, while contemporary economics may not be procapitalist, it surely tends to be promarket. Mainstream economists may favor income redistribution, but they will prefer to carry it out in ways that least disrupt the efficient workings of markets (for example, they will prefer the use of taxes and transfers to direct interference with wage scales). A few of them may even favor greater public ownership of industry, but if so they will prefer market socialism to centralized planning. On the whole, mainstream economists probably tend to be more moderate in their politics and more favorably disposed toward liberal society than most other social scientists or intellectuals.

Nonetheless, contemporary economics is not immune from the general tendency of value-free social science to undermine the theoretical foundations of liberal democracy.[55] For Smith political economy was the science of wealth, and it remained subordinate to the larger science of the legislator. Despite the central importance attributed to wealth by the older political economy, the economic realm was still understood as part of a larger moral and political whole. Contemporary economic science, however, not only has emancipated itself from any concern with moral and political ends but no longer views its proper subject matter as confined to the sphere of wealth. It purports to be able to deal with practically the full range of human behavior and decisions.

The intellectual imperialism spawned by this enlarged view of its range has had some positive effects. Economists have brought a welcome rigor and clarity to many questions of public policy for which their methods are appropriate. But the reliance of economics on mathematics typically leads economists to ignore or undervalue the significance of nonquantifiable considerations. And the overriding concern of the economist with efficiency in achieving given ends tends to blind him to the deeper moral and political issues that so often underlie public policy debate.

Value-free economic science has enriched our appreciation of the technical virtues of markets, but it has only fostered skepticism or indifference regarding the political and moral case for capitalism. Indeed, value-free economics constitutes the final break on the level of theory between the tradition of political economy and the comprehensive view of liberal democracy of the American founders.

12
Reflections on Marxism and America

W. R. Newell

Marxism has always been both close to and far from the American experience. More than most countries, the United States and the Soviet Union had what may be termed theoretical foundings. Their origins are not shrouded in myth but claim a certain kind of scientific insight. Both countries espouse universal principles of equality and freedom and claim that these principles can be beneficially extended to other peoples. Both countries thus see themselves as "mankind's last best hope" and even in their rivalry acknowledge each other as the great (if flawed) alternative.

The tension between the two countries and the principles they represent is, of course, proverbial. The Soviet version of Marxism claims to have achieved the unity of theory and practice, meaning that it has resolved, at least in principle, every problem of political life. Americans, by contrast, are, as Tocqueville observed, natural Cartesians[1]—they are instinctively skeptical of any overarching theory claiming to integrate individual freedom with the requirements of state and society. Hence, while the U.S. Constitution sees the protection of rights as exhausting the legitimating purpose of government, the Soviet Constitution both guarantees rights and requires duties to the collective good.[2] Moreover, in protecting rights, the Soviet Union claims to have transcended the American tendency to identify rights with property rights. Altogether, whereas the American founding presents the rights of man as constituting a natural truth that is permanent like other natural phenomena, the Soviet political system claims to embody a basic historical advancement over this Enlightenment understanding of politics.

The tension between the two systems also stems from the fact that America represents something of a scandal for Marxism, a symbol of what Richard Lowenthal has called the "missing" revolution. According to Marx, America reveals the essence of the modern state "in its completely developed form."[3] But for this very reason America should, more than most nations, manifest the contradictions that yield the path to socialism—the transcendence of "political" freedom by "social" freedom. But Marxism as a political movement has been least successful in America of all the developed industrial nations and has arguably lost its appeal in European countries precisely as they lost their vestigial traces of feudalism and progressed through capitalism—progressed, as one might say, along the route America had already traveled. The New Deal forestalled what Marxists took to be the inevitability of capitalism's economic collapse; and in the mixture of market forces, redistributive social welfare programs, and fiscal fine-tuning by governments characteristic of American and European development after World War II, the Marxist understanding of alienation was driven from the material world into the spiritual, leaving the existence of a real-world proletariat in doubt. Lenin gave way to Adorno; Old Left to New.

Nevertheless, the success of Keynesian economics in preempting the breakdown of capitalism is not a decisive refutation of Marxism. For Marx never embraced—indeed he strenuously rejected—the idea that socialism's appeal would be invalidated by capitalism's success at enriching the workers. Reformism of the Keynesian or social democratic kind he anticipated and rejected as merely "better payment for the slave."[4] I argue in this essay that the core of Marxism's appeal is the yearning for wholeness, for an existence that unites personal and collective satisfaction. Capitalism and its depredations are the most important symptoms of the lack of this wholeness, but they are only symptoms. The collapse and supersession of capitalism are inevitable to Marx not because of a narrowly empirical development that can be predicted like the weather. These breakdowns are inevitable because capitalism must function by robbing man of a wholeness whose lack is, in the long run, unbearable to our species. The real scandal afforded to Marxism by the American experience is not so much its economic success as Americans' apparent unawareness of this unbearable schism in their lives. Natural Cartesians that they are, they seem content with fragmentation, with parceling themselves out among their private, economic, and public pursuits. Such ultimate meaning as existence may possess they are largely content to find in private family or love life, in religion, or even in hobbies and leisure, looking on the political system as a means to these private satisfactions.

The continuing encounter between America and Marxism is stimulated by another development, an ironic counterpoint to America's failure to manifest the contradictions yielding to socialism. This is the spread of Marxism in the countries least likely, according to Marx's analysis of modern development, to foster socialism, beginning with the Soviet Union. Thus in our century, even as America defied Marx's view that class conflict will intensify as the modern state advances, America took on the role of the bourgeoisie vis-à-vis the new proletariat of the developing nations, the "backyard of the world." Thus, just when Marxism was a dead letter once and for all in American domestic politics, in its ever more complicated international relations America had repeatedly to encounter Marxism and Marxist-based critiques of its role in the wider world.

Of course, the Soviet version of Marxism has never been a faithful reflection of Marx's real doctrine. Moreover, people can reasonably disagree over whether or to what degree the experiences of Cuba, China, or other nations claiming to be Marxist are genuinely in accordance with, or have helped develop, Marxism as a political philosophy. It is arguable that the official versions of Marxism elaborated by these states are increasingly irrelevant to their actual functioning. In my view, however, the attempt to calibrate precisely a Marxist regime's faithfulness to Marxist philosophy misses the main point (as well as being hopelessly controversial). To my mind the real question is this: Why is it that, of all the versions of socialism available since the nineteenth century, Marx's version is the one that is repeatedly embraced, avowed, refashioned, or betrayed? Or, to put the converse, why does this collection of political beliefs continue to be called, believed in, rhetorically manipulated, and acted on as Marxism when it has been modified, bowdlerized, and compromised seemingly beyond recognition? It is the perdurance of the claim to be Marxist that is the impressive continuum behind these changes. In the rest of this essay, I suggest some reasons for Marxism's remarkable plasticity as an omnium-gatherum of economic, psychological, and cultural dissatisfactions with liberal democracy of the American kind. This plasticity is, I believe, not merely the consequence of the many kinds of regimes and movements that have avowed that they are Marxist but at the core of Marx's political philosophy.[5]

Labor, Alienation, and the Proletariat

The central ideas of Marx's political philosophy concern alienation, the proletariat, and the labor theory of value. According to Marx, human beings produce commodities by investing their labor in the materials provided by nature. But by labor Marx means something much broader than the Lockean, utilitarian understanding. Labor embraces the full range of man's creative potentiality, not only technical but artistic and intellectual abilities. Labor thus entails the means to biological survival but is not reducible to it. By laboring we express our creativity and embody it in the objects we produce, achieving a kind of aesthetic unity between our talents and their external realization that we may enjoyably "contemplate."[6] "Alienation" occurs when I am ripped out of this unity of self and object. This is the state of affairs under capitalism, where the surplus value of my creations beyond their capacity to sustain my biological existence is transferred to another person who controls my access to the means of production. When we live as "species-being," our material needs are integrated with our fullest range of self-expression. Capitalism perverts this gestalt of integrated energies, reducing man's technical, artistic, and theoretical capacities to the service of biological existence alone. Species-being declines into "the animal kingdom of man."[7]

For Marx, then, alienation cannot be properly understood apart from species-being, since this latter concept expresses the unified existence that we have lost under capitalism. The meaning of species-being is complex and controversial, but it is perhaps easier to say what it is not. It is not an ideal in the Kantian sense but an existential, integrated, fully lived, or "sensuous" kind of being. It is communal but an immanent communality. By this I mean that, unlike the kind of community that the ancient political philosophers thought might be achieved through elaborate statecraft and a lifelong education in civic virtue, the communality of species-being is released by the removal of capitalism's impediments to it. It is a free, spontaneous association of individuals because there is no need to compel it by political means. But neither is it a blissfully ignorant anarchism like the golden age of Rousseau's state of nature. Because Marx is a materialist—though not a reductive materialist—he believes that while people need not be reduced to living for the sake of survival, neither can they transcend or evade the bodily necessities and the productive techniques developed throughout history to serve them. After the socialist revolution, the productive apparatus of the capitalist epoch will be retained to provide permanently for everyone's material needs. To dismantle this technological apparatus would only rekindle the centuries-long competition for economic survival and domination in a natural environment of scarcity that had culminated in the miseries of capitalism.

Marx's socialism may accordingly be described as the stateless organization of labor without surplus value. Marxism is notorious, especially in light of the Russian Revolution, for its lack of detail about what kind of political institutions and constitutional safeguards should be established after the revolution. This was not an oversight of Marx, who was a tireless and brilliant analyst of political affairs, but rather stems from his conviction that the whole subject matter of politics will disappear after the brief "transition" from the dictatorship of the proletariat to socialism. For politics to Marx means the monopoly of state power by a predominant class and as such cannot take place under socialism.

Marx viewed the industrial working class, the "proletariat," as the prime sufferer of capitalist exploitation, the prospective majority class of mankind, and mankind's future redeemer. As early as 1843 Marx was sure that this characteristically modern class could be shown to embody the dehumanizing course of modernity as a whole. Believing this critique of modernity to be borne out by the experience of a living group of the worst off gave him a powerful theoretical and empirical fulcrum with which to analyze the workings of the political and economic systems. Marx endowed the proletariat with a concept central to German idealism, that man is a self-maker, a creator *ex nihilo* enmeshed in the world he has progressively transformed. Hegel had viewed history as a process (*Geist* or spirit) that continually crucified and recreated itself, centering on man as the locus for its cycles of dissolution and resurrection. Marx transferred this dynamic power from the process of history to the purely human, flesh-and-blood struggles of the workers. In his vision of the proletariat's development, it suffers the dissolution of all fixity and security, losing its ties to premodern caste and religion, ultimately losing its property and the very means of survival. But in the agony of its suffering it mirrors the creative drive of history itself and will later do freely what it now passively undergoes. Rather than suffer the loss of every security, it will experience the freedom of untrammeled creativity.[8]

According to the labor theory of value, the bourgeoisie must progressively impoverish the proletariat to finance the expansion of capitalism. Since the proletariat, ever increasing in size, lacks the income to buy what capitalism produces, the result is an economic crisis of overproduction and underconsumption, leading to further impoverishment until, on the verge of starvation, the proletariat revolts. The proletariat is ready and able to exercise political power to effect the transition to socialism because the experience of factory work under capitalism has taught it how to discipline and organize itself while the collapse of the capitalist economy has taught it how to exist without private property. This is how the bourgeoisie acts unwittingly as its own "gravedigger." One of the most original features of Marxism is that, whereas the other great exploration of communism in the history of political philosophy, Plato's *Republic*, concluded that self-interest and bodily desire made communism virtually impossible, Marx believes that communism will be brought about precisely by the fullest development of self-interest and bodily desire. Socialism, the least competitive epoch, is brought about by capitalism, the most competitive.

This helps us to understand a characteristic and important paradox of Marx's thinking: his ability to combine a remarkably hard-headed acuity about the power struggles and selfish interests masked by the modern state with an apparent naiveté about how people will act after the transition to socialism. Even granting that the proletariat will exercise its dictatorial power during the transition phase only for as long as it takes to dismantle the remains of the bourgeoisie's control, someone outside the Marxist standpoint naturally wonders why avarice, vanity, and competitiveness will not start all over again under socialism. For Marx, as much as it is senseless to expect altruism from people living within the distorting limitations of capitalism, it is axiomatic that, once history has liberated people from the system that functions on alienation and exploitation, people will shed every motive for aggressive behavior. Simply put, Marx (in this respect a follower of Rousseau) believes that people do not want to be competitive and ambitious but are compelled to be in a dog-eat-dog world. This shows the very limited sense in which Marx's is an empirical theory, at least in the instrumentalist Anglo-American view of empiricism.

The laws of economics, Marx believed, enable us to understand capitalism. But when the authentic species-being immanent within the repressive system governed by those laws emerges into "social" freedom, those laws and the assumption in which they are grounded of an egoistic, compulsively selfish individualism will lose their validity. This is why, to amplify an earlier point, Marx has little to say about the psychology of political ambition or the dangers of tyranny inherent in a party presuming to exercise dictatorial power after the revolution.[9] Russian Marxists living to see the rise of Stalin learned through bitter experience how unhelpful Marx was in this regard. For Marx the traditional concerns of political philosophy with how to identify and condemn tyrannical ambition and distinguish it from true statesmanship were, however well motivated, symptomatic of what stood in the way of man's final liberation from all such oppression. Once the liberation takes place, the need for such knowledge will vanish along with the dangers it was meant to cope with.

Rights and the Liberal State

Some of Marx's most revealing observations about the United States occur in his essay *On the Jewish Question*. The purpose of this essay is to dissuade Jews from being content with the extension of civil rights by states like France and Germany in the process of shedding their former identification with Christianity. For Marx it is not so much the restriction of religious freedom by the state as the existence of religion itself that is "a defect," since belief in God and an otherworldly salvation sums up the greatest possible alienation of man from his own creative powers. Marx concedes that the pursuit of the right to worship as one chooses without loss of other rights is in a sense a struggle against religion itself, especially in European countries where some "semblance" of an established church remains. But in Marx's view the institution of a purely secular state and the universal freedom of worship, far from weakening religion, intensifies it by freeing its energies from the responsibilities of governing, removing the state's restriction of some creeds on behalf of its own, and leaving each individual to the undistracted enjoyment of his own religious "whim and caprice."[10] Thus, paradoxically, in a secular liberal state religion flourishes as never before.

It was in demonstrating this paradox that Marx found the experience of the United States so valuable:

> It is only in the free states of North America . . . that the Jewish question loses its *theological* significance and becomes a truly *secular* question. Only where the state exists in its completely developed form can the relation of . . . the religious man in general to the political state appear in a pure form.

Quoting Beaumont and Tocqueville, Marx continues:

> There are even some states in North America in which "the constitution does not impose any religious belief or practice as a condition of political rights." And yet, "no one in the U.S. believes that a man without religion can be an honest man." And North America is preeminently the country of religiosity.[11]

The evidence furnished by America confirms for Marx a key principle of his theory. America shows the furthest point to which the political state can advance: the recognition and protection of such inalienable rights as freedom of worship. Since in this "perfected democracy" religion is only strengthened by being disestablished and privatized and since religion ("the opium of the people") must be abolished, religious tolerance as practiced in America reveals the fundamental limitations of politics:[12]

> If we find in the country which has attained full political emancipation that religion not only continues to *exist*, but is *fresh* and *vigorous*, this is proof that the existence of religion is

> not at all opposed to the perfection of the state. But since the existence of religion is the existence of a *defect,* the source of this defect must be sought in the *nature* of the state itself.[13]

Thus Marx concludes: "To be *politically* emancipated from religion is not to be finally and completely emancipated from religion, because political emancipation is not the final and absolute form of *human* emancipation."[14]

The deficiency of liberal democracy revealed by religious rights is borne out, Marx argues, by the other "rights of man" championed by Thomas Paine and made the basis of the American founding. The state properly speaking reveals its distinct character only in modern times, when it supersedes feudalism by unpacking religious faith and the power of property from political authority. In a sense, property was more powerful when the wealthy were also dukes and bishops. But in a more important sense, Marx argues, the rights of property are liberated by being privatized and universalized, since people can now pursue wealth undistractedly and limitlessly, without any sense of obligation to others. Whereas feudalism conflated personal wealth with political authority, the modern state claims to represent impersonally a community of free and equal individuals. But the formal equality of rights guaranteed by the impersonality of the liberal state masks the lived reality of liberal society, a "war of all against all" (Marx uses Hobbes's famous phrase) where the inequality of result expands without limit. The possession of rights—the occasion of so much reverence for the American Revolution—Marx believes to be nothing grander than the pursuit of wealth, in which the greediest and boldest triumph. It is not merely a particular interpretation or application of rights but the very concept of rights—the identification of freedom with rights—that is defective, amounting to the social and political institutionalizing of alienation:[15] "Liberty as a right of man is not founded on the relations between man and man, but rather upon the separation of man from man. . . . The liberty of man [is] regarded as an isolated monad, withdrawn into himself."[16]

The community of equal citizens that the liberal state claims to represent is thus a ghostly abstraction in contrast with the growing real inequality of bourgeoisie and workers. It is not a life of high-minded public service but the energy and talent of the successful bourgeois that are admired—he "is considered the *true* and *authentic* man."[17] In other words, Marx would say, if we must choose between the life of Gordon Gecko and the kind of citizenship described in civics textbooks, the alienation typified by the Wall Street bandit at least has some guts and style as opposed to the alienation typified by the League of Women Voters. That the existence of the rapacious bourgeois is recognized as, and really is, the most authentic way of life in a liberal democracy shows, for Marx, how far we are from the unity of the ideal and sensuous that will blossom through "social" emancipation. Behind the idealistic camouflage of the rights of man, the liberal state serves the interests of the bourgeoisie. This is a prime instance for Marx of how our communal capacities as species-beings are reduced to mere means for the perpetuation of man's "partial being" as a producer and consumer of commodities.[18] As Europe and the rest of the world progress toward the form of the state already perfected in America, the contradiction between the ghostly, unrealizable "ought" of the liberal ideal of citizenship and the vicious, degrading "is" of the competition for property will become unbearable. America points the way to the supersession of liberalism and therewith of politics altogether:

> Human emancipation will only be complete when the real, individual man has absorbed into himself the abstract citizen; when as an individual man, in his everyday life, in his work, and in his relationships, he has become a *species-being;* and when he has recognized and organized his own powers as *social* powers so that he no longer separates this social power from himself as *political* power.[19]

How far does Marx's understanding of liberal democracy accord with the self-understanding of the framers of the American Constitution? The emphasis on property rights is certainly borne out by *Federalist* No. 10, where James Madison, echoing John Locke, identifies protecting the "different and unequal faculties of acquiring property" as the "first object of government." For Marx this would be a clear indication that the other rights secured by the Constitution were derivative from this most important material interest of the bourgeoisie. In Marx's view of the historical evolution of capitalism, the bourgeoisie endows the workers with these rights so as to destroy their traditional ties to caste, village, and church and gather them together in the cities for factory work.

It is far from clear, however, that Madison, let alone Thomas Jefferson, understood property rights to be the cause and basis of the other rights of worship, free speech, due process, and self-government, even though they considered property rights very important. The Enlightenment thinkers such as Montesquieu and Locke from whom the framers derived their new science of politics never argued that property was the cause and basis of all other rights. The fundamental right, the first law of nature, was the freedom of every individual from arbitrary treatment, especially by despotic governments, and its practice entailed the right to acquire property, worship, express a political opinion, move about, emigrate, and educate or amuse oneself as one wished, as long as others' rights were not invaded. Locke particularly favored property rights among these various dividends of individual liberty because of the social and political stability he believed they engendered in contrast with claims to rule based on divine right. But he also championed religious toleration and more flexible approaches to education and child rearing. Montesquieu valued the rise of the middle class in England because the pursuit of property was a palpable demonstration that individual liberty was flourishing in other spheres as well. If more people were devoting their energies to commerce, fewer people were absorbed in religious hatreds or the feudal pursuit of martial honor. In sum, while Marx views the rights of man as derivative from the right to property, liberal political philosophy treats the right to property as one among a number of liberties that derive from, demonstrate, actualize, and reinforce the fundamental right to freedom from tyranny. Liberalism permits capitalism, not the reverse.

Progress, Community, and the Liberal State

During Marx's lifetime, European conservatives began to identify America with modernity at its most soulless.[20] "Amerika" came to stand for the corrosive forces of science and industry threatening the fabric of traditions that bound together an ancient people. In contrast, Marx can sometimes sound like an untroubled champion of modernization, unabashedly pointing to America's advances over Europe. Marx detested the romantic conservatives' nostalgia for a premodern *völkisch* community as furnishing yet another way for the bourgeoisie to camouflage the real function of the state as the instrument of its economic interests. He wanted the workers to lose their remaining illusions about the compatibility of capitalism with older loyalties to the organic hierarchy of the feudal community. One of his reasons for regarding America as "the most perfect example of the modern state" was that, with its absence of a feudal heritage to retard or cosmeticize the victory of bourgeois self-interest, the masses could not cling to these nostalgic traces of throne and altar. "The . . . American writers all express the opinion that the state exists only for the sake of private property, so that this fact has penetrated into the consciousness of the normal man."[21] When we tear away these shards of the *ancien régime,* Marx argues, we see that capitalism is relentlessly creating a labor force that will be global in extent and whose division of labor is as

In dilating on the "horror" of the polis, Hamilton has in mind not only the Tories among his readers who doubted that enough Americans possessed the education and character needed for republican self-government. He is also trying to dampen the enthusiasm for the ancient republics manifested by those who wanted a more democratic and egalitarian society than the authors of the *Federalist* had in mind. Within a few years the radical wing of the French Revolution would try to create a kind of Sparta in Paris with the authority to level differences in wealth and teach people to rise above their venal impulses. They were inspired by Rousseau's vision of the polis—not, as in Plato's and Aristotle's ideal states, a self-governing aristocracy but an egalitarian collective whose leveling of extremes of wealth and austere morals would approximate in civil society the absolute equality of all human beings in the state of nature. Throughout the *Federalist* Hamilton and Madison defend the new Constitution against both the Tory preference for a community of aristocratic virtue and the radical vision of an egalitarian community aimed at "reducing mankind to a perfect equality . . . perfectly equalized and assimilated in their possessions, their opinions and their passions."

Rather than try to control the "causes" of vice by subordinating self-interest to a cohesive political community, *Federalist* No. 10 suggests letting the clash of interests regulate its own bad "effects." There will be too many diverse and geographically extended factions in America for any group of them to coalesce for long enough or in enough numbers to exercise power despotically over the others. Rather than equip government with the power to improve human character, the framers wished to dilute government so as to deny anyone the capacity to tyrannize. *Federalist* No. 10 is perhaps the most anticommunitarian treatise ever written, designing a system that will repeatedly, almost mechanically, frustrate what the framers viewed as the natural urge of people to wield political power for their own advantage and dress it up with mendacious claims to superior virtue.

The "bourgeois republic," then, as Marx called America,[24] frustrates tyranny of the large-scale, terrible kind by routinizing it into a universal, endless series of minor victories over others in commerce. Locke, Montesquieu, and the framers considered this a great victory for liberty because it channels the most belligerent aspects of human nature into relatively benign and negotiable commercial interests and, in addition to the safeguards provided by representative political institutions, allows us to exercise our other freedoms without fear of harm from those around us. But Marx echoes Rousseau's great protest—that the bourgeois era causes this mundane competitiveness to eat into each one of us heart and soul, dominating our existences. We may no longer be in danger of the lash or gibbet for being on the wrong side of a religious zealot or monarch. But we have also been robbed of any feeling of obligation to others or any sense that society respects faith or probity above avarice. Although Marx saw no possibility of restoring any version of Greek or Roman virtue, he does, like Rousseau, appeal to those who consider liberal individualism to have truncated the human spirit. In this sense he feeds the longing for a restored polis that the framers wished to dampen, which had its American adherents in 1788 and which some have continued to mourn as the "lost" revolution.[25]

At the same time Marx rejects in principle the ancient political philosophers' belief that vice could be transcended by the optimal state. Because he believes in economic and scientific progress and is to this extent an Enlightenment thinker, Marx accepts the hardheaded view characteristic of the framers that the ancient polis, and all states in reality, have existed to serve selfish interests, whatever they may preach about upholding the standards of a virtuous community. The liberal state "perfects" the historical development of the state because, while earlier states were created when some classes gained the upper hand over other classes, in modern society every individual has the right to try to take advantage of others. By universalizing the tyrannical impulse, albeit to disperse it so widely as to prevent anyone from successfully becoming a tyrant, the liberal state for Marx reveals on a universal scale the essence of politics since the beginning of history—domination. Marxism's goal, therefore, is not the achievement of a good state to remedy the vices of an imperfect state. Its goal is the transcendence of all states through the transcendence of the final state, liberal democracy.

The Core Claim of Marxism

As the foregoing considerations begin to show, Marx's economic analysis, notwithstanding its frequent brilliance, does not adequately explain Marxism's appeal. Already in Marx's lifetime technology was forestalling the need to extract ever more surplus value from the workers' labor by increasing the efficiency of that labor. The redistribution of income through social welfare programs forestalled the crisis of overproduction and underconsumption by providing the workers with more purchasing power. As a matter of strict empirical observation, then, the labor theory of value was refuted by the course of the industrial democracies' development. In a way these forestalling measures were a real tribute to Marx. The bourgeoisie, one might say, was warned and took the warning seriously. At the same time, if

Marx's appeal rested on his foreseeing a cataclysm for the bourgeoisie that the bourgeoisie took measures to prevent, we would only remember him as a rather prominent nineteenth-century social theorist like Emile Durkheim—historically interesting but not of great contemporary relevance.

The liberal democracies have a fairly good record in appeasing economic dissatisfaction, at least over the long run, and even many "quality of life" objections to the aridity of bourgeois existence have been met by providing more discretionary income for private avocations. Yesterday's yippie is today's yuppie, yesterday's head shop today's herb dispensary. As long as the equality of opportunity is periodically renewed by some curtailment of the established inequality of result, even initially radical challenges to the liberal ethos are usually ploughed back into the soil of economic self-advancement.

Be that as it may, I do not think Marx, were he brought back to life today, would be dismayed by these apparent failures of his theory as a matter of empirical prediction. Marx lived through many of capitalism's permutations and did not view history as a rigidly deterministic sequence. Regardless of these shifts and starts, he remained transfixed by what he saw as the great either-or that the whole course of modern history was preparing and would sooner or later make manifest: intensifying woe and despair as the prelude to the great reversal of unprecedented happiness and fulfillment. This is sometimes misunderstood by those who think that Marxism is primarily competing with capitalism on capitalism's own terms of increasing economic opportunity. The varieties of Marxism do claim that they will triumph economically in the long run. But the core claim is different, more radical, and cannot be disproved by any criterion of measurable economic performance alone.[26]

The core is "socialism," which for Marx means the unity of the sensuous and ideal; of individual and collective satisfaction; of the private and public interest—in sum, the unity of nature and freedom. To reach this core, we have to bear in mind Marxism's origins in German Idealism and Romanticism, with which it shares a number of characteristic thought structures. The Enlightenment made a fundamental distinction between man as a natural being motivated by self-preservation and man as a free being capable of willing himself to rise above the natural inclinations and establish his autonomy. In the New World this distinction helped the individual to throw off the shackles of religious and political authorities claiming to integrate the natural and moral dimensions of human life in some objective teleological order. Americans were, to recall Tocqueville's observation, Cartesian selves who invented themselves every day in a cheerful bustle of innovation and enterprise.

In Europe, however, the split in man between his natural and free sides was considered true but deeply troubling, a sign that modern man was alone in the world, cut adrift from any mooring in the harmonious orderings of nature or tradition. While the American founders were content to encourage a balance of civic freedom and material self-interest, expecting that each would temper the other, the Europeans were scandalized at the lack of a unifying third term and tended to drive the poles of nature and freedom further apart as they reflected on the most extreme reaches of each. Schiller looked for an aesthetic unity between the individual and a larger culture that would avoid both the debased materialism that he believed came with philosophies, like Locke's, that stress man's natural side and the tendency of philosophies of freedom, like Kant's and Fichte's, that encourage a kind of fanaticism in which the will strives to overcome every natural limitation. This search for unity culminated in the longing for a "third condition," as Schiller expressed it, that would unite spontaneity and feeling with will and autonomy—the millenarian longing characteristic, in different but related ways, of Marx, Nietzsche, Heidegger, and today, some of the German Greens.[27]

Hegel warned that this millenarian longing for the transcendence of alienation had to be tempered by an appreciation for the degree to which human happiness—even in the future, and certainly now—is, in the real world of experience, always intermixed with avarice, vanity, and belligerence. Even at the end of history, therefore, a political state with laws and police will be needed to balance the public and private goods. Marx's connection to Hegel is attested to by a long tradition of commentary and by some of Marx's terminology, but it is important to see how very different their philosophies are in this respect. For Hegel man's pursuit of fulfillment in history can never be entirely divorced from either the idealistic or the nasty dimensions of human behavior. Because we are free from nature, Hegel argues, we have to be alienated. This feeling of Pascalian loneliness in an empty cosmos is modern man's cross to bear but also a sign of our spiritual strength and superiority to ancient peoples like the Greeks who felt at home in the world. History is permeated, however, with the power of divine forgiveness and reconciliation, preventing the present and even the darker ages of the past from being nothing but struggles for domination.

Marx regarded the Hegelian synthesis as too consoling and too much of a compromise with alienation. He took the belief in God to sum up all of man's alienated creativity, a force not in harmony with human development (as Hegel believed) but standing in pure contradiction to it. For Marx alienation is not (as Hegel believed) a price that a maturely self-conscious individual knows he must pay for his freedom from the superstitions and tyrannies of the past but an agonizing separation from our unity with nature and our fellow men that must be totally negated. His response, accordingly, is to drive the poles of the Hegelian synthesis apart and radicalize each one. He radicalizes the view of history to date into nothing but a power struggle between masters and slaves, haves and have-nots. He purifies the elements of communality and reconciliation that Hegel believed mitigated this struggle throughout history by locating them in the future era of socialism. After the withering away of the political, the social will flower. All mankind will then enjoy the unity of will and feeling that Schiller thought could be approached through the delicate and gradual cultivation of aesthetic education. Indeed, rather than a successor to Hegelianism, Marxism can be more accurately described as the transposition of the aesthetic unity in cultural life evoked by Schiller to the plane of the actual liberation of mankind through revolution from all alienating social and political forces. For Schiller the "third condition" was only a hope for deliverance in the future. For Marx precisely the worst excesses of natural desire and fanatical will power in the present guarantee the achievement of this deliverance for everyone.

I have discussed the capacity of Marx's thought for containing, within a comprehensive critique of liberalism, sharply contrasting, even contradictory assessments: (1) radical skepticism about all current claims to be serving the public good combined with a view of future man as lacking all belligerence and vanity; (2) acceptance of and admiration for the forces of industrial and scientific progress combined with contempt for bourgeois vulgarity and regret at the loss of rooted communities. Marxism, like the wider German philosophy in which it originated, appeals to those who want both the fruits of liberal autonomy and a sense of belonging to a community worthy of affection and respect—a synthesis of unselfish freedom and unforced duties.

The polarity between the political and the social, thematically rooted in the structure of Marx's thought, is the source of these sharp contrasts. For Marx the political is the sphere of will, domination, exploitation, and the conquest of nature. The power of creation *ex nihilo,* the power of the Fichtean self that pursues its freedom through the limitless reconstruction of nature, Marx traces as history's terrible engine of revolutionary upheaval and transformation. Beyond this dark night, and because of it, awaits our release as sensuous beings freely communing through our labor.

The comprehensiveness of these poles and the tension between them helps to explain why Marx's philosophy, energized by his immense talents as a political observer, is so flexible and can survive so many specific refutations by events. Marxism is not a utopian socialism like the ideal community planned by Dühring because not only does the real world not make it difficult to believe in the ideal one, but the worst outcome of the real is needed to actualize the ideal.[28] Thus Marx does not need to appeal to man's higher sentiments to demonstrate the possibility of socialism and can explore the muck of politics in the fullest factual detail without endangering the counterfactual goal. To put it another way, Marx is against liberalism but in favor of modernization and the unedifying analysis of politics as driven by self-interest. He thus fights what he understood as political economy and what we might now term behavioralism on their own ground—their pride in the imperative to empirical and analytical clarity unbefuddled by moralism and sentimentality—without being limited by the liberal-individualist ontology in which these "neutral" assumptions are grounded. This combination of contraries surely helps to explain Marxism's appeal in this century in the developing world as a rhetoric of modernization that does not necessarily require political and economic pluralism and is compatible with the priority of community over rights. Marxism has understandably had appeal for countries whose colonial rulers often destroyed preliberal sources of communal tradition, failed to create a liberal democracy in their stead, and then departed, having thrust upon those countries the imperative to catch up with the international economy as quickly as possible.

The irony here is that Marxism, whose original aim was transcendence of the state, is transformed into a manifesto for state building. In the case of Stalinism, the most extreme and tragic variant of Marxism as an imperative to modernization "from above," this involved a horrific inversion of the political and social poles of Marx's philosophy. In Marx's most coherent version of the transition to socialism, when the political revolution occurred, the proletariat would already, under capitalism, have swelled to constitute the vast majority of people, while the productive apparatus needed to end scarcity would already have been largely developed. The material and characterological bases for a classless society would thus have been largely engendered during the late stage of capitalism. Marx warned that if the political revolution for socialism was too far in advance of this socioeconomic development, the result could only be the imposition of equality by *force majeure*—the expropriation and extermination of the unequal classes, as in the Terror of Robespierre.[29]

Stalinism fully bore out this warning. According to Stalinism, since the political revolution preceded Russia's socioeconomic maturation, the state must confiscate the peasants' property to finance rapid industrialization (thus completing the economic modernization that would have taken place under capitalism) and simultaneously achieve, by political fiat, the ideal of a classless society. The result was a program of state terror to be equaled only by the Nazis. Stalin's view, however, was that the Soviet Union was only experiencing in a concentrated way the destruction that capitalism had had centuries to carry out as it uprooted the *ancien régime* and assimilated premodern classes into the proletariat. This is where the inversion of Marx's dialectic occurs. For Marx the bourgeoisie's conscious exploitation unconsciously produces the very opposite of its intention, the preconditions for socialism. In Stalinism the state consciously enacts the process that Marx believed history had unconsciously effected: progress toward the greatest happiness by means of the greatest oppression. Since the development of capitalism had, over centuries, caused the peasantry in Europe to vanish, Stalinists reasoned, why not use the state to hasten history forward in Russia by the deliberate liquidation of classes known from capitalism's unfolding elsewhere to be doomed by history anyway?[30]

In Stalinism, then, the revolutionary ruthlessness that, Marx taught, had enabled the bourgeoisie to create capitalism and, undesignedly, the bases for socialism is enlisted in the service of designedly creating socialism. The Fichtean drive to reconstruct nature and human nature is no longer, as for Marx, history's dark prelude to the flowering of species-being—to the release of the human personality from the historically imposed compulsion to aggression. It is the will to power of the "builders of socialism" themselves as they carry out the titanic destruction that Marxism had revealed to be the engine of historical advancement.

Plainly, therefore, Marx's philosophy is not responsible for Stalinism in a causal sense. Indeed, it warned against such a dangerous, deluded path to the classless society. At the same time, I would argue that Marx's explosion of the Hegelian synthesis of freedom and alienation left his philosophy intrinsically vulnerable to further radicalizations of its political pole—the "scientistic" dimension of Marxism (to use Habermas's term) that serves as an imperative for the technological mastery of nature and human nature.[31] By depicting politics as the pursuit of power bereft of any mitigating bonds of communality and obligation in the present so as to preserve the socialist future from any compromise with alienation in the present, Marx made his philosophy vulnerable to manipulation by tyrants like Stalin, who could claim to be employing the ruthlessness of politics as uncovered by Marx himself to hasten the transcendence of the political.

I began this chapter by observing that Marxism has always been both close to and far from the American experience. Today America watches with a mixture of optimism and uncertainty as the new Soviet leadership moves to dismantle the Stalinist legacy and release the energies of private enterprise and a degree of ethnic, cultural, and intellectual pluralism. In this way and to this extent, it appears finally to be admitting Marx's contention that socialism can succeed only when it is rooted in the material conditions and technical culture characteristic of an advanced capitalist society like America. Whereas Stalinism methodically crushed individual liberties from above, the new leadership summons them forth. But—this must be noted—it summons them forth from above, in a methodical way, with limits on how much of the previous orthodoxy is open to criticism and change. In this way the leadership attempts to preserve the Soviet state's long-term commitment, inextricable from the legitimacy of its authority, to the political goals of classlessness and community without which, in Marx's view, modern economic productivity like America's could at best produce better payment for the slave. Can this new synthesis of social and political goals succeed? So far both optimism and doubt have been justified by turns. Only one thing is certain: America's long encounter with Marxism is not yet over.

13
Freud and the American Constitution

Joel Schwartz

When Freud arrived in the United States for his first and only visit, to deliver a set of lectures at Clark University in 1909, he is said to have been surprised at the warmth and enthusiasm of the reception he received. He is reported to have said that "they [the Americans] do not know that we are bringing them the plague."[1]

Freud's statement suggests that psychoanalytic doctrine is in crucial respects incompatible with American principles and practices as understood by him. His belief that psychoanalysis would be a plague upon America has certainly not been shared by all Americans, however. Psychoanalytic doctrine has instead received a remarkably warm welcome in America, the country in which it has had the most pervasive impact. It therefore comes as no surprise that Freud's influence has recently been held to be the most prominent cause of the differences between what Americans characteristically believe today and what they characteristically believed at the time of Tocqueville's visit to America in 1831.[2] Freud's influence, and that of his psychoanalytic rivals and disciples, is clearly reflected in the extraordinary prevalence of psychological jargon in contemporary American speech: consider the ubiquity today of words such as *Oedipus complex, sibling rivalry, extrovert, introvert, compulsive, sublimation, death wish, Freudian slip,* and *inferiority complex.*[3]

The Appeal of Psychoanalysis

It is not obvious why psychoanalysis has achieved its remarkably influential status in America: for it presents itself as a therapy, and its therapeutic efficacy is very much subject to dispute. We can begin to explain the American interest in psychoanalysis with the assistance of Tocqueville, who argues that psychological introspection appeals to democratic human beings: "Democratic peoples may amuse themselves by looking at nature, but it is about themselves that they are really excited."[4] In an egalitarian society, in which easily observable differences between people become less prominent and different people can appear to be so many interchangeable parts, each individual, Tocqueville suggests, will be inclined to focus on the part that he knows best and that concerns him most—himself. The general appeal of psychological introspection, however, cannot by itself explain the appeal of its specifically psychoanalytic variant. As it happens, a second Tocquevillian observation can help us deal with this objection: for he speaks of Americans' materialistic preoccupation with "caring for the . . . needs of the body" and of their countervailing spiritual tendency, which causes them to "launch out into the world of spirits for fear of being held too tightly bound by the body's fetters."[5] These two somewhat contradictory proclivities capture much of the appeal of psychoanalysis, in which man is primarily understood as a creature of bodily (and especially sexual) impulses but also as a creature about whom there is something spiritual, even mystical (the unconscious). Psychoanalysis presents itself as a science that uncovers the hidden depths of man and thereby restores a certain profundity, perhaps even poetry, that had been missing from the prosaic and excessively rationalistic psychologies that preceded it. Its appeal to Americans should therefore not be especially surprising; purporting to be the poetic materialistic science of man's unconscious depths, psychoanalysis can be said to complement economics, the prosaic materialistic science of his conscious surface. Economics explains the American search for wealth; the appeal of psychoanalysis stems from the inchoate recognition that there must be something more to life than wealth.

What we are specifically concerned with, though, is more the consequences of psychoanalytic influence than its causes. From the perspective of the founders, is psychoanalytic doctrine understood correctly as a plague? This is not an easy question to answer, because the perspective of the founders is most obviously political, whereas the political implications of psychoanalysis are hardly apparent. One would not go to an analyst in search of advice about the comparative merits of bicameral as opposed to unicameral legislatures or federal as opposed to centralized government.

Political Implications of Psychoanalytic Doctrine

Psychoanalytic doctrine, nevertheless, does have important political implications, which have filtered down into the American popular consciousness. Some of them are more compatible with the founders'

ity; whereas political power, which is unnatural, arises from voluntary conventions or agreements in which governors are chosen so that the subjects choosing them may be benefited by being secured in the possession and use of their property.

It is noteworthy that Freud rejects this distinction, at least with respect to our unconscious minds. For Freud's depiction of the unconscious suggests that the liberal distinction between the paternal and the political in a sense is untenable. All authority is in essence paternal authority: "The father is the oldest, first, and for children the only authority, and from his autocratic power the other social authorities have developed in the course of the history of human civilization."[17] Of the many "Freudian slips" that Freud himself committed and then discussed, the most politically significant and symptomatic is his substitution in a Latin inscription of the word *patriae* for *publicae*: for Freud, what is the people's is essentially the fatherland or the father's land.[18]

It would be wrong to exaggerate the importance of this implicit Freudian critique of Lockean liberalism. If Freud is not Locke, neither is he Robert Filmer. His argument is entirely descriptive, not normative: he says only that people do tend to treat their leaders like fathers, not at all that they should. In fact, he clearly disapproves of their tendency to do so. Furthermore, Freud's influence has obviously not led to the emergence in America of any sort of reactionary movement opposed to limited constitutional government, advocating the restoration of patriarchal authority in its stead. In general, it is noteworthy that the antidemocratic implications of Freud's thought have been ignored in America, whereas its extreme democratic implications, as we will see, have been exaggerated; if America has been Freudianized, it is also true that Freud has been Americanized or democratized.

Nevertheless, the psychoanalytic suggestion that people want fathers, not political leaders, does in one respect have important implications, which have influenced the way in which Americans think about politics. For if it is true that what we really want is a father, then no political leader can truly satisfy us, for none of them is our father. This is one of the many reasons for the existence of a tremendous pessimism about politics at the heart of psychoanalytic doctrine. In many ways it suggests that no political alternative can ultimately be satisfactory; all political alternatives, regardless of the differences among them, must in fundamental respects be unsatisfactory.

This is the contention of *Civilization and Its Discontents*, which is probably Freud's best known and most influential work of social theory. There he asserted that all social orders arouse discontents, because they all require us to repress our sexual and aggressive instincts. Implicit in this view is the suggestion, antithetical to the founders' position, that the difference between tyrannical and legitimate governments is less than fundamental. What is most important about government is instead a characteristic shared by all governments, regardless of the conceivable differences among them—the fact that they all necessarily frustrate human needs in addition to satisfying them.[19] The negative characteristics common to all governments would appear to be more important than the negative characteristics unique to tyrannical governments, which make possible the distinction between legitimate and tyrannical governments. Similarly, Freud's account of the origins of politics, in *Totem and Taboo,* explains that man's emotional attitude to all social order is necessarily ambivalent, because social order was made possible by a violent crime, the murder of the primal father, for which man feels remorse. The Lockean account of the origins is designed to provide us with a standard of legitimacy, to indicate why legitimate civil society represents an improvement over the state of nature, and to explain how legitimate civil society satisfies human needs, while justifying our rebellion against illegitimately arbitrary rule. By contrast, Freud's account of the origins dispenses with the question of legitimacy by suggesting that no political alternative can satisfy our antithetical unconscious urges both to submit and to rebel.

In this respect Freud can be and has been taken to counsel a general resignation or indifference to politics. This sort of apolitical pessimism is a prominent aspect of Freud's impact upon contemporary intellectual opinion in America, making Freud one source (although hardly the only source) of a generalized disaffection from and lack of interest in politics that prevails in many nonradical circles today. His influence is reflected in the widespread belief that political questions are irrelevant to the deepest yearnings of the human soul. Freud's psychology is apolitical, perhaps antipolitical; it may not be coincidental that he referred to it as a "depth-psychology,"[20] a psychology that plumbs the depths of the soul. Implicit in this characterization may be the suggestion that more rationalistic rival psychologies, which place a greater emphasis on the importance of politics than does Freud's, do not get beneath the surface of things, do not address the true profundities, and can therefore be regarded as "shallow" psychologies.

One source of Freud's belief that public life is inherently unsatisfactory is his emphasis upon the importance of sexual pleasure, which he correctly understood as a private, antipolitical pleasure.[21] For Freud, human sexuality exemplifies the strength of the bodily passions, which demand satisfaction and impel men to act in self-interested ways to attain it. In this respect Freud can be understood as an heir to the tradition of unsentimental and "realistic" psychologists that includes figures such as Locke, Montesquieu, and Madison, not as its opponent. In the manner of this tradition, Freud asserted that men's happiness is attainable primarily through the acceptance of their self-interested and bodily nature and not through the struggle against it. Thus his contention that humans should not attempt to be "more noble-minded than their [bodily] constitution allows" and that they would be "more healthy" if they could be "less good"[22] is in certain respects reminiscent of Madison's injunction against relying on "moral [or] religious motives," and his related recognition that, since men are not "angels," self-interested "ambition must be made to counteract ambition."[23] These similarities point to a partial affinity between liberalism and psychoanalytic doctrine that is both genuine and important: psychoanalysis like liberalism supports a greater liberation of the natural self-interested human passions from what are thought to be artificial constraints; psychoanalysis like liberalism accepts the fact that the interests of competing human beings will conflict and advocates bringing the conflict into the open, as opposed to attempting to deny it by smothering it.[24]

Furthermore, even Freud's hedonism, evident in his assertion that "every action" is "a means to the reproduction of pleasure,"[25] can be understood as a development of the psychological position maintained by some of the philosophers (notably Locke) who influenced the founders.[26] Nevertheless, it is also obvious that Freud's hedonism differs in important ways from that of Locke, in that the pleasure that Freud emphasized is primarily (at times it seems almost exclusively) sexual pleasure. In this respect Freud's influence upon America has been enormous and all-pervasive. America today, as opposed to the America of the founders, is the land of sexual liberation. Conceivably sexual liberation is the "plague" that Freud thought he was bringing to America; in any event, Freud is probably the thinker whom most Americans think of as the intellectual founder of sexual liberation.

Liberation and Morality

There is considerable evidence in support of the popular perception of Freud as an advocate of sexual liberation. Freud harshly criticized what he called " 'civilized' sexual morality,"[27] in which sexual relations were restricted to heterosexual monogamous intercourse within marriage for purposes of reproduction.[28] Freud contended instead that "in man the sexual drive does not originally serve the purposes of reproduction at all, but has as its aim the gaining of particular kinds of pleasure."[29] In many, although not all, sectors of the American populace, Freud's understanding that sexuality is more in the service of pleasure than in that of procreation has obviously come to predominate over and to replace the understanding of sexuality that, he argued, previously prevailed.

Because he believed that sexuality is primarily in the service of pleasure, "sexual morality as defined by society, in its most extreme form that of America," struck Freud in 1915 as "very contemptible"; by contrast he favored "an infinitely freer sexual life."[30] It is not, however, altogether clear how free Freud thought infinite freedom should be. For Freud's treatment of sexuality is in one respect quite reminiscent of Marx's treatment of economics: just as Marx has much to say about the horrors of economic oppression, but next to nothing to say to illuminate how a society free from economic oppression would function, so did Freud catalog the costs of sexual repression at considerable length, while never very clearly stating exactly what he envisioned as sexual liberation. And the difficulty posed by Freud's vagueness on this point is greatly increased when one realizes that in the very essay in which he criticized "'civilized' sexual morality," he also asserted that "masturbation vitiates the character through *indulgence*" and that the varieties of nongenital intercourse "are ethically objectionable, for they degrade the relationship of love between two human beings from a serious matter to a convenient game, attended by no risk and no spiritual participation."[31] These are not comments that are likely to be cited approvingly in the *Playboy* philosophy.

The conservatism of these statements can seem quite surprising today; at least until the AIDS epidemic mandated a tactical retreat by its shock troops, the sexual revolution had far outstripped Freud in its proclamation of a democracy of all the orifices. It is tempting to say that the sexual revolution, like earlier revolutions, has had difficulty outgrowing its oral stage; hence it has devoured Freud, its intellectual father.

Freud's statements are conservative in that they clearly express an ethical concern as well as, and overriding, a hedonistic one. For Freud, freer sexuality was supposed not just to provide men and women with a greater number of intense and harmless pleasures but also in some way to elevate them morally. This ethical concern of Freud's is expressed most clearly in his critique of the consequences of sexual repression:

> I have not gained the impression that sexual abstinence helps to bring about energetic and self-reliant men of action or

> original thinkers or bold emancipators and reformers. Far more often it goes to produce well-behaved weaklings who later become lost in the great mass of people that tends to follow, unwillingly, the leads given by strong individuals.[32]

Freud believed that sexual repression helped to produce dependency and conformity, and therefore he hoped that liberating man's sexuality would help to elevate man's moral character, by promoting a greater measure of independence and self-reliance. With the benefit of hindsight it is possible to suggest that sexual liberation has not really yielded this anticipated moral dividend. Nor is it altogether surprising that it should have failed to do so, for there is no reason why unthinking conformity cannot exist among the promiscuous quite as easily as it does among the prudish.

Freud was certainly right to suggest that there is no necessary correlation between sexual abstinence and energy, self-reliance, and originality. As opposed to this, though, one can also argue that there is a plausible correlation between sexual promiscuity, self-indulgence, and personal irresponsibility. One can in fact argue this on Freud's own grounds, for Freud himself pointed to a correlation between the easy achievement of sexual satisfaction and an increase in the personality disorder to which he gave the name of narcissism.[33] Thus it is no accident that the characteristic personality disorder of our time is not the hysteria that evidently proliferated throughout sexually repressed Vienna but rather the narcissism that has evidently proliferated in sexually liberated, "laid-back" America.[34]

Finally, even on hedonistic grounds one can question the desirability of sexual liberation gone to extremes. Here too one can quote Freud against the very development that he set in motion:

> If sexual freedom is unrestricted from the outset the result is no better [than if the quest for sexual pleasure is frustrated]. It can easily be shown that the psychical value of erotic needs is reduced as soon as their satisfaction becomes easy. . . . In times in which there were no difficulties standing in the way of sexual satisfaction. . . love became worthless and life empty.[35]

It would be wrong to suggest that sexual liberation has left nothing but disaster in its wake and to deny that it has enabled thoroughly decent people to take increased satisfaction in altogether harmless pleasures. It would also be wrong to suggest that the greater measure of sexual freedom (made possible partly by more easily available contraceptive devices) involves a simple rejection and not a development of the founders' principles,[36] for the " 'civilized' sexual morality" that Freud denounced was a product of Christianity more than it was a product of the secular teaching of natural rights to which the founders were principally indebted. Nevertheless, even leaving aside AIDS—as well as the tremendous increases in the number of illegitimate births, with whose baleful consequences contemporary American social policy seems altogether unequipped to deal—one can still suggest that the sexual liberation that Freud helped bring about (his personal misgivings notwithstanding) and that has so markedly altered the character of American society in our lifetime has produced problems as well as solving them.

Freud's misgivings about the possible consequences of sexual liberation indicate that he was a most reluctant revolutionary; his critique of society and his praise for the instincts that society represses go only so far and no further. One important consequence of Freud's work, however, has been a succession of more radical apostates from Freud and reinterpreters of him, who have attempted in different ways (in the name of his own principles) to outdo him, to go further than he did, and to be more consistently revolutionary than he was. Figures such as Wilhelm Reich, Herbert Marcuse, Norman O. Brown, and R. D. Laing have rejected many of the nuances and qualifications that are built into Freud's doctrine and have expounded a doctrine with radically antinomian and egalitarian implications. Freud himself was decidedly conservative in cultural and moral matters and a devoted admirer of England's (though not America's) liberal politics. It is therefore noteworthy that much of Freud's intellectual impact in America has been on the radical left, in the service of doctrines that are profoundly antithetical to liberal politics.

Freud's doctrine was designed, however ambivalently, to preserve the traditional standards that proclaim the superiority of reason to impulse and sanity to madness, rather than to jettison them. These standards are in many respects rejected in radicalized revisions of his doctrine. Reason is no longer thought to be superior to the impulses it restrains; instead, impulse is at least the equivalent of reason, if not its superior (in that the satisfaction of impulse is held to be "authentic," whereas its restraint is held to be hypocritical). Similarly, Laing held madness to be superior to sanity, because madness is an "authentic" response to a civilization that is itself thought to be mad, whereas "sanity" is said to represent a willfully self-deceiving blindness to the hideous character of that civilization.

Freud's own views, it need hardly be said, are undoubtedly more sober, more moderate, more compatible with the moral requisites of liberal society than are those of his radical successors. Undeniably, however, the radical revisions of Freud's doctrine derive in some respects from the original. Freud himself was far from being a radical egalitarian, but many of his arguments can be used to serve radical egalitarian ends. Thus Freud himself called into question the difference between sanity and madness, arguing "that the borderline between the normal and the abnormal in nervous matters is a fluid one, and that we are all a little neurotic."[37] He suggested that we are in fundamental respects creatures dominated by impulses beyond rational control, in that "we are 'lived' by unknown and uncontrollable forces [that is, the id],"[38] so that "*the ego is not master in its own house.*"[39] He implied that morality is a latter-day, less authentic derivative of immorality, in that "the pre-existence of strong 'bad' impulses in infancy is often the actual condition for an unmistakable inclination towards 'good' in the adult."[40] One aspect of Freud's doctrine can therefore seem to justify a radically egalitarian and antinomian assault upon the standards of morality and rationality that liberal society presupposes and upon the self-control that a liberal democracy requires at least in some measure of its citizens.

As I have already suggested, however, this assault can draw only upon one aspect of his doctrine and must disregard much else in it. Thus, with respect to normality, Freud wrote that "equal care must be taken . . . to avoid two sources of error—the Scylla of underestimating the importance of the repressed unconscious, *and* the Charybdis of judging the normal *entirely* by the standards of the pathological."[41] He claimed that "we cannot in practical life do without the distinction between normal and pathological,"[42] even though "that distinction . . . possesses only a conventional value."[43] Similarly, he contended that "psycho-analysis has never said a word in favour of unfettering drives that would injure the community."[44] Instead, he suggested that "the work of psycho-analysis puts itself at the orders of precisely the highest and most valuable cultural trends, as a better substitute for the cultural repression."[45] Even when most critical of the burdens that social life places upon individuals, Freud rejected antinomianism, asserting that "integration in, or adaptation to, a human community appears as a scarcely avoidable condition which must be fulfilled before [the] aim of happiness can be achieved."[46] Far from being an opponent of civilized social life, Freud instead spoke of "our [Freud's? all psychoanalysts'? all mankind's?] appointed task of reconciling men to civilization."[47]

The above quotations are all well taken, and yet there is still a sense in which Freud's radical critics and reinterpreters may have a point. Freud did believe in standards; but it is not, finally, altogether clear how he could have justified his belief. This problem emerges when one considers a passage in his *Introductory Lectures on Psycho-*

Analysis: "We call [the] process [wherein a sexual aim is replaced with a nonsexual one] 'sublimation,' in accordance with the general estimate that places social aims higher than the sexual ones, which are at bottom self-interested."[48] Freud appeared to be content to accept the "general estimate," without fully considering the ways in which his postulates may render that estimate problematic. Why, on Freud's grounds, are social aims "higher" than sexual ones? Why, on his grounds, is it a critique of sexual aims to say that they are "at bottom self-interested"? Freud, who believed that "what is moral is self-evident,"[49] did not think it necessary to answer these questions. In practice, Freud's attitude is far more consonant with the requirements of liberal society than is the attitude of his radical critics and reinterpreters; but in theory, one can wonder whether they may not have thought through some of the troubling implications of his teaching more consistently than he did himself.

The left-wing reinterpretations of Freud—which envision a radically egalitarian society in which self-restraint will be unnecessary and in which all impulses can be satisfied without provoking conflict—are and are intended to be incompatible with liberal conceptions of politics and psychology. Freud's influence, however, is manifest not only or even primarily in this revolutionary coloration; it is also manifested far more prominently in the American fascination with the many different sorts of therapies that stem more or less directly from his discoveries.

The Fascination with Therapy

Many more Americans have certainly been affected far more deeply by their experiences with the various therapies—in addition to classical psychoanalysis, one can mention analytic psychotherapy, Jungian analysis, human potential, Gestalt psychology, *est*, and primal therapy, to name only a few—than by psychoanalytic radicalism. As opposed to psychoanalytic radicalism, Americans' great interest in therapy (to which the constant presence of self-help books on best-seller lists also attests) appears not to challenge liberal society in principle, in that the desire for mental health and emotional stability is presumably compatible with the goals of liberal society.

The prevalence of therapy, however, seems to point to a mass insecurity within liberal society: everyone wants to be happy and healthy, but virtually no one is confident that he is. Why this mass insecurity should characterize liberal democratic societies is an interesting question, to which Tocqueville once again can help us respond. He predicted this insecurity a century and a half ago, claiming that democratic man is "overwhelmed by a sense of his insignificance and weakness" and tends to get lost in the crowd, in whose midst he is "isolated and defenseless."[50] Conceivably this sense of isolation is at the root of the various psychological maladies that therapists are called on today to cure.

It is also worth noting that Tocqueville spoke of the democratic fascination with practical and applied science, stemming from the democrats' belief that it can "chang[e] their lot and better it."[51] It is clearly on this practical level, as a therapy, that psychoanalysis has most intrigued Americans: if psychoanalytic doctrine provides the theoretical explanation for the discontents that American civilization is thought necessarily to engender, psychoanalytic therapy and its variants are thought to provide a palliative if not a cure for them. The American interest in therapy in particular would therefore derive from the American confidence in the power of science generally, in that therapy presupposes the patients' confidence that the therapist possesses a science that will enable them to live more healthily and happily. This is, of course, a remarkable power with which to credit anyone; it is especially remarkable in view of the questionable efficacy of psychotherapy.

In many ways one is tempted to reject out of hand the contemporary fascination with therapy, because what people seem to want out of therapy so often points to a demeaning and trivialized understanding of life. To refer to Tocqueville yet again, one can suggest that the fascination with therapy is a manifestation of a characteristically democratic disorder, the propensity to stretch "the scope of human perfectibility . . . beyond reason."[52] To the extent that therapy is expected to put an end to psychic conflicts and unhappiness, its goal is simply ill conceived. For conflict and unhappiness are not signs of a diseased or neurotic life but instead represent a significant portion of the contents of normal life. Psychological health does not guarantee happiness; among therapies probably only lobotomy puts an end to disappointment and frustration.[53] Guilt feelings do not always indicate neurosis; they may instead be an appropriate response to past shameful behavior, with which the commendable resolution to behave better in the future can begin. To the extent that the fascination with therapy bespeaks a desire to live a life without conflict and guilt, it aims not at a happy and healthy human life, but at an amoral and subhuman life.

Therapists who claim too much for their therapies should be regarded as charlatans, and patients who understand so little about life as to believe them are fittingly their dupes. Rejecting a grandiose understanding of the powers of psychotherapy based on an impoverished understanding of the complexities of life, however, need not imply a rejection of psychotherapy altogether. For its goals can be presented much more cautiously, modestly, and believably. As it happens, this more modest presentation resembles Freud's; as outlined by him, the goals of psychotherapy are rather unexceptionable. In Freud's view, the aim of the treatment is merely "to make [the patient] as efficient and as capable of enjoyment as is possible"[54] or to win back for him "some degree of capacity for work and enjoyment."[55] According to another formulation, "What analysis achieves for neurotics is nothing other than what normal people bring about for themselves without its help."[56] These goals, it should be noted, are quite consistent with the founders' expectations for Americans' lives. On the basis of the founders' views, how could, why should, anyone object to a treatment that attempts to restore to people the capacity to lead decent, happy, productive private lives? Such private lives were not the only possibility to be offered to citizens within the American regime as the founders envisioned it, but they were presumably the lives that the founders expected the great majority of Americans to live within. My argument here presupposes, of course, that psychotherapy can be an effective means to the limited ends of efficiency and enjoyment; but then it is also altogether consonant with the founders' understanding of the regime that prospective patients be left free to make the decision about its efficacy or inefficacy on their own.

Conclusion

We are thus left with the question with which we began: from the founders' perspective, did Freud bring us the plague or did he not? This question remains a perplexing one. As we have seen, in some respects accepting Freud's doctrine necessitates rejecting the theory underlying the founders' political project (even though in other respects Freud's doctrine can be regarded as a development and elaboration of it). The theoretical tension, however, appears to be greater than the practical one. For in practice it is obvious that many people have no difficulty in affirming both the truth of psychoanalysis and the validity of the principles of liberal democracy. It is interesting that this should be so; that it is so does not testify simply to the human capacity (to which Freud himself so often called attention) to believe two incompatible things at the same time.

For it is not at all clear that accepting the truth of Freud's postulates requires one simply to reject other views, such as the founders', with which they appear in part to conflict. This is because Freud can be more or less compatible with the founders' understanding in practice, depending on the extent to which one thinks that Freud's theories explain everything. I have suggested that in some cases Freud undoubtedly extended the applicability of his theories beyond what one would like to think of as their appointed sphere. But it is important to realize that often Freud also made comparatively modest claims concerning the explanatory validity of his theories: "Psycho-analysis has never claimed to provide a complete theory of human mentality in general, but only expected that what it offered should be applied to supplement and correct the knowledge acquired by other means."[57] Elsewhere he wrote:

> Psycho-analysis alone cannot offer a complete picture of the world. . . . Psycho-analysis is to be described as a psychology of the id (and of its effects upon the ego). In each field of knowledge, therefore, it can make only *contributions*, which require to be completed from the psychology of the ego.[58]

Almost all the criticisms of Freud that I have made from the perspective of the founders are valid only to the extent that Freud asserted the dominance of the unconscious over our mental life; to the extent that he asserted that the unconscious merely *affects* our mental life but does not necessarily *control* it, Freud's perspective is much more compatible with that of the founders. Freud and the founders can coexist much more readily to the extent that Freud really did believe (in the words of the well-known anecdote) that at times a cigar is just a cigar.

Even if Freud's influence has not brought a plague upon the founders' house, though, it would be hard to argue that it has simplified its living arrangements. In a famous passage, Freud asserted that all political aspirations are unrealizable (and hence that the founders' political aspirations were unrealizable). "It almost looks as if analysis were the third of those 'impossible' professions in which one can be sure beforehand of achieving unsatisfying results. The other two, which have been known much longer, are education and government."[59] On the one hand, Freud's influence has probably not made "government" under the principles of the American Constitution significantly more "impossible"; on the other hand, it is also unlikely that it has helped to make it easier.

14
Pragmatism and the U.S. Constitution

James H. Nichols, Jr.

Pragmatism is the only philosophical school whose correlative adjective is used to praise political character and style of action. A statesman is never praised as stoic (although a private individual may be), let alone epicurean. But to call a statesman pragmatic is to indicate that he is not rigidly doctrinaire, excessively ideological, or lost in clouds of idealism; he can compromise reasonably to achieve real, though less than perfect, goals. During the past thirty years, as the end of ideology has receded into the dimmer future, the term "pragmatic" is used less exclusively for purposes of praise; one can now be blamed for unprincipled pragmatism. Yet it remains a generally favorable term, while political usage has brought forth another pejorative term for those deficient in pragmatism: "true believers."

Pragmatism stands out, from the other ways of thinking discussed in this volume, as distinctively American in two ways. On the one hand, it appears to be the only native American school of philosophical thought. In this regard, the palm for philosophical originality (as well as for being neglected) is generally awarded to Charles Peirce.[1] On the other hand, pragmatism seems to have given systematic intellectual expression to distinctively American elements of experience and to an archetypically American approach to life; in this regard, it is hard to say whether the first rank belongs to John Dewey, "in the profoundest sense . . . the philosopher of America,"[2] or to the more vivid and eloquent writer who first popularized the pragmatic movement, William James. Today one asserts less confidently and sweepingly than thirty years ago that pragmatism reflects *the* American way of thinking; yet its intellectual legacy remains strong, and no alternative has come near to attaining pragmatism's status in American life.[3]

A half-century before the emergence of pragmatism, Tocqueville observed that philosophy is paid less attention in the United States than elsewhere in the civilized world and that "the Americans have no school of philosophy peculiar to themselves."[4] He nonetheless discerned a philosophical method common to almost all Americans, whose chief traits he characterized thus:

> To escape from the spirit of system, the yoke of habit . . .; to take tradition only as information and existing facts only as a useful study to show how to do things differently and better; . . . to strive for results without getting entangled in the means and to look through forms to the basis of things—such are the principal traits of what I would call the American philosophical method.[5]

Tocqueville goes on to develop other features of American thinking in some detail, such as our attachment to ideas of progress and human perfectibility and our greater zeal for practically useful applications of science than for meditative inquiry into abstract theory. Tocqueville's depiction of American tendencies bears a striking resemblance to the main features of pragmatism (with the one important exception that, whereas Tocqueville emphasizes the contribution made by individual self-reliance to the American mode of thinking, Peirce and others emphasize the importance of the community of inquirers).

Whether one looks forward from Tocqueville's standpoint or back from the present, then, pragmatism seems distinctively American. Both then and now, however, it is no less distinctively American to take pride in American political institutions and to revere the Constitution.[6] Reflection on the relation of pragmatism to the Constitution and the thought underlying it might thus shed some especially revealing light on the American political and intellectual condition.

This relation immediately comes to sight as complex: pragmatism attacks fundamental substantive aspects of the founders' thinking, while it nonetheless seems to praise and to imitate key features of the mode of thinking that produced the Constitution. It criticizes the individualist natural rights philosophy of leading founders and calls into question the permanent validity of basic constitutional forms; but it follows the experimentalism, openness to political innovation, and general progressivism of the founders and seems in basic ways to wish to carry forward their political and social goals. To explore these matters in more detail, I propose first to examine critiques by pragmatism of the thought underlying the Constitution, next to consider the political and social goals at which pragmatism seems to aim, and finally to present some concluding reflections on this complex relationship. I shall move from the doubtless rash endeavor to speak of pragmatism in general to the firmer ground of considering Dewey's writings in particular, since he deals with political and social matters more extensively and more influentially than other pragmatists, with but an occasional reference to similar or contrasting positions advanced by James.

Critiques of the Constitution's Intellectual Basis

The pragmatist, according to James, is resolutely opposed to "a lot of inveterate habits dear to professional philosophers." He turns away from abstraction, "from verbal solutions, from bad *a priori* reasons, from fixed principles, closed systems, and pretended absolutes and origins" and looks toward "last things, fruits, consequences, facts." James goes on to describe Dewey's pragmatistic, "instrumental" view of truth as meaning *"that ideas (which themselves are but parts of our experience) become true just in so far as they help us to get into satisfactory relation with other parts of our experience."*[7] Pragmatism favors an open, skeptical search for helpful truths. It distrusts absolutist conceptual orders, permanent verities, and fixed, rigid, or ready-made conceptions. Dewey's pragmatic approach seeks in all domains of human concern to follow the example, as he understands it, of the intelligent method pursued with dramatic success in the natural sciences.

For our present purpose of reflecting on the relation between pragmatism and the Constitution, the most evidently important place to begin is with Dewey's critical rejection of those basic conceptions of the Declaration of Independence that provide the philosophical foundation for the kind of self-government whose institutions are framed in detail by the Constitution. That laws of nature and of nature's God should guide our political action, that the individual has inalienable natural rights, that the individual is prior to government so that legitimate government needs to rest on a social contract, that the primary purpose of government is securing individuals' rights—all these self-evident truths of the Declaration are rejected as opinions not firmly supported by pragmatist inquiry. Dewey realizes the significance of thus calling into question "the 'ideology' of which the Declaration of Independence is the classic expression." He asks:

> If belief in natural rights and natural law as the foundation of free government is surrendered, does the latter have any other moral basis? . . . The democratic tradition, call it dream or call it penetrating vision, was so closely allied with beliefs about human nature and about the moral ends which political institutions should serve, that a rude shock occurs when

> these affiliations break down. Is there anything to take their place, anything that will give the kind of support they once gave?[8]

I shall return to these questions in the concluding section of this essay; for now the point is to establish Dewey's full awareness of the weighty political issues raised by the movement of thought away from the founders' convictions.

On this level of fundamental conception, Dewey most fully develops and most frequently restates a critique of the founders' individualist conception of man. He asserts that this earlier liberalism "bequeathed to later social thought a rigid doctrine of natural rights inherent in individuals independent of social organization"; it was individualistic "in the sense in which individualism is opposed to organized social action."[9] It conceived of individuality

> as something ready-made, already possessed, and needing only the removal of certain legal restrictions to come into full play. It was not conceived as a moving thing, something that is attained only by continuous growth. Because of this failure, the dependence in fact of individuals upon social conditions was made little of.[10]

Or again:

> The real fallacy lies in the notion that individuals have such a native or original endowment of rights, powers and wants that all that is required on the side of institutions and laws is to eliminate the obstructions they offer to the "free" play of the natural equipment of individuals.[11]

In contrast with this early liberal conception of the natural individual apart from society, Dewey argues that—apart from certain biological structures—the individual does not have much that characterizes him: "the actual 'laws' of human nature are laws of individuals in association, not of beings in a mythical condition apart from association." Accordingly, the idea of opposition between individuals and society is "wholly unjustified."[12] The older idea of the individual as something given is a misleading abstraction; in fact, "social arrangements, laws, institutions . . . are means of *creating* individuals."[13]

Dewey's critical rejection may in part be taken as an assertion of pure common sense against an oversimplified version (not to say a straw man) of the older view of the individual. On the level of philosophical argumentation, he appears to attribute the decisive refutation of this older view to Hegel:

> In Hegel's philosophy of history and society culminated the efforts of a whole series of German writers—Lessing,

> Herder, Kant, Schiller, Goethe—to appreciate the nurturing influence of the great collective institutional products of humanity. For those who learned the lesson of this movement, it was henceforth impossible to conceive of institutions or of culture as artificial. It destroyed completely—in idea, not in fact—the psychology that regarded "mind" as a ready-made possession of a naked individual by showing the significance of "objective mind"—language, government, art, religion—in the formation of individual minds.[14]

As one would expect from someone who learned the Hegelian lesson, Dewey develops his critique of that older concept of individualism with a more particularly historical account of the concept's origin, use, and decline. "The earlier liberals lacked historic sense and interest." This lack for a while had "an immediate pragmatic value" in the fight against reactionaries, "the opponents of social change," by undermining appeals to "origin, precedent, and past history."[15] But in the longer run the liberals' historically conditioned ideas lost their value and, falsely upheld as "timeless truths," became obstacles to further beneficial social adaptation to changed circumstances. The individualist philosophy triumphed just when "the individual was counting for less in the direction of social affairs, at a time when mechanical forces and vast impersonal organizations were determining the frame of things."[16]

The proper task of intellect is historically conditioned, according to Dewey: "the genuine work of the intellectual class at any period" is "to detect and make articulate the nascent movements of their time."[17] And again, "the task of future philosophy is to clarify men's ideas as to the social and moral strifes of their own day," with full consciousness of the historically relative character of its activities and objects, in contrast with earlier philosophy's mistaken metaphysical claim to deal with ultimate and absolute reality.[18] One needs now to discard the old opposition of individual and society in order to elaborate a new conception of individuality in a more corporate, collectivized, and cooperative society. The task at hand is "reconstruction of the ways and forms in which men unite in associated activity."[19] "The problem of constructing a new individuality consonant with the objective conditions under which we live is the deepest problem of our times."[20]

Dewey treats the idea of liberty similarly to that of individuality. According to the view of earlier liberals such as the founders, Dewey argues, liberty is a naturally "ready-made possession" of individuals, and its most dangerous enemy is government. Overlooking the Declaration's principle that governments are instituted "to secure these rights," Dewey asserts that "not till the second half of the nineteenth century did the idea arise that government might and should be an instrument for *securing* and extending the liberties of individuals."[21] Against the earlier notion of liberty as something mainly negative (freedom from coercion), legal, political, fixed, and formal, Dewey calls for a positive, expansive, growing notion of liberty. He criticizes the earlier liberals for failing to distinguish "between purely formal or legal liberty and effective liberty of thought and action" and favors the idea that liberty "is something to be achieved."[22] For Dewey freedom "consists in a trend of conduct that causes choices to be more diversified and flexible, more plastic and more cognizant of their own meaning, while it enlarges this range of unimpeded operation." We must seek freedom "in something which comes to be, in a certain kind of growth; in consequences, rather than in antecedents."[23] Dewey sometimes enlarges the concept of freedom so far as to include pretty much all kinds of power, as in the following:

> Freedom from restriction, the negative side, is to be prized only as a means to a freedom which is power: power to frame purposes, to judge wisely, to evaluate desires by the consequences which will result from acting upon them; power to select and order means to carry chosen ends into operation.[24]

Dewey's revised view of the individual and expanded concept of liberty, together with his open-ended and experimental approach to truth, have the consequence that no definitively true assertions can be made about the proper relation between individuals and their political society or about the best form of government. Most generally, "the relation of individual freedom to organization is seen to be an experimental affair. It is not capable of being settled by abstract theory."[25] Given the far-reaching changes that have occurred in human history and may be presumed to continue to occur in the future, even the most basic principles of right political organization cannot reasonably be considered true once for all.

Dewey does not hesitate to point out how this way of thinking calls into question the most basic constitutional provisions and forms. Indeed, he often warns against treating the Constitution or general legal principles with excessive respect. He invokes Thomas Jefferson's democratic thinking to warn us against "the idolatry of the Constitution as it stands that has been sedulously cultivated."[26] Democracy "cannot be conceived as a consecration of some form of government which has already attained constitutional sanction."[27] Or more generally:

> Failure to recognize that general legal rules and principles are working hypotheses, needing to be constantly tested by the way in which they work out in application to concrete situations, explains the otherwise paradoxical fact that the slogans of the liberalism of one period often become the bulwarks of reaction in a subsequent era.[28]

Far from accepting this rational pragmatic view of legal and constitutional forms, the mass of men are given to "a truly religious idealization of, and reverence for, established institutions; for example in our own politics, the Constitution, the Supreme Court, private property, free contract, and so on. The words 'sacred' and 'sanctity' come readily to our lips when such things come under discussion."[29]

In the founders' thought, the original social contract or compact is the source of constitutional forms and the means by which the people confer powers and impose limits on government. For Dewey such a contract is mythical, at best a half-truth or symbol; it is a "theory whose falsity may easily be demonstrated both philosophically and historically," but it is nonetheless "of great worth as a symptom of the direction of human desire."[30] It points, however, toward a truth: "The truth of which the social compact was a symbol is that social institutions as they exist can be bettered only through the deliberate interventions of those who free their minds from the standards of the order which obtains."[31]

The search for improvement involves skeptical inquiry into the most basic of our constitutional institutions, to see whether they remain advantageous in the light of ever-changing historical circumstances. "There is no sanctity in universal suffrage, frequent elections, majority rule, congressional and cabinet government. These things are devices evolved in the direction in which the current was moving."[32] Dewey does not often specify what new political institutions might serve as better replacements for the old; one rare example that he does give is "supplementation [of the present forms of representative government] by political agencies that represent definitely economic social interests, like those of producers and consumers."[33] In a further-reaching but institutionally still vaguer suggestion, he advocates "the substitution of the intelligence that is exemplified in scientific procedure" for the sort of public discussion we now have. Our present public discussion does mark a decisive advance over despotic government, but it tends to become partisan propaganda and to be merely symbolic rather than to deal substantively with our real social problems. "Approximation to use of scientific method in investigation and of the engineering mind in the invention and projection of far-reaching social plans is demanded."[34]

Not only forms and institutions but also the purposes and functions of government should never be considered settled once for all but should be subjected to continuous pragmatic reconsideration and reconstruction. The limits of state action must vary with circumstances, such as those that cause activities to have public consequences; the scope of a state's functions is "something to be critically and experimentally determined."[35] This pragmatic position could lead to either expanding or narrowing the limits of state action; in facing the American scene where ideas of earlier liberalism still held sway over the people, Dewey clearly considered it certain that more positive state action was needed. Thus, for example, he welcomed Jeremy Bentham's rejection of natural rights as removing "the obstacle to positive action by the state whenever it can be shown that the general well-being will be promoted by such action" and noted with evident regret in his discussion of the utilitarians that the United States "lagged more than a generation behind Great Britain in promotion of social legislation."[36]

That Dewey could welcome social experiments with practices far different indeed from those prevalent in the United States appears most vividly from his generally laudatory comments in 1929 on Soviet Russia.[37] He observed there "the sense of a vast human revolution that has brought with it . . . an outburst of vitality, courage, confidence in life" and found that the effort evinced "a faith in human nature which is democratic beyond the ambitions of the democracies of the past."[38] The efforts in education especially interested him, and he observed "an enormous constructive effort taking place in the creation of a new collective mentality; a new morality I should call it, were it not for the aversion of Soviet leaders to all moral terminology."[39] The whole effort could most helpfully be viewed, he wrote, as "an enormous psychological experiment in transforming the motives that inspire human conduct."[40] Capitalist ideologues and Marxist dogmatists believed the experiment doomed to fail or to prevail, respectively; Dewey was fascinated and open-minded as to the outcome. While not finding the Soviets' aversion to moral terminology ominous, he nonetheless had some awareness of the costs of such experimentation; he considered it "an experiment, by all means the most interesting one going on upon our globe—though I am quite frank to say that for selfish reasons I prefer seeing it tried in Russia rather than in my own country."[41]

Political and Social Goals of Dewey's Pragmatism

Taken in isolation, Dewey's critiques of the founders' political thought could lead one to view pragmatism as hostile to the whole constitutional system. But if one looks at the broader context of the goals at which Dewey's political, moral, and educational writings aim, one could plausibly argue that they attempt to preserve and to perfect what is most valuable in American constitutionalism.

Since, in Dewey's view, historical developments have brought about fundamental changes in the conditions of human life (especially during the past few centuries when science has been applied to technological inventions affecting modes of production, transportation, and communication), political thinking and practice must be constantly revised if the basic purposes of American constitutionalism, of liberalism, are to be preserved. Rigid adherence to dogmas and institutions that worked in the past may produce disaster in the present or future, with the consequent loss of those core values—such as democracy and the free and equal opportunity to develop one's capacities—to which liberal constitutionalism was dedicated. Thus Dewey puts himself on the side of those who "urge that preservation of democratic institutions requires just that extension of governmental functions which to the authors of our tradition was the enemy to be fought."[42] Unintelligent traditionalism can produce what it most abhors, revolution. "The belief in political fixity, of the sanctity of some form of state consecrated by the efforts of our fathers and hallowed by tradition, is one of the stumbling-blocks in the way of orderly and directed change; it is an invitation to revolt and revolution."[43] The Constitution and the thought underlying it must be constantly criticized and revised, to preserve its vital and valid core; a pragmatic approach is necessitated even by a conservative goal.

The key realm where even mere preservation cries out for pragmatic reconstruction of political thinking, institutions, and policies is the economy. Eighteenth-century notions of individual liberty and of the forms and scope of government may have been efficacious, roughly suitable, and progressive in American circumstances then, but now economic life is dominated in crucial respects by large corporate entities, in the face of whose power the weak individual endowed with formal economic liberties may be able to accomplish little for himself. New relations between politics and economics—most dramatically illustrated by the corporation, a creature of legislatures and courts—have made older determinations of rights and duties obsolete. These aimed at "maintaining peaceful relations between persons as persons," whereas now "large combinations have largely replaced individual persons as the units of effective action."[44] Since "freedom is unreal which does not have as its basis an economic command of environment"[45] and since economic forces and structures increasingly escape the individual's power of effective action, real liberty for individuals "will require social control of economic forces in the interest of the great mass of individuals."[46] The "elimination" of the older economic and political individualism "will liberate imagination and endeavor for the task of making corporate society contribute to the free culture of its members. Only by economic revision can the sound element in the older individualism—equality of opportunity—be made a reality."[47]

Without spelling out in great detail what a revised political economy should be or just how, politically, we can best get to it, Dewey unambiguously calls for greatly increased public control of the economy. Only thus can the benefits of the scientific and industrial revolutions be spread more widely than to the "relatively small class" of "industrial entrepreneurs," who "have reaped out of all proportion to what they sowed." We need "organized social reconstruction that puts the results of the mechanism of abundance at the free disposal of individuals"; contemporary liberals must see that "socialized economy is the means of free individual development as the end."[48] Dewey does not only demand redistribution just for the sake of greater equality of benefits; he wants us to reorient our political thinking more deeply by recognizing that uncontrolled private economic power in our day can be as detrimental to liberty in various spheres of ordinary life as the "unchecked control of political power." Earlier liberals devoted their greatest efforts to guarding against unchecked political power; in our times we must make similar exertions against unchecked private economic power. And, of course, he urges us to support appropriate public measures against such dangers to liberty. Whereas "beneficiaries of the established economic regime" seek through organizations called Liberty Leagues "to perpetuate the harsh regimentation of millions of their fellows," public power should intervene with appropriate social legislation to ameliorate such unfree conditions of work.[49] To take another example: the founders, deeming a free press crucial to liberal democracy, designed constitutional fences against the danger they perceived, namely, that of governmental censorship; for us, however, the greatest threat to a free press may well be economic factors tending toward centralization.[50]

That corporate society should "contribute to the free culture of its members," that "socialized economy is the means" toward the end of "free individual development"—these and myriad similar statements suggest that Dewey's social and political goals go beyond economic justice through redistribution or socialism, as well as beyond mere preservation in changed circumstances of liberal constitutionalism's valuable core. Dewey sketches the extent and reach of these goals while giving an account of John Stuart Mill's struggles with the problem of achieving freedom:

> The problem of democracy was seen to be not solved, hardly more than externally touched, by the establishment of universal suffrage and representative government. . . . The problem of democracy becomes the problem of that form of social organization, extending to *all* the areas and ways of living, in which the powers of individuals shall not be merely released from mechanical external constraint but shall be fed, sustained and directed.[51]

The substantive areas of life concerning which society may take active measures and the goals that society may seek to attain cannot be defined once for all: they are unlimited. All kinds of circumstances change, and every change can bring new public problems to light; no solution to a problem, however adequate, can prevent novel problems from arising unpredictably soon thereafter. A domain of activity or circumstance at one time reasonably left free of public control may subsequently require it, as we have seen Dewey argue most notably for economic life and as is best exemplified in our own day by environmental issues. Whenever people experience obstacles, dissatisfactions, painful frustrations, or the hope of satisfying new desires, one may be able to make a reasonable case that society should take public action. These human passions and plans attain no final satisfaction—the solution to one problem or the fulfillment of one new hope creates a new situation in which new problems and hopes will arise. No ultimate end or final perfection calls forth these varying passions, nor does any fixed intelligible hierarchy put them in order. In Hobbes's memorable formulation, what men seek, felicity, is "a continual progress of the desire, from one object to another; the attaining of the former, being still but the way to the latter."[52]

With such a view of the human condition (not to say human nature), what can one rely on for the rational guidance of life, particularly political life? The American founders took their bearings from the inalienable natural rights with which, they believed, all men were equally endowed and to secure which was the proper business of government. For Dewey, as we have seen, this approach taken by early liberalism became unconvincing and undesirable, each doubly: the concept of an intelligible fixed nature of man had been discredited philosophically by the Hegelian interpretation of man's historical becoming and scientifically by the Darwinian teaching on evolution; the doctrine of natural rights set up crippling obstacles in the way of adequate adaptation to change and imposed unacceptably low limits on the goals of governmental action.

The founders did not ignore human ends beyond the securing of natural rights through government, nor did they think (as Dewey sometimes seems to suggest) that the isolated individual left to himself could adequately achieve all those other ends; they did, however, assert that the *fundamental* task of government was to secure natural rights, and they left the bulk of other human goals to society as distinct from government, that is, to individuals, families, churches, and other nongovernmental associations and organizations. Dewey finds this constraining direction of government toward the ends of natural rights unpersuasive for all the reasons just reviewed; for these same reasons he finds the Hobbesian endeavor to subordinate all rational governance to self-preservation, to avoiding violent death, to dispelling fear for one's security, still more unsatisfactory.

Reasonable guidance of society, for Dewey, must come not from the Hobbesian goal of self-preservation alone or from the natural rights of man as understood by the founders but from the goal of growth itself, the development of human capacities for satisfaction and self-actualization. Not some final perfection to be attained or produced but the process itself of growing, developing, seeking, testing, and learning is the highest value toward the advancement of which all our rational plans should be directed.

Dewey's criterion of growth bears important resemblances to Hobbes's standard of self-preservation: for Dewey as for Hobbes no utmost aim or greatest good could fulfill all our striving; and as Hobbes proceeds thence to take his bearings from preserving the individual's ability to seek satisfactions of whatever sorts, so Dewey posits growth itself as the sovereign consideration. But one must not underestimate the differences. Hobbes looks above all to the negative pole, violent death; the dominating passion that gives reason a firm direction aims at avoiding the greatest evil. Dewey, by contrast, stresses the positive goals implicit in the idea of growth (and in this respect his argument converges with Aristotle's positive conception of happiness as certain activities). Furthermore, Hobbes's whole orientation rests on fundamental assertions about human nature. Dewey, however, as we have seen, rejects claims for definitive knowledge of human nature: the goal of growth is meant to be open-ended, infinite, in contrast with the limits inherent in knowledge of any being's nature (and in this respect, of course, he diverges even more from Aristotle than from Hobbes). The significant thing is

> the process of growth, of improvement and progress. . . . The end is no longer a terminus or limit to be reached. It is the active process of transforming the existent situation. Not perfection as a final goal, but the ever-enduring process of perfecting, maturing, refining is the aim in living. . . . Growth itself is the only moral "end."[53]

Our common idea of growth comes from observing nature: acorns sprout, the sprouts become saplings, and the saplings eventually grow to mature oak trees, which in turn produce new acorns; the baby becomes a child, a youth, a mature adult. Dewey's conception of human growth, as indeterminate and open-ended, differs radically from such natural examples, being itself rooted in a historicist conception of man such as Hegel's (with a determinate end of history removed). Growth as the highest human value is thus conceived, paradoxically, as something non-natural or even preternatural or as a transcending, an overcoming, a conquest of nature; perhaps one should rather say that growth is conceived in the manner of Darwinian nature rather than nature as commonly experienced (but a Darwinian nature into which rational planning can be integrated).

However that may be, this open-ended conception of growth has certain advantages: it makes sense of our love of novelty, our hope for a different and better future, and our faith in progress. Furthermore, it avoids some problems associated with more traditional distinctions between means and ends: if the human end is conceived as too remote from current experience and possibilities, it can hardly guide us effectively; if the human end is too near and easily achieved, it cannot do justice to our higher aspirations; most important, we cannot reasonably claim to have adequate and definitive knowledge of the highest human fact, *the* goal of human development. In accordance with his conception of growth, Dewey rejects the traditional dichotomy of means and ends in favor of a continuum. Our intellectual processes of valuing and our deliberations toward action always take ends and means together—no rational thinking takes place concerning intrinsic or absolute ends in abstraction from or unrelated to the means for attaining them. Similarly, no end that we attain is final; rather it is part of a new context that supplies the means for moving on to further ends.[54]

The deepest problem attaching to Dewey's conception of open-ended growth involves how, in separation from the ordinary view of nature, we can distinguish healthy growth from changes for the worse, such as malignant tumors or overall decay. One is tempted to say that ordinary sane experience of changes informs us adequately whether we have grown and developed or sickened and decayed; and Dewey does often seem to follow just such common-sense judgment. Such judgment, however, seems ultimately to rely on the ordinary notion of nature (in accordance with which growth is finite and toward a given end) that Dewey rejects. Dewey's conception seems both to need nature as a guide and to insist on rejecting it. A revealing illustration of this dilemma occurs in a sympathetic discussion by

Dewey of Jefferson's democratic convictions. For Jefferson, of course, the commitment to democracy takes root in the rational doctrine of natural rights. Rejecting natural rights, Dewey says we must

> translate the word "natural" into *moral*. . . . [Jefferson's] fundamental beliefs remain unchanged in substance if we forget all special associations with the word *Nature* and speak instead of ideal aims and values to be realized—aims which, although ideal, are not located in the clouds but are backed by something deep and indestructible in the needs and demands of humankind.[55]

Most of us, speaking in common-sense ways, would have no trouble identifying what is "deep and indestructible in the needs and demands of humankind" with human nature, but Dewey's philosophy does not let him do so. Accordingly he tries to elaborate another way to distinguish growth from decay: growth is what enables still more growth to follow as an ever-enduring process. Apart from any problem of circularity, the ultimate test for growth as distinct from decay seems thus to emerge as perpetuation or survival, and we fall back into the very Hobbesian position above which the higher goal of growth sought to elevate us (or rather to a Hobbesian position modified in the light of historicist philosophy and evolutionary science). Concerning Dewey's theoretical treatment of the ultimate criteria of evaluation, it may not be too harsh to judge that "pragmatic theory . . . wanders hopelessly between subjective satisfaction of desire and the test of survival."[56]

Turning back from these difficult philosophical problems, we observe that, since a human being's rationally directed growth can sensibly be called education, we can properly single out education as the highest or most comprehensive theme of Dewey's moral, political, and social thought. Just as growth is the only moral end, so likewise "there is nothing to which education is subordinate save more education."[57] Alternatively, we could say that Dewey's highest theme is threefold: science, education, and democracy, with education in the center like the keystone of an arch. In this crucial respect his thought closely resembles the Enlightenment convictions of the founders. As Dewey points out, "The devotion of democracy to education is a familiar fact."[58] Unlike some democratic theorists of this century who appear to think that appropriate procedures and institutions can ensure successful democracy however selfish, ignorant, and debased the citizenry, Dewey joins the founders in holding democracy's devotion to education indispensable.

Indeed, it can fairly be said that Dewey gives greater emphasis to the crucial importance of education than the founders did, because of how he understands certain key features of modern life. Rural inhabitants of the past understood most things that affected their lives through direct experience; despite his much more numerous separate items of information, the modern city dweller does not. Many influences on our lives are remote and unknown: "We are at the mercy of events acting upon us in unexpected, abrupt, and violent ways."

> The average person is surrounded today by readymade intellectual goods as he is by readymade foods, articles, and all kinds of gadgets. He has not the personal share in making either intellectual or material goods that his pioneer ancestors had. Consequently they knew better what they themselves were about.

These changes affect "the cultural conditions involved in the maintenance of freedom."[59] Consciously planned education is needed more than ever before if we are to be an informed public capable of intelligent judgment rather than a mass manipulated by propaganda and if we are to be able to deal with the complex problems of our political economy and society. "The future of democracy is allied with the spread of the scientific attitude. It is the sole guarantee against wholesale misleading by propaganda. More important still, it is the only assurance of the possibility of a public opinion intelligent enough to meet present social problems."[60]

Science, education, and democratic society are linked together most frequently in Dewey's well-known demand for scientific approaches to be used in handling democracy's social problems. He calls for the divorce of natural science from humanity to be overcome: the natural sciences' goals must be directed to relieving human woes, and natural science should provide "the technique of social and moral engineering."[61] Dewey wants the "potential alliance between scientific and democratic method" to be consummated "in the techniques of legislation and administration."[62] Positing this social goal as the most important task for contemporary philosophy, he intends his pragmatism to extend and complete the Baconian scientific project in the manner that will benefit human life the most.[63]

In Dewey's hopes for progress from science, a moral dimension is always crucial. The production of superior material artifacts cannot be the measure of science's worth to a society, for a society's success turns on the kind of people it produces. As Dewey asks, "How can there be a society really worth serving unless it is constituted of individuals of significant personal qualities?" The great worth of democracy accordingly lies above all in the opportunities it provides for development—that is, again, for education. "If democracy has a moral and ideal meaning, it is that a social return be demanded from all and that opportunity for development of distinctive capacities be afforded all."[64] Science itself must be guided by the moral purpose of democracy at its best, and one can no longer take this guidance simply for granted. One cannot hold the simple Enlightenment faith "that assured advance of science will produce free institutions by dispelling ignorance and superstition," for "a more adequate science of human nature might conceivably only multiply the agencies by which some human beings manipulate other human beings for their own advantage," a possibility actualized to a novel degree in totalitarian states.[65]

While on the one hand science must be led by democratic morality, on the other, as we have seen already, democracy needs science, especially new applications of the scientific approach to moral and social problems. "If [science] is incapable of developing moral techniques which will determine these relations [which human beings, severally and in groups, sustain to one another] . . . not only democracy but all civilized values are doomed."[66] The hope for fruitful harmony between science and democracy is given plausibility by the observable character of a genuine morale to be found among free scientific inquirers: "fairmindedness, intellectual integrity, the will to subordinate personal preferences to ascertained facts and to share with others what is found."[67] Democracy needs to be infused with this moral scientific spirit. A certain kinship between democracy and science, consisting in such shared traits as experimental innovativeness, openness, and devotion to progress and eminently displayed in such persons as Jefferson, makes their cooperative harmony a reasonable hope as well as an indispensable goal. The most needful education would foster the advance of science and democracy together toward a better future.[68]

Conclusion

Let me begin some concluding reflections on the relation between American constitutionalism and Dewey's pragmatism with a general observation about how Dewey treats the founders' thought. In a word, his treatment is usually superficial, for reasons that are easily understood in the context of his thought as a whole. Since he takes a historicist view of human development, with special emphasis on scientific progress, he has no expectation of finding any superior political wisdom in the past and hence no incentive to seek a detailed, probing, sympathetic interpretation in depth of any past thinking. His pressing concerns turn on contemporary problems, and he discusses the past to grasp just so much historical background as he considers necessary to handle the present situation. In the social realm that I have chiefly dealt with, Dewey wishes mainly to grasp and to critique dominant contemporary political opinions—as given expression in such places as Supreme Court opinions and party platforms—rather than fully to probe the best thinking of a Jefferson or a James Madison.

He sometimes distinguishes between simpler common opinions and the more sophisticated thinking of some of the founders. Thus: "The maintenance of democratic institutions is not such a simple matter as was supposed by some of the founding fathers—although the wiser among them realized how immensely the new political experiment was favored by external circumstances." Likewise, whereas much American opinion blurs the real influence of economic factors on culture and politics, "Madison as well as Jefferson was quite aware of the connection [of economics and politics] and of its bearing upon democracy." And again: "The founders of American political democracy were not . . . unaware of the necessity of cultural conditions for the successful working of democratic forms."[69] Nonetheless, most of the time Dewey criticizes simple dogmatic versions or offshoots of the founders' thought, and a Jefferson or a Madison could have much to say in response to such criticism without having to change his basic position. Consequently, certain pressing social problems, which Dewey urges on our attention as necessitating the abandonment of old constitutional doctrines, could in fact be handled well within the framework of the founders' constitutionalism. After all, as Dewey sometimes notes, innovative experimentalism characterizes to no small degree the thought of many a prominent founder.

Does Dewey's position as a whole, with the full extent of public social policies he advocates, nonetheless amount to a fundamental break with the way of thinking that underlies our Constitution? One could argue that it does, along the following lines. Dewey calls for a new kind of social engineering without delineating any limits beyond which it should not go. What is more, he frequently suggests that all areas of life may potentially need to be publicly directed, and he repeatedly argues against any clear conception of rights belonging to human individuals by nature that government must respect and secure. Quite to the contrary, the open-ended conception of human beings and of social forms invites social experiments and engineering that might ride roughshod over individual liberties, in the name of whatever concern happened at the time to be most intensely felt.

Perhaps "the dogma of fixed unchangeable types and species"[70] is called into question by recent developments in science, which thus also pose theoretical problems for the doctrine of natural rights; but without a dominant public belief in such rights, grounds for reasonable confidence that our liberties are secure may fail. Jefferson, after all, questioned whether even the rational conviction in natural rights could suffice in the absence of belief in divine sanction: "And can the liberties of a nation be thought secure when we have removed their only firm basis, a conviction in the minds of the people that these liberties are of the gift of God? That they are not to be violated but with his wrath?"[71] If weakened belief in divine sanction for liberties threatens the security of their tenure, what must become of that security when people call natural rights themselves into question and even doubt the existence of a clearly definable human nature?

Dewey's evident impatience with doctrinal obstacles to the kinds of social experiments he favors, together with frequent oversimplification and belittling of individualist views opposed to his own, increases one's uneasiness at the future toward which pragmatic social engineering might lead. In this respect—probably less for philosophically fundamental reasons than because of personal temperament and emphasis—James provokes less alarm than Dewey. On the one hand, James does not display hostility to individualism; quite to the contrary, his *Varieties of Religious Experience* focuses on individual religious experience to the virtually complete neglect of religion's organized, social, collective dimensions. More important, if more elusive: James seems more truly and deeply open to views opposed to his own, less quick to dismiss them as currently irrelevant products of circumstances that no longer obtain. To give just one important example, James argues that both skepticism and religious faith are living options:

> In either case we *act*, taking our life in our hands. No one of us ought to issue vetoes to the other, nor should we bandy words of abuse. We ought, on the contrary, delicately and profoundly to respect one another's mental freedom: then only shall we bring about the intellectual republic; then only shall we have that spirit of inner tolerance without which all our outer tolerance is soulless.[72]

Whatever may be the status of this difference between Dewey and James, certainly Dewey is fully aware that the abandonment of natural rights poses a deep problem for the basis of democratic liberties.[73] His own social thought, while removing the older basis, seeks to provide new benefits and assurances. On the positive side, of course, Dewey points society toward providing a greater range of rights or liberties, reinterpreted in the more extensive and positive manner that we have already considered. On the negative side—that is, with a view to preventing coercion, manipulation, or tyranny—

Dewey counts on the self-correcting character of pragmatism itself, with such attributes of scientific inquiry as truly objective consideration of consequences, genuinely open-minded experimental testing of hypotheses, and deeply rooted commitment to freedom of thought, discussion, and inquiry.

This pragmatic scientific approach should keep us away not only from chance and magic or exhortation and preaching, but also from "a fanaticism that will force the realization of preconceived ends at any cost."[74] It should, in short, prevent our straying from the democratic path into totalitarianism. That Dewey himself practiced what he preached in this regard can be nicely illustrated by the contrast between his generally favorable remarks in 1929 on the Soviet experiment, quoted above, and the following judgments based on fuller information and reflection published in 1939. In the chapter "Totalitarian Economics and Democracy," Dewey presents harsh criticism of the monolithic Marxist theory applied by the Soviets and expresses deeper appreciation of the value of existing democratic forms. Concerning Marxism he notes the irony that

> the theory which has made the most display and the greatest pretense of having a scientific foundation should be the one which has violated most systematically every principle of scientific method. What we may learn from this contradiction is the potential alliance between scientific and democratic method and the need of consummating this potentiality in the techniques of legislation and administration.[75]

Still more interesting, not least for the rare opportunity it affords to see an important thinker correct an earlier error, the following passage merits quotation at length:

> Democratic methods are proved, even if they lack adequate substance, to be indispensable to effecting economic change in the interest of freedom. In common with many others, I have from time to time pointed out the harmful consequences the present regime of industry and finance has upon the reality of democratic ends and methods. I have nothing to retract. But conditions in totalitarian countries have brought home the fact, not sufficiently realized by critics, myself included, that the forms which still exist encourage freedom of discussion, criticism and voluntary associations, and thereby set a gulf between a country having suffrage and popular representation and a country having dictatorships, whether of the right or left.[76]

Dewey's pragmatism rejects the foundational principles of American constitutionalism. It therefore lessens the settled sense of security in the functions, structures, and limits of government. Correlatively, as open-endedly progressive, it is constitutionally incapable of reaping the social and political benefits of habitual veneration for long-established principles. By maintaining a truly open-minded, experimental devotion to free inquiry, however, Dewey's pragmatism can guard against political excesses and fanatic dogmatism. Nothing prevents it from fully appreciating real beneficial consequences of America's experiment in constitutional self-government. And, above all through reflection on the moral kinship between science and democracy, it can provide reasons of its own for valuing constitutional democratic forms. Averse though he is to stating eternal verities, Dewey nonetheless ventures a strong generalization near the end of *Freedom and Culture:* "If there is one conclusion to which human experience unmistakably points it is that democratic ends demand democratic methods for their realization."[77]

15
Existentialism and Democracy

Werner J. Dannhauser

A discussion of the relation between existentialism and democracy—understood here as *liberal* democracy—should begin with the realization that it is easier to come to grips with democracy than with existentialism.

We understand democracy well enough to be able to dispense with any formal definition of it. Its very name, referring to rule of the many, provides a good deal of information, and we have no trouble recognizing a democracy when we come across one. Attempting to discover whether a given regime can be called democratic, we know we must see whether or not it enjoys majority rule along with minority rights. We look for a form of government dedicating itself to the principles of equality and liberty. We understand that democracy entails certain institutions like independent judiciaries and legislatures that are more than rubber stamps. It also involves respect for laws and legalities; we look for certain procedures such as free elections. What is more, and perhaps most important for present purposes, democracy has a local habitation and a name; we can study the United States of America, examine its authoritative documents like the Declaration of Independence and discussions of it in important theoretical works like Tocqueville's *Democracy in America*. We have no unusual difficulty, then, in recognizing a democracy when we see one, though at times a marginal case, like Mexico, may perplex us. We have, however, no difficulty in seeing when regimes are something else; for example, we know that neither Albania nor Paraguay is a democracy.

When, by way of contrast, we attempt to come to grips with existentialism,[1] we encounter problems all along the way. The term *democracy* reveals a good deal; the term *existentialism* reveals next to nothing. If we are told that existentialism is a doctrine according to which existence precedes essence, we still know next to nothing, except existentialism's academic guise. We can, of course, pursue the deeper meaning of that formula and learn that existentialists maintain that human existence precedes human essence and that man is the animal without a nature who makes himself.[2] While such statements convey meaning, especially to students of the history of political philosophy, they still will not enable anybody to "situate" existentialism, especially not in politically relevant terms.

If we try to avoid such difficulties by simply beginning to read existentialist texts, new problems arise—and not merely because the two thinkers most profoundly influential on existentialism, Kierkegaard and Nietzsche, precede the existence of existentialism as a philosophical school or movement. Thus most people would agree that Heidegger and Sartre are the two leading existentialists of the twentieth century, but both rejected that label, so that when we treat them as existentialists, we run the danger of trying to understand them better than they understand themselves, or at least differently. We take no risks calling Camus an existentialist, because he called himself one; but here we face the problem that Camus is commonly, and not altogether unfairly, considered a thinker of the second rank.

Although the study of Nietzsche and Kierkegaard as the fountainheads of existentialism circumvents such difficulties, it does not dispose of problems associated with the history of existentialism. Where do we begin? Antecedents have been discovered in the pre-Socratics, the Book of Job, Montaigne, Pascal, Rousseau, and Hegel.[3] It appears that existentialism had a long, distinguished, and tangled past long before it acquired a name, probably in 1929.[4]

Considerations of this sort may lead us, momentarily at least, to doubt whether existentialism really exists in any meaningful sense—it seems to have neither a nature nor a history. Moreover, in the realm of ideas, we tend to define things by beginning to demarcate them from what they are *not*. For example, our understanding of the soul can plausibly begin with the vague realization that it is something that is not body. Similarly, we can usually start to understand an "ism" by showing that it is incompatible with all sorts of other isms, the way idealism can be set against materialism.

The trouble with existentialism is, however, that it comes to sight as compatible with everything under the sun. Two examples will suffice to make this point, and perhaps to undercut it by bringing us closer to the core of existentialism.

Christian Existentialism

In October 1945, Jean-Paul Sartre gave a lecture in Paris entitled "Existentialism Is a Humanism." More than any other single event in the history of existentialism, this lecture imposed itself on the public consciousness. It put existentialism on the map, as it were.[5] Sartre candidly proclaimed his—and existentialism's—atheism. In this he was doing no more than following Nietzsche, whose Zarathustra is most famous for proclaiming the death of God.

Since the death of God, especially the death of the Christian God, constitutes the starting point of the existentialist analysis of our human predicament, it would appear that a Christian (or Jewish) existentialist is an impossibility, or at least a contradiction in terms. Yet once we draw this conclusion, we can look up and find millions of Christian existentialists. What is more, religious thinkers from Pascal and Kierkegaard to Marcel and Buber figure prominently in any pantheon of existentialist thought.

What, then, is to be done with the religious dimension of existentialism? It will not do simply to ignore it, but the following considerations may justify our bracketing of it. On the whole, and to caricature, religious existentialism divides into two parts: an analysis of a universe bereft of God and a leap of faith out of, or beyond, that world. Politics deals with this world, so we can here shortchange an otherworldly aspect of a body of thought. Moreover, precisely because it devotes so much energy to delineating a godless universe, the religious part of existentialism comes under suspicion. When Pascal, for example, described the world as an "infinite sphere, the center of which is everywhere, the circumference nowhere," he had to abstract from Genesis 1, according to which the world is no such thing.[6] Religious existentialism pretends that there is no account of creation in the Bible, no insistence on the world's being a cosmos rather than a chaos. Advocating an atheistic existentialism, the young Sartre asserted that even if there were a God, it would make no difference. Religious existentialists assert that God exists, but it is not quite clear what difference that makes.[7]

When studying the relation between existentialism and democracy, we also do well to remember that religious existentialists do not often speak of the social aspects of religion. Following Kierkegaard, who argued for Christ and against churches, they have very little to say about religion as a mediating structure in society, dwelling almost exclusively on the individual's individual encounter with a mysterious God.

Marxist Existentialism

Having realized that there are religious existentialists even though in some sense there are not supposed to be, we must also take a glance at the problem posed by the existence of Marxist existentialists.

Marxism and existentialism seem obviously incompatible, indeed diametrically opposed. Existentialism stresses subjectivity in contradistinction to Marxism's objectivity. Marxists sometimes deride the irrationalism of existentialists, who in turn denigrate the arid and dehumanizing rationalism of Marxists. Marxism is almost relentlessly optimistic, holding as it does that mankind sets itself only such tasks as it can solve; existentialism equates optimism with shallowness. Existentialists criticize Marxists for their materialism, while Marxists criticize existentialists for their idealism—and both have a point. Marxism's strong suit is its focus on the collective; existentialism specializes, as it were, in the solitary individual. Marxists speak of the end of alienation, while existentialists posit the permanent loneliness of man. Existentialists stress freedom where Marxists see determinism.

These contrasts, which could be multiplied at will, are not arbitrary. In fact, almost all of them have been taken either from a distinguished Marxist like Lukács or from the young Sartre.[8] As is well known, Sartre himself would eventually find it possible to reconcile what he had previously held to be irreconcilable, writing a huge book that intermeshed the principles of existentialism with those of Marxism.[9] Moreover, his practice followed his principles, as he came more often than not to side with the Soviet Union in its struggle with the theory and practice of liberal democracy.

Once more we see that in messy reality the mind might find much that is difficult to conceive. So full is our present world of Marxist existentialists that if we were forced to classify today's existentialism as either a left-wing or a right-wing phenomenon, we would most likely put it on the Left. If then existentialism can accommodate itself to Marxism, however strained such an accommodation may be, we must wonder about its kinship, or lack of kinship, with democracy.

Since existentialism can make peace with both Christianity and Marxism, we may be understandably suspicious that it is compatible with absolutely everything. That, in turn, would lead us to doubt that it is a coherent doctrine or unified body of thought. And indeed, we could do worse than to approach existentialism as a persuasion rather than as a systematic philosophy, a mood rather than a full articulation of reality.

Such an understanding of existentialism should not be confused with an underestimation of its significance. In spite of its vagueness, or perhaps because of it, existentialism is a pervasive modern phenomenon, especially among the thoughtful. In 1948, Karl Löwith, still the best guide to the literature of existentialism, wrote:

> We are all existentialists, some consciously, some willy-nilly, and some without knowing it, because we are all more or less caught in the predicament of being "modern" by living in an epoch of dissolution of former beliefs and certainties. Even those who have never read a line of Heidegger, Jaspers, or Sartre are so familiar with such typical categories of existential philosophy as "contingency" and "finiteness" of our existence, "anxiety" and "care" and all that which Jaspers calls "extreme situations" that they can hardly imagine a normalcy apart from mediocrity.[10]

More than forty years after they were written, these words remain persuasive.

The Existential Perspective

The existentialist perspective influences our general perspective of all things; it suffuses the awareness. Its special efficacy may have to do with its closeness to art. (In this connection we should remember that Nietzsche and Heidegger both wrote poetry, that Camus as well as Sartre were distinguished dramatists and novelists.) Having brought an appreciation of existentialism's significance to its views on politics in general and democracy in particular, we must, however, quickly add that existentialism's most obvious stance in such matters hovers between the apolitical and the antipolitical. Four brief glimpses into the realm of existentialist art will clarify the point.

The film *Devil in the Flesh* came to these shores at roughly the same time that Camus and Sartre were beginning to become fashionable in the United States. In its powerful last scene, the grief-stricken hero walks through a crowd of jubilant Parisians. He mourns the death of his beloved, to whom, it almost goes without saying, he was not married. Oblivious to the clamor of the surrounding throng, he cares nothing for the fact that it is November 11, 1918, that his country has just survived and concluded its greatest war. France's victory means nothing to him as private griefs blot out public affairs.

The second example comes from prerevolutionary Russia, from Dostoevski's *Notes from Underground,* published in 1864. Its protagonist, the precursor of any number of existentialist heroes and antiheroes, cares very little for the world surrounding him, which matters far less to him than the humiliation, or the diseased liver, from which he suffers. The novel is a document of one man's vanity and self-absorption, a man who casts derision not only on his own society, but even, and especially, on the progressive world beyond

Russia. The Crystal Palace of London, a monument to the century's technological aspirations, becomes something of a personal foe to him.[11]

The spiritual descendant of Dostoevski's protagonist in Sartre's *Nausea,* Antoine Roquentin has no more basic sensation than revulsion; indeed many a wag has said of him that his motto is "I am nauseated, therefore I am." Roquentin loathes nature, and he loathes man. His well-nigh universal disgust makes all things equal to him, equally repulsive. Therefore, we ought not to be surprised when "at the end of an empty Sunday," Roquentin surveys the political scene. He thinks fleetingly of "Communists and Nazis shooting it out in the streets of Berlin. Unemployed pounding the pavements of New York. . . ." Roquentin could not care less about how the street fights of Berlin will be resolved or how the United States will cope with the Depression, though it is 1932 and the end of Roquentin's France is already in sight.[12]

Finally, we may look at a scene in Camus's *The Stranger,* that perennial favorite of undergraduates in America. Meursault has murdered an Arab, with no compelling reason for doing so. Arrested, he faces an examining magistrate: "He [the magistrate] began by asking bluntly if I'd loved my mother. 'Yes' I replied, 'like everybody else.' " The reader knows that Meursault has been prompted by his lawyer to answer affirmatively. Camus mocks the public authorities by presenting them as inauthentic boors who insist on conventional feelings and who view the hero as a moral monster. (He had fired five consecutive shots at his victim.)[13]

In all these works, public authority appears as a shadowy impediment to the modest pleasures really available to man: making love, swimming, basking in the sun—in general the innocent joys of the body. While the political things seem to keep men from being happy, it is not altogether certain that existentialists cherish happiness as a goal. Their superhero, Zarathustra, in his very last speech asks, "Am I concerned with *happiness?* I am concerned with my *work.*"[14]

Existentialist skepticism about happiness assumes several forms. It may simply involve the conviction that happiness cannot be attained by pursuing it but may attend, or grace, the pursuit of one's work. It can also, however, manifest a kind of Kantian distrust of following the inclinations rather than fervent commitment to a great task. If we were to argue against such objections that happiness is simply what all men pursue by definition—the beginning of Aristotle's discussion in the *Ethics*—the typical existentialist response would probably be that whatever happiness is, it is something that must be sought in the private realm.

That rejoinder points to a deep disdain for public life as such. The existentialist aversion to politics has something to do with the fact that politics deals with the many, while existentialism, to repeat, specializes in the solitary individual. In this sense, existentialism betrays itself as elitist, even in its left-wing forms. It harbors distrust for the many, or, in the language better suited to liberal democracy, the people.

Elitism appears in another antipolitical guise as well. Politics necessarily devotes much of its energies to the ordinary problems of ordinary people, to "bread and butter" issues, and to routine regulations of routine affairs. The typical existentialist finds such things boring, which is to say that he raises aesthetic objections to political problems.

None of what has been described should be taken to mean that existentialists are simply immune to the attractions of the social. The very notion of loneliness implies a yearning for the warmth and comfort of human contact, for community. Community, though, is what liberal democracy finds itself unwilling and unable to provide, at least in existentialist eyes. Community belongs to the world of the polis, and existentialism in some ways is a reaction to the impossibility of the polis in modernity.[15] Therefore, existentialism tends either to yearn "for the good old days" when life was simpler and nobler or to dedicate itself to a postmodern future in which humanity transcends its present miseries. It endorses the politics of yesterday and the politics of tomorrow, whereas democracy represents the politics of today, the paltry present.

Existential Politics

Trying to articulate the existentialist mood, we observe a compound of nostalgia for the past, yearning for the future, discontent with the present. Such feelings find liberal democracies to be the most fertile soil for their perpetuation. Existentialism flourishes most in liberal democracies; whereas such democracies may not always honor philosophical sentiments of this kind, they indulge them even when they do not nourish them.

The very fact that democracies safeguard a distinction between the public and the private provides solace for existentialism. The typical democrat may well hold the existentialist view of the world in contempt, but he will almost certainly think that a world view is a man's own business. It should not therefore occasion any surprise that films like *Devil in the Flesh* and novels like *Nausea* and *The Stranger* adorn the cultures of democracies. *Notes from Underground* is an exception, to be sure, but only a partial one. Its protagonist obviously loathes democratic Britain more than undemocratic Mother Russia.

We exaggerate very little in maintaining that when the Left assumes political power, it has no use for existentialists. Marxism may in principle adopt from existentialism some of its dissections of alienation, but the "real life" existentialist is more likely to be found in the Gulag Archipelago, imprisoned for being a hooligan, a wrecker, or the perpetrator of some other hideous crime against socialism.[16] Similarly, the Right persecutes existentialists as decadents, purveyers of diseased culture, degenerates. In this respect the Nazi condemnation of Expressionist art may be more revealing than Heidegger's rectorship of the University of Freiburg in Hitler's Germany.

The democratic indulgence of existentialist self-indulgence elicits no great surge of gratitude from existentialists; at most it stimulates a shrug of acknowledgment. The typical existentialist simply ignores political matters, a luxury that can be enjoyed in very few countries in this century. Be that as it may, even when existentialism does not castigate the political as mere diversion, it is likely to disdain it.

A perusal of existentialist literature provides sufficient proof. We look in vain—and feel like a fool for looking at all—for an existentialist work on voting, a treatise on legislatures, or a study of party politics. Although we can barely imagine an existentialist comparison of the puberty rites of two tribes, it would be absurd to expect a card-carrying existentialist to compare the constitutions of two modern democratic states.

At this point we may detect a kinship between existentialism and the Left, for a card-carrying Marxist can also be imagined as denying any significant difference between written constitutions. But the Left retains a relationship with modern democratic politics by virtue of its interest in economics, the importance of which for the democratic state nobody will deny. By contrast, existentialists show themselves to be indifferent not only to modern politics but also to modern economics, and that indifference points to a kinship between existentialism and the Right. We can point to a great economic work of the Left, *Das Kapital;* we can point to a great economic work of the center, *The Wealth of Nations;* we cannot point to a great economic work of the Right.

Existentialism may have next to nothing to say about political or economic man, but it has a great deal to say about social man. "Existentialist sociology" is not an oxymoron. Indeed, to the extent that sociology refuses to surrender to the lure of quantification and mindless surveys, to the extent that it yearns to be "humanistic," to that very extent does it show itself to be influenced by existentialism in general and by Nietzsche in particular. Such names as Georg Simmel and Max Scheler come readily to mind, as well as the phenomenological sociology of Alfred Schutz and his followers. That does not refute our contention that existentialism is nonpolitical, at least in regard to democracy. After all, sociology studies *society* in conscious contradistinction to the state, and more often than not it tacitly assumes that politics does not matter all that much.

We do well to admit, however, that our attempts to "situate" existentialism encounter a problem when it comes to sociology. One name practically "covers" the problem: Max Weber, who in some ways *must* be understood as an existentialist sociologist. He presents us with a problem, not least because we have identified existentialism with the poetic, and Max Weber is nothing if not prosaic. Nevertheless he knew his Nietzsche, had stared into the abyss of nihilism, described modern disenchantment, and steadfastly maintained that men were at least as much moved by what they held to be sacred as by economic considerations. A man who could say he became a social scientist to see how much he could suffer is a man who has imbibed existentialist thought.

One can plausibly maintain that Weber's sociology bears the same relation to his existentialist predilections as does the Christianity of Christian existentialists to *their* existentialism. It is a reaction, perhaps an overcoming and perhaps a denial. Moreover, sociologists have been more influenced by Weber's response than by his stimulus, paying more attention to his methodological disquisitions, elaborate taxonomic schemes, and things like his reflections on bureaucracy than to his understanding of the human situation as such. Nevertheless, it is safer to think of Max Weber in the way we have introduced him into the discussion: a problem.[17]

Less problematical is the political engagement of prominent thinkers associated with existentialism. Heidegger's disgraceful accommodations to, and compromises with, National Socialism, do not change the fact that the topics of morality and politics are not the focus of his *magnum opus, Being and Time,* and that one may plausibly argue that Heidegger regards politics as superstructure.[18] Similarly, Sartre's manifold apologies for Communist brutality do not change the fact that his *magnum opus, Being and Nothingness,* is not a work of political philosophy. In this respect one can fruitfully contrast both Heidegger and Sartre with Plato, whose two longest dialogues, *The Republic* and *The Laws,* deal overtly with political things and who never wrote a dialogue in which politics was simply peripheral.

Nietzsche

The search for existentialist writings on politics leads inevitably to Friedrich Nietzsche. He wrote at least two books in which the political plays a primary role, *Beyond Good and Evil: Prelude to a Philosophy of the Future* and *On the Genealogy of Morals: A Polemic*. Their very titles reveal something of existentialism's view of politics. The first title looks forward to a new and decisively different kind of politics and morality, in a book which equates the political with the moral.[19] The second title announces a treatment of the dubious past of morality and politics. Both books treat political matters in historical perspective and deny the efficacy of any other treatment. The significance of history for any and all existentialist understanding of politics should become clear as our exposition proceeds.

When turning to Nietzsche for illumination of the relationship between existentialism and democracy, we must beware of facile prejudgments, no matter how reasonable they may be. He is not disqualified from shedding light on this topic because he undoubtedly bears some responsibility for fascism. In this context we should remember that he preceded the advent of fascism and that to some extent it is possible to separate Nietzsche the diagnostician of the crisis of his time, which to some extent remains our time, from Nietzsche the prescriber of cures that may well be worse than the diseases he describes. We should also be cautious about prematurely placing Nietzsche in opposition to the apolitical and antipolitical strands of existentialism described earlier.

Nietzsche in fact describes himself as "the last unpolitical German," and much of his writing casts disdain on politics as such, in the best existentialist mode. The following aphorism is rather typical:

> *Apart*—Parliamentarism—that is, public permission to choose between five basic political opinions—flatters and wins the favor of all those who would like to *seem* independent and individual, as if they fought for their opinions. Ultimately, however, it is indifferent whether the herd is commanded to have one opinion or permitted to have five. Whoever deviates from the five public opinions and stands apart will always have the whole herd against him.[20]

Such utterances, and Nietzsche divested himself of a goodly number of them, show that the emphasis on the solitary individual is alive and well in Nietzsche. Indeed, it flourishes to such an extent that Nietzsche's influence has been more evident on the artists than on the political thinkers of this century. What distinguishes Nietzsche's thought most markedly from that of more simplistic existentialists, however, is that in him the emphasis on the creative individual coexists in a fruitful, perhaps unresolvable, tension with an emphasis on "great politics."[21] He thus once more points thought to the tension, articulated by his great predecessor Rousseau, between the citizen and the bohemian.

On the way to the heart of Nietzsche's politics and his critique of democracy, we should recognize two additional stumbling blocks.

First, the historical cast of Nietzsche's thought, to which we have already alluded, leads him to equate democracy rather cavalierly with modernity as such. Thus he can alternately refer to economism as a modern and as a democratic phenomenon. Now a case *can* be made that modernity is essentially democratic, that the kind of democracy we confront is essentially modern, or both. The stumbling block consists more often than not in Nietzsche's refusal to spell out what is inherently plausible or at least arguable. Therefore he may criticize certain features of life that afflict modern democracies as well as antidemocracies and still refer to them as democratic. Economism, as a matter of fact, is a good example, for obviously both the Soviet Union and the United States are vulnerable to the charge of excessive materialism. The second stumbling block resembles the first. It is constituted by Nietzsche's seemingly incurable tendency to paint with very broad brush strokes and to sacrifice the charm of specificity to the charm of dazzling generalizations. Moreover, he prefers assertion to argument. Attending this mode of his thinking are an almost total absence of distinctions between kinds and degrees of democracy and a nearly complete lack of interest in the United States. In this respect he is again reminiscent of Rousseau, who was much more fascinated by the American Indians than by their conquerors.

Nietzsche thinks of democracy as an exemplification of slave morality. His perspectivism precludes him from classifying moralities as either true or false; for him there are no moral phenomena, only moral interpretations of phenomena.[22] Moralities are creations, originally the creations of herds, or ways of looking at the world that enable one to cope with the world. Basically there are two fundamental ways: that of the strong who do what they will and that of the weak who suffer what they must. In master moralities are affirmations of strength by the strong, as opposed to slave moralities, with their rejection of strength by the weak. Democracy is obviously a form of slave morality.[23]

Master morality is a celebration of vigor by the vigorous; slave morality represents an essentially negative reaction to it. Whereas masters distinguish between the good—roughly an expression and glorification of instincts—and weakness, which they dismiss contemptuously as the bad, slaves reject the innocent cruelty of masters as evil. Slaves are preoccupied with evil, thinking of good mainly as passivity intermingled with humility. Nietzsche tries not to judge simplistically between the two moralities: eagles cannot help being eagles, and lambs cannot help being lambs. Indeed, it is slavish democrats who do the judging. They maintain that both the strength of eagles and the impotence of lambs are voluntary, hence their lamblike yet bitter moralism.

That moralism becomes most venomous when it encounters any sign of the beautiful or noble. Master morality is obviously a morality that involves aristocracy. For Nietzsche democracy is not only vile in itself but vile because it renders impossible the splendors of the aristocratic life. He had learned from Tocqueville the fundamental impossibility of preserving the magnificence of aristocracy in the face of modern pressures, but he was not resigned to sanction, as was Tocqueville, the victory of democracy on the grounds that it was, when all was said and done, more just.

He thus condemns democracy for spelling the end of the kind of magnificence one associates with the martial virtues, chivalry, and lofty manners. Nietzsche's condemnation can become quixotic, because he does not really anticipate a return to the "good old days" and because the future he desires will owe quite as much to the cunning of slaves as it will to the magnanimity of masters. But his realization that the past of serfs and princes is irretrievably lost does not detract from his loathing of democracy. In fact, one of the many things with which democracy can be charged is its clinging to certain discredited aspects of the past. Democracy is the bad interim between a good past and a better future.

Democracy's most obvious tie to the past is not fully conscious, consisting of its inheritance of discredited Christianity. On the one hand, democracy's indisputable link to the Enlightenment leads it to foster atheism; on the other hand, it attempts to further Christian morality even while it sacrifices the Christian God. Democracy fails to assess Christianity correctly, failing to see, as Nietzsche does, that Christianity entails democracy in various ways. It begins a rebellion of slaves against the morality of masters by turning pride into a vice and humility into a virtue. It spreads a potent idea of equality by understanding all men as equal in two decisive respects, as sinners and as children of God. It even spawns the Enlightenment by producing the modern scientist, who with his ascetic devotion to truth is a secularized monk. In short, democracy is not only the heir of Christianity but its fulfillment.

To cherish all men as equal before God, to hold each soul to be infinitely and hence equally precious, is for Nietzsche to cater to the vulgar many at the expense of the precious few. As secularized Christianity, democracy threatens the well-being and ultimately the very existence of the exceptional man—the "genius of the heart,"[24] the authentic solitary individual so cherished by Nietzsche in particular and by existentialism in general. The typical existentialist does not deny the existence of excellence but thinks of it as vulnerable, frail, easy to stunt.

Therefore, suspicion of democracy and democracy's ethics is fully warranted. If we take our bearings by the many, we accommodate our standards to the meanest capacities. We produce a flatland of the imagination. Democracy inevitably means mediocrity, partly because the high shrivels when treated indifferently by those too low to understand the high, partly because the grace of the well begotten produces active resentment among the less favored.

We have previously mentioned the historical cast of the existentialist imagination. When it dwells on the dreadful mediocrity of democratic life, its gloom is all the greater because it holds such mediocrity to be inevitable. It is not only a necessary byproduct of democratic ways but a necessary development. Like individuals, political societies and whole civilizations grow old. Their vigor and their very will to live decline. They become senile; they wither. When Spengler wrote of the decline of the West, he was heavily indebted to Nietzsche and acknowledged as much.[25] The West that was declining featured democracy as its most typical and pervasive political arrangement. Democracy equals old age with its odor of impending death and it makes us yearn for the exuberance of youth. Nietzsche was a philosopher, not a rhetorician, and so are all of the best existentialists. Their critique of democracy is not a cartoonlike depiction of its shortcomings and dreadful effects. They understand its uses and even its attractions. In this respect, too, Nietzsche remains instructive. One does well to ponder the fact that he assigned democracy a most striking lineage, ultimately tracing it back to Socrates and the Socratic destruction of nobility. Socratism—likened by Nietzsche to the plebeian outlook of mankind—saved Western civilization from the orgiastic destructiveness associated with Dionysian excesses.[26] That was long ago, before the advent of Christianity; in fact, it goes a way toward explaining the advent of Christianity.

Historically, then, democracy has been on the side of life against the forces of dissolution and disintegration, albeit on the side of low, ignoble life against the forces of higher life. It continues to be the agent of mildness, of gentle living, of unspectacular decencies, of soft manners that can at times be pleasing and that always foster peaceful sentiments along with harmonious living. These assets may not amount to all that much when judged from the perspective of world-historical heroism, and they may not be enough when we consider the needs of the present time. They are not simply negligible, however, and the existentialists do not simply neglect them.

Moreover, democracy can be understood as useful for the preparation of mankind's glorious future. According to Nietzsche, that future will belong to the superman,[27] that synthesis of statesman, poet, philosopher, and saint, the Roman Caesar with the soul of Christ. Although the superman can, of course, be envisioned as a solitary individual, more likely he will be responsible for the future of the whole human race. He will rule: rulers need a people to rule, and democracy does yeoman service in preparing an ideal people for the superman to rule. It socializes mankind, implanting in it the qualities that make it easy to govern. A democratic people may fall like ripe fruit into the hands of the genius of the heart, who will mold it like clay.

Existential Critique of the Declaration of Independence

Obviously, such an understanding of democracy runs counter to the way democracy understands itself. Since that self-understanding appears most clearly in the basic documents of democracy, it may be useful to construct an existentialist critique of the single most authoritative statement of democratic principles, the Declaration of Independence. The first sentence alone contains a multitude of offenses to the creed of existentialism:

> When in the course of human events, it becomes necessary for one people to dissolve the political bands which have connected them with another, and to assume among the powers of the earth, the separate and equal station to which the laws of Nature and of Nature's God entitle them, a decent respect to the opinions of mankind requires that they should declare the causes which impel them to the separation.

The Declaration of Independence, then, begins with a reference to "Nature and Nature's God." It goes on to state that men have rights because their "Creator" endows them with rights, and it concludes with a reference to the reliance of the signers on "the protection of Divine Providence," a trust that helps them to pledge their honor, which they regard as "sacred."

We have previously noted the centrality of the saying that "God is dead" to an existentialist analysis of the human predicament. Nietzsche's proclamation means many different things, but among them it is surely of paramount importance that *belief* in God is dead; religion is no longer the binding social force it once was. On this level, it does not matter much whether the author of the Declaration of Independence, Thomas Jefferson, and its signers, referred to religion because they thought of it as true or because they thought of it as useful. Religion diminishes in usefulness because belief in its truth becomes ever more difficult to sustain. Since, however, such belief provides the grounding for so much of what follows, the arguments of the Declaration of Independence become mostly groundless. They cease to be a viable rallying cry for the forces of democracy.

Nor will it do to think that the Declaration used pious language to impress upon its readers some teaching based on nature rather than on God. We can, indeed, maintain that Nature's God is a far cry from the God of Abraham, the God of Isaac, and the God of Jacob. The founders of this nation may well have subscribed to modern teachings of natural rights and based themselves more on Hobbes and Locke than on the Ten Commandments and the Sermon on the Mount. Such a stratagem would not be decisive, according to an existentialist analysis, simply because appeals to nature have become fully as dubious, as untenable, as appeals to God. Nietzsche's Zarathustra moves inexorably from proclaiming that God is dead to proclaiming that "*all* gods are dead."[28] He means that all transcendent standards have ceased to be viable. Nature may exist in the sense of meaningless givens; it may even exist as a wild, demonic force that can be occasionally emulated and often admired; but it is no longer a nature that is teleological. It has become senseless to think in terms of the laws of nature, and nature does not "entitle" a people to a separate and equal station among the powers of the earth—or to anything else.

A "decent respect to the opinions of mankind" becomes doubly problematical with the death of God. If we take it seriously, we must resign ourselves to debase the higher by submitting it to the judgment of the lower. Politics does that continually and ritualistically; it therefore affronts aesthetic delicacy as well as intellectual probity, two cardinal existentialist virtues. In past ages we might resign ourselves to catering to the vulgar with lies—"holy lies"[29]—in order to keep them more or less contentedly in their place. That was always distasteful, but with the spread of atheism, it becomes ridiculous because it becomes ineffectual. The lessons of atheism become ever more influential on the opinions of mankind.

To put it a bit crudely, the self-evident truths to which the Declaration of Independence appeals have seen better days. They were never eternal and immutable truths to begin with, because such truths do not exist, but they were compelling myths, which is to say that they were lies agreed upon. Now, however, the agreement has disintegrated. We may try to cherish them yet as ideals, or as myths especially precious to us because they are our own, but myths are fully efficacious only if one mistakes them for truth. At the very least, adhering to a discredited myth entails the sacrifice of honesty.

Hence, today it behooves honest men to admit and assert that men are not created equal. Such equality refers to a common element in what it means to be human, to an essence, but it is no longer credible to believe in essences—or in a God all of whose children are equal by virtue of being His children. We must come to terms with the brute fact that men are unequal because they vary so much in strength—it does not matter in this respect whether the inequality lies in physical force or spiritual cunning.

Similarly, we can no longer indulge our faith in a creator who endows us with anything. Rights cease to be "unalienable" when we comes to realize they are not conferred by a nonhuman, superhuman power. They dwindle from entitlements to mere assertions of force or power. It is safer to comprehend human beings as organisms that have no right to life but instead are bundles of energy *determined* to live. An emphasis on a right to life, moreover, encourages a mean-spirited resolve to preserve life, whereas the existentialist hero believes in squandering life.

The other two rights are not deserving of adulation either. Liberty may simply be an illusion that is necessarily engendered by the will in action. Even if it is more than that, a necessary precondition for the will's functioning, its dignity depends on *what* men choose, what and how vigorously they will. As for the pursuit of happiness, it too easily degenerates into a search for "wretched contentment."[30] Existentialists, as we have seen, can rival Kantians in their distrust of happiness.

Existentialism tends to see all assertions of rights as being a kind of ludicrous posturing. Human beings can easily pretend, to themselves as well as to others, that they come to the struggle for existence well equipped, as though God or nature had provided them with an imposing armature against misfortune. Such pretense may cause men to forget their nakedness in a world they never made, but it cannot very well conceal—from others or themselves—their terrible vulnerability.

Nobody and nothing exist to endow men with rights, so it involves illusion to institute governments to secure what has no basis in reality, namely rights. Existentialism does believe that governments *are* in fact instituted among men. Man is not by nature a political animal. But existentialism draws a conclusion from the social contract different from that suggested by the Declaration of Independence. In the latter, the supersession of nature amounts to a great human triumph over chaos. Existentialism, by contrast, attempts the strange feat of celebrating chaos. In the process it renames chaos as the primal creative force, superior in its demonic splendor to the arbitrary construct we call government. Existentialism tends to denigrate liberal democracy as conventional, resorting to a deeply problematic appeal to an unruly, unteleological nature.

When we observe the wildness of nature, which finds expression in the dark promptings of human nature, we experience a good measure of contempt for the "safety and happiness" government supposedly effects. When a thinker like Nietzsche counsels men to live dangerously,[31] he advises them to steer deliberately clear of a life of safety, to court risk and seek out the very things that render life unpredictably hazardous.

The Declaration of Independence chooses the predictable in every possible way, as can be seen by its emphasis on law, indeed by its tendency to equate the tyrannical with the illegal. A government of laws is a government that respects procedures, that believes in doing business and its citizens' doing business through the proper channels. That means it decisively rejects, or at least subordinates, the extraordinary in favor of the ordinary. The best of human beings as well as the best of their deeds and speeches is not what readily runs through established channels.

The efficacy of law depends totally on its applicability to all men. From an existentialist perspective, therefore, law deals with the common as opposed to the individual, the exceptional. It refuses to respect persons because its essence depends on that refusal. We may thus contend that all law, all constitutional government, betrays a democratic bias. It regulates the things of concern to all men, as opposed to exceptional men. Insofar as all politics is tilted toward the democratic, it must counter the existentialist tilt toward the exceptional.

We can state that tension from a slightly different angle. In an important way the viewpoint of existentialism and the viewpoint of politics share a preference for action over contemplation. Politics *means* doing things that affect the polis, the political community; and existentialism distrusts—in fact, it rejects—the idea of pure mind, of a disembodied devotion to gazing at objects in order simply to let them *be*. The kind of politics that existentialism favors, however, in its contemplative rejection of contemplation, cannot very well be democratic politics. The existentialist tribute to the life in action issues in a panegyric not to presidents or heads of parliaments but to men of action defined in a suitably vague way. When Camus seeks to sketch models of excellence, he turns not to chiefs of government or legislative leaders but to what he calls conquerors.[32]

To read the Declaration of Independence is to confront a most sober document. That sobriety emanates from a conscious resolve to obey the dictates of prudence. Thinking of prudence, or practical wisdom, as its paragon intellectual virtue does not demean either its intention or its effect. On the level of moral virtue, the equivalent of prudence is moderation. The Declaration of Independence secured for the world a regime that has no superior either in antiquity or in modernity for its moderation. A sober view of the world engendered a sober republic dedicated to producing sober men. Existentialism, however, disdains to hide its partiality for Dionysus, the god of drunkenness.

Existential Critique of the Bourgeois Man

Different regimes produce different kinds of human beings. The most telling thing about democracies, as well as the most important thing for purposes of daily life, is the kinds of people they help to shape: democracies engender democratic man.[33]

That is not what he is called in existentialist literature, however. Most often he appears there as *bourgeois man,* a petty creature of consummate vanity, a bore of no vision and no appreciation of the visionary as such, a philistine when it comes to art and a hypocrite when it comes to morality. Existentialists condemn democracies because they produce too many such men, elect them to office, and altogether fail to see what is wrong with them. That is why the most intense existential loathing may well direct itself not at tyrants of the Left and Right, not at great criminals, cruel adventurers, or irresponsible charlatans, but at the middle-class people who live in suburbs, hold down ordinary jobs, and plunge into debt to put their children through college.

One finds Nietzsche's most vivid single depiction of this creature in *Thus Spoke Zarathustra,* where he appears as "the last man," who no longer understands love, creativity, yearning, or that which used to educe reverence. The last man's only real longing is for comfortable self-preservation. He prefers warmth to heat, acquaintanceships to friendships, compromise to conflict, entertainment to deep involvement, and numbness to a sensitivity that might possibly involve pain. He cares neither for ruling nor for obeying, and he rather likes being like everybody else: he cultivates mockery for all that is great. He has due regard for health of the body but would scarcely understand even the notion of health of the soul.[34]

Such a sorry excuse for a genuine human being becomes necessary not on the basis of vices indulged by democracies but on the basis of the very virtues they cultivate. To the extent, for example, that modern man is economic man—to a very considerable extent—he must practice thrift, frugality. Even when thrift does not curdle into stinginess, it diminishes man, whose most noble possibilities have much more to do with exuberance and squandering. Similarly, as commercial man, the citizen of a liberal democracy must cultivate industriousness, which necessarily dwindles into a mechanical routinization that becomes fatal to nobility.

The existentialist argues that all the ordinary virtues of the petit bourgeoisie make men petty, so what is needed is a transvaluation of values that will result in a transfiguration of such ordinary virtues. Whereas justice, for example, has always contained a democratic tendency in that all men must be treated as equals before the law, a new justice must appear, which takes its bearing by *inequality,* forthrightly granting special privileges to those happy few who require special treatment if only because their appearance is so rare among the mass of mankind.

The wisdom cultivated by democracies leaves much to be desired. It consists mostly of calculation, of balancing credits against debits, and it can be said to be prosaic from principle in that the bourgeois conception of life has little use for the imagination. The wisdom that existentialism extols, by contrast, soars beyond the confines of logic; it attempts to divorce thinking from reason itself; it abandons prose for poetic flights of fancy, reestablishes the old notion of divine madness, and celebrates itself as *wild* wisdom.

When such a view of the virtues comes to moderation, it confronts the fact that moderation defeats all attempts to transfigure or transvalue it. Moderation, as it were, demands to be treated moderately. It thrives only in a subdued atmosphere, as the restraining influence on courage. Hence existentialist literature makes no plausible attempt to transfigure or transvalue moderation. Instead, it constantly mocks moderation, exposing its vulnerability again and again—moderation being vulnerable because it fails to generate excitement—and ultimately dismissing it as merely another word for mediocrity.[35]

Courage fares much better; in fact it becomes the primary and almost the sole human virtue. The elevation of courage takes two forms. First, courage no longer elicits distrust because of its obvious connection to martial harshness and possible ties to cruelty. The rejection of moderation means that courage is allowed to strut the stage in full glory. Second, courage now becomes not only a moral virtue concerned with the proper stance toward fear but also an intellectual virtue concerned with the proper stance toward the unpalatable truths the thinking man is fated to discover. While the existentialist hero may be intemperate, he has the fortitude to face down his foes and to look into the abyss without blinking; his courage is all.

Courage always relates to war. Even intellectual courage suggests *wrestling* with the truth rather than enjoying it. Democracies do not extol courage over moderation in part because of their deep commitment to peace over war. Only the most doctrinaire leftists deny the reality of that commitment; democracies are justly famous for preferring butter to guns.

The democratic attachment to peace may strike us as banal simply because it becomes ever harder to find anybody attached to war. It is worthwhile, however, to consider both the fact that the love of peace runs very deep in democracies and that it connects democracy to an ancient, classical way of looking at the world.

The love of peace means more than a preference for the creature comforts of domesticity over the bracing life of the barracks. It can, and philosophically does, run so deep that it bases itself on a preference for rest over motion. Ultimately, peace "makes sense" because (only because?) all change seeks an end in a permanence above and beyond change, because becoming finds fulfillment in being, because action acknowledges the superiority of the contemplation of what neither needs change nor responds to it readily: a world that is good, a cosmos.

For present purposes, it must suffice to describe this view of the world in a way that must sound uncomfortably rosy and childish. Perhaps the fact that it comes across as childish and rosy attests to the inroads existentialism has made on our consciousness. Classical philosophy, which held to some notion of the universe like the one we have so crudely sketched above, was not on that account oblivious to what our denuded idea of reality calls the real world. To see that, we need only consider the way it accepts the near-inevitability of war, or the way it deals with the problem of slavery, or its unflinching treatment of tyranny. Yet, while appreciating the harsh imperatives of politics, classical philosophy attempts to see them as part of a world that sustains excellence.

The existentialist temperament, as we have seen, finds no ground for solace in its contemplation of the world. The existence of the good strikes existentialism as a quirk, a jest without a jester. Be that as it may, existentialism finds in democracy's love of peace a decayed adherence to a discredited classical philosophy, an illicit and ultimately futile journey to shrines that no longer have the power to grant comfort.

This does not mean that today's existentialists can be identified by their ferocious bellicosity. More likely they prefer peace to war, like just about everybody else, but their praise of striving once more reveals a debt to Nietzsche, perhaps the last great thinker who had some kind words for war.[36]

Conclusion

To appreciate contemporary liberal democracy, we have to appreciate the somewhat soft virtues connected with muddling through. Democracies tend to paper over hard choices and to bury all either-or issues in murkiness. The friction between liberty and equality, the tension between church and state, the battle among irreconcilable virtues—all become subject to a morass of compromise. Such a way of managing life is bound to affront the existentialist sensibility so attached to the idea of striving for all, to preferring all or nothing to the middle ground preempted by democracy.

So the existentialist has difficulty in pledging his full allegiance to democracy's flag. It strikes him as unworthy of his full devotion, possibly because it rarely asks for it. He swears by resoluteness and commitment, whereas democracy encourages a patriotism based on rational self-interest.

It would then seem that an existentialist democrat comes close to being a contradiction in terms. Yet we must conclude with the simple fact that existentialists who are democrats can easily be found in today's world. The existentialist democrat resembles the Christian gentleman in being very hard to understand in theory and very easy to observe in real life. Indeed, Löwith's remarks, cited earlier, that today we are all existentialists, suggest as much.

When we look for today's existentialists in liberal democracies, we should begin with those who find themselves *really* unable to believe in the principles enunciated by the Declaration of Independence. Does that not include most cultivated human beings today? But they can point to no viable substitute for those principles; they find themselves unable to provide a grounding in theory for decent practice. Does that not include most cultivated human beings today? These questions are not necessarily rhetorical, but they are surely hard to answer negatively.

Today's existentialists may, in response to "the fix" in which they find themselves, cultivate a bemused sense of the absurd when it comes to liberal democracy. They may cherish some uneasy acceptance of "the benign indifference of the universe"[37] and live out their lives in a kind of reserved loyalty to democracy. Their detachment may even come within hailing distance of the stance of those ancients who managed to strive for human excellence while remaining tolerably good citizens, who saw the soundness of saying: Sparta has fallen to our lot; let us adorn it.

16
Social Science and the Constitution

Harvey C. Mansfield, Jr.

But it is not to be denied that the portraits (the advocates of despotism) have sketched of republican government were too just copies of the originals from which they were taken. If it had been found impracticable to have devised models of a more perfect structure, the enlightened friends to liberty would have been obliged to abandon the cause of that species of government as indefensible. The science of politics, however, like most other sciences, has received great improvement.

FEDERALIST 9

Our fifth proposition is that in so far as there is any general protection in human society against the deprivation by one group of the freedom desired by another, it is probably not to be found in constitutional forms. It is to be discovered, if at all, in extra-constitutional factors.

ROBERT DAHL, A Preface to Democratic Theory

Here is a very distinct contrast. On the one hand is the political science of the American Constitution given credit by the author of *The Federalist* for a saving contribution to republican government, without which the friends of liberty would have had to abandon its cause. On the other is a nearly complete dismissal of the importance of our Constitution, together with the political science, which, according to *The Federalist*, made it possible. The weight of the contrast is on the importance of constitutional models or forms. Although Robert Dahl declares his support for the American "system" because of its peculiar "extra-constitutional factors," he does indeed abandon republican government as a *cause*—that is, as an example for the rest of mankind.[1] Since, for him, the Constitution is not the cause of American political behavior, in the sense of determining it, it is not a cause, or end, that he or we should be devoted to promoting or should recommend to the world. Dahl calls the extraconstitutional factors "social prerequisites,"[2] from which we receive a hint about why his political science, in contrast to that of *The Federalist,* is generally regarded as a branch of "social science."

Political Science versus Social Science

What, then, is the full extent of the contrast between *The Federalist*'s political science and American social science today? What are the various differences in method and results, and how do they combine to make the one science the creator and savior of the Constitution and the other its detractor and indifferent observer? To carry out this inquiry, we are aided by the critique that Dahl himself made of "Madison's political science" in *A Preface to Democratic Theory* (1956). Although American social science is not at all preoccupied with its history, it has one nonetheless.[3] It has roots in the German philosophy it despises as a priori and in the Scottish political economy that its liberal majority considers inhumane.[4] It has an embarrassing ancestor in Arthur F. Bentley, whose antics in *The Process of Government* (1908) seem now to mock the modern battalions of sophisticated scientific explorers like the imitations of an ape in a tree. It has a prophet and propagandist in Harold Lasswell, who set forth in the 1930s all the promises of social science for an earthly paradise of safety, income, and deference and displayed an imagination not yet equaled by his successors. Dahl's book, however, was published in the heyday of American social science, shortly after World War II, at its moment of greatest organized ambition as opposed to imaginary heights, when it decided it wanted to rule the universe—of departments of political science in American universities.

Dahl's book has been criticized by defenders of Madison (among whom I count myself), but his good humor under attack has kept him true to his intent, which was progressive rather than exegetical. One should be grateful for a founding document of American social science that seeks to displace *The Federalist* rather than ignore it or merely disparage it. Other social scientists, having left to Dahl the task accomplished or attempted in this document, have thereby left to him the mantle of founder. Social science is now as diverse as any other successful movement of thought in a liberal democracy—I mean successful in its political, not its scientific objectives. Since I cannot cover it all, I shall concentrate on Dahl's *Preface* because of its foundational character and on the "public choice" school. That school, we shall see, makes a nice contrast with the "reflection and choice" claimed for the Constitution by *The Federalist.* But before considering how social science relates itself to the Constitution, we need to remind ourselves of the role and character of political science in *The Federalist.*

The Political Science of 'The Federalist'

Political science, we have already seen, is not merely in the background of the Constitution, providing implicit assumptions; it is expressly acknowledged in *The Federalist* and given credit for making the Constitution possible. This should help recall to us that liberalism in its origin was primarily a doctrine of political science. Although liberalism was based on rights and interests, it was not primarily a doctrine—as we often suppose today—asserting that men should have their rights guaranteed and their interests satisfied. Liberalism was originally about self-government in which men attempt to exercise their rights and pursue their interests by themselves, in freedom. The manner in which they exercise rights and pursue interests—the *forms* of self-government—were as important as the securing of rights and interests, because rights and interests had to be secured *freely.* So although liberalism began its reasoning from prepolitical rights and interests in a state of nature, it always looked forward to the constitution of government under which rights and interests would be exercised and pursued politically, in constitutional channels. Liberalism was originally a doctrine of constitutionalism discovered and set forth by political science.

The Constitution can be said to be based on "liberalism" (in a generic sense that bears little relation to today's "liberals") because it puts liberty over virtue as did the original seventeenth-century liberals, Hobbes (not himself a constitutionalist), Spinoza, and Locke. This does not mean that the Constitution has nothing to do with virtue. On the contrary, the Constitution uses virtue, relies on it, and attempts to call it forth both from the people at large and from the more virtuous among the people.[5] Moreover, *Federalist* 51 asserts that "justice is the end of government." But by this it meant that justice will always be *demanded* by the people and that government must respond to this demand.[6] Similarly, *Federalist* 55 supposes that there is sufficient virtue among men for self-government. But it is not the business of government, or of the federal government (which will become more powerful than state governments), to cultivate virtue and to improve souls.[7] Thus the Constitution is based on a kind of behavioralism. It relies on what can be expected in human behavior rather than exhorting to deeds that can only be wished for. What can be expected, however, is not the worst or even the lowest common denominator: it is a modicum of virtue in the people and outstanding virtue in a few, both of these cooperating with, and under the direction of, an insistence on liberty that can be found in the nature of every human being and cultivated in a free people.

What can be expected in human behavior is not the same as what has been seen. *The Federalist* makes it quite clear that the Constitution is not based on past experience. Past experience is almost entirely discouraging to a new republic, for republics, both ancient and modern, have lived alternately in the extremes of tyranny and anarchy. They have been weak abroad as well as unstable at home. Previous "celebrated authors" in modern political science, too much impressed by this experience or unable to overcome it, have been unfriendly to republics and have based their constitutions on monarchies, in recognition of the fact that the modern state was everywhere the work of a monarchy.[8] The Constitution, therefore, is avowedly an "experiment."[9] It is a departure; as the application of a new theory or hypothesis, its success is not ensured. It is an experiment to see, as we learn on the first page of *The Federalist*, "whether societies of men are really capable or not of establishing good government from reflection and choice, or whether they are forever destined to depend for their political constitutions on accident and force."

Reflection and choice: what do these mean here? We may begin with choice because, we shall see, the reflection necessary to free government concerns mainly the bounds to choice. Choice is not merely will. Although choice begins from a will, it is a reasoned will with inconsistencies and momentary inclinations refined out. Government by choice is settled and stable; when it changes, it does so deliberately by design and for a definable purpose. Such a government is even capable, through its executive, of undertaking "extensive and arduous enterprises."[10] Reflecting "the deliberate sense of the community,"[11] it is as much opposed to governments by popular will alone as to monarchies, both of which belong to the company of constitutions depending on "accident and force." Certainly the "passions" of the public "ought to be controlled and regulated by the government."[12] The element of will in choice gives it a grounding in the universal human insistence on having things one's own way, but if that will were unaccompanied by reason, it would bring anarchy (accident) and tyranny (force). The work of reason is to give direction and solidity to the insistence of will, both to elevate it above whim and to settle it into determination. In this view the American Constitution does after all attempt to improve men's souls, but the method peculiar to it is to elicit reason from the people rather than to impose it on them.

The Constitution, therefore, is not a mixed constitution giving different classes separate powers in accordance with the sense of honor or faculty of reasoning that they might be expected to oppose to popular will. The Constitution is "wholly popular," which means that *all* its branches are derived from the people.[13] But since all branches are *derived* from the people, none of them *is* the people (as with the democratic assemblies of ancient republics); and the wholly popular Constitution is thereby "wholly elective."[14] The American Constitution establishes the first republic that derives all powers from the people but also the first that withdraws all powers from the people. The people's choice is to be governed by those whom they choose in "elections." Government by choice, as explained in *The Federalist,* appears as a species of the genus, government by consent, but it is equally opposed to pure democracy on the one hand and government by a single act of consent, on the other.

The single act of consent is a species of government by consent invented and elaborated by Thomas Hobbes. Hobbes had criticized the ancient democracies for being actual oligarchies ruled by whoever could sway the passions of the people, the demagogues. He thought it necessary to seek the consent of the people; but to prevent them from having any active share in the government, he conceived that they must consent once, and once only, to the absolute power of a sovereign. A choice that cannot change, however, is not a settled or determined choice. It is not a choice at all, but a submission. While repeating Hobbes's criticism of demagogues[15] and accepting his conclusion that government must be withdrawn from the people, *The Federalist* maintains a middle ground between demagogues and Thomas Hobbes in government by choice through elections and the structure of government. This middle is constituted by the choice of a people in its constitution, for a *constitution* is lacking in both pure democracy and Hobbesian sovereignty.

Americans, with their "republican genius,"[16] were of course not drawn to Hobbes's solution. They preferred the constitutional tradition revived by Locke and Montesquieu. But in making their Constitution wholly popular, they improved on Locke and Montesquieu with a demonstration by experiment that the people are capable of self-government without the aid of a hereditary monarchy or senate. Such "aid" is both accident and force when juxtaposed to the choice of the people, for only a wholly popular constitution is wholly elective. Nonrepublican and mixed constitutions depend on the accident of heredity and, when they are not lucky, on force.[17] Thus the American Constitution, by republicanizing the constitutional tradition of Locke and Montesquieu, perfects the liberal constitution of consent into a republican constitution of choice. But most Americans were instinctively republicans; through practice and prejudice they were captives of a republican tradition hostile to monarchy and to mixed constitutions. They had no difficulty in supporting a wholly popular constitution, for the state constitutions they had spontaneously (undeliberately) adopted after 1776 were wholly popular.[18] They were not, however, wholly elective, even though they made ample use of "elections," because they did not establish, through extensive size and separation of powers, the necessary and proper distinction between the people's will and their intention or choice or "election."[19] Since most Americans were instinctive republicans, the primary rhetorical and political task of the framers of the Constitution was to constitutionalize the republican tradition. They did this by republicanizing the constitutional tradition, which was the primary feat of their political science. But to republicanize the constitutional tradition, *The Federalist* had to soften republican hostility to institutions outside the republican tradition. The essential political distinction in *The Federalist,* therefore, is that between democracy and republic, a distinction *within* republicanism. Although today such a distinction may seem "conservative," it is endorsed and explained principally by the "liberal" Madison in *Federalist* 10, 14, and 39, as well as implied by the "conservative" Hamilton in *Federalist* 9.[20] The usual opposition between republic and monarchy or aristocracy, characteristic of both constitutional political science and republican polemics, hardly appears in *The Federalist* because republican Americans do not need it and will in fact be harmed by it.[21] For the essential difficulty of the Constitution, only partly revealed in *The Federalist,* is that certain nonrepublican institutions and practices in bad odor with republicans must be appropriated from the constitutional tradition and made republican to make good the distinction between democracy and republic. For *The Federalist,* the republican tradition is the problem, and the constitutional tradition, the solution.

The republican tradition, with its dependence on a small territory, a homogeneous people, and cultivated virtues, exaggerates the extent of human choice. Those seemingly choice-worthy qualities are too easily transformed in practice into weakness, majority faction, and aggression or intolerance.[22] The task of "reflection" in political science, then, is to take account of things in nature and by chance that cannot be chosen and to match them with things that can be chosen. Since, for example, a republic cannot choose to avoid foreign relations, it must be large enough to succeed in them. Since it cannot choose a human nature that will keep the homogeneous majority from domineering the minority, it must have a diverse people. And since it cannot expect that virtue will always come out moderate instead of self-righteous, it must encourage interest and ambition. A republic, then, must be taught to choose what, abstractly, it would not have chosen—precisely to found government by choice. A large, diverse, commercial republic is a more deliberate and rational choice than a small republic chosen from the republican tradition (and out of Anti-Federalist sentiment) because with such a republic, a people does not try to choose everything. Prompted and taught by reflection, it chooses to limit choice.

To choose to limit choice in this way might be called *constitutionalizing or formalizing behavior.*[23] It would be fine if one could solve all the problems for which men consent to government simply by establishing a republic, that is, a republican form of government. A people could then use its form of choice to choose how to deal with the world. But certain necessities of the kinds mentioned above—foreign enemies, the human desire to domineer, and the human interest in security—intervene. Then a choice arises over how to deal with these necessities: to keep them out of the constitution, so that the choice to be republican remains pure and noble, if frequently frustrated; or to bring them into the constitution, anticipating so far as possible necessities before they arise. *The Federalist* praises the American Constitution for anticipating necessities.

According to *The Federalist,* the republican form is so far from solving all problems that it itself is the main problem in a republic. For the republican form of the republican tradition suggests that every majority produced by that form is legitimate and wholesome, which is far from the case. Thereby the republican form conceals the factiousness of a domineering majority and the usurpations of the legislature in which it dominates.[24] The form makes people believe that the main danger to republican government comes from an aristocratic minority desiring to rule, when in fact the very establishment of the form has made this danger both unlikely and easy to defeat. Republicanism, in its assertiveness as well as in its complacency, is too attached to the republican form. It was necessary, then, for the framers of the Constitution to bring to republicans, smugly satisfied with the republican form, an awareness of the actual behavior of republican majorities. Up to 1787 in ancient and modern history, republican majorities, while adhering formally to the republican form, had destroyed republics with their actual behavior.

Thus we find in the political science of *The Federalist,* as in social science today, a certain dismay with the naiveté of republican citizens and a central concern with the difference between forms of government and actual behavior. But in considering how to give effect to this concern, *The Federalist* wanted to maintain respect for republicanism, partly out of deference to its obvious force in America, but also because it had in view another, opposite concern. Having been too much attached to the republican form, the people might become too little attached to it. Perhaps even through remedies adopted to counter the first danger, the people might fall into the second. In that case, the Constitution might seem to become an instrument, a mere means to an end outside itself. If all human behavior, including that of republican majorities, is self-interested, then any political form, even the republican, will be maintained only so long as it seems to promote the self-interested ends of individuals or groups. Yet if republican government is to be obeyed, it must be seen to be over the people whom it controls,[25] not as a mere factor in their calculations. It must be something they prize as worthy for its own sake, an authority for them, which they even venerate.[26] How can a people venerate a constitution it regards as a mere instrument? How will it defend that constitution? This was the difficulty on which Hobbes's political science foundered: a sovereign consented to and for the sake of self-preservation will be abandoned, when danger comes, for the same end of self-preservation. A republican people could also abandon the republican form for the sake of security with a conquering despot or an all-powerful government if it had no attachment to the form as such, if it had no republican genius or spirit. Therefore, despite the delusions inspired by the republican form in its traditional sense, Publius takes care to maintain that the new Constitution is "strictly republican."[27]

The problem faced by the political science of *The Federalist* was this: on the one hand, one must never question "that fundamental principle of republican government which admits the right of the people to alter or abolish the established Constitution whenever they find it inconsistent with their happiness."[28] Yet on the other hand, when this right is admitted, it seems to imply that the people can do what they like with the Constitution and that republican government and the rule of law continue only at their option for their convenience. This problem may reflect an ambivalence in choice itself between the human desire to choose for oneself, protected by the right of choice, and the rationality in choice that distinguishes it from mere will. Too rational a choice may seem to foreclose choice; too choosy a choice may seem to demean it.

As soon as one states the problem in this way, however, the solution adopted in *The Federalist* begins to reveal itself. Government by choice, we have seen, must take account of the actual behavior of men in which they frequently subordinate their choice, and the republican form that protects it, to their interest in security. As *Federalist* 51 reminds us in the famous passage defending the Constitution's appeal to the interest of an officeholder—or its *constitutionalizing* of self-interest—men are not angels. But the same human nature that keeps men from being angels prevents them from being messengers or slaves of higher authority and inspires them to insist on their freedom. Those who demand that forms of government be judged by actual behavior must admit that men do actually insist on their freedom as well as their interest and that they will often go to great trouble, against their interest, merely to have things their own way—or even to *feel* they have had their own way.[29] The Constitution, according to *The Federalist,* adopts both motives of interest and motives of freedom. It appeals to the interested behavior of men even as it seeks to satisfy the universal necessity of security and the need some feel of attaining an ambition.[30] The Constitution also takes account of the universal human need for the "liberty which is essential to political life"[31] as well as "that honorable determination which animates every votary of freedom to rest all our political experiments on the capacity of mankind for self-government."[32]

Regarding one's interest, the Constitution is a means to an end outside itself. It provides avenues for the pursuit of one's interest in its political offices, in the rights it guarantees, including the right to vote, in a national commerce, and in a free economy. Regarding one's freedom, however, the Constitution becomes an end in itself in which the people provide for their interests through self-government. Self-government in this respect is not merely a means to men's happiness but an essential part of it, since to live as a slave however rich or famous would be inhuman and dishonorable. The republican forms of the Constitution, which allow free pursuit of one's interest, make the Constitution an end in itself as well as a means to private ends because it satisfies the "capacity of mankind for self-government." In *The Federalist,* though, the Constitution becomes an end *as well as* a means. To forget that the Constitution is a means to the people's happiness would exaggerate the power of human choice to the point of supposing that men could form a permanent arrangement regardless of necessities that might arise. It would also diminish choice (in accordance with the ambivalence of choice noted above) by implying that the right of the people to choose a government, once exercised, no longer exists. Thus *The Federalist* emphasizes several times the sovereignty of "absolute necessity," hence of substance over form in politics; it declares the "transcendant law of nature and of nature's God . . . that the safety and happiness of society are the objects at which all political institutions aim and to which all such institutions must be sacrificed."[33] This necessity was the substance of *The Federalist*'s case against the Articles of Confederation and in a general sense, as we have seen, against all previous republics.

Yet again, the choice for a new constitution must not be made lightly for transient partisan advantage, as if a constitution were a disposable convenience, made for obsolescence. A new constitution must be made "by some solemn and authoritative act" to show respect for mankind's capacity for self-government.[34] To make it work requires an "honorable determination" (as we say today, a commitment), rather than a hasty, passionate decision or a cool, standoffish calculation of what it may do for me. A constitution needs loyalty as opposed to ignorant enthusiasm or a temporary investment, and insofar as it satisfies our capacity for self-government, it deserves loyalty even when the benefits are unclear or far off. To allow the people's happiness to become an overspecific standard by which to criticize the output of the Constitution on a daily basis—like a misery index for the health of the economy—would be to ignore the fact that the very working of the Constitution, apart from its policies, is part of the people's happiness. Government by choice prizes choosing as much as the things chosen.

The ambivalence of the Constitution as a means and as an end in itself can be seen in the various statements on the ends of the Constitution in *The Federalist*. It is not enough, in the first place, that the Constitution merely be republican; it must aim at, and achieve, ends that are beyond republicanism and that therefore put republicanism to a test, in keeping with the experimental, as well as the instrumental, character of the American Constitution. For a people wholly absorbed in republicanism cannot convincingly recommend republican government to the rest of mankind, who may not be so absorbed. These ends beyond republicanism in *The Federalist* (carefully described and analyzed by David F. Epstein[35]) are justice and the public good. Justice is respect for private rights and is the end of "civil society" as well as government; the duty of government is the "protection," not the perfection, of men's diverse faculties, especially but not only in regard to property.[36] The public good is the end only of government; hence it is narrower than justice. The concern of government for the public good, however, amounts to "pursuing" or "promoting."[37] The public good consists first of all in safety,[38] for which government needs both "energy" and "stability"[39]—two modes of political power that are neutral as to regime, not necessarily republican. Promoting prosperity and commerce is the other element in the public good to receive mention.[40]

Yet if these are ends beyond republicanism, so that republican government cannot attain them merely by being republican, they are not altogether separated from republicanism. The ends in themselves seem designed to maximize the choice of ways of life left to the people. Justice is mainly the prevention of crime, a negative duty for government; and the public good, though positive, is limited to those activities such as national defense and general welfare that allow or make it easy for people to lead their own lives.[41] Liberal individualism and republicanism, two erstwhile enemies, are shown how to make friends with each other as government by the people's choice is revealed, in the Constitution, to be the government that leaves the most choice to the people. Republican government that formalizes the behavior that people insist on, their living in security and their having a choice, will also be the limited government that liberals have wished for and sometimes found but never been able to cheer for. The "true test of a good government," according to *Federalist* 68, is "its aptitude and tendency to produce a good administration." This would be recognized today as a behavioral test of government—of what it can produce or show. Yet Hamilton introduces it by disagreeing with the "political heresy" that says that only fools contest for forms of government.[42] The republican form—of the American Constitution—has an aptitude and tendency to produce a good administration of the ends of government. The Constitution achieves these ends indirectly by the tendency of its form rather than directly through indoctrination in the ends or imposition of a way of life.

What, then, is the general character of the republican form of the Constitution as *The Federalist* explains it? It is to establish government by choice by introducing forms that take account of behavior arising from necessity or from human nature, not from choice—representative government with separation of powers in a large, diverse country. This paradox is required by the human insistence on free choice and the natural limits to such choice. By constitutionalizing the limits to choice, the Constitution secures choice better than all previous republics, according to *The Federalist*. Thus in embracing the imperial size and representative structure previously thought fatal to republics, the Constitution is said to provide a "republican remedy" for the diseases of republican government,[43] though it might be more accurate to speak of a *republicanized* remedy when referring to the "more permanent" parts of the government—the Senate, the executive, and the judiciary—which seem to operate by their own choice apart from the people's.

It is in the nature of a form, however, to leave open the content or behavior that it formalizes. A constitutional form, whether it is an institution such as the presidency or a right such as the right to vote, leaves open whether the president will provide an effective administration and the voter prefer "fit characters" to demagogues. Thus, once one incorporates into the Constitution the necessity for a strong executive and the necessity to avoid pure democracy, a choice of how to deal with those necessities is established. Behavior thus formalized is no longer simply determined by necessity, so long as the Constitution is successful in developing an *aptitude and tendency* to good administration; a poorly made constitution will of course aggravate troubles by spreading the delusion of choice. For example, in explaining the separation of powers, a republican device in origin, *The Federalist* shows at first (*Federalist* 47–51) that separate powers must be independent; and to be independent, each power must have means of defense, especially the more permanent powers. Thus, contrary to republican tradition, separation of powers compels Americans to abandon the supremacy of the legislature. The traditional republican form of a dominant legislature is made to face necessity and to do so by accepting a necessity—the self-interest that officeholders will predictably connect to the constitutional rights of their offices (*Federalist* 51). But then, as *The Federalist* goes on to explain and defend each of the three branches, it becomes clear that much more can be expected of officeholders than a merely stubborn defensiveness toward one another: virtue in congressmen (*Federalist* 55), character and moderation in senators (*Federalist* 62, 63), energy in the president (*Federalist* 70), and knowledge and judgment in the judiciary (*Federalist* 78). How far one can expect these qualities varies with the office and finally remains uncertain;[44] altogether, one can speak only of an "aptitude and tendency" to produce them, argued by *The Federalist* not from the character of a certain class expected to hold the Constitution's offices but from the formal characteristics (term, appointment, and powers) of the offices.[45] As befits an experimental Constitution, there is no guarantee of success. No constitution of a government by choice could guarantee success without depriving the people of choice or demeaning their choice to mere whim. All it can do is to set up a tendency to responsible government,[46] in a new sense of "responsible" now somehow familiar to us as "choosing to be responsible for," rather than merely "responsive to," the people.[47] The Constitution exists in its aptitude and tendency, as conceived by political science, to elevate the will of the people to their intention; the achievement is up to us.

The Social Science Model

Our social science will not tolerate the indeterminacy of a situation in which the Constitution may or may not achieve its end. Social science wants a guarantee that it will do so. Where social science cannot find certainty in the individual case (as often happens), it insists on a calculation of statistical probability to discount that uncertainty. It would never be satisfied with the shrug of the shoulders in the ordinary man's "probably" or with the careful forbearance in *The Federalist*'s "aptitude and tendency." Social science objects, therefore, to the use of terms or ideas over which people disagree; social science will replace these vague, contestable ideas with agreed-upon definitions, so that social science can progress without always having to go back to reconsider old disputes. Social science will be cumulative, which means that the advance of knowledge will necessarily go together with agreement on its findings. Social science proceeds by causing consent to itself; as science, it is not only irrefutable but also undeniable. And what is it that can neither be refuted nor denied? The facts of behavior, as opposed to the promises, the "oughts," the open authorizations of formal statements, especially those in a constitution. Hence the first rule of social science is, *Behavioralize the formal.* Always look for the actual behavior resulting from a formal authorization or definition, and when you catch people at what they do—for you must watch what they do rather than listen to what they say—you will have a truth that will gain agreement.

Behavioralizing the Formal. In the first chapter of *A Preface to Democratic Theory,* Dahl behavioralizes the forms and formalities of the Constitution and the formalized explanations of *The Federalist.* Beginning with his chapter title, "Madisonian Democracy"—for who can say that the founders or Publius had a consistent intention?—Dahl cuts both of them down to size. The forms of the Constitution can be summarized as the separation of powers (including federalism, which gives separated powers to the states and the federal government), but since one can prevent tyranny without this device (as in Great Britain[48]) and since one cannot surely prevent tyranny with it, one must seek the social conditions of behavior that make separation of powers work or fail to work. Whereas the constitutional device is indeterminate because it depends on the chances that founders will discover it and get it accepted, and then that it will be used sensibly and constructively rather than stubbornly and obstructively, the social conditions are determinate because they do not depend on human intentions. If they did, then one would have to wait to see how men dealt with their conditions, and political science would have to abandon prediction as the test of its success and return to retrospective praise and blame. Whether these conditions "work," Dahl points out, cannot be judged by using terms such as *tyranny* or *faction,* because those terms are subject to partisan definition and therefore "remain mere untestable assertions."[49] The first rule of social science requires a reduction of boastful rhetoric, of ambiguous terms, and of offices defined by their supposed functions—in sum, of the formal—to its actual results, its unarguable meaning, and its testable operation.[50]

This reduction, however, is not enough; it is only half the story. To guarantee the working of a political system, social science cannot allow things to happen as they will, for this too would be a surrender to chance. Social science must show that it can replace faulty, bombastic explanations with realistic, operational ones; it must project into the future, and to do this it must develop models with the capacity to predict. Historical explanations are cluttered with historical circumstances, thus always to some extent accidental. True explanation is universal, and the best test of universal knowledge is not being surprised by an unexpected event; for a social scientist, to admit surprise is to confess a culpable ignorance. Models with the capacity to predict, then, are universal conditions cleansed of their historical manifestations, which are accidental and arbitrary: these models are *formal*. Hence the second rule of social science is a reversal of the first: *formalize the behavioral*. Always state the behavior one has found in a form that guarantees its universality.[51] To generalize is not enough, because generalizations have exceptions and the chance exception may change everything in a particular case. Only a formalization that does not merely add up particular instances can discount, and therefore overcome, the particularity of those instances.

Formalizing the Behavioral. When the social scientist formulates his pattern or model, he is freed of dependence on accidental fact while free, too, of ambiguous values. He can project into the future without waiting for events to occur, yet also without "prescribing" what he merely likes or wishes. He can be contemptuous of both historian and philosopher (as traditionally understood), while at the same time claiming to be both empirical and formal. When a social scientist claims to be both of these things, he is talking out of both sides of his mouth. From one side he deflates phony formalities pretending to transcend reality; from the other he condemns "journalists" who are satisfied with particulars and do not know the methods of formalizing. This paradox of aggressive humility combined with calculated hubris is the essence of a social scientist. It is true that he might be embarrassed to say which comes first, the fact or the model. For how can we check our model with the facts, if we cannot find facts unless we first have a model? And how can we generate a realistic model unless we first have facts? This difficulty (which cannot be resolved by uttering the phrase "ideal type") reveals an ambiguity in "behavioral" and "formal." If the one can be so readily converted to the other, perhaps they are not so clearly distinct from one another as behavioral science supposes when it insists that we progress from political responsibility (which may or may not appear) to scientific explanation (which is determinate and guaranteed).

After Dahl has behavioralized the formal, by resolving constitutional forms into the behavior they wrongly claim to cause, he proceeds to formalize the behavioral. He introduces the model of "polyarchy" with which, through subtle elaboration in several books, he has come to be identified. "Polyarchy," not the Constitution, supplies the categories in which American politics is to be understood or, more precisely, its "conditions." Instead of learning, with the help of *The Federalist,* what we *ought* to do to make the Constitution work, we are told what we *shall* do, given the conditions of the American polyarchy. If the American polyarchy does not function according to one's preference, one can—under certain conditions—change the conditions that make it what it is and must be. But in the view of Dahl, one cannot make a constitution.

To make a constitution, one must make a comprehensive choice, a choice to limit choice, in our case a settled intention solemnized in a written document to which constitutional officers take an oath. Such a choice is a choice above other choices establishing a fundamental law above ordinary laws; and it is therefore to some degree unconditioned insofar as it is intended to shape and anticipate conditions and to do so in a characteristic mode. In the view of social science, a people cannot make a constitution because by its conditioning it has only one suitable constitution, the one it already has. In the view of *The Federalist,* however, a people, to its enduring cost and shame, may choose not to make a choice, through willfulness or bad advice or both: one cannot be certain about it.

In the analysis proposed here, *The Federalist* bears a considerable resemblance to modern social science, and it is no wonder that many social scientists, despite their criticism, feel at home when they read it. *The Federalist* behavioralizes the formal by compelling the republican genius to face the facts of republican experience, and it formalizes the behavioral by bringing those facts and the necessities they represent into the form of the Constitution. Publius, though, corrected the republican principle out of fidelity to it; he was concerned to sustain the dignity of man's capacity for self-government by establishing the first successful republic. With its basis in the human desire and capacity for self-government, *The Federalist* formalizes the formal in us: our insistence on running our own lives even against our interests; our refusal to be bound by conditions that make us merely dependent, responsive creatures; and our belief in the possibility of honor and sacrifice. These things are "formal" because they are powerful in us regardless of our "preferences"; they constitute a desire for *self*-government independent of what we may think government is good for. Although this formality of the will is often seen in stubborn and angry actions, precisely those actions confirm our capacity to rise above our interests; and although they can lead us in self-righteous idiocy to demean and even cast away our freedom, this formality is the basis of freedom in our nature.

Assisted Choice. Since Publius respects this desire for freedom, *The Federalist* offers a new republican political science to assist the choice of a free people. Consistent with republicanism, it can do no more than *assist* that choice; it cannot replace that choice or make it unnecessary by discovering the conditions determining how and when it would be made. *The Federalist* also finds a place, in its political science, for the founders and their fame ("the ruling passion of the noblest minds") as men without whom American politics would not be as it is today.[52] A free people, it appears, cannot choose a constitution for itself spontaneously or automatically; it needs to be assisted by political science and by statesmen and by each in a manner so as not to exclude the assistance of the other. Dahl, however, finds no place in his model for a constitution; a well-drawn constitution and able statesmen to establish it are not among the conditions of polyarchy, even in the book he wrote to set forth the conditions of *becoming* a polyarchy.[53] In another book Dahl discusses the making of the American Constitution and concludes that the founders created a framework that could be either a democratic or an aristocratic republic. He implies, however, that this indeterminacy was a fault to be corrected.[54]

In general, social science has had little or nothing to say about the American Constitution, constitutions, or constitutionalism. It does not accept that any difference exists between the founding of a constitution and ordinary politics, or that ordinary politics could be affected by the making or not making of a constitution. In keeping with Dahl's belief that the American political system is "endless bargaining," the Constitutional Convention of 1787 has been interpreted as an instance of bargaining and its outcome explained by the theory of voting coalitions, to wit, "an explanatory framework for the operation, impact and characteristic process of conflict in a serial decision-making situation."[55] If anything has been left to statesmanship by this theory, William Riker will take it away, in his talkathon Greek, with "heresthetics," the art of political strategy.[56] Such a framework, supplemented by such an art, both dissolves and replaces the Constitution by behavioralizing and formalizing. Social science not merely assists a free people in constitution making, but it takes over their choice, first telling them that constitutions do not matter and then showing them the conditions that will in fact determine their behavior, that is, their lives. And to judge from the social scientists, the American people do not need their founders.

This conclusion has to be drawn from what the social scientists have said; they are not men of great ambition for themselves personally. Although their theories would replace the Constitution, they themselves do not want to overturn it. Indeed, on the great issue in deciding upon the Constitution according to *The Federalist,* whether to have democracy or a republic (with representation and extensive size), the social scientists are all with Publius. In the late 1960s social scientists were accused of being defenders of the status quo and made to suffer furious assaults on their integrity by advocates of "participatory democracy" (who, in turn, retained many of the fundamental features of the American Constitution). Dahl assumes, too, that a polyarchy will have a strong executive, an independent judiciary, and something like a Bill of Rights.[57] For all their disregard of constitutional forms, social scientists seem to work, as it were, next to the Constitution, but oblivious of the shadow it casts on their work. If American politics is "endless bargaining,"[58] for example, is this not partly because the formality of separation of powers requires it? And are not the terms of bargaining partly determined by the formal, constitutional powers of the several institutions? In general, is not the "extra-constitutional" partly determined by the constitutional?

Institutions. Recently, social science has rediscovered the importance of "institutions," impressed (it is said) by the obvious difference in behavior (and success) of the Democratic party before and after the McGovern-Fraser reforms of 1970 while none of the underlying conditions had changed. But to understand the "institutions," one would have to return to the Constitution that instituted them and raise the question of intent: has the institution evolved according to its original intention? In the case of parties, not mentioned in the Constitution, one would have to see whether they were nonetheless intended, and for what; and whether the founders of parties had intentions to improve the Constitution or merely tactics to manipulate or circumvent it. In general, one would have to ask, is government by constitution possible, or does the comprehensive intention it constitutes waste away through the accidents of history? Dahl attributes the survival of the American Constitution to its being "frequently adapted to fit the changing social balance of power,"[59] but he does not give it credit even for adaptability. He does not think that the fundamental problem it should have addressed was that of *majority* faction; much more than this he fears *minority* faction from some source of oligarchy and therefore welcomes above all else the democratization of the Constitution.[60] In company with social scientists in general, he takes the conventional republican or democratic citizen's view, opposed in *The Federalist,* that the enemies of popular government are much more dangerous than its vices, if indeed it has any vices other than a disposition to tolerate its enemies. What is needed from social science is reflection parallel and rival to that in *The Federalist* to show why the people's reason should endorse, rather than seek to dominate or moderate, its will. What we get instead is an analysis attempting to determine what conditions the people's will, which simply assumes that the people ought to have what they want.

Will and Reason. Social science does not accept the distinction essential to *The Federalist* between the people's will and its reason or intention. It takes note, as we have seen typically, that we have no *assurance* from the working of the Constitution that popular will must become a reasoned intention. An aptitude to refine the people's will or a tendency in that direction is not enough, since what the Constitution does it must do unfailingly and indisputably. Therefore, instead of wasting time on the study of promised tendencies in the Constitution frequently not delivered in fact—not to mention reflection on what the people's reason as opposed to its will might be—social science turns to a search for the *determinants* of popular will. In *The Federalist* the formal orders of the Constitution are described as having a tendency to further justice and the public good; hence they are praised in the act of describing. Politicians who read *The Federalist* and citizens who hear what it says will learn, in the subdued, nonhortatory way explained above, what is expected of them and what can be hoped from them. In particular, they will learn that republics are in need of seemingly nonrepublican institutions and that popular will must be checked and improved in its own interest to become something more reasonable than it frequently, temporarily is. The political science of *The Federalist* is, therefore, practical and edifying. It provides a guide—though one without passion or elaboration—for action toward something better, toward the good. But although political science of this kind may offer guidance to politicians and citizens, it is not universal, necessary, and exact—precisely because it partly depends on politicians and citizens to make it actual.

To achieve the determinacy of a science that is universal, necessary, and exact, social science looks beneath the popular will rather than beyond it, for what determines or correlates with popular will cannot be will. Social science reduces the people's will to nonwill, whereas *The Federalist* elevates it to an intention. It does seem that any attempt to understand the people's will leads above it or below it. Social science goes below, to find out why people will as they do—because of their income, sex, race, and the like. Most social scientists approve of constitutional checks on popular will, since such checks are based on a calculation of self-interest, a more determinate and predictable motive than virtue. But they could not say why they approve of them. In practice their theories belie their sense of responsibility and their political acumen and result in a powerful but peculiar democratism. They see that the forms of the Constitution do not surely elevate popular will, as intended; they believe their analyses show that the only things surely elevated by those forms are certain groups, for example, property holders. The consequence of social science, then, is to debunk those allegedly public-spirited minorities, actually self-serving, who try to justify their prominence, actually dominance, by claiming to refine the people's will or to contribute to the public good. These are "elites." When social science rejects the explanatory value of the constitutional in favor of the extraconstitutional, it necessarily denies the political contribution of those who claim to use the constitutional forms as intended. In particular, it refutes the claim in *The Federalist* that the nonrepublican parts of the Constitution serve the republican whole: hence the democratism of social science, revealed in a Beardian view of the Constitution—not requiring the researches of Beard—as a shelter and headquarters for the privileged few.

Yet this is a peculiar democratism, because it does not, cannot, support the claim to rule of the people as a whole. For social science discloses a democracy without a people—that is, a democracy in which the people are not a whole. The people could be a whole only if their will made sense as an intention, only if they have a common good, but since there is no guarantee of this, one must seek the determinants of their will as we have seen. In seeking the determinants of their will, however, social science dissolves that will into wills; different groups in the people have wills differently determined. Not only is there no common good, but even "majority rule is mostly a myth" because majorities are nothing but self-seeking minorities in combination.[61] They are, to use the technical term, "coalitions." (Publius too spoke of majorities composed of minorities, but he was always ready to judge them by the standards of justice and the public good.) The minority or minorities that prevail do so arbitrarily and, considering the lack of a common good, necessarily so. Yet, considering the same lack, no other minority or minorities would win out any less arbitrarily. The elites that social science discovers dominating the people are both necessarily arbitrary and arbitrarily necessary. They cannot be justified yet cannot be imagined away: an elite-cursed democracy! Some social scientists try to wriggle out of this bind by settling for the status quo (though not defending it); others, by hoping that when all the elites except the social scientists have been melted away, a genuine people will be found in the pot.

Dahl seems to think he has got around this difficulty when he brings up, as opposed to constitutional forms, elections and political competition.[62] These operate against a background of "underlying consensus" that is "prior to politics" (hence extraconstitutional) to save the American system from falling under the rule laid down by the Italian Gaetano Mosca that every society has a ruling class. Not minority rule in America, Dahl says, but minorities' rule. Just a moment, Professor Dahl! What guarantee do we have that minorities will not compete to establish rival schemes of oppression or collaborate on one? How do we know that they will accept the result of an election? An election is a constitutional form[63] bestowing popular approval on a government that it simultaneously withdraws from direct popular rule, as we have seen. An election is an essentially aristocratic device (because it presupposes that, as opposed to selection by lot, some people are better than others—a point to be learned from Aristotle[64]). It was appropriated by the founders of a representative, constitutional republic to help combat the vices of republics. Although elections do not always produce fit characters, or even soft, compassionate characters, let us hear some applause from social scientists for a nonrepublican constitutional form that often works and for the courage and perspicacity of those who saw how to use it on behalf of republics. As for the "underlying consensus," it is indeed political, though originally—yet surely not now—distinct from the details of the American Constitution. It is not merely a "social prerequisite" but a political one too. And what guarantee is there that the consensus will not justify slavery, to use Dahl's own example?[65] If one can dissolve "majority rule" into myth, one can do the same for consensus.

Surveys. It is time to consider surveys. The survey is an extraconstitutional form, invented and propagated by social science, which has had a considerable, as yet unmeasured, effect on American politics and society. If we wished to decide whether social science is of assistance to American democracy, as Publius asserts his political science has come to the aid of American republicanism, we would have to judge whether this most outstanding innovation of social science has made the working of American democracy easier or harder. Its tendency is probably to promote the democratism discussed above. Surveys of popular opinions and attitudes resemble elections but apparently have a contrary effect. Instead of asking, as in elections, who should be entrusted with government and for what ends, they encourage people to believe that their current opinions and attitudes should be immediately adopted by their government. Otherwise, why ask? Or is it that survey data will be highly useful to power-seeking politicians who want to take advantage of what people feel?

Certainly surveys are at odds with the idea of representative government as it appears in *The Federalist*. There, representative government is presented as an attempt by popular authorization to create scope to govern; but surveys have the effect (if not the intent) of closing this space. Surveys create pressure on governments to produce immediate results, sooner even than the next election. Moreover, they foster a mode of thinking (the misery index) that makes elections turn on immediate results or promises thereof. Politicians are encouraged to seek popularity and to do so they are given scientific means to make carefully modulated appeals to various and conflicting sections of the electorate. Citizens learn nothing useful; it does not help them to judge the political questions they face to discover that a certain percentage of other citizens of one type or another agrees or disagrees with them. Social science in this aspect and as a whole is practical for politicians who want to manipulate and appear complaisant, but it is not edifying. Nor, apparently, do these devices of popularity actually make government more popular. They seem rather to breed dissatisfaction as the people are taught to demand popularity and to produce cause for dissatisfaction as government is distracted into seeking popularity. In studying behavior as opposed to intention, social science specializes in the discovery of unintended consequences. With its surveys social science appears to have had some unintended consequences of its own for the working of the Constitution.

Public Choice Theory

Rather than ask the opinion of a scientifically sampled respondent—a formalized but still real human being—social science has discovered that it is possible to infer (with a certain mathematical sophistication) the choice of a rational individual without ever approaching a real human being. It is even possible, as James Buchanan and Gordon Tullock have shown, to conceive the rules a rational individual would choose for making choices and thus to model a rational constitution.[66] This is the achievement of "formal theory," so called to denote its distance from the arithmetic of actual measurement, including today a thriving school of "public choice" theorists. These social scientists study politics with the conceptual tools of welfare economics and especially of game theory, a mathematics originally applied to economics by von Neumann and Morganstern.[67] Although the origin and character of this theorizing are economic, its adepts and pioneers differ over just how closely politics resembles economics. To speak of the pioneers, William Riker (in *The Theory of Political Coalitions,* 1962) says that politics is essentially conflict, whereas economics is essentially compromise; to use the term of game theory that has passed into popular lingo, politics is "zero-sum" (one player's winnings are another's losses).[68] But Anthony Downs (*An Economic Theory of Democracy,* 1957) and Buchanan and Tullock (*The Calculus of Consent,* 1962) believe that the compromise achievable in economics can also be got in politics; so politics is nonzero sum, and all can gain from it.[69] Those holding political compromise possible have been joined by theorists of international relations who conclude that politics among nations is essentially more irenic than it sometimes appears to be. Are we then left with a decision, made prior to scientific inquiry, over whether politics is peace or war? To avoid this embarrassment, it appears we must go with Riker. His assumption that politics is war is more determinate because it covers all cases; one can derive peace from war (since to seek peace is rational behavior) but not war from peace. The experience of peaceable economic exchange on which the others rely may be derivative and hence deceptive, because it depends on political peace. If so, it might be better to understand economic exchange as a device of politics, undertaken for political motives such as keeping government limited, rather than politics as an extension of economics. Riker, while revealing the most political perspicacity of these theorists, does not go so far, but in the main point he aligns himself with Hobbes (*De Cive,* 1642).[70]

The Federalist attempts in its understanding of government by choice to do justice to both the people's will and their reason; this is the main task of the Constitution. While constitutional government must be by consent to recognize the human insistence on choice, it must also refine and elevate consent to face the necessity of providing good administration. The difficulty of making consent rational while keeping it choosy accounts for the indeterminacy of the constitutional system: government by choice depends on the chance that peoples and governments will choose well. There is no getting around the dependence of choice on chance.[71] But this is precisely what the public choice theorists attempt to do. They want to provide "theoretical determinacy," the "logical foundations of constitutional democracy" (Buchanan and Tullock),[72] "a generalized yet realistic behavior rule for a rational government" (Downs),[73] "precision of statement" (Riker,[74] typically less optimistic). The consequence, we can see, is disastrous for the understanding (and perhaps also for the practice) of public choice. The twin but opposite evils that *The Federalist* wanted to avoid are both embraced by the theorists of public choice: their models are both so rational as to foreclose choice and so choosy as to demean it.

Instead of bringing together will and reason (which is a problematic undertaking, hence unscientific in their view), these social scientists keep them apart for the purpose of modeling undisturbed by this difficulty—that is, the main difficulty—and then hope at the end for a magical reconciliation. They begin with people's choices, including everything from the deliberate to the whimsical (for how could one define the difference scientifically?); these are also called "interests" or "preferences," and they add up to "utility." In common with the current usage of economists, this "utility" has almost nothing to do with what is useful. It is merely what you think to be useful, when "useful" means "good" or, rather, apparently good; the most useless luxury is part of your "utility" if you show by your behavior that you want it. Thus utility loses the realism in the power to puncture and deflate spurious ideals that made it attractive, or useful, to the first utilitarians.[75] Similarly, "interest" is no longer the realistic alternative to passion, and "preference," to insistence. All utilitarian realism must be sacrificed to the greater, postutilitarian necessity of relativism, because no social scientist now believes he can surely say what is realistic. Hence it becomes realistic to refuse to say what is realistic. What if the founders had adopted this attitude toward the Articles of Confederation or the republican tradition, both of which they thought to be unrealistic? The public choice theorists leave "choices" undefined and uncriticized and move to "rational behavior" as the means to the ends given to them, however foolish or self-destructive.

Once the ends are given, the theorists take possession of the means with their modeling. A model of choice is no longer a choice; it shows how choice must necessarily proceed. Such a model, as Riker says, "permits one to transcend the obstacle of the existence of choice."[76] Choice is an obstacle to reason because there is always the chance, often a good chance, that it will not in fact be exercised according to reason. A "leap over choice"[77] is thus a leap over chance. The rationality of choice is then within the competence of the social scientist and is his to play and romp with (since the habit of abstraction makes social scientists light-headed) without interference from those who have set the ends to which he will supply the means. The democratism with which the analysis began—all ends are equal—gives way suddenly to the expertise of social science so that Buchanan and Tullock, for example, can make a logical constitution without holding a constitutional convention and a vote of ratification. Their expertise in modeling takes over from the actual consent of the people because they can show what the people, if rational, *would* have consented to. For actual majority rule, they substitute "conceptual unanimity."[78]

Social scientists occupy an office similar to that of Hobbes's sovereign. Once authorized to find the rational means to the people's ends, they brook no interference from those who might want to specify the means as well as the ends. The people can reset the problem by changing their ends, but they cannot insert their opinion as to which model will best achieve them. The people do not, in effect, have the right "to alter or to abolish it, and to institute new government, laying its foundation on such principles, and organizing its powers in such form, as to them shall seem most likely to effect their safety and happiness." For if they were to have such a right and exercise it, they would not get what they want! Social science with its expertise in modeling can guarantee choice, that is, get the people what they want, only if the people do not exercise their choice of getting what they want in their own way. From this result we see that the initial aloof objectivity of social science in seeming not to care what the people's wants were and whether they were good was actually the only way of getting them what they want, which is also the most effectual way of caring for them. To have offered a frown at the meaner and more bizarre wants of the people would have been attempting to set their reason against their will with no sure prospect of victory for either and the likelihood of a tense debate. The trick, then, is to leave the people their will and take away their reason; then social science can bring its reason to serve their will, showing them their inconsistencies and telling them how to get more of what they want.[79] The value neutrality of social science is the best or only means by which government can bring value to the people. And how do we ensure the loyalty of social scientists to democracy rather than to some other model?[80] Pay them more! The most mercenary servant is the most reliable.

Despite their fondness for the word "process" and their reverence for such precursors of public choice as Arthur Bentley (*The Process of Government*, 1908) and David Truman (*The Governmental Process*, 1951), the public choice theorists have no justification for the actual processes of government, in America or elsewhere, except as they approximate the contours of their models.[81] Those models are the contrivance of a scientific or theoretical reason that does not care whether it reaches its destination through human beings who reason; in fact, as we have seen, the way is surer if the model does not depend on them. So the various functions that *The Federalist* expects from appropriate constitutional offices and forms—deliberation from the House of Representatives, experience from the Senate, duration from the executive, stability from the judiciary, and refinement of popular will through elections—do not appear in public choice models. These functions are nontheoretical helps to reason or aspects of practical reason, which make reason effective in the practical world of politics where it has to contend with unreason, as opposed to the laboratory or library where these nontheoretical aspects are hindrances to reason.

So public choice adopts an attitude of theoretical disdain for both the functions and the men who perform them. It understands the constitutional offices only as negative checks on a majority (as in *Federalist* 51), not as positive contributions to a majority (as in later sections of *The Federalist* on the three branches); for it, a "qualified" majority means one that is checked, not one that is capable. Deliberation is logrolling, and bargaining is "bribery."[82] But according to *Federalist* 51 the defensive strongholds of the separated powers are manned by the ambitious; such people do not exist in theories of public choice (except, once again, for Riker, who makes tenuous allowance for leaders[83]). *Homo politicus,* the rational individual, is a consumer like *homo economicus.*[84] He is concerned for the costs of decision making. That there might actually be a type of human being called "politician" who likes politics and that the few of this type might be both useful and dangerous to the many who care less for politics are problems that do not appear or are not themes in theories of public choice. They do speak of the "intensity" of preferences, since they have no other way to speak of what is noble or higher in rank except as multiplication of what is banal or mundane.[85] With this much admired makeshift they run the risk of underestimating the danger (so well appreciated in *Federalist* 10) as well as the contribution of "intensity" to democracy. And most notoriously, those theories cannot explain why people take the trouble to vote.[86]

Conclusion

In sum, public choice and social science in general cannot understand why the Constitution should be an end in itself; they see it only as a means to an end.[87] They do not see anything admirable in *self*-government, that is, good government from reflection and choice rather than from accident and force. Under the name of choice, social science promotes government from reflection and accident, its reflection on what democratic peoples happen to want. If peoples could get their wants satisfied by other governments, social science would have no objection; and, it would say, if democratic peoples want to insist on self-government, let that be added to their accidental wants.[88] In the argument presented here, social science begins its objection to constitutional forms from the fact that their working depends on chance. But at the end of all its ingenious conceits fashioned to overcome this chance, it appears as the servant of a people that by historical chance wants to govern itself.

Social scientists are for the most part innocent of philosophy. They have, of course, absorbed the subjectivity of utility and with it have accepted the necessity that their positivism—the naive alliance of science and human good—become a logical positivism or philosophy of science that promises much less. They have surely heard of Thomas Kuhn's *The Structure of Scientific Revolutions,* and some of them must have noted, more wryly than gloatingly, the political character of the behavioral revolution since World War II that has transformed political science into social science. But social scientists have not yet penetrated to the Nietzschean critique of science lying behind Kuhn's book; that critique says that science depends on a prescientific insight and hence concludes that science itself is a historical accident. One can say, however, that the materials for the discovery of this critique and for the greater self-understanding to which it would lead lie within social science and are concentrated in its treatment of the Constitution or lack thereof.

I am aware that I have dealt with only a few books in social science and those not the most recent, but I am persuaded that they are neither incidental nor obsolete. Social science is all around us; it is a rubric that covers many diverse individuals and activities. Yet precisely because of this diversity, its general and remarkable inattention to the Constitution cannot be accidental. Those who want to take refuge in this diversity still have to take thought for what they are involved in. If they should come to have doubts, the political science of *The Federalist* beckons as an attractive and impressive alternative.

17
Neoconstitutionalism? Rawls, Dworkin, and Nozick

Clifford Orwin and James R. Stoner, Jr.

As the previous chapters of this volume have stressed, theoretical developments of the nineteenth and early twentieth centuries have proved unkind to constitutionalism. Yet the past twenty years have witnessed a resurgence of apparently liberal and constitutional theorizing in America, as teeming as it was unexpected. Where Locke, Adam Smith, Kant, Bentham, and the Mills failed, countless professors have lately conceived new hopes of succeeding, at placing liberalism on a new and sound theoretical basis, from which it would shine forth resplendently in all its superiority to the alternatives. Such theorists have combined an aggressive up-to-dateness with an avowed return to the roots of the liberal (and constitutional) tradition. Whatever their disagreements among themselves, they have joined in assuring us in this epoch of the constitutional bicentennial that, yes, we can have it all.

Here we will treat three of the best-known names—John Rawls, Ronald Dworkin, and Robert Nozick. Rawls is the father of almost all such neoliberal theorists, of Dworkin and Nozick as of a host of lesser figures, and the special protector of their redistributionist wing. Dworkin has gladdened that wing with a theory of constitutional adjudication. Nozick, in contrast, is the restorer of libertarianism and so holds special allure for friends of free enterprise.

As members of opposing camps of the same school, the three thinkers have much in common. Each presents as his great step forward what might look like a long step back: the rejection of utilitarianism in favor of the sanctity of individual rights. In constructing his new individualism, moreover, each rummages widely through the old, refurbishing such items as the state of nature (Nozick) and the original contract (Rawls). Each seeks to renew in his way just what Bentham was sure that he had persuaded us was "nonsense on stilts," the tradition of liberal natural right animating the American founding.

The means that each offers to this end are eclectic, now reminding us of Locke, now of Kant, now of games that game theorists play. They join both Locke and Kant in their commitment to notions of right or justice. Whereas utilitarian liberals reject justice as the standard in favor of maximizing utility (thus compelling themselves to derive the just from the useful) and Hayekian libertarians reject it in favor of liberty, Rawls and Nozick offer "theories of justice." Each then presents his system as the zenith and perfection of the liberal tradition, surpassing utilitarianism and economism in founding liberalism on justice, surpassing Locke and Jefferson (and Kant) in placing justice itself on a new, theoretically sound foundation. Yes, it does sound too good to be true.

Rawls and the Redistributive State

The influence of Rawls on current liberalism is pervasive. Perhaps that is equally true of its influence on him. His arguments vindicate every project that currently divides those whom journalists call "liberals" from "old liberals," "neoconservatives," or whatever name captures liberals who have failed to keep up.

Since Rawls is a system builder, we must begin with the principal elements of his theoretical structure as a whole. These elements are well known by now, but for the sake of clarity we will summarize them. The central conception of the theory is the "original position," a hypothetical situation in which human beings choose a conception of justice under conditions deemed fair.[1] These conditions include the motivational assumption of mutual disinterest and the epistemological assumption of the "veil of ignorance," the requirement that no one know anything particular about himself—his social position, his natural talents, his values, even his sex—although everyone is allowed, indeed required, to know certain general principles of social theory and human psychology. Ignorant of anything distinctive about themselves, the parties make their choice on the basis of what is the same in all of them, namely, the capacity for moral personality, which Rawls defines as the ability to form a conception of one's good and to have a sense of justice. Moral personality in the original position exists only as a potential; the parties do not yet know what their conceptions of the good are, and they cannot have a sense of justice until they have created justice, which is precisely what they are in the original position to do. They seek justice not out of any fellow feeling or common sense of good but because cooperation is impossible without it. Cooperation is a problem because human interests differ widely, but fortunately Rawls discovers that there are certain things that everyone wants no matter what his larger goals in life. These he calls the "primary goods," and they include "rights and liberties, opportunities and powers, income and wealth," and, he adds later, the "social bases of self-respect" (92). The primary goods are what enable each of us to live by principles of justice and to choose freely his own way of life.

Having defined the original position and the problem of choice it presents, Rawls proceeds to specify the conception of justice its inmates would pick. Since each is ignorant of his particular nature and social standing, no one can know he is not among the worst endowed, and since one's entire life prospects are at stake, no one would risk his happiness and indeed his moral personality itself by choosing to define justice by the principles of utilitarianism, which would maximize the well-being of only the greatest number, much less by the principle of perfection, which would maximize the achievement of the best endowed. Rather, the parties would choose Rawls's "two principles":

> • Each person has an equal right to a fully adequate scheme of equal basic liberties which is compatible with a similar scheme of liberties for all.
>
> • Social and economic inequalities are to satisfy two conditions. First, they must be attached to offices and positions open to all under conditions of fair equality of opportunity; and second, they must be to the greatest benefit of the least advantaged members of society.[2]

The first principle has priority over the second, meaning that equal liberty can be restricted only for the sake of liberty, not for economic or social benefits; and within the second principle, fair equality of opportunity cannot be compromised for the sake of increasing social wealth.

Rawls names his theory "justice as fairness" or "the contract doctrine" to contrast it with utilitarianism, which he understands to be its main rival in contemporary political philosophy. Justice as fairness is a deontological rather than a teleological theory, meaning that it defines justice independently of any prior standard of the good rather than making justice a means of achieving the general welfare. Rawls wants to preserve justice in a world where questions of value are thought to be relative.[3] This he does by beginning with human beings as beings capable of moral personality, capable of having values, and then constructing substantive principles of justice out of this bare fact. The parties in the original position do not choose justice for its own sake but because they think it will make possible cooperation and thus enhance their good; nevertheless, the right remains prior to the good since it is embodied in the conditions of fairness that constitute the original position. Rawls's theory is deontological because it is an argument from the original position, and because it begins from the mere fact of moral personality rather than from any assumptions about the human good.

Strictly speaking, however, the original position is not the beginning point of Rawls's philosophy; its conditions are not self-evident facts of an elusive moral reality. Rather, the original position is one of several structural components of a theory designed both to reflect and to clarify certain data, and these data are our "considered judgments," our most deeply held and carefully weighed moral convictions, such as our beliefs in religious freedom, in racial equality, and in the moral arbitrariness of the natural distribution of talents. Considered judgments form the "provisional fixed points" in Rawls's "moral geometry" (20, 121), but in ordinary life our convictions clash, both within each one of us and between us. The aim of a theory of justice is to foster agreement, both within and without. The moral philosopher seeks the theory that best accounts for his moral convictions, but if some of his convictions remain unexplained by this theory, he can adjust them so that they become consistent. If, however, one feels too strongly about the unaccounted-for convictions to abandon them, one can adjust the theory to create a "better fit." Rawls coins the term "reflective equilibrium" to describe this interplay between moral theory and the convictions that it justifies but that also call the theory into being in the first place (19–21, 48–53, 577–87). Reflective equilibrium is the background to or foundation of Rawls's theory of justice, for it explains the epistemological status of the moral theory itself. Critics have accused Rawls of having manipulated the original position to predetermine the choice of principles made in it, but to raise this charge as an objection to his theory is to mistake the meaning of reflective equilibrium. Rawls openly admits to having designed the original position to generate its consequences (20–22, 514). Having generalized from his conviction supporting religious tolerance to ideals of a pluralistic society and of the individual within it, he uses the device of the original position to specify how the ideal society is ordered and what its members believe. To call the original position a device is not to imply that the argument establishing it or the argument it establishes is arbitrary. For Rawls insists that the conditions of the original position are conditions that "we do in fact accept."

Rawls's original position generates his two principles of justice, and these in turn, his version of constitutionalism. Much could be (and has been) said both about what goes into the original position and about what comes out of it.[4] We will make just three points particularly relevant to our topic.

Rawls presents himself as the restorer of the contractarian tradition, which means the restorer of something like the state of nature, out of which the contract emerges and from which it takes its bearings. The state-of-nature teaching is essential to early constitutionalism. It articulates both men's natural needs and the natural obstacles to their satisfaction. It is these obstacles that men oppose with the artifice of constitutional government: avoidance of them dictates and limits its legitimate ends. Rejected by Bentham, the state of nature and the social contract have long ceased to carry any weight within the constitutionalist tradition. (The problems attendant upon their rejection have been explored in earlier chapters of this volume.) Rawls's restoration of these notions after nearly two centuries thus appears quite remarkable. Appearances can deceive.

Rawls's "original position" is anything but man's original condition. Not the state of nature, it is at most a state of mind. Instead of presenting man's world as it is, prior to his efforts to improve upon it, it is itself an artifice for effecting improvement. Imaginary and unimaginable, it is as far from Locke's state of nature as a game theory workshop is from Colonel Mengistu's Ethiopia. Lacking the reality, it lacks the urgency of the state of nature of Hobbes or Locke. Such urgency as it claims is moral rather than prudential (where the moral, again contra Locke, is understood as wholly apart from the prudential). Rather than lifting the veil of convention to reveal the truth about nature (and hence the necessity and limits of convention), the original position is itself a convention that by means of the "veil of ignorance" abstracts from our natural awareness of the world.[5]

The original position presents itself as heir to the state of nature because it is prepolitical and results in a contract that reflects each contractor's self-concern. Yet it would be a mistake to assume that Rawls agrees with the founders of constitutionalism that self-concern is the foundation of sound politics. Rawls praises justice as the first virtue of political society, and for him no more than for Kant is justice to be derived from self-concern. The original position is Rawls's device for arriving at the content of justice; it is subsequent to our commitment to justice which therefore owes nothing to it. So too it results from rather than in our acceptance of "justice as fairness" and the peculiar notion of fairness to which Rawls subscribes. Its place in Rawls's argument is much less fundamental than the place of the state of nature in Locke's. Fundamental are the (moral) conditions that define the original position, those conditions that Rawls insists that we do in fact accept as the common moral currency of liberal society.[6]

That brings us to our second point. Because he claims to bring order out of the clash of opinions, Rawls can liken himself to Socrates (49). But Socrates appealed not to men's "considered judgments" (read "entrenched prejudices") but from these to the truth; he began with the reigning opinions of his day because like all opinions they afforded some scant access to the steep path of truth—which, however, led far beyond those opinions and implied radical challenges to them. In a word, he appealed from convention to nature. In this, at least, the fathers of constitutionalism followed him: "the laws of nature and nature's God," their theoretical point of departure, rest on a claim to see the moral world as it is, through eyes cleansed of the encrusted errors of premodern opinion.

Rawls, by contrast, can invoke neither reason nor nature. While his system is not arbitrary *in relation to* our alleged "considered judgments," these last are themselves, in Rawls's view, ultimately arbitrary. His seeming Socratism masks a radical conventionalism (which is to say a radical relativism) far removed from the positions of both Socrates and the American founders.[7] Rawls can appeal to the views that journalistic "liberals" hold today, and he can argue, if unpersuasively, that liberals in the broader sense must for the sake of consistency share these views. He cannot claim, however, that these opinions enjoy any standing in the world or that he is more than just the deft interpreter of an ultimately groundless climate of opinion.[8] He thus displays the pervasive impotence of relativistic political theory. Unable to ground belief in liberal ways, he must nonetheless presume it—even as his inability to ground it subverts it.

If Rawls might appear conservative in sticking with a liberalism that has slipped its moorings, his interpretation of its principles is "liberal" in the journalistic sense, or even somewhat to the left of it. As today's "liberals" are not yesterday's, so Rawls's liberalism is markedly different from the founders' constitutional republicanism. One big difference bears on the political significance of natural inequalities of human capacity.

Constitutionalism has traditionally held that such disparities should be allowed their play (always respecting, of course, the primary equality of human rights): indeed, that one of man's primary rights is to equal protection of the fruits of his exertion of his (unequal) capacities. According to Rawls, however, government must rather respect "our" considered judgment that natural inequalities are morally arbitrary, and that so too are all such disparities of achievement as result from them. As Rawls tells it, "we" believe that since no one can be said to have earned his natural capacities (including even his diligence), no one is entitled to raise a claim to have earned anything by their exercise. In short (Rawls's fallacy), every basis of a claim to desert must itself have been deserved, which must involve us in an infinite regress. This also contradicts Rawls's argument that justice is owed equally to all men because of their (presumed) equal capacity for "moral personality," for this (natural and universal) capacity is no more deserved and so no less "arbitrary" than any other.[9]

In asserting this position, so crucial to the design of the "original position" and so of his argument as a whole, Rawls can claim to speak for us only if "we" are a handful of professors who have not thought through its nihilistic consequences. As Rawls admits, this argument, while allegedly the consummation of liberal thought on natural inequalities, involves a decisive break with previous liberal notions, including that of "equal opportunity" (65–75). It also eviscerates the commitment to limited government so central to constitutionalism. For Publius natural inequalities and the economic inequalities that arise from them figure politically as the fountainhead of majority faction, that gravest of ills endemic to popular governments. A great object in constitution making is to curb the power of such faction and its perennial tendency to oppress the few to the detriment of all. By confining government to the equal protection of unequal capacities, we limit it to employing the fruits of those capacities only insofar as the protection of the capacities themselves demands it; it is above all this project that yields what the founders meant by the general welfare.[10]

For Rawls, in contrast, the inviolability of the person does not extend to his faculties (which are conceived as in effect external to him). On the contrary, that very inviolability *requires* the most thoroughgoing redistribution of the fruits of these faculties. In an extraordinary inversion of the original constitutionalist understanding, Rawls limits government to only such protection of unequal faculties as is of benefit to the least advantaged. To be sure, Rawls cannot say how much protection is required by way of incentive for the gifted to produce for the sake of the rest of us. That is for the economists to determine, weighing the trade-off between equality and efficiency. Still, the principle of the thing (Rawls's "difference principle") is hardly one of "limited government" in economic matters.

We may in fact conceive Rawls as the theorist par excellence of the transition from the welfare state to the redistributive state.[11] The former taxes private property to relieve specific ills attendant upon that unequal distribution of property that is the inevitable consequence of the protection of private property. The redistributive state, by contrast, would deny the legitimacy of unequal distribution as such (except, if we follow Rawls, insofar as inequalities were to the benefit of the least advantaged). It would by the same token deny the privacy of property as such. Such a state would treat property instead as a "social product," the distribution of which rests by right with society as a whole, and so with the state—upon which it is incumbent to distribute that property as equally as possible (pending, perhaps, the difference principle). In two perhaps contradictory words, we might describe Rawls's project as redistributive constitutionalism. Maintaining liberal (and constitutional) forms, he lends them a novel substance.

In his approach to constitutionalism, then, Rawls is no Rexford Tugwell, offering us a new institutional blueprint with the *i*'s dotted and the *t*'s crossed. What he expounds are the broad implications of regarding constitutionalism as a vehicle for his principles of justice. Rawls offers a "four-stage sequence" by which the two principles are fashioned into actual, workable institutions and practices governing everyday life. In this sequence the initial stage, or original position, is followed by the stage of the "constitutional convention," at which the form of government is chosen and basic rights and liberties are guaranteed; then by the legislative stage, at which policy is made regarding the distribution of wealth and opportunities; and finally by the stage involving "the application of rules to particular cases by judges and administrators, and the following of rules by citizens generally" (199). At the successive stages, the "veil of ignorance" is gradually lifted. The veil is gone, and participants are fully aware at the final stage of application, while members of the constitutional convention and the legislature know "the relevant general facts" about their society, "its natural circumstances and resources, its level of economic advance and political culture, and so on," though they remain ignorant of their own interests (197). Rawls states explicitly that the four-stage sequence, like the original position, is hypothetical, that it is meant as a model for moral argument rather than as a description of actual political practice or institutions (197, n. 2).[12] The sequence provides a framework to organize the judgments citizens have to make concerning the justice of social policies, the constitutional arrangements for reconciling conflicting opinions, and the limits of the obligation to obey the law.

The implications of the four-stage sequence for constitutionalism are at once problematic and revealing, and they come to light above all in Rawls's treatment of the judiciary. In the initial formulation of the sequence, the judicial task appears squarely placed in the final stage of application. Once judges are given the power to define constitutional limitations on legislative action, however, courts assume as well the role of the "constitutional convention," and Rawls's discussion in a recent article of judicial definition of constitutional rights makes it clear that he intends for them to assume this role.[13] The problem becomes even more complex as one works through Rawls's distinction between the constitutional and the legislative stages. The task of the former is to devise institutions for the day-to-day functioning of government. Its choices are guided on the one hand by the procedural demands included in the two principles of justice and on the other hand by the project of engineering the political process so that it becomes most likely to lead to a just outcome. The constitution, in other words, must be both just in itself and productive of justice. These two aims, however, might well conflict. Among the basic liberties protected by the first principle of justice is political liberty, the right of each to participate equally in political decisions and therefore to have such decisions made by a simple majority vote. In actuality, though, majorities are liable to produce unjust legislation, making the task of constitutional design that of determining in which cases functions can safely be left to majority decision and in which cases justice demands institutional and legal limits on majority rule.

Under certain conditions, then, political liberty must be compromised. This in itself proves no obstacle in Rawls's theory, for one liberty can be limited for the sake of others. The priority of the first principle of justice over the second requires that compromises of any liberty not be made for the sake of economic gain; except in underdeveloped societies, only another liberty can limit a liberty (542–43). What is essential, Rawls has since explained, is that the "central range of application" of each liberty be secured within a "workable constitutional arrangement."[14] Provided a "central range" is preserved for majority rule, constitutional limitations are in order to protect the other basic liberties Rawls enumerates: "freedom of thought and liberty of conscience; freedom of association; and the freedom defined by the liberty and integrity of the person, as well as by the rule of law."[15] In the scheme Rawls sketches, majority rule finds its place in a legislature devoted to the distribution of economic opportunities and rewards, while the basic liberties are protected by constitutional provision. Though conflated in ideal circumstances, the constitutional and legislative stages turn out to correspond in their tasks to the dictates of the first and second principles of justice, respectively (199). While conceived through a hypothetical agreement among abstract moral beings, the two principles of justice outline the division between the realms of constitutional adjudication and legislative authority that has evolved in American jurisprudence since the New Deal and World War II.

Rawls indeed says that the division of labor between the constitutional and legislative stages corresponds to the division between the two principles, but he adds that this correspondence works "roughly." Such roughness ought to be expected, since he argues that the determination of legislative power and constitutional limits cannot be made a priori but must be worked out empirically, so to speak, through "moving back and forth between the stages of the constitutional convention and the legislature" (198). But the "roughness," in fact, runs deeper, for several reasons. First, the political liberties guaranteed by the first principle must not only receive formal protection but also have their "fair value" secured in practice. It is not enough, for instance, that all be guaranteed the right to free speech; they must also be provided reasonably effective means for making themselves heard, through campaign finance laws and the like (224–27). This requirement of "fair value" illustrates one way in which the first principle not only precedes but also controls the second, although Rawls appears content to leave the security of the "fair value" of political liberty to legislative action, asking of the judiciary only that it not interfere.[16]

The second breach in the distinction between the two principles and thus in the distinction between the constitutional and the legislative stages involves what Rawls terms the primary good of self-respect. Self-respect or, more precisely, the social bases of self-respect are the most problematic of the primary goods in *A Theory of Justice*. In the accounts of primary goods early in the volume, self-respect is mentioned only as an afterthought; its meaning is defined and its status defended only in the final part of the book. Moreover, self-respect is the only one of the primary goods that Rawls does not explicitly assign to either the first or the second of his principles. These textual oddities appear to occur not because self-respect is too unimportant to interfere with constitution building but, on the contrary, because its influence is too pervasive to provide a determinate starting point for defining the basic structure. Fortunately, or rather through the ingenuity of reflective equilibrium, the two principles established to ensure a just distribution of the other primary goods turn out to secure individuals' self-respect as well. According to Rawls, this is primarily accomplished by the guarantee of equal liberties; individuals allowed to choose their own way of life and assured of their status as equal participants in the community will respect themselves, regardless, say, of their income or the prestige accorded their occupation (422, 544–46, 536). Rawls is aware, though, that equal liberties will not always be enough. In addition to frustrating equal political participation, great disparities in wealth and prestige may cause those at the lower end to lose their sense of their own worth. In this case, their envy of the privileged is justified, and an upper limit on wealth can justly be imposed, regardless of the implication for efficiency as defined by the second principle (534). At least one of Rawls's commentators has used this limit imposed on private wealth by the needs of self-respect as a justification for judicially established constitutional welfare rights, and in a recent article Rawls has referred to this argument with apparent approbation.[17]

Rawls's blurring of the distinction between the two principles and thus between the constitutional and the legislative stages reveals the underlying difficulty in his suggestion that the constitutional stage can be embodied institutionally in the courts. Ambiguous constitutional provisions and principles demand definition, and the difficulty with Rawls's formulation, as indeed the difficulty with the self-understanding of the modern Supreme Court, is that it does not squarely face the old issue of how and by whom the Constitution is to be defined and enforced. In Rawls's conceptual scheme this task belongs to the stage of the constitutional convention, but if in practice the constitutional stage is performed by the courts, they are put in the anomalous position, on the one hand, of determining the constitutional limits on legislative action, while, on the other, being themselves the principal institutional check on the legislature. The courts, in other words, would be both the architect of the constitutional framework and a part of that framework; they would define their own function, which is practically to say that they would be without limits, except insofar as judges are limited by their acceptance of the principles of justice. Although today we often take for granted that authoritative interpretation of the whole Constitution belongs exclusively to the judiciary, Rawls's analytical scheme illustrates how radical an assumption this is. It is hard to see how the concept of a judiciary that sets its own limits is compatible with any definition of constitutionalism as limited government, much less with a scheme that claims to preserve for majority rule "a central range of application." If the constitutional stage is indeed the exclusive province of the courts, political liberty appears relegated to the secondary task of economic regulation, although in light of both the demands for the "fair value" of political liberties and the requirements of self-respect, the legislature does not have free rein even in economic matters. In any event, if the courts sit as "constitutional conventions," judges are left not only the responsibility of protecting the fundamental things but also the authority to determine what is fundamental.

It is not apparent from the surface of Rawls's book that he intends so dramatic a judicial function. His most extensive remarks on judicial review in *A Theory of Justice* appear to stress the limits of that power rather than its possibilities. These remarks occur, significantly, in the context of his discussion of civil disobedience. Rawls defines civil disobedience, in contradistinction to conscientious refusal, as a political action, the open breaking of a law as a means of addressing the community's sense of justice in order to achieve reform. He introduces it as "one of the stabilizing devices of a constitutional system . . . along with such things as free and regular elections and an independent judiciary empowered to interpret the constitution (not necessarily written)" (383). His theory of civil disobedience is meant to be a constitutional theory, and he compares the advance it makes upon existing constitutionalism to the improvement of modern upon medieval constitutionalism: whereas modern constitutional government institutionalized the sovereignty of the people instead of simply declaring the supremacy of law, the constitutionalism of civil disobedience fosters justice by making possible direct appeal by a citizen to the public mind instead of simply relying on institutional mechanisms (385–86). In this context, Rawls presents judicial review not as an alternative to civil disobedience but rather as its analogue. Drawing on Alexander Bickel's account of the politics of judicial review, he argues that not the Supreme Court but public opinion is the final court of appeal in constitutional matters. For Rawls, this is not only a matter of fact but an issue of right: the doctrine of equal rights means that "each person must indeed make his own decision" concerning the demands of justice; in politics as in science, "everyone is autonomous yet responsible"; "equals accepting and applying reasonable principles need have no established superior" (389–90). In short, when judges strike down laws on constitutional grounds, they do nothing different in kind from the person who engages in civil disobedience. Both appeal to the same sovereign, and both find the success of their action dependent upon its judgment. The constitutional stage in Rawls's theory, then, would appear to be exercised by the community at large. When courts engage in constitutional argument, it is as participants in public discussion rather than as authoritative arbiters of last resort (390).

While this argument about judicial review and civil disobedience cuts against the most exaggerated claims made on behalf of judicial review by its supporters, it nevertheless offers no determinate guidance concerning the proper extent of the judicial role. Civil disobedience is an extraordinary remedy and indeed can succeed in focusing public attention on a particular injustice only if it remains extraordinary. The more ordinary route by which an individual or a small group of individuals may succeed in bringing an injustice to public attention is still through the courts. The courts even have a role to play in civil disobedience, for they must often decide whether those engaging in it ought to be punished. Indeed, Rawls's account provides a backhanded justification for active judicial review: since the courts' "conception of the constitution must, if it is to endure, persuade the major part of the citizens of its soundness," any precedent that endures can be presumed to have won popular acceptance (390). Of course, what the whole discussion of judicial review in this context somewhat disingenuously overlooks is the fact that court decisions not only influence the public mind but have authoritative force to reorder the lives of individuals and larger institutions. However analogous the role of Supreme Court justices and civilly disobedient individuals in proposing constitutional theories that may eventually win over public opinion, in the short run the individual can only protest, while the Court issues orders and decrees. To be sure, Rawls declares his interest to lie not in the short but in the long run (222, compare 587). But in political life the short run matters, certainly to those directly affected by judicial decisions but also in setting the direction of the long-run course. Indeed, in constitutional affairs, the "short run" can last a generation or more, as the experience of the early twentieth century confirms, especially since on the federal level constitutional amendment in practice requires the support of much more than a majority. Rawls's passing over this distinction between the immediate and the ultimate significance of constitutional interpretation by the judiciary indicates the inadequacy of his explicit treatment of the conflict between judicial review and democracy.

There is, however, a strain in Rawls, muted but persistent, which seems to tend against too ready an acquiescence in rule by judges. If, as he so resoundingly asserts in expounding his doctrine of political community, the "collective activity of justice is the pre-eminent form of human flourishing" (529), then popular self-government might yet deserve some special status in his eyes. In fact, Rawls does raise this possibility, particularly in his discussion of political liberties or, more precisely, the liberties of equal political participation. He mentions but refuses to adopt the traditional liberal doctrine that the rights of private life are more fundamental than political rights, that the latter are merely instrumental to the former (201–2, 229–30). Although he also refuses to endorse the reverse, he does hint on several occasions at a certain priority of the political. He notes, for example, the connection between political participation and moral development. Drawing on Mill's account of how political liberty provides an "education to public spirit," he remarks that political freedoms "strengthen men's sense of their own worth, enlarge their intellectual and moral sensibilities, and lay the basis for a sense of duty and obligation upon which the stability of just institutions depends." In short, "equal political liberty is not solely a means," or rather, is a means not solely to just legislation but to the self-respect that comes from being part of a larger community, from participating in justice in Rawls's enlarged sense of the term. The liberties of equal political participation develop and themselves embody the autonomy of the individual citizen (234, compare 221–22).[18] If elsewhere Rawls appears a remote descendant of the liberalism of the founders, here at least he also sounds an echo of their republicanism.

On close examination, however, even Rawls's celebration of political liberty is less enthusiastic than it initially seems, and the realm for judicial intervention in politics expands correspondingly. Although participation in a just society involves the individual in a "far more comprehensive good" than any private life can offer by itself, the life of active citizenship remains for Rawls only one way of life among many. Whatever the special place of politics in a well-ordered society, Rawls denies that the principle of participation "define[s] an ideal of citizenship" or "lay[s] down a duty requiring all to take an active part in political affairs" (227). In the end, despite the rhetoric of community and some flirtation with a special place for politics, Rawls assigns priority to the side of moral personality that chooses an individual good over the side that involves a sense of justice. Or rather, he assumes that the sense of justice can be sufficiently cultivated and exercised in the ordinary course of everyday life, even if one withdraws from the political arena where questions concerning the justice of the basic structure of society are debated.

Moreover, what appears to be the strongest argument in favor of a special place for the liberties of equal participation—that these liberties "mirror" the equality and autonomy of the parties in the original position—likewise turns out upon scrutiny to disclose the limits of politics in Rawls's scheme. Unlike earlier social contract theories, which require that all members of society be party to the fundamental agreement, Rawls's "contract" in the original position is among representative moral persons. In fact, since by donning the veil of ignorance the parties lose all that makes them distinctive, it is difficult to see why in principle his contract is a contract at all rather than the conclusion of a single mind.[19]

What is remarkable is not that the original position fails as a paradigm for how politics actually is but that Rawls intends it as a model for how politics ought to be. The representative nature of the parties in the original position is of course mirrored by actual legislative representatives, but, like the parties in the original position, representatives ought to be ignorant of their own interests and of any interests peculiar to their constituents. Since by *interests* Rawls includes not only economic interests but also religious, ethnic, and cultural beliefs, his ideal of representation requires that human beings overcome nearly every cleavage that leads to partisanship in the political world. Moreover, his ideal politics is not only without interests but without ambition as well. He writes that in a well-ordered society "no one is inclined to look beyond the constitutional affirmation of equality for further political ways of securing his status" (544). Purged of interests even in the broadest sense and of the ambition of those who might articulate and guide them, politics in the well-ordered society reduces to the activities of voting and talking, activities that individuals can engage in as "private citizens." It is altogether characteristic that Rawls classifies freedom of association under the rights of private life, the rights that enable the individual to pursue his own good, rather than among the rights essential to the political dispute over justice.[20]

Of course, Rawls intends the original position to outline politics only in ideal circumstances. He is well aware that in a less-than-well-ordered society political men and women are moved not only by a sense of justice but also by interest and ambition, enmity and loyalty. Nevertheless, even "ideal theory" presents itself as a guide for less-than-ideal situations; the two principles of justice are meant to bind us here and now, and contemporary political institutions are to be designed to make these principles as effective as possible. The "politics" of the original position, then, serves as a model not only for the well-ordered society but also for us today. This can be seen in Rawls's account of civil disobedience. Like a party to the original contract, the civilly disobedient individual acts autonomously, without regard to previously established law, and addresses his argument directly to the other individuals in society outside established institutional channels. Civil disobedience, however, succeeds only in extraordinary circumstances. In everyday affairs, the politics of the original position is most closely duplicated not in the battles and compromises of partisan electoral, legislative, and executive politics as we know them but in the activities of courts. Here partisanship is expected to be absent; people approach the state not in aggregates but as individuals; and they make their claims as reasoned arguments according to specified procedural constraints. More especially, the sort of reasoning that takes place in the original position depicts the judicial process as classically portrayed. Judges, detached from their own interests and free of any personal bias toward one of the parties, are to reach individual decisions on the basis of legal arguments alone; they are under no compulsion to compromise their principles to achieve consensus with their colleagues, and trading votes would be an open breach of duty. Indeed, as experts in procedure and detachment, judges might seem not only to represent the original position but also to be capable of consciously recreating it through their own efforts, of thinking themselves through the original position and its subsequent stages to determine *de novo* what is just. Or rather, since the original position is only the mediate beginning point of Rawls's theory, one might argue that judicial detachment lends itself well to the experiments in reflective equilibrium that underlie his whole moral philosophy. As expressed by one scholar who advocates the use of Rawls's philosophy to guide adjudication, "'reflective equilibrium' perhaps offers a paradigm of judicial review."[21]

Despite the rhetoric of democratic community and participation, then, Rawls's theory, when applied to the actual circumstances of the contemporary United States, opens the door for an expansive use of the judicial power in the service of justice as he defines it. Although ultimately checked by the need for popular acceptance of their opinions, perhaps expressed especially through the technique of civil disobedience, courts have a wide range for their task of defining and protecting individual rights. Rawls's egalitarianism constrains him to treat equal democratic participation as an ideal, but until the well-ordered society has arrived, the safety of egalitarian justice depends upon granting unequal political power to the educated and trustworthy few. His equivocation concerning the judicial role reflects his sense of the inherent tension in inegalitarian enforcement of egalitarian justice.

Dworkin and Radical Equality

Ronald Dworkin boldly asserts what Rawls leaves us to tease from his theory: the need for an activist judiciary to confer justice upon political life. Of our three writers he is the one most directly concerned with the processes of constitutional government. He begins, moreover, with a critique of legal positivism—of a position that, by inspiring "legal realism," has played a goodly part in the debunking of constitutionalism. Even so, this enemy of its enemies proves not to be constitutionalism's friend.

Dworkin develops his critique of positivism by expounding and refuting its three tenets: (1) that the law is a set of rules, identified by "their pedigree or the manner in which they were adopted and developed"; (2) that when a case is not covered by a rule of law, it must be decided by a judge "exercising his discretion"; and (3) that legal obligation is limited to those circumstances governed by valid legal rules.[22] His strategy is to refute the first and the third by examining the situation covered by the second, judicial resolution of "hard cases." A hard case is one that is not clearly covered by a legal rule, or one in which the rules that seem to apply conflict, or one in which the outcome that seems dictated by the applicable rule is plainly unjust. (Clearly, "hard cases" include constitutional cases.) In such cases, Dworkin argues, judges reach their decision not by the exercise of a mysterious discretion or purely preferential choice but by the application of "legal principles" (22–39). Unlike rules, which apply in all-or-nothing fashion, dictating one or the other determinate outcome, legal principles have weights that incline a hard decision one way or another. What distinguishes Dworkin's theory from that of the positivists (and "legal realists") is his assertion that the principles judges invoke are strictly legal and that the indeterminacy of the outcomes they demand reflects not their extralegal character but the deep complexity of legal argument (35–39). Principles as well as rules constitute the law, and this is so not because of any doctrine of speculative metaphysics but because as members of a legal system we speak and act as though it were so.

Dworkin insists, moreover, that his approach reflects a deeper structure in our moral lives. Legal principles are at the same time moral and as such bear implications beyond themselves. A larger theory of law is implicit in legal principles, and because those legal principles are moral principles, a theory of political morality, indeed a political philosophy, is also implicit in legal principles. From what presents itself merely as conceptual clarification, Dworkin's larger project emerges: the subsuming of law under the scepter of political philosophy. A constitution, too—whether we conceive it as a statement of rules or of principles—can be cogent (and therefore fully authoritative) only inasmuch as it implies a political philosophy: an appeal to the Constitution is necessarily an appeal to such a philosophy.

Since Dworkin agrees with Rawls that the starting point of moral theory is the fact of living in a particular society, the relevant sources of law for the "philosophic judge" are the various sources of law in his society: the constitution, statutes, legal precedents and practices, and the like (36, 41, 105–49). Legal theory seeks principles that can bind all these into a coherent and consistent whole. This will of course prove impossible, a great boon for Dworkin, as it provides the crack through which a moral theory will slip to become law. It is by means of his moral theory that Dworkin proceeds from his theory of law and judging to his "favored interpretation" of American law, which is ipso facto one of American constitutionalism. In the American context, at least, "principles" prove to consist exclusively of individual rights, in contrast with "policies" or collective goals (82–83, 91).

Dworkin proceeds to specify what sort of rights he means to protect. Although he argues that rights must be defined in response to the threats the individual faces, he offers a "favored form of argument for political rights, which is [their] derivation from the abstract right to concern and respect taken to be fundamental and axiomatic" (xiv–xv). Dworkin is aware that this "principle" requires interpretation, that it is a "concept" of which there might be various more precise "conceptions" (127, 134–35, 351–52). He interprets it as protecting freedom of speech and of the press, as allowing affirmative action, and as securing "free choice in personal and sexual relations" (277). Above all, he argues, it is not a right to liberty simply, for the liberty of each must be restrained to preserve the liberties of others. Rather it is the right to equality—though including rights to certain equal liberties—because equality best expresses the autonomy of individuals in the choice of their own conceptions of the good. He claims that the right to equal concern and respect is the most radical concept of equality that exists (182). He also presents it as grounding the only truly "liberal" theory of law (vii).

Dworkin discovers this right through an examination of Rawls's philosophy, especially the original position, a device "well designed to enforce the abstract right to equal concern and respect" (181). Well designed though it be, Dworkin discards the device, and with it the cumbersome indirectness of Rawls's procedure, its rococo complexity and creakiness, which leave it vulnerable at so many points. Dworkin is Rawls made simple, that is, the Rawlsian principle concisely stated and applied directly to political life (182).

By sticking in his thumb and pulling out the plum of a right to equal concern and respect, Dworkin facilitates the transformation of a theory of justice into one of law and the entrusting of justice to the judiciary. He has his political theory and insists that the first duty of government is to act on a consistent political theory. Indeed, he insists that this is precisely what "taking rights seriously" means (186). It is a short step from "articulate consistency" as the preeminent political requirement to courts as the preeminent political institution. The task of articulating consistent rules and principles of law has long been assigned to the judicial function. By insisting against the positivists that law is as much a matter of principles as of rules and further that all political principle is a matter of law, Dworkin can argue that his judges must be rulers simply because they are judges: the supremacy of principle in law implies the supremacy of judges in politics.

Dworkin would not entrust all questions to the courts, of course, only matters of principle; questions of policy he would leave to legislatures (85). He sometimes speaks as if this would leave legislatures with extensive powers, but as he proceeds, the realm of the legislative shrinks. For one thing, the distinction between principles and policies is not simple and absolute. Indeed both are at root policies or, to preserve Dworkin's terms, "political aims," of which rights are individuated and policies or goals collective (82–83, 91). Similarly, principles or rights can be created as part of any public policy; indeed, this would seem to occur whenever a policy is enacted into law and its enforcement turned over to the courts. One might, moreover, take the security of individual rights as a collective goal, thus making the enforcement of principle a public policy (82–84, 294–300). Thus do popular bodies enjoy a role in the definition and enforcement of rights; Dworkin applauds, for example, the Civil Rights Act of 1964 and the wide variety of "affirmative action" programs enacted by legislative or quasi-legislative authorities around the country (223–39). This power cuts both ways, however, for if legislatures may establish policies to enforce principles, courts might find that the enforcement of principles, which is their special task, requires them to make policy. Court-ordered busing as well as legislated civil rights earns Dworkin's praise (345). Indeed, since the courts have primary authority in matters of principle and since they have the final say anyway in its application to particular cases, courts can or must refashion legislative policies to conform to their views of what principle requires. Since all laws beyond the simplest rules are ambiguous, according to Dworkin, the interpretation of statutes necessarily depends upon principles of a larger legal theory, and while fidelity to legislative intent is one such principle, such intent is also often ambiguous, leaving judges to make an independent assessment based on political theories of their own (107–10). As for collective goals, Dworkin's final position is that they must consist not in a notion of public good but only in a coincidence of private interests—unless they are goals for the enforcement of principles (232–39, 274–77, 357–58).

On questions of principle or rights, then, judges, according to Dworkin, are supreme. Indeed to leave custody of such rights with the majority would be to annul them, since rights in Dworkin's understanding are precisely rights against the majority (85). In reaching judgment on matters of principle, judges must not vote merely their personal preferences, but they can vote no more than their own best judgment of what the law requires—where the law includes community morality rationalized into a consistent theory (124–30). To remit decisions on matters of individual rights to the majority would be to suppose the ordinary voter a better judge of arguments of principle than lawyers and judges, who are specially trained in such matters and compelled to articulate their reasons in opinions subject to public scrutiny. Dworkin finds this supposition implausible, and to the objection that judges err, he replies that that is no argument against their trying not to (129–30). Besides, if "any other particular group" in society has "better facilities of moral argument," "then it is the process of selecting judges, not the techniques of judging they are asked to use, that must be changed" (130). He speaks as if this were just another recommendation for procedural reform and not half the problem of constitutional government in a nutshell. Since Dworkin thinks judges can be philosophers or at least trained by philosophers, he is oblivious to the fundamental principle of constitutionalism that the human propensity to overreach must be opposed not by exhortation to perfection but by limits on the power invested in any individual or group.

Nor in the end does Dworkin set much store by consent, that other pillar of constitutionalism. Like Rawls (and Kant before him), he holds that one shows sufficient concern for the right of consent by taking it hypothetically: since he presumes that human beings consent to being ruled by reason, the force of law belongs to the best conclusions that reason can devise.[23] Since the reasoners par excellence are judges, the practical consequence of Dworkin's theory is a government of courts. Where rights are trumps (xi), it is judges who take the tricks.

Nozick and the Minimal State

Of our three writers, only Robert Nozick stands on what journalists would call the right. Since that is the place where the fewest American intellectuals would be caught dead, Nozick, while an acknowledged phenomenon, has found less favor than Rawls and Dworkin. As an enterprising supporter of enterprise, however, he probably enjoys a better reputation than they with many readers of the present volume—with reason. Especially in his critique of Rawls and of redistributive policies generally, he strikes many brilliant blows for common sense and limited government. His cleverness and audacity, moreover, pose endless challenges to complacency. In the end, however, as we will argue, Nozick, however congenial, offers not a solution but a libertarian variant of the problem, where the problem is the falling out between liberalism (in the generic sense) and constitutionalism.

If Nozick is a libertarian, he is one with a difference. Typically libertarians—Friedrich von Hayek is a distinguished example—have rejected the propriety of justice as the political standard, alleging its incoherence and incompatibility with the priority of liberty. (This we may regard as at the very least a rhetorical weakness in their argument: few human beings are willing to abandon their insistence on justice.[24]) Nozick, however, follows Rawls in asserting the absolute priority of justice—and then sets out to demonstrate that what justice demands is precisely libertarian liberty. His book, consequently, is divided into three parts, each of which explores a different implication of Nozick's revision of Rawls: part one, which vindicates the "minimal state" against those (anarcho-libertarians) who contend for less; part two, which defends it against those ("liberals" in the journalistic sense and leftists) who contend for more; and part three, "Utopia," which admonishes those who fail to find such a state "inspiring."[25]

As Rawls argues that the liberal state of today does too little, Nozick argues that it does much too much. Indeed, borrowing our terms from Rawls (65–74), as Rawls achieves the transition from the second to the third and final epoch of liberalism (from "equality of opportunity" to "democratic equality" as expressed in the "difference principle"), Nozick urges a return from the second stage to the first (the "system of natural liberty"). Nozick's audacious book is in fact largely a rejoinder to Rawls. Where the one discounts inequalities of human capacity, the better to recognize equal "moral personhood," the other reinterprets "moral personhood" with results much friendlier to the inequalities of human capacity. And while Rawls, as we have seen, proposes an "original position" worlds apart from the state of nature, Nozick, departing from every other liberal thinker since Bentham, actually invokes a "state of nature" (as well as a theory of property rights), which alludes repeatedly to Locke's. His argument thus first comes to sight as a unique and ambitious attempt to restore something like the Lockean conclusions on the basis of something like the Lockean arguments. Just as with Rawls, however, these overtones of early liberal moral realism prove misleading: Nozick's argument is "idealistic" to the core.

In fact Nozick presents himself as taking Rawls seriously, that is, as sticking by Rawls's principles, which Rawls himself unwittingly abandons. Nozick too stresses the repulsiveness of utilitarianism; he too would rescue a quasi-Kantian moralism from the perplexities of

Kant's metaphysics. His cry, like Rawls's, is the inviolability of the person, its status as end in itself. And like Rawls's his case for this is shaky enough to seem almost frivolous.

Briefly, Nozick argues from the separateness of our existences to their inviolability (33–35). No one can rightly subordinate another's radically separate life to his own; in deference to its separateness, he must treat the other as an end in himself. This does not mean that we owe each other any favors, but it does mean that in our mutual dealings we must all respect certain "side constraints" or "thou-shalt-nots." These Nozick does not specify completely, but basically thou shalt not deny another his rights to life, liberty, and property. He has a right to require no less—as do you to offer no more. To compel you to offer more would violate the side constraints by treating *you* as a means to *his* ends.

Is separate, however, really sacred? A slug's existence is as separate as yours or mine; is it as sacred? (In fact, Nozick devotes most of his exposition of the moral foundations of his system to a plea for vegetarianism.) In any case separateness is the wrong route to take to moral obligation. (According to Kant such obligation depends upon our membership in the *community* of rational beings.) If my life is mine and yours is yours, what is yours to me—if not something to be made use of by me?

Nozick tries again by invoking something distinctively human, our capacity to form a life plan (compare Rawls); it is this capacity that lends "meaning" to our lives (48–51). No one meaning of life is given to us as human beings to guide us in forming our plans; rather we create our own several meanings precisely *by* forming plans. For each of us then his own plan is authoritative; it is authoritative because it is his. The primary human good is self-assertion.

From this it follows, Nozick suggests, that each of us must restrain his self-assertion within certain bounds, out of respect for the self-assertion of others. But this does not follow at all. It is with meaning as with separateness (our meanings being separate): if the meaning of my life abides in my life plan, what are your lives to me but grist for my mill? This is also, of course, how you would view mine. In a world of beings so separate that each is free to name his own meaning, the natural state of those beings is war.

Nozick needs to argue with Hobbes and Locke that although self-assertion is the name of the game, morality is the best policy. Or he needs to argue with Kant that mere self-assertion is meaningless, that we can lend meaning (dignity) to our lives only by submitting to the moral law. Instead he wants to have it both ways: the unqualified primacy of the self links hands with an unconditional moral law. From the pseudo-Nietzschean premise we jump to the pseudo-Kantian conclusion.

None of this is new. Nozick serves up, with exotic garnishes, the typical non sequitur of contemporary liberalism: self-expression is primary; therefore we have to be nice. The difference is that the implications that he derives from it are libertarian. Only Nozick concludes that the "Kantian principle" of the sanctity of the individual proscribes (rather than demands) social programs, that indeed it strictly precludes all states beyond the minimal one. It does so because all schemes of justice, however otherwise dissimilar, that benefit some at the expense of others treat the latter as a means to the former rather than as ends in themselves (167–74). While Nozick's arguments are many and ingenious, it is ultimately on his interpretation of this "Kantian principle" that all else rests. It is the more regrettable, then, that even granting Nozick his impossible leap from self-assertion to morality, his argument is far too vague to support his specifically libertarian conclusions.[26]

Be this as it may, Nozick's argument, like Rawls's, is moral rather than prudential, with the twist that, according to him, the only moral obligations are negative ones. It is morality that demands that we get off the backs of others and that they (the state included) vacate ours. The pressing question is whether even the minimal state is morally defensible.

So it is that Nozick offers an account of the genesis of the state that aims at vindicating its legitimacy. It is this account that begins from something like Locke's state of nature (3–25)—only from something like it, though, because Nozick's state of nature resembles in the decisive respect its Rawlsian counterpart rather than its Lockean one: it is avowedly hypothetical. Nozick presents his pseudo-state of nature as the best condition among men that can be reasonably expected in the absence of a state, arguing that if such a condition can be shown to require the minimal state, then so a fortiori must any worse case.

Unlike Locke's state of nature, then, Nozick's is no such thing—no such account of man's true natural condition. Nor is Nozick's moral law anything like Locke's natural one, although Nozick sometimes calls it that. Locke's natural law is not extended to his state of nature but arises from it: it articulates the harsh code that nature imposes upon those who would tame it. Nozick's law, by contrast, descends upon the "state of nature" from without, resting only upon the weak arguments already discussed. So while Locke exerts himself to show that in vindicating certain rights the state makes itself preeminently useful to all, Nozick seeks to confirm its goals as morally binding on all.

Not that Nozick is unmindful that men in the state of nature would require some sort of protection from their fellows. He argues, however, that this need could be met by wholly voluntary, noncoercive, and nonredistributive "protective agencies," each offering protection for a fee to (only) those clients who signed up for it (12–25). But how then should we proceed, morally speaking, from these associations to the state (even the minimal state), which, in providing protection to all at the expense of those who are able to pay for it, practices coercive redistribution and makes of some lives means to the ends of others (26–28)? How should we derive, from merely negative "side constraints," a positive obligation, enforceable by the state, to contribute to the defense of other people's rights?

Nozick argues, with great ingenuity and at great length, that principles of compensation for risk oblige a dominant protective agency serving customers to become a state serving (and compelling) all (54–119). Briefly, he contends that such an agency would enjoy the right, in settling disputes between its clients and outsiders, to impose on the outsiders procedures of adjudication acceptable to the clients. In so doing, however, the agency denies the outsiders the protection of such procedures as *they* may regard as reliable. It thus subjects them to risk, thereby violating a side constraint, for which the agency must compensate them by offering them the same impartial protection vis-à-vis its clients as it offers to clients vis-à-vis them. Q.E.D.: the minimal state is a moral imperative, and the anarcho-libertarian objectors are confounded (114–15).

There are at least two things wrong with this argument. The first is that lurking beneath Nozick's pyrotechnics on compensation and risk is an unstated (and unsupported) denial of a necessary consequence of the Lockean teaching (to which Nozick subscribes) that men are originally free and equal. That consequence is the right of each to be judge in his own case, with apologies to no one.

Nozick would compel his insiders to defer to the judgment of the outsiders (by compensating them for flouting it) even while he grants those insiders the right to flout it. According to Locke, however, man, being free and equal, is rightfully judge in his own case both of his own needs and of his duties to others, except (as under civil government) where he has consented to relinquish that right. As I owe the other no deference, so I owe him nothing for withholding it. The decision to submit to a common judge (that is, civil government) must therefore be a matter of prudence rather than one of obligation.[27] The conclusion, again, necessarily follows from accepting men as naturally free and equal. It is indeed a necessary implication of understanding government as based on consent (rather than on such a prior obligation as would render consent superfluous).

The second thing wrong with Nozick's argument is that while it allegedly vindicates the minimal state, what it in fact justifies falls far short of that. Nozick's state would not be entitled to protect all within its borders in their dealings with all—the least (if also the most) that we demand of the minimal state—but merely some (the paid-up members) in their dealings with all, and the rest only in their dealings with some. Mayhem among nonclients is no affair of this state; indeed, in squandering its funds to suppress it, it would be bruising the rights of the paying customers. Only in the quarrels of the nonclients with the valued clients of the state would outsiders be entitled to its (scrupulously impartial) offices.

To see what nonsense this is, we need only consider these hypothetical headlines from successive issues of the Nozicksburg *Utopia–Herald:* "Bloodbath Rages among Nonclients, Protective Agency Cordons Off Area," and "Bloodbath Spills Over into Clients' Neighborhood: Mob Assured of Due Process." Nozick's clients and nonclients are not citizens of the same state or even members of the same people: they are foreigners, one group of which elects to treat the other according to a super–Geneva Convention. But anyone who can imagine a protection-for-hire outfit that holds the lives of nonclients so cheap when they fall out among themselves and so dear when they clash with its clients, has as good an imagination as Nozick.

On reflection, then, Nozick's account serves merely to confirm that American constitutionalism, following Locke, begins at the right place: with the prudential (not moral) necessity that each human being seek the full protection of political society. The anarcho-libertarian position of which Nozick is so indulgent asserts the impropriety of the coercion practiced by even the most minimal state, but such coercion would be improper only if it were unnecessary. In fact, as the founders agreed, government must wield compulsion for the same reason that submission to some form of government is compulsory: because men's wills are naturally diverse and refractory. Coercion is legitimate wherever it rests on consent, and consent to government is of necessity consent to the prospect of coercion.

So, then, while both the founders and Nozick reject government except where founded on consent, they understand consent quite differently. The founders interpret it politically: "no taxation without representation." I consent to abide by the decision of a majority of the legislature (which "represents" me); its authority rests on my consent and supersedes it. "Consent" legitimates majority rule expressed through representative government.

Nozick, however, interprets consent literally and hence unpolitically. I personally must consent to every disposition of my property: all taxation is theft (167–74)—well, not quite *all* taxation. As we have seen, taxation in support of the ends of the "minimal" state is not proscribed but obligatory and so may be levied without my consent. So while for the founders all taxation is presumptively legitimate if properly enacted by a legislature resting on consent acting within the bounds of a constitution adopted by the people, for Nozick it is presumptively larcenous—except where substantively legitimate because morally obligatory—in which case consent is superfluous. Nozick's doctrine of legitimate compulsion is both more and less stringent than that of the founders. It is each in a way that displays its inferiority to theirs.

According to Nozick, again, we are morally obliged, consent to it or not, to bear the expenses required to maintain the "minimal" state. Beyond that, unanimity is required; there must be no coercion of the recalcitrant. In whom is vested the right, however, to decide whether a given expenditure is in fact required? (This is a question that is as sure to be contentious in a "minimal" state as in any other.) Does the individual citizen have that right? In that case, he is no citizen, as we forthwith return to the very anarchy that Nozick rejects. Or (the only alternative) does "the state" have the right, more precisely our elected representatives (as constitutionalism would have it)—or our hired gun (as Nozick would)—to whom we the people have delegated the right to speak for us as a people? Political consent or anarchy—there is no third option.

Political consent, as expressed, shaped, and perpetuated by a constitution, is one aspect of the founders' scheme for establishing effective popular self-government. Ultimately Nozick is indifferent to constitutionalism because like Rawls and Dworkin he is indifferent to the existence of peoples. "We the Board of Directors of the Glendale Protection Agency, Inc., in order to serve our clients more efficiently . . ." is no way to begin a preamble. The dignity and authority of a constitution depend upon that of its people: it represents that people's considered decision about the forms by which it will govern itself. It is the work of individuals only insofar as they speak to and for a people.

Publius would of course have agreed with Nozick that government originates to vindicate the rights of individuals. It is to exercise these rights effectively that men form political societies, which is what the Lockean tradition means by peoples. Precisely to secure these rights, however, the people must supersede the individual as the authoritative judge of the rights of each; and, moreover, the government that the people establishes must (if only as its fiduciary) supersede the authority of the people itself. That peoples should exist is, while the result of choice, a matter of necessity; that they should govern themselves is a matter of right; that they should do so constitutionally, one of both safety and dignity.

The question for constitutionalism, then, is not only whether a given government respects individual rights but also whether the form of that government represents the considered, uncoerced choice of a people, as well as whether it is a form by which that people continues to govern itself. None of these questions is practically separable from the others. For Nozick, however, the legitimacy of a given state is identical with its "minimality." A tyranny that enforced his side constraints (and no more than his side constraints) would be as fully legitimate as any other state that did.[28] A people is free to govern itself neither less nor more than "minimally," and where "minimality" is practiced, the question of popular consent is moot.

Nozick, indeed, looks askance at peoples; representative democracy leaves him cold. He coins the word *demoktesis*, "ownership of the people, by the people, and for the people," to describe the "modern [democratic] state, with its vast panoply of powers over its citizens" (290). He offers an account of how such a state might evolve spontaneously and so unobjectionably, from an original "minimal" state: this account is sufficiently fanciful to imply the illegitimacy of all actual modern democracies (276–90). As this passage comprises Nozick's only discussion of popular government as such, we hesitate to ascribe to him "that honorable determination which animates every votary of freedom, to rest all our political experiments on the capacity of mankind for self-government."[29]

Nozick's discussion of *demoktesis* caps part two of his book, "Beyond the Minimal State." Here, again, Nozick, having earlier established to his satisfaction that the minimal state is obligatory, denies that a more than minimal one is permissible. It is this part that contains, in our opinion, the foremost achievements of Nozick's book. His critique of Rawls's argument on desert and of the structure of the original position (183–231), his dramatization of the massive coercion implicit in welfarist principles of distribution (160–65), his brilliant sendup of the alleged "right to a say in the decisions that affect one's life" (268–71): these, among other features, are trenchant and funny and well worth the price of admission. They defend, in their way, limited government; in so doing they might buttress someone's case for constitutionalism.

Given limited space, however, we will dwell primarily on Nozick's treatment of property, which anchors part two and provides yet another obvious point of comparison with the outlook of the founders. Indeed, Nozick might seem to agree with *Federalist* 10 that the "protection of [different and unequal faculties of acquiring property] is the chief end of government." In fact, the sanctity of property à la Nozick far exceeds anything proclaimed by Publius or Locke.

Nozick treats property in the course of propounding his "entitlement theory of justice," the main positive argument of part two. Perhaps we should call it his main prophylactic argument, intended to preempt all possible cases for a "more than minimal" state.

Nozick offers his entitlement theory as the alternative to "patterned principles" of justice. Adherents of any one of the latter conceive justice as a certain pattern of distribution (whether according to merit, need, marginal contribution, maximum utility, or the like). "To each according to . . ." expresses a patterned principle and implies regulation of the holdings of each according to the standard in question. Nozick's fighting words are "to each his own," where no patterned principle obtrudes on the determination of one's own (150–64).

Nozick offers several witty criticisms of "patterned principles," but the one that matters is that these necessarily trample his "side constraints." Because no pattern exists that equally gratifies all life plans, patterned principles procure the good of some people at the expense of others. Only the entitlement theory of justice is compatible with honoring Nozick's side constraints, precisely because it alone rests on no patterned principle. The strongest case for the theory is thus a negative one, and what underlies Nozick's seemingly ultra-Lockean conclusions are his same pseudo-Kantian premises.

According to Nozick the entitlement theory offers not a "patterned" but a "procedural" or "historical" principle of justice: a person is sufficiently entitled to something by the fact that he has it, having come by it in some way other than wresting it from others who had it. He is entitled to what he has justly acquired (no one having previously acquired it) and to what he has justly obtained from others who had justly acquired it or justly obtained it from others who. . . . (By "justly" we always mean "without infringing side constraints.") Only where the knee bone is not connected to the thigh bone and so on back to the original acquisition, or where that original acquisition was itself illicit, is the status quo in any way unjust and in need of rectification.

Nozick fully specifies neither the principles of justice in acquisition nor those of justice in transfer. These last, however, seem to resemble the precepts of the Uniform Commercial Code, as expanded to cover cases of giving as well as selling. What is crucial is that these rules never cede under any circumstances to some other, "patterned" principle: only procedural principles crimp our freedom of transfer.

It is similarly only procedural principles which limit our freedom to acquire, to gain title to something to which no one has previously been entitled. Nozick here provides his second discussion of Locke; indeed his own system includes what he dubs a "Lockean proviso" (174–82). This proviso limits our freedom to acquire, with reference of course not to any pattern but merely to the ubiquitous side constraints. (Nor does the "Lockean proviso" sketch the dictates of self-interest in the face of nature's niggardliness: as always Nozick gives us Kant in Locke's clothing.)

While Nozick, however, offers an account of those transgressions that nullify ownership where acquisition would otherwise create it, he never explains how it is that acquisition creates it. Given his insistence that property is no less sacrosanct—that is to say, no less unconditionally one's own—than life and liberty, this is a pressing question. How does something external to a person become as much "his own" as he himself is?

Locke, of course, has an answer to this question. Because a person's body and its labor are properly his own and because it is labor that makes for 99.9 percent of the value of the world, the labor that he invests in a quasi-worthless object not his own makes it 100 percent his own. Such, at least, is the origin of property, and all subsequent title is derived from it, whether by the willing exchange of the fruits of one's labor or by that of one's labor power.[30]

Nozick flirts with but appears to reject this answer (174–75). He seems to overlook the crucial point, Locke's labor theory of value. This latter is crucial because it links Locke's argument from the ownership by each of his body and labor to his argument from the prospective general good of mankind. Labor, as the source of the value of the world, improves it, not just for the laborer but for everyone; but this improvement depends upon the incentive to labor that only private property provides.[31] Characteristically, Nozick, following Rawls, eschews all such merely "utilitarian" trash. He ends up, however, providing no real account of the infusion of the "me" into "mine." He is much better on the question of why what is mine is not yours.

Let us briefly mention Nozick's third principle of justice, that of rectification (152–53). If history proves less than spotless in matters of acquisition and transfer, then rectification is not only appropriate but obligatory. While we may admire Nozick's purity of heart, it does not detract from the fatuity of a principle that, as Harvey C. Mansfield, Jr., has put it, would force us "to give the country back to the Indians even if they now owned most of it."[32] Presumably Nozick is aware, as Locke was following Hobbes, that "there is scarce a commonwealth in the world, whose beginnings can in conscience be justified."[33] He differs from Locke in his moralistic unwillingness to face the necessary harshness of beginnings—and the necessity of the more productive rescuing the earth from the less so.

In cases where history is one of flagrant transgressions of his principles, Nozick sanctions the temporary implementation of Rawls's difference principle as the avenging angel of rectification (230–31). This surrender is as puzzling as it is supine: after three generations of massive redistribution in American society, one might rather expect that Nozick's prescription for rectification would be "make the poor pay."

According to Nozick, then, property is in principle sacred. It is only in practice that it is theft. With friends like Nozick the propertied might grow nostalgic for friends like Locke.[34]

In part three of his work, "Utopia," Nozick argues that the minimal state is not only obligatory but inspiring. He thereby launches a counterattack against the utopianism of the Left, as well as against our tendency to assume that nowadays the Left has a corner on utopianism. This section is important to us because only here does Nozick sketch the kind of society that might arise on the basis of the minimal state; only here do we glimpse the human vision animating his libertarianism. It is also only here that we encounter Nozick's version of self-government, consideration of which is clearly necessary to locate him vis-à-vis constitutionalism. As one of us has discussed Nozick's "Utopia" at some length elsewhere, we will do so only briefly here.[35]

Nozick's libertarian state would provide a "framework for utopia," where utopia designates (among other things) an attempt at a self-sufficient community. Like quite a few other contemporary liberal thinkers, Nozick is anxious to combine liberty with community. His state (the "framework") is libertarian, thereby leaving us free to form communities: one state, a thousand and one ways of life.

Suppose, however, that we reformulate that: one ideology, a thousand and one ways of life. Is that really a tenable position? Each of the diverse communities would have to be in fact a libertarian community, so as not to violate the "framework." There would be no diversity among them at this fundamental level. Each, indeed, would necessarily subvert itself as a community by its Nozickian acknowledgment of the primacy of every individual as such to every community as such. So many communities, each professing the same authoritative principles, and individualistic ones at that—would these be anything but minor variations on the same profoundly individualistic society?

And would such an individualistic society provide fertile ground for devotion to community or to the ends that constitute true communities? Oddly, Nozick seems to foresee a society in which acquisition is sacred but which would not be an acquisitive society, in which the individual is sacred but which would not be an individualistic society. He needs a lesson from Tocqueville on the prospects for utopian communities—indeed, for any form of devotion to the nonmaterial—in a modern egalitarian society. At best, Nozick mistakes the "counterculture" for the culture.

Nozick offers "Utopia" to establish that a libertarian society would be not only just but "inspiring." Unfortunately, this goal is predicated on a falsehood, one that Nozick shares with Rawls and most other current liberal thinkers. Liberalism, to hear them tell it, is neutral regarding ways of life, and it is just this that is inspiring about it—not its way of life, because liberalism fosters no way of life. Anyone who can believe this can, like these theorists, believe anything. The truth would seem to be that liberalism fosters a way of life—the commercial way of life—but that liberal theorists no longer find it inspiring.[36]

Here what Locke united Nozick has put asunder, severing the just (acquisition, commerce, investment) from the inspiring (his utopian cloud-cuckoo-land). Nozick cannot present the conquest of nature as inspiring because he does not present nature as a tyrannical master. And although he adverts in stirring terms to the nobility of political freedom (328), he does not mean constitutionalism. For him the communities are the arenas of self-government, and the constitution (which he relegates to a footnote, 353 n. 13), just an ingenious contraption for keeping the state off their backs—while still enabling it to keep them off the backs of their members.

Can we really agree, though, that Nozick's communities practice self-government? Not of the popular sort, unless we deem each a separate people. Do they practice the local sort, then? Not all of the communities are local or, for that matter, comprehensive in their concerns; what Nozick means by a community is a voluntary association of whatever sort. Even were all these communities perched on lofty crags, however, we could not admit that what they practiced was self-*government*. They are, again, voluntary associations, which, however vital for educating citizens for self-government, fall far short of practicing it themselves. True self-government implies sovereignty, that one's word, as uttered through the government, is law. In Nozick's as in every liberal society, legislative authority rests not with the "communities" or private sphere but with the public: the state or "framework." What is ultimately authoritative precisely *within* his communities is, as we have seen, only the limits to community imposed by the framework. These only are enforceable: all else is counsel; these are command.

In effect, while Nozick's communities may practice self-counsel, government in his Utopia need not be self-government. Nowhere does Nozick argue that his side constraints imply a right to self-government. If, then, the sole test of state legitimacy is respect for these side constraints, we could, in principle at least, let George govern, where he is the benevolent-despot-for-a-fee of the local protective agency rechristened "minimal state."[37] At no point in Nozick's schema does the community at large or people accept and wield responsibility for itself as a whole; ideally, indeed, there is no community at large, just an impersonal institutional framework. A constitution is then on the order of a blueprint for this framework (329–30). It is not a form—the decisive form—of self-government but merely a device for leaving people free to disport themselves in the private sphere.

Nozick then offers us a constitution on a different plane from that on which he offers us "self-government." By the latter he means the direct self-government in small communities that Publius had so roundly rejected. Like many products of the 1960s, Nozick is too impressed with "community" to locate self-government in anything so vast and distant as a people speaking only through its representatives. Yet he shares enough of Publius' good sense not to trust these communities of his actually to govern. What constitutionalism would join—self-government and the extended people—Nozick would sunder—only to end up by returning government, if not to the people, then to the "framework."

As Nozick is indifferent to the people, so is he to those ambitious few whom a people needs as partners in self-government. His libertarian model of politics as an exchange among rational actors presents leadership as entrepreneurship: some sell us apples, some sell protection. Nozick is blind to the necessity for successful politics of men who rise above concern with wages through a not wholly selfless concern with the good of the political whole. Like most libertarians (and like Rawls), Nozick grasps the problems with, but not the promise of, political men. As for making ambition counteract ambition, he comes to cluck at that passion (306, compare 272), not to tap it.

Nozick then leaves off just about where constitutionalism comes in. Must not a "framework" that is to be responsible for the people also be responsible to it? And does not the dignity of genuine self-government—of a people governing itself in the only way that a people prudently can, through the binding decisions of its elected representatives—eclipse that of the spurious autonomy that Nozick vests in his communities?

Conclusion

Our three thinkers are liberals in the broad pervasive sense in which the founders themselves were such; all seek, moreover, to combine effective self-government with effective restraints on government. All then can claim, however loose the fit, the mantle of constitutionalism; each sets out to restore and refit it for our day. It is important, therefore, to grasp just what in constitutionalism eludes them.

The problem lies, we think, with the perfect relativism concerning the good on which our thinkers seek (unsuccessfully) to erect a perfect dogmatism concerning justice. To this is related their reduction of the supreme political goal to the preservation of subpolitical rights (which they obfuscate but do not qualify by their homage to participation and community).

Yes, American constitutionalism recognizes a certain indeterminacy of the human good. Its theoretical charter, the Declaration of Independence, is famous for proclaiming "the pursuit of happiness" rather than any form of happiness defined. To this end, the Constitution protects certain individual rights, and it has long been established that the judiciary has a crucial role in realizing this protection. The protection of rights, however, is not the sole aim of the government established by the Constitution, even if it is the foremost, as the Declaration claims. Although "to establish justice" is among the first aims enumerated in the Constitution's preamble, it is not alone, nor can the others be reduced to it. The aims of "insur[ing] domestic tranquillity, provid[ing] for the common defense, [and] promot[ing] the general welfare," entrusted to the political branches, surely affect the protection of rights but just as surely go beyond rights. This is self-evidently true of the mandate to promote general welfare, and for our thinkers to reduce American constitutionalism to securing individual rights and avoiding definition of the good, they must scrupulously ignore this clause. Moreover, the aims of union and liberty, which frame the list, represent an ideal of public spiritedness and republicanism that points beyond the preservation of a realm of private autonomy toward an active and democratic political life.

The complex structure of powers in American government suggests a complex structure of values underlying it. If the judiciary reflects a certain concept of individual rights, the political branches in their different ways suggest a concept of the public good. Unlike the theories of justice expounded by Rawls, Dworkin, and Nozick, the complex structure of American constitutionalism seeks not to overcome but to balance these competing aspects of political life and political morality, to balance the claims of individual rights and public good.

As we celebrate the bicentennial of our Constitution, would-be defenders of constitutionalism find themselves in a parlous state. The experience of the past two centuries is with them, and the thought of those centuries is against them. Not much comfort is to be had from our three authors. To be sure, they make a heroic effort to bring liberal democratic thinking up to date. Marxism they more or less ignore, and the existentialism that has touched them all is heavily watered. Idealism, historicism, and utilitarianism, however, as well as relativism, economism, and social science—all these figure in their arguments, sometimes only to be rejected, but more often to be co-opted. As we have seen, Rawls, Dworkin, and Nozick all present themselves as both restorers and perfecters of the older liberal tradition grounded in the sanctity of the individual and in the principles of self-government flowing therefrom. The first question, as we have seen, is how firmly they grasp the way this tradition understood itself, in particular how it understood itself at the beginning. The second is whether their response to the challenges to this tradition is not to beat those challenges by joining them, thereby securing for constitutionalism a Pyrrhic victory, if any.

Notes

Chapter 2: The Philosophic Understandings of Human Nature Informing the Constitution

1. References to the *The Federalist* will be to Clinton Rossiter's edition (New York: New American Library, 1961).

2. *The Basic Writings of Thomas Paine* (New York: Willey Book Co., 1942), p. 148.

3. Quoted from Philip B. Kurland and Ralph Lerner, *The Founders' Constitution*, 5 vols. (Chicago: University of Chicago Press, 1986), vol. 1, pp. 3–4. Compare Lord Acton's remarks, in his "Influence of America," *Essays in the History of Liberty*, 2 vols., ed. J. Rufus Fears (Indianapolis: Liberty Press, 1985), vol. 1, pp. 200–203:

> These early authors of American independence were generally enthusiasts of the British Constitution, and preceded Burke in the tendency to canonise it, and to magnify it as an ideal exemplar for nations. . . . When these men found that the appeal to the law and the constitution did not avail them, that the king, by bribing the people's representatives with the people's money, was able to enforce his will, they sought a higher tribunal, and turned from the laws of England to the law of Nature, and from the king of England to the King of kings. . . . The primitive fathers of the United States began by preferring abstract moral principle to the letter of the law and the spirit of the Constitution. But they went further. . . . In their appeal to the higher law the Americans professed the purest Whiggism. . . . By their closer analysis, and their fearlessness of logical consequences, they transformed the doctrine and modified the party. The uprooted Whig, detached from his parchments and precedents, his leading families and historic conditions, exhibited new qualities; and the era of compromise made way for an era of principle.

4. The speech was delivered November 24, 1787; I have used the text as found in Randolph G. Adams, ed., *Selected Political Essays of James Wilson* (New York: Alfred A. Knopf, 1930), pp. 163ff.

5. The best explicit interpretative discussion of the *Spirit of the Laws* among the founders (and one of the most penetrating brief interpretations of

Montesquieu ever written) is that of Carter Braxton, the great Virginia statesman and signer of the Declaration of Independence: "An Address to the Convention of the Colony and Ancient Dominion of Virginia on the Subject of Government in General, and Recommending a Particular Form to Their Attention," published in June of 1776 anonymously or "by a Native of this Colony." The essay is a direct reply to John Adams's "Thoughts on Government," published previously the same year, and demonstrates cogently Adams's misunderstanding of Montesquieu—a misunderstanding that continued to be shared by some founders. For both Adams's and Braxton's essays, see Charles S. Hyneman and Donald S. Lutz, eds., *American Political Writing during the Founding Era 1760–1805,* 2 vols. (Indianapolis: Liberty Press, 1983), vol. 1, pp. 328–39 and 401–9.

6. *Spirit of the Laws,* bk. 11, chap. 2. All translations from Montesquieu are my own; the only available English translation of the *Spirit of the Laws,* by Thomas Nugent, is extremely inaccurate, unreliable, and often misleading. I have used the Pléiade edition of the works of Montesquieu: Roger Caillois, ed., *Oeuvres complètes,* 2 vols. (Paris: Gallimard, 1951).

7. Ibid., bk. 3, chaps. 4 and 5; and bk. 5, chap. 8.

8. Ibid., bk. 5, chap. 19; compare William Blackstone, *Commentaries on the Laws of England,* bk. 1, chap. 2, sec. 2.

9. *Spirit of the Laws,* bk. 5, chap. 6.

10. Ibid., bk. 20, chap. 2.

11. Ibid., bk. 20, chap. 1.

12. "Of the Populousness of Ancient Nations," in *Essays: Moral, Political, and Literary,* ed. Eugene Miller (Indianapolis: Liberty Press, 1985), p. 408.

13. Ibid., p. 414.

14. "Of Civil Liberty," in *Essays: Moral, Political, and Literary,* p. 93.

15. "Of the Populousness of Ancient Nations," p. 416.

16. "Of Civil Liberty," and "Of Commerce," in *Essays: Moral, Political, and Literary,* pp. 86, 259, 262–63.

17. "Idea of a Perfect Commonwealth," in *Essays: Moral, Political, and Literary,* pp. 526–28.

18. *Fame and the Founding Fathers* (New York: W. Norton, 1974), chaps. 3 and 4.

19. Compare Hume's "Idea of a Perfect Commonwealth," pp. 520–26.

20. *The Federalist,* No. 2, p. 38.

21. Ibid., No. 84, pp. 514–15.

22. Compare *The Federalist,* No. 55, p. 346.

23. *The Federalist,* No. 9, pp. 71–72.

24. In his remarkable "Defense of the *Spirit of the Laws*"—*a tour de force* of evasiveness, wit, and gentle polemic—Montesquieu felt compelled to reply to a passionate and sometimes penetrating Christian critic who focused, in part, on Montesquieu's bold opening discussion of God and creation. To the critic's objection that Montesquieu in effect denied the unfathomable Biblical God in saying that "creation, which might seem an arbitrary act, presupposes rules as invariable as the fatality taught by atheists," Montesquieu replied that he "was speaking in no way about causes, nor comparing causes, but speaking about

effects, and comparing effects . . . thus it is absolutely necessary that the phrase mean: creation, which might seem at first to have to produce variable rules of motion, has produced such as are as invariable as the fatality taught by atheists" ("Defense of the *Spirit of the Laws,*" Part 1, sec. 1, Objection and Response 3 [pp. 1124–25 of the Pléiade ed.]). This dazzlingly clever reply of course does not refer to or explain what Montesquieu could have meant when he said that "the laws according to which [God] created are those according to which he preserves." But it also does not meet the core difficulty. For suppose that Montesquieu were speaking only of effects (the nature of the created universe), and not causes (the creative act by which the universe was brought about): how could he know or claim to know the invariable nature of the effect if he did not know or claim to know the nature of the cause? How could he know that the laws of motion, or the laws determining the natures of the created beings, cannot be varied—miraculously interrupted, suspended, contradicted—by the creator if he did not know the necessities that bind the creator?

25. Compare the characterization of Plutarch in "Defense of the *Spirit of the Laws,*" part 1, sec. 1, Objection and Response 2, p. 1124.

26. See *Guide for the Perplexed,* part two.

27. *Spirit of the Laws,* Preface.

28. Ibid.

29. Consider here *The Persian Letters.*

30. *Spirit of the Laws,* bk. 1, chap. 1, end; and bk. 24, chap. 11.

31. *Politics* 1252a26ff.

32. *Anangkē:* ibid., 1252a26.

33. See especially *Spirit of the Laws,* bk. 5, chaps. 2 (with which compare bk. 14, chap. 7), 11, and 19 ("Second Question").

34. Ibid., "Author's Warning," and bk. 3, especially chaps. 1 and 4.

35. Ibid., bk. 19, chap. 27, p. 575.

36. Ibid.

37. Compare Aristotle, *On the Soul* 433a15ff.: "the object at which desire aims [*to orekton*] is the cause of motion, and it is on account of this that thought [*dianoia*] is set in motion; for it is this that is the ruling beginning or cause [*archē*] of thought: the object at which desire aims."

38. Consider, above all, the way Montesquieu speaks of fear, and its relation to preservation, in bk. 1, chap. 2. The primordial fear is linked to preservation, or focused by the thought of death, only after the intervention of "ideas" which are not intrinsic to the primordial passion. Contrast Locke, *Two Treatises of Government,* bk. 1, sec. 86. Rousseau was to seize on this, as on many other elements in the Montesquieuian account, and argue in effect that Montesquieu had failed to develop fully, or push to their logical conclusions, his insights: if man by nature possesses no conception of death, why should the fundamental sentiment be one of terror?

39. *Spirit of the Laws,* bk. 1, chap. 1.

40. Ibid., bk. 1, chap. 2.

41. Compare "Defense of the *Spirit of the Laws,*" part one, sec. 2, Objections and Responses 3 and 6, pp. 1130–31.

42. Compare and contrast Plato's *Laws* 790e–791a and context.
43. Compare also *Spirit of the Laws,* bk. 5, chap. 11, end.
44. See ibid., bk. 26, chap. 14.
45. Ibid., bk. 1, chap. 3.
46. *The Federalist,* No. 51, pp. 324–25.
47. *Spirit of the Laws,* bk. 30, chap. 19.
48. Ibid.
49. Ibid.
50. Ibid., bk. 12, chap. 6.
51. Ibid., bk. 10, chap. 3.
52. Ibid., bk. 10, chaps. 2 and 3; bk. 15, chap. 17; bk. 24, chap. 6; bk. 26, chaps. 3 and 7.
53. Ibid., bk. 16, chap. 12; bk. 26, chap. 3.
54. Ibid., bk. 6, chap. 13; bk. 10, chap. 2.
55. Ibid., bk. 26, chap. 7.
56. Ibid., bk. 1, chap. 1.
57. See, for example, ibid., bk. 26, chap. 14.
58. Ibid., bk. 10, chap. 3.
59. Ibid., bk. 1, chap. 1.
60. Ibid.
61. Ibid., bk. 6, chaps. 9, 16, 19; bk. 12, chap. 4.
62. Ibid., bk. 6, chap. 9.
63. Ibid., bk. 26, chap. 1; cf. bk. 10, chap. 3.
64. See especially ibid., bk. 19.
65. Ibid., bk. 1, chap. 3.
66. Ibid., bk. 8, chap. 21; bk. 14, chaps. 5 and 8.
67. Ibid., bk. 15, chaps. 7 and 8.
68. Ibid., Preface, end.
69. "Some Thoughts Concerning Reading and Study for a Gentleman," in James L. Axtell, ed., *The Educational Writings of John Locke* (Cambridge, Eng.: University Press, 1968), p. 400.
70. *Two Treatises,* bk. 2, sec. 42.
71. *Social Contract,* bk. 3, chap. 8.
72. Contrast Locke's *Two Treatises of Government,* bk. 1, secs. 47–48, 55, 88–91, 93, 97, 98, 101; bk. 2, secs. 52ff.
73. Contrast Locke, ibid., bk. 2, sec. 142.
74. See Locke, ibid., bk. 2, chap. 19, especially sec. 225; and compare sec. 192.
75. See especially *The Federalist,* No. 49.
76. See Antoine Destutt de Tracy, *Commentary and Review of Montesquieu's Spirit of the Laws* (Philadelphia: William Duane, 1811). For Jefferson on Destutt de Tracy and Montesquieu, see, for example, Letter to William Duane of January 22, 1813, in Adrienne Koch and William Peden, eds., *The Life and Selected Writings of Thomas Jefferson* (New York: Random House, The Modern Library, 1944), pp. 625–26; and Letter to John Adams of January 11, 1817, in Lester J. Cappon, ed., *The Adams-Jefferson Letters,* 2 vols. (Chapel Hill: University of North Carolina Press, 1959), vol. 2, pp. 505ff. On Hume, see Jefferson's

Letter to [George Washington Lewis?] of October 25, 1825, in Koch and Peden, eds., *The Life and Selected Writings of Thomas Jefferson*, pp. 723–26.

77. *The Federalist*, No. 49, p. 313; compare No. 22, p. 146.

78. In *Selected Political Essays of James Wilson*, pp. 181, 196–97, and 199–200; and Jonathan Eliot, ed., *The Debates in the Several State Conventions, on the Adoption of the Federal Constitution*, 5 vols. (Philadelphia: J. B. Lippincott, 1907), vol. 2, p. 456.

79. Bk. 1, chap. 2, sec. 1; hereafter, references to the works of John Locke will be to the following editions, with titles abbreviated as indicated:

SCCLI = *Some Considerations of the Consequences of the Lowering of Interest, and Raising of the Value of Money*, in *Several Papers Relating to Money, Interest, and Trade* [etc.] (London: Churchill, 1696).

RC = *The Reasonableness of Christianity, as Delivered in the Scriptures:* reference will be to paragraphs, as numbered in the abridged edition of I. T. Ramsey (Stanford: Stanford University Press, 1958), except where that edition omits the passage cited, in which case the page number of the 1824 edition, published in London by Rivington et al., will be cited.

NL = the unpublished manuscript of Locke's untitled disputations on natural law, cited by disputed question and folio page number (I have supplemented von Leyden's occasionally inadequate edition of the Latin text, and his often inaccurate translation, published under the misleading title *Essays on Natural Law* [Oxford: Clarendon Press, 1958], with the critical philological comments of Leo Strauss, "Locke's Doctrine of Natural Law," in *What Is Political Philosophy?* [Glencoe, Ill.: The Free Press, 1959], pp. 197–220, and by an as yet unpublished translation by Jenny and Diskin Clay, edited by Robert Horwitz, which the latter was kind enough to show me).

LCT = *A Letter Concerning Toleration: Latin and English Texts Revised*, ed. M. Montuori (The Hague: Martinus Nijhoff, 1963).

TT = *Two Treatises of Government*, ed. Peter Laslett (New York: New American Library, 1965); cited by book (that is, treatise) and section number.

STCE = *Some Thoughts Concerning Education*, in *The Educational Writings of John Locke*, ed. James Axtell (Cambridge: Cambridge University Press, 1968); cited by section number.

CU = *Of the Conduct of the Understanding*, 2d ed., ed. Henry Fowler (New York: Burt Franklin, 1971); cited by section number.

ECHU = *An Essay Concerning Human Understanding*, ed. Peter Nidditch (Oxford: Clarendon Press, 1979); cited by book, chapter, and section number.

In all quotations, italics are Locke's own unless otherwise noted (for the importance Locke attached to his italicization, see Laslett's Introduction to TT, pp. 21–22).

80. RC, pp. 34–83, esp. 59, 70, 82–83 (all on Jesus' "concealment of himself," his "reservedness" in "perplexing" and "rendering unintelligible" his "meaning" to his initial or careless hearers), para. 238 (on the way "the rational and thinking part of mankind" kept the "truth locked up . . . as a secret," and on the manner of writing of Plato and Aristotle, who "were fain, in their outward professions and worship, to go with the herd, and keep to their religion established by law"). See also the discussion of how to read, or

"the true key of books" in CU, 20, as well as 24 (p. 56), 35, and 42. See ECHU I iv 8, II xxi 20, III ix 3ff. See the passages collected in John Dunn, "Justice and Locke's Political Theory," *Political Studies* 16 (1968), pp. 68–87, p. 70 n. 1. Compare Leo Strauss, *Natural Right and History* (Chicago: University of Chicago Press, 1953), pp. 206ff.; Richard Cox, *Locke on War and Peace* (Oxford: Oxford University Press, 1960), pp. 1–44; C. B. Macpherson, *The Political Theory of Possessive Individualism: Hobbes to Locke* (Oxford: Oxford University Press, 1962), p. 7. Michael Zuckert has presented a conclusive rebuttal of the few sustained scholarly attempts that have been made to explain away the overwhelming evidence for Locke's use of a covert style of writing: "The Recent Literature on Locke's Political Philosophy," *Political Science Reviewer* 5 (1975): 271–304, and "Of Wary Physicians and Weary Readers: The Debates on Locke's Way of Writing," *Independent Journal of Philosophy* 2 (1978), pp. 55–66. As far as I have been able to determine, Zuckert's detailed critical discussions of the issue and the literature have thus far gone unanswered and even unchallenged. Especially striking is Richard Ashcraft's failure to join the issue, in his recent five-hundred-page tome, *Revolutionary Politics and Locke's Two Treatises of Government* (Princeton: Princeton University Press, 1986).

81. TT I 7, 110.

82. See my *Spirit of Modern Republicanism: The Moral Vision of the American Founders and the Philosophy of Locke* (Chicago: University of Chicago Press, 1988), part three.

83. TT I 92. Compare TT I 39 and the opening of the fifth chapter of the *Second Treatise*, on property as "meat," that is, "Venison" as well as "Fruit."

84. Compare ECHU II xx 5.

85. TT I 38.

86. Compare TT I 22, 23, 24, 39.

87. TT I 39.

88. See especially Leviticus 3: 16–17, 17:10–11, 25:23; consider also Numbers 11.

89. *The Laws of War and Peace* II, chaps. 2 and 3. Helpful for the Christian background is Ernst Troeltsch, *The Social Teaching of the Christian Churches*, trans. Olive Wyon (Chicago: University of Chicago Press, 1976), 116–18, 137, 152–53, 260, 411n., with its many illuminating references, especially to Thomas Aquinas. See also C. B. Macpherson, *Democratic Theory: Essays in Retrieval* (Oxford: Oxford University Press, 1973), pp. 17 and 126ff. G. E. Alymer, "The Meaning and Definition of 'Property' in Seventeenth-Century England," *Past and Present* 86 (1980), pp. 87–97, esp. 95, has presented a case for the truly amazing speed with which Locke's conception of property permeated and radically transformed English common law. By 1704 (six years after publication of the *Two Treatises!*) Locke's notions began to appear as the standard or orthodox notions in legal commentary. I believe it is safe to surmise that Locke's influence on the legal and hence political thinking of the American colonists in subsequent years, by way of this transformation in legal thinking, was enormous.

90. Locke reproduces this traditional outlook, in part, in NL XI, 112–13. For a helpful discussion of the still-vibrant echoes of this older view in

eighteenth-century America, see Forrest McDonald, *Novus Ordo Seclorum: The Intellectual Origins of the Constitution* (Lawrence, Kans.: University Press of Kansas, 1985), pp. 98–99.

91. TT II 57.

92. TT I 86–87.

93. TT II 4, 6, 7.

94. TT II 6–7.

95. See especially TT II 21, 176, 241.

96. TT II 7–9, 87, 128.

97. TT II 13.

98. TT II 123; compare 124–27.

99. TT II 6.

100. For divine power and wisdom as opposed to divine goodness and bounty, see especially RC para. 228.

101. TT II 25–26; compare STCE 116.

102. Locke speaks even more frankly a few pages later, when he explains the natural law dictating that each individual may intervene to punish anyone who threatens or injures another: when someone is threatened, a third party "joyns with him in his Defence, and espouses his Quarrel: it being reasonable and just I should have a right to destroy that which threatens me with Destruction" (TT II 16). Compare Robert Goldwin, "John Locke," in L. Strauss and J. Cropsey, eds., *History of Political Philosophy,* 2d. ed. (Chicago: University of Chicago Press, 1972), pp. 457–58.

103. TT II 23.

104. TT II 11, 16.

105. TT II 27.

106. See TT I 86 and II 44.

107. TT II 26–28.

108. Contrast Grotius II ii 2, 3, 6, and 11.

109. See especially TT II 28.

110. Compare Grotius II ii 6, and Strauss, *Natural Right and History,* pp. 247–48.

111. TT II 27.

112. TT II 32.

113. Compare TT II 32, 35, 36, with 26.

114. TT II 34.

115. TT II 35.

116. TT II 36–39.

117. TT II 111.

118. TT II 51.

119. See Troeltsch, *Social Teaching of the Christian Churches,* pp. 115–18, 137, 153, 411.

120. Compare TT I 46–47; and RC, opening paragraphs.

121. TT II 36–37, 94, 110, 111.

122. TT II 36.

123. TT II 37, 41.

124. TT II 42–43.

125. TT II 45.
126. TT II 42.
127. TT II 43.
128. TT II 48.
129. TT II 49.
130. TT II 50.
131. TT II 2, 24, 28, 29, 41, 77; all to be read in the light of II 85. Compare Macpherson's helpful discussion in *Political Theory of Possessive Individualism*, pp. 215ff. and 282.
132. TT II 41.
133. TT II 36, 37, 38, 42, 43, 45.
134. See especially TT II 41 and LCT 82–85.
135. Compare Strauss, *Natural Right and History*, p. 245: "Locke's thought is perfectly expressed by Madison's statement: 'The protection of different and unequal faculties of *acquiring* property is the first object of government'—*The Federalist*, No. 10."
136. TT I 42, II 42, 50.
137. Compare TT II 40, 43, 44, with I 33.
138. See Robert Brown, *The Nature of Social Laws: Machiavelli to Mill* (Cambridge: Cambridge University Press, 1984), pp. 58–64; Harvey C. Mansfield, Jr., "On the Political Character of Property in Locke," in A. Kontos, ed., *Powers, Possessions, and Freedom: Essays in Honor of C. B. Macpherson* (Toronto: University of Toronto Press, 1979), p. 38; Karen I. Vaughn, *John Locke: Economist and Social Scientist* (Chicago: University of Chicago Press, 1980), esp. pp. 115–21; and Vernon Parrington, *The Colonial Mind 1620–1800* (New York: Harcourt, Brace, 1954), pp. 274–75. According to Brown (p. 58), Locke is the first thinker to apply the term "law" to economic regularities, conceived as scientific laws in the modern sense.
139. TT II 28, 30, 35, 37, 38, 42, 45, 50; compare II 3 and Vaughn, *John Locke: Economist and Social Scientist*, pp. 121–22, as well as Macpherson, *Political Theory of Possessive Individualism*, pp. 299–300.
140. SCCLI 13.
141. TT II 42.
142. Contrast Hooker, *Laws of Ecclesiastical Polity*, bk. 1, chap. 10, sec. 2.
143. TT II 94; compare 3, 85, 123–24, 134, 137, 138, 139, and LCT 14–18, 82–86.
144. See especially TT II 38 and 45; cf. 74, 127, and 105: "Government is hardly to be avoided amongst Men that live together."
145. Despite what Locke sometimes seems to say, for instance at LCT 82–85.
146. ECHU I iii 2, 8–9.
147. ECHU I iii 12.
148. ECHU I iii 9; compare II xxviii 14–15 and NL II 28–29, IV 38, VII 66ff., especially 72–73. For the importance of the notion of the conscience and its innate principles in English thought prior to Locke, see John W. Yolton, *John Locke and the Way of Ideas* (Oxford: Oxford University Press, 1956), pp. 31–35.
149. ECHU I iii 4.

150. ECHU I iii 4.
151. STCE 143.
152. RC, para. 245.
153. ECHU II xxi 41, 43, 68; compare also 59.
154. ECHU I iii 6.
155. ECHU II xxi 42.
156. ECHU II xxi 65.
157. ECHU II xxi 55.
158. STCE 103–5, 110, 119; compare 35 and 109: "Children who live together often strive for Mastery, whose Wills shall carry it over the rest."
159. ECHU I iii 3, 9, 13; compare NL XI 116 and IV 42: "Those who have no other guide than nature herself, those among whom the dictates of nature are least corrupted by positive regulations concerning morals, live ignorant of any law, as if they had to take no account at all of what is right and proper."
160. ECHU II xii 1; compare Strauss's *Natural Right and History,* p. 249.
161. ECHU I iv 12, 18.
162. ECHU III xi 16 and IV iii 18; compare *Spirit of the Laws,* bk. 1, chap. 1.
163. TT I 58.
164. ECHU II xxi 31–46, 71; compare II xx 6.
165. ECHU II xxi 64.
166. ECHU II xx 7.
167. ECHU II xxi 51, 52.
168. TT I 86.
169. ECHU II xxvii, especially 9, 17, 26.
170. TT I 88.
171. TT I 86, 88.
172. TT I 87, 97; ECHU I i 5.
173. TT II 6, 128.
174. TT II 11: my italics; compare also 16 and 172.
175. TT II 16; compare 135.
176. STCE 116.
177. ECHU I iii 4, 5, 12; IV iii 18; TT II 142.
178. Contrast especially Plato's *Laws* 788aff. and *Republic* 376eff., and Xenophon's *Education of Cyrus* as a whole.
179. STCE 14; ECHU I iii 22; cf. I iv 12; II xxi 69; and II xxxiii entire.
180. STCE 33, 36, 38, 45, 48, 50, 52, 55, 63, 75, 77, 90, 103, 107, 139, 200.
181. STCE 78; contrast Aristotle's *Nicomachean Ethics* 1128b10–35.
182. STCE 56.
183. STCE 73, 76, 103, 108, 118, 128, 130, 148, 167.
184. See especially STCE 46 and 63.
185. See especially STCE 69.
186. See the references to education at TT I 90, 93; II 56, 59, 61, 65, 67, 68, 69, 170.
187. TT I 44ff.
188. TT I 50–51.
189. 1 Corinthians 11:3, 14:33–35; Ephesians 5:22; Titus 2:5; 1 Timothy 2:9–15; 1 Peter 3:1–7.

190. Compare, for example, Grotius, Prolegomena 40 and 46, as well as II v 1 and 12; Richard Hooker, *Laws of Ecclesiastical Polity,* I v as well as viii 1, 3, 5, 7, and especially xi 4; contrast Locke's NL V as a whole, as well as VI 60–61.
191. TT I 47.
192. TT I 52.
193. TT I 54.
194. TT I 53.
195. TT I 55.
196. TT I 88, 96, 98; cf. 123, 126; but see 59 end: contrast Grotius II v 8. Compare Blackstone's *Commentaries,* bk. I, chap. 15: "Our law considers marriage in no other light than as a civil contract. . . . And, taking it in this civil light, the law treats it as it does all other contracts . . ."; but consider the modifications of this principle Blackstone is compelled to introduce in the body of the same chapter, and see note 242 below.
197. TT I 47.
198. ECHU I iii 12; compare RC 143 and NL VII 73–74.
199. TT I 57–58; my italics.
200. TT I 97; compare II 63, 75, 107, and STCE 34, 99, 107.
201. ECHU I iii 12.
202. STCE 34.
203. TT I 88.
204. TT I 97; contrast 56.
205. TT II 70; ECHU II xi 7.
206. Which we can find conveniently summarized again in Grotius, especially in II viii 3ff.; see also Blackstone's *Commentaries,* bk. 1, chap. 16, sec. 1, subsec. 1.
207. TT I 90.
208. TT I 88, 92, 93.
209. TT I 87.
210. TT II 65.
211. Compare Strauss, *Natural Right and History,* pp. 218–19.
212. TT I 91; compare 90, 95, 111, 115.
213. TT II 52.
214. TT II 53.
215. TT II 55; compare 66, 67, 74.
216. TT II 58.
217. TT II 59.
218. TT II 63.
219. TT II 64.
220. Compare TT II 49: "In the beginning all the World was *America,* and more so than it is now."
221. TT II 65.
222. TT II 68.
223. Robert Goldwin, "Locke on Property" (Ph.D. diss., University of Chicago, 1963), p. 26; compare STCE 99.
224. TT II 69.
225. TT II 72, 73; contrast Plato's *Laws* 922cff.

226. Compare TT II 73 and 120.

227. Forrest McDonald (*Novus Ordo Seclorum,* p. 11) quotes the 1776 Virginia act abolishing entail on estates, an act which attacks entail as an improper restriction of the parents' liberty to arrange their own last wills; the act advances as its justification the perfect Lockean argument that such restriction on parents' freedom to dispose of their property after death "does injury to the morals of youth, by rendering them independent of and disobedient to their parents."

228. TT II 77.

229. TT II 78.

230. TT II 77; compare 86. Patriarchy may be the general practice, but, against the Bible, Locke will not let us forget the equally right or natural possibility of matriarchy.

231. TT II 79–81.

232. TT II 80, 81.

233. TT II 79.

234. TT II 49; compare 108.

235. TT II 65.

236. TT II 82.

237. Compare TT I 47.

238. TT II 80.

239. TT II 81.

240. TT II 82.

241. TT II 83; contrast Blackstone's *Commentaries,* bk. 1, chap. 15, sec. 3.

242. TT II 80.

243. STCE 9; see also 6, 37, 70, 152; contrast the spirit of English law, as summarized by Blackstone in the closing paragraph of his account of marriage law: *Commentaries,* bk. 1, chap. 15, end: "We may observe, that even the disabilities, which the wife lies under, are for the most part intended for her protection and benefit. So great a favourite is the female sex of the laws of England."

244. TT II 94, 105, 112.

245. See especially TT II 123–27; compare Goldwin, "John Locke," p. 458.

246. TT I 92.

247. TT II 90.

248. TT II 137.

249. TT II 225; compare 13, 91.

250. TT II 90; compare 163.

251. TT II 89; compare 90 end; 14; and Goldwin, "John Locke," p. 454.

252. TT II 123.

253. Hobbes, *Leviathan* chap. 13.

254. Compare Strauss, *Natural Right and History,* pp. 230–31.

255. For a full discussion, see Cox, *Locke on War and Peace.*

256. TT II 118; compare 191.

257. TT II 122.

258. TT II 119–22.

259. TT II 95.

260. LCT 14–17; my translation.
261. *Commentaries*, bk. 1, chap. 1; see also bk. 4, chap. 4, beginning.
262. LCT 44–45, 70–71.
263. Compare especially TT II 163.
264. Letter to Joseph Priestly of March 21, 1801, in Koch and Peden, eds., *Life and Selected Writings of Thomas Jefferson*, p. 562.
265. TT II 149.
266. Goldwin, "John Locke," p. 481; TT II 94, beginning, and 225.
267. TT II 96.
268. TT II 129–30, 168, 208.
269. TT II 225.
270. TT Preface.
271. "Of the Original Contract," in *Essays: Moral, Political, and Literary*, pp. 472–73.
272. LCT 98–99; my translation.
273. TT II 192.
274. Letter to Joseph Priestly of March 21, 1801, in Koch and Peden, eds., *Life and Selected Writings of Thomas Jefferson*, pp. 562–63.
275. For William Blackstone's adaptation, and transplantation into the common law, of Locke and Montesquieu, see Herbert J. Storing's penetrating discussion, "William Blackstone," in Strauss and Cropsey, eds., *History of Political Philosophy*.

Chapter 3: The Political Theory of the Constitution

1. Declaration of Independence.
2. *The Works of James Wilson*, edited by Robert Green McCloskey, 2 vols. (Cambridge, Mass.: Belknap Press of Harvard University Press, 1967), vol. 2, p. 765.
3. *Commentaries on the Constitution: Public and Private* (hereafter, *Commentaries*), 4 vols. to date, edited by John P. Kaminski and Gaspare J. Saladino, vols. 13–16 of *The Documentary History of the Ratification of the Constitution* (Madison: State Historical Society of Wisconsin, 1981–), vol. 2, p. 232.
4. *The Federalist Papers*, by Alexander Hamilton, James Madison, and John Jay, edited by Clinton Rossiter (New York: New American Library, 1961), No. 2, p. 37.
5. *Works of Wilson*, vol. 2, p. 765.
6. *Federalist* No. 51, p. 322.
7. *Federalist* No. 23, p. 155.
8. *Federalist* No. 51, pp. 324–25; *Commentaries*, vol. 1, p. 525, and vol. 2, p. 232; *Works of Wilson*, vol. 2, p. 765.
9. *Federalist* No. 51, p. 322; and No. 15, p. 110.
10. Thomas Hobbes, *Leviathan*, edited by C. B. Macpherson (Harmondsworth, Eng.: Penguin Books, 1968), chap. 13, pp. 184–85.
11. Brutus, in *Commentaries*, vol. 1, p. 525.
12. John Locke, *Second Treatise*, in *Two Treatises of Government*, edited by

Peter Laslett, revised edition (New York: New American Library, 1965), chap. 9, sec. 128, p. 397.

13. See *Federalist* No. 6, p. 54: the causes of hostility include both the love of power *and* the desire of equality and safety.

14. *Federalist* No. 6, p. 59.

15. *Commentaries,* vol. 2, pp. 348, 336.

16. Hobbes, *Leviathan,* chap. 13, pp. 184–85.

17. A Landholder, in *Commentaries,* vol. 2, p. 336.

18. Wilson Nicholas, in *The Debates in the Several State Conventions on the Adoption of the Federal Constitution,* edited by Jonathan Elliot, 5 vols., second edition (Philadelphia, Penn.: J. B. Lippincott, 1896), vol. 3, p. 358.

19. *Federalist* No. 6, pp. 56–57.

20. *Federalist* No. 15, p. 109.

21. Gouverneur Morris, in *The Records of the Federal Convention of 1787* (hereafter, *Records*), edited by Max Farrand, revised edition in 4 vols. (New Haven, Conn.: Yale University Press, 1966), vol. 1, p. 43.

22. *Federalist* No. 3, p. 44.

23. *Federalist* No. 15, p. 112.

24. *Works of Wilson,* vol. 2, p. 766.

25. *Federalist* No. 7; No. 6, p. 59.

26. Hobbes, *Leviathan,* chap. 13, p. 188.

27. See ibid., chap. 17, p. 223.

28. Constitution, Preamble.

29. Compare "the indispensable necessity of government" (*Federalist* No. 2, p. 37) with the *"utility of the UNION"* (*Federalist* No. 1, p. 36).

30. Centinel, in *Commentaries,* vol. 3, p. 389.

31. *Records,* vol. 2, p. 666; see *Commentaries,* vol. 1, p. 525.

32. *Records,* vol. 2, p. 666.

33. *Commentaries,* vol. 2, p. 140.

34. *Works of Wilson,* vol. 2, p. 767.

35. Montesquieu, *De l'esprit des lois,* in *Oeuvres complètes,* vol. 2, edited by Roger Caillois (Paris: Gallimard, 1951) (Pléiade edition), book 11, chap. 3, p. 395.

36. Constitution, Preamble.

37. *Federalist* No. 51, pp. 324–25.

38. *Records,* vol. 1, p. 533.

39. *Federalist* No. 10, p. 78; see *Works of Wilson,* vol. 2, p. 767.

40. Samuel Savage, in *Commentaries,* vol. 4, p. 334.

41. John Locke, *A Letter Concerning Toleration* (Indianapolis, Ind.: Bobbs-Merrill, 1955), p. 47.

42. A Landholder, in *Commentaries,* vol. 4, p. 473.

43. Locke, *Letter Concerning Toleration,* p. 47.

44. See John Rawls, *A Theory of Justice* (Cambridge, Mass.: Harvard University Press, 1971), p. 74.

45. Locke, *Second Treatise,* chap. 5, sec. 27, p. 328.

46. Ibid., sec. 50, p. 344.

47. *Federalist* No. 10, p. 79.

48. See Madison's 1792 essay "Parties," in *The Papers of James Madison*, edited by William T. Hutchinson and others (Chicago, Ill.: University of Chicago Press, 1962–), vol. 14, p. 197.

49. Brutus, in *Commentaries*, vol. 2, p. 425.

50. *Federalist* No. 10, p. 84.

51. A Landholder, in *Commentaries*, vol. 4, p. 473.

52. *Records*, vol. 2, p. 344.

53. "Republican Distribution of Citizens" (1792), in *Papers of Madison*, vol. 14, pp. 244–46.

54. A Landholder, in *Commentaries*, vol. 4, p. 473.

55. *Records*, vol. 2, p. 606.

56. *Records*, vol. 1, p. 605.

57. *Works of Wilson*, vol. 2, pp. 776–77.

58. *The Complete Anti-Federalist*, edited by Herbert Storing, 7 vols. (Chicago, Ill.: University of Chicago Press, 1981), vol. 6, no. 12, para. 10.

59. *Records*, vol. 2, p. 616.

60. Philadelphiensis, in *Commentaries*, vol. 2, p. 351.

61. Ibid., emphasis added.

62. *Federalist* No. 10, p. 77.

63. *Pamphlets on the Constitution of the United States*, edited by Paul Leicester Ford (Brooklyn, N.Y.: 1888), p. 46, emphasis altered.

64. William Blackstone, *Commentaries on the Laws of England*, facsimile of the first edition of 1765–1769, 4 vols. (Chicago, Ill.: University of Chicago Press, 1979), vol. 1, book 1, chap. 1, p. 122. But Blackstone's application of this principle excuses an act that Madison regarded as unjust, an arbitrary restriction on men's "free use of their faculties and free choice of occupations." According to Blackstone, "the statute of king Charles II, which prescribes . . . a dress for the dead, who are all ordered to be buried in woollen; is a law consistent with public liberty, for it encourages the staple trade, on which in great measure depends the universal good of the nation" (ibid.). In contrast, Madison lamented "the spirit of legislation where a manufacturer of linen cloth is forbidden to bury his own child in a linen shroud, in order to favour his neighbour who manufactures woolen cloth" ("Property" [1792], in *Papers of Madison*, vol. 14, p. 267).

65. Locke, *Second Treatise*, chap. 9, sec. 130, p. 398.

66. Adam Smith, *Lectures on Jurisprudence*, edited by R. L. Meek, D. D. Raphael, and P. G. Stein (Indianapolis, Ind.: Liberty Classics, 1982), p. 5.

67. *Records*, vol. 1, p. 18.

68. See *Commentaries*, vol. 1, pp. 360–61, 382.

69. *Pamphlets on the Constitution*, pp. 46–47.

70. *Commentaries*, vol. 2, p. 270.

71. John Locke, *First Treatise*, in *Two Treatises of Government*, chap. 9, sec. 92, p. 247.

72. Hobbes, *Leviathan*, chap. 30, p. 376.

73. *Federalist* No. 12, p. 91.

74. See Locke, *Second Treatise*, chap. 5, sec. 42, p. 340; and Adam Smith, *An Inquiry into the Nature and Causes of the Wealth of Nations*, edited by R. H.

Campbell and A. S. Skinner, 2 vols. (Indianapolis, Ind.: Liberty Classics, 1981), vol. 1, book 4, chap. 5b, p. 540.

75. Madison, in *Debates in the Several State Conventions*, vol. 3, p. 538.

76. *Federalist* No. 43, p. 272.

77. *Federalist* No. 10, p. 78, and No. 51, p. 324; see Smith, *Lectures on Jurisprudence*, p. 5.

78. Virginia Plan, in *Records*, vol. 1, p. 21.

79. A Freeman, in *Commentaries*, vol. 3, p. 458.

80. See Hamilton's definition of 1774, according to which "[a free] man is governed by the laws to which he has given his consent, either in person, or by his representative." *The Papers of Alexander Hamilton*, edited by Harold C. Syrett (New York: Columbia University Press, 1961–), vol. 1, p. 47.

81. Hamilton, in *Records*, vol. 1, p. 467; and Pinckney, in ibid., p. 402.

82. *Federalist* No. 23, p. 153.

83. *Records*, vol. 2, pp. 329–30.

84. *Federalist* No. 25, p. 165.

85. Brutus, in *Commentaries*, vol. 1, pp. 414 and 526.

86. Ibid., p. 415; see *Records*, vol. 1, p. 465.

87. *Federalist* No. 8, p. 66.

88. Locke, *Second Treatise*, chap. 7, sec. 87, p. 367.

89. *Federalist* No. 37, p. 226.

90. *Federalist* No. 62, p. 381.

91. *Records*, vol. 2, p. 198; compare p. 199.

92. *Federalist* No. 64, p. 393.

93. *Federalist* No. 62, p. 380.

94. *Baltimore Maryland Gazette*, in *Commentaries*, vol. 1, p. 112.

95. *Commentaries*, vol. 1, p. 100.

96. Virginia Plan, in *Records*, vol. 1, p. 21.

97. *Records*, vol. 1, pp. 54, 256.

98. *Federalist* No. 16, p. 116.

99. *Federalist* No. 70, p. 423.

100. *Records*, vol. 4, p. 18.

101. Hobbes, *Leviathan*, chap. 18, pp. 232–33.

102. Locke, *Second Treatise*, chap. 12, sec. 147, pp. 411–12.

103. Ibid., chap. 14.

104. *Federalist* No. 70, p. 423.

105. *Records*, vol. 2, p. 318.

106. *Federalist* No. 74, p. 449.

107. *Federalist* No. 40, pp. 252–53.

108. John Mercer, in *Complete Anti-Federalist*, vol. 5, no. 5, para. 10.

109. *Debates in the Several State Conventions*, vol. 4, p. 95; compare *Commentaries*, vol. 3, p. 238.

110. *Federalist* No. 68, p. 414.

111. *Federalist* No. 57, p. 350.

112. *The Republic of Plato*, translated by Allan Bloom (New York: Basic Books, 1968), book 6, 501a-e.

113. *Federalist* No. 62, p. 380, emphasis added.

114. *Federalist* No. 3, p. 45.
115. Hobbes, *Leviathan*, chap. 25.
116. Montesquieu, *De l'esprit des lois*, book 8, chap. 16, p. 362.
117. *Federalist* No. 10, p. 78; and No. 71, p. 432.
118. *Federalist* No. 57, p. 350.
119. *Federalist* No. 63, p. 387.
120. These included doubts about whether a popular vote for president would scatter among too many candidates, and a desire to give the states a role in electing officers.
121. Brutus, in *Commentaries*, vol. 2, p. 300.
122. *Federalist* No. 10, pp. 82–83.
123. *Federalist* No. 68, p. 414.
124. *Records*, vol. 1, p. 366.
125. Ibid., p. 422. Other arrangements—the bicameral legislature and presidential veto—were also intended to discourage passionate haste and encourage careful deliberation. See *Commentaries*, vol. 1, p. 299; and *Federalist* No. 71, p. 432.
126. *Records*, vol. 1, p. 380.
127. Ibid., p. 387.
128. Ibid. See *Records*, vol. 2, p. 288.
129. Montesquieu, *De L'Esprit des Lois*, book 5, chap. 3, p. 275.
130. Madison, in *Records*, vol. 1, p. 389.
131. Ibid., p. 392 (Yates's notes of Madison's speech, a more extreme statement than appears in Madison's own notes).
132. *Federalist* No. 63, p. 383.
133. *Federalist* No. 51, p. 321, emphasis added.
134. *Federalist* No. 70, pp. 427–28.
135. *Records*, vol. 2, pp. 119–20.
136. Ibid., p. 105.
137. *Federalist* No. 72, p. 437.
138. Ibid.
139. G. Morris, in *Records*, vol. 2, p. 53.
140. *Federalist* No. 72, p. 437.
141. *Federalist* No. 51, p. 322.
142. Hamilton, in *Debates in the Several State Conventions*, vol. 2, p. 252.
143. Benjamin Rush, in *Commentaries*, vol. 1, p. 48.
144. Webster, in *Pamphlets on the Constitution*, p. 60.
145. Brutus, in *Commentaries*, vol. 1, pp. 419–20.
146. *Records*, vol. 1, pp. 406–7.
147. *Federalist* No. 27, p. 174.
148. Hamilton, in *Debates in the Several State Conventions*, vol. 2, p. 254.
149. *Federalist* No. 49, p. 314; David Hume, "Of the First Principles of Government," in *Essays: Moral, Political and Literary* (London: Oxford University Press, 1963), p. 29.
150. Hobbes, *Leviathan*, chap. 30, p. 376.
151. *Republic of Plato*, book 2.
152. An Old Whig, in *Commentaries*, vol. 1, p. 501.

153. *Commentaries*, vol. 2, p. 491; bracketed material supplied by the editors of *Commentaries*.
154. *Federalist* No. 11, p. 91; and No. 51, p. 324.
155. Montesquieu, *De L'Esprit des Lois*, Preface, p. 230.
156. *Federalist* No. 26, p. 169.
157. *Federalist* No. 49, pp. 314–15.
158. *Records*, vol. 2, p. 126.
159. *Federalist* No. 51, p. 322.
160. Brutus, in *Commentaries*, vol. 1, p. 526; see Locke, *Second Treatise*, chap. 7, sec. 91, p. 370.
161. Brutus, in *Commentaries*, vol. 2, pp. 302–3.
162. *Commentaries*, vol. 2, pp. 265–66.
163. *Federalist* No. 55, p. 346.
164. *Federalist* No. 57, p. 350.
165. *Federalist* No. 51, p. 323.
166. Wilson, in *Commentaries*, vol. 1, p. 339.
167. Madison, in *Records*, vol. 1, p. 53.
168. *Federalist* No. 39, p. 245.
169. Brutus, in *Commentaries*, vol. 1, p. 526.
170. Lee, in *Ratification of the Constitution by the States*, edited by Merrill Jensen, 2 vols. to date, vols. 2–3 of *The Documentary History of the Ratification of the Constitution* (Madison: State Historical Society of Wisconsin, 1976–), vol. 1, p. 337.
171. *Commentaries*, vol. 4, p. 380.
172. A Countryman, in *Commentaries*, vol. 2, p. 296.
173. *Federalist* No. 36, p. 223.
174. Marcus, in *Commentaries*, vol. 4, p. 428; see *Federalist* No. 40, pp. 252–54.
175. A True Friend, in *Commentaries*, vol. 2, p. 376.
176. *Federalist* No. 23, p. 153.
177. *Federalist* No. 84, p. 515.
178. *Commentaries*, vol. 2, p. 401.
179. *Commentaries*, vol. 3, p. 199.
180. A Countryman, in *Commentaries*, vol. 2, p. 173.
181. *Federalist* No. 23, p. 156.
182. Sherman, in *Commentaries*, vol. 2, p. 387.
183. *Federalist* No. 28, p. 180.
184. *Federalist* No. 49, p. 316.
185. Brutus, in *Commentaries*, vol. 2, p. 122.
186. Ibid., p. 300.
187. *Federalist* No. 25, p. 164.
188. *Federalist* No. 3, p. 43.
189. *Debates in the Several State Conventions*, vol. 2, p. 116; *Records*, vol. 2, p. 629.
190. A True Friend, in *Commentaries*, vol. 2, p. 376.
191. *Records*, vol. 1, pp. 152–53.
192. *Federalist* No. 45, p. 291.

193. *Federalist* No. 46, p. 298.
194. *Federalist* No. 51, p. 322.
195. *Federalist* No. 57, p. 351.
196. *Federalist* No. 72, p. 437.
197. *Federalist* No. 51, p. 322.
198. Locke, *Second Treatise*, chap. 12, sec. 143, p. 410.
199. *Federalist* No. 57, p. 352.
200. *Federalist* No. 48, p. 308.
201. Ibid.
202. Mason, in *Records*, vol. 1, p. 86.
203. G. Morris, in *Records*, vol. 2, p. 76.
204. One reason for permitting two-thirds of the House and Senate to override the veto was to prevent the veto from becoming a device by which the executive could simply dictate to the legislature. Franklin claimed that in Pennsylvania "the negative of the Governor was constantly made use of to extort money. No good law whatever could be passed without a private bargain with him" (*Records*, vol. 1, p. 99).
205. *Records*, vol. 2, p. 78; see Madison, in *Records*, vol. 1, p. 139.
206. Madison, in *Records*, vol. 1, p. 421.
207. *Records*, vol. 1, p. 48. Franklin may have been an exception, but Farrand thinks not (ibid., p. 48, n.9).
208. *Records*, vol. 2, pp. 298–99.
209. *Commentaries*, vol. 3, pp. 513–14; *Federalist* No. 81, p. 482.
210. The judicial role is also less modest than the executive's veto in that the latter can be overridden by a two-thirds vote in Congress.
211. Hamilton suggests (*Federalist* No. 78) that the judiciary can drag its feet in applying unjust laws to particular cases, but not that it can overtly strike them down.
212. *Records*, vol. 2, pp. 73–75.
213. Ibid., p. 376.
214. *Federalist* No. 81, pp. 484–85.
215. *Federalist* No. 70, p. 430.
216. *Records*, vol. 2, p. 67.
217. Franklin, in *Records*, vol. 2, p. 65.
218. *Records*, vol. 2, pp. 550–52.
219. *Federalist* No. 37, p. 227.
220. *Federalist* No. 51, p. 324.
221. *Papers of Madison*, vol. 9, p. 357.
222. *Records*, vol. 1, p. 182.
223. Locke, *Second Treatise*, chap. 7, sec. 87, p. 367.
224. *Records*, vol. 1, p. 422.
225. *Federalist* No. 71, p. 432.
226. Madison, in *Records*, vol. 1, p. 422.
227. *Federalist* No. 73, p. 445.
228. Madison, in *Records*, vol. 1, p. 108.
229. Williamson, in *Records*, vol. 2, p. 376.
230. *Papers of Madison*, vol. 12, p. 207 (1789).

231. *Federalist* No. 78, p. 470.

232. *Federalist* No. 51, pp. 323–24. Madison was willing to hope that a bill of rights would have an educational effect on the majority but was not willing to rely on that prospect. Although "paper barriers" seem "too weak," "yet, as they have a tendency to impress some degree of respect for them, to establish the public opinion in their favor, and rouse the attention of the whole community, it may be one means to controul the majority from those acts to which they might be otherwise inclined" (*Papers of Madison*, vol. 12, pp. 204–5, 1789).

233. *Federalist* No. 10, pp. 79, 78.

234. G. Morris, in *Records*, vol. 1, p. 552.

235. A Federal Republican, in *Commentaries*, vol. 2, p. 260.

236. Brutus, in *Commentaries*, vol. 2, p. 122.

237. Madison, in *Records*, vol. 1, p. 428.

238. Webster, in *Pamphlets on the Constitution*, p. 40.

239. Ibid., p. 41n.

240. Hamilton, in *Debates in the Several State Conventions*, vol. 2, p. 318.

241. *Federalist* No. 51, p. 325.

242. *Records*, vol. 2, p. 451.

243. Hamilton, in *Debates in the Several State Conventions*, vol. 2, p. 305.

244. Lee, in *Commentaries*, vol. 2, p. 372.

245. *Federalist* No. 22, pp. 147–48. Some founders hoped, and some feared, that requiring two-thirds of the Senate to ratify treaties would protect particular interests (see Gerry, in *Records*, vol. 2, p. 541; and Morris, in ibid., p. 548). That provision was also defended on the grounds that, with the House of Representatives excluded for the sake of secrecy (ibid., p. 538), the Senate's small numbers made bribery a danger, and its apportionment meant that a majority of the Senate might represent a minority of the people (ibid., p. 548).

246. Montesquieu, *De l'esprit des lois*, book 11, chap. 6, p. 401.

247. Madison, in *Records*, vol. 1, p. 422.

248. I say mildly because not all property holders are wealthy.

249. Madison, in *Records*, vol. 2, p. 204n.

250. *Records*, vol. 2, pp. 201–2.

251. *Records*, vol. 1, p. 179.

252. Ibid., p. 466.

253. Fabius, in *Commentaries*, vol. 5 (forthcoming), document 716 (quoted from a typescript generously made available by the editors of *Commentaries*).

254. *Records*, vol. 1, p. 486.

255. Ibid., p. 580.

256. Mason, in *Records*, vol. 2, p. 370.

257. Lansing, in *Records*, vol. 1, p. 337.

258. *Records*, vol. 2, p. 548.

259. Agrippa, in *Complete Anti-Federalist*, vol. 4, no. 6, para. 17.

260. Ibid., para. 16.

261. *Commentaries*, vol. 1, p. 476.

262. Ibid., pp. 418–19.

263. A Citizen of New Haven, in *Commentaries*, vol. 3, pp. 280–81.

264. Ibid., p. 281.

265. Montesquieu, *De l'esprit des lois,* book 9, chap. 1, p. 370.

266. *Commentaries,* vol. 1, p. 447.

267. *Federalist* No. 10, p. 83. Although Madison gave this argument its clearest formulation, at least two other speakers at the Convention (Mason and Sherman) seem to have shared his view. See *Records,* vol. 2, pp. 273, 450.

268. *Records,* vol. 1, p. 407; see *Debates in the Several State Conventions,* vol. 2, p. 46.

269. *Records,* vol. 1, p. 154.

270. G. Morris, in *Records,* vol. 2, p. 439.

271. Madison himself regarded these provisions as an inadequate substitute for a congressional veto over the state legislatures, because majority factions in states would not confine themselves to the particular injustices that could be anticipated and defined in the Constitution's text (see *Records,* vol. 2, p. 589).

272. *Federalist* No. 72, p. 437.

273. *Federalist* No. 30, p. 191.

274. *Federalist* No. 22, p. 148.

275. Declaration of Independence.

276. Butler, in *Records,* vol. 1, p. 125.

277. *Federalist* No. 37, p. 227.

278. *Federalist* No. 22, p. 152; Declaration of Independence.

279. Locke, *Second Treatise,* chap. 1, sec. 1, p. 308.

280. Ibid., chap. 8, sec. 98, pp. 376–77.

281. Declaration of Independence.

282. Hobbes, *Leviathan,* chap. 19, pp. 239–40.

283. Wilson, in *Records,* vol. 2, p. 125.

284. *Federalist* No. 78, p. 470.

285. Blackstone, *Commentaries on the Laws of England,* vol. 1, book 1, chap. 3, p. 183.

286. Hume, "Of the Original Contract," in *Essays,* pp. 457–59.

287. Gerry, in *Records,* vol. 2, p. 89.

288. Ellsworth, in *Records,* vol. 2, p. 91.

289. Madison, in *Records,* vol. 1, pp. 122–23.

290. King, in *Records,* vol. 2, p. 92.

291. *Federalist* No. 1, p. 33.

292. Jean-Jacques Rousseau, *Du Contract social,* in *Œuvres complètes,* vol. 3, edited by Marcel Raymond (Editions Gallimard: Bibliothèque de la Pléiade, 1964), book 2, chap. 7, p. 381.

293. Ibid., p. 383.

294. *Records,* vol. 1, pp. 87, 288.

295. *Federalist* No. 1, p. 34.

296. Randolph, in *Records,* vol. 1, p. 88.

297. *Federalist* No. 1, p. 35.

298. *Records,* vol. 1, p. 214; see *Commentaries,* vol. 3, pp. 438, 498.

299. *Federalist* No. 49, p. 314.

300. *Federalist* No. 31, p. 194; *Commentaries,* vol. 1, p. 330.

301. *Records,* vol. 1, pp. 125, 491.
302. Madison, in *Records,* vol. 1, p. 215.
303. *Federalist* No. 40, p. 253.
304. *Federalist* No. 71, p. 432.
305. Butler, in *Commentaries,* vol. 1, p. 352.
306. *Federalist* No. 40, p. 253; No. 37, p. 230.
307. *Commentaries,* vol. 1, p. 352.
308. Martin, in *Records,* vol. 2, p. 364.
309. Wilson, in *Records,* vol. 1, p. 587.
310. G. Morris, in *Records,* vol. 1, p. 588.
311. Sherman, in *Records,* vol. 2, p. 369. Some argued that the Constitution was an improvement over the status quo regarding slavery; for example, its implication that the slave trade would be banned in twenty years laid a "solid foundation . . . for exploding the principles of negro slavery" (An American Citizen, in *Commentaries,* vol. 1, p. 432).
312. In this case, the problem might seem to be caused by an incomplete practice of consent, that is, the fact that the slaves were excluded from the ratification process. But the possibility that slaves who could vote might have been outvoted anyway means that partiality complicates consent for any society not perfectly united, that is, for any society.
313. Madison, in *Commentaries,* vol. 3, pp. 327–28.
314. See *Records,* vol. 1, p. 530; *Commentaries,* vol. 4, p. 71.
315. *Records,* vol. 1, p. 452.
316. R. Livingston, in *Debates in the Several State Conventions,* vol. 2, p. 209.
317. An Old Whig, in *Commentaries,* vol. 1, p. 500.
318. Madison, in *Records,* vol. 1, p. 314.
319. See *Records,* vol. 1, p. 324.
320. Montesquieu, *De l'esprit des lois,* book 9, chap. 1, p. 369.
321. *Records,* vol. 2, p. 475.
322. Ibid., pp. 469, 477.
323. By Madison's calculation, even the smallest ten states would constitute a majority of the American population (see *Records,* vol. 2, p. 469); so most likely combinations of nine should have as well. The nine-state rule was more likely to thwart a consenting majority than to empower a consenting minority.
324. Paradoxically, this aspect of the procedure might seem to imply that America was not yet a single society of individuals or of states; but if that were the case, only one state, not nine, would be needed to institute the Constitution. A nine-state union would have represented the majority's decision to dissolve the old society, and a unanimous consent by a smaller group to create a new one; but a thirteen-state ratification (which some founders correctly calculated would be promoted by a nine-state requirement) makes clear that the preexisting society intended to perpetuate itself by adopting a better form of government.
325. *Federalist* No. 14, p. 100; No. 65, p. 396.
326. Declaration of Independence.
327. *Federalist* No. 71, p. 432.

328. *Records,* vol. 1, p. 339.
329. *Commentaries,* vol. 1, p. 419.
330. *Federalist* No. 37, pp. 226, 227.
331. Blackstone, *Commentaries on the Laws of England,* vol. 1, Introduction, sec. 2, pp. 48–49.
332. Curtius, in *Commentaries,* vol. 1, p. 269.
333. An American Citizen, in *Ratification by the States,* vol. 2, p. 140.
334. *Federalist* No. 70, p. 423.
335. *Records,* vol. 2, p. 202.
336. Ibid., pp. 202–3.
337. Ibid., p. 204.
338. Ibid., p. 208.
339. *Records,* vol. 1, p. 145.
340. *Records,* vol. 4, pp. 17–18.
341. Madison, in *Records,* vol. 2, p. 236.
342. An American Citizen, in *Commentaries,* vol. 1, p. 432.
343. *Northampton Hampshire Gazette, in Commentaries,* vol. 1, p. 517.
344. Wilson, in *Records,* vol. 1, p. 375.
345. R. Livingston, in *Debates in the Several State Conventions,* vol. 2, p. 293.
346. Franklin, in *Records,* vol. 2, p. 249.
347. Wilson, in *Records,* vol. 2, p. 237; see p. 491.
348. See *Commentaries,* vol. 2, pp. 184–85.
349. *Commentaries,* vol. 3, p. 545.
350. Ibid.
351. Pinckney, in *Records,* vol. 1, p. 398.
352. Aristotle, *The Politics,* translated by Carnes Lord (Chicago, Ill.: University of Chicago Press, 1984), book 3, chap. 10, p. 100.
353. Cato, in *Commentaries,* vol. 2, pp. 428–29.
354. *Records,* vol. 2, p. 123.
355. *Federalist* No. 71, p. 432.
356. Madison, in *Records,* vol. 1, p. 72. This fact makes elective monarchies "turbulent and unhappy"—indicating that even interest will not be secure if pride is not given its due.
357. *Records,* vol. 1, p. 321; see vol. 2, p. 10.
358. Madison's contrast between justice and safety was formulated by Luther Martin as a contrast between pride and freedom. Martin thought "the feelings of *pride* and *ambition* . . . ought not to be gratified at the expence of *freedom*" (*Commentaries,* vol. 3, p. 250). In contrast to the view that human freedom includes the proud, ambitious claim to an equal share in rule, Martin indicates that the "freedom" he has in mind is what Madison called safety: the avoidance of the *"foot* on *our necks"* that proportional representation would confer on the larger states (ibid., p. 253).
359. *Records,* vol. 2, p. 207.
360. *Records,* vol. 1, p. 487.
361. Pinckney, in *Records,* vol. 1, p. 398.
362. *Federalist* No. 39, p. 240.
363. *Federalist* No. 63, p. 387.

364. *Commentaries*, vol. 1, p. 47.
365. *Debates in the Several State Conventions*, vol. 2, p. 253.
366. Ibid., p. 302.
367. *Works of Wilson*, vol. 2, p. 778.
368. Madison, in *Records*, vol. 1, p. 138.
369. *Federalist* No. 10, p. 79.
370. *Federalist* No. 50, p. 320.
371. *Debates in the Several State Conventions*, vol. 2, p. 252.
372. Iredell, in *Debates in the Several State Conventions*, vol. 4, p. 97.
373. *Federalist* No. 76, p. 455; No. 58, p. 360; No. 55, p. 342.
374. *Federalist* No. 58, p. 360.
375. *Du conract social*, bk. 3, chap. 15, p. 430.
376. *Federalist* No. 8, p. 68.
377. *Federalist* No. 49, p. 314.
378. *Federalist* No. 51, p. 322.
379. *Federalist* No. 49, p. 315.
380. *Federalist* No. 10, p. 81.
381. *Federalist* No. 9, p. 72.
382. According to Fisher Ames, having the Senate elected directly by the people would "totally obliterate the federal features of the Constitution. What would become of the state governments, and on whom would devolve the duty of defending them against the encroachments of the federal government?" (*Debates in the Several State Conventions*, vol. 2, p. 46).

Chapter 4: Jefferson's Pulse of Republican Reformation

1. Thomas Jefferson, "Autobiography," in *The Works of Thomas Jefferson*, ed. Paul Leicester Ford ("Federal Edition"; New York: G. P. Putnam's Sons, 1904–5), vol. 1, pp. 66–67; hereafter cited as *Works*.

2. The text of the 126 bills reported by the Committee of Revisors, along with much useful editorial matter, is in *The Papers of Thomas Jefferson*, ed. Julian P. Boyd et al. (Princeton: Princeton University Press, 1950–), vol. 2, pp. 305–665; hereafter cited as *Papers*. Bills will be cited by number parenthetically in the text. Most of Virginia's seventeenth- and eighteenth-century laws are collected in the edition of William W. Hening, *The Statutes at Large; Being a Collection of All the Laws of Virginia* (Richmond, 1809–23); hereafter cited as Hening. For present purposes I accept the conclusions to which Boyd was led in trying to determine the extent of Jefferson's responsibility for the revisal; *Papers*, vol. 2, pp. 319–21. An asterisk marks bills not attributed by Boyd to Jefferson.

3. See William Wirt, *The Letters of the British Spy* (Chapel Hill: University of North Carolina Press, 1970), pp. 231–32 (also cited in *Papers*, vol. 2, pp. 534–35); and Jackson Turner Main, "Government by the People: The American Revolution and the Democratization of the Legislatures," *William and Mary Quarterly*, 3d ser., vol. 23 (1966), pp. 396, 402–3, 407.

4. In entitling others, who live in states that are "parties to the American

confederation," to the rights, privileges, and immunities of free Virginians, Bill No. 55 is careful to specify only free white inhabitants, "paupers, vagabonds and fugitives from justice excepted."

The liberalization of practice implicit in Bill No. 55's offer of naturalization to "all white persons" is easily overlooked. See the traces of Jefferson's argument and pen in his revision of Pendleton's earlier naturalization bill of October 1776 "for the encouragement of Foreign Protestants to settle in this Countrey"; *Papers*, vol. 1, pp. 558–59.

5. Thomas Jefferson, *Notes on the State of Virginia*, ed. William Peden (Chapel Hill: University of North Carolina Press, 1954), p. 118; hereafter cited as *Notes on Virginia*. By the terms of his 1776 draft of a constitution Jefferson would have had the state provide "every person of full age" with more than enough land in the country to qualify as an elector; *Papers*, vol. 1, pp. 358, 362. In both his 1783 draft of a constitution and his 1794 notes for a constitution Jefferson would have guaranteed the right to vote to anyone enrolled in the militia; see ibid., vol. 6, p. 296; and Jefferson, *Works*, vol. 8, p. 159.

6. Act for the Revision of the Laws, October 1776, 9 Hening, pp. 175–77 (reprinted in *Papers*, vol. 1, pp. 562–63).

7. This is no empty gesture, paired as it is with a major change in a basic institution of the Virginia polity; see *Papers*, vol. 2, p. 582 n, and vol. 1, pp. 361, 606–7.

8. Compare 6 Hening, p. 478 (1755), and *Papers*, vol. 2, p. 423 n. See also *Notes on Virginia*, pp. 133–34, for the praise of local relief and local caring.

9. *Papers*, vol. 1, pp. 344, 352–53, 362–63; *Notes on Virginia*, pp. 164–65. The revisal's policy regarding the inheritance of property is treated in the following section.

10. Here, John Quincy Adams asserted (January 18, 1831), lies buried one of the main reasons Jefferson displayed uncharacteristic conservatism in opposing Pendleton's proposal that the revisers begin by abolishing the entire existing system of laws and then replace them with an institute of their own design. To have gone along with this plan would have meant, among other things, that the revisers would be restoring slavery after having purged it from the statute books. Speaking in their own names they would be assuming "to themselves all the odium of establishing it as a positive institution, directly in the face of all the principles they had proclaimed." But while coolly noting (January 29, 1831) that Jefferson "had not the spirit of martyrdom," Adams nonetheless never doubted that the same Jefferson "could not, or would not, prostitute the faculties of his mind to the vindication of that slavery which from his soul he abhorred"; Charles Francis Adams, ed., *Memoirs of John Quincy Adams, Containing Portions of His Diary from 1795 to 1848* (Philadelphia: J. B. Lippincott, 1874–77), vol. 8, pp. 283–85, 299–300. Adams's reading of motives, confided to the pages of his diary, is rendered more sinister by John T. Noonan, Jr., who faults Jefferson and Wythe less for "not attempting the impossible"—abolishing slavery altogether—than for shabbily camouflaging their personal responsibility for its continuance; John T. Noonan, Jr., *Persons and Masks of the Law: Cardozo, Holmes, Jefferson, and*

Wythe as Makers of the Masks (New York: Farrar, Straus and Giroux, 1976), pp. 49–54. As the following pages make clear, this is not my reading of the matter.

Even the status of the reported bill is at issue. Was it "a mere digest of the existing laws," a decoy introduced with a view to a later and more timely liberalizing amendment? (See Jefferson, "Autobiography," *Works*, vol. 1, p. 76; *Notes on Virginia*, pp. 137–38.) Or, rather, was it already, as Boyd would have it, "a definite proposal for a system of gradual emancipation"? (See the judicious remarks in *Papers*, vol. 2, pp. 472–73 n.)

11. Jefferson calculated the 1782 ratio of free inhabitants to slaves "nearly as 11 to 10," while adding immediately that natural increase "under the mild treatment our slaves experience" was furthering "this blot in our country"; *Notes on Virginia*, p. 87.

12. In his "Draught of a Fundamental Constitution for the Commonwealth of Virginia" of 1783, Jefferson would have forbidden the General Assembly "to permit the introduction of any more slaves to reside in this state, or the continuance of slavery beyond the generation which shall be living on the 31st. day of December 1800; all persons born after that day being hereby declared free"; *Papers*, vol. 6, p. 298. The silent presumption—and, for Jefferson, foregone conclusion—was that this massive change would be followed by the wholesale emigration and colonization of blacks elsewhere. For Jefferson's underlying justification, see *Notes on Virginia*, pp. 138–143.

13. Edmund Burke to Henry Dundas, April 9, 1792, in *Selected Letters of Edmund Burke*, ed. Harvey C. Mansfield, Jr. (Chicago: University of Chicago Press, 1984), pp. 297–300; and Noonan, *Persons and Masks of the Law*, p. 52.

14. *Notes on Virginia*, p. 138.

15. Jefferson to David Rittenhouse, July 19, 1778, *Papers*, vol. 2, pp. 202–3.

16. Cited in ibid., p. 346 n.5.

17. "Proposed Resolution for Rotation of Membership in the Continental Congress," July 1, 1776, ibid., vol. 1, p. 411. See also ibid., vol. 2, p. 17 n, and Jefferson's bill for regulating the appointment of delegates to Congress, as enacted, 9 Hening, p. 299 (1777).

18. Needless to say, the act of 1745 on which much of Bill No. 33 is modeled had made no provision for public disclosure of salaries (5 Hening, p. 326).

19. Compare Bill No. 5 with 9 Hening, pp. 267, 313–14 (1777), 11 Hening, pp. 477, 494 (1784); and see *Papers*, vol. 2, p. 355 n.3.

20. Jefferson to George Wythe, March 1, 1779, *Papers*, vol. 2, p. 235. On Jefferson's possible authorship of this, the most egregious restraint of trade in the revisal, see ibid., p. 589 n.2.

21. Jefferson, "Autobiography," pp. 58–59. Of considerable value in asserting this revolutionary intent are the comments of St. George Tucker, ed., *Blackstone's Commentaries: With Notes of Reference, to the Constitution and Laws, of the Federal Government of the United States; and of the Commonwealth of Virginia* (Philadelphia, 1803); see especially vol. 2, p. 119 n.14, and vol. 2, app. n.B, pp. 18–24, 27–28, where the talk is repeatedly of utter incompatibility, dramatic opposition, and irreconcilability, when comparing rules that are "the off-

spring of feudal barbarism and prejudice" with "the policy and intention of the framers of our law." (My citation is to the volume and page numbers standard for editions of Blackstone.) A close study of wills, court records, and other transactions suggests that recourse to these feudal devices was not as widespread in Virginia as has been imagined; C. Ray Keim, "Primogeniture and Entail in Colonial Virginia," *William and Mary Quarterly,* 3d ser., vol. 25 (1968), pp. 545–86. Their cumulative effect, however, might have been or become significant.

22. *Papers,* vol. 1, pp. 560–62; 9 Hening, pp. 226–27 (1776). Since by a law of 1727 Virginia had annexed slaves to the land, rendering them too subject to limitations in tail (4 Hening, pp. 225–26), later abolitions of entail covered both land and slaves.

23. See the language of the preamble to Jefferson's earlier bill in *Papers,* vol. 1, p. 560.

24. John Locke, *Two Treatises of Government,* bk. 1, sec. 90.

25. This point is somewhat blurred in Boyd's otherwise excellent statement in *Papers,* vol. 1, pp. 330–31. The immediately relevant provisions in Jefferson's 1776 drafts of a constitution are in ibid., pp. 344, 352–53, 362–63. The most striking of Jefferson's assessments of the work of revisal is in Jefferson, "Autobiography," pp. 77–78.

26. See Jefferson's first draft of a constitution, *Papers,* vol. 1, p. 345; and Tucker, *Blackstone's Commentaries,* vol. 2, p. 244 n.4.

27. *Papers,* vol. 2, p. 506 n.4; see also Jefferson to Pendleton, August 26, 1776, ibid., vol. 1, p. 505. My discussion in this and the following paragraph draws on material in ibid., vol. 2, pp. 504–6 n.

28. Compare Tucker, *Blackstone's Commentaries,* vol. 4, pp. 60–62, 436, with Thomas Jefferson, *Reports of Cases Determined in the General Court of Virginia. From 1730, to 1740; and from 1768 to 1772* (Charlottesville, 1829), app., pp. 137–42 (the latter is reprinted in Jefferson, *Works,* vol. 1, pp. 453–64). A possible explanation that dissolves this incongruity and renders Jefferson's treatment of religion more consistent than the text allows would see this provision in Bill No. 64 as another instance of his self-proclaimed rational hostility to priestcraft. By this account the revisal is willing to promote diverse religions provided they are stripped of any civil powers and are respectful of civil necessity and the reason of the people.

29. Jefferson's account of how the House of Burgesses, alarmed by news of the passage of the Boston Port Act, came to proclaim a day of fasting, humiliation, and prayer appears in Jefferson, "Autobiography," pp. 11–12. (The resolution itself, May 24, 1774, is in *Papers,* vol. 1, pp. 105–6.) Jefferson's narrative is more than sufficient evidence of the chasm separating Robert Carter Nicholas, who introduced the resolution, and Jefferson, who could recall how he and his political allies "rummaged over" precedents, "cooked up" a resolution, and picked Nicholas to be its mover on account of his "grave & religious character."

30. See 3 Hening, pp. 72–73 (1691), 138–39 (1696), 360–61 (1705).

31. 12 Hening, pp. 336–37.

32. Jefferson would have discriminated between public and private donations. Where church property was traceable to public levies—"contributions on the people independent of their good will"—he would have reserved the clerical incumbents' "rights to such Glebe lands during their lives" but no longer. Private donations might be enjoyed perpetually; see *Papers*, vol. 1, pp. 530–33, and 9 Hening, p. 165 (1776).

33. See *Papers*, vol. 2, p. 423 n; and Charles Ramsdell Lingley, *The Transition in Virginia from Colony to Commonwealth* (New York: Columbia University, 1910), pp. 200–211.

34. 4 Hening, pp. 42–45.

35. Compare the old law—3 Hening, pp. 150 (1696), 441–42 (1705); 4 Hening, pp. 245–46 (1730); 6 Hening, pp. 81–82 (1748)—with the later reluctant accommodations—10 Hening, pp. 361–63 (1780); 11 Hening, pp. 281–82 (1783), 503–4 (1784). It is not surprising that Bill No. 86 never got beyond a second reading.

Agitation over the marriage law was incessant at this time. See William Taylor Thom, *The Struggle for Religious Freedom in Virginia: The Baptists*, "Johns Hopkins University Studies in Historical and Political Science," Ser. 18, Nos. 10–12 (Baltimore: The Johns Hopkins Press, 1900), pp. 62–63, 66–75; William Henry Foote, *Sketches of Virginia, Historical and Biographical (First Series)* (Philadelphia, 1850), pp. 329–40; and Hamilton J. Eckenrode, *Separation of Church and State in Virginia: A Study in the Development of the Revolution*, "Special Report of the Department of Archives and History, Virginia State Library" (Richmond, 1910), pp. 66–73.

36. Of the 126 bills in the revisal, only seven have preambles: No. 7* (giving emergency powers to the governor and council), No. 64 (proportioning crimes and punishments), No. 79 (for the more general diffusion of knowledge), No. 80 (amending the charter of the College of William and Mary), No. 82 (establishing religious freedom), No. 112 (providing help for paupers in their suits), and No. 120* (changing to the Gregorian calendar). Most (or arguably, all) of these bear Jefferson's unmistakable mark. On the function of legislative preludes, see Plato, *Laws*, 722D–723D.

37. *Notes on Virginia*, p. 148. Had this bill been enacted, Jefferson mused some thirty-five years later, "our work [of laying "the axe to the root of Pseudo-aristocracy"] would have been compleat"; letter to John Adams, October 28, 1813, in Lester J. Cappon, ed., *The Adams-Jefferson Letters: The Complete Correspondence between Thomas Jefferson and Abigail and John Adams* (Chapel Hill: University of North Carolina Press, 1959), vol. 2, pp. 389–90.

38. *Notes on Virginia*, p. 146. Julian P. Boyd asserts that elitism of this kind "never became and possibly could not become an explicit object of any democratic society"; *Papers*, vol. 2, p. 534 n. Jefferson clearly thought otherwise. He chose to proclaim rather than conceal his judgment that popular government could not possibly do without the very thing that threatened it—the talents and ambitions of its rarest types. In this respect Jefferson did not differ from other founders as politically diverse as John Adams, Alexander Hamilton, James Madison, and George Washington. Jefferson, however,

chose to defend this policy in terms that stressed what today's jargon would call its cost effectiveness. The reluctance of the legislature to establish, and then of the county governments to implement, a public education system suggests that Jefferson did not mistake the obstacle to success.

39. *Notes on Virginia,* p. 148.

40. "The historical introduction is soured by an unworthy and unnecessary resentment of the past for not being what Jefferson would have liked it to be, and this biliousness seems to have affected the author as he worked on the body of the text so that his habitual lucidity for once escaped him and the whole draft reads like a parody of those acts of which he himself had complained" [then quoting from Jefferson, "Autobiography," p. 70]; J. E. Morpurgo, *Their Majesties' Royall Colledge: William and Mary in the Seventeenth and Eighteenth Centuries* (Williamsburg: College of William and Mary in Virginia, 1976), p. 185.

41. *Papers,* vol. 2, pp. 325, 599 (Bill No. 102, opening), 320–21.

42. The breadth and sweep of Jefferson's reasoning here ought to be compared with the cautious arguments of opposing counsel in *Bracken* v. *The Visitors of William & Mary College,* 3 Call's Reports (Va.) 573 (1790), esp. pp. 590 (John Taylor), and 592–94 (John Marshall).

43. Jefferson, "Autobiography," pp. 75–76; *Notes on Virginia,* pp. 147–48, 150–51.

44. Classifications were not a matter that Jefferson took lightly. See the perceptive discussion by Douglas L. Wilson in "Sowerby Revisited: The Unfinished Catalogue of Thomas Jefferson's Library," *William and Mary Quarterly,* 3d ser., vol. 41 (1984), pp. 619–25.

45. "Autobiography," p. 75; *Notes on Virginia,* p. 149; *Papers,* vol. 2, p. 203.

46. The revisal's silence about freedom of political opinion and of the press must at least be noted. To the extent that it touches on these concerns, it is in the form of requiring assurances of fidelity to the commonwealth from electors, civil officials, militia officers, clerics, lawyers, teachers, and professors. In his 1776 drafts of a constitution Jefferson would have guaranteed that printing presses be free, limiting exceptions to private action for private injury; *Papers,* vol. 1, pp. 344–45, 353, 363. But consider this ardent revolutionary's uncertain thoughts about "seditious preaching or conversation against the authority of the civil government"; ibid., pp. 344, 347 n.10, 353.

47. By this account, No. 79 (more general diffusion of knowledge), No. 80 (William and Mary), No. 81 (public library), and No. 82 (religious freedom) belong together as serving a single intention—enabling free men to be their own best guardians of their rights. Alternatively, No. 82 would be the first of a series of bills devoted to supporting religion and including No. 83 (saving Anglican church property), No. 84 (punishing disturbers of religious worship and Sabbath breakers), No. 85* (appointing days of public fasting and thanksgiving), and No. 86* (annulling marriages prohibited by the Levitical law). It is possible to assert that the arrangement of the 126 bills is not simply random without being obliged to account for all its details and without being driven to overingenious explanations. As sensible and conscientious draftsmen, the

revisers took the trouble to group bills bearing on related topics before presenting the legislature with the results of their labors of two and one-half years. This is not to say that the logic of their groupings is always obvious. In support of the reading offered in my text, consider James Madison to Thomas Jefferson, January 22, 1786, quoted in ibid., vol. 2, p. 549 n.

48. Differences between the bill as proposed and the act as adopted (12 Hening, pp. 84–86) are detailed in the numbered notes in *Papers*, vol. 2, pp. 552–53.

49. Jefferson's notes on Locke and Shaftesbury are in *Papers*, vol. 1, pp. 544–50; Adam Smith, *An Inquiry into the Nature and Causes of the Wealth of Nations*, ed. Edwin Cannan (New York: Modern Library, 1937), pp. 743–45. For the textual emendation, see *Papers*, vol. 2, p. 552 n.5.

50. On the sole authority of Jefferson's later gloss, these two phrases from the preamble of Bill No. 82 are to be read as appositional, leading one to wonder what that religion is; see *Papers*, vol. 2, p. 552 n.3.

The limits of a legislative sanction probably account for the absence from the report of the Committee of Revisors of the two most prominent pieces of Virginian lawmaking. Neither the Declaration of Rights (9 Hening, pp. 109–12) nor the Constitution of 1776 (9 Hening, pp. 112–19) is proposed for reenactment. They figure only as the report's last word, so to speak, as the most visible and notable exceptions listed in the bill repealing earlier acts of Parliament and of the General Assembly (No. 126*). In making these particular exceptions, the revisers in effect only reasserted Jefferson's belief that those necessary but extralegal actions of the interregnum legislature exposed Virginians to "the hazard of having no fundamental rights at all." A proper basis could not be found in ordinary acts of legislation: "To render a form of government unalterable by ordinary acts of assembly, the people must delegate persons with special powers"; *Notes on Virginia*, pp. 121–25. Thus leaving those foundations of Virginian liberty in place without reenacting them was tantamount to declaring that only an authority superior to that of any legislature, the authority or personal consent of the people, could set matters on a solid and proper footing. This is a persistent Jeffersonian theme; see *Papers*, vol. 1, pp. 347, 354, 357, 364, and vol. 6, pp. 294–95.

51. See Jefferson's "Declaration of Independence," *Papers*, vol. 1, pp. 318, 426.

Chapter 5: The Social Theory of the Founders

1. References to the debates at the federal convention are by date to facilitate reference to either Madison's *Notes of Debates in the Federal Convention of 1787* (New York: W. W. Norton, 1969) or *The Records of the Federal Convention of 1787*, ed. Max Farrand, 4 vols. (New Haven: Yale University Press, 1966). Abbreviations and contractions have been spelled out and some punctuation altered.

2. J. Franklin Jameson, *The American Revolution Considered as a Social*

Movement (Princeton: Princeton University Press, 1967); compare p. 27 to pp. 32–39.

3. Madison may have added this footnote, together with one asserting that he spoke to aid Dr. McClurg, whom he held in particular regard and who was unaccustomed to public debate, because while Madison said then behind closed doors that he was "not apprehensive of being thought to favor any step towards monarchy" he was later apprehensive of precisely that when facing the prospect of publication and recalling how Hamilton had long suffered from leaked accounts of his allegedly monarchic plan. But Madison's original record of his contribution to the debate indicates that he was primarily supporting executive independence and doubted the propriety of the proposal for a tenure of good behavior though "respect for the mover entitled his proposition to a fair hearing and discussion, until a less objectionable expedient should be applied for guarding against a dangerous union of the Legislative and Executive departments."

4. This curious episode is not mentioned in Charles C. Thatch's *The Creation of the Presidency 1775–1789* (Baltimore: Johns Hopkins University Press, 1969); receives one sentence in Farrand's *The Framing of the Constitution of the United States* (New Haven: Yale University Press, 1913), p. 117; and appears in Clinton Rossiter's *1787: The Grand Convention* (New York: Mentor Books, 1968), p. 216, only as McClurg's having somehow put his foot in his mouth.

5. Later when defending the reeligibility of the president in the original Constitution in *Federalist* No. 72, Hamilton invoked "the love of fame, the ruling passion of the noblest minds, which would prompt a man to plan and undertake extensive and arduous enterprises for the public benefit."

6. Jefferson on "those who labor in the earth" as "the chosen people of God," in Query XIX of *Notes on the State of Virginia,* in *The Portable Thomas Jefferson,* ed. Merrill D. Peterson (New York: Viking, 1975), p. 217.

7. *The Political Writings of John Adams,* ed. George A. Peek, Jr. (Indianapolis: Bobbs-Merrill, 1954), p. 115.

8. "Democracy and *The Federalist:* A Reconsideration of the Framers' Intent," *American Political Science Review,* vol. 53 (1959) pp. 52–68, p. 59 n. 8.

9. Farrand, *Records of the Federal Convention of 1787,* vol. 2, p. 204 n. 17.

10. Marvin Meyers, ed., *The Mind of the Founder: Sources of the Political Thought of James Madison* (Hanover, N.H.: University Press of New England, 1981), pp. 393–400.

11. Ibid., pp. 406–08.

12. Ibid., 397.

13. Ibid., pp. 397, 407–08.

14. Diamond, "Democracy and *The Federalist,*" p. 66.

15. *The Papers of James Madison,* ed. Robert A. Rutland et al. (Chicago: University of Chicago Press, 1977), vol. 10, p. 213.

16. Meyers, *Mind of the Founder,* p. 413. See also Mason (May 31).

17. Morton J. Frisch, ed., *Selected Writings and Speeches of Alexander Hamilton* (Washington, D.C.: American Enterprise Institute, 1985), pp. 209–10.

Chapter 6: The Scottish Enlightenment and the Liberal Political Tradition

1. Compare Garry Wills, *Inventing America* (New York: Doubleday, 1978); *Explaining America* (New York: Doubleday, 1980); Henry F. May, *The Enlightenment in America* (Oxford: Oxford University Press, 1976); Douglas Sloan, *The Scottish Enlightenment and the American College Ideal* (New York: Teachers College Press, 1971); and Morton White, *The Philosophy of the American Revolution* (Oxford: Oxford University Press, 1978).

2. Compare Gladys Bryson, *Man and Society: The Scottish Enquiry of the Eighteenth Century* (Princeton: Princeton University Press, 1945), p. 1; Henry Thomas Buckle, *On Scotland and the Scotch Intellect* (Chicago: University of Chicago Press, 1970), pp. 238–244; S. A. Grave, *The Scottish Philosophy of Common Sense* (Oxford: Clarendon Press, 1960), p. 1; Friedrich von Hayek, *Individualism and the Economic Order* (London: Routledge & K. Paul, 1949), pp. 3–13; Wills, *Inventing America,* pp. 187–190, 232, 292; and Nichole Phillipson, "The Scottish Enlightenment," in *The Enlightenment in National Context,* ed. Roy Porter and Mikulas Teich (Cambridge: Cambridge University Press, 1981), pp. 19–40.

3. For indications of the internal disputes among the thinkers of the Scottish Enlightenment, see *The Correspondence of Adam Smith,* ed. Ernest Campbell Mossner and Ian Simpson Ross (Oxford: Clarendon Press, 1977), pp. 164, 169, 34, in particular. See also Dugald Stewart's *Account of the Life and Writings of Thomas Reid, Works* (London), vol. 10, pp. 251–259.

4. May, *Enlightenment in America,* p. 344.

5. Compare James McCosh, *The Scottish Philosophy* (New York: AMS Press, 1975), pp. 2–7.

6. Compare note 2.

7. J. G. A. Pocock, *The Machiavellian Moment* (Princeton: Princeton University Press, 1975), pp. 493–505; *Virtue, Commerce and History* (Cambridge: Cambridge University Press, 1985), especially chap. 2; *Wealth and Virtue: The Shaping of Political Economy in the Scottish Enlightenment,* ed. Istvan Hont and Michael Ignatieff (Cambridge: Cambridge University Press, 1983). For a good summary of the major tenets of the civic humanist tradition as understood by these scholars, see John Robertson, "The Scottish Enlightenment at the Limits of the Civic Tradition," pp. 138–139; for Pocock's own formulation, see Hont and Ignatieff, eds., *Wealth and Virtue,* pp. 235–236.

8. Compare James Moore and Michael Silverthorne, "Gershom Carmichael and the Natural Jurisprudence Tradition in Eighteenth Century Scotland," and Donald Winch, "Adam Smith's 'Enduring Particular Result,'" in Hont and Ignatieff, eds., *Wealth and Virtue,* pp. 73–88, 253–270. Also see Moore and Silverthorne, "Natural Sociability and Natural Rights in the Moral Philosophy of Gershom Carmichael," *Philosophers of the Scottish Enlightenment,* ed. V. Hope (Edinburgh: Edinburgh University Press, 1984), pp. 1–13. For Pocock's response, see "Cambridge Paradigms and Scotch Philosophers," in Hont and Ignatieff, eds., *Wealth and Virtue,* pp. 235–252.

9. McCosh, *Scottish Philosophy,* pp. 28–29.

10. Dugald Stewart, *Works,* vol. 1, p. 216.

11. Ibid., p. 484; see also pp. 246, 251, 479, 551; Stewart cites Locke's political and educational writings, as well as the *Essay concerning Human Understanding,* as having great influence over the Scots.

12. See Francis Hutcheson, *Illustrations upon the Moral Sense and Inquiry into the Original of our Ideas of Beauty and Virtue, Works* (Hildesheim: 1917), vols. 1–2; David Hume, *Enquiry Concerning the Principles of Morals,* chap. 1, appendix 1; Adam Smith, *Theory of Moral Sentiments* (Oxford: Clarendon Press, 1976); Henry Home, Lord Kames, *Essays on the Principles of Morality and Natural Religion* (Hildesheim: G. Olms Press, 1976); Adam Ferguson, *An Essay on the History of Civil Society* (Edinburgh: Edinburgh University Press, 1966), pt. 1, sec. 4; Thomas Reid, *Essays on the Active Powers of the Human Mind* (Cambridge, Mass.. MIT Press, 1969), nos 3, 5; Reid, however, understands moral approval to be closer to a rational insight or intuition than to a sense or feeling, as does Ferguson in a later work (*Principles of Moral and Political Science* [New York: 1977], pt. 2, chap. 2, sec. 3). For a useful examination of the history of this concept, see David D. Raphael, *The Moral Sense* (Oxford: Oxford University Press, 1947).

13. For a discussion of this, see Thomas L. Pangle's chapter in this volume.

14. Anthony, Earl of Shaftesbury, *Characteristics of Men, Manners, Opinions, Times,* Treatise 4.

15. See Hutcheson's *System of Moral Philosophy* (New York: A. M. Kelley, 1968), vol. 1, pp. 52, 59, 61–62; *Inquiry,* preface, iii-xi, pp. 109, 245. In what follows, see *Inquiry,* pp. 103–6, 129–31; Hutcheson, *System,* 1, pp. 61–79.

16. Hutcheson, *Inquiry,* p. 160.

17. Ibid., p. 162; compare also pp. 289–91.

18. Hutcheson, *System,* 1, pp. 268, 271–74.

19. Ibid., p. 293.

20. Ibid., p. 178.

21. Ibid., pp. 145, 268–69, 286–7; *Inquiry,* p. 195–220.

22. McCosh, *Scottish Philosophy,* pp. 30–31, 34, 70–72, 74–75; Raphael, *Moral Sense,* pp. 33–41; and Hutcheson, *System,* 1, p. 58: "And 'tis pretty plain that *reason* is only a subservient power to our ultimate determinations; either of perception or will . . . . Reason can only direct to the means or compare two ends previously constituted by some other immediate powers."

23. Compare David Hume, *Enquiry,* sec. 9, part 1; *Treatise of Human Nature* (Oxford: Oxford University Press, 1978), p. 591; Adam Smith, *Theory of Moral Sentiments,* pp. 23–24, 262–64, 300–5.

24. See Smith's critique of Hutcheson's doctrine of the moral sense, *Theory of Moral Sentiments,* pp. 321–27; also see Hume's *Treatise,* pp. 574–91.

25. Smith, *Theory of Moral Sentiments,* p. 108.

26. Ibid., p. 110.

27. Ibid., p. 13.

28. See John Locke, *Essay Concerning Human Understanding,* bk. 2, chap. 28, sec. 10–12; Jean-Jacques Rousseau, *Discourse on the Origin and Foundation of*

Inequality among Mankind (New York: St. Martin's Press, 1967), pp. 200–3, 256. If Smith differs at all from these thinkers, it is perhaps in his greater optimism regarding the power of these social sentiments to tame self-love in the majority of men.

29. See Locke, *Essay*, bk. 2, chap. 21, secs. 31–46. Compare with *Theory of Moral Sentiments*, pp. 181–85.

30. Hutcheson had also considered the possibility that morality was founded upon "sympathy" but had rejected this alternative because of its hedonistic implications. See Hutcheson, *Inquiry*, 140–43; Hutcheson, *System*, book 1, pp. 47–50. Also see "A Letter to Dr. Adam Smith" and "Letters on Infidelity," in *The Works of the Right Reverend George Horne* (London: 1818), vol. 4, pp. 329–421; see also Phillipson, "The Scottish Enlightenment," pp. 36–38.

31. See Wills, *Inventing America;* Carolyn Robbins, *The Eighteenth Century Commonwealthmen* (Cambridge, Mass.: Harvard University Press, 1959), pp. 185–95; Winch, "Adam Smith's 'Enduring Particular Result' "; John P. Diggins, *The Lost Soul of American Politics* (Chicago: University of Chicago Press, 1984), pp. 10–11, 33–34, 42–43, 80, 84. Ronald Hamowy's review of Wills, *William and Mary Quarterly*, vol. 36, pp. 503–23, and vol. 37, pp. 535–40, provides a partial corrective to this view.

32. One should also note the importance of Scottish and continental writers on natural jurisprudence, expecially Carmichael and Pufendorf, as influences on Hutcheson's work. The outline of Hutcheson's *System* is virtually identical to Pufendorf's *On the Law of Nature and Nations.*

33. Hutcheson, *System of Moral Philosophy*, vol. 1, p. 283.

34. Ibid., p. 282.

35. Ibid., p. 287.

36. Ibid., p. 292.

37. Ibid., pp. 299–300.

38. Ibid., p. 300.

39. Ibid., p. 324.

40. Ibid., p. 321.

41. Ibid., p. 258.

42. Ibid., vol. 2, p. 212.

43. Ibid., pp. 214–15.

44. Ibid., p. 212.

45. Ibid., p. 279.

46. Ibid., p. 269.

47. Ibid., p. 282.

48. Ibid., p. 317.

49. Ibid., p. 315.

50. David Hume, *Essays, Moral, Political, and Literary* (Indianapolis: Liberty Classics, 1985), pp. 32–42, 465–93.

51. Ibid., pp. 490–91.

52. Also see Smith, *Lectures on Justice, Police, Revenue and Arms* (Oxford: Clarendon Press, 1896), pp. 11–15; Ferguson, *Principles*, bk. 2, pp. 244–47, 289–92.

53. Smith, *Theory of Moral Sentiments*, pp. 50–61, 227–34; Ferguson, *Princi-*

ples, pp. 256–70; Hume, *Essays,* p. 39. Also, *Federalist* No. 49; John Adams, *Discourse on Davila,* pp. 2–13; Smith's influence on Adams's work was extensive.

54. See Dugald Stewart's comments on the influence of Montesquieu, *Works,* vol. 1, pp. 192–93.

55. See A. O. Hirschman, *The Passions and the Interests* (Princeton: Princeton University Press, 1977); Thomas L. Pangle, *Montesquieu's Philosophy of Liberalism* (Chicago: University of Chicago Press, 1973), chap. 9.

56. See, for example, E. G. West, "The Political Economy of Alienation, Karl Marx and Adam Smith," *Oxford Economic Papers,* vol. 21, pp. 1–23.

57. See Joseph Cropsey, *Polity and Economy: An Interpretation of the Principles of Adam Smith* (The Hague: M. Nijhoff, 1957) for a full discussion.

Chapter 7: Rousseau—The Turning Point

1. *Social Contract,* bk. 2, chaps. 8–10.

2. *Social Contract,* bk. 1, chap. 6 note, and *Emile,* trans. Allan Bloom (New York: Basic Books, 1979), pp. 39–41.

3. *Discourse on the Origins of Inequality,* pt. 2. Compare *Social Contract,* bk. 1, chap. 9.

4. *Discourse on the Arts and Sciences,* in Roger and Judith Masters, eds., *Two Discourses* (New York: St. Martin's Press, 1964), p. 51.

5. *Social Contract,* bk. 1, chap. 6.

6. Ibid., chap. 8.

7. Ibid.

8. Ibid., bk. 2, chap. 9, bk. 3, chap. 12.

9. Ibid., bk. 3, chap. 15.

10. Ibid., bk. 2, chap. 7.

11. Ibid., bk. 2, chap. 8. Compare *Emile,* "Profession of Faith of a Savoyard Vicar," pp. 266–313.

12. Edmund Burke, "Letter to a Member of the National Assembly," in Peter J. Stanlis, ed., *Selected Writings and Speeches* (Garden City, N.Y.: Doubleday & Co., 1963), pp. 511–13.

13. *Social Contract,* bk. 1, chap. 8.

14. There were strands of utopian socialism that still looked toward the establishment of small communities of the kind Rousseau prescribed. Their most notable expression was the kibbutzim in Israel, founded by Russian Jews influenced by Tolstoy, who was a most ardent admirer of Rousseau.

Chapter 8: Utilitarianism and the Constitution

1. Jeremy Bentham, *An Introduction to the Principles of Morals and Legislation,* ed. J. H. Burns and H. L. A. Hart (London: Athlone, 1970), p. 309.

2. Jeremy Bentham, "Preface Intended for the Second Edition of the *Fragment on Government*" (1822), in *A Comment on the Commentaries and a*

Fragment on Government, ed. J. H. Burns and H. L. A. Hart (London: Athlone Press, 1977), pp. 502–3.

3. In addition to Bentham, I will be discussing James Mill, John Austin, and John Stuart Mill—the so-called classical utilitarians. John Stuart Mill will have a peripheral place, for the many changes in his views, not least on the doctrine of utility, make him unrepresentative of the utilitarian political theory associated with Bentham. Although there was a distinctive utilitarian political theory, there were enough differences among various utilitarians and enough changes in the political outlook of any one of them to justify referring to particular utilitarians rather than to utilitarianism. David Hume will not be included, for although he had an important place in the development of utilitarianism as an ethical theory, because his politics were so very different from those of Bentham and his followers, it would be difficult in a small space to deal with the connections between the Constitution and utilitarian political theory so broadly defined that it included Hume as well as Bentham and his disciples. Bentham's distance from Hume is indicated by his criticism of Hume's use of the term "utility," although Bentham acknowledged that Hume was the first to give utility a central place in a discussion of ethics. See "Article on Utilitarianism," *Deontology Together with a Table of the Springs of Action and Article on Utilitarianism,* ed. Amnon Goldworth (Oxford: Oxford University Press, 1983), pp. 289–90, 322–23. Of course, there were affinities between Hume and James Madison with regard to politics. See Douglass Adair, *Fame and the Founding Fathers* (New York, 1974), pp. 93–106; and Garry Wills, *Explaining America: The Federalist* (Garden City: Doubleday, 1981), pp. 20–21 and passim.

4. Jeremy Bentham, *Plan of Parliamentary Reform* (1817), in *Works,* ed. John Bowring (Edinburgh: William Tait, 1843), vol. 3, pp. 447, 560; see also p. 472; and *Radicalism Not Dangerous* (1819–1920), in *Works,* vol. 3, p. 612. Bentham said the belief that democracy led to anarchy was a disease and America was the cure. See *Jeremy Bentham to His Fellow-Citizens of France, on Houses of Peers and Senates* (1830), in *Works,* vol. 4, p. 449.

5. Bentham to President Andrew Jackson, June 14, 1830, *Correspondence of Andrew Jackson,* ed. John Spencer Bassett (Washington: Carnegie Institution, 1929), vol. 4, p. 146. For evidence of Austin's favorable opinions about America at a time when he had already adopted utilitarianism, see his "Primogeniture," *Westminster Review,* vol. 2 (October 1824), pp. 507, 550–51.

6. Jeremy Bentham, *Constitutional Code* (Edinburgh: William Tait, 1827), in *Works,* vol. 9, p. 123.

7. Bentham, *Introduction to Morals and Legislation,* p. 311. Bentham's criticism of the Declaration of Independence was incorporated in his friend John Lind's *An Answer to the Declaration of the American Congress* (London, 1776); see pp. 119–20; Bentham to Lind, September 2, 1776, *Correspondence of Jeremy Bentham,* ed. T. L. S. Sprigge (London: Athlone Press, 1968), vol. 1, pp. 341–44 (this letter gives a line-by-line analysis of the Preamble to the Declaration); Bentham, *Works,* vol. 1, pp. 247–48; vol. 10, pp. 54, 57, 62–63; and H. L. A. Hart, "Bentham and the United States of America," *Journal of Law and Economics,* vol. 19 (October 1976), pp. 550–51. Bentham wanted to visit America and

thus tried to get an appointment as assistant to George Johnstone, one of the commissioners sent in 1778 to negotiate with the American Congress. He was unsuccessful, as Adam Ferguson had already accepted the appointment. See Bentham, *Correspondence,* vol. 2, p. 94, n. 2. Bentham's views on America are also discussed in Hart, "Bentham and the United States," pp. 547–68; Gertrude Himmelfarb, "Bentham versus Blackstone," in *Marriage and Morals among the Victorians* (New York: Knopf, 1986), pp. 94–110; Charles W. Everett, "Introduction to 'Anti-Senatica' by Jeremy Bentham," in *Smith College Studies in History,* vol. 11 (July 1926), pp. 209–20; Charles W. Everett, "Bentham in the United States of America," in George W. Keeton and Georg Schwarzenberger, eds., *Jeremy Bentham and the Law* (London: Stevens, 1948), pp. 185–201; Chilton Williamson, "Bentham Looks at America," *Political Science Quarterly,* vol. 70 (1955), pp. 543–51; Paul Palmer, "Benthamism in England and America," *American Political Science Review,* vol. 35 (October 1941), pp. 855–71; and Peter J. King, *Utilitarian Jurisprudence in America: The Influence of Bentham and Austin on American Legal Thought in the Nineteenth Century* (New York: Garland Publishers, 1986).

8. John Austin, *The Province of Jurisprudence Determined* (1832), ed. H. L. A. Hart (London: Weidenfeld and Nicolson, 1965), pp. 254, 258–62. On Austin's utilitarianism, see Mill's comment: "Of all views I have yet seen taken of the utilitarian scheme, I like Austin's best, in his book on *The Province of Jurisprudence;* but even that falls very far short of what is wanted," in Mill to John Pringle Nichol, October 14, 1834, *Earlier Letters of John Stuart Mill, 1812–1848,* ed. Francis Mineka, in Mill, *Collected Works* (Toronto: University of Toronto Press, and Routledge and Kegan Paul, 1963), vol. 12, p. 236. Austin became an enthusiast for constitutionalism once he turned against utilitarianism. See his *Plea for the Constitution* (London: John Murray, 1859), pp. 37–38, 41; and Lotte Hamburger and Joseph Hamburger, *Troubled Lives: John and Sarah Austin* (Toronto: University of Toronto Press, 1985), pp. 174–75, 181–84.

9. Bentham, *Fragment on Government* (1776), in *A Comment and a Fragment,* pp. 485–86. Bentham allowed an exception; the supreme governor's authority was indefinite, he said, "unless where limited by express convention." This was not an allusion to constitutional limitations arising from custom, however, for in a footnote he indicated that it referred to reduction of authority as a result of a treaty between states or from an international organization. Ibid., pp. 484, 484n; see also Himmelfarb, "Bentham versus Blackstone," p. 103. Hart contends that Austin was more emphatic than Bentham about the illegality of constitutional limitations. See "Bentham and the United States," pp. 551–52; and *Essays on Bentham* (London: Oxford University Press, 1982), pp. 108–9, 222–32.

10. Jeremy Bentham, "Anarchical Fallacies; Being an Examination of the Declaration of Rights Issued during the French Revolution," in *Works,* vol. 2, p. 515; see also p. 494.

11. Bentham, *Introduction to Morals and Legislation,* pp. 308–9. Of course Bentham acknowledged the existence of constitutional law, but for him it only

defined offices and jurisdictions without establishing effective limitations. Ibid., p. 308.

12. See, for example, James Mill, *An Essay on Government* (New York: Library of Liberal Arts, 1955), p. 48.

13. Austin, *Province of Jurisprudence,* p. 79. John Stuart Mill quoted this passage with approval. See "Austin's Lectures on Jurisprudence," *Tait's Edinburgh Magazine,* vol. 2 (December 1832), p. 348.

14. Austin, *Province of Jurisprudence,* pp. 126–27, 133–43, 149–50, 209, 257–58. Austin would have opposed constitutional limitations even if they originated in a positive morality shaped by a science of ethics. If the limitations were justified by the same science of ethics that was also the source of positive law, it would be pointless to have them serve as checks on positive law, for constitutionalism had meaning only when it invoked standards that were independent from and "higher" than the laws it judged.

15. Alexander Hamilton, James Madison, and John Jay, *The Federalist,* with an introduction by Edward Mead Earle (New York: Modern Library, n.d.), No. 84, p. 561. Madison was cautiously favorable to a bill of rights but was uncertain about its effectivenss in all circumstances. See Madison to Jefferson, October 17, 1788; and Madison to George Eve, January 2, 1789, in *The Writings of James Madison,* ed. Gaillard Hunt (New York: G.P. Putnam's Sons, 1904), vol. 5, pp. 271–74, 319–21.

16. Bentham, "Anarchical Fallacies," *Works,* vol. 3, pp. 500–502, 522–24. He also called the usage "a moral crime," p. 524; use of the phrase "natural rights" was "nonsense upon stilts," p. 501. See also *Works,* vol. 10, p. 45; Bentham to John Lind, September 2, 1776, *The Correspondence of Jeremy Bentham,* vol. 1, p. 343; Bentham to Brissot de Warville, mid-August 1789, in *Correspondence of Jeremy Bentham,* ed. A. T. Milne (London: Athlone Press, 1981), vol. 4, pp. 84–85. On the use of the language of rights in America, see *Introduction to Morals and Legislation,* p. 310.

17. Austin said, "There are no rights but those which are the creatures of law," in *Lectures on Jurisprudence, or the Philosophy of Positive Law,* ed. Robert Campbell, 4th ed. (London: John Murray, 1873), vol. 1, p. 354. See also James Mill, "Jurisprudence," *Supplement to the Fourth, Fifth, and Sixth Editions of the Encyclopaedia Britannica* (Edinburgh, 1824), vol. 5, pp. 143–44.

18. Bentham, "Anti-Senatica," p. 265. Bentham also pondered, "perhaps after all the old men are dead that labored to form the federal Constitution and it . . . rests only on its own merit the probability is that it will be changed and the power of the federation much limited."

19. Austin, *Province of Jurisprudence,* pp. 246–47; John Austin, "Centralization," *Edinburgh Review,* vol. 85 (January 1847), p. 222. On American government, see *Province of Jurisprudence,* pp. 250–51; "Centralization," pp. 228–29.

20. Austin, "Centralization," pp. 223, 236–55 passim. On Bentham's view, see M. I. Zagday, "Bentham and the Poor Law," in *Jeremy Bentham and the Law,* pp. 62–63.

21. John Stuart Mill, "De Tocqueville on Democracy in America" (1840), *Essays on Politics and Society,* in *Collected Works,* vol. 18, pp. 169–70.

22. John Stuart Mill, *Considerations on Representative Government*, in *Collected Works*, vol. 19, pp. 534–37, 539–45, 555. For a somewhat equivocal but not incompatible statement of his position, see *On Liberty*, in *Collected Works*, vol. 18, pp. 309–10.

23. *Federalist* No. 37, p. 229. *The Federalist* is being used as the most sophisticated explanation of the ideas that shaped the Constitution and as an authoritative explanation of the Constitution as understood by the most influential of the framers. Madison in 1825 said it was "an Authority to which appeal is habitually made by all and rarely declined or denied by any, as evidence of the general opinion of those who framed and those who accepted the constitution of the U[nited] States on questions as to its genuine meaning"; and that it "may fairly enough be regarded as the most authentic exposition of the text of the federal Constitution, as understood by the Body which prepared and the Authority which accepted it." See Madison to Jefferson, February 8, 1825, *Writings of James Madison*, vol. 9, pp. 219, 221. In referring to Publius, the differences among the authors of *The Federalist* are being ignored, as they do not have a bearing on the contrast with utilitarianism.

24. Bentham, "Anarchical Fallacies," *Works*, vol. 2, p. 520. "Divide et impera." Madison also used the phrase: "If the same sect form a majority and have the power, other sects will be sure to be depressed. Divide et impera, the reprobated axiom of tyranny, is under certain qualifications, the only policy, by which a republic can be administered on just principles." Madison to Jefferson, October 24, 1787, *Writings of James Madison, Works*, vol. 5, p. 31.

25. Bentham to President Andrew Jackson, June 14, 1830, *Correspondence of Andrew Jackson*, vol. 4, p. 149. John Adams, *A Defence of the Constitutions of the United States of America* (Philadelphia: Hall and Sellers, 1787), may be taken as a criticism of Bentham and the utilitarians, for although it was directed against Turgot, Mably, and Price, its purpose was to undermine their view, which was shared by Bentham, that the American Constitution was defective because of the separation of powers.

26. *Federalist* No. 47, p. 313. Mill thought that the principle of separation ought to be sacrificed so that the chief executive could be appointed by the representative body, that is, by the majority party in the legislature. See *Representative Government*, pp. 524–25.

27. William Blackstone, *Commentaries on the Laws of England* (1765), ed. Stanley N. Katz (Chicago: Univ. of Chicago Press, 1979), vol. 1, p. 51. See also Corinne Comstock Weston, *English Constitutional Theory and the House of Lords, 1556–1832* (New York: Columbia University Press, 1965), pp. 123–41; and Francis D. Wormuth, *The Origins of Modern Constitutionalism* (New York: Harper, 1949), pp. 174–76.

28. James Mill, *Essay on Government*, p. 65. The affinities between separation of powers and mixed government doctrines are also suggested by the Anti-Federalists' use of the language of mixed government doctrine in their criticisms of the way the separation principle was applied in the new Constitution. The presidency was associated with monarchy and the Senate with aristocracy.

29. Bentham, "Anti-Senatica," pp. 234, 264; see also Bentham, *Works,* vol. 4, p. 448. Mill, however, praised the American second chamber. See *Representative Government,* p. 559.

30. Bentham, *Fragment on Government,* p. 488. See also Hart, *Essays on Bentham,* p. 232.

31. Austin, *Province of Jurisprudence,* p. 191; and *Lectures on Jurisprudence,* vol. 2, pp. 548, 641, 649–52.

32. Mill, "De Tocqueville on Democracy in America" (1835), in *Collected Works,* vol. 18, pp. 66–67; *Representative Government,* pp. 556–57.

33. Herbert J. Storing, *What the Anti-Federalists Were For* (Chicago: University of Chicago Press, 1981), p. 64; *Federalist* No. 83, pp. 538–55; No. 84, pp. 555–58. See also Roscoe Pound, *The Development of Constitutional Guarantees of Liberty* (New Haven: Yale University Press, 1963), pp. 55–111. Compare Bentham: "For constitutional legislation, [the Americans] had in view no better approved guidance than that which was afforded them by the anility and servility of [Blackstone]," in *Jeremy Bentham to His Fellow-Citizens, Works,* vol. 4, p. 448.

34. Jeremy Bentham, *Papers Relative to Codification and Public Instruction: Including Correspondence with the Russian Emperor, and Divers Constituted Authorities in the American United States,* in *Works,* vol. 4, pp. 456, 460, 485–87.

35. Austin, "Primogeniture," pp. 524, 544. Austin changed his views on common law much later. See *Plea for the Constitution.*

36. James Mill, "Summary Review of the Conduct and Measures of the Imperial Parliament," *Parliamentary Review* (London, 1826), p. 777.

37. Bentham, *Papers Relative to Codification,* pp. 453, 461, 467, 484. See also pp. 479, 507–14; and *Works,* vol. 11, pp. 40–42. Although Bentham had American disciples, they were few in number and without widespread influence, especially before 1850. See Charles W. Everett, "Bentham in the United States"; and Palmer, "Benthamism in England and America."

38. Bentham, *Introduction to Morals and Legislation,* p. 11; "Anarchical Fallacies," *Works,* vol. 2, p. 497. See also *Works,* vol. 9, p. 5.

39. James Mill, *Essay on Government,* p. 56.

40. *Federalist* No. 6, p. 27; No. 15, pp. 92, 94; No. 34, p. 206; No. 51, p. 337; No. 55, p. 365; No. 76, p. 495. Madison in the Virginia convention could have been responding to Bentham: "I go on this great republican principle, that the people will have virtue. . . . Is there no virtue among us? If there be not, we are in a wretched situation. No theoretical checks, no form of government, can render us secure. To suppose that any form of government will secure liberty or happiness without any virtue in the people, is a chimerical idea." *The Debates in the Several State Conventions, on the Adoption of the Federal Constitution, as Recommended by the General Convention at Philadelphia in 1787,* ed. Jonathan Elliot (Washington, 1836), vol. 3, pp. 536–37.

41. *Federalist* No. 10, pp. 55–56; No. 37, p. 231; No. 60, p. 390.

42. James Mill, "Constitution: Summary Review," *Parliamentary History and Review* (London, 1826), p. 773.

43. James Mill, *Essay on Government,* pp. 79–80.

44. Austin, *Province of Jurisprudence,* pp. 53–58.

45. *Letters of the Right Hon. Sir George Cornewall Lewis, Bart. to Various Friends*, ed. Gilbert Frankland Lewis (London: Longmans, 1870), p. 105–6.

46. Bentham, *Fragment on Government*, pp. 491–92.

47. James Mill, *Analysis of the Phenomena of the Human Mind* (London, 1829), vol. 2, p. 187. See also Bentham, *Plan of Parliamentary Reform*, *Works*, vol. 3, pp. 445–46, 502, 527.

48. Some have mistakenly held that James Mill was exclusively a spokesman for middle-class interests, and it has been claimed that evidence can be found in a well-known passage in which Mill made a flattering observation about the middle class. The passage, however, shows that, far from defending a suffrage restricted to the middle class, he was trying to appease fears of universal suffrage by pointing out that those in the middle rank will shape the outlook and votes of those in lower ranks: "There can be no doubt that the middle rank . . . is that portion of the community of which, if the basis of representation were ever so far extended, the opinion would ultimately decide. Of the people beneath them a vast majority would be sure to be guided by their advice and example." James Mill, *Essay on Government*, p. 90.

49. Bentham, *Plan of Parliamentary Reform*, p. 446. Not all utilitarians were majoritarian at all times. Austin, although he had been a defender of full democracy, became skeptical of majorities in the *Province of Jurisprudence;* and John Stuart Mill, under the influence of Austin and the St. Simonians, also did so (circa 1829–1830).

50. *Federalist* No. 22, p. 141; No. 49, p. 327; No. 52, p. 343; see also No. 39, pp. 243–44; No. 53, p. 353; No. 57, pp. 370–71. Publius held, however, that it was unnecessary to have representation of all classes, that representatives will be responsible to constituents regardless of class differences, and that merchants were the natural representatives of artisans and manufacturers. See No. 35, pp. 213–16.

51. Ibid., No. 10, pp. 54, 57–58; No. 15, p. 92; No. 37, p. 232.

52. Ibid., No. 51, pp. 337, 339.

53. Ibid., No. 34, p. 204; No. 37, pp. 224–25, 229–30; No. 60, p. 389.

54. Ibid., No. 52, p. 343; No. 56, p. 368.

55. Ibid., No. 37, p. 226; No. 63, pp. 410–11; No. 70, p. 456. Adair makes a much larger claim for the role of history in the founders' thinking and conduct. See Adair, *Fame and the Founding Fathers*, pp. 109, 107–23 passim. His own analysis rather supports Publius's more modest claim that history was like a beacon warning about dangers without showing how to avoid them. Adair shows that by looking to the past the framers increased their sensitivity to such problems as class conflict (pp 116–17), reemergence of monarchy (pp. 118–19), stability (p. 115), and Balkanization of the union (p. 118). While Adair seems correct in saying that "history, scientifically considered, thus helped *define* . . . the nature of the crisis of 1787 for these leaders and their audience," one may doubt his argument that it "also determined in large part the 'reforms' that, it could be predicted, would end the crisis" (p. 97). This latter claim denies to the framers the wisdom and inventiveness that elsewhere Adair is glad to allow them (for example, p. 135). For an account of the

awareness of limitations on the use of history among the founders and their contemporaries, see Meyer Reinhold, *Classica Americana,* in *The Greek and Roman Heritage in the United States* (Detroit: Wayne State University Press, 1984), pp. 104–7.

56. *Federalist* No. 70, p. 457.

57. Ibid., No. 9, pp. 48–49; No. 37, pp. 227, 231; No. 51, pp. 335–37; No. 77, p. 502.

58. Ibid., No. 9, pp. 48–49; No. 51, p. 337; see also No. 47, p. 313.

59. Ibid., No. 6, pp. 32–33; No. 8, p. 47; No. 28, p. 171; No. 46, p. 309; No. 60, p. 389; No. 84, p. 562.

60. Ibid., No. 28, p. 170; No. 34, p. 206; see also No. 15, pp. 93, 95; No. 18, pp. 107, 112; No. 43, pp. 283–84; No. 68, p. 442. For Bentham on the American Revolution, see *Works,* vol. 10, p. 57; for Austin on the American Revolution, see *Province of Jurisprudence,* pp. 56–57.

61. *Federalist* No. 6, p. 32; No. 29, p. 180; No. 34, p. 203; No. 84, p. 555. See also No. 37, p. 231; No. 43, p. 284; No. 51, p. 341.

62. Ibid., No. 6, p. 27; No. 41, p. 260; No. 85, pp. 570–71. See also No. 38, p. 239; No. 65, p. 428.

63. Bentham, *Fragment on Government,* p. 448; and Himmelfarb, "Bentham versus Blackstone," p. 109.

64. James Mill, "Theory and Practice," *London and Westminster Review,* vol. 3 (April 1836), pp. 223–34; see also Austin, *Province of Jurisprudence,* pp. 49–50.

65. John Stuart Mill, *Autobiography,* in *Collected Works,* vol. 1, pp. 67, 69, 111. The historian Grote and Molesworth, the editor of Hobbes's works, shared these views.

66. Thomas Babington Macaulay, "Mill on Government" (March 1829), "Westminster Reviewer's Defence of Mill" (June 1829), and "Utilitarian Theory of Government" (October 1829), in *Miscellaneous Writings* (London: Longmans, 1860), vol. 1, pp. 282–395.

67. John Stuart Mill, "Rationale of Representation" (July 1835), in *Collected Works,* vol. 18, p. 42.

68. *Federalist* No. 9, p. 47; No. 63, p. 410.

69. Quoted from Bentham manuscripts in Douglas G. Long, *Bentham on Liberty: Jeremy Bentham's Idea of Liberty in Relation to His Utilitarianism* (Toronto: Univ. of Toronto Press, 1977), p. 173.

70. Bentham, "Anarchical Fallacies," p. 493.

71. Austin, *Province of Jurisprudence,* p. 269.

72. Bentham, *Fragment on Government,* p. 485; Long, *Bentham on Liberty,* p. 204; and Himmelfarb, "Bentham versus Blackstone," p. 106.

73. Long, *Bentham on Liberty,* p. 205; Bentham, *Principles of Penal Law,* in *Works,* vol. 1, pp. 574–75; and Bentham, *Liberty of the Press and Public Discussion,* in *Works,* vol. 2, pp. 277–80. Bentham pointed to the United States as a place where liberty of the press was allowed by law (p. 280).

74. Long, *Bentham on Liberty,* pp. 198, 206; see also pp. 196, 198–206 passim. Bentham's "vision of utilitarian society embodied the idea of a near-unanimity of wills founded upon a near-homogeneity of individual personalities. A community rendering undeviating obedience to the dictates of

utility would represent at one and the same time the apotheosis of majority tyranny in J. S. Mill's terms" (p. 118). Long points to a close affinity between Bentham and B. F. Skinner in *Walden Two* (pp. 214, 216). Richard A. Posner has discussed "Bentham's legacy to totalitarian regimes" in "Blackstone and Bentham," *Journal of Law and Economics*, vol. 19 (October 1976), p. 599.

75. Long, *Bentham on Liberty*, p. 215.

76. Alexis de Tocqueville, *Democracy in America*, ed. Phillips Bradley (New York: Knopf, 1945), vol. 1, p. 270. Tocqueville, however, shared Bentham's skepticism about mixed government (ibid.). On Tocqueville's use of *The Federalist*, see James T. Schleifer, *The Making of Tocqueville's Democracy in America* (Chapel Hill: Univ. of North Carolina Press, 1980), chap. 7.

77. George Bentham, "Autobiography," vol. 2, pp. 364, 404–5, Library, Royal Botanic Gardens, Kew.

78. Bentham, *Introduction to Morals and Legislation*, p. 12.

79. Austin, "Centralization," pp. 244, 251–52. Austin knew Tocqueville; they may have met during Tocqueville's visit to England in 1835 and perhaps were introduced by John Stuart Mill or by Henry Reeve, the first translator of the *Democracy* into English, who was the nephew of Austin's wife, Sarah. The Austins certainly were in touch with Tocqueville when they lived in Paris from 1843 until 1848.

80. John Stuart Mill, "De Tocqueville on Democracy in America" (1835), pp. 80, 86.

81. This theme occupied Book IV of Tocqueville's work; Mill quoted Book IV once, but not on this theme. Mill, "De Tocqueville on Democracy in America" (1840), pp. 156, 191–96, 200.

82. John Stuart Mill, *On Liberty*, p. 219. For an example of the commonly held view that Mill and Tocqueville thought alike on this matter, see David Spitz, "Freedom and Individuality: Mill's *Liberty* in Retrospect," in Mill, *On Liberty: Annotated Text Sources and Background Criticism*, ed. David Spitz (New York: Norton, 1975), p. 235.

83. Mill, *On Liberty*, pp. 219, 220.

84. *Federalist* No. 9, p. 47; see also No. 38, p. 242: "A dissolution or usurpation is the dreadful dilemma to which [a government] is continually exposed."

85. Richard M. Gunmere, "The Classical Ancestry of the United States Constitution," *American Quarterly*, vol. 14 (1962), pp. 6–9. John Adams emphasized the importance of Polybius as one "whose writings were in the contemplation of those who framed the American constitutions." Gilbert Chinard, "Polybius and the American Constitution," *Journal of the History of Ideas*, vol. 1 (1940), pp. 43, 53, 57. In summarizing Plato's teachings, John Adams emphasized Plato's analysis of the changes in regimes that came from "revolutions of governments into one another," especially the move from a democracy turned licentious into a condition of order turned tyrannical. See *A Defence of the Constitutions*, pp. 188, 200, 203.

86. Blackstone, *Commentaries on the Laws of England*, vol. 1, p. 123.

87. Adams, *A Defence of the Constitutions*, pp. v, 382. Gordon Wood's argument that the rationale for Adams's views in his *Defence of the Constitutions*

was obsolete does not have a bearing on this feature of his argument, which was shared by Publius. See *The Creation of the American Republic, 1776–1787* (Chapel Hill: University of North Carolina Press, 1969), pp. 574–92.

88. *Federalist* No. 28, p. 170; No. 34, p. 206; No. 68, p. 442. *Records of the Federal Convention of 1787,* vol. 1, p. 318; see also vol. 3, p. 547. *Debates of the Several State Conventions,* vol. 3, p. 399. To describe Shays's Rebellion, James Wilson used words from Horace: "We walked on ashes concealing fire beneath our feet," in Gunmere, "Classical Ancestry," p. 5.

89. Gunmere, "Classical Ancestry," pp. 10, 13–15; *Federalist* No. 1, pp. 5–6; No. 8, p. 44; see also No. 18, pp. 107, 112; No. 80, p. 517.

90. *Federalist* No. 37, p. 227; No. 63, p. 411.

91. James Mill, "Periodical Literature, Edinburgh Review," *Westminster Review,* vol. 1 (January 1824), p. 218.

Chapter 9: Idealism

1. For a discussion of this tendency in the early years of the republic, see Alexis de Tocqueville, *Democracy in America,* trans. George Lawrence, ed. J. P. Mayer (Garden City, N.Y.: Doubleday & Co., 1969), p. 534.

2. This feature of idealism was particularly attractive to prominent American thinkers of the nineteenth century, including Ralph Waldo Emerson, Charles Sanders Peirce, and Josiah Royce. See, for example, Royce's lengthy discussions of Kant, Fichte, and Hegel in a series of popular lectures delivered at Harvard University and later published under the title *The Spirit of Modern Philosophy* (New York: Dover, 1983). Royce, who called himself a "metaphysical idealist," writes:

> The world . . . is such stuff as ideas are made of. Thought possesses all things. But the world isn't unreal. It extends infinitely beyond our private consciousness, because it is the world of universal mind. . . . Absolutely the only thing sure from the first about this world . . . is that it is intelligent, rational, orderly, essentially comprehensible, so that all its problems are somewhere solved, all its darkest mysteries are known to the supreme Self (p. 381).

Although Victorian moral uplift may have given way to "new age healing," optimistic appeals to the "universal spirit in all of us" have not gone out of style.

3. See, for example, the "Second Preface" of Kant's *Critique of Pure Reason,* trans. Norman Kemp Smith (London: MacMillan & Co., 1929).

4. The essentials of this teaching are laid down in Immanual Kant, *Groundwork of the Metaphysics of Morals,* trans. H. J. Paton (New York: Harper and Row, 1964); and the *Critique of Practical Reason,* trans. Lewis White Beck (Indianapolis: Bobbs-Merrill, 1956).

5. See, for example, Kant, *Groundwork,* pp. 403, 411.

6. Ibid., p. 393f.

7. Ibid., p. 433.

8. Immanual Kant, *Metaphysical Elements of Justice*, trans. John Ladd (Indianapolis: Bobbs-Merrill, 1965), pp. 34, 71.

9. Kant, *Justice*, p. 43f.

10. "On the Common Saying 'This May Be True in Theory but It Does Not Apply in Practice,'" in *Kant's Political Writings*, ed. Hans Reiss (Cambridge: Cambridge University Press, 1971), p. 73.

11. "Perpetual Peace," in *Kant on History*, ed. Lewis White Beck (Indianapolis: Bobbs-Merrill, 1963), p. 126.

12. See John Locke, *Second Treatise of Government*, chap. 5.

13. "Theory and Practice," Kant, p. 75. According to Kant, the state may provide for the poor as a security measure, not out of respect or any particular claims on their part.

14. Kant, *Justice*, p. 97.

15. In addition to that of John Rawls and his school, see the influential thought of the constitutional theorist, Herbert Wechsler.

16. Kant, "Perpetual Peace," p. 114.

17. Ibid., p. 112.

18. Kant, *Groundwork*, p. 100.

19. Immanual Kant, *Anthropology from a Pragmatic Point of View*, trans. Mary J. Gregor (The Hague: Martinus Nijhoff, 1974), p. 190.

20. For an extended treatment of this theme, see Fichte's *Science of Ethics* [*Das System der Sittenlehre*], vol. 4 of *Fichtes Werke*, ed. I. H. Fichte (Bonn: Adolph-Marcus, 1834–36), hereafter cited as *F.W.* See also the (not always literal) English translation published in 1897 by A. E. Kroeger, who was affiliated with the St. Louis Hegelians discussed below.

21. Efficacy *(Wirksamkeit)* is a major theme of the *Grundlage des Naturrechts nach Prinzipien der Wissenschaftslehre*, *F.W.*, vol. 3. See also the sometimes misleading translation by Kroeger, *The Science of Right* (London: Routledge and Kegan Paul, 1970).

22. *F.W.*, vol. 3, p. 402.

23. Ibid., pp. 185–86. See n. 3.

24. Ibid., vol. 4, pp. 432–44.

25. Thus despite the brief flowering of the labor movement in America as a broad-based social and moral cause, it has only too easily become just another bread-and-butter interest group.

26. *Hegel's Philosophy of Right*, trans. T. M. Knox (London: Oxford University Press, 1952), preface.

27. Ibid.

28. *Natural Law: The Scientific Way of Treating Natural Law, Its Place in Moral Philosophy, and Its Relation to the Positive Sciences of Law*, trans. T. M. Knox (Philadelphia: University of Pennsylvania Press, 1975).

29. Hegel, *Philosophy of Right*, no. 124.

30. Ibid., nos. 238, 253.

31. Ibid., no. 158ff.

32. Tocqueville, *Democracy in America*, vol. 2, chap. 12.

33. Hegel, *Philosophy of Right*, no. 176.

34. Ibid., no. 324.

35. Ibid., no. 258 addition.

36. From a Hegelian perspective, the three constitutional branches overlap functionally as well as "checking and balancing" one another and thus display an articulated unity that is not merely mechanical but "organic."

37. The so-called St. Louis Hegelians published the influential *Journal of Speculative Philosophy.* They included among their number a lieutenant governor of Missouri and the first U.S. secretary of education. That many of the public universities founded during this period looked to the German rather than to the British model is further testimony both to the impact of German immigration and to the high regard of many educated Americans for German *Wissenschaft.*

Chapter 10: Historicism and the Constitution

1. James Madison, *The Federalist* (New York: Modern Library, n.d.), No. 51, p. 337.

2. Ibid., No. 10, p. 55.

3. Ibid., p. 61.

4. Alexis de Tocqueville, *Democracy in America,* trans. Henry Reeve (New York: Vintage Books, 1945), vol. 2, p. 183; and Charles Dickens, *The Life and Adventures of Martin Chuzzlewit* (New York: Charles Scribner's Sons, 1901), pp. 220ff.

5. Harry V. Jaffa, *Crisis of the House Divided* (New York: Doubleday, 1959), pp. 26–27.

6. Ronald Dworkin, *Taking Rights Seriously* (Cambridge, Mass.: Harvard University Press, 1977), pp. 176–77.

7. Benjamin N. Cardozo, *The Nature of the Judicial Process* (New Haven, Conn.: Yale University Press, 1921), p. 135.

8. Harper v. Virginia Board of Elections, 383 U.S. 663 (1966) at 669.

9. Carl Becker, *Detachment and the Writing of History,* ed. Phil L. Snyder (Ithaca, N.Y.: Cornell University Press, 1958), p. 45.

10. Ibid., p. 48.

11. Ibid., p. 56.

12. Ibid., p. 75.

13. Carl Becker, *Everyman His Own Historian* (New York: F. S. Crofts, 1935), pp. 237–39.

14. Carl Becker, *The Heavenly City of the Eighteenth Century Philosophers* (New Haven, Conn.: Yale University Press, 1932).

15. Carl Becker, *The Declaration of Independence* (New York: Knopf, 1942), p. iv.

16. Ibid., p. 277.

17. Ibid.

18. Ibid., p. 28.

19. Ibid., p. 57.

20. Ibid., p. 133.

21. Ibid., p. 279.

22. Ibid., p. 265.
23. Ibid., p. xvi.
24. Ibid., p. 278.
25. Ibid., p. 279.
26. Ibid., p. 233.
27. While a Kierkegaard or a Tertullian might argue that faith in God might be maintainable in the teeth of the evidence, faith is hardly maintainable for things of this world.
28. M. E. Bradford, "Dividing the House: The Gnosticism of Lincoln's Political Religion," *Modern Age*, vol. 23 (1979), pp. 10–23, is a good example, as is his "A Better Guide Than Reason: The Politics of John Dickinson," *Modern Age*, vol. 21 (1977), p. 47.
29. Friedrich Hebbel, *Agnes Bernauer* (Stuttgart: Reclam, 1962), act 5, sc. 10, p. 97. "Wir müssen das an sich Wertlose stempeln und ihm einen Wert beilegen, wir müssen den Staub über den Staub erhöhen."
30. Cf. M. E. Bradford, "The Heresy of Equality: Bradford Replies to Jaffa," *Modern Age*, vol. 20 (1976), esp. p. 68.
31. Ibid., p. 70; and Bradford, "Dividing the House," p. 21.
32. Henry Pachter, *Weimar Etudes* (New York: Columbia University Press, 1982), p. 136.
33. Ibid., pp. 136–37.
34. Aristotle, *The Politics*, Book 2, chaps. 9–12.
35. Max Weber, "Politics as a Vocation," *From Max Weber: Essays in Sociology*, ed. H. H. Gerth and C. Wright Mills (Oxford: Oxford University Press, 1967), p. 77.
36. Thomas Hobbes, *The Leviathan*, ed. C. B. Macpherson (New York: Penguin, 1982), pt. 4, chap. 46, p. 686.
37. John Locke, *An Essay Concerning Human Understanding*, ed. Peter H. Nidditch (Oxford: Oxford University Press, 1975), p. 265.
38. Ibid., p. 266.
39. David Hume, *A Treatise of Human Nature*, ed. T. H. Green and T. H. Grose (London: Longmans, Green and Co., 1890), vol. 2, p. 233.
40. David Hume, "An Enquiry Concerning the Principles of Morals," *The Philosophical Works*, ed. T. H. Green and T. H. Grose (Aalen: Scientia Verlag, 1964), vol. 4, pp. 206–7.
41. Ibid., p. 207.
42. Ibid.
43. Hume, *A Treatise*, p. 245.
44. Ibid., pp. 243–44.
45. Hume, "An Enquiry," p. 260.
46. Hume, *A Treatise*, p. 359.
47. Ibid.
48. Edmund Burke, *Reflections on the Revolution in France* (with Thomas Paine, *The Rights of Man*) (New York: Doubleday, 1961), p. 71.
49. Ibid., p. 72.
50. Ibid.
51. Ibid., p. 74.

52. Ibid.

53. Leo Strauss, *Natural Right and History* (Chicago: University of Chicago Press, 1965), p. 303.

54. Burke, *Reflections,* p. 89.

55. Edmund Burke, "An Appeal from the New to the Old Whigs," *The Works of Edmund Burke,* rev. ed. (Boston: Little, Brown and Company, 1865), vol. 4, p. 173.

56. Burke, *Reflections,* p. 30.

57. Ibid., p. 90.

58. Edmund Burke, "First Letter on a Regicide Peace," *Works,* vol. 5, p. 235.

59. Cited in Strauss, *Natural Right and History,* p. 318. Cf. also p. 314 for the discussion of the relation of the "local and accidental" to history in Burke's thought.

60. Jean-Jacques Rousseau, *The First and Second Discourses,* ed. Roger D. Masters, trans. Roger D. and Judith Masters (New York: St. Martin's Press, 1964), p. 102.

61. Leopold von Ranke, "Einleitung zur historisch-politischen Zeitschrift" (Introduction to the *Historical-Political Journal), Sämmtliche Werke* (Collected Works), 2d ed. (Leipzig: Duncker & Humblot, 1873), vol. 49, p. 3: "Diese neue Scholastik ist bemüht, die reale Welt nach ihren Schulmeinungen einzurichten" ("This new scholasticism seeks to arrange the real world according to its school opinions").

62. Johann Gottfried Herder, "Auch eine Philosophie der Geschichte zur Bildung der Menschheit" ("Another Philosophy of History for the Education of Humanity"), *Herders Werke* (Berlin: Aufbau-Verlag, 1964), vol. 2, p. 302. "Niemand in der Welt fühlt die Schwäche des allgemeinen Charakterisierens mehr als ich . . . . Wer bemerkt hat, was es für eine unaussprechliche Sache mit der Eigenheit eines Menschen sei" ("No one in the world feels the weakness of general characterization more than I . . . whoever has noticed what an inexpressible thing the particularity of a human being is").

63. Ranke, *Sämmtliche Werke,* vol. 49, pp. 3–4. "Ein reines Urtheil ist nur möglich, wenn man Jedweden nach dessen eigenem Standpunkt, nach dem ihm innewohnenden Bestreben würdigt." See too in Ranke, "Über die Verwandschaft und den Unterschied der Historie und der Politik" ("On the relationship and distinction between history and politics"), *Sämmtliche Werke,* vol. 24, p. 285, his celebration of the joy of the study of history once it has given up trying to force events into a single, predetermined pattern.

64. Herder, "Ideen zur Philosophie der Geschichte der Menschheit" ("Ideas towards the philosophy of the history of humanity"), Works (*Werke*), vol. 4, appendix from the drafts for the ninth book, p. 467: "Jeder Staat als solcher ist eine Maschine" ("Every state as such is a machine"). Cf. F. M. Barnard, ed., *Herder on Social and Political Culture* (Cambridge, Eng.: Cambridge University Press, 1969), p. 324 n. 18, for an enlightening comment on this passage.

65. Barnard, *Herder on Social and Political Culture,* pp. 325–26.

66. Ranke, "Deutsche Geschichte im Zeitalter der Reformation" (German

History in the Age of the Reformation), *Sämmtliche Werke,* vol. 5, p. 102. "Unsere deutsche Geschichte ist nun einmal in diesem Zeitalter gleichsam die allgemeine Geschichte" ("Our German history in this age is now for once also universal history").

67. Ranke, *Die Römischen Päpste* (The Roman Popes), *Sämmtliche Werke,* vol. 38, p. 3.

68. Ranke, "Einleitung zur historisch-politischen Zeitschrift" ("Introduction to the *Historical-Political Journal*"), *Sämmtliche Werke,* vol. 49, p. 4. "Von der Doktrin würde man auf die Forderung der Sache, von den eingebildeten Bedürfnissen auf das Positive zurückkommen" ("From the doctrines one would return to promoting the substance, from the imagined needs one would return to the positive").

69. Ibid. "Die Einsichtigen aller Zeiten wussten wass gut und gross, wass erlaubt und Rechtens, was Fortschritt und Verfall ist. In grossen Zügen ist es in den menschlichen Brust geschrieben: ein einfaches Nachdenken genügt, um es aufzufassen."

70. Ranke, "Über die Verwandschaft und den Unterschied der Historie und der Politik" ("On the relationship and distinction between history and politics"), *Sämmtliche Werke,* vol. 24, p. 285. "Als den Kern und das tieffste Geheimnis der Begebenheiten in sich aufzunehmen und bei einen oder dem andern Volke zu beobachten, wie die menschlichen Dinge gegründet werden, Kräfte gewinnen, wachsen und gedeihen."

71. Ibid., p. 287. "Das vor Augen Liegende zu beobachten, und daraus durch Nachdenken die Geheimnisse entfernliegenden Ursachen zu erschliessen."

72. Ranke, *Deutsche Geschichte im Zeitalter der Reformation* (German history in the Age of the Reformation), *Sämmtliche Werke,* vol. 1, p. 3. "In wie fern der Staat zu gründen ist, macht sich ein eigenthümliches Prinzip geltend, ebenfalls geistiger Natur, das auch seine innere Notwendigkeit hat, in bestimmten Formen sich ausspricht, besondere Bildungen hervortreibt, eine unbedingte Freiheit in Anspruch nimmt."

73. R. G. Collingwood, *The Idea of History* (Oxford: Oxford University Press, 1962), pp. 282ff.

74. Richard Hofstadter, "The Founding Fathers: An Age of Realism," in Robert H. Horwitz, ed., *The Moral Foundations of the American Republic,* 3d ed. (Charlottesville: University of Virginia Press, 1986), p. 74, expresses this view, though, like a Beckerian liberal patriot, with great sadness. "Modern humanistic thinkers who seek for a means by which society may transcend eternal conflict and rigid adherence to property rights as its integrating principles can expect no answer in the philosophy of balanced government as it was set down by the Constitution-makers of 1787."

75. The fact that irresponsible result-oriented administration now often is undertaken by the judicial branch and indeed presents itself as a *check* on executive prerogative does not contradict the fundamental point. Compare Jeremy Rabkin, *Judicial Compulsions* (New York: Basic Books, 1989).

76. John Stuart Mill, "On Liberty," in *Three Essays* (Oxford: Oxford University Press, 1975), pp. 16, 87, 105.

77. Richard Falk, "Trusting Khomeini," *New York Times*, February 16, 1979.

78. Leo Strauss, *Philosophy and Law*, trans. Fred Baumann (Philadelphia: Jewish Publication Society, 1987), p. 111n.

79. Herder, "Abhandlung über den Ursprung der Sprache" ("Essay on the origin of language"), *Werke*, vol. 2, p. 90.

80. Ibid. "Entweder er hat das ganze Ding Sprache schon vor der ersten Seite seines Buchs erfunden vorausgesetzt, oder ich finde auf jeder Seite Dinge, die sich gar nicht in der Ordnung einer bildenden Sprache zutragen konnten."

81. Ibid., p. 91. "Kurz, es entstanden Worte, weil Worte da waren, ehe sie da waren."

82. Ibid., pp. 91–92.

83. Rousseau, *First and Second Discourses*, pp. 119–26.

84. Herder, *Werke*, vol. 2, p. 98. "Man nenne diese ganze Disposition seiner Kräfte, wie man wolle: Verstand, Vernunft, Besinnung usw. . . ."

85. Ibid., p. 97.

86. Ibid., p. 98. "Wenn man die Namen nicht für abgesonderte Kräfte oder für blosse Stufenerhöhungen der Tierkräfte annimt, so gilts mir gleich."

Chapter 11: Capitalism

1. Karl Marx, *Capital* (New York: Modern Library, 1906), Author's Preface to the Second Edition, pp. 17–20.

2. Mark Blaug, *Economic Theory in Retrospect*, 3d ed. (Cambridge: Cambridge University Press, 1978), p. 199.

3. Adam Smith, *The Wealth of Nations*, ed. Edwin Cannan (Chicago: University of Chicago Press, 1976), vol. 1, p. 449.

4. Adam Smith, *The Theory of Moral Sentiments*, ed. D. D. Raphael and A. L. Macfie (Oxford: Oxford University Press, 1976), p. 342.

5. Adam Smith, *Lectures on Jurisprudence*, ed. R. L. Meek, D. D. Raphael, and P. G. Stein (Oxford: Clarendon Press, 1978), pp. 6–7. In all quotations from this volume, I have modernized the spelling.

6. In an "Advertisement" to the sixth edition (1790) of the *Theory of Moral Sentiments*, where Smith notes that "various occupations" have prevented him from writing the discourse on jurisprudence promised at the conclusion of this work, he states, "In the *Enquiry concerning the Nature and Causes of the Wealth of Nations*, I have partly executed this promise: at least so far as concerns police, revenue, and arms." The inclusion of arms must refer to the discussion "Of the Expence of Defence," chap. 1, pt. 1, of book 5, "Of the Revenue of the Sovereign or Commonwealth," of the *Wealth of Nations*. A similar brief discussion "of the Expence of Justice" also appears under the heading of revenue (that is, in book 5), although Smith does not refer to it in the Advertisement. See *Theory of Moral Sentiments*, p. 3.

7. Smith, *Lectures on Jurisprudence*, p. 331.

8. Smith, *Theory of Moral Sentiments*, p. 341.

9. Plato, *The Laws* 740a–745b.

10. Jean-Jacques Rousseau, *Discours sur les Sciences et les Arts* (First Discourse) in *Oeuvres Complètes* (Paris: Bibliothèque de la Pleiade, 1964), vol. 3, p. 19. Cf. Montesquieu, *The Spirit of the Laws*, book 3, sec. 3. Rousseau wrote the article "Political Economy" in the *Encyclopèdie*. Given Rousseau's adherence to the ancient view that subordinated wealth to virtue, it is not surprising that Joseph Schumpeter concludes that this article "contains next to no economics." Joseph A. Schumpeter, *History of Economic Analysis* (New York: Oxford University Press, 1954), p. 139.

11. Smith, *Wealth of Nations*, vol. 2, p. 208.

12. The same holds true for Smith's more distinguished successors among the English classical economists. See Lionel Robbins, *The Theory of Economic Policy in English Classical Political Economy* (London: Macmillan, 1952), pp. 34–67.

13. Smith, *Wealth of Nations*, vol. 1, pp. 344–45.

14. Ibid., p. 493. Compare vol. 2, pp. 48–49.

15. Ibid., vol. 2, pp. 49–50.

16. Ibid., vol. 1, p. 367.

17. Ibid., pp. 362–65. These conclusions must to some extent be qualified in the light of Smith's discussion of the need for publicly sponsored education as a means of combating the cowardice and "gross ignorance and stupidity" that, in a commercial society, afflict the great body of the people "unless government takes some pains to prevent it." Ibid., vol. 2, pp. 282–338. Yet the vehemence of Smith's critical comments in these passages does not lead him to call into question his advocacy of commercial society. And the measures he recommends to counteract the corrupting aspects of commercial society fall into the category not of traditional moral or religious education but of "enlightenment": elementary instruction in reading, writing, and mathematics for the common people; the encouragement of public diversions to "correct whatever was unsocial or disagreeably rigorous in the morals" of popular religious sects; and learning in science and philosophy ("the great antidote to the poison of enthusiasm and superstition") for the middle and upper classes. Moreover, it should be noted that Smith's discussion of education comes under the heading of "revenue" rather than "police." That is, education is treated not in terms of the ends of political society but as an expense of a kind legitimately borne by the sovereign "because the profit could never repay the expence to any individual or small number of individuals, though it may frequently do much more than repay it to a great society." Ibid., p. 209. In short, the theoretical framework in which Smith's discussion of education appears already presupposes the desirability of extending the sphere of private commercial enterprise as far as it may effectively go.

18. John Locke, *Two Treatises of Government*, ed. Peter Laslett (New York: New American Library, 1965), p. 395 (italics in the original).

19. Ibid., pp. 327–44. This brief account necessarily truncates and oversimplifies Locke's exceedingly careful and complex argument. For a fuller interpretation, see the essay by Thomas Pangle in this volume and the following studies: Leo Strauss, *Natural Right and History* (Chicago: University of Chicago Press, 1953), pp. 234–48; C. B. Macpherson, *The Political Theory of*

Possessive Individualism (Oxford: Oxford University Press, 1962), pp. 194–220; and Robert Goldwin, "John Locke," in Leo Strauss and Joseph Cropsey, eds., *History of Political Philosophy* (Chicago: Rand McNally, 1972), pp. 460–70.

20. Smith, *Wealth of Nations*, vol. 1, p. 2.

21. Compare ibid., pp. 15–16, with Locke, *Two Treatises*, p. 43.

22. For a discussion of the founders' views of these matters, see Marc F. Plattner, "American Democracy and the Acquisitive Spirit," in Robert A. Goldwin and William A. Schambra, eds., *How Capitalistic Is the Constitution?* (Washington, D.C.: American Enterprise Institute, 1982), pp. 1–21.

23. Adrienne Koch and William Peden, eds., *The Life and Selected Writings of Thomas Jefferson* (New York: Modern Library, 1944), p. 496.

24. *The Federalist* (New York: New American Library, 1961), No. 9, p. 72. Cf. Smith, *Wealth of Nations*, vol. 2, pp. 139ff., 243–44. See also Smith, *Lectures on Jurisprudence*, pp. 270ff.

25. On Smith's views regarding republicanism, see Joseph Cropsey, *Polity and Economy: An Interpretation of the Principles of Adam Smith* (The Hague: Martinus Nijhoff, 1957), pp. 64–70. Cropsey notes that Holland had a hereditary *stadtholder* and thus was not regarded by the authors of *The Federalist* as a republic in the strict sense. For an expression of the superiority of monarchy to "some modern republics" with regard to liberty, see *Wealth of Nations*, vol. 2, pp. 229–30.

26. Smith, *Lectures on Jurisprudence*, pp. 315–25, 401–4. Compare David Hume, "Of the Original Contract," in *Political Essays*, ed. Charles W. Hendel (Indianapolis: Library of Liberal Arts, 1953), pp. 43–61, and David Hume, *A Treatise of Human Nature*, ed. L. A. Selby-Bigge (Oxford: Clarendon, 1896), book 3, secs. 8–10.

27. Hume, *Treatise of Human Nature*, book 3, sec. 2.

28. Smith, *Lectures on Jurisprudence*, pp. 105, 399, 401, 458; cf. p. 398.

29. John Bowring, ed., *The Works of Jeremy Bentham* (New York: Russell and Russell, 1962), vol. 1, *A Fragment on Government*, pp. 261–72, and vol. 2, *Anarchical Fallacies*, p. 501.

30. Alfred Marshall, *Principles of Economics*, 8th ed. (New York: Macmillan, 1949), app. B, p. 760. Lionel Robbins also expresses the view that Bentham's influence on subsequent economic thought has generally been underestimated (*English Classical Political Economy*, pp. 38–39). Robbins, it should be added, includes Hume along with Smith among the English classical economists and emphasizes the disjunction between this utilitarian school and the natural rights school of political economy represented by the physiocrats. Ibid., pp. 2, 46–49.

31. Albert Venn Dicey, *Lectures on the Relation between Law and Public Opinion in England* (London: Macmillan, 1948), p. 309. See also pp. 171–75.

32. Jeremy Bentham, *Principles of the Civil Code*, in Bowring, *Works of Jeremy Bentham*, vol. 1, pp. 302, 305.

33. Marshall, *Principles of Economics*, p. 760.

34. Bentham, *Principles of the Civil Code*, pp. 307–12.

35. John Stuart Mill, *Principles of Political Economy*, ed. W. J. Ashley (London: Longmans, Green & Co., 1920), p. 115.

36. Ibid., p. 697. See also pp. 881ff.

37. Ibid., p. 780. See also p. 938.

38. Ibid., pp. 211–12, 805.

39. Dicey, although he asserts that laissez faire was "practically the most vital part of Bentham's legislative doctrine," recognizes that "laissez faire is not from a logical point of view an essential article of the utilitarian creed." Indeed, he devotes a short chapter, "The Debt of Collectivism to Benthamism," to showing that British socialists of the early twentieth century adopted and redirected Benthamite principles. *Law and Public Opinion in England*, pp. 146–47, 303, 310.

40. Schumpeter, *History of Economic Analysis*, p. 531.

41. Henry Sidgwick, *The Principles of Political Economy*, 3d ed. (London: Macmillan, 1901), p. 516. The first edition was published in 1883.

42. Frank Hyneman Knight, *The Ethics of Competition* (Chicago: University of Chicago Press, 1935), p. 56n.

43. F. A. Hayek, *The Constitution of Liberty* (Chicago: Gateway, 1972), p. 441.

44. Knight, *The Ethics of Competition*, p. 56.

45. Arthur M. Okun, *Equality and Efficiency: The Big Tradeoff* (Washington, D.C.: Brookings Institution, 1975), p. 44.

46. John Rawls, *A Theory of Justice* (Cambridge: Harvard University Press, 1971), p. 15.

47. Ibid., p. 101. It is worth noting that although Rawls professes to be returning to the tradition of individual rights and the social contract, his teaching is closer in crucial respects to the utilitarian tradition of the economists. The clearest evidence of this is his rejection out of hand of the idea of a right to the fruits of one's labor.

48. Locke, *Two Treatises of Government*, pp. 328–29. See also pp. 340–41.

49. The Lockean justification of economic inequality, shared by the American founders, does not demand laissez faire or preclude government policies aimed at assisting the needy. It is incompatible, however, with government policies explicitly aimed at redistribution of income. For an analysis of the redistributionist doctrines of Okun and Rawls and of the dangers redistributionism poses for liberal democracy, see Marc F. Plattner, "The Welfare State vs. the Redistributive State," *The Public Interest*, vol. 55 (Spring 1979).

50. See Hayek, *The Constitution of Liberty*, pp. 89, 93–95; and Milton Friedman, *Capitalism and Freedom* (Chicago: University of Chicago Press, 1962), pp. 164, 166.

51. Hayek, *The Constitution of Liberty*, pp. 93–100; Friedman, *Capitalism and Freedom*, pp. 161–66.

52. Hayek, *The Constitution of Liberty*, pp. 85ff.; Friedman, *Capitalism and Freedom*, p. 195. Note that the titles of these two works call attention to the central place their authors give to freedom.

53. Hayek, *The Constitution of Liberty*, p. 100. For a further discussion of the views of Hayek, Friedman, and other free-market economists on questions of economic justice, see Marc F. Plattner, "The New Egalitarianism," in Peter

Berger, ed., *Modern Capitalism,* vol. 1, *Capitalism and Equality in America* (Lanham, Md.: Hamilton Press, 1987), pp. 259–76.

54. Lionel Robbins, *An Essay on the Nature and Significance of Economic Science,* 2d ed. (London: Macmillan, 1962), p. 24.

55. See Harvey Mansfield, Jr., "Social Science and the Constitution," this volume.

Chapter 12: Reflections on Marxism and America

1. Alexis de Tocqueville, *Democracy in America,* ed. Phillips Bradley (New York: Vintage Books, 1945), vol. 2, p. 4.

2. David F. Roth and Paul V. Warwick, *Comparative Politics: Diverse States in an Interdependent World* (New York: Harper and Row, 1989), pp. 190–91. For the Soviet viewpoint, see V. Afanasyev, M. Makarova, and L. Minayev, *Fundamentals of Scientific Socialism* (Moscow: Progress Publishers, 1969), pp. 285–89.

3. Karl Marx, "On the Jewish Question," p. 28. Unless otherwise indicated, all references to Marx's writings are to Robert C. Tucker, ed., *The Marx-Engels Reader* (New York: W. W. Norton, 1972).

4. Marx, "Economic and Philosophic Manuscripts of 1844," p. 66.

5. This is not the place for a discussion of the large secondary and interpretive literature on Marx and Marxism. The best general work, in my view, is still Shlomo Avineri's *The Social and Political Thought of Karl Marx* (Cambridge: Cambridge University Press, 1975). For further bibliography and a most lucid discussion of some of the ethical ambiguities and political implications of Marxism, see Steven Lukes, *Marxism and Morality* (Oxford: Oxford University Press, 1987).

6. Marx, "Economic and Philosophic Manuscripts of 1844," p. 62.

7. Avineri notes the centrality of Marx's notion of labor as humane creative potential throughout all the periods of his thought (*Social and Political Thought of Marx,* pp. 232–33).

8. Marx, "Contribution to the Critique of Hegel's Philosophy of Right," pp. 22–23.

9. See the discussion in Lukes, *Marxism and Morality,* pp. 45–46, 98–99.

10. Marx, "On the Jewish Question," p. 33.

11. Ibid., pp. 28–29.

12. Ibid., p. 37; and Marx, "Critique of Hegel's Philosophy of Right," p. 12.

13. Marx, "On the Jewish Question," p. 29.

14. Ibid., p. 30.

15. See Lukes, *Marxism and Morality,* pp. 78–79.

16. Marx, "On the Jewish Question," p. 40.

17. Ibid., p. 41.

18. Ibid.

19. Ibid., p. 44.

20. Fritz Stern, *The Politics of Cultural Despair* (Berkeley: University of California Press, 1974), pp. 130–31, 196–97.

21. Marx, "The German Ideology," p. 151.

22. Marx, "Manifesto of the Communist Party," pp. 337–38.

23. This may shed some light on the paradox identified by Lukes:

> Is there not a contradiction between the image of *community,* or even of a community of communities, on the one hand, and that of society as a gigantic factory on the other? For Marx was also the author of the idea, taken up by Kautsky and Lenin, that society as a whole could be organized on the basis of the division of labour, socially controlled and regulated. (*Marxism and Morality,* pp. 91–92)

24. Marx, "The Eighteenth Brumaire of Louis Bonaparte," p. 444.

25. See, for example, Hannah Arendt, *On Revolution* (New York: Viking Press, 1965), pp. 252–59, 283–85; and J. G. A. Pocock, *The Machiavellian Moment* (Princeton, N.J.: Princeton University Press, 1975), pp. 506–52.

26. See Lukes's argument that Marxist reasoning is primarily perfectionist and only secondarily utilitarian (*Marxism and Morality,* pp. 71–99, 144).

27. Friedrich Schiller, *On the Aesthetic Education of Man,* trans. Reginald Snell (New York: Frederick Ungar, 1974), pp. 23–37. See also Bernard Yack, *The Longing for Total Revolution* (Princeton, N.J.: Princeton University Press, 1986), pp. 146–81.

28. As "The German Ideology" puts it: "Communism is for us not a *state of affairs* which is to be established, an *ideal* to which reality will have to adjust itself. We call communism the *real* movement which abolishes the present state of things." Quoted in Avineri, *Social and Political Thought of Marx,* p. 222. See Lukes, *Marxism and Morality,* pp. 38–47.

29. Marx, "On the Jewish Question," p. 34.

30. See Robert Conquest, *The Harvest of Sorrow: Soviet Collectivization and the Terror Famine* (New York: Oxford University Press, 1987), pp. 24, 65–70, 105, 119, 145, 170–71, 233.

31. Habermas criticizes Marx for failing to distinguish between the modes of reasoning appropriate to hermeneutical and critical reflection and the instrumentalist reasoning appropriate to the natural sciences, technology, and the organization of labor. See the discussion in Richard J. Bernstein, *The Restructuring of Social and Political Theory* (Philadelphia: University of Pennsylvania Press, 1976), pp. 185–95.

Chapter 13: Freud and the American Constitution

1. The anecdote is recounted in *In Dora's Case,* Charles Bernheim and Claire Kahane, eds. (New York: Columbia University Press, 1985), p. 31.

2. Richard Reeves, *American Journey: Traveling with Tocqueville in Search of Democracy in America* (New York: Simon and Schuster, 1982), pp. 52–53, 122–23, 198–200.

3. A lengthier list of such terms is provided by Martin Gross, *The Psychological Society* (New York: Random House, 1978), p. 15.

4. Alexis de Tocqueville, *Democracy in America,* trans. George Lawrence, ed. J. P. Mayer (Garden City, N.Y.: Doubleday-Anchor, 1969), vol. 2, part 1, chap. 17, p. 484.

5. Ibid., vol. 2, part 2, chaps. 10 and 12, pp. 530, 535.

6. See *Totem and Taboo,* essay 4, in *The Standard Edition of the Complete Psychological Works of Sigmund Freud,* ed. James Strachey et al. (London: The Hogarth Press, 1953–1974), vol. 13, p. 157 (hereafter referred to as *SE*): "The problems of social psychology . . . prove soluble on the basis of one single concrete point—man's relation to his father."

7. Consider in this context Lincoln's discussion in the Cooper Union Address of "our fathers that framed the Constitution" and his statement in the Gettysburg Address that "our fathers brought forth . . . a new nation" in 1776. See *The Political Thought of Abraham Lincoln,* ed. Richard N. Current (Indianapolis: Bobbs-Merrill, 1967), pp. 140, 284.

8. See, for example, *Totem and Taboo,* essay 4, in *SE,* vol. 13, p. 152, where Freud speaks of "the two driving factors, the son's sense of guilt [toward his father] and the son's rebelliousness [against him]."

9. See Barbara Tuchman, "Can History Use Freud? The Case of Woodrow Wilson," *The Atlantic* (February 1967), p. 40: "The psychoanalytic fraternity . . . have greeted this posthumous work of the Master as if it were something between a forged First Folio and the Protocols of Zion."

10. Sigmund Freud and William Bullitt, *Thomas Woodrow Wilson, Twenty-eighth President of the United States: A Psychological Study* (Boston: Houghton Mifflin, 1966), p. 106.

11. Ibid., p. 54.

12. Ibid., pp. 59–60.

13. See ibid., p. 88: "Lodge entered Wilson's life as a person in authority: a father representative." See also pp. 181, 283–84.

14. The psychohistorical orientation has become popular in part because of its affinity with the extreme egalitarian trends that I discuss below. The motive for psychoanalyzing the purportedly "great man" can easily be to cut him down to size: to demonstrate that he is really not great, that he achieved what he did only because of his love for his mother or his hatred for his father, hence that he is not fundamentally our superior. See Hegel's prescient critique of psychobiography before the fact, in *The Philosophy of History,* trans. J. Sibree (New York: Dover, 1956), pp. 31–32: "This [that is, Hegel's] mode of considering [great men] also excludes the so-called 'psychological' view, which—serving the purposes of envy most effectually—contrives so to refer all actions to the heart . . . as that their authors appear to have done everything under the impulse of some passion . . . and on account of these passions to have been not moral men. . . . What pedagogue has not demonstrated of Alexander the Great—of Julius Caesar—that they were instigated by such passions, and were consequently immoral?—whence the conclusion immediately follows that he, the pedagogue, is a better man than they,

because he has not such passions; a proof of which lies in the fact that he does not conquer Asia."

15. See Paul Roazen, *Freud: Political and Social Thought* (New York: Vintage, 1970), p. 22: "Political figures matter to history not because of their psychic conflicts, but for what they managed to accomplish in spite of these problems. The investigation of the psychic level can only be justified insofar as it helps us to understand the nature and limitations of the accomplishments themselves."

16. John Locke, *The Second Treatise of Government* (Indianapolis: Bobbs-Merrill, 1952), chap. 1, sec. 2. See also chap. 6, sec. 71, and chap. 15, sec. 170.

17. *The Interpretation of Dreams*, chap. 5, sec. B, in *SE*, vol. 4, p. 217. Locke would not have disagreed with the strict import of Freud's statement, since he maintained (*Second Treatise*, chap. 6, sec. 76) that "the natural fathers of families by an insensible change became the politic monarchs of them too." But Locke would have disagreed with the implications that Freud derives from his statement. Although Locke agrees with Freud that in the past the political evolved out of the paternal, Locke nevertheless claims that in the present we can qualitatively distinguish between the political and the paternal. Such a distinction is far more problematical in Freud's view, one feature of which is that the past is immortal within the unconscious: "In mental life nothing which has once been formed can perish . . . everything is somehow preserved and . . . in suitable circumstances . . . can once more be brought to light" (*Civilization and Its Discontents*, chap. 1, in *SE*, vol. 21, p. 69). In Freud's view, therefore, the unconscious is perennially and ineluctably inclined to equate the statement that "the political once evolved out of the paternal" with the statement that "the political is still the paternal."

18. *Interpretation of Dreams*, chap. 6, sec. F, in *SE*, vol. 5, p. 423.

19. Freud's failure to differentiate among various kinds of civil society is seemingly but not really remedied in one of the most influential Freudian works written since Freud's death—Herbert Marcuse's *Eros and Civilization: A Philosophical Inquiry into Freud* (New York: Vintage, 1955). Marcuse recognized that Freud's concept of civilization obliterates potentially useful distinctions among various sorts of societies. But he was no more interested than was Freud in classifying actually existing regimes; instead, as in Freud, all existing regimes are grouped together under the rubric of repressive societies, to which Marcuse contrasted the hypothetical nonrepressive society of the future. To understate, one can say that Marcuse's account of political authority in the nonrepressive society is not illuminating. See p. 206: "Knowledge of the available means for creating a humane existence for all is no longer confined to a privileged elite. The facts are all too open, and the individual consciousness would safely arrive at them if it were not methodically arrested and diverted." Those in search of a reinterpretation of Freud in which political insights are added to psychoanalytic ones will not find what they are looking for in Marcuse.

20. See especially *The Question of Lay Analysis*, chap. 7, in *SE*, vol. 20, p. 248: "As a 'depth-psychology,' a theory of the mental unconscious [psychoanalysis] can become indispensable to all the sciences which are concerned

with . . . [human civilization's] major institutions such as . . . the social order."

21. See *Totem and Taboo,* essay 2, in *SE,* vol. 13, p. 74: "Sexual needs are not capable of uniting men in the same way as are the demands of self-preservation. Sexual satisfaction is essentially the private affair of each individual."

22. " 'Civilized' Sexual Morality and Modern Nervous Illness," in *SE,* vol. 9, p. 191.

23. Alexander Hamilton, James Madison, and John Jay, *The Federalist Papers,* ed. Clinton Rossiter (New York: New American Library, 1961), No. 10, p. 81; and No. 51, p. 322.

24. See especially Freud's statement in "The Future Prospects of Psycho-Analytic Therapy," in *SE,* vol. 11, p. 150. He speaks there of the effect that he hopes the enlightenment of society by psychoanalysis will have on neurotics: their "flight into illness," he hopes, will be barred, so that "they will have to be honest, confess to the instincts that are at work in them, face the conflict, fight for what they want, or go without it."

25. *Jokes and Their Relation to the Unconscious,* chap. 6, in *SE,* vol. 8, p. 180. Toward the end of his career, in light of his new emphasis on what he called the death instinct, Freud came to qualify the priority that he had previously ascribed to the hedonistic character of mental processes. But even Freud's later psychology, which goes *beyond* the pleasure principle, still implies that most human actions are explicable *on the basis of* the pleasure principle.

26. Compare John Locke, *An Essay Concerning Human Understanding* (New York: Dover, 1965), book 2, chap. 20, sec. 2: "Things . . . are good or evil, only in reference to pleasure or pain." See also book 2, chap. 20, sec. 3; chap. 21, secs. 41–43.

27. " 'Civilized' Sexual Morality and Modern Nervous Illness," p. 181.

28. Ibid., p. 189.

29. Ibid., p. 188.

30. Letter to James J. Putnam, July 8, 1915, in *The Letters of Sigmund Freud,* ed. Ernst L. Freud, trans. Tania and James Stern (New York: Basic Books, 1975), p. 308.

31. " 'Civilized' Sexual Morality and Modern Nervous Illness," pp. 199–200. The emphasis is Freud's.

32. " 'Civilized' Sexual Morality and Modern Nervous Illness," pp. 196–97.

33. See *Group Psychology and the Analysis of the Ego,* chap. 10, in *SE,* vol. 18, p. 124: "The possibility of [sexual] satisfaction without any need for delay . . . allow[s] . . . narcissism always to rise to its full height."

34. The psychoanalytic prophet of narcissism is the late Heinz Kohut, who was perhaps the most theoretically innovative and influential of contemporary analysts; its popularizer is the radical cultural critic Christopher Lasch, author of *The Culture of Narcissism: American Life in an Age of Diminishing Expectations* (New York: Norton, 1979).

35. "On the Universal Tendency to Debasement in the Sphere of Love," in *SE,* vol. 11, pp. 187–88.

36. Consider in this context the encouragement given to technological

innovations by the eighth paragraph of sec. 8 of Art. I of the Constitution, which authorizes Congress "to promote the Progress of Science and useful Arts, by securing for limited Times to . . . Inventors the exclusive Right to their . . . Discoveries."

37. *The Psychopathology of Everyday Life,* chap. 12, in *SE,* vol. 6, p. 278.

38. *The Ego and the Id,* chap. 2, in *SE,* vol. 19, p. 23.

39. "A Difficulty in the Path of Psycho-Analysis," in *SE,* vol. 17, p. 143. The emphasis is Freud's.

40. "Thoughts for the Times on War and Death," essay 1, in *SE,* vol. 14, p. 282. Note that the quotation marks surrounding *good* and *bad* are Freud's. See also "The Claims of Psycho-Analysis to Scientific Interest," part 2, sec. E, in *SE,* vol. 13, p. 160: "Our highest virtues have grown up, as reaction-formations and sublimations, out of our worst dispositions."

41. *Group Psychology and the Analysis of the Ego,* chap. 12, in *SE,* vol. 18, p. 138. The emphases are mine.

42. Freud's "Introduction" to Freud and Bullitt, p. xvi.

43. *An Outline of Psycho-Analysis,* chap. 8, in *SE,* vol. 23, p. 199.

44. "The Resistances to Psycho-Analysis," in *SE,* vol. 19, p. 219.

45. *Five Lectures on Psycho-Analysis,* fifth lecture, in *SE,* vol. 11, p. 53.

46. *Civilization and Its Discontents,* chap. 8, in *SE,* vol. 21, p. 140.

47. *The Future of an Illusion,* chap. 8, in *SE,* vol. 21, p. 44.

48. Lecture 22, in *SE,* vol. 16, p. 345.

49. Letter to Putnam, July 8, 1915, in *The Letters of Sigmund Freud,* p. 308.

50. Tocqueville, *Democracy in America,* vol. 2, part 1, chap. 2, p. 435.

51. Ibid., vol. 2, part 1, chap. 10, p. 462.

52. Ibid., vol. 2, part 1, chap. 8, p. 454.

53. In this respect it is worth noting that Freud's own views of therapy were notably more sensible than these, in part perhaps because Freud was no democrat and not much of a believer in human perfectibility: for Freud, the goal of therapy (as described in *Studies on Hysteria,* part 4, in *SE,* vol. 2, p. 305) is only to "succeed in transforming . . . hysterical misery into common unhappiness."

54. The first of the "Two Encyclopaedia Articles," on "Psycho-Analysis," in *SE,* vol. 18, p. 251.

55. "Recommendations to Physicians Practicing Psycho-Analysis," in *SE,* vol. 12, p. 119. See also Erik H. Erikson, *Identity and the Life Cycle* (New York: International Universities Press, 1959), p. 96: "Freud was once asked what he thought a normal person should be able to do well. . . . [He] simply said, *'Lieben und arbeiten'* ('to love and to work')."

56. "Analysis Terminable and Interminable," sec. 3, in *SE,* vol. 23, p. 225.

57. *On the History of the Psycho-Analytic Movement,* chap. 3, in *SE,* vol. 14, p. 50.

58. "A Short Account of Psycho-Analysis," sec. 5, in *SE,* vol. 19, p. 209. The emphasis is the translator's. Note, however, Strachey's editorial comment: "Freud seems, in this passage, to be imposing unusual restrictions on the scope of psychoanalysis." In other words, Strachey may believe that in

Freud's usual view psychoanalysis alone perhaps *can* offer a "complete" picture of the world. Note also that Freud goes on in this passage to say that psychoanalysis's "contributions often contain the essence of the facts."

59. "Analysis Terminable and Interminable," sec. 7, in *SE,* vol. 23, p. 248. The quotation marks around *impossible* are Freud's.

Chapter 14: Pragmatism and the U.S. Constitution

1. The interesting suggestion that Peirce's philosophy amounts to an American philosophical Declaration of Independence from British nominalism has recently been made by Josiah Lee Auspitz in "The Greatest Living American Philosopher," *Commentary,* vol. 76, no. 6 (December 1983), p. 59.

2. George Herbert Mead writing in 1930, quoted by Charles Morris, *The Pragmatic Movement in American Philosophy* (New York: George Braziller, 1970), p. 8.

3. David A. Hollinger provides a thoughtful analysis of the place of pragmatism in American life and in historians' interpretations in "The Problem of Pragmatism in American History," *Journal of American History,* vol. 67, no. 1 (June 1980), pp. 88–107.

4. Alexis de Tocqueville, *Democracy in America,* trans. George Lawrence (Garden City, N.Y.: Doubleday, 1969), vol. 2, part 1, chap. 1, p. 429; see also chaps. 8, 10, 20.

5. Ibid., p. 429; I have altered the translation toward greater literalness in a few places.

6. Gabriel A. Almond and Sidney Verba, *The Civic Culture* (Boston: Little, Brown and Co., 1965), pp. 64–65.

7. William James, *Pragmatism* (Indianapolis, Ind.: Hackett, 1981), pp. 28–30; emphasis in the original.

8. John Dewey, *Freedom and Culture* (New York: G. P. Putnam's Sons, 1979 [originally 1939]), pp. 4–5.

9. John Dewey, *Liberalism and Social Action* (New York: G. P. Putnam's Sons, 1935), pp. 4–5.

10. Ibid., p. 39.

11. John Dewey, "Philosophies of Freedom," in *Philosophy and Civilization* (New York: Minton, Balch and Co., 1931), p. 281.

12. Dewey, *Liberalism,* p. 41.

13. John Dewey, *Reconstruction in Philosophy* (Boston: Beacon Press, 1948 [originally 1920]), p. 194.

14. John Dewey, *Democracy and Education* (New York: Macmillan Co., 1916), p. 69.

15. Dewey, *Liberalism,* p. 32.

16. John Dewey, *The Public and Its Problems* (New York: Henry Holt and Co., 1927), pp. 96–97.

17. Dewey, *Liberalism,* p. 12.

18. Dewey, *Reconstruction,* pp. 26–27.

19. Dewey, *The Public,* p. 192.

20. John Dewey, *Individualism Old and New* (New York: Minton, Balch and Co., 1930), p. 32.

21. Dewey, *Liberalism,* pp. 5–6 (emphasis added), 26.

22. Ibid., pp. 34, 26.

23. Dewey, "Philosophies of Freedom," p. 291.

24. John Dewey, *Experience and Education* (New York: Macmillan Co., 1938), p. 74; the strong emphasis on intelligence is worth noting and characteristic. So too in *Human Nature and Conduct* (New York: Henry Holt and Co., 1922), p. 304: "Intelligence is the key to freedom in act."

25. Dewey, *Human Nature,* p. 307.

26. Dewey, *Freedom,* p. 158. Contrast Madison's appreciation of "that veneration which time bestows on everything, and without which perhaps the wisest and freest governments would not possess the requisite stability." *The Federalist Papers,* ed. Clinton Rossiter (New York: New American Library, 1961), No. 49, p. 314.

27. Dewey, *Reconstruction,* p. 209.

28. John Dewey, "Logical Method and Law," in *Philosophy,* p. 139.

29. Dewey, *The Public,* pp. 169–70. Ten pages earlier Dewey called habit "the mainspring of human action" and quoted James at length on the social consequences of habit ("stated once for all by James"); in the present passage Dewey more characteristically dwells on habit as an obstacle to progress rather than society's "most precious conservative influence" (p. 159, quoting James).

30. Dewey, *Reconstruction,* p. 44.

31. John Dewey, *Experience and Nature* (New York: Dover Books, 1958 [reprint of second edition, 1929]), p. 218.

32. Dewey, *The Public,* p. 145.

33. Dewey, *Liberalism,* p. 86.

34. Ibid., pp. 70–73.

35. Dewey, *The Public,* pp. 73–74.

36. Dewey, *Liberalism,* pp. 18–19. See *Reconstruction,* p. 180: "Utilitarianism has marked the best in the transition from the classic theory of ends and goods to that which is now possible."

37. *John Dewey's Impressions of Soviet Russia and the Revolutionary World* (New York: Bureau of Publications, Teachers College, Columbia University, 1964, reprint edition).

38. Ibid., pp. 49, 60.

39. Ibid., p. 72.

40. Ibid., p. 102.

41. Ibid., p. 103.

42. Dewey, *Freedom,* p. 56.

43. Dewey, *The Public,* p. 34.

44. Dewey, *Freedom,* pp. 68–69.

45. Dewey, *Human Nature,* p. 306.

46. Dewey, *Liberalism,* p. 34.

47. Dewey, *Individualism,* p. 72.

48. Dewey, *Liberalism*, pp. 75, 89–90.
49. Ibid., pp. 36, 33.
50. Dewey, *Freedom*, p. 41.
51. Dewey, *Liberalism*, p. 31, emphasis added.
52. Thomas Hobbes, *Leviathan*, ed. Michael Oakeshott (New York: Collier Books, 1962) chap. 11, first paragraph.
53. Dewey, *Reconstruction*, p. 177.
54. Dewey treats the general topics of values, means, and ends most coherently and extensively in *Theory of Valuation* (Chicago: University of Chicago Press, 1939), written for the *Foundations of the Unity of Science* unit of a projected *International Encyclopedia of Unified Science;* see especially pp. 26–28, 34–35, 40–49, 55–56; see also *Reconstruction*, pp. 38, 51–52, 73, 115, 177; and *Democracy*, pp. 89–91, 124.
55. Dewey, *Freedom*, p. 156.
56. William, Y. Elliott, *The Pragmatic Revolt in Politics* (New York: Macmillan Co., 1928), p. 63.
57. Dewey, *Democracy*, p. 60.
58. Ibid., p. 101.
59. Dewey, *Freedom*, pp. 44–46.
60. Ibid., pp. 148–49.
61. Dewey, *Reconstruction*, p. 173.
62. Dewey, *Freedom*, pp. 101–2.
63. Dewey, *Reconstruction*, pp. 26, 36–38, 43, 125; and *Liberalism*, p. 87.
64. Dewey, *Democracy*, p. 142; see also p. 300; and *Reconstruction*, p. 198.
65. Dewey, *Freedom*, pp. 131, 171.
66. Ibid., p. 154.
67. Ibid., p. 148.
68. In Richard Rorty's recent restoration of pragmatism to higher philosophical respectability, Dewey's faith in scientific methods and confidence in the mutual support of democracy and science seem to evanesce. Rorty's decidedly postmodernist Dewey "was at his best when he emphasized the similarities between philosophy and poetry, rather than when he emphasized those between philosophy and engineering"; *Consequences of Pragmatism* (Minneapolis: University of Minnesota Press, 1982), p. 56, n.38. Richard J. Bernstein writes, I believe correctly, that "the 'aesthetic' strain in Rorty has become more and more pronounced" ("One Step Forward, Two Steps Backward: Richard Rorty on Liberal Democracy and Philosophy," *Political Theory*, vol. 15, no. 4 [November 1987], p. 541). Rorty's current pragmatism would seem to offer less possible guidance to democracy than Dewey's (as I have interpreted Dewey).
69. Dewey, *Freedom*, pp. 20, 8, 40. It is in this work that Dewey expresses his highest level of respect for the founders' thinking, especially Jefferson's.
70. Dewey, *Reconstruction*, p. 75.
71. Thomas Jefferson, *Notes on the State of Virginia*, Query 18 in *The Portable Jefferson*, ed. Merrill D. Peterson (Harmondsworth, Eng.: Penguin Books, 1977), p.215.
72. William James, "The Will to Believe," in *Pragmatism and Other Essays*

(New York: Washington Square Press, 1963), p. 213.

73. See above all the passage from *Freedom and Culture* cited in note 8.

74. Dewey, *Reconstruction*, p. 73.

75. Dewey, *Freedom*, pp. 101–2.

76. Ibid., pp. 93–94. Referring to Peirce, Auspitz makes an apt point that holds for Dewey as well: "Insofar as it bears on politics, pragmatism consists simply in understanding the meaning of a doctrine in terms of its practical effects. Thus if, for instance, a given view of the state carries with it the need for wholesale liquidation of populations, suppression of freedoms, and regimentation of everyday life, these are not, pragmatically considered, 'means' to an 'end'; rather, they are the 'meaning' of the doctrine itself." ("Greatest Living American Philosopher," p. 61.)

77. Dewey, *Freedom*, p. 175.

Chapter 15: Existentialism and Democracy

1. The most reliable guide to the perplexities of existentialism is Karl Löwith, *Nature, History and Existentialism*, ed. Arnold Levison (Evanston, Ill.: Northwestern University Press, 1966).

2. The best introductory formulation of the tenets of existentialism by an existentialist is Jean-Paul Sartre, "Existentialism Is a Humanism," in *Existentialism from Dostoevsky to Sartre*, ed. Walter Kaufmann (New York: Meridian Books, 1956), pp. 287–312.

3. The most useful historical background to existentialism can be found in William Barrett, *Irrational Man* (New York: Doubleday Anchor Books, 1962). See especially chap. 2, "The Sources of Existentialism in the Western Tradition," pp. 69–119.

4. In that year, F. H. Heinemann published *Neue Wege der Philosophie*, which introduced the term *Existenzphilosophie*. See his later *Existentialism and the Human Predicament* (New York: Harper Torchbooks, 1958), p. 1.

5. See above, note 2. For the historical setting of postwar existentialism see Paul Johnson, *Modern Times: The World from the Twenties to the Eighties* (New York: Harper Colophon Books, 1983), pp. 575–76. Also see George Lichtheim, *Europe in the Twentieth Century* (New York: Praeger, 1972), pp. 366–69.

6. Blaise Pascal, *Pensées*, in *Pensées and the Provincial Letters* (New York: Modern Library, 1941), fragment 72.

7. Religious existentialism is unjustly neglected in this essay. The single most manifest omission is a neglect of the thought of Kierkegaard. To the limited extent that Kierkegaard concerned himself with democracy, he is a critic of it from the far right. The best statement of his politics appears in Karl Löwith, *Wissen, Glaube und Skepsis (Knowledge, Faith, and Skepticism)* (Göttingen: Vandenhoeck & Ruprecht, 1956), pp. 49–67. Those seeking a representative later text of religious existentialism do well to begin with Gabriel Marcel, *Being and Having: An Existentialist Diary* (New York: Harper Torchbooks, 1965).

8. An indispensable collection of material is George Novack, ed., *Existentialism versus Marxism: Conflicting Views on Humanism* (New York: Delta Books, Dell Publishing Company, 1966). See especially pp. 67–162.

9. The book was *Critique de la raison dialectique.* The most competent critique of it can be found in Raymond Aron, *Marxism and the Existentialists* (New York: Harper & Row, 1969), pp. 111–76. For an example of the political journalism of Sartre, see *The Ghost of Stalin,* trans. Martha Fletcher (New York: George Braziller, 1968). It is unrepresentative, however, in that here he writes in opposition to the Soviet Union, protesting the 1956 invasion of Hungary.

10. Löwith, *Nature, History, and Existentialism,* p. 31. Jaspers, mentioned in this quotation, will also and unjustly be omitted from consideration in this essay. The best starting point for the study of Jaspers is his *Existentialism and Humanism,* ed. Hanns E. Fischer (New York: Russell F. Moore Co., 1952). Also see Nino Langiulli, ed., *The Existentialist Tradition: Selected Writings* (New York: Anchor Books, 1971), pp. 157–85, for excerpts and a good bibliography. Consider as well Judith N. Shklar, *After Utopia: The Decline of Political Faith* (Princeton: Princeton University Press, 1957). The chapter "The Romanticism of Defeat: The Unhappy Consciousness," pp. 108–63, includes some appraisals of Jaspers.

11. Feodor Dostoevski, *Notes from Underground,* trans. Mirra Ginsburg (New York: Bantam Books, 1974). See especially pp. 36–42.

12. Jean-Paul Sartre, *Nausea,* trans. Lloyd Alexander (New York: New Directions, 1964). See especially pp. 55–56.

13. Albert Camus, *The Stranger,* trans. S. Gilbert (New York: Knopf, 1946). See especially p. 184.

14. Friedrich Nietzsche, *Thus Spoke Zarathustra.* Zarathustra says this in the final chapter of the final part, "The Sign," echoing what he said in the first speech of that part, "The Honey Sacrifice." See *The Portable Nietzsche,* ed. and trans. Walter Kaufmann (New York: Viking Press, 1954), pp. 349, 439.

15. This idea, and others too numerous to acknowledge specifically, was suggested to me by my teacher, Leo Strauss.

16. See Aleksandre I. Solzhenitsyn, *The Gulag Archipelago* (New York: Harper and Row, 1973–1974), 3 vols. One cannot read this account without realizing that when there is any basis at all for the arrest of prisoners it is more likely than not for being what in the West might be considered eccentric, or lonely, or "alienated."

17. The two works by Max Weber himself that most clearly illustrate the problem are his two famous lectures, "Politics as a Vocation" and "Science as a Vocation." They can be found in *From Max Weber: Essays in Sociology,* trans. and ed. by H. H. Gerth and C. Wright Mills (New York: Oxford University Press, 1946), pp. 77–156. Also see Karl Löwith, *Max Weber and Karl Marx,* trans. Hans Fantel (London: George Allen & Unwin, 1982). Consult Robert Eden, *Political Leadership and Nihilism: A Study of Weber and Nietzsche* (Tampa, Fla.: University Presses of Florida, 1983), especially pp. 36–71, 134–210.

18. A comprehensive discussion of Heidegger's political philosophy—or lack of one—can be found in Mark Blitz, *Heidegger's Being and Time and the Possibility of Political Philosophy* (Ithaca, N.Y.: Cornell University Press, 1981).

Heidegger's closest contact with what is usually understood as political philosophy probably comes in his reflections on technology as a characteristically modern human endeavor. See Martin Heidegger, *The Question Concerning Technology and Other Essays,* trans. William Lovitt (New York: Harper Torchbooks, 1977).

19. Friedrich Nietzsche, *Beyond Good and Evil: Prelude to a Philosophy of the Future,* trans. Walter Kaufmann (New York: Vintage Books, 1966). See aphorism 211, p. 136.

20. Friedrich Nietzsche, "Ecce Homo," in *On The Genealogy of Morals and Ecce Homo,* trans. Walter Kaufmann (New York: Viking Books, 1967), p. 225; *The Gay Science,* trans. Walter Kaufmann (New York, Viking Books, 1974), aphorism 174, p. 202.

21. See, for example, Nietzsche, *Beyond Good and Evil,* aphorism 208, p. 131. Kaufmann translates—or, rather, mistranslates—the term as "large-scale politics."

22. Ibid., aphorism 108, p. 85.

23. See ibid., aphorism 212, pp. 137–39; aphorisms 260–61, pp. 204–9. Also see the first essay of Nietzsche in *On the Genealogy of Morals,* " 'Good and Evil,' 'Good and Bad,' " pp. 24–56.

24. See Nietzsche, *Beyond Good and Evil,* aphorism 295, pp. 233–36.

25. In the 1922 preface to the revised edition of *The Decline of the West,* Oswald Spengler writes that he owes "practically everything" to Goethe and Nietzsche (New York, Alfred A. Knopf, 1926), trans. Charles Francis Atkinson, 2 vols. See vol. 1, p. xiii.

26. Friedrich Nietzsche, *The Birth of Tragedy,* trans. Walter Kaufmann (New York: Vintage Books, 1967). See especially secs. 11–15, pp. 73–98.

27. See Nietzsche, *Thus Spoke Zarathustra,* "Zarathustra's Prologue," pp. 124–28. The whole first section of the book is relevant to Nietzsche's teaching of the superman, pp. 137–90. Kaufmann ill-advisedly translated the German *Ubermensch* (superman) as "overman."

28. Ibid., p. 191.

29. Friedrich Nietzsche, *Twilight of the Idols,* trans. R. J. Hollingdale (Baltimore: Penguin Books, 1968), pp. 55–59.

30. Nietzsche, *Thus Spoke Zarathustra,* pp. 125–27.

31. Nietzsche, "Ecce Homo," pp. 326–27.

32. Albert Camus, *The Myth of Sisyphus and Other Essays,* trans. Justin O'Brien (New York: Vintage Books, 1960), pp. 62–68.

33. The *locus classicus* for the discussion of democratic man is, of course, Plato, *Republic,* Book 8, 555a–562c.

34. Nietzsche, *Thus Spoke Zarathustra,* pp. 128–31.

35. Ibid., pp. 279–84. The chapter is called, fittingly enough, "On Virtue That Makes Small."

36. Ibid., pp. 155–58. This speech, "On War and Warriors," contains Zarathustra's celebrated quip: "You say it is the good cause that hallows even war? I say unto you: it is the good war that hallows any cause" (p. 159). Similar examples, in Nietzsche's own voice, are not hard to find.

37. Camus, *The Stranger,* p. 154. Also see Camus's *The Rebel: An Essay of*

Man in Revolt, trans. Anthony Bower (New York: Vintage Books, 1958), pp. 302–6.

Chapter 16: Social Science and the Constitution

1. Robert A. Dahl, *A Preface to Democratic Theory* (Chicago, Ill.: University of Chicago Press, 1956), pp. 149–51.

2. Ibid., p. 135.

3. See Bernard Crick, *The American Science of Politics* (Berkeley, Calif.: University of California Press, 1959).

4. Jeffrey T. Bergner, *The Origin of Formalism in Social Science* (Chicago, Ill.: University of Chicago Press, 1981).

5. *The Federalist,* Clinton Rossiter, ed. (New York: New American Library, 1961), 6, p. 59; 10, p. 81; 15, p. 106; 36, p. 224; 55, pp. 345–46; and 57, pp. 350, 353. See David F. Epstein, *The Political Theory of the Federalist* (Chicago, Ill.: University of Chicago Press, 1984), intro.; and *The Federalist Concordance,* T. S. Engeman, E. J. Erler, and T. B. Hofeller, eds. (Middletown, Conn.: Wesleyan University Press, 1980).

6. *Federalist* 51, p. 324; Epstein, *Political Theory of the Federalist*, pp. 144–46.

7. Compare Plato, *Laws* 650b; Aristotle, *Nicomachean Ethics* 1102a8–17.

8. *Federalist* 9, pp. 72–73; 10, p. 77; 14, pp. 100–101. Probably Locke, Montesquieu, Hume, and others who took the British constitution for their model of political liberty are meant.

9. *Federalist* 14, p. 104; 39, p. 240. Useful inheritances are, of course, acknowledged by *The Federalist,* and "experiment" is not always used in a good sense. See *Federalist* 49, p. 315.

10. *Federalist* 72, p. 437.

11. *Federalist* 71, p. 432; 63, p. 384.

12. *Federalist* 49, p. 317.

13. *Federalist* 14, p. 100; 39, p. 241.

14. *Federalist* 65, p. 396; 63, p. 387.

15. *Federalist* 1, p. 35; 6, p. 54; 10, p. 79; 55, p. 342.

16. *Federalist* 37, p. 227; 66, p. 403.

17. *Federalist* 39, pp. 240–41; 51, p. 324.

18. See Jack N. Rakove, *The Beginnings of National Politics* (Baltimore, Md.: Johns Hopkins University Press, 1982), p. 388.

19. On the first page of *The Federalist* Publius speaks of the danger of a "wrong election" by Americans as to the proposed Constitution.

20. See Epstein, *The Political Theory of The Federalist*, pp. 118–25.

21. Note the references to "a handful of tyrannical nobles" within a republic, in *Federalist* 39, p. 241, and to the "hereditary or self-appointed authority" that is rejected in *Federalist* 51, p. 324.

22. See the argument by which Montesquieu progressively exposes these defects of the virtuous ancient republics: *Spirit of the Laws*, 4.7, 8; 5.6; 6.9; 7.10; 8.2; 9.1; 11.4.

23. For the notion of constitutionalizing I am indebted to Herbert J.

Storing and also to Gerald Stourzh; see Stourzh, "Fundamental Laws and Individual Rights in the Eighteenth Century Constitution," Claremont Bicentennial Essay, no. 5 (1984), pp. 14–15.

24. "When a majority is included in a faction, the form of popular government . . . enables it to sacrifice to its ruling passion or interest both the public good and the rights of other citizens." *Federalist* 10, p. 80.

25. "You must first enable the government to control the governed," *Federalist* 51, p. 322.

26. *Federalist* 49, p. 314.

27. *Federalist* 39, p. 240; also 10, p. 80.

28. *Federalist* 78, p. 469.

29. When social scientists question the rationality of voting, they point out that it is in your interest to take a "free ride," that is, to let someone else exercise your freedom.

30. *Federalist* 51, p. 322.

31. *Federalist* 10, p. 78.

32. *Federalist* 39, p. 240. Epstein's book makes a theme of this "honorable determination," as opposed to the one-sided interpretation of *The Federalist*, based on a quick reading of *Federalist* 10 and 51, as promoting self-interest only; *The Political Theory of The Federalist*, intro. and chap. 4.

33. *Federalist* 43, p. 279; also 28, p. 180; 40, p. 254; 45, p. 289; 51, p. 325.

34. *Federalist* 78, p. 470.

35. *The Political Theory of The Federalist*, pp. 40–44, 59–85, 162–66.

36. *Federalist* 10, p. 78; 51, p. 325.

37. *Federalist* 45, p. 289; 57, p. 350.

38. *Federalist* 3 and 23.

39. *Federalist* 37, p. 226.

40. *Federalist* 12 and 30.

41. Epstein, *The Political Theory of the Federalist*, pp. 85, 163.

42. Ibid., p. 165. See also Gerald Stourzh, *Alexander Hamilton and the Idea of Republican Government* (Stanford, Calif.: Stanford University Press, 1970), p. 83.

43. *Federalist* 10, p. 84.

44. For the presidency, see *Federalist* 68, p. 414.

45. Epstein, *The Political Theory of The Federalist*, p. 166.

46. *Federalist* 63, p. 383.

47. Epstein, *The Political Theory of The Federalist*, pp. 179–84; see *Federalist* 70, p. 424.

48. Dahl, *A Preface to Democratic Theory*, p. 21. Great Britain does indeed have a separation of powers: the judiciary is separate, and members of Parliament who are in the cabinet and outside it have very different functions and powers. So I dispute this "fact" of Dahl's. See also Robert A. Dahl, *Dilemmas of Pluralist Democracy* (New Haven, Conn.: Yale University Press, 1982), pp. 28, 65–66.

49. Yet in a joint work Dahl and Lindblom describe the "First Problem of Politics" as enabling citizens to "keep their rulers from becoming tyrants." When it comes to facing facts, they can recognize tyranny, the enemy of

polyarchy; they have more difficulty in understanding faction, the disease of polyarchy. Robert A. Dahl and Charles E. Lindblom, *Politics, Economics and Welfare,* 2d ed. (Chicago, Ill.: University of Chicago Press, 1976), pp. 273, 295–97. For them, the disease of polyarchy is nothing but its imperfection, which results from concessions to inequality or tyranny.

50. This consequence of the first rule is counteracted, as will be seen in regard to "utility," by the social science relativism that accepts wishful, boastful "preferences" in the place of solid "interests." But the reason for this is that "interests," which were originally discovered in order to avoid argument, have been found to be arguable after all. In the current phrase "revealed preferences," *revealed* represents the behavioral element, the preferences one acts upon; but "preference" in its ordinary sense is so flabby and concessive that social scientists still speak of interest (for example, the national interest) in contexts where some insistence is likely.

51. Behavioralizing the formal, formalizing the behavioral: this is but a restatement of Galileo's resolutive-compositive method. See Thomas Hobbes, *De Cive,* preface.

52. See Douglass Adair, *Fame and the Founding Fathers,* T. Colbourn, ed. (New York: Norton, 1974); *Federalist* 72, p. 437.

53. Robert A. Dahl, *Polyarchy: Participation and Opposition* (New Haven, Conn.: Yale University Press, 1971), p. 203. Dahl and Lindblom seem ready to promote the cause of polyarchy, but then their recommendation is lost in the elaboration of the "necessary conditions" of polyarchy that make the recommendation superfluous, *Politics, Economics and Welfare,* pp. 275–323.

54. Robert A. Dahl, *Pluralist Democracy in the United States* (Chicago, Ill: Rand McNally, 1967), chap. 2; *A Preface to Democratic Theory,* p. 150.

55. Calvin C. Jillson, "Constitution-Making: Alignment and Re-Alignment in the Federal Convention of 1787," *American Political Science Review,* vol. 75 (1982), p. 598.

56. William H. Riker, "The Heresthetics of Constitution-Making: The Presidency in 1787, with Comments on Determinism and Rational Choice," *American Political Science Review,* vol. 78 (1984), pp. 1–16. Despite Riker's insistence (or is it merely a preference?), the role for choice is not "fully preserved" in his heresthetics; see Aristotle, *Nicomachean Ethics* 1112a13–1112b12, 1140a32–1140b2.

57. In *Polyarchy* Dahl speaks of a hypothetical innovator who might wish to establish a polyarchy; he is prudently advised to consult the familiar experience of "the most durable representative democracies"! *Polyarchy,* pp. 215, 227.

58. Dahl, *A Preface to Democratic Theory,* p. 150.

59. Ibid., p. 143.

60. See Robert A. Dahl, "On Removing Certain Impediments to Democracy in the United States," and the critique by James W. Ceaser, "In Defense of Republican Constitutionalism: A Reply to Dahl," in Robert H. Horwitz, ed., *The Moral Foundations of the American Republic,* 3d ed. (Charlottesville, Va.: University Press of Virginia, 1986). Also, Robert A. Dahl, "Procedural Democracy," in P. Laslett and J. Fishkin, eds., *Philosophy, Politics and Society,* 5th series

(New Haven, Conn.: Yale University Press, 1979), pp. 97–133; *Who Governs?* (New Haven, Conn.: Yale University Press, 1961), pp. 1–4; *Dilemmas of Pluralist Democracy,* chap. 5.

61. Dahl, *A Preface to Democratic Theory,* p. 133. Dahl and others take note in this regard of Kenneth J. Arrow's voters' paradox, which argues that imprecision in determining a majority denies it reality; Dahl, *Dilemmas of Pluralist Democracy,* p. 139. William H. Riker, *Liberalism against Populism* (San Francisco, Calif.: W. H. Freeman, 1982), pp. 236–38.

62. Dahl, *A Preface to Democratic Theory,* pp. 54, 124, 132.

63. Perhaps even by Dahl's definition, ibid., p. 135. See Anthony Downs's phrase "duly constituted election," *An Economic Theory of Democracy* (New York: Harper, 1957), p. 25.

64. Aristotle, *Politics* 1294b8; see Julien Freund, *L'Essence du Politique* (Paris: Sirey, 1951), p. 329.

65. Dahl, *A Preface to Democratic Theory,* pp. 133, 143. Slavery, needless to say, is a political question. See also Dahl, *Dilemmas of Pluralist Democracy,* pp. 91–93.

66. James M. Buchanan and Gordon Tullock, *The Calculus of Consent: Logical Foundations of Constitutional Democracy* (Ann Arbor, Mich.: University of Michigan Press, 1962). This model does not presuppose any difference between a constitutional intention and an ordinary political one, and it does not claim that ordinary politics would be affected by the actual making of its merely logical constitution.

67. John von Neumann and Oskar Morganstern, *The Theory of Games and Economic Behavior* (Princeton, N.J.: Princeton University Press, 1944, 2d ed., 1947).

68. William Riker, *The Theory of Political Coalitions* (New Haven, Conn.: Yale University Press, 1962), pp. 22, 30.

69. Downs, *An Economic Theory of Democracy,* pp. 11, 74; Buchanan and Tullock, *The Calculus of Consent,* pp. 23–24.

70. Riker, *The Theory of Political Coalitions,* pp. 31, 210. Buchanan refers to Spinoza as a precursor, but Spinoza, who was not an economist, believed in the natural right of big fish to swallow little fish, Buchanan and Tullock, *The Calculus of Consent,* pp. 312–13.

71. Aristotle, *Physics* 197a7–8.

72. Buchanan and Tullock, *The Calculus of Consent,* p. 5 and subtitle.

73. Downs, *An Economic Theory of Democracy,* p. 3.

74. Riker, *The Theory of Political Coalitions,* p. 8.

75. In Hume, utility promotes solid "social virtues" over dubious "eminent qualities," *An Enquiry Concerning the Principles of Morals,* secs. 2, 5. In Bentham, utility is contrasted to "sentiment" or "caprice," *An Introduction to the Principles of Morals and Legislation,* chap. 1. And even in J. S. Mill, where "utility" is greatly expanded, it is recommended by contrast to transcendental theories, *Utilitaranism,* chap. 3.

76. Riker, *The Theory of Political Coalitions,* p. 8.

77. Ibid., p. 15.

78. Buchanan and Tullock, *The Calculus of Consent,* p. 5.

79. Ibid., p. 33.

80. See Downs, *An Economic Theory of Democracy,* p. 11, who notes that political rationality is not necessarily democratic.

81. Buchanan and Tullock, *The Calculus of Consent,* pp. 286, 301; Dahl, *A Preface to Democratic Theory,* p. 151; Riker, *The Theory of Political Coalitions,* p. 243 (end).

82. Buchanan and Tullock, *The Calculus of Consent,* p. 191; Dahl, *A Preface to Democratic Theory,* p. 68.

83. Riker, *The Theory of Political Coalitions,* chaps. 5, 9.

84. Downs, *An Economic Theory of Democracy,* p. 7. Edward C. Banfield, in reproof of Downs, defines *homo economicus* the old-fashioned way, as one who seeks to make money, *Here the People Rule: Selected Essays* (New York: Plenum Press, 1985), chap. 20.

85. Lindblom distinguishes "volitions" from preferences as having been influenced or determined by the attempt to persuade. But which—influenced or determined? As merely influenced, they are beyond the reach of social science; as determined, they are no more than different preferences. Charles E. Lindblom, *Politics and Markets* (New York: Basic Books, 1977), pp. 134–43.

86. Downs, *An Economic Theory of Democracy,* chap. 14; Buchanan and Tullock, *The Calculus of Consent,* p. 133. Howard Margolis has remarked on this anomaly in *Selfishness, Altruism and Rationality* (Cambridge: Cambridge University Press, 1982). He is an excellent critic of public choice from within. Steven E. Rhoads is the same from outside; see *The Economist's View of the World* (Cambridge: Cambridge University Press, 1985).

87. See Buchanan and Tullock, *The Calculus of Consent,* pp. 283, 285, for a failed attempt to understand a constitution as an end in itself.

88. Ibid., p. 11, where it is unclear whether the rational individual is truly a human possibility or merely a postulate of "Western philosophical tradition."

Chapter 17: Neoconstitutionalism? Rawls, Dworkin, and Nozick

1. John Rawls, *A Theory of Justice* (Cambridge: Belknap Press of Harvard University, 1971). Subsequent references to this volume will appear in parentheses in the text.

2. We cite these principles as Rawls (re-) formulates them in "The Basic Liberties and Their Priority," Sterling M. McMurrin, ed., *The Tanner Lectures in Human Values,* vol. 3 (1982), pp. 1, 5.

3. On whether he has succeeded at this, Brian Barry, *The Liberal Theory of Justice* (Oxford: Clarendon Press, 1973), pp. 121–27; Leon H. Craig, "Contra Contract: A Brief against John Rawls' *Theory of Justice,*" *Canadian Journal of Political Science,* vol. 8 (1975), pp. 71–75; and David Lewis Schaefer, *Justice or Tyranny? A Critique of John Rawls's Theory of Justice* (Port Washington, N.Y.: Kennikat Press, 1979), pp. 49–51.

4. See, for example, Barry, *Liberal Theory,* pp. 10–127; Benjamin Barber,

"Justifying Justice: Problems of Psychology, Measurement, and Politics in Rawls," *American Political Science Review,* vol. 69 (1975), pp. 663–74; Craig, "Contra Contract," pp. 66–71; Michael P. Zuckert, "Justice Deserted: A Critique of Rawls' *A Theory of Justice,*" *Polity,* vol. 13 (1981), pp. 466–83; "Liberalism and Nihilism: Contemporary Constrained Performance Theories of Justice," *Constitutional Commentary,* vol. 2 (1985), pp. 395–98; and Michael J. Sandel, *Liberalism and the Limits of Justice* (New York: Cambridge University Press, 1982). Also noteworthy is Nozick's critique of Rawls's design of the original position, to which we shall be referring below.

5. Allan Bloom, "John Rawls vs. the Tradition of Political Philosophy," *American Political Science Review,* vol. 69 (1975), pp. 651–53; Schaefer, *Justice or Tyranny?* pp. 20–41; Harvey C. Mansfield, Jr., *The Spirit of Liberalism* (Cambridge: Harvard University Press, 1978), pp. 90–96.

6. Zuckert, "Justice Deserted," pp. 467–75; and Zuckert, "Liberalism and Nihilism," p. 395.

7. Bloom, "Rawls vs. the Tradition," p. 649; Schaefer, *Justice or Tyranny?* pp. 92–97, 99.

8. Such ambiguity on this point as might have haunted *A Theory of Justice* has been dispelled by Rawls's subsequent elaborations of his thought. On this, see William A. Galston, "Moral Personality and Political Theory: John Rawls's 'Dewey Lectures,'" *Political Theory,* vol. 10 (1982), pp. 510–14.

9. Compare Robert Nozick, *Anarchy, State, and Utopia* (New York: Basic Books, 1974), pp. 213–31; Mansfield, *Spirit of Liberalism,* pp. 97–98; Schaefer, *Justice or Tyranny?* pp. 52–56; Zuckert, "Justice Deserted," pp. 457–77, and "Liberalism and Nihilism," p. 399; Galston, "Moral Personality," pp. 506–9; and Clifford Orwin, "Welfare and the New Dignity," *The Public Interest,* vol. 71 (1983), pp. 91–95.

10. On this, see David F. Epstein's discussion in this volume.

11. We owe this distinction to Marc F. Plattner, "The Welfare State vs. the the Redistributive State," *The Public Interest,* vol. 55 (1979), pp. 28–48; he discusses Rawls on pp. 34–48.

12. On the shortcomings of Rawls's constitutionalism as a guide to statesmen, see Barry, *Liberal Theory,* pp. 134–53; Schaefer, *Justice or Tyranny?* pp. 45–47; and Ronald Moore, "Rawls on Constitution-Making," J. Roland Pennock and John W. Chapman, eds., *Constitutionalism* (*Nomos* 20) (New York: New York University Press, 1979).

13. Rawls, "Basic Liberties," pp. 55–60.

14. Also compare "Basic Liberties," p. 11.

15. Rawls, "Social Unity and Primary Goods," A. K. Sen and Bernard Williams, eds., *Utilitarianism and Beyond* (New York: Cambridge University Press, 1982), pp. 159, 162.

16. Rawls, "Basic Liberties," pp. 76–78.

17. Frank Michelman, "In Pursuit of Constitutional Welfare Rights: One View of Rawls' *Theory of Justice,*" *University of Pennsylvania Law Review,* vol. 121 (1973), pp. 990–91. Compare Rawls, "Basic Liberties," p. 54, n.46.

18. Also compare Rawls, "Basic Liberties," pp. 42–43.

19. Sandel, *Limits of Justice,* chap. 4, especially pp. 131–32.

20. Rawls, "Basic Liberties," p. 47.

21. Michelman, "Pursuit," p. 1018.

22. Ronald Dworkin, *Taking Rights Seriously,* expanded ed. (Cambridge: Harvard University Press, 1978), p. 17. Subsequent references to this volume will appear in parentheses in the text. This "expanded edition" includes an appendix in which Dworkin jousts with selected critics; see also Thomas Pangle, "Rediscovering Rights," *The Public Interest,* vol. 50 (1978), pp. 157–60.

23. Compare Michael Walzer, "Philosophy and Democracy," *Political Theory,* vol. 9 (1981), pp. 387–97.

24. Compare Plattner, "Welfare State," pp. 45–47, and his parallel discussion in his contribution to the present volume.

25. All references in the text are to Nozick, *Anarchy, State and Utopia* (above, note 9). For an anthology of criticism of this work, see Jeffrey Paul, ed., *Reading Nozick* (Totawa, N.J.: Rowman and Littlefield, 1981).

26. On the weakness of Nozick's foundations, compare Mansfield, *Spirit of Liberalism,* pp. 103–4; Zuckert, "Liberalism and Nihilism," pp. 404–6.

27. Locke, *Second Treatise of Government,* secs. 7–13, 16–21.

28. See Ellen Frankel Paul, "The Time-Frame Theory of Governmental Legitimacy," in J. Paul, ed., *Reading Nozick,* pp. 270–5, who argues precisely this but believes, mistakenly in my opinion, that she is arguing against Nozick rather than with him.

29. *Federalist* 39.

30. Locke, *Second Treatise,* chap. 5, especially secs. 27–30, 34–38, 40–44.

31. Ibid., secs. 46–50.

32. Mansfield, *Spirit of Liberalism,* p. 102.

33. Hobbes, *Leviathan,* "A Review and Conclusion." Compare Locke, *Second Treatise,* secs. 25, 26, 33, 99, 101, 103 (end), 107, 110, 112, 115, 162, 175, 176, 186, 211 (Mansfield, *Spirit of Liberalism,* p. 102 and note 43).

34. For thoughtful critiques of Nozick's theory of property, see Mansfield, *Spirit of Liberalism,* pp. 101–3; and, from the left, G. A. Cohen, "Robert Nozick and Wilt Chamberlain: How Patterns Preserve Liberty," *Erkenntnis,* vol. 11 (1977), pp. 5–23; Ron Replogle, "Natural Rights and Distributive Justice," *Canadian Journal of Political Science,* vol. 17 (1984), pp. 65–86; Edward Andrew, "Inalienable Rights, Alienable Property, and Freedom of Choice," ibid., vol. 18 (1985), pp. 529–50.

35. Clifford Orwin, "Robert Nozick's Libertarian Utopia," *This World,* vol. 9 (1984), pp. 84–89.

36. Compare Tocqueville, *Democracy in America,* II, ii, chaps. 10, 11, 17–19; iii, chap. 19.

37. See above, pp. 203–4.

Index

A Note on the Book

*This book was edited by Dana Lane,
Ann Petty, Andrea Posner, and Trudy Kaplan of the
publications staff of the American Enterprise Institute.
The text was set in Palatino, a typeface designed by Hermann Zapf.
Coghill Book Typesetting Company, of Richmond, Virginia,
set the type, and Edwards Brothers Incorporated,
of Ann Arbor, Michigan, printed and bound the book,
using permanent acid-free paper.*

The AEI Press is the publisher for the American Enterprise Institute for Public Policy Research, 1150 17th Street, N.W., Washington, D.C. 20036: *Christopher C. DeMuth,* publisher; *Edward Styles,* director; *Dana Lane,* editor; *Ann Petty,* editor; *Andrea Posner,* editor; *Teresa Fung,* editorial assistant (rights and permissions). Books published by the AEI Press are distributed by arrangement with the University Press of America, 4720 Boston Way, Lanham, Md. 20706.

The American Enterprise Institute for Public Policy Research

Founded in 1943, AEI is a nonpartisan, nonprofit, research and educational organization based in Washington, D.C. The Institute sponsors research, conducts seminars and conferences, and publishes books and periodicals.

AEI's research is carried out under three major programs: Economic Policy Studies; Foreign Policy and Defense Studies; and Social and Political Studies. The resident scholars and fellows listed in these pages are part of a network that also includes ninety adjunct scholars at leading universities throughout the United States and in several foreign countries.

The views expressed in AEI publications are those of the authors and do not necessarily reflect the views of the staff, advisory panels, officers, or trustees. AEI itself takes no positions on public policy issues.

Library of Congress Cataloging-in-Publication Data

Confronting the Constitution : the challenge to Locke, Montesquieu, Jefferson, and the Federalists from utilitarianism, historicism, Marxism, Freudianism, pragmatism, existentialism— / [edited] by Allan Bloom.

p. cm.

ISBN 0-8447-3699-6 (alk. paper)

1. Political science—United States—History. 2. Liberalism—History. 3. Natural law—History. 4. United States—Constitutional law—Philosophy. I. Bloom, Allan David, 1930– .

JA84.U5C62 1990

342.73′029—dc20 89-27830

CIP